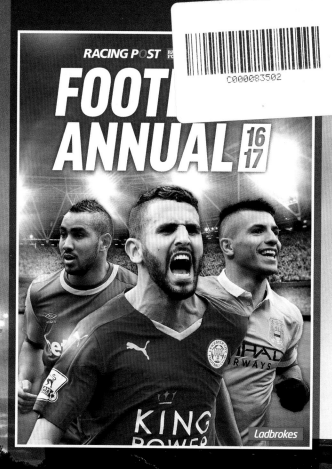

Editor *Dan Sait*

Contributors *Joe Champion, Paul Charlton, Dan Childs, Michael Cox, Steve Davies, Alex Deacon, Danny Hayes, Glenn Jeffreys, Mark Langdon, James Milton, Kevin Pullein*

Data editor *Chris Mann*

Cover design *Jay Vincent*

Published in 2016 by Racing Post Books

27 Kingfisher Court, Hambridge Road, Newbury, Berkshire, RG14 5SJ

Copyright © 2016 Racing Post Books

A catalogue record for this book is available from the British Library.

ISBN 978-1-910498-51-4

Printed and bound in Great Britain by Buxton Press

CONTENTS

2015/2016 STATS

HENRIKH MKHITARYAN
B DORTMUND ▶ MAN UNITED

NATIONALITY	Armenian
POSITION	Midfield
AGE	27
HEIGHT	5'8"
APPS	44
GOALS	18

	W	D	L	WIN%
MATCHES WITH SUB APPEARANCES NOT INCLUDED				
	32	6	6	**73%**
MATCHES WITHOUT				
	4	3	1	**50%**

MKHITARYAN WHO?

GET SET FOR THE NEW SEASON WITH OUR IN-DEPTH DATABASE OF PLAYER, TEAM AND COMPETITION STATS, PLUS EXPERT ADVICE FROM THE BETTING BOFFINS AT RACING POST SPORT

EDITOR'S INTRODUCTION

The last year has seen many of football's accepted truisms unravel. Leicester sunk the idea that only big clubs win the Premier League. Bournemouth and Watford bridged with ease the supposed chasm between first and second tiers. Wales, Iceland and a continent of enthralled neutrals scoffed at the idea that the European Championships would suffer for its expansion.

Merely a freak of a season, or is something bigger afoot? Will the established order regain a footing in 2016-17 or is this the dawn of a new capricious era in football? It's a conundrum that bettors must figure out quickly.

True, we won't suddenly be swamped with 5,000-1 winners – in part because bookies will now think twice before again offering such odds. But in years to come will we look back at Leicester's success and simply see the first of many occasions when a lesser side dealt the established elite a bloody nose? Shock title successes by relegation candidates are sure to remain a rarity, but the massive television revenues now floating about hint at a trend rather than a blip. And it certainly suggests that the big boys must be wiser in their spending if they are to avoid being caught by the chasing pack.

If 2015-16 taught us anything, perhaps it is that football is rediscovering its appreciation of teamwork. Leicester, Wales, Iceland and Tottenham are a few of those who overachieved and all produced eye-catching performances from ordinary-looking squads. None of the managers involved had been heralded as geniuses but each crafted a fine team with relatively limited resources. Is old-fashioned teamwork threatening to undermine the cult of the celebrity manager?

We should soon find out as the Premier League has become a mecca for elite coaches, and for them there is no excuse for failure. If the biggest clubs with the greatest pull and the best managers cannot restore the status quo, then the game really could be on the cusp of a refreshing era of relative chaos.

That need not concern bettors as the shrewd judge thrives when plotting a course through confusion. And we can offer many of the finest minds in the game to help unravel the punting puzzles ahead, kick-starting your season over the following pages and keeping you ahead of the game daily in the Racing Post and weekly in the Racing & Football Outlook. Here's hoping another enthralling and profitable campaign to come.

Dan Sait

A unique season can still provide punting pointers

1 Dreams really can come true

It still feels strange to call Leicester the English champions, but the 5,000-1 ante-post shots didn't just win the Premier League – they thrashed the elite clubs and had a ten-point buffer to Arsenal.

It was unrealistic for most punters to pick Leicester out as potential title winners in August but it was interesting to see how little faith bookies had in the underdogs despite their superb early-season results.

Jamie Vardy broke the Premier League record for scoring in consecutive matches, Riyad Mahrez was turning opposition full-backs inside-out, and yet Leicester were still 250-1 when they hit the summit in November and were still 11-1 at Christmas. It was not until Leicester won at the Etihad in early February that bookmakers even rated them favourites.

Sometimes dreams do come true and there were a lot of people thinking Leicester couldn't win the league purely because they were one of the smaller teams.

2 Managers make a big difference

Sunderland swapped Dick Advocaat for Sam Allardyce in October but Newcastle held on to Steve McClaren until March. Sunderland survived their relegation battle and Newcastle didn't.

Put simply, had McClaren gone earlier Newcastle would probably still be a Premier League side. And with so many top coaches now in England's top flight it is imperative clubs get their managerial selection correct.

Newcastle failed to do that and McClaren took a team who should have finished in mid-table down to the Championship.

The very best players may not want to come to England but the managers do. And with Pep Guardiola, Jurgen Klopp, Jose Mourinho and Antonio Conte among those now in England you need a manager who can stand toe-to-toe with those big guns.

3 Harry Kane is not a one-season wonder

It was fair for punters to question whether Harry Kane would be able to repeat his first-season form for Tottenham but he actually improved his tally to 25 goals in the second campaign to take the Golden Boot at 14-1.

Kane became only the 12th player to score 20 or more Premier League goals in successive seasons and is in elite company alongside Sergio Aguero, Luis Suarez, Robin van Persie, Carlos Tevez, Thierry Henry, Ruud van Nistelrooy, Jimmy Floyd Hasselbaink, Alan Shearer, Robbie Fowler, Les Ferdinand and Andy Cole.

4 Not such a big step up

Playoff winners Norwich went back down but Bournemouth and Watford easily preserved their top-flight status.

Bournemouth suffered an early-season injury crisis but still stayed clear of relegation and Watford were never in the bottom three.

The Hornets even reached an FA Cup semi-final without getting sucked into trouble.

5 Saints are a superbly run club

Southampton continue to see their managers and star players depart but results remain excellent and Saints fully deserved to qualify for Europe.

Manager Ronald Koeman has gone to Everton but something is right off the pitch and their recruitment continues to pay off, just as it did last season when they successfully replaced Toby Alderweireld and Morgan Schneiderlin.

Forget 5,000-1 shots – if you're after thrills, steam into those 1-1,000 Blues

T here is, of course, only one place to start a betting review of the 2015-16 football season. It's difficult to comprehend such an astonishing, historic achievement and it still hasn't fully sunk in even as we approach the start of a new campaign. Rest assured, though, it did happen – after 114 years, Hibernian really did win the Scottish Cup.

Once the Hibs hysteria had finally died down, it was time to reflect on a half-decent betting story south of the border.

Leicester's Premier League triumph has been labelled as one of sport's greatest fairytales but perhaps the best way to tell the Foxes' story is through cold, hard, unsentimental ante-post odds.

The headline-grabbing price was the 5,000-1 about Claudio Ranieri's men winning the title but they were also 1,000-1 for a top-four finish while Jamie Vardy landed the place money for Golden Boot backers at 500-1.

One bookmaker reported that Ranieri's appointment had prompted a gamble on Leicester to be relegated and they kicked off the season just 3-1 for the drop and 1-5 to finish in the bottom half.

The media relished tales of Leicester fans who had £5 or £10 bets at massive prices although mainstream journalists struggled to quantify the scale of the shock. Apparently Leicester's title win was less likely than Elvis Presley riding Shergar to victory in the Greyhound Derby – or, indeed, Shergar riding Elvis – when the only thing required to put it into context was the fact that LEICESTER CITY WON THE FLIPPING PREMIER LEAGUE!

One consequence of 5,000-1 shots winning the top flight is that every other team's successes look, well, a bit rubbish.

But let's guzzle a can of some dubious energy drink, force an insincere grin across our jaded faces and listlessly applaud some of the other 2015-16 champions.

In the Championship, Burnley proved the value of speculating to accumulate after splashing out £9m on Brentford's Andre Gray in August. The striker duly landed the Golden Boot at odds of 20-1 and the 14-1 Clarets went up as champions.

Wigan, 7-1 ante-post, saw off the impressive challenges of Burton (33-1) and Walsall (40-1) in League One while Barnsley reminded punters not to write off their pre-season bets too soon. The Tykes, bottom of the division on November 28, went on a wonderful run culminating in a win over Millwall in the playoff final and queues of punters clutching hastily-Sellotaped betting slips formed outside Yorkshire betting shops.

Down in League Two, Northampton (16-1) flirted with administration before surging to the title and Bristol Rovers striker Matty Taylor picked up the Golden Boot in his first season in the Football League. The Gas man may as well just change his name by deed poll to 'the new Jamie Vardy'.

There wasn't much Leicester spirit elsewhere in Europe as whatever you call the opposite of underdogs – overdogs? – dominated proceedings. Juventus, Bayern

*Mrs Milton stuck the Corgi
on a Chelsea top-half finish*

Munich, Barcelona and Paris Saint-Germain all won their divisions – PSG seemed to have the French league mathematically wrapped up by mid-November – and you could have chucked Celtic and Rangers into that short-priced accumulator too.

A far more profitable strategy was simply to back West Ham in every Premier League game. The Hammers' excellent record against the bigger teams, especially away from home, meant a £1 bet on them every week would have produced a seasonal profit of £37.90.

Slaven Bilic's side were such a great team to follow that even if you'd backed both them and Aston Villa to win every game you'd have come out £9.93 ahead. That's purely hypothetical, of course – if anyone had

actually been betting on Villa to win every weekend, their friends, family and social workers would have been duty-bound to stage an intervention shortly after Christmas.

The miracle of Leicester is bound to have an effect on punters' and bookmakers' attitudes to the 2016-17 season. Fans of smaller clubs will be inspired to throw a fiver at their team winning the league and bookies will adjust their prices accordingly. Still, I'm happy with my 16-1 about the Hull-Burnley straight forecast.

The pursuit of 5,000-1 winners shouldn't distract us from value bets at shorter prices. Take Chelsea last season, for example. The Blues were 1-1,000 ante-post for a top-ten finish and they did it in style, finishing, er, tenth. A winner's a winner.

HOW THEY BET 2016-17

Premier League winner

	b365	Bright	Coral	Hills	Lads	Power
Man City	9-4	9-4	9-4	2	12-5	9-4
Man United	7-2	7-2	7-2	7-2	7-2	7-2
Arsenal	11-2	6	11-2	6	6	11-2
Chelsea	13-2	6	6	6	11-2	6
Liverpool	8	8	8	9	8	9
Tottenham	7	8	7	7	7	8
Leicester	28	25	28	25	25	20
West Ham	100	80	80	80	66	80
Everton	100	100	100	66	100	80
Southampton	100	100	100	100	100	100
Stoke	500	500	400	500	350	500
Crystal Palace	750	750	500	750	500	500
Swansea	1000	750	500	1000	500	1000
Middlesbro'	1000	1000	1000	1000	1000	1000
Bournemouth	1000	1000	500	750	750	1000
Burnley	1500	1000	1000	1000	1000	1000
Hull	1500	1000	1000	1000	1000	500
Sunderland	1000	1000	1000	1000	1000	1000
Watford	1000	1000	750	1000	1000	1000
West Brom	1500	1000	1000	1000	1000	1000

Win or each-way

Premier League relegation

	b365	Bright	Coral	Hills	Lads	Power
Burnley	5-6	10-11	5-6	10-11	5-6	4-5
Hull	5-6	5-6	1	8-11	5-6	5-6
Middlesbro'	5-4	5-4	13-10	5-4	5-4	11-10
Watford	15-8	5-2	9-4	9-4	2	23-10
West Brom	2	7-4	9-4	2	2	2
Bournemouth	11-4	11-4	10-3	10-3	3	11-4
Sunderland	4	3	5-2	3	11-4	23-10
Swansea	4	7-2	4	4	4	7-2
Crystal Palace	11-2	5	5	11-2	5	4
Stoke	10	8	10	9	9	13-2
Leicester	16	16	14	20	16	12
Southampton	20	20	20	20	20	25
Everton	25	25	20	25	20	18
West Ham	33	33	25	33	22	25
Tottenham	500	500	250	500	250	500
Liverpool	250	600	200	250	250	500
Chelsea	500	500	300	750	500	500
Man United	500	500	300	750	750	500
Arsenal	500	750	500	500	500	500
Man City	1000	1000	500	1000	1000	500

Win only

Championship winner

	b365	Bright	Coral	Hills	Lads	Power
Newcastle	7-4	2	21-10	15-8	15-8	2
Aston Villa	8	9	9	9	8	8
Norwich	9	9	10	9	10	9
Derby	12	12	12	11	11	10
Brighton	14	12	12	12	12	12
Sheffield Wed	16	16	16	14	16	16
Wolves	16	16	16	16	16	16
Brentford	33	25	25	25	25	25
Cardiff	33	25	28	20	25	25
Fulham	33	25	28	25	33	25
Reading	33	25	33	20	25	25
QPR	33	28	28	25	28	25
Leeds	40	33	33	33	28	25
Bristol City	40	40	33	25	40	33
Ipswich	33	33	28	25	25	40
Huddersfield	40	33	28	33	40	33
Wigan	40	25	20	25	28	33
Nottm Forest	40	25	33	25	25	25
Blackburn	66	40	33	66	40	33
Birmingham	66	40	40	33	40	40
Preston	66	33	33	50	40	40
Barnsley	100	66	66	66	50	50
Rotherham	150	100	80	100	66	66
Burton	250	100	80	150	100	50

Win or each-way

League One winner

	b365	Bright	Coral	Hills	Lads	Power
Sheffield Utd	6	6	6	13-2	6	6
Millwall	11	10	9	10	10	11
Charlton	8	9	11	9	12	10
MK Dons	12	12	12	10	10	11
Bradford	12	10	12	10	11	11
Bolton	14	14	11	14	11	11
Coventry	14	14	16	16	16	14
Oxford United	16	14	14	14	12	11
Peterborough	16	14	12	16	14	14
Scunthorpe	20	20	14	16	16	16
Bristol Rovers	16	20	20	14	16	14
Walsall	25	16	25	20	18	14
Northampton	28	20	20	20	16	18
Gillingham	25	20	25	20	20	25
Wimbledon	33	33	33	33	25	33
Rochdale	40	25	33	33	25	16
Chesterfield	40	40	50	50	33	33
Fleetwood	33	33	33	40	33	50
Shrewsbury	40	50	40	50	40	50
Southend	33	40	40	40	33	33
Swindon	50	40	40	40	33	33
Bury	33	50	40	50	40	25
Port Vale	66	50	50	50	50	40
Oldham	66	40	50	66	66	40

Win or each-way

League Two winner

	b365	Bright	Coral	Hills	Lads	Power
Portsmouth	9-2	4	4	4	4	4
Doncaster	9	7	7	11-2	13-2	9
Luton	10	10	9	10	9	8
Leyton Orient	10	10	9	11	11	7
Plymouth	14	10	14	12	12	14
Cambridge	16	14	14	12	14	12
Carlisle	14	18	14	20	16	18
Blackpool	16	20	20	20	16	20
Colchester	20	20	18	16	16	16
Cheltenham	20	20	20	20	16	18
Notts County	25	25	25	20	16	20
Wycombe	25	20	25	20	18	20
Grimsby	20	25	22	20	20	20
Mansfield	25	25	20	25	25	18
Crewe	33	25	33	25	28	20
Accrington	25	25	33	25	25	25
Exeter	33	33	40	33	28	25
Yeovil	40	40	33	50	40	40
Barnet	40	40	33	40	40	33
Hartlepool	33	50	33	33	40	50
Stevenage	50	50	50	50	40	33
Crawley	80	50	66	66	50	50
Morecambe	100	66	66	66	66	50
Newport Co	100	66	66	66	80	66

Win or each-way

National League winner

	b365	Bright	Coral	Hills	Lads	Power
Forest Green	9-2	5	9-2	9-2	9-2	-
Tranmere	13-2	13-2	7	6	6	-
Eastleigh	7	7	13-2	8	8	-
Dagenham & R	10	10	10	10	9	-
Wrexham	10	10	9	10	11	-
York City	12	12	10	11	11	-
Lincoln	14	16	16	10	16	-
Dover	16	16	18	14	14	-
Barrow	16	16	20	12	12	-
Gateshead	20	20	16	20	20	-
Braintree	20	20	25	25	18	-
Macclesfield	33	33	28	33	25	-
Torquay	33	33	33	33	25	-
Aldershot	40	33	40	40	33	-
Bromley	33	33	33	40	40	-
Chester	50	33	40	33	33	-
Maidstone	50	50	50	40	40	-
Solihull	50	50	50	40	40	-
Woking	40	33	50	33	33	-
Boreham W	50	66	40	66	66	-
Sutton Utd	50	50	66	40	40	-
Guiseley	66	66	66	80	80	-
Southport	50	66	50	80	66	-
North Ferriby	100	100	66	100	80	-

Win or each-way

Scottish Premiership winner

	b365	Bright	Coral	Hills	Lads	Power
Celtic	1-4	1-4	1-4	1-4	1-4	1-4
Rangers	7-2	7-2	4	3	3	7-2
Aberdeen	16	16	16	12	12	14
Hearts	40	33	50	33	33	40
Motherwell	250	200	250	150	175	150
St Johnstone	250	200	200	150	200	150
Dundee	500	200	250	150	200	150
Inverness	500	250	500	250	250	375
Ross County	500	500	250	250	250	250
Hamilton	1000	1000	500	250	500	475
Kilmarnock	1000	1000	500	250	500	500
Partick	1000	1000	300	250	500	250

Win or each-way

Scottish Championship winner

	b365	Bright	Coral	Hills	Lads	Power
Hibernian	11-10	5-4	11-8	11-8	5-4	5-4
Dundee Utd	11-4	9-4	9-4	2	9-4	9-4
Falkirk	11-2	7	5	7	6	6
Dunfermline	10	11	11	11	11	12
St Mirren	10	14	14	14	12	14
Raith Rovers	20	14	14	16	16	16
Morton	33	25	40	25	28	33
Queen of Sth	40	25	25	25	25	33
Ayr	66	33	33	33	33	40
Dumbarton	100	50	66	50	50	66

Win or each-way

Scottish League One winner

	b365	Bright	Coral	Hills	Lads	Power
Alloa	11-4	-	5-2	7-2	11-4	7-2
Peterhead	4	-	9-2	4	4	4
Livingston	-	-	4	3	10-3	3
Airdrie	11-2	-	5	5	9-2	5
Stranraer	6	-	5	9-2	11-2	11-2
East Fife	12	-	11	14	10	12
Albion Rovers	14	-	16	20	16	20
Brechin	20	-	14	25	20	20
Queens Park	16	-	25	25	22	25
Stenhousemuir	25	-	33	25	28	33

Win or each-way

Scottish League Two winner

	b365	Bright	Coral	Hills	Lads	Power
Clyde	5-2	3	-	3	11-4	3
Arbroath	5	5	-	9-2	9-2	9-2
Forfar	9-2	9-2	-	5	11-2	5
Cowdenbeath	5	11-2	-	9-2	9-2	9-2
Elgin	6	6	-	7	6	5
Annan	12	7	-	7	6	6
Stirling	12	12	-	12	10	12
Berwick	16	12	-	12	10	10
Edinburgh City	25	25	-	-	25	25
Montrose	33	25	-	25	22	25

Win or each-way

Mark Langdon
RP Football Editor

What was your best bet of last season?
Next! It was a mainly dismal ante-post saved somewhat by backing Barnsley for promotion at 25-1 just as they got hot

Give us your Yankee for the top four English divisions
Each-way as all of them are so competitive – Arsenal, Derby, Millwall and Plymouth

Can another unfancied side break into the top four, or was 2015-16 a one-off?
I doubt it. All of the mid-ranked teams have more money but the big clubs have fixed their managerial issues spectacularly

How will the English teams perform in Europe?
They did quite well last term with Liverpool reaching a final and Man City the semis. They don't have the really special players like Messi, Ronaldo and Suarez but I expect them to go close without winning

Can you envisage any upsets in World Cup qualification?
Not particularly as the seeding makes it so much easier for the big boys. Hungary could be value up against Portugal and Switzerland

If you had just one bet all season, what would it be?
Bayern to win the Champions League under European Cup specialist Carlo Ancelotti, who will concentrate more on that than the Bundesliga. They've come close in recent years and don't have a weakness in any position. New signings Mats Hummels improves the defence and Renato Sanches is one of the world's best teenagers

Dan Childs
Racing Post tipster

What was your best bet of last season?
Burnley to be top Championship north-west team at 6-5. The Clarets finished a massive 31 points ahead of Preston North End, who were their closest challengers

Give us your Yankee for the top four English divisions
Premier League: Liverpool
Championship: Newcastle
League One: Bradford
League Two: Portsmouth

Can another unfancied side break into the top four, or was 2015-16 a one-off?
I can't see it happening this time around. Leicester have the Champions League to contend with, West Ham's home form may suffer with the move to the Olympic Stadium and Southampton must get used to another new manager

How will the English teams perform in Europe?
Leicester are top seeds and could make the knockout stage given a kind draw. Arsenal and Tottenham will struggle to get further than the quarter-finals but Manchester City are potential challengers if the right signings are made

Can you envisage any upsets in World Cup qualification?
Spain are not certainties to win Group G. Italy defeated them at Euro 2016 and may eclipse them in qualifying

If you had just one bet all season, what would it be?
Newcastle to win the Championship. They should be unstoppable with Rafa Benitez at the helm

Steve Davies
Racing Post tipster

What was your best bet of last season?
The then criminally under-rated Hammers at 11-1 to win at Manchester City

Give us your Yankee for the top four English divisions
Manchester City, Newcastle, Charlton and Portsmouth

Can another unfancied side break into the top four, or was 2015-16 a one-off?
I think they can (though don't necessarily think they will). The state of the transfer market has changed so much that middle-ranked sides like West Ham, Southampton and Leicester are now picking up top-class stars. So why can't Stoke, Swansea or another team do likewise?

How will the English teams perform in Europe?
I would be astonished if there is an English winner of either competition. Three out of four to get through the Champions League group phase, just two – Southampton and Manchester United – getting into the last 32 of the Europa League

Can you envisage any upsets in World Cup qualification?
Romania are a team on the up and could eclipse Poland and Denmark in Group E. There were also hints from Turkey, with one or two classy youngsters emerging, that they could be a force in Group I

If you had just one bet all season, what would it be?
Southampton to finish in the bottom half. These summer firesales will eventually have an impact and the appointment of Claude Puel doesn't inspire

Kevin Pullein
Betting expert

What was your best bet of last season?
I stake my bets so the difference between winning and losing is always about the same, so no bet means much more to me than any other. What gives me pleasure is finishing a season with more money than I had when it started

Give us your Yankee for the top four English divisions
I only bet singles. My one ante-post single is Chelsea

Can another unfancied side break into the top four, or was 2015-16 a one-off?
They can but probably will not. The difference in spending power between the richest Premier League clubs and others is about the same as it used to be. With the new television deal everyone's income will rise. And spending power is what usually drives success

How will the English teams perform in Europe?
Perhaps not quite as well as usual in the Champions League because their standard seems lower. Usually England gets the best results after Spain

Can you envisage any upsets in World Cup qualification?
Yes – but not what they will be!

If you had just one bet all season, what would it be?
My one ante-post bet is Chelsea to win the Premier League at 13-2. Two seasons ago they were champions. Last season was an aberration. Nearly always nowadays they perform at a level that should give them a better than 13-2 chance

Dan Sait
RFO Football Editor

What was your best bet of last season?
My Championship tips went well with Burnley promoted at 9-2 and Bolton relegated at 6-1. And laying QPR game-by-game paid off nicely, too. If only Boro could have nicked the title...

Give us your Yankee for the top four English divisions
Arsenal or Tottenham (the only half-reasonably priced teams in a genuinely wide-open race), Newcastle, Millwall, Portsmouth

Can another unfancied side break into the top four, or was 2015-16 a one-off?
If you count Liverpool and Spurs, then yes. Of the genuine outsiders, I'll be interested to see how Everton go under new ownership and management

How will the English teams perform in Europe?
I fancy a strong challenge in the Europa League, but Leicester and Tottenham's inexperience could show in the Champions League. I'd be surprised if Man City can repeat their semi-final showing but surely Arsenal must end their last 16 hoodoo

Can you envisage any upsets in World Cup qualification?
Ireland at 11-2 to win Group D as the top four look much of a muchness. And 3-1 about Iceland finishing in the top two of Group I is interesting. Croatia should win that section but Ukraine, Turkey, Finland and Kosovo are all very beatable

If you had just one bet all season, what would it be?
Newcastle to win the Championship. I just can't see how they won't do it

Bradley Addison
Ladbrokes trader

What was your best bet of last season?
Sunderland to win at Selhurst Park at 6-1. Crystal Palace were the shortest price for a Premier League match in their history at 8-15. They had been in good form against those around them but that's all it was, form

Give us your Yankee for the top four English divisions
Liverpool, Newcastle, Peterborough, Doncaster

Can another unfancied side break into the top four, or was 2015-16 a one-off?
The Premier League's distribution of wealth is narrowing and the result could be a more level playing field. The days of the established top four may be long gone

How will the English teams perform in Europe?
Business as usual. Progression to the latter stages of both competitions but ultimately outmanoeuvred by European counterparts

Can you envisage any upsets in World Cup qualification?
It's looking ominous for Brazil – currently sitting outside of the qualification places, they are in real danger of not qualifying for the World Cup for the first time in their history

If you had just one bet all season, what would it be?
Sell Man United points on the spreads. The lines look far too high for what I expect to be another very competitive season – I don't expect the eventual winner to get many more than 75 points, let alone the second favourites

Mouthwatering managerial mix set to make life tricky for Premier League punters

The Premier League bills itself as the world's most unpredictable league and the ante-post odds for 2016-17 support that claim. In Ligue 1, just one team is under 10-1 for the title. In the Bundesliga and La Liga there are two, and in Serie A three. In England, there are six sides under 10-1 – Man City, Man United, Arsenal, Chelsea, Tottenham and Liverpool. And that doesn't even include the champions, Leicester.

It's not simply the race itself which is unpredictable but many of the individual favourites themselves. Three of the anticipated top four – Manchester City, Manchester United and Chelsea – have new managers, and while all are title-winners with established reputations, their approach won't be entirely as expected.

New Manchester City boss Pep Guardiola, for example, was cast as an ideologue at Barcelona, a coach who preached possession football by overloading the central midfield zone. Yet when he arrived at Bayern Munich, Guardiola surprised everyone by basing his team around speedy wingers and increasingly emphasised crossing to two aerially dominant centre-forwards.

Guardiola will evolve at City. He's rarely had a pure speedster upfront like Sergio Aguero, an energetic, technical midfielder like Ilkay Gundogan or a counter-attacking number ten like Kevin De Bruyne. Guardiola is more adaptable than many believe.

Chelsea manager Antonio Conte took Juventus to three straight Serie A titles and became renowned for favouring a 3-5-2 system, but that is far from his default approach. Giorgio Chiellini, Leonardo Bonucci and Andrea Barzagli were all top-class centre-backs, so a three-man defence was logical – as was sticking with that system when he coached the same players for Italy.

But when Conte initially took charge of Juventus he tried to play an attack-minded 4-2-4 system, which involved pressing aggressively and playing with plenty of width. Considering Roman Abramovich stresses the need for entertainment, Conte will presumably revert to something nearer that philosophy.

Then there's Jose Mourinho, hardly a newcomer to Premier League football. The former Chelsea manager has developed a reputation as a defensive-minded coach but he has often built perfectly attacking teams, particularly in his days at Real Madrid and in the first half of Chelsea's 2014-15 title-winning campaign.

While Mourinho's initial impact in the Premier League was popularising deep defending, quick counter-attacking and playing a no-nonsense defensive midfielder, Mourinho has learned to play more open, attacking football to meet the demands of supporters. In particular, he's been happy to give relatively free roles to the likes of Wesley Sneijder, Cristiano Ronaldo and Eden Hazard, allowing them to develop their attacking game and dominate their side.

United will be well-organised but not necessarily defensive – and probably no different in style to the later Sir Alex Ferguson years.

We know roughly what to expect from

Arsene Wenger's Arsenal, Mauricio Pochettino's Tottenham and Jurgen Klopp's Liverpool, although all three will be forced to adapt their approach after disappointing ends to their respective 2015-16 campaigns.

Wenger has acknowledged the need to strengthen the spine of his side and Arsenal's improvement might come primarily from new signings after he neglected to add a single outfielder to his squad last summer. Granit Xhaka is a tough-tackling midfielder, while Wenger has clearly been determined to sign attackers who offer something different to his existing options.

Pochettino's Tottenham improved their attacking play significantly in the second half of last season, creating chances through incisive passing combinations rather than simply by pressing high up the pitch and regaining possession quickly. Indeed, that relentless pressing resulted in their tiredness during the closing weeks of 2015-16 and we might witness a more patient, intelligent Tottenham this time around.

Klopp, meanwhile, has been able to recruit his own players, which is crucial.

Last term felt like something of a wasted season for Liverpool, even though they reached two cup finals, as Klopp was applying his old Borussia Dortmund approach to players who didn't suit that style.

With younger, more energetic and dynamic players, Klopp should be capable of introducing the high-tempo football he became famed for. More than Guardiola or Conte, he does appear to have a very defined approach.

Finally, there's Leicester, who start the campaign as the side to beat and will encounter opponents playing extremely deep to deny Jamie Vardy space to break into, having learned from underestimating them last season. Claudio Ranieri's side will need to evolve their game, adding more creativity to break down organised teams.

To varying extents all seven sides will have changed their style from last season, and all seven have a shot at winning the title. It is perhaps appropriate that in the season that marks the Premier League's silver anniversary, it has never been trickier to predict who will take home the silverware.

Forget about form when it comes to betting on both to score

L ee is hunched over a coupon writing bets. He backs both teams to score. The matches he chooses carefully. He looks for teams with form – teams who scored and conceded in a high proportion of past games. Then he bets that they will score and concede today.

When the results come in, Lee scrunches his receipt and throws it away. Every week he is disappointed then confused. He cannot understand why teams who scored and conceded so often in the past seem to score and concede much less often in the future. I might as well pick matches with a pin, he thinks.

He would probably be better off if he did. What Lee does sounds reasonable. It seems to make sense. Like a lot of other bad ideas.

Assuming the future will resemble the past can be a good idea if there is evidence that what happened before happens again. When you are betting on both teams to score, there is not.

Both teams scored in 50 per cent of Premier League games played in the last 20 seasons, 1996-97 to 2015-16. No matter how often a team scored and conceded in the first half of a season, the proportion of games in which they scored and conceded in the second half of that season was rarely far from 50 per cent.

Take teams who scored and conceded in 68 per cent of their games in the first half of a season. What happened in the second half? They scored and conceded in 52 per cent of their games. Or teams who scored and conceded in 32 per cent of their games in the first half of a season. In the second half of the season they scored and conceded in 48 per cent of their games.

Both teams to score form is almost as useless as coin-tossing form. Imagine there was an annual coin-tossing tournament with a prize for whoever got heads most often. Stats from last year would give you no idea of what might happen this year.

Michael J Mauboussin, head of global financial strategies at Credit Suisse, wrote a book called The Success Equation. It was subtitled: Untangling Skill and Luck in Business, Sports, and Investing. Mauboussin said: "Statistics are widely used in a range of fields. But rarely do the people who use statistics stop and ask how

useful they really are."

When betting on both teams to score in a football match the right answer is: statistics are hardly any use at all.

Mauboussin would say that both teams to score statistics have low persistence. Persistence is a measurement of the extent to which what happens in the present is similar to what happened in the past.

Two things influence the chance of both teams scoring – the difference in ability between the teams and the total number of goals. The smaller the difference in ability the more likely it becomes that both will score. The larger the number of goals in a match the more likely it becomes that both teams will score at least once.

Annoyingly, one influence tends to counteract the other. The smaller the difference in ability between teams, other things being equal, the lower the number of goals. The higher the number of goals in a match, as a rule, the wider the difference in ability between teams. As one influence increases the likelihood of both teams scoring, the other reduces it.

The prospect of both teams scoring does not vary much from game to game. Despite this, or because of it, or in the absence of any knowledge of it, both teams to score is one of the most popular markets.

To make a profit betting on both teams to score you need to be lucky or to find odds that are bigger than they should be. Don't count on being lucky. Odds can be too big if a market has not taken into account something it should have – or because it has taken into account something it should not have.

Perhaps the best strategy, then, is to look for matches where the odds suggest there is a lower than usual chance of both teams scoring. Often these will involve teams with a poor record of scoring and conceding. But as you now know, there is no valid reason to think that will continue.

June 2016

Tuesday 28-29	Champions League first qualifying round, first leg
Thursday 30	Europa League first qualifying round, first leg

July 2016

Tuesday 5-6	Champions League first qualifying round, second leg
Thursday 7	Europa League first qualifying round, second leg
Sunday 10	Euro 2016 final, Paris
Tuesday 12-13	Champions League second qualifying round, first leg
Thursday 14	Europa League second qualifying round, first leg
Friday 15	Champions League third qualifying round draw
	Europa League third qualifying round draw
	Scottish League Cup group stage, matchday one
Tuesday 19-20	Champions League second qualifying round, second leg
	Scottish League Cup group stage, matchday two
Thursday 21	Europa League second qualifying round, second leg
Saturday 23	Scottish League Cup group stage, matchday three
Tuesday 26-27	Champions League third qualifying round, first leg
	Scottish League Cup group stage, matchday four
Thursday 28	Europa League third qualifying round, first leg
Saturday 30	Scottish League Cup group stage, matchday five

August 2016

Tuesday 2-3	Champions League third qualifying round, second leg
	Scottish Challenge Cup first round
Thursday 4	Europa League third qualifying round, second leg
Friday 5	Champions League playoff round draw
	Europa League playoff round draw
	Start of Dutch Eredivisie season
Saturday 6	Start of Football League season
	Start of National League season
	FA Cup extra preliminary round
	Start of Scottish Professional Football League season
Sunday 7	FA Community Shield
	Leicester City v Manchester United
Tuesday 9	Scottish League Cup second round
	League Cup first round
Wednesday 10	Uefa Super Cup, Trondheim
	Real Madrid v Seville
Friday 12	Start of French Ligue 1 season
Saturday 13	Start of Premier League season
	Scottish Cup first preliminary round
	Start of Portuguese Primeira Liga season (to be confirmed)
Tuesday 16-17	Champions League playoff round, first leg
	Scottish Challenge Cup second round
Thursday 18	Europa League playoff round, first leg
Saturday 20	FA Cup preliminary round
	Start of Italian Serie A season
Sunday 21	Start of Spanish Primera Liga season
Tuesday 23-24	Champions League playoff round, second leg
	League Cup second round
Thursday 25	Champions League group stage draw
	Europa League playoff round, second leg
Friday 26	Europa League group stage draw
	Start of German Bundesliga season
Monday 29 (week commencing)	International friendlies
	Ireland v Oman
	Football League Trophy first round

September 2016

Saturday 3	FA Cup first qualifying round
	Scottish Cup second preliminary round
	Scottish Challenge Cup third round
Sunday 4	World Cup qualifiers
	Czech Republic v Northern Ireland
	Malta v Scotland
	Slovakia v England
Monday 5	World Cup qualifiers
	Serbia v Ireland
	Wales v Moldova
Saturday 10	FA Vase first qualifying round
Tuesday 13-14	Champions League group stage, matchday one
Thursday 15	Europa League group stage, matchday one
Saturday 17	FA Cup second qualifying round
Tuesday 20-21	League Cup third round
	Scottish League Cup quarter-finals
Saturday 24	FA Vase second qualifying round
	Scottish Cup first round
Tuesday 27-28	Champions League group stage, matchday two
Thursday 29	Europa League group stage, matchday two

October 2016

Saturday 1	FA Cup third qualifying round
Tuesday 4	Football League Trophy second round
Thursday 6	World Cup qualifiers
	Austria v Wales
	Ireland v Georgia
Saturday 8	World Cup qualifiers
	England v Malta
	Northern Ireland v San Marino
	Scotland v Lithuania
	FA Trophy preliminary round
	Scottish Challenge Cup fourth round
Sunday 9	World Cup qualifiers
	Moldova v Ireland
	Wales v Georgia
Tuesday 11	World Cup qualifiers
	Germany v Northern Ireland
	Slovakia v Scotland
	Slovenia v England
Saturday 15	FA Cup fourth qualifying round
Tuesday 18-19	Champions League group stage, matchday three
Thursday 20	Europa League group stage, matchday three
Saturday 22	FA Vase first round
	Scottish Cup second round
	Scottish League Cup semi-finals
Tuesday 25	League Cup fourth round
Saturday 29	FA Trophy first qualifying round

November 2016

Tuesday 1-2	Champions League group stage, matchday four
Thursday 3	Europa League group stage, matchday four
Saturday 5	FA Cup first round
Monday 7 (week commencing)	International friendlies
Tuesday 8	Football League Trophy third round

Friday 11	World Cup qualifiers
	England v Scotland
	Northern Ireland v Azerbaijan
Saturday 12	World Cup qualifiers
	Austria v Ireland
	Wales v Serbia
	FA Trophy second qualifying round
	FA Vase second round
	Scottish Challenge Cup quarter-finals
Tuesday 22-23	Champions League group stage, matchday five
Thursday 24	Europa League group stage, matchday five
Saturday 26	FA Trophy third qualifying round
	Scottish Cup third round
Sunday 27	Scottish League Cup final
Tuesday 29	League Cup fifth round

December 2016

Saturday 3	FA Cup second round
	FA Vase third round
Tuesday 6-7	Champions League group stage, matchday six
	Football League Trophy area semi-finals
Thursday 8	Europa League group stage, matchday six
	Fifa Club World Cup begins, Japan
Saturday 10	FA Trophy first round
Monday 12	Champions League last 16 draw
	Europa League last 32 draw
Sunday 18	Fifa Club World Cup final

January 2017

Saturday 7	FA Cup third round
	FA Vase fourth round
Tuesday 10	League Cup semi-final, first leg
Saturday 14	Africa Cup of Nations begins, Gabon
	FA Trophy second round
Saturday 21	Scottish Cup fourth round
Tuesday 24	League Cup semi-final, second leg
	Football League Trophy area final, first leg
Saturday 28	FA Cup fourth round
	FA Vase fifth round

February 2017

Saturday 4	FA Trophy third round
Sunday 5	Africa Cup of Nations final
Tuesday 7	Football League Trophy area final, second leg
Saturday 11	Scottish Cup fifth round
Tuesday 14-15	Champions League last 16, first leg
Thursday 16	Europa League last 32, first leg
Saturday 18	FA Cup fifth round
	FA Vase sixth round
	Scottish Challenge Cup semi-finals
Tuesday 21-22	Champions League last 16, first leg
Thursday 23	Europa League last 32, second leg
Friday 24	Europa League last 16 draw
Saturday 25	FA Trophy fourth round
Sunday 26	League Cup final

March 2017

Saturday 4	Scottish Cup quarter-finals
Tuesday 7-8	Champions League last 16, second leg
Thursday 9	Europa League last 16, first leg

Saturday 11	FA Cup sixth round
	FA Trophy semi-final, first leg
	FA Vase semi-final, first leg
Tuesday 14-15	Champions League last 16, second leg
Thursday 16	Europa League last 16, second leg
Friday 17	Champions League quarter-final draw
	Europa League quarter-final draw
Saturday 18	FA Trophy semi-final, second leg
	FA Vase semi-final, second leg
Monday 20 (week commencing)	International friendlies
Friday 24	World Cup qualifiers
	Ireland v Wales
Saturday 25	Scottish Challenge Cup final
Sunday 26	World Cup qualifiers
	England v Lithuania
	Northern Ireland v Norway
	Scotland v Slovenia

April 2017

Sunday 2	Football League Trophy final
Tuesday 11-12	Champions League quarter-final, first leg
Thursday 13	Europa League quarter-final, first leg
Tuesday 18-19	Champions League quarter-final, second leg
Thursday 20	Europa League quarter-final, second leg
Friday 21	Champions League semi-final draw
	Europa League semi-final draw
Saturday 22-23	FA Cup semi-finals
	Scottish Cup semi-finals
Saturday 29	National League season ends
	Scottish Premiership splits

May 2017

Tuesday 2-3	Champions League semi-final, first leg
Thursday 4	Europa League semi-final, first leg
Saturday 6	Football League season ends
	Scottish Championship, League One, League Two seasons end
Tuesday 9-10	Champions League semi-final, second leg
Thursday 11	Europa League semi-final, second leg
Saturday 13	National League North & South playoff finals (to be confirmed)
Sunday 14	National League Premier playoff final
Sunday 21	Premier League season ends
	FA Trophy final
	FA Vase final
	Scottish Premiership season ends
Tuesday 24	Europa League final, Stockholm
Saturday 20	League One playoff final
Saturday 27	FA Cup final (to be confirmed)
	Scottish Cup final
Sunday 28	League Two playoff final
Monday 29	Championship playoff final

June 2017

Saturday 3	Champions League final, Cardiff
Monday 5 (week commencing)	International friendlies
Saturday 10	World Cup qualifiers
	Azerbaijan v Northern Ireland
	Scotland v England
Sunday 11	World Cup qualifiers
	Ireland v Austria
	Serbia v Wales

PREMIER LEAGUE

European break can help Reds go all the way in the Premier League title race

T he landscape of English football has changed in the wake of Leicester's title triumph and an unpredictable 2016-17 race could go the way of Liverpool, who are ready to take major strides in their first full season under Jurgen Klopp, writes Dan Childs. Several smaller clubs will be thinking of doing a Leicester, including Leicester themselves who will find it easier to attract a higher quality of player now they can offer Champions League football.

Two potential challengers who don't have European football to worry about are Chelsea and Liverpool.

Chelsea are the shorter price of the pair but it is hard to fancy a Blues side who look in need of a major rebuild under Antonio Conte. Jose Mourinho was part of the problem at Stamford Bridge last season and there was an improvement under Guus Hiddink, but Chelsea remained way short of the standards they set in 2014-15. Getting back to that level will be tough because older players like Cesc Fabregas and John Terry are past their best and others, such as Oscar, Eden Hazard and Nemanja Matic, have a lot to prove after a disappointing 12 months.

Turning Chelsea around may take more than one season but the revival at Liverpool is already gaining traction.

The Reds finished on 60 points (ten more than Chelsea) but that tally would have been higher had Klopp not been concentrating on the Europa League in the closing weeks of the season. As the season progressed, Liverpool became less reliant on the injury-prone Daniel Sturridge and began to see better performances from Philippe Coutinho, Divock Origi and Roberto Firmino.

Even at this stage Origi may not be ready to play up front week-in, week-out but he is ready to take the weight off Sturridge's shoulders and that could be key to Liverpool

having a much-improved season.

Both Manchester clubs are expected to improve but, as is the case with Chelsea, there are deep-rooted problems that need to be addressed.

There are question marks over the spine of Manchester City's side which Pep Guardiola may find difficult to address. And Jose Mourinho may have to conduct a massive clearout at Manchester United where Ander Herrera, Marouane Fellaini, Bastian Schweinsteiger, Memphis Depay and Morgan Schneiderlin have been major disappointments.

That leaves the north London challenge which could be strong with Arsenal and Tottenham looking to build on second- and third-place finishes.

The Gunners' problem is that they have one way of playing and it often leads to defeat whenever their passing game fails to click. Not since 2007-08 have they mustered more than 80 points and that is the level of consistency they must get back to.

Tottenham have never gained more than 72 points in the Premier League but there is the potential for their talented young side to improve. They have a very strong first team but the squad may need beefing up, having been exposed in the Europa League tie against Borussia Dortmund and during the suspension-hit Premier League run-in.

Key to the data

The table next to every team profile shows head-to-head data for every side they will have to play in the league this season.

1 Every team the club will play in the league in the order they finished last season

2 Results of last season's league meetings **W** win **D** draw **L** loss. Where there was more than one league meeting, the latest is at the right. Regular season only

3 Head-to-head results over the last six seasons at the club's own ground. **P** games played **W** wins **D** draws **L** losses **OV** games with over 2.5 total goals **UN** games with under 2.5 total

goals **BS** games in which both teams scored **CS** number of clean sheets for the home side

4 Promoted and relegated teams shown in fawn in the order in which they finished last season

5 League finishes over the last three seasons

6 Over and under 2.5 and both sides to score stats, including rank in club's division last season. The bar chart shows, horizontally, from top to bottom and rounded to the nearest 5 per cent, the division high, the profiled club and the division low

Leading scorers Numbers in brackets show first goals then 'anytime' goals

	2015-16		Last six seasons at home							
	H	A	P	W	D	L	OV	UN	BS	CS
Leicester	2		3	1	1	0	2	1	0	
Arsenal	L	L	1	0	0	1	0	1	0	0
Tottenham	L		1	0	0	1	0	1	0	0
Man City	W	L	1	0	0	1	1	0	0	0
Man United	W	W	1	1	0	0	1	0	0	0
Southampton	W		2	1	0	1	1	1	1	1
West Ham	L	W	1	0	0	1	1	0	1	0
Liverpool			1	0	0	1	1	0	1	0
Stoke	L		1	0	0	1	1	0	1	0
Chelsea	L		1	0	0	1	0	1	0	0
Everton	W		1	0	1	0	1	0	1	0
Swansea	W	L	1	1	0	0	1	0	1	0
Watford			3	1	2	0	3	2	1	
West Brom	L		1	0	1	0	0	1	1	0
Crystal Palace	W		1	0	1	0	0	1	0	1
Bournemouth										
Sunderland	W	D	1	1	0	0	0	1	1	0
Burnley			1	0	1	0	0	1	1	0
Middlesbrough			2	1	1	0	1	1	0	2
Hull										

Season	Division	Pos	P	W	D	L	F	A	GD	Pts
2015-16	Premier League	18	38	11	9	18	45	67	-22	42
2014-15	Championship	1	46	26	12	8	98	45	+53	90
2013-14	Championship	10	46	18	12	16	67	66	+1	66

Over/Under 58%/42% 4th   **Both score** 61%/39% 3rd

Bournem...

ARSENAL

Nickname: The Gunners
Colours: Red and white
Ground: Emirates Stadium   **Capacity:** 60,260
Tel: 020-7704-4000   www.arsenal.com

Last season was a missed opportunity for Arsenal, who will hope to go one better and land a first league title since 2004.

Their consistency – 20 successive top-four finishes – is a quality many of their rivals would love to replicate but the danger of finishing outside of the Champions League spots looks greater than ever given the level of competition.

Arsene Wenger's transfer priority must be to add potency to an attack which has lacked a reliable focal point in recent seasons. Despite impressive contributions from Mesut Ozil and Alexis Sanchez, Arsenal were not always free-scoring last term and ended up with 65 league goals – their lowest tally since 2006-07.

They were prone to being caught on the counter but have beefed up the midfield with the capture of Granit Xhaka.

Longest run without a loss: 10
Longest run without a win: 4
Highest/lowest league position: 1/4
Clean sheets: 18
Yellow cards: 42 **Red cards:** 4
Average attendance: 59,963
Players used: 25
Leading scorer: O Giroud 16 (6,13)

2015-16	H	A	Last six seasons at home							
			P	W	D	L	OV	UN	BS	CS
Leicester	W	W	2	2	0	0	2	0	2	0
Arsenal										
Tottenham	D	D	6	3	2	1	3	3	5	1
Man City	W	D	6	2	3	1	2	4	3	2
Man United	W	L	6	2	2	2	3	3	3	3
Southampton	D	L	4	3	1	0	1	3	1	3
West Ham	L	D	5	4	0	1	3	2	2	2
Liverpool	D	D	6	2	3	1	2	4	3	2
Stoke	W	D	6	6	0	0	3	3	2	4
Chelsea	L	L	6	1	3	2	2	4	2	3
Everton	W	W	6	4	2	0	2	4	3	3
Swansea	L	W	5	1	1	3	2	3	2	1
Watford	W	W	1	1	0	0	1	0	0	1
West Brom	W	L	6	5	0	1	3	3	2	4
Crystal Palace	D	W	3	2	1	0	1	2	2	1
Bournemouth	W	W	1	1	0	0	0	1	0	1
Sunderland	W	D	6	3	3	0	3	3	3	3
Burnley			1	1	0	0	1	0	0	1
Middlesbrough			-	-	-	-	-	-	-	-
Hull			2	1	1	0	1	1	1	1

Season	Division	Pos	P	W	D	L	F	A	GD	Pts
2015-16	Premier League	2	38	20	11	7	65	36	+29	71
2014-15	Premier League	3	38	22	9	7	71	36	+35	75
2013-14	Premier League	4	38	24	7	7	68	41	+27	79

Over/Under 50%/50% 14th   **Both score** 42%/58% 19th

Key stat: Arsenal are unbeaten in their last ten Premier League fixtures, although five of those matches were drawn

2015-16 Premier League appearances

	P	G	Y	R
M Arteta	0 (9)	0	1	-
H Bellerin	36	1	3	-
J Campbell	11 (8)	3	-	-
S Cazorla	15	0	3	1
P Cech	34	0	-	-
C Chambers	2 (10)	0	2	-
F Coquelin	21 (5)	0	6	1
M Debuchy	2	0	-	-
M Elneny	9 (2)	0	3	-
M Flamini	12 (4)	0	3	-
Gabriel Paulista	18 (3)	1	4	1
K Gibbs	3 (12)	1	-	-
O Giroud	26 (12)	16	2	-
A Iwobi	8 (5)	2	-	-
L Koscielny	33	4	3	-
P Mertesacker	24	0	1	1
N Monreal	36 (1)	0	1	-
D Ospina	4	0	-	-
A Oxlade-Chamberlain	9 (13)	1	-	-
M Ozil	35	6	4	-
A Ramsey	29 (2)	5	4	-

	P	G	Y	R
A Sanchez	28 (2)	13	1	-
T Walcott	15 (13)	5	-	-
D Welbeck	7 (4)	4	1	-
J Wilshere	1 (2)	0	-	-

Olivier Giroud scored 16 goals for the Gunners

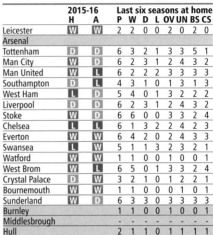

BOURNEMOUTH

Nickname: The Cherries
Colours: Red and black
Ground: Dean Court **Capacity:** 11,464
Tel: 0844-576-1910 www.afcb.co.uk

Bournemouth survived despite taking just one point from their final five games and suffering dreadful luck on the injury front, but they will hope to push on in their second Premier League season.

Callum Wilson and Max Gradel spent most of 2015-16 on the sidelines and will be looking forward to contributing more. A fully-fit Wilson would certainly make a difference up front, but Bournemouth's main problem was keeping goals out of their own net – their open, attacking style often resulted in them being caught out at the back and a goals-conceded tally of 67 was the joint-second highest in the division.

Eddie Howe will be reluctant to change the Cherries' positive approach but defensive enhancements are necessary if his team is to become tougher to beat.

Longest run without a loss: 6
Longest run without a win: 8
Highest/lowest league position: 11/19
Clean sheets: 7
Yellow cards: 53 **Red cards:** 1
Average attendance: 11,183
Players used: 28
Leading scorer: J King 6 (1,6)

	2015-16	Last six seasons at home							
	H	A	P	W	D	L	OV	UN	BS CS
Leicester	D	D	2	0	1	1	0	2	1 0
Arsenal	L	L	1	0	0	1	0	1	0 0
Tottenham	L	L	1	0	0	1	1	0	1 0
Man City	L	L	1	0	0	1	1	0	0 0
Man United	W	L	1	1	0	0	1	0	1 0
Southampton	W	L	2	1	0	1	1	1	1 1
West Ham	L	W	1	0	0	1	1	0	1 0
Liverpool	L	L	1	0	0	1	1	0	1 0
Stoke	L	L	1	0	0	1	1	0	1 0
Chelsea	L	W	1	0	0	1	1	0	1 0
Everton	D	L	1	0	1	0	1	0	1 0
Swansea	W	D	1	1	0	0	1	0	1 0
Watford	D	D	3	1	2	0	0	3	2 1
West Brom	D	W	1	0	1	0	0	1	1 0
Crystal Palace	D	W	1	0	1	0	0	1	0 1
Bournemouth									
Sunderland	W	D	1	1	0	0	0	1	0 1
Burnley			1	0	1	0	0	1	1 0
Middlesbrough			2	1	1	0	1	1	0 2
Hull			-	-	-	-	-	-	- -

Season	Division	Pos	P	W	D	L	F	A	GD	Pts
2015-16	Premier League	16	38	11	9	18	45	67	-22	42
2014-15	Championship	1	46	26	12	8	98	45	+53	90
2013-14	Championship	10	46	18	12	16	67	66	+1	66

Over/Under 58%/42% 4th   **Both score** 61%/39% 3rd

Key stat: Bournemouth had the second-worst home record in the Premier League last season. Only Aston Villa picked up fewer points on their own patch

2015-16 Premier League appearances

	P	G		Y	R		P	G		Y	R
B Afobe	12 (3)	4		-	-	T Rantie	0 (3)	0		-	-
R Allsop	0 (1)	0		-	-	M Ritchie	33 (4)	4		5	-
H Arter	21	1		7	-	A Smith	22 (9)	2		5	-
A Boruc	32	0		2	-	J Stanislas	17 (4)	3		1	-
S Cook	36	4		5	-	A Surman	38	0		4	-
C Daniels	37	3		2	-	L Tomlin	3 (3)	0		1	-
S Distin	9 (3)	0		-	-	C Wilson	9 (4)	5		-	-
T Elphick	11 (1)	1		1	-						
A Federici	6	0		-	-						
S Francis	38	0		5	1						
D Gosling	28 (6)	3		6	-						
L Grabban	4 (11)	0		2	-						
M Gradel	11 (3)	1		1	-						
J Iturbe	0 (2)	0		-	-						
Y Kermorgant	0 (7)	0		-	-						
J King	24 (7)	6		1	-						
S MacDonald	0 (3)	0		-	-						
T Mings	0 (1)	0		-	-						
G Murray	6 (13)	3		2	-						
E O'Kane	6 (10)	0		2	-						
M Pugh	15 (11)	3		1	-						

Callum Wilson's injury blunted Bournemouth

BURNLEY

Nickname: The Clarets
Colours: Claret and blue
Ground: Turf Moor **Capacity:** 22,546
Tel: 0871-221-1882 www.burnleyfootballclub.com

Sean Dyche is a great believer in continuity but he may have to make some major changes if he is to steer Burnley to safety in the top flight.

Keeping a settled squad was the right approach last season and the Clarets reaped the reward by winning automatic promotion with a game to spare.

Now the challenge is to build on that and avoid a repeat of 2014-15, when a physical, hard-working Burnley side were relegated from the Premier League.

Burnley lacked the necessary quality two seasons ago and without some bold moves in the transfer market they run the risk of following the same path.

Playing 4-4-2 was an effective tactic in the second tier, but it may prove costly in the top flight as teams with greater quality will dominate them in midfield.

Longest run without a loss: 23
Longest run without a win: 6
Highest/lowest league position: 1/7
Clean sheets: 20
Yellow cards: 50 **Red cards:** 0
Average attendance: 16,250
Players used: 25
Leading scorer: A Gray 23 (7,17)

	2015-16		Last six seasons at home							
	H	A	P	W	D	L	OV	UN	BS	CS
Leicester			5	1	0	4	2	3	1	1
Arsenal			1	0	0	1	0	1	0	0
Tottenham			1	0	1	0	0	1	0	1
Man City			1	1	0	0	0	1	0	1
Man United			1	0	1	0	0	1	0	1
Southampton			2	1	1	0	0	2	1	1
West Ham			2	0	1	1	2	0	2	0
Liverpool			1	0	0	1	0	1	0	0
Stoke			1	0	1	0	0	1	0	1
Chelsea			1	0	0	1	1	0	1	0
Everton			1	0	0	1	1	0	1	0
Swansea			2	1	0	1	1	1	1	0
Watford			4	1	3	0	2	2	3	1
West Brom			1	0	1	0	1	0	1	0
Crystal Palace			4	2	1	1	1	3	2	2
Bournemouth			1	0	1	0	0	1	1	0
Sunderland			1	0	1	0	0	1	0	1
Burnley										
Middlesbrough	D	L	5	1	2	2	1	4	2	1
Hull	W	L	5	4	0	1	1	4	0	4

Season	Division	Pos	P	W	D	L	F	A	GD	Pts
2015-16	Championship	1	46	26	15	5	72	35	+37	93
2014-15	Premier League	19	38	7	12	19	28	53	-25	33
2013-14	Championship	2	46	26	15	5	72	37	+35	93

Over/Under 46%/54% 11th **Both score** 48%/52% 17th

Key stat: Burnley are unbeaten in their last 23 league fixtures. They last tasted defeat when losing 3-0 at Hull on Boxing Day

2015-16 Championship appearances

	P	G		Y	R
S Arfield	46	8		5	-
A Barnes	1 (7)	0		1	-
J Barton	37 (1)	3		9	-
G Boyd	42 (2)	5		2	-
T Darikwa	21	1		1	-
M Duff	23 (1)	0		1	-
L Dyer	0 (3)	0		-	-
A Gray	41	23		2	-
T Heaton	46	0		-	-
R Hennings	3 (23)	1		-	-
D Jones	39 (2)	1		2	-
L Jutkiewicz	3 (2)	0		-	-
M Keane	44	5		3	-
M Kightly	12 (6)	0		2	-
C Long	1 (9)	0		1	-
M Lowton	25 (2)	1		4	-
D Marney	7 (5)	0		3	-
B Mee	46	2		9	-
M Sordell	0 (3)	0		-	-
J Tarkowski	2 (2)	0		-	-
M Taylor	1 (26)	4		-	-

	P	G		Y	R
F Ulvestad	1 (4)	0		1	-
S Vokes	39 (4)	15		1	-
J Vossen	3 (1)	0		-	-
S Ward	23 (1)	1		2	-

Sean Dyche brought Burnley straight back up

CHELSEA

Nickname: The Blues
Colours: Blue
Ground: Stamford Bridge   **Capacity:** 41,798
Tel: 0207-958-2190   www.chelseafc.com

A new era dawns for Chelsea, who are preparing for their first season without European football since 1996-97.

Chelsea's fall from grace last term was truly spectacular as they mustered just 50 points – a drop off of 37 points from the previous campaign.

Improvement is likely under Antonio Conte but it may not be sufficient to get Chelsea into title or top-four contention.

Jose Mourinho made a complete hash of the first three months of Chelsea's 2015-16 campaign, but his removal has not solved all of the club's problems.

Conte inherits an ageing squad and recovery could take longer than expected.

Manchester United are an example of how difficult it can be to arrest a sudden decline in performance and Chelsea may have to go through a similar process.

Longest run without a loss: 15
Longest run without a win: 4
Highest/lowest league position: 9/17
Clean sheets: 9
Yellow cards: 60 **Red cards:** 5
Average attendance: 41,517
Players used: 28
Leading scorer: D Costa 12 (6,11)

2015-16	H	A	Last six seasons at home P	W	D	L	OV	UN	BS	CS
Leicester	D	L	2	1	1	0	0	2	1	1
Arsenal	W	W	6	5	0	1	3	3	2	4
Tottenham	D	D	6	3	3	0	5	1	3	3
Man City	L	L	6	3	2	1	3	3	3	2
Man United	D	D	6	3	2	1	4	2	5	1
Southampton	L	W	4	1	2	1	3	1	4	0
West Ham	L	L	5	3	2	0	2	3	1	4
Liverpool	L	D	6	1	2	3	3	5	0	
Stoke	D	L	6	5	1	0	2	4	2	4
Chelsea										
Everton	D	L	6	4	2	0	3	3	4	2
Swansea	D	L	5	4	1	0	3	2	3	2
Watford	D	D	1	0	1	0	1	0	1	0
West Brom	D	W	6	4	2	0	4	2	3	3
Crystal Palace	L	W	3	2	0	1	2	1	2	1
Bournemouth	L	L	1	0	0	1	0	1	0	0
Sunderland	W	L	6	4	0	2	5	1	4	1
Burnley			1	0	1	0	0	1	1	0
Middlesbrough			-	-	-	-	-	-	-	-
Hull			2	2	0	0	0	2	0	2

Season	Division	Pos	P	W	D	L	F	A	GD	Pts
2015-16	Premier League	10	38	12	14	12	59	53	+6	50
2014-15	Premier League	1	38	26	9	3	73	32	+41	87
2013-14	Premier League	3	38	25	7	6	71	27	+44	82

Over/Under 63%/37% 2nd   **Both score** 63%/37% 2nd

Key stat: Chelsea won just five home league games last season – the joint-second lowest tally in the league alongside Bournemouth

2015-16 Premier League appearances

	P	G	Y	R		P	G	Y	R
T Abraham	0 (2)	0	-	-	Ramires	7 (5)	2	1	-
C Azpilicueta	36 (1)	2	7	-	L Remy	3 (10)	1	-	-
A Begovic	15 (2)	0	-	-	J Terry	24	1	3	2
G Cahill	21 (2)	2	2	-	F Tomori	0 (1)	0	-	-
J Clarke-Salter	0 (1)	0	-	-	B Traore	4 (6)	2	-	-
D Costa	27 (1)	12	8	-	Willian	32 (3)	5	5	-
T Courtois	23	0	1	2	K Zouma	21 (2)	1	-	-
J Cuadrado	0 (1)	0	-	0					
C Fabregas	33 (4)	5	5	-					
R Falcao	1 (9)	1	1	-					
E Hazard	25 (6)	4	2	-					
B Ivanovic	33	2	5	-					
Kenedy	4 (10)	1	-	-					
R Loftus-Cheek	4 (9)	1	-	-					
N Matic	28 (5)	2	5	1					
M Miazga	2	0	1	-					
J Mikel	19 (6)	0	6	-					
Oscar	20 (7)	3	4	-					
A Pato	1 (1)	1	-	-					
Pedro	24 (5)	7	3	-					
B Rahman	11 (4)	0	1	-					

Diego Costa got 12 goals in a miserable season

Nickname: The Eagles
Colours: Red and blue
Ground: Selhurst Park **Capacity:** 25,456
Tel: 020-8768-6000 www.cpfc.co.uk

Crystal Palace suffered an alarming decline in performance over the second half of last season but that doesn't necessarily mean they are set for a tough time in 2016-17.

The FA Cup proved a major distraction for Palace in the final few months. They saved some of their best performances for the cup, winning 2-1 at Southampton and 1-0 at Tottenham, and showed they remain a force to be reckoned with when fully focused on the task at hand.

Manager Alan Pardew is a very safe pair of hands and has no need to make drastic alterations unless the plan is to turn Palace into top-six challengers.

Top of the shopping list will be a new striker. Connor Wickham often flatters to deceive and Dwight Gayle has been sold to Newcastle.

Longest run without a loss: 6
Longest run without a win: 14
Highest/lowest league position: 4/16
Clean sheets: 8
Yellow cards: 61 **Red cards:** 2
Average attendance: 24,703 **Players used:** 30
Leading scorer: Y Bolasie 5 (2,4), Y Cabaye 5 (2,5), S Dann 5 (3,5), C Wickham 5 (1,1)

	2015-16 H	2015-16 A	Last six seasons at home P	W	D	L	OV	UN	BS	CS
Leicester	L	L	5	2	1	2	3	2	3	1
Arsenal	L	D	3	0	0	3	2	1	2	0
Tottenham	L	L	3	1	0	2	2	1	2	0
Man City	L	L	3	1	0	2	1	2	1	0
Man United	D	L	3	0	1	2	1	2	1	1
Southampton	W	L	4	1	0	3	1	3	1	1
West Ham	L	D	4	1	1	2	3	1	3	1
Liverpool	L	W	3	1	1	3	0	3	0	0
Stoke	W	W	3	2	1	0	1	2	2	1
Chelsea	L	W	3	1	0	2	2	1	1	1
Everton	D	D	3	0	2	1	0	3	0	2
Swansea	D	D	4	1	1	2	1	3	0	2
Watford	L	W	4	2	0	2	4	0	3	1
West Brom	W	L	3	2	0	1	1	2	1	1
Crystal Palace										
Bournemouth	L	D	1	0	0	1	1	0	1	0
Sunderland	L	D	3	1	0	2	2	1	2	0
Burnley			4	2	2	0	1	3	1	3
Middlesbrough			3	2	0	1	1	2	1	1
Hull			5	2	2	1	1	4	1	3

Season	Division	Pos	P	W	D	L	F	A	GD	Pts
2015-16	Premier League	15	38	11	9	18	39	51	-12	42
2014-15	Premier League	10	38	13	9	16	47	51	-4	48
2013-14	Premier League	11	38	13	6	19	33	48	-15	45

Over/Under 50%/50% 14th **Both score** 53%/47% 9th

Key stat: No Crystal Palace player scored more than five league goals last season

2015-16 Premier League appearances

	P	G		Y	R		P	G		Y	R
M Adebayor	7 (5)	1		1	-	P N'Diaye Souare	34	0		6	1
P Bamford	0 (6)	0		-	-	J Puncheon	31	2		3	-
H Boateng	0 (1)	0		-	-	B Sako	11 (9)	2		1	-
Y Bolasie	23 (3)	5		2	-	J Speroni	2	0		-	-
Y Cabaye	32 (1)	5		7	-	J Ward	30	2		4	-
F Campbell	4 (7)	0		1	-	C Wickham	15 (6)	5		1	-
M Chamakh	1 (9)	0		1	-	W Zaha	30 (4)	2		5	-
S Dann	35	5		7	-						
D Delaney	32	2		2	-						
D Gayle	8 (8)	3		2	1						
B Hangeland	7	0		2	-						
W Hennessey	29	0		1	-						
M Jedinak	16 (11)	0		6	-						
M Kelly	11 (2)	0		3	-						
J Ledley	11 (8)	1		1	-						
Lee Chung-Yong	4 (9)	1		-	-						
A Mariappa	7	0		-	-						
J McArthur	26 (2)	2		5	-						
A McCarthy	7	0		-	-						
G Murray	2	0		-	-						
J Mutch	7 (13)	0		-	-						

Palace's season ended in Wembley heartbreak

EVERTON

Nickname: The Toffees
Colours: Blue and white
Ground: Goodison Park **Capacity:** 39,571
Tel: 0870-442-1878 www.evertonfc.com

Continuity has often been Everton's watchword but that may all change now that Farhad Moshiri has taken a controlling stake in the club.

Everton have long craved an injection of funds but the immediate priority must be to get more out of the current squad – with the exception of Chelsea, few teams underperformed more than the Toffees last season.

Simply doing the basics better would have made a huge difference and former manager Roberto Martinez has to take some of the blame as his team lost far too many games against the run of play.

Poor home form also needs addressing. They wrapped up the home schedule with wins over Bournemouth and Norwich but ended with just six league wins at Goodison – the lowest since 2000-01.

Longest run without a loss: 6
Longest run without a win: 7
Highest/lowest league position: 5/12
Clean sheets: 10
Yellow cards: 47 **Red cards:** 5
Average attendance: 38,163
Players used: 31
Leading scorer: R Lukaku 18 (4,14)

	2015-16		Last six seasons at home							
	H	A	P	W	D	L	OV	UN	BS	CS
Leicester	L	L	2	0	1	1	2	0	2	0
Arsenal	L	L	6	1	2	3	3	3	3	1
Tottenham	D	D	6	3	2	1	2	4	3	2
Man City	L	D	6	3	1	2	2	4	3	2
Man United	L	L	6	3	1	2	3	3	1	3
Southampton	D	W	4	3	1	0	2	2	3	1
West Ham	L	D	5	3	1	1	3	2	3	2
Liverpool	D	L	6	1	4	1	2	4	3	2
Stoke	L	W	6	3	0	3	2	4	1	3
Chelsea	W	D	6	4	0	2	3	3	3	3
Everton										
Swansea	L	D	5	2	2	1	2	3	2	3
Watford	D	D	1	0	1	0	1	0	1	0
West Brom	L	W	6	2	2	2	2	4	2	3
Crystal Palace	D	D	3	0	1	2	2	1	3	0
Bournemouth	W	W	1	1	0	0	1	0	1	0
Sunderland	W	L	6	4	0	2	3	3	2	2
Burnley			1	1	0	0	0	1	0	1
Middlesbrough			-	-	-	-	-	-	-	-
Hull			2	1	1	0	1	1	2	0

Season	Division	Pos	P	W	D	L	F	A	GD	Pts
2015-16	Premier League	11	38	11	14	13	59	55	+4	47
2014-15	Premier League	11	38	12	11	15	48	50	-2	47
2013-14	Premier League	5	38	21	9	8	61	39	+22	72

Over/Under 58%/42% 4th **Both score** 55%/45% 6th

Key stat: Only one of Everton's 11 wins last season came against a team that finished in the top eight

2015-16 Premier League appearances

	P	G	Y	R		P	G	Y	R
L Baines	16 (2)	2	-	-	K Mirallas	10 (13)	4	1	2
R Barkley	36 (2)	8	4	-	S Naismith	4 (6)	3	1	-
G Barry	32 (1)	1	6	1	O Niasse	2 (3)	0	-	-
M Besic	7 (5)	0	1	-	L Osman	2 (7)	0	-	-
T Browning	3 (2)	0	1	-	B Oviedo	12 (2)	0	-	-
T Cleverley	17 (5)	2	1	-	S Pienaar	0 (4)	0	-	-
S Coleman	27 (1)	1	4	-	J Robles	13	0	1	-
T Davies	1 (1)	0	-	-	J Stones	31 (2)	0	3	-
G Deulofeu	16 (10)	2	2	-					
K Dowell	1 (1)	0	-	-					
R Funes Mori	24 (4)	4	4	1					
B Galloway	14 (1)	0	2	-					
D Gibson	2 (5)	0	3	-					
T Hibbert	0 (1)	0	-	-					
T Howard	25	0	1	-					
P Jagielka	21	0	-	-					
J Kenny	0 (1)	0	-	-					
A Kone	16 (9)	5	1	-					
A Lennon	17 (8)	5	1	-					
R Lukaku	36 (1)	18	3	-					
J McCarthy	29	2	6	1					

Romelu Lukaku scored 18 league goals

HULL

1904

Nickname: The Tigers
Colours: Amber and black
Ground: The KC Stadium   **Capacity:** 25,404
Tel: 0870-837-0003   www.hullcityafc.net

Playoff victors have the least amount of time to prepare for a step up and Hull must be careful not to follow in the footsteps of QPR and Norwich, who were relegated a year after their Wembley wins.

Steve Bruce's side were inconsistent last term but produced a big display when it mattered in the playoff final.

Their defensive record of 35 goals conceded was as good as Burnley's, and understandably so because centre-backs Curtis Davies and Michael Dawson are both former England internationals. But they were less convincing in attack and relied too much on Abel Hernandez, who scored just four goals in 25 games in his debut Premier League season.

Hernandez will have to do much better this season or Hull could find themselves dragged into a relegation battle.

Longest run without a loss: 11
Longest run without a win: 5
Highest/lowest league position: 1/5
Clean sheets: 20
Yellow cards: 59 **Red cards:** 1
Average attendance: 17,279
Players used: 27
Leading scorer: A Hernandez 20 (8,18)

	2015-16		Last six seasons at home							
	H	A	P	W	D	L	OV	UN	BS	CS
Leicester	4	1	1	2	1	3	1	1
Arsenal	2	0	0	2	2	0	1	0
Tottenham	2	0	1	1	1	1	2	0
Man City	2	0	0	2	1	1	1	0
Man United	2	0	1	1	1	1	1	1
Southampton	3	0	0	3	0	3	0	0
West Ham	3	1	1	1	1	2	1	1
Liverpool	2	2	0	0	1	1	1	1
Stoke	2	0	2	0	0	2	1	1
Chelsea	2	0	0	2	1	1	1	0
Everton	2	1	0	1	0	2	0	1
Swansea	3	2	0	1	0	3	0	2
Watford	3	1	1	1	1	2	1	1
West Brom	2	1	1	0	0	2	0	2
Crystal Palace	5	1	2	2	0	5	1	2
Bournemouth	-	-	-	-	-	-	-	-
Sunderland	2	1	1	0	0	2	1	1
Burnley	W	L	5	1	0	4	2	3	1	1
Middlesbrough	W	L	4	3	0	1	3	1	2	2
Hull								

Season	Division	Pos	P	W	D	L	F	A	GD	Pts
2015-16	Championship	4	46	24	11	11	69	35	+34	83
2014-15	Premier League	18	38	8	11	19	33	51	-18	35
2013-14	Premier League	16	38	10	7	21	38	53	-15	37

Over/Under 35%/65% 22nd   **Both score** 37%/63% 23rd

Key stat: Hull have lost only one of their last 24 home league games

2015-16 Championship appearances

	P	G	Y	R		P	G	Y	R
C Akpom	19 (17)	3	2	-	D Meyler	20 (8)	2	3	-
S Aluko	8 (17)	3	-	-	M Odubajo	45	0	8	1
A Bruce	9 (3)	1	1	-	N Powell	0 (3)	0	-	-
S Clucas	39 (9)	6	5	-	A Robertson	44 (1)	3	5	-
C Davies	40 (2)	2	4	-	R Snodgrass	21 (6)	4	2	-
M Dawson	35	1	7	-	R Taylor	1 (3)	0	-	-
M Diame	34 (7)	10	2	-					
A Diomande	3 (8)	3	-	-					
A Elmohamady	31 (10)	3	2	-					
I Hayden	3 (9)	1	5	-					
A Hernandez	37 (5)	21	3	-					
T Huddlestone	27 (13)	2	4	-					
C Jahraldo-Martin	0 (1)	0	-	-					
E Jakupovic	5	0	-	-					
N Jelavic	3 (1)	1	-	-					
B Lenihan	1	0	-	-					
J Livermore	36 (1)	4	9	-					
G Luer	0 (2)	0	-	-					
H Maguire	17 (7)	0	4	-					
S Maloney	8 (12)	1	-	-					
A McGregor	44	0	1	-					

Hull were deserved winners in the playoff final

LEICESTER

Nickname: The Foxes
Colours: Blue
Ground: King Power Stadium **Capacity:** 32,312
Tel: 0844-815-6000 www.lcfc.co.uk

Uncharted territory beckons for Leicester, who have a title defence and a first ever Champions League adventure to look forward to.

They could make an impact in the Champions League group stage because as English champions they are placed in pot one so will avoid Europe's elite clubs.

However, they are likely to be distracted from domestic matters and any loss of focus could be damaging for a side which has worked so hard at getting the fine details just right.

They also relied heavily on certain key individuals and a lot will depend on how much of their title-winning squad remains intact.

Do well in the transfer market and a top-four push is possible. Get it wrong and they could drop into the bottom half.

Longest run without a loss: 12
Longest run without a win: 3
Highest/lowest league position: 1/8
Clean sheets: 15
Yellow cards: 51 **Red cards:** 3
Average attendance: 32,013
Players used: 23
Leading scorer: J Vardy 24 (12,19)

	2015-16		Last six seasons at home							
	H	A	P	W	D	L	OV	UN	BS	CS
Leicester										
Arsenal	L	L	2	0	1	1	1	1	2	0
Tottenham	D	W	2	0	1	1	1	1	2	0
Man City	D	W	2	0	1	1	0	2	0	1
Man United	D	D	2	1	1	0	1	1	2	0
Southampton	W	D	3	3	0	0	1	2	1	2
West Ham	D	W	3	1	1	1	3	0	3	0
Liverpool	D	L	2	1	0	1	1	1	1	1
Stoke	W	D	2	1	0	1	1	1	0	1
Chelsea	W	D	2	1	0	1	2	0	2	0
Everton	W	W	2	1	1	0	2	0	2	0
Swansea	W	W	3	3	0	0	2	1	1	2
Watford	W	W	5	3	1	1	4	1	4	1
West Brom	D	W	2	0	1	1	1	1	1	0
Crystal Palace	W	W	5	2	1	2	2	3	2	2
Bournemouth	D	W	2	1	1	0	1	1	1	1
Sunderland	W	W	2	1	1	0	1	1	1	1
Burnley			5	2	3	0	3	2	3	2
Middlesbrough			4	2	2	0	1	3	1	3
Hull			4	2	2	0	2	2	3	1

Season	Division	Pos	P	W	D	L	F	A	GD	Pts
2015-16	Premier League	1	38	23	12	3	68	36	+32	81
2014-15	Premier League	14	38	11	8	19	46	55	-9	41
2013-14	Championship	1	46	31	9	6	83	43	+40	102

Over/Under 53%/47% 7th   **Both score** 58%/42% 4th

Key stat: Leicester are unbeaten in their last 15 Premier League home fixtures

2015-16 Premier League appearances

	P	G	Y	R
M Albrighton	34 (4)	2	4	-
D Amartey	1 (4)	0	-	-
Y Benalouane	0 (4)	0	1	-
J Dodoo	0 (1)	0	-	-
D Drinkwater	35	2	4	-
N Dyer	0 (13)	1	1	-
C Fuchs	30 (2)	0	4	-
D Gray	1 (11)	0	-	-
R Huth	35	0	8	-
G Inler	3 (2)	0	-	-
N Kante	33 (4)	1	3	-
A King	9 (15)	2	2	-
A Kramaric	0 (2)	0	-	-
R Mahrez	36 (1)	17	1	-
W Morgan	38	2	3	-
S Okazaki	28 (8)	0	1	-
J Schlupp	14 (10)	1	4	-
K Schmeichel	38	0	2	-
D Simpson	30	0	3	1
L Ulloa	7 (22)	6	-	-
J Vardy	36	24	5	1

	P	G	Y	R
M Wasilewski	3 (1)	0	2	-
R de Laet	7 (5)	1	1	-

Claudio Ranieri was crowned king of Leicester

LIVERPOOL

Nickname: The Reds
Colours: Red
Ground: Anfield **Capacity:** 45,276
Tel: 0151-263-2361 www.liverpoolfc.tv

Losing the Europa League final was a bitter pill for Liverpool to swallow and it will be interesting to see how they react.

Having no European football is a blow to the club's finances but will reduce the players' workload and make it easier for them to focus on the Premier League.

The jury is still out on whether Jurgen Klopp is the long-term answer to Liverpool's problems but there have been encouraging signs under the German.

Getting to the Europa League final was a major achievement and the undoubted highlight was the 5-4 aggregate win over Borussia Dortmund which demonstrated Liverpool's ability to compete with one of the strongest teams on the continent.

However, Liverpool's league results tailed off and an eighth-place finish was below the club's expectations.

Longest run without a loss: 6
Longest run without a win: 4
Highest/lowest league position: 6/10
Clean sheets: 11
Yellow cards: 64 **Red cards:** 3
Average attendance: 44,058
Players used: 34
Leading scorer: Roberto Firmino 10 (4,8)

	2015-16		Last six seasons at home							
	H	A	P	W	D	L	OV	UN	BS	CS
Leicester	W	L	2	1	1	0	1	1	1	1
Arsenal	D	D	6	1	3	2	4	2	5	0
Tottenham	D	D	6	3	2	1	3	3	3	2
Man City	W	W	6	4	2	0	5	1	4	2
Man United	L	L	6	2	1	3	3	3	4	1
Southampton	D	L	4	2	1	1	1	3	2	1
West Ham	L	L	5	3	1	1	3	2	1	3
Liverpool										
Stoke	W	W	6	4	2	0	1	5	1	5
Chelsea	D	W	6	2	2	2	3	3	4	1
Everton	W	D	6	3	3	0	4	2	2	4
Swansea	W	L	5	4	1	0	3	2	2	3
Watford	W	L	1	1	0	0	0	1	0	1
West Brom	D	D	6	3	1	2	3	3	3	1
Crystal Palace	L	W	3	1	0	2	3	0	3	0
Bournemouth	W	W	1	1	0	0	0	1	0	1
Sunderland	D	W	6	2	4	0	4	2	4	2
Burnley			1	1	0	0	0	1	0	1
Middlesbrough			-	-	-	-	-	-	-	-
Hull			2	1	1	0	0	2	0	2

Season	Division	Pos	P	W	D	L	F	A	GD	Pts
2015-16	Premier League	8	38	16	12	10	63	50	+13	60
2014-15	Premier League	6	38	18	8	12	52	48	+4	62
2013-14	Premier League	2	38	26	6	6	101	50	+51	84

Over/Under 53%/47% 7th **Both score** 55%/45% 6th

Key stat: Liverpool are unbeaten in their last 12 home matches since losing 1-0 to Stoke in the second leg of their League Cup semi-final

2015-16 Premier League appearances

	P	G	Y	R		P	G	Y	R
J Allen	8 (11)	2	-	-	D Origi	7 (9)	5	-	-
C Benteke	14 (15)	9	2	-	C Randall	2 (1)	0	-	-
A Bogdan	2	0	-	-	R Firmino	24 (7)	10	1	-
C Brannagan	1 (2)	0	-	-	J Rossiter	0 (1)	0	-	-
E Can	28 (2)	1	9	-	M Sakho	21 (1)	1	1	-
S Canos	0 (1)	0	-	-	M Skrtel	21 (1)	1	5	-
S Caulker	0 (3)	0	-	-	B Smith	3 (1)	0	2	1
P Chirivella	1	0	-	-	K Stewart	6 (1)	0	1	-
N Clyne	33	1	6	-	D Sturridge	11 (3)	8	-	-
P Coutinho	24 (2)	8	2	1	K Toure	9 (5)	1	1	-
J Flanagan	5	0	1	-	D Ward	2	0	-	-
J Gomez	5	0	3	-					
J Henderson	15 (2)	2	1	-					
J Ibe	12 (15)	1	-	-					
D Ings	3 (3)	2	1	-					
Joao Teixeira	0 (1)	0	-	-					
A Lallana	23 (7)	4	2	-					
D Lovren	22 (2)	0	2	-					
Lucas	21 (6)	0	8	-					
S Mignolet	34	0	2	-					
J Milner	28	5	10	1					
A Moreno Perez	28 (4)	1	3	-					
O Ojo	5 (3)	0	-	-					

Roberto Firmino top scored with just ten goals

MANCHESTER CITY

Nickname: The Citizens
Colours: Sky blue and white
Ground: Etihad Stadium   **Capacity:** 54,693
Tel: 0870-062-1894   www.mcfc.co.uk

Pep Guardiola has been appointed with the aim of taking Manchester City to the pinnacle of European football but it is the Premier League where there is greater room for improvement.

City finished 15 points behind Leicester and only secured Champions League football with the help of a massive leg up from West Ham, who beat Man United 3-2 in their final Upton Park fixture.

Many pundits have put City's poor league results down to the players not putting a shift in for Manuel Pellegrini, but that argument looks overly simplistic.

There were major structural problems with the City team, including the failing fitness of Vincent Kompany and ageing legs of Yaya Toure. Replacing those two giants will be tough and City will have to be smart with their transfer dealings.

Longest run without a loss: 7
Longest run without a win: 3
Highest/lowest league position: 1/4
Clean sheets: 16
Yellow cards: 61 **Red cards:** 0
Average attendance: 54,000
Players used: 25
Leading scorer: S Aguero 24 (5,15)

2015-16	H	A	P	W	D	L	OV	UN	BS	CS
Leicester	L	D	2	1	0	1	1	1	1	1
Arsenal	D	L	6	2	2	2	3	3	3	1
Tottenham	L	L	6	5	0	1	5	1	4	2
Man City										
Man United	L	D	6	3	1	2	2	4	2	3
Southampton	W	L	4	4	0	0	3	1	3	1
West Ham	L	D	5	4	0	1	3	2	3	2
Liverpool	L	L	6	4	1	1	6	0	4	2
Stoke	W	L	6	5	0	1	4	2	0	5
Chelsea	W	W	6	4	1	1	2	4	2	3
Everton	D	W	6	3	2	1	2	4	3	3
Swansea	W	D	5	5	0	0	4	1	2	3
Watford	W	W	1	1	0	0	0	1	0	1
West Brom	W	W	6	6	0	0	5	1	2	4
Crystal Palace	W	W	3	3	0	0	2	1	0	3
Bournemouth	W	W	1	1	0	0	1	0	1	0
Sunderland	W	W	6	4	2	0	6	0	4	2
Burnley			1	0	1	0	1	0	1	0
Middlesbrough	-	-	-	-	-	-	-	-	-	-
Hull			2	1	1	0	0	2	1	1

Season	Division	Pos	P	W	D	L	F	A	GD	Pts
2015-16	Premier League	4	38	19	9	10	71	41	+30	66
2014-15	Premier League	2	38	24	7	7	83	38	+45	79
2013-14	Premier League	1	38	27	5	6	102	37	+65	86

Over/Under 66%/34% 1st   **Both score** 50%/50% 11th

Key stat: Manchester City took three points from a possible 24 in their matches against teams who finished in the top five positions

---

2015-16 Premier League appearances

	P	G		Y	R
S Aguero	29 (1)	24		1	-
W Bony	13 (13)	4		1	-
W Caballero	3 (1)	0		-	-
B Celina	0 (1)	0		-	-
G Clichy	12 (2)	0		-	-
K De Bruyne	22 (3)	7		2	-
F Delph	8 (9)	2		-	-
M Demichelis	10 (10)	0		3	-
Fernandinho	31 (2)	2		8	-
Fernando	17 (7)	2		4	-
J Hart	35	0		-	-
K Iheanacho	7 (19)	8		1	-
A Kolarov	25 (4)	3		3	-
V Kompany	13 (1)	2		5	-
E Mangala	23	0		8	-
Manu Garcia	0 (1)	0		-	-
S Nasri	4 (8)	2		3	-
J Navas	24 (10)	0		1	-
N Otamendi	30	1		9	-
P Roberts	0 (1)	0		-	-
B Sagna	27 (1)	0		4	-

	P	G		Y	R
D Silva	22 (2)	2		1	-
R Sterling	23 (8)	6		1	-
Y Toure	28 (4)	6		3	-
P Zabaleta	12 (1)	0		3	-

Sergio Aguero stood out for disappointing City

MANCHESTER UNITED

Nickname: The Red Devils
Colours: Red and white
Ground: Old Trafford
Tel: 0870-442-1994

Capacity: 75,765
www.manutd.com

United entered the winner's enclosure for the first time since the Alex Ferguson era by claiming last season's FA Cup but have their eyes fixed on bigger prizes after luring Jose Mourinho to Old Trafford.

A pursuit of the Champions League trophy will have to wait but United expect to feature prominently in the Premier League title race and are giving Mourinho freedom to reshape the squad.

Mourinho has a history of making an immediate impact, taking league titles in his first year at Porto, Chelsea and Inter, but might need a little more time to put United back at the top of English football.

Never in his career has Mourinho taken on a club outside of the top four and the rebuild at United looks tricky as many underperforming players are on massive contracts and will be hard to shift.

Longest run without a loss: 7
Longest run without a win: 6
Highest/lowest league position: 1/6
Clean sheets: 18
Yellow cards: 66 **Red cards:** 1
Average attendance: 75,335
Players used: 33
Leading scorer: A Martial 11 (3,9)

	2015-16 H	A	Last six seasons at home P	W	D	L	OV	UN	BS	CS
Leicester	D	D	2	1	1	0	1	1	2	0
Arsenal	W	L	6	5	1	0	3	3	4	2
Tottenham	W	L	6	4	0	2	4	2	2	4
Man City	D	W	6	2	1	3	5	1	4	1
Man United										
Southampton	L	W	4	1	1	2	1	3	2	0
West Ham	D	L	5	4	1	0	3	2	2	3
Liverpool	W	W	6	5	0	1	6	0	4	1
Stoke	W	L	6	6	0	0	5	1	4	2
Chelsea	D	D	6	2	3	1	2	4	3	2
Everton	W	W	6	4	1	1	2	4	2	3
Swansea	W	L	5	4	0	1	3	2	3	2
Watford	W	W	1	1	0	0	0	1	0	1
West Brom	W	L	6	3	1	2	2	4	2	3
Crystal Palace	W	D	3	3	0	0	0	3	0	3
Bournemouth	W	L	1	1	0	0	1	0	1	0
Sunderland	W	L	6	5	0	1	2	4	1	4
Burnley			1	1	0	0	1	0	1	0
Middlesbrough			-	-	-	-	-	-	-	-
Hull			2	2	0	0	2	0	1	1

Season	Division	Pos	P	W	D	L	F	A	GD	Pts
2015-16	Premier League	5	38	19	9	10	49	35	+14	66
2014-15	Premier League	4	38	20	10	8	62	37	+25	70
2013-14	Premier League	7	38	19	7	12	64	43	+21	64

Over/Under 45%/55% 19th   **Both score** 39%/61% 20th

Key stat: United never finished lower than third in their last 22 seasons under Alex Ferguson. In three seasons since, they haven't finished higher than fourth

2015-16 Premier League appearances

	P	G	Y	R		P	G	Y	R
D Blind	35	1	2	-	M Schneiderlin	25 (4)	1	3	-
C Borthwick-Jackson	6 (4)	0	-	-	B Schweinsteiger	13 (5)	1	3	-
M Carrick	22 (6)	0	4	-	L Shaw	5	0	1	-
M Darmian	24 (4)	1	8	-	C Smalling	35	0	8	-
M Depay	16 (12)	2	2	-	L Valencia	8 (6)	0	1	-
M Fellaini	12 (6)	1	2	-	G Varela	3 (1)	0	1	-
T Fosu-Mensah	2 (6)	0	1	-	J Weir	0 (1)	0	-	-
J Hernandez	0 (1)	0	6	-	J Wilson	0 (1)	0	-	-
A Herrera	17 (10)	3	4	-	A Young	11 (7)	1	5	-
A Januzaj	2 (3)	1	1	-	D de Gea	34	0	-	-
P Jones	6 (4)	0	-	-					
W Keane	0 (1)	0	-	-					
J Lingard	19 (6)	4	4	-					
D Love	0 (1)	0	-	-					
A Martial	29 (2)	11	2	-					
J Mata	34 (4)	6	5	1					
P McNair	3 (5)	0	-	-					
A Pereira	0 (4)	0	2	-					
N Powell	0 (1)	0	-	-					
M Rashford	11	5	-	-					
M Rojo	15 (1)	0	3	-					
S Romero	4	0	-	-					
W Rooney	27 (1)	8	4	-					

Anthony Martial impressed upon his arrival

MIDDLESBROUGH

Nickname: Boro
Colours: Red and white
Ground: Riverside Stadium   **Capacity:** 34,998
Tel: 0844-499-6789   www.mfc.co.uk

Middlesbrough's seven-year exile from the Premier League is over but they have a massive battle on their hands to re-establish themselves in the top flight.

Goalscorers are invaluable at this level and Boro lack genuine quality up front.

Uruguayan Cristhian Stuani was their top marksman with just 11 goals in all competitions and he is preparing for his first taste of English top-flight football.

Jordan Rhodes is a more natural talent and has been prolific in the second and third tiers, but he may lack the pace and power to make an impact at the top level.

Defensively, Boro look better prepared. Centre-back Daniel Ayala possesses the physicality and composure required to lead the back line and 28-year-old attacking left-back George Friend finally gets to play at the level his talent deserves.

Longest run without a loss: 10
Longest run without a win: 5
Highest/lowest league position: 1/6
Clean sheets: 22
Yellow cards: 66 **Red cards:** 2
Average attendance: 23,605
Players used: 27
Leading scorer: D Nugent 8 (4,8)

2015-16	H	A	Last six seasons at home							
			P	W	D	L	OV	UN	BS	CS
Leicester	4	0	2	2	3	1	3	1
Arsenal	-	-	-	-	-	-	-	-
Tottenham	-	-	-	-	-	-	-	-
Man City	-	-	-	-	-	-	-	-
Man United	-	-	-	-	-	-	-	-
Southampton	1	1	0	0	1	0	1	0
West Ham	1	0	0	1	0	1	0	0
Liverpool	-	-	-	-	-	-	-	-
Stoke	-	-	-	-	-	-	-	-
Chelsea	-	-	-	-	-	-	-	-
Everton	-	-	-	-	-	-	-	-
Swansea	1	0	0	1	1	0	1	0
Watford	5	2	2	1	3	2	4	1
West Brom	-	-	-	-	-	-	-	-
Crystal Palace	3	2	1	0	2	1	2	1
Bournemouth	2	0	2	0	1	1	1	1
Sunderland	-	-	-	-	-	-	-	-
Burnley	W	D	5	4	0	1	2	3	2	2
Middlesbrough										
Hull	W	L	4	3	1	0	1	3	1	3

Season	Division	Pos	P	W	D	L	F	A	GD	Pts
2015-16	Championship	2	46	26	11	9	63	31	+32	89
2014-15	Championship	4	46	25	10	11	68	37	+31	85
2013-14	Championship	12	46	16	16	14	62	50	+12	64

Over/Under 37%/63% 20th   **Both score** 35%/65% 24th

Key stat: Middlesbrough had the meanest defence in the top four tiers of English football last season, conceding 31 goals in 46 league games

2015-16 Championship appearances

	P	G		Y	R		P	G		Y	R
A Adomah	36 (7)	6		1	-	J Stephens	0 (1)	0		-	-
F Amorebieta	11 (2)	0		5	-	C Stuani	20 (16)	7		4	-
D Ayala	34 (1)	3		7	-	Y Wildschut	1	0		-	-
A Clayton	41 (2)	1		13	-	B Zuculini	3 (2)	0		-	-
C De Pena	3 (3)	0		3	-	R de Laet	9 (1)	0		-	-
S Downing	40 (5)	3		1	-	J de Sart	0 (2)	0		-	-
D Fabbrini	14 (8)	4		4	-						
A Forshaw	9 (20)	2		-	-						
G Friend	39 (1)	1		2	-						
D Fry	7	0		-	-						
B Gibson	32 (1)	1		5	1						
T Kalas	19 (7)	0		1	-						
Kike	10 (9)	4		1	-						
D Konstantopoulos	46	0		-	-						
G Leadbitter	39 (2)	4		11	-						
E Nsue	37 (3)	3		2	-						
D Nugent	24 (14)	8		3	1						
G Ramirez	15 (3)	7		1	-						
A Reach	3 (1)	1		-	-						
J Rhodes	13 (5)	6		1	-						
E Sola	1 (1)	0		1	-						

Four of Stuani's 11 goals came in the League Cup

SOUTHAMPTON

Nickname: The Saints
Colours: Red and white
Ground: St Mary's Stadium **Capacity:** 32,689
Tel: 0845-688-9448 www.saintsfc.co.uk

Southampton continue to make progress irrespective of who manages the club, and Saints' next target will be to improve on the 63 points achieved last term.

Involvement in the Europa League last season did not extend beyond the qualifying rounds, but they go straight into the group stage this time and it will be interesting to see how they cope with the demands of Thursday night football.

There is depth to the squad and Saints were strong in attack, with Graziano Pelle, Shane Long and Sadio Mane all hitting double figures last season.

Success will again lead to interest in their key men – Mane and Pelle have already left – but they coped well with the sales of Nathaniel Clyne and Morgan Schneiderlin last term and are experts in replacing departees with new star men.

Longest run without a loss: 6
Longest run without a win: 5
Highest/lowest league position: 6/13
Clean sheets: 12
Yellow cards: 60 **Red cards:** 6
Average attendance: 30,399
Players used: 26
Leading scorer: G Pelle 11 (4,9) S Mane 11 (1,8)

	2015-16		Last six seasons at home							
	H	A	P	W	D	L	OV	UN	BS	CS
Leicester	D	L	3	1	1	1	1	2	1	1
Arsenal	W	D	4	2	2	0	2	2	2	2
Tottenham	L	W	4	0	1	3	3	1	3	0
Man City	W	L	4	2	1	1	3	1	3	0
Man United	L	W	4	0	1	3	3	1	4	0
Southampton										
West Ham	W	L	5	2	3	0	0	5	1	4
Liverpool	W	D	4	2	0	2	3	1	2	0
Stoke	L	W	4	1	2	1	1	3	2	1
Chelsea	L	W	4	1	1	2	3	1	3	0
Everton	L	D	4	2	1	1	2	2	0	3
Swansea	W	W	4	2	1	1	1	3	2	1
Watford	W	D	2	2	0	0	1	1	0	2
West Brom	W	D	4	2	1	1	2	2	0	3
Crystal Palace	W	L	4	4	0	0	1	3	1	3
Bournemouth	W	L	2	2	0	0	2	0	2	2
Sunderland	D	W	4	1	2	1	1	3	2	1
Burnley			2	2	0	0	0	2	0	2
Middlesbrough			1	1	0	0	1	0	0	1
Hull			3	3	0	0	2	1	2	1

Season	Division	Pos	P	W	D	L	F	A	GD	Pts
2015-16	Premier League	6	38	18	9	11	59	41	+18	63
2014-15	Premier League	7	38	18	6	14	54	33	+21	60
2013-14	Premier League	8	38	15	11	12	54	46	+8	56

Over/Under 50%/50% 14th   **Both score** 50%/50% 11th

Key stat: Southampton have improved their points tally in each of the last three seasons

2015-16 Premier League appearances

	P	G	Y	R
C Austin	2 (5)	1	-	-
R Bertrand	32	1	6	-
S Caulker	1 (2)	0	-	-
J Clasie	20 (2)	0	5	-
K Davis	1	0	-	-
S Davis	31 (3)	5	4	-
J Fonte	37	2	4	1
F Forster	18	0	-	-
P Gazzaniga	2	0	-	-
Juanmi	0 (12)	0	-	-
S Long	23 (5)	10	2	-
S Mane	30 (7)	11	5	2
C Martina	11 (4)	1	1	-
G Pelle	23 (7)	11	6	-
G Ramirez	0 (3)	0	-	-
H Reed	0 (1)	0	-	-
J Rodriguez	3 (9)	0	1	-
O Romeu	17 (12)	1	7	-
C Soares	23 (1)	0	3	-
M Stekelenburg	17	0	-	-
D Tadic	27 (7)	7	2	-

	P	G	Y	R
M Targett	13 (1)	0	1	-
V Wanyama	29 (1)	1	6	3
J Ward-Prowse	14 (19)	2	5	-
M Yoshida	10 (10)	1	-	-
V van Dijk	34	3	2	-

Graziano Pelle led a potent Saints front line

STOKE

Nickname: The Potters
Colours: Red and white
Ground: Bet365 Stadium
Tel: 0871-663-2008

Capacity: 27,740
www.stokecityfc.com

A measure of Stoke's progress is the fact that last season's ninth place was greeted with no great fanfare.

It was the third-successive ninth place the Potters have registered, remaining as high as they have finished in any top-flight campaign since 1974-75.

They also went close to silverware, losing to Liverpool in a League Cup semi-final penalty shootout, and put in some impressive performances against the big fish, registering home wins over Chelsea, Manchester City and Manchester United.

The January raid for Gianelli Imbula suggests Stoke's ambition is undiminished and there may yet be scope for them to get among the battle for European places.

But the Potters were the lowest scorers of the top 12 teams so a striker is sure to be high on their summer shopping list.

Longest run without a loss: 4
Longest run without a win: 6
Highest/lowest league position: 7/17
Clean sheets: 10
Yellow cards: 52 **Red cards:** 4
Average attendance: 27,483
Players used: 27
Leading scorer: M Arnautovic 11 (5,9)

2015-16	H	A	Last six seasons at home P	W	D	L	OV	UN	BS	CS
Leicester	D	L	2	0	1	1	1	1	1	0
Arsenal	D	L	6	3	3	0	2	4	3	3
Tottenham	L	D	6	2	0	4	5	1	3	1
Man City	W	L	6	1	4	1	1	5	4	2
Man United	W	W	6	2	2	2	2	4	4	1
Southampton	L	W	4	1	2	1	3	1	4	0
West Ham	W	D	5	2	2	1	3	2	4	0
Liverpool	L	L	6	4	0	2	3	3	3	2
Stoke										
Chelsea	W	D	6	2	2	2	2	4	2	2
Everton	L	W	6	2	3	1	1	5	3	2
Swansea	D	W	5	3	2	0	2	3	3	2
Watford	L	W	1	0	0	1	0	1	0	0
West Brom	L	L	6	1	3	2	1	5	2	3
Crystal Palace	L	L	3	1	0	2	3	0	3	0
Bournemouth	W	W	1	1	0	0	1	0	1	0
Sunderland	D	L	6	2	3	1	1	5	3	2
Burnley			1	0	0	1	1	0	1	0
Middlesbrough			-	-	-	-	-	-	-	-
Hull			2	2	0	0	0	2	0	2

Season	Division	Pos	P	W	D	L	F	A	GD	Pts
2015-16	Premier League	9	38	14	9	15	41	55	-14	51
2014-15	Premier League	9	38	15	9	14	48	45	+3	54
2013-14	Premier League	9	38	13	11	14	45	52	-7	50

Over/Under 53%/47% 7th

Both score 47%/53% 14th

Key stat: Stoke have not kept a clean sheet in their last ten Premier League away fixtures

2015-16 Premier League appearances

	P	G	Y	R		P	G	Y	R
C Adam	12 (10)	1	6	1	J Walters	18 (9)	5	1	-
I Afellay	24 (7)	2	3	1	G Whelan	37	0	6	-
M Arnautovic	33 (1)	11	2	-	M Wilson	1 (3)	0	-	-
P Bardsley	9 (2)	0	1	-	P Wollscheid	30 (1)	0	2	-
M Biram Diouf	12 (14)	5	3	-	M van Ginkel	8 (9)	0	-	-
J Butland	31	0	-	-					
G Cameron	27 (3)	0	-	1					
P Crouch	4 (7)	0	-	-					
S Given	3	0	1	-					
J Haugaard	4 (1)	0	-	-					
G Imbula	14	2	6	-					
S Ireland	0 (13)	0	2	-					
G Johnson	25	0	1	-					
Joselu	10 (12)	4	-	-					
B Krkic	22 (5)	7	2	-					
M Muniesa	12 (3)	0	2	-					
P Odemwingie	0 (5)	0	-	-					
E Pieters	35	0	10	-					
X Shaqiri	27	3	3	-					
R Shawcross	20	0	3	1					
S Sidwell	0 (1)	0	-	-					

Marko Arnautovic lit up the Britannia Stadium

SUNDERLAND

Nickname: Mackems/The Black Cats
Colours: Red and white
Ground: Stadium of Light   **Capacity:** 48,707
Tel: 0191-551-5000   www.safc.com

Sunderland have had to perform rescue missions in each of the last four seasons and could be set for another rough ride if Sam Allardyce leaves for the England job.

No Black Cats' manager has been in charge for a full campaign since Steve Bruce in 2009-10, and Allardyce had seemed set to buck the trend.

Few gave Sunderland a chance of survival when Big Sam arrived in October but he did a fantastic job. January signings Wahbi Khazri and Jan Kirchhof were inspired bits of business and Allardyce got the very best out of Jermain Defoe, who finished on 15 league goals.

If the club can hold on to Allardyce then Sunderland should steer clear of further relegation worries. Lose him late in the summer, though, and a struggling club starts the season on the back foot.

Longest run without a loss: 6
Longest run without a win: 9
Highest/lowest league position: 17/20
Clean sheets: 7
Yellow cards: 66 **Red cards:** 2
Average attendance: 42,150
Players used: 31
Leading scorer: J Defoe 15 (4,12)

	2015-16		Last six seasons at home							
	H	A	P	W	D	L	OV	UN	BS	CS
Leicester	L	L	2	0	1	1	0	2	0	1
Arsenal	D	L	6	0	2	4	2	4	3	1
Tottenham	L	L	6	0	2	4	4	2	4	1
Man City	L	L	6	4	0	2	1	5	1	4
Man United	W	L	6	1	2	3	2	4	3	1
Southampton	L	D	4	1	2	1	2	2	3	0
West Ham	D	L	5	2	2	1	3	2	3	2
Liverpool	L	D	6	1	1	4	1	5	2	1
Stoke	W	D	6	5	1	0	2	4	2	4
Chelsea	W	L	6	1	1	4	5	1	5	1
Everton	W	L	6	2	3	1	2	4	3	2
Swansea	D	W	5	1	3	1	1	4	2	3
Watford	L	D	1	0	0	1	0	1	0	0
West Brom	D	L	6	1	3	2	3	3	3	3
Crystal Palace	D	W	3	0	2	1	2	1	2	1
Bournemouth	D	L	1	0	1	0	0	1	1	0
Sunderland										
Burnley			1	1	0	0	0	1	0	1
Middlesbrough			-	-	-	-	-	-	-	-
Hull			2	0	0	2	1	1	1	0

Season	Division	Pos	P	W	D	L	F	A	GD	Pts
2015-16	Premier League	17	38	9	12	17	48	62	-14	39
2014-15	Premier League	16	38	7	17	14	31	53	-22	38
2013-14	Premier League	14	38	10	8	20	41	60	-19	38

Over/Under 53%/47% 7th   **Both score** 55%/45% 6th

Key stat: Sunderland's last seven league defeats have all come against teams who finished in the top half of the Premier League

2015-16 Premier League appearances

	P	G	Y	R		P	G	Y	R
F Borini	22 (4)	5	6	-	J O'Shea	23 (5)	0	2	-
W Brown	6	0	1	-	C Pantilimon	17	0	3	-
L Cattermole	27 (4)	0	8	-	J Pickford	2	0	-	-
S Coates	14 (2)	0	4	-	T Robson	1	0	-	-
J Defoe	28 (5)	15	3	-	J Rodwell	9 (13)	1	5	-
S Fletcher	11 (5)	4	-	-	O Toivonen	9 (3)	0	1	-
J Gomez	5 (1)	0	-	-	D Watmore	7 (16)	3	-	-
D Graham	4 (6)	0	-	-	D Yedlin	21 (2)	0	2	-
R Greenwood	1	0	-	-	P van Aanholt	33	4	2	-
G Honeyman	0 (1)	0	1	-					
A Johnson	11 (8)	2	3	-					
B Jones	23 (1)	1	8	-					
Y Kaboul	22 (1)	0	4	1					
W Khazri	13 (1)	2	3	-					
J Kirchhoff	14 (1)	0	-	-					
L Kone	15	2	4	1					
S Larsson	6 (12)	0	2	-					
J Lens	14 (6)	3	4	1					
Y M'Vila	36 (1)	1	1	-					
V Mannone	19	0	2	-					
A Matthews	0 (1)	0	-	-					
D N'Doye	5 (6)	1	2	-					

Jermain Defoe came to Sunderland's rescue

SWANSEA

Nickname: The Swans
Colours: White
Ground: Liberty Stadium
Tel: 01792-616-600

Capacity: 20,745
www.swanseacity.net

Swansea are preparing for a sixth-successive season in the top flight and do so under new ownership after Americans Jason Levien and Steve Kaplan bought a controlling stake in the club.

What the change of ownership will mean in the long term remains to be seen. However, the stated immediate priority is to keep change to a minimum, so head coach Francesco Guidolin stays on and chairman Huw Jenkins remains in control of the club's day-to-day affairs.

Resisting the temptation to make swift changes looks wise. Swansea regressed slightly last term but their 47-point tally was their joint-second highest of the Premier League era.

They should do no worse next term as long as key players like Gylfi Sigurdsson and Ashley Williams stick with the club.

Longest run without a loss: 4
Longest run without a win: 7
Highest/lowest league position: 11/18
Clean sheets: 9
Yellow cards: 60 **Red cards:** 1
Average attendance: 20,660
Players used: 27
Leading scorer: A Ayew 12 (2,11)

	2015-16		Last six seasons at home							
	H	A	P	W	D	L	OV	UN	BS	CS
Leicester	L	L	3	2	0	1	1	2	0	2
Arsenal	L	W	5	2	0	3	4	1	3	0
Tottenham	D	L	5	0	2	3	4	1	5	0
Man City	D	L	5	1	2	2	2	3	3	2
Man United	W	L	5	2	1	2	3	2	4	0
Southampton	L	L	4	0	1	3	0	4	0	1
West Ham	D	W	4	1	3	0	1	3	1	3
Liverpool	W	L	5	2	2	1	2	3	2	2
Stoke	L	D	5	3	1	1	2	3	2	2
Chelsea	W	D	5	1	2	2	1	4	2	1
Everton	D	W	5	0	2	3	2	3	2	1
Swansea										
Watford	W	L	2	1	1	0	0	2	1	1
West Brom	W	D	5	4	0	1	4	1	2	3
Crystal Palace	D	D	4	1	3	0	1	3	3	1
Bournemouth	D	W	1	0	1	0	1	0	1	0
Sunderland	L	D	5	1	3	1	3	2	3	2
Burnley			2	2	0	0	0	2	0	2
Middlesbrough			1	1	0	0	0	1	0	1
Hull			3	1	2	0	1	2	3	0

Season	Division	Pos	P	W	D	L	F	A	GD	Pts
2015-16	Premier League	12	38	12	11	15	42	52	-10	47
2014-15	Premier League	8	38	16	8	14	46	49	-3	56
2013-14	Premier League	12	38	11	9	18	54	54	0	42

Over/Under 53%/47% 7th
▬▬▬▬▬▬▬▬▬▬

Both score 53%/47% 9th
▬▬▬▬▬▬▬▬▬▬

Key stat: Swansea achieved just four away league wins last season – the lowest tally since their debut Premier League campaign in 2011-12

2015-16 Premier League appearances

	P	G		Y	R
J Amat	5 (3)	0		-	-
A Ayew	34	12		5	-
M Barrow	6 (16)	1		-	-
K Bartley	3 (2)	0		2	-
L Britton	19 (6)	0		4	-
J Cork	28 (7)	1		3	-
N Dyer	0 (1)	0		-	-
Eder	2 (11)	0		-	-
M Emnes	1 (1)	0		-	-
L Fabianski	37	0		1	-
L Fer	9 (2)	0		2	-
F Fernandez	32	1		3	-
J Fulton	0 (2)	0		-	-
B Gomis	18 (15)	6		-	-
M Grimes	1	0		-	-
Ki Sung-Yueng	21 (7)	2		4	-
S Kingsley	4	0		-	-
J Montero	14 (9)	0		-	-
K Naughton	19 (8)	0		2	1
K Nordfeldt	1	0		-	-
A Paloschi	7 (3)	2		2	-

	P	G		Y	R
A Rangel	20 (3)	0		6	-
W Routledge	22 (6)	2		3	-
J Shelvey	14 (2)	1		5	-
G Sigurdsson	32 (4)	11		6	-
N Taylor	33 (1)	0		4	-
A Williams	36	2		8	-

Andre Ayew proved an impressive free signing

TOTTENHAM

Nickname: Spurs
Colours: White and navy blue
Ground: White Hart Lane
Tel: 0870-420-5000

Capacity: 36,284
www.tottenhamhotspur.com

Champions League qualification was the aim for Tottenham last season but they ended up being disappointed with third.

No wins in their last four games meant 2015-16 ended on a low and highlighted a lack of depth when key men Dele Alli and Mousa Dembele were unavailable.

However, now that the dust has settled there is a realisation of just how far the club has come in a short space of time.

The English midfield core of Alli and Eric Dier is only likely to get better and there are diminishing doubts about the qualities of Harry Kane, who backed up a stunning 2014-15 campaign by topping the Premier League scoring charts.

The new stadium will need paying for but nobody seems in a rush to leave and there is a real chance of the Londoners going from strength to strength.

Longest run without a loss: 14
Longest run without a win: 4
Highest/lowest league position: 2/8
Clean sheets: 13
Yellow cards: 72 **Red cards:** 0
Average attendance: 35,733
Players used: 24
Leading scorer: H Kane 25 (9,17)

	2015-16		Last six seasons at home							
	H	A	P	W	D	L	OV	UN	BS	CS
Leicester	L	D	2	1	0	1	1	1	1	0
Arsenal	D	D	6	3	2	1	5	1	5	0
Tottenham										
Man City	W	W	6	2	1	3	4	2	4	1
Man United	W	L	6	1	4	1	3	3	3	3
Southampton	L	W	4	3	0	1	2	2	2	2
West Ham	W	L	5	2	2	1	4	1	3	1
Liverpool	D	D	6	3	1	2	5	1	2	2
Stoke	D	W	6	2	3	1	4	2	4	2
Chelsea	D	D	6	1	4	1	2	4	5	1
Everton	D	D	6	3	3	0	2	4	3	3
Swansea	W	D	5	5	0	0	3	2	3	2
Watford	W	W	1	1	0	0	0	1	0	1
West Brom	D	D	6	1	4	1	1	5	4	1
Crystal Palace	W	W	3	2	1	0	0	3	0	3
Bournemouth	W	W	1	1	0	0	1	0	0	1
Sunderland	W	W	6	5	1	0	3	3	4	2
Burnley			1	1	0	0	1	0	1	0
Middlesbrough			-	-	-	-	-	-	-	-
Hull			2	2	0	0	0	2	0	2

Season	Division	Pos	P	W	D	L	F	A	GD	Pts
2015-16	Premier League	3	38	19	13	6	69	35	+34	70
2014-15	Premier League	5	38	19	7	12	58	53	+5	64
2013-14	Premier League	6	38	21	6	11	55	51	+4	69

Over/Under 55%/45% 6th   **Both score** 58%/42% 4th

Key stat: Tottenham were the only team who failed to win in the opening four games and the last four games of last season.

2015-16 Premier League appearances

	P	G	Y	R
T Alderweireld	38	4	3	-
D Alli	28 (5)	10	7	-
N Bentaleb	2 (3)	0	1	-
T Carroll	4 (15)	1	3	-
N Chadli	10 (19)	3	1	-
B Davies	14 (3)	0	3	-
M Dembele	27 (2)	3	3	-
E Dier	37	3	10	-
C Eriksen	33 (2)	6	2	-
Heung-Min Son	13 (15)	4	-	-
H Kane	38	25	5	-
E Lamela	28 (6)	5	9	-
H Lloris	37	0	-	-
R Mason	8 (14)	1	3	-
C N'Jie	0 (8)	0	-	-
J Onomah	0 (8)	0	-	-
A Pritchard	0 (1)	0	-	-
D Rose	24	1	7	-
A Townsend	0 (3)	0	-	-
K Trippier	5 (1)	1	1	-
J Vertonghen	29	0	5	-

	P	G	Y	R
M Vorm	1	0	-	-
K Walker	33	1	7	-
K Wimmer	9 (1)	0	2	-

Harry Kane took the golden boot with 25 goals

WATFORD

Watford

Nickname: The Hornets
Colours: Yellow and red
Ground: Vicarage Road   **Capacity:** 20,910
Tel: 0845-442-1881   www.watfordfc.co.uk

Watford have taken stick for showing a lack of loyalty to their managers, but the club is well run by owner Gino Pozzo as he looks to establish them at the top level.

Quique Sanchez Flores did his job to steer the Hornets to safety but there was an alarming downturn in performances in 2016 and Flores's expensive January recruits, Mario Suarez and Nordin Amrabat, were largely ineffective.

New manager Walter Mazzarri boasts an impressive CV and his counter-attacking style will not depart much from the tactics employed by Flores.

What will change is the formation – from a back four to a back three – but there is sufficient quality to make it work and exciting new faces are sure to arrive as Watford reap the benefits of their owners' renowned scouting network.

Longest run without a loss: 5
Longest run without a win: 6
Highest/lowest league position: 7/15
Clean sheets: 11
Yellow cards: 74 **Red cards:** 3
Average attendance: 20,498
Players used: 25
Leading scorer: O Ighalo 15 (6,12)

	2015-16		Last six seasons at home							
	H	A	P	W	D	L	OV	UN	BS	CS
Leicester	L	L	5	3	0	2	4	1	3	0
Arsenal	L	L	1	0	0	1	1	0	0	0
Tottenham	L	L	1	0	0	1	1	0	1	0
Man City	L	L	1	0	0	1	1	0	1	0
Man United	L	L	1	0	0	1	1	0	1	0
Southampton	D	L	2	0	1	1	1	1	0	1
West Ham	W	L	2	1	0	1	1	1	0	1
Liverpool	W	L	1	1	0	0	1	0	0	1
Stoke	L	W	1	0	0	1	1	0	1	0
Chelsea	D	D	1	0	1	0	0	1	0	1
Everton	D	D	1	0	1	0	0	1	1	0
Swansea	W	L	2	1	0	1	1	1	1	1
Watford										
West Brom	D	W	1	0	1	0	0	1	0	1
Crystal Palace	L	W	4	0	2	2	1	3	2	0
Bournemouth	D	D	3	1	2	0	1	2	2	1
Sunderland	D	W	1	0	1	0	1	0	1	0
Burnley			4	1	2	1	3	1	4	0
Middlesbrough			5	4	0	1	3	2	3	2
Hull			3	0	1	2	2	1	3	0

Season	Division	Pos	P	W	D	L	F	A	GD	Pts
2015-16	Premier League	13	38	12	9	17	40	50	-10	45
2014-15	Championship	2	46	27	8	11	91	50	+41	89
2013-14	Championship	13	46	15	15	16	74	64	+10	60

Over/Under 47%/53% 17th   **Both score** 45%/55% 16th

Key stat: Watford failed to win any of their 12 matches against teams that finished in the Premier League's top six

2015-16 Premier League appearances

	P	G	Y	R		P	G	Y	R
A Abdi	25 (7)	2	4	-	J Paredes	7 (10)	0	1	-
N Ake	20 (4)	1	4	1	S Prodl	19 (2)	2	5	-
N Amrabat	4 (8)	0	2	1	M Suarez	8 (7)	0	2	-
I Anya	17 (11)	0	-	-	B Watson	31 (4)	2	4	-
G Arlauskis	0 (1)	0	-	-					
V Behrami	14 (7)	0	3	1					
S Berghuis	0 (9)	0	2	-					
M Britos	24	0	7	-					
E Capoue	33	0	7	-					
C Cathcart	34 (1)	0	3	-					
T Deeney	36 (2)	13	6	-					
A Diamanti	0 (3)	0	-	-					
H Gomes	38	0	4	-					
A Guedioura	3 (15)	0	2	-					
J Holebas	11	0	2	-					
V Ibarbo	0 (4)	0	-	-					
O Ighalo	36 (1)	15	4	-					
J Jurado	27	0	3	-					
M Layun	2 (1)	1	-	-					
A Nyom	29 (3)	0	8	-					
O Oulare	0 (2)	0	-	-					

Ighalo and Deeney got 28 of Watford's 40 goals

WEST BROM

WEST BROMWICH ALBION

Nickname: The Baggies/Throstles/Albion
Colours: Navy blue and white
Ground: The Hawthorns **Capacity:** 26,768
Tel: 0871-271-1100 www.wba.co.uk

West Brom survived despite scoring just 34 goals, but a more enterprising style of play may be needed if they are to avoid another relegation battle in 2016-17.

Manager Tony Pulis has never been relegated, but his methods may not be as effective as they once were and are likely to attract scepticism from fans who are becoming frustrated at the dour football.

Pulis could argue that last season was a case of job done in difficult circumstances given the lack of contribution from want-away striker Saido Berahino.

However, Berahino's value has dropped substantially meaning any future sale of the player may not deliver the funds needed to reshape the West Brom squad.

Last summer's big signing Salomon Rondon scored nine goals in 34 games but must do better if Albion are to progress.

Longest run without a loss: 4
Longest run without a win: 9
Highest/lowest league position: 10/16
Clean sheets: 11
Yellow cards: 65 **Red cards:** 3
Average attendance: 24,348
Players used: 28
Leading scorer: J Rondon 9 (8,9)

	2015-16		Last six seasons at home							
	H	A	P	W	D	L	OV	UN	BS	CS
Leicester	L	D	2	0	0	2	2	0	2	0
Arsenal	W	L	6	1	2	3	4	2	5	0
Tottenham	D	D	6	0	3	3	3	3	4	0
Man City	L	L	6	0	1	5	4	2	3	1
Man United	W	L	6	1	2	3	5	1	4	1
Southampton	D	L	4	2	1	1	0	4	0	3
West Ham	L	D	5	1	2	2	3	2	2	2
Liverpool	D	D	6	2	3	1	2	4	3	2
Stoke	W	W	6	2	0	4	3	3	2	1
Chelsea	L	D	6	3	1	2	4	2	4	2
Everton	L	W	6	2	1	3	1	5	2	2
Swansea	D	L	5	2	1	2	2	3	3	1
Watford	L	D	1	0	0	1	0	1	0	0
West Brom										
Crystal Palace	W	L	3	2	1	0	2	1	2	1
Bournemouth	L	D	1	0	0	1	1	0	1	0
Sunderland	W	D	6	5	1	0	4	2	2	4
Burnley			1	1	0	0	1	0	0	1
Middlesbrough			-	-	-	-	-	-	-	-
Hull			2	1	1	0	0	2	1	1

Season	Division	Pos	P	W	D	L	F	A	GD	Pts
2015-16	Premier League	14	38	10	13	15	34	48	-14	43
2014-15	Premier League	13	38	11	11	16	38	51	-13	44
2013-14	Premier League	17	38	7	15	16	43	59	-16	36

Over/Under 37%/63% 20th   **Both score** 45%/55% 16th

Key stat: West Brom scored fewer than two goals in 15 of their final 17 Premier League fixtures of 2015-16

2015-16 Premier League appearances

	P	G		Y	R
V Anichebe	3 (7)	0		-	-
S Berahino	17 (14)	4		-	-
C Brunt	20 (2)	0		7	-
J Chester	9 (4)	0		5	-
C Dawson	38	4		3	-
J Evans	30	1		4	-
S Field	0 (1)	0		-	-
D Fletcher	38	1		3	-
B Foster	15	0		1	-
C Gamboa	0 (1)	0		1	-
C Gardner	20 (14)	3		5	-
S Gnabry	0 (1)	0		-	-
R Lambert	5 (14)	1		2	-
J Leko	3 (2)	0		-	-
J Lescott	2	0		-	-
G McAuley	34	1		4	1
J McClean	28 (7)	2		7	1
C McManaman	2 (10)	0		2	-
J Morrison	17 (1)	3		3	-
B Myhill	23	0		2	-
J Olsson	25 (3)	1		5	-

	P	G		Y	R
S Pocognoli	0 (1)	0		-	-
A Pritchard	0 (2)	0		-	-
T Roberts	0 (1)	0		1	-
J Rondon	30 (4)	9		1	1
Sandro	5 (7)	0		-	-
S Sessegnon	21 (4)	2		1	-
C Yacob	33 (1)	0		8	-

Plenty of defences were undone by Rondon

WEST HAM

Nickname: The Hammers/Irons
Colours: Claret and blue
Ground: Olympic Stadium   **Capacity:** 60,010
Tel: 020-8548-2748   www.whufc.com

West Ham are hoping their move to the Olympic Stadium can help them join the elite of English football and have every reason to be optimistic as they begin their second season under Slaven Bilic.

Hammers' owners David Gold and David Sullivan took a gamble last summer in replacing Sam Allardyce with Bilic and the move paid off handsomely.

West Ham again have Europa League football to look forward to, but this time it's a result of improved performances rather than Uefa's Fair Play rankings.

However, improving on seventh may be tough in the short term. Better players may want to come to a club with a bigger stadium, but West Ham will lose the advantage of playing at Upton Park where the intimidating atmosphere often made life very tough for visiting sides.

Longest run without a loss: 10
Longest run without a win: 8
Highest/lowest league position: 3/8
Clean sheets: 11
Yellow cards: 58 **Red cards:** 5
Average attendance: 34,930
Players used: 28
Leading scorer: A Carroll 9 (1,7) D Payet 9 (1,8)

	2015-16		Last six seasons at home							
	H	A	P	W	D	L	OV	UN	BS	CS
Leicester	L	D	3	2	0	1	2	1	2	1
Arsenal	D	W	5	0	1	4	5	0	4	0
Tottenham	W	L	5	3	0	2	1	4	1	3
Man City	D	W	5	1	2	2	4	1	4	1
Man United	W	D	5	1	2	2	3	2	4	0
Southampton	W	L	5	3	1	1	4	1	5	0
West Ham										
Liverpool	W	W	5	3	0	2	4	1	4	1
Stoke	D	L	5	1	3	1	1	4	2	2
Chelsea	W	D	5	2	0	3	4	1	3	0
Everton	D	W	5	0	2	3	3	2	5	0
Swansea	L	D	4	3	0	1	2	2	2	2
Watford	W	L	2	1	1	0	1	1	2	0
West Brom	D	W	5	1	4	0	3	2	5	0
Crystal Palace	D	W	4	0	2	2	2	2	2	1
Bournemouth	L	W	1	0	0	1	1	0	1	0
Sunderland	W	D	5	2	2	1	4	1	4	3
Burnley			2	1	0	1	1	1	1	1
Middlesbrough			1	0	1	0	0	1	1	0
Hull			3	3	0	0	3	0	2	1

Season	Division	Pos	P	W	D	L	F	A	GD	Pts
2015-16	Premier League	7	38	16	14	8	65	51	+14	62
2014-15	Premier League	12	38	12	11	15	44	47	-3	47
2013-14	Premier League	13	38	11	7	20	40	51	-11	40

Over/Under 63%/37% 2nd   **Both score** 66%/34% 1st

Key stat: West Ham lost just three games at Upton Park last season. Only Leicester and Manchester United lost fewer home league fixtures

2015-16 Premier League appearances

	P G		Y	R
Adrian	32	0	1	1
M Antonio	23 (3)	8	3	-
S Byram	2 (2)	0	3	-
A Carroll	13 (14)	9	2	-
J Collins	16 (3)	0	3	1
A Cresswell	37	2	1	-
J Cullen	0 (1)	0	-	-
E Emenike	5 (8)	0	-	-
M Jarvis	0 (3)	0	-	-
N Jelavic	1 (12)	1	1	-
C Jenkinson	13 (7)	2	3	1
C Kouyate	34	5	5	1
M Lanzini	23 (3)	6	3	-
M Maiga	0 (3)	0	-	-
V Moses	13 (8)	1	-	-
M Noble	37	7	8	1
K Nolan	1 (1)	0	-	-
P Obiang	11 (13)	0	2	-
A Ogbonna	27 (1)	0	5	-
R Oxford	3 (4)	0	-	-
D Payet	29 (1)	9	3	-

	P G		Y	R
D Randolph	6	0	-	-
W Reid	24	1	5	-
D Sakho	18 (3)	5	3	-
A Song	8 (4)	0	1	-
J Tomkins	23 (2)	0	4	-
E Valencia	10 (9)	4	1	-
M Zarate	9 (6)	3	1	-

Payet and Bilic were both big hits at West Ham

Premier League stats 2015-16

Key Points in all tables (except the league table) do not include any deductions imposed by the league.
POS H A Overall league position, rank from home games only, rank from away games only **Sup** Average
match supremacy **GFA** Goals For Average **GAA** Goals Against Average **PGA** Points Gained Average

Premier League 2015-16				Home				Away						
Pos	H	A		P	W	D	L	F	A	W	D	L	F	A	GD	Pts
1	1	1	Leicester (CL)	38	12	6	1	35	18	11	6	2	33	18	+32	81
2	3	3	Arsenal (CL)	38	12	4	3	31	11	8	7	4	34	25	+29	71
3	5	2	Tottenham (CL)	38	10	6	3	35	15	9	7	3	34	20	+34	70
4	4	5	Man City (CL)	38	12	2	5	47	21	7	7	5	24	20	+30	66
5	2	9	Man Utd (EL)	38	12	5	2	27	9	7	4	8	22	26	+14	66
6	6	7	Southampton (EL)	38	11	3	5	39	22	7	6	6	20	19	+18	63
7	7	4	West Ham (EL)	38	9	7	3	34	26	7	7	5	31	25	+14	62
8	8	6	Liverpool	38	8	8	3	33	22	8	4	7	30	28	+13	60
9	11	11	Stoke	38	8	4	7	22	24	6	5	8	19	31	-14	51
10	13	8	Chelsea	38	5	9	5	32	30	7	5	7	27	23	+6	50
11	15	10	Everton	38	6	5	8	35	30	5	9	5	24	25	+4	47
12	9	16	Swansea	38	8	6	5	20	20	4	5	10	22	32	-10	47
13	14	14	Watford	38	6	6	7	20	19	6	3	10	20	31	-10	45
14	17	15	West Brom	38	6	5	8	20	26	4	8	7	14	22	-14	43
15	18	13	Crystal Palace	38	6	3	10	19	23	5	6	8	20	28	-12	42
16	19	12	Bournemouth	38	5	5	9	23	34	6	4	9	22	33	-22	42
17	12	17	Sunderland	38	6	6	7	23	20	3	6	10	25	42	-14	39
18	10	19	Newcastle (R)	38	7	7	5	32	24	2	3	14	12	41	-21	37
19	16	18	Norwich (R)	38	6	5	8	26	30	3	2	14	13	37	-28	34
20	20	20	Aston Villa (R)	38	2	5	12	14	35	1	3	15	13	41	-49	17

Best attack

		GF	GFA
1	Man City	71	1.87
2	Tottenham	69	1.82
3	Leicester	68	1.79
4	Arsenal	65	1.71
5	West Ham	65	1.71
6	Liverpool	63	1.66
7	Southampton	59	1.55
8	Chelsea	59	1.55
9	Everton	59	1.55
10	Man Utd	49	1.29
11	Sunderland	48	1.26
12	Bournemouth	45	1.18
13	Newcastle	44	1.16
14	Swansea	42	1.11
15	Stoke	41	1.08
16	Watford	40	1.05
17	Crystal Palace	39	1.03
18	Norwich	39	1.03
19	West Brom	34	0.89
20	Aston Villa	27	0.71

Best defence

		GA	GAA
1	Tottenham	35	0.92
2	Man Utd	35	0.92
3	Leicester	36	0.95
4	Arsenal	36	0.95
5	Man City	41	1.08
6	Southampton	41	1.08
7	West Brom	48	1.26
8	Liverpool	50	1.32
9	Watford	50	1.32
10	West Ham	51	1.34
11	Crystal Palace	51	1.34
12	Swansea	52	1.37
13	Chelsea	53	1.39
14	Stoke	55	1.45
15	Everton	55	1.45
16	Sunderland	62	1.63
17	Newcastle	65	1.71
18	Bournemouth	67	1.76
19	Norwich	67	1.76
20	Aston Villa	76	2

Top scorers

	Team	Goals scored
H Kane	Tottenham	25
S Aguero	Man City	24
J Vardy	Leicester	24
R Lukaku	Everton	18
R Mahrez	Leicester	17
O Giroud	Arsenal	16
J Defoe	Sunderland	15
O Ighalo	Watford	15
T Deeney	Watford	13
A Sanchez	Arsenal	13
A Ayew	Swansea	12
D Costa	Chelsea	12
M Arnautovic	Stoke	11
S Mane	Southampton	11
A Martial	Man Utd	11
G Pelle	Southampton	11
G Sigurdsson	Swansea	11
G Wijnaldum	Newcastle	11
D Alli	Tottenham	10
R Firmino	Liverpool	10
S Long	Southampton	10

Over 2.5 goals

	H	A	%
Man City	16	9	66%
Chelsea	12	12	63%
West Ham	11	13	63%
Everton	12	10	58%
Bournemouth	10	12	58%

Under 2.5 goals

	H	A	%
West Brom	10	14	63%
Man Utd	12	9	55%
Watford	10	10	53%
Aston Villa	11	9	53%
Saints, Palace, Arsenal			50%

Both to score

	H	A	%
West Ham	13	12	66%
Chelsea	14	10	63%
Bournemouth	11	12	61%
Leicester	10	12	58%
Tottenham	10	12	58%

Both not to score

	H	A	%
Man Utd	6	9	61%
Arsenal	7	9	58%
Aston Villa	8	9	55%
Watford	8	9	55%
West Brom	10	7	55%

Premier League results 2015-16

	Arsenal	Aston Villa	Bournemouth	Chelsea	Crystal Palace	Everton	Leicester	Liverpool	Man City	Man United	Newcastle	Norwich	Southampton	Stoke	Sunderland	Swansea	Tottenham	Watford	West Brom	West Ham
Arsenal		4-0	2-0	0-1	1-1	2-1	2-1	0-0	2-1	3-0	1-0	1-0	0-0	2-0	3-1	1-2	1-1	4-0	2-0	0-2
Aston Villa	0-2		1-2	0-4	1-0	1-3	1-1	0-6	0-0	0-1	0-0	2-0	2-4	0-1	2-2	1-2	0-2	2-3	0-1	1-1
Bournemouth	0-2	0-1		1-4	0-0	3-3	1-1	1-2	0-4	2-1	0-1	3-0	2-0	1-3	2-0	3-2	1-5	1-1	1-1	1-3
Chelsea	2-0	2-0	0-1		1-2	3-3	1-1	1-3	0-3	1-1	5-1	1-0	1-3	1-1	3-1	2-2	2-2	2-2	2-2	2-2
Crystal Palace	1-2	2-1	1-2	0-3		0-0	0-1	1-2	0-1	0-0	5-1	1-0	1-0	2-1	0-1	0-0	1-3	1-2	2-0	1-3
Everton	0-2	4-0	2-1	3-1	1-1		2-3	1-1	0-2	0-3	3-0	3-0	1-1	3-4	6-2	1-2	1-1	2-2	0-1	2-3
Leicester	2-5	3-2	0-0	2-1	1-0	3-1		2-0	0-0	1-1	1-0	1-0	1-0	3-0	4-2	4-0	1-1	2-1	2-2	2-2
Liverpool	3-3	3-2	1-0	1-1	1-2	4-0	1-0		3-0	0-1	2-2	1-1	1-1	4-1	2-2	1-0	1-1	2-0	2-2	0-3
Man City	2-2	4-0	5-1	3-0	4-0	0-0	1-3	1-4		0-1	6-1	2-1	3-1	4-0	4-1	2-1	1-2	2-0	2-1	1-2
Man United	3-2	1-0	3-1	0-0	2-0	1-0	1-1	3-1	0-0		0-0	1-2	0-1	3-0	3-0	2-1	1-0	1-0	2-0	0-0
Newcastle	0-1	1-1	1-3	2-2	1-0	0-3	2-0	1-1	3-3			6-2	2-2	0-0	1-1	3-0	5-1	1-2	1-0	2-1
Norwich	1-1	2-0	3-1	1-2	1-3	1-1	1-2	4-5	0-0	0-1	3-2		1-0	1-1	0-3	1-0	0-3	4-2	0-1	2-2
Southampton	4-0	1-1	2-0	1-2	4-1	0-3	2-2	3-2	4-2	2-3	3-1	3-0		0-1	1-1	3-1	0-2	2-0	3-0	1-0
Stoke	0-0	2-1	2-1	1-0	1-2	0-3	2-2	0-1	2-0	2-0	1-0	3-1	1-2		1-1	2-2	0-4	0-2	0-1	2-1
Sunderland	0-0	3-1	1-1	3-2	2-2	3-0	0-2	0-1	0-1	2-1	3-0	1-3	0-1	2-0		1-1	0-1	0-1	0-0	2-2
Swansea	0-3	1-0	2-2	1-0	1-1	0-0	0-3	3-1	1-1	2-1	2-0	1-0	0-1	0-1	2-4		2-2	1-0	1-0	0-0
Tottenham	2-2	3-1	3-0	0-0	1-0	0-0	0-1	0-0	4-1	3-0	1-2	3-0	1-2	2-2	4-1	2-1		1-0	1-1	4-1
Watford	0-3	3-2	0-0	0-0	0-1	1-1	0-1	3-0	1-2	1-2	2-1	2-0	0-0	1-2	2-2	1-0	1-2		0-0	2-0
West Brom	2-1	0-0	1-2	2-3	3-2	2-3	2-3	1-1	0-3	1-0	1-0	0-1	0-0	2-1	1-0	1-1	1-1	0-1		0-3
West Ham	3-3	2-0	3-4	2-1	2-2	1-1	1-2	2-0	2-2	3-2	2-0	2-2	2-1	0-0	1-0	1-4	1-0	3-1	1-1	

Record when first to score

		P	W	D	L	F	A	Sup	PGA	Pts
1	Man Utd	22	18	3	1	37	13	+1.09	2.6	57
2	Norwich	10	8	2	0	20	11	+0.90	2.6	26
3	Leicester	26	21	3	2	52	21	+1.19	2.5	66
4	Man City	20	16	3	1	53	17	+1.80	2.5	51
5	Arsenal	24	18	4	2	49	15	+1.42	2.4	58
6	Southampton	20	15	2	3	45	17	+1.40	2.4	47
7	Stoke	18	13	4	1	32	16	+0.89	2.4	43
8	West Ham	19	13	5	1	39	16	+1.21	2.3	44
9	Watford	15	11	2	2	26	13	+0.87	2.3	35
10	Liverpool	23	14	8	1	49	26	+1.00	2.2	50
11	Tottenham	22	14	6	2	46	17	+1.32	2.2	48
12	Swansea	14	9	4	1	22	10	+0.86	2.2	31
13	Newcastle	12	8	2	2	25	22	+0.25	2.2	26
14	Everton	17	10	6	1	41	16	+1.47	2.1	36
15	Bournemouth	16	10	4	2	28	21	+0.44	2.1	34
16	C Palace	14	9	2	3	21	15	+0.43	2.1	29
17	Chelsea	20	11	6	3	46	27	+0.95	2	39
18	West Brom	15	9	3	3	22	16	+0.40	2	30
19	Sunderland	15	8	6	1	29	17	+0.80	2	30
20	Aston Villa	7	3	1	3	8	12	-0.57	1.4	10

Record when keeping a clean sheet

		P	W	D	F	Sup	PGA	Pts
1	Leicester	15	13	2	24	+1.6	2.7	41
2	Arsenal	18	14	4	32	+1.78	2.6	46
3	Liverpool	11	9	2	20	+1.82	2.6	29
4	Norwich	5	4	1	5	+1	2.6	13
5	Tottenham	13	10	3	23	+1.77	2.5	33
6	Southampton	12	9	3	18	+1.5	2.5	30
7	West Ham	11	8	3	16	+1.45	2.5	27
8	Man Utd	18	13	5	21	+1.17	2.4	44
9	Man City	16	11	5	31	+1.94	2.4	38
10	Stoke	10	7	3	9	+0.9	2.4	24
11	Sunderland	7	5	2	12	+1.71	2.4	17
12	Watford	11	7	4	12	+1.09	2.3	25
13	West Brom	11	7	4	7	+0.64	2.3	25
14	Chelsea	9	6	3	13	+1.44	2.3	21
15	Swansea	9	6	3	7	+0.78	2.3	21
16	Newcastle	8	5	3	8	+1	2.3	18
17	Everton	10	6	4	17	+1.7	2.2	22
18	Bournemouth	7	4	3	8	+1.14	2.1	15
19	C Palace	8	4	4	5	+0.63	2	16
20	Aston Villa	6	3	3	4	+0.67	2	12

THE CHAMPIONSHIP

Impressive Newcastle too strong to suffer the curse of the failing favourites

S econd-tier favourites are notoriously unreliable but Newcastle can become the first Championship jolly to oblige since 2002, writes Dan Sait. While still a volatile division, the size and vast spending power of a handful of leading Championship clubs suggest that the lesser sides will find it increasingly difficult to compete and Newcastle have so much in their favour that they are hard to oppose even at odds of 2-1.

Owner Mike Ashley has made plenty of mistakes on Tyneside but his even his most ardent critics will acknowledge that landing Rafa Benitez represents a real coup. To persuade a man of Benitez's calibre to roll up his sleeves and scrap in the second tier sends out a powerful signal and the way in which Newcastle finished 2015-16 suggests they should thrive at a lower level.

Benitez's early signings look impressive. Several players who were getting regular top-tier action – among them Matt Richie, Dwight Gayle and Atletico's Jesus Gamez – have been persuaded to drop a division, and the club's recent experience in bouncing back from relegation will count in their favour.

The six behind Newcastle in the market all deserve respect. Aston Villa are boosted by a recent takeover and Wolves also look set for a summer sale, but there is plenty of rebuilding needed at both clubs so 2016-17 could come too soon for the midlands pair.

Derby should again be in the mix but are hard to trust after three successive promotion failures, and Norwich are tricky to gauge at this stage as there will be plenty of comings and goings at Carrow Road and it would be no surprise if the Canaries made a slow start.

But Sheffield Wednesday and Brighton are worth backing for promotion at 9-2 and 4-1 respectively. Wednesday are stable, have been investing heavily and will feel they

belong in the promotion mix having reached the playoff final in May. Brighton have regained the progressive look they acquired prior to the ill-advised appointment of Sami Hyypia in June 2014, and replacement Chris Hughton rarely disappoints at this level.

The relegation market is fascinating. Promoted Burton rightly head the market – their form tailed off alarmingly after manager Jimmy Floyd Hasselbaink left last season and they are a small club playing at this level for the first time – but aside from the Brewers the market looks wide open.

Wigan are 9-1 for an immediate return to the third tier, which looks too big. The Latics finished just two points above Burton last term and while they have recent experience at this level and more money to spend, Wigan being almost nine times the Brewers' price for relegation simply cannot be right.

Barnsley finished 13 points behind Wigan last term and seem another likely candidate, but they impressed in navigating the playoffs expertly and are a little too short at 10-3.

Instead try Blackburn at 11-2. There are so many negatives creeping out of Ewood Park that Rovers must be considered relegation candidates, even if only for trading purposes. The owners are losing money through the club, the fans have lost faith and new gaffer Owen Coyle hasn't had a good run in any of his last three managerial posts.

The capture of Rafa Benitez looks a real coup for Newcastle

ASTON VILLA

AVFC

Nickname: The Villans
Colours: Claret and blue
Ground: Villa Park (42,785)
Tel: 0121-327-2299   www.avfc.co.uk

Villa were shambolic as they slipped from the top flight for the first time in 29 years, winning just three matches and recording a pitiful goal difference of minus 49.

But the sale of the club to Tony Xia does promise an upturn in fortunes, even if some of his claims seem a little fanciful.

It's hard to believe Villa really will rank alongside Barca within five years, but billionaire Xia is still a big step up from Randy Lerner and he looks ready to back Roberto di Matteo in the transfer market.

Longest run without win/loss: 19/3
High/low league position: 18/20
Clean sheets: 6 **Yellows:** 76 **Reds:** 3
Avg attendance: 35,200 **Players used:** 29
Leading scorer: J Ayew 7 (1,7)
Key stat: In the top seven leagues, the closest any side came to matching Villa's record of just 27 goals scored was Welling, who scored 35

	2015-16 H	2015-16 A	Last six seasons at home P	W	D	L	OV	UN	BS	CS
Newcastle	D	D	6	1	3	2	2	4	3	3
Norwich	W	L	4	3	1	0	2	2	3	1
Aston Villa										
Brighton			-	-	-	-	-	-	-	-
Derby			-	-	-	-	-	-	-	-
Sheffield Weds			-	-	-	-	-	-	-	-
Ipswich			-	-	-	-	-	-	-	-
Cardiff			1	1	0	0	0	1	0	1
Brentford			-	-	-	-	-	-	-	-
Birmingham			1	0	1	0	0	1	0	1
Preston			-	-	-	-	-	-	-	-
QPR			3	1	2	0	3	0	3	0
Leeds			-	-	-	-	-	-	-	-
Wolves			2	0	1	1	0	2	0	1
Blackburn			2	2	0	0	2	0	2	0
Nottm Forest			-	-	-	-	-	-	-	-
Reading			1	1	0	0	0	1	0	1
Bristol City			-	-	-	-	-	-	-	-
Huddersfield			-	-	-	-	-	-	-	-
Fulham			4	1	2	1	2	2	3	1
Rotherham			-	-	-	-	-	-	-	-
Wigan			3	1	1	1	1	2	1	1
Burton			-	-	-	-	-	-	-	-
Barnsley			-	-	-	-	-	-	-	-

Season	Division	Pos	P	W	D	L	F	A	GD	Pts
2015-16	Premier League	20	38	3	8	27	27	76	-49	17
2014-15	Premier League	17	38	10	8	20	31	57	-26	38
2013-14	Premier League	15	38	10	8	20	39	61	-22	38

Over/Under 47%/53% 17th   **Both score** 45%/55% 16th

BARNSLEY

Nickname: Tykes
Colours: Red and white
Ground: Oakwell (23,287)
Tel: 01226-211-211   www.barnsleyfc.co.uk

Barnsley fans had to buckle up last term as an awful start had them bottom going into December but a meteoric rise then saw them into the playoff spots by March.

The Tykes were arguably lucky to meet already-promoted Wigan on the final day to secure a top-six place but were superb in the playoffs, thrashing Walsall 6-1 on aggregate and calmly seeing off Millwall.

Paul Heckingbottom has made a fine start to his managerial career but faces a real test of his promise at a higher level.

Longest run without win/loss: 8/7
High/low league position: 6/24
Clean sheets: 16 **Yellows:** 79 **Reds:** 2
Avg attendance: 8,532 **Players used:** 36
Leading scorer: S Winnall 21 (5,15)
Key stat: Barnsley have won 19 of their last 27 competitive matches and lost just three

	2015-16 H	2015-16 A	Last six seasons at home P	W	D	L	OV	UN	BS	CS
Newcastle			-	-	-	-	-	-	-	-
Norwich			1	0	0	1	0	1	0	0
Aston Villa			-	-	-	-	-	-	-	-
Brighton			3	1	2	0	1	2	1	2
Derby			4	1	2	1	2	2	4	0
Sheffield Weds			2	0	1	1	0	2	1	0
Ipswich			4	0	3	1	2	2	4	0
Cardiff			3	0	0	3	2	1	2	0
Brentford			-	-	-	-	-	-	-	-
Birmingham			3	0	0	3	3	0	2	0
Preston			2	1	1	0	0	2	1	1
QPR			2	0	0	2	1	1	1	0
Leeds			4	3	0	1	2	2	2	1
Wolves			1	1	0	0	1	0	1	0
Blackburn			2	0	1	1	2	0	2	0
Nottm Forest			4	2	1	1	2	2	3	1
Reading			3	0	1	2	1	2	1	0
Bristol City			4	2	1	1	3	1	3	1
Huddersfield			2	1	0	1	1	1	1	0
Fulham			-	-	-	-	-	-	-	-
Rotherham			-	-	-	-	-	-	-	-
Wigan	L	W	2	0	0	2	1	1	0	0
Burton	W	D	1	1	0	0	0	1	0	1
Barnsley										

Season	Division	Pos	P	W	D	L	F	A	GD	Pts
2015-16	League 1	6	46	22	8	16	70	54	+16	74
2014-15	League 1	11	46	17	11	18	62	61	+1	62
2013-14	Championship	23	46	9	12	25	44	77	-33	39

Over/Under 54%/46% 8th   **Both score** 52%/48% 10th

BIRMINGHAM

Nickname: Blues
Colours: Blue
Ground: St Andrews (29,409)
Tel: 0844-557-1875   www.bcfc.com

Birmingham were always on the fringes of the playoff places without ever looking the most likely to sneak into the top six. However, a repeat of their 2014-15 tenth-place finish confirmed Blues have at least stabilised following a worrying period of turmoil at the club.

Whether they can now push on could depend on both their ability to hold on to highly rated manager Gary Rowett and the completion of the sale of the club, but Blues fans should now be looking up.

Longest run without win/loss: 6/6
High/low league position: 2/10
Clean sheets: 16 **Yellows:** 78 **Reds:** 1
Avg attendance: 17,396 **Players used:** 28
Leading scorer: C Donaldson 11 (5,8)
Key stat: Birmingham's goals-scored tally has dropped in each of the last four seasons

	2015-16 H	A	Last six seasons at home P	W	D	L	OV	UN	BS	CS
Newcastle			1	0	0	1	0	1	0	0
Norwich			1	0	1	0	0	1	0	1
Aston Villa			1	0	1	0	0	1	1	0
Brighton	L	L	5	1	2	2	2	3	2	2
Derby	D	W	5	1	3	1	4	1	4	0
Sheffield Weds	L	L	4	1	1	2	2	2	2	1
Ipswich	W	D	5	2	2	1	3	2	3	1
Cardiff	W	D	4	1	2	1	0	4	1	2
Brentford	W	W	2	2	0	0	1	1	1	1
Birmingham										
Preston	D	D	1	0	1	0	1	0	1	0
QPR	W	L	2	1	0	1	1	1	1	0
Leeds	L	W	5	2	1	2	2	3	3	2
Wolves	L	D	4	1	1	2	2	2	3	0
Blackburn	D	L	5	1	3	1	3	2	4	1
Nottm Forest	L	D	5	2	1	2	3	2	3	1
Reading	W	W	4	3	0	1	3	1	3	1
Bristol City	W	D	3	2	1	0	2	1	2	1
Huddersfield	L	D	4	0	1	3	1	3	2	0
Fulham	D	W	3	0	1	2	1	2	2	0
Rotherham	L	D	2	1	0	1	1	1	1	0
Wigan			3	1	1	1	1	2	1	1
Burton			-	-	-	-	-	-	-	-
Barnsley			3	0	2	1	1	2	2	0

Season	Division	Pos	P	W	D	L	F	A	GD	Pts
2015-16	Championship	10	46	16	15	15	53	49	+4	63
2014-15	Championship	10	46	16	15	15	54	64	-10	63
2013-14	Championship	21	46	11	11	24	58	74	-16	44

Over/Under 37%/63% 20th   **Both score** 46%/54% 18th

BLACKBURN

Nickname: Rovers
Colours: Blue and white
Ground: Ewood Park (31,154)
Tel: 0871-702-1875   www.rovers.co.uk

Paul Lambert voluntarily departed the Blackburn dugout at the end of the season stating that the club needed help. Owners Venky's then reportedly turned down an offer for investment, but their club debts now run to over £104 million and it's hard to see how Rovers' slide will halt without boardroom-level changes.

Incoming manager Owen Coyle joined having left MLS side Houston Dynamo bottom of the Western Conference and that follows failures at Wigan and Bolton.

Longest run without win/loss: 9/8
High/low league position: 11/23
Clean sheets: 14 **Yellows:** 92 **Reds:** 4
Avg attendance: 15,996 **Players used:** 33
Leading scorer: J Rhodes 10 (2,8)
Key stat: Blackburn scored just seven first-half goals away from home in 2015-16

	2015-16 H	A	Last six seasons at home P	W	D	L	OV	UN	BS	CS
Newcastle			2	0	1	1	0	2	0	1
Norwich			2	1	0	1	1	1	1	1
Aston Villa			2	1	1	0	0	2	1	1
Brighton	L	L	4	0	2	2	1	3	2	0
Derby	D	L	4	1	2	1	1	3	2	2
Sheffield Weds	D	L	4	1	2	1	2	2	2	2
Ipswich	W	L	4	4	0	0	1	3	1	3
Cardiff	D	L	3	0	2	1	1	2	3	0
Brentford	D	W	2	0	1	1	1	1	2	0
Birmingham	W	D	5	2	2	1	1	4	3	2
Preston	L	W	1	0	0	1	1	0	1	0
QPR	D	D	3	2	1	0	1	2	2	1
Leeds	L	W	4	2	1	1	2	2	2	2
Wolves	L	D	5	1	0	4	3	2	2	1
Blackburn										
Nottm Forest	D	D	4	1	2	1	2	2	1	2
Reading	W	L	3	2	1	0	2	1	2	1
Bristol City	D	W	2	1	1	0	1	1	1	1
Huddersfield	L	D	4	1	2	1	0	4	0	3
Fulham	W	L	4	3	1	0	3	1	3	1
Rotherham	W	W	2	2	0	0	1	1	1	1
Wigan			4	3	0	1	3	1	3	0
Burton			-	-	-	-	-	-	-	-
Barnsley			2	2	0	0	2	0	2	0

Season	Division	Pos	P	W	D	L	F	A	GD	Pts
2015-16	Championship	15	46	13	16	17	46	46	0	55
2014-15	Championship	9	46	17	16	13	66	59	+7	67
2013-14	Championship	8	46	18	16	12	70	62	+8	70

Over/Under 33%/67% 24th   **Both score** 43%/57% 22nd

BRENTFORD

Nickname: The Bees
Colours: Red and white
Ground: Griffin Park (12,763)
Tel: 0845-3456-442   www.brentfordfc.co.uk

It was no shock to see Brentford slip back last season. They arguably overachieved in 2014-15 following promotion and the subsequent loss of key players and, more importantly, manager Mark Warburton was always likely to prove detrimental.

Marinus Dijkhuizen was sacked after eight games but replacement Dean Smith – appointed two months later – had fans fearing relegation after a run of ten defeats in 13. The Bees rallied well in the end but remain a difficult side to judge.

Longest run without win/loss: 4/6
High/low league position: 8/20
Clean sheets: 8 **Yellows:** 81 **Reds:** 3
Avg attendance: 14,016 **Players used:** 29
Top scorers: A Judge 14 (3,11) L Vibe 14 (3,12)
Key stat: Seven of Brentford's 19 league wins came in the final nine games of the season

	2015-16 H	A	Last six seasons at home P	W	D	L	OV	UN	BS	CS
Newcastle			-	-	-	-	-	-	-	-
Norwich			1	0	0	1	1	0	0	0
Aston Villa			-	-	-	-	-	-	-	-
Brighton	D	L	3	1	1	1	1	2	1	1
Derby	L	L	2	1	0	1	2	0	2	0
Sheffield Weds	L	L	4	1	1	2	2	2	2	2
Ipswich	D	W	2	0	1	1	2	0	2	0
Cardiff	W	L	2	1	0	1	2	0	2	0
Brentford										
Birmingham	L	L	2	0	1	1	0	2	1	0
Preston	W	W	4	3	0	1	2	2	2	2
QPR	W	L	1	1	0	0	1	0	1	
Leeds	D	D	2	1	1	0	0	2	1	1
Wolves	W	W	3	2	0	1	3	0	0	2
Blackburn	L	D	2	1	0	1	1	1	1	0
Nottm Forest	W	W	2	1	1	0	2	0	2	0
Reading	L	W	2	1	0	1	2	0	2	0
Bristol City	D	W	2	1	1	0	1	1	2	0
Huddersfield	W	W	4	2	0	2	3	1	2	0
Fulham	W	D	2	2	0	0	2	0	1	1
Rotherham	W	L	3	2	0	1	2	1	1	1
Wigan			1	1	0	0	1	0	0	1
Burton			-	-	-	-	-	-	-	-
Barnsley			-	-	-	-	-	-	-	-

Season	Division	Pos	P	W	D	L	F	A	GD	Pts
2015-16	Championship	9	46	19	8	19	72	67	+5	65
2014-15	Championship	5	46	23	9	14	78	59	+19	78
2013-14	League 1	2	46	28	10	8	72	43	+29	94

Over/Under 65%/35% 1st   **Both score** 61%/39% 2nd

BRIGHTON

Nickname: The Seagulls
Colours: Blue and white
Ground: Community Stadium (27,500)
Tel: 01273-695-400   www.seagulls.co.uk

Brighton spent much of the first half of the season at the top of the table and were bitterly disappointed to miss out on automatic promotion on goal difference. A win in either of their last two games would have sent them up, and the hangover carried over to the playoffs.

But the club is in great shape. Solid in defence, good to watch and the joint-highest scorers, they proved 2014-15 was a blip under Sami Hyypia. Chris Hughton is a far steadier hand on the tiller.

Longest run without win/loss: 7/21
High/low league position: 1/6
Clean sheets: 17 **Yellows:** 77 **Reds:** 4
Avg attendance: 21,580 **Players used:** 30
Leading scorer: T Hemed 17 (5,12)
Key stat: Brighton improved their goals-scored tally from 44 in 2014-15 to 72 in 2015-16

	2015-16 H	A	Last six seasons at home P	W	D	L	OV	UN	BS	CS
Newcastle			-	-	-	-	-	-	-	-
Norwich			1	0	0	1	0	1	0	0
Aston Villa			-	-	-	-	-	-	-	-
Brighton										
Derby	D	D	5	3	1	1	2	3	3	2
Sheffield Weds	D	D	5	2	2	1	1	4	1	3
Ipswich	L	W	5	2	1	2	2	3	2	1
Cardiff	D	L	4	0	4	0	1	3	3	1
Brentford	W	D	3	2	0	1	1	2	0	2
Birmingham	W	W	5	3	1	1	2	3	3	1
Preston	D	D	1	0	1	0	0	1	0	1
QPR	W	D	2	2	0	0	1	1	0	2
Leeds	W	W	5	3	2	0	3	2	2	3
Wolves	L	D	3	1	1	0	3	1	1	
Blackburn	W	W	4	2	2	0	1	3	2	2
Nottm Forest	W	W	5	2	1	2	2	3	2	3
Reading	W	D	4	1	2	1	1	3	2	1
Bristol City	W	W	3	3	0	0	1	2	1	2
Huddersfield	W	D	5	2	2	1	3	2	3	2
Fulham	W	W	2	1	0	1	2	0	1	1
Rotherham	W	L	2	1	1	0	1	1	2	0
Wigan			2	1	0	1	1	1	1	1
Burton			-	-	-	-	-	-	-	-
Barnsley			3	2	0	1	2	1	2	1

Season	Division	Pos	P	W	D	L	F	A	GD	Pts
2015-16	Championship	3	46	24	17	5	72	42	+30	89
2014-15	Championship	20	46	10	17	19	44	54	-10	47
2013-14	Championship	6	46	19	15	12	55	40	+15	72

Over/Under 54%/46% 4th   **Both score** 54%/46% 9th

BRISTOL CITY

Nickname: The Robins
Colours: Red and white
Ground: Ashton Gate (21,804)
Tel: 0871-222-666 www.bcfc.co.uk

Last season felt like a hangover from a celebratory 2014-15 for Bristol City as they never got higher than 17th, went out of both cups at the first hurdle and sacked manager Steve Cotterill rather hastily.

But there was no shame in the Robins spending a season consolidating their position back in the second tier and they never looked in any danger of relegation after Cotterill's replacement, 35-year-old Lee Johnson, led them on a three-match winning run in early February.

Longest run without win/loss: 6/4
High/low league position: 17/24
Clean sheets: 11 **Yellows:** 63 **Reds:** 3
Avg attendance: 16,301 **Players used:** 31
Leading scorer: J Kodjia 19 (6,15)
Key stat: There were 2.96 goals per game at Ashton Gate last season – only Fulham's Craven Cottage saw more action

	2015-16 H	A	P	W	D	L	OV	UN	BS	CS
Newcastle	-	-	-	-	-	-	-	-	-	-
Norwich			1	0	0	1	1	0	0	0
Aston Villa	-	-	-	-	-	-	-	-	-	-
Brighton	L	L	3	0	1	2	1	2	0	1
Derby	L	L	4	1	1	2	1	3	2	1
Sheffield Weds	W	L	2	1	1	0	1	1	2	0
Ipswich	W	D	4	2	0	2	3	1	2	0
Cardiff	L	D	4	2	0	2	3	1	2	1
Brentford	L	D	2	0	0	2	2	0	2	0
Birmingham	D	L	3	0	1	2	0	3	0	1
Preston	L	D	4	0	2	2	1	3	3	0
QPR	D	D	2	0	2	0	0	2	2	0
Leeds	D	L	4	0	1	3	3	1	2	0
Wolves	W	L	3	1	0	2	2	1	2	1
Blackburn	L	D	2	0	0	2	1	1	1	0
Nottm Forest	W	W	4	2	1	1	1	3	1	3
Reading	L	L	3	1	0	2	1	2	1	1
Bristol City										
Huddersfield	W	W	2	1	0	1	2	0	1	1
Fulham	L	W	1	0	0	1	1	0	1	0
Rotherham	D	L	2	0	1	1	1	1	2	0
Wigan			-	-	-	-	-	-	-	-
Burton			-	-	-	-	-	-	-	-
Barnsley			4	2	2	0	3	1	3	1

Season	Division	Pos	P	W	D	L	F	A	GD	Pts
2015-16	Championship	18	46	13	13	20	54	71	-17	52
2014-15	League 1	1	46	29	12	5	96	38	+58	99
2013-14	League 1	12	46	13	19	14	70	67	+3	58

Over/Under 50%/50% 8th   **Both score** 50%/50% 14th

BURTON

Nickname: The Brewers
Colours: Yellow and black
Ground: Pirelli Stadium (6,912)
Tel: 01283-565938 www.burtonalbionfc.co.uk

The feelgood factor from their 2014-15 League Two title success proved a catalyst for Burton to record impressive back-to-back promotions, but while it may seem churlish to criticise such a performance there must be concerns over the Brewers' form over the second half of the season.

Jimmy Floyd Hasselbaink won 13 of his 20 games in charge (65 per cent) but after he left for QPR that figure collapsed to 44 per cent under returning manager Nigel Clough.

Longest run without win/loss: 6/8
High/low league position: 1/4
Clean sheets: 22 **Yellows:** 64 **Reds:** 3
Avg attendance: 5,704 **Players used:** 25
Leading scorer: L Akins 12 (5,10)
Key stat: Burton scored just 57 goals last season – Bradford were the only top-ten team in League One to score fewer

	2015-16 H	A	P	W	D	L	OV	UN	BS	CS
Newcastle	-	-	-	-	-	-	-	-	-	-
Norwich	-	-	-	-	-	-	-	-	-	-
Aston Villa	-	-	-	-	-	-	-	-	-	-
Brighton	-	-	-	-	-	-	-	-	-	-
Derby	-	-	-	-	-	-	-	-	-	-
Sheffield Weds	-	-	-	-	-	-	-	-	-	-
Ipswich	-	-	-	-	-	-	-	-	-	-
Cardiff	-	-	-	-	-	-	-	-	-	-
Brentford	-	-	-	-	-	-	-	-	-	-
Birmingham	-	-	-	-	-	-	-	-	-	-
Preston	-	-	-	-	-	-	-	-	-	-
QPR	-	-	-	-	-	-	-	-	-	-
Leeds	-	-	-	-	-	-	-	-	-	-
Wolves	-	-	-	-	-	-	-	-	-	-
Blackburn	-	-	-	-	-	-	-	-	-	-
Nottm Forest	-	-	-	-	-	-	-	-	-	-
Reading	-	-	-	-	-	-	-	-	-	-
Bristol City	-	-	-	-	-	-	-	-	-	-
Huddersfield	-	-	-	-	-	-	-	-	-	-
Fulham	-	-	-	-	-	-	-	-	-	-
Rotherham			3	1	1	1	1	2	2	1
Wigan	D	W	1	0	1	0	0	1	1	0
Burton										
Barnsley	D	L	1	0	1	0	0	1	0	1

Season	Division	Pos	P	W	D	L	F	A	GD	Pts
2015-16	League 1	2	46	25	10	11	57	37	+20	85
2014-15	League 2	1	46	28	10	8	69	39	+30	94
2013-14	League 2	6	46	19	15	12	47	42	+5	72

Over/Under 39%/61% 21st   **Both score** 37%/63% 23rd

CARDIFF

Nickname: The Bluebirds
Colours: Blue
Ground: Cardiff City Stadium (26,847)
Tel: 02920-221-001   www.cardiffcityfc.co.uk

The Bluebirds spent the entire season on the fringes of the playoff places but never looked serious promotion contenders due to their inability to string together a run of consistent form.

Russell Slade didn't do a bad job and his side were particularly solid at home, losing just twice in Cardiff. But the lack of a ruthless second-tier goalscorer cost them the chance to nick points in tight games and new gaffer Paul Trollope has been quick to hunt new striking talent.

Longest run without win/loss: 4/6
High/low league position: 6/10
Clean sheets: 14 **Yellows:** 79 **Reds:** 4
Avg attendance: 17,881 **Players used:** 29
Leading scorer: A Pilkington 9 (3,7)
Key stat: Cardiff only twice strung together consecutive wins – a three-match run in August and a two-game run in February

	2015-16		Last six seasons at home							
	H	A	P	W	D	L	OV	UN	BS	CS
Newcastle			1	0	0	1	1	0	1	0
Norwich			3	2	0	1	3	0	3	0
Aston Villa			1	0	1	0	0	1	0	1
Brighton	W	D	4	1	1	2	2	2	2	1
Derby	W	L	5	3	1	1	2	3	3	1
Sheffield Weds	D	L	3	2	1	0	2	1	2	1
Ipswich	W	D	5	2	2	1	2	3	2	2
Cardiff										
Brentford	W	L	2	1	0	1	2	0	2	0
Birmingham	D	L	4	3	1	0	1	3	2	2
Preston	W	D	2	1	1	0	1	1	2	0
QPR	D	D	2	0	2	0	1	1	1	1
Leeds	L	L	5	3	1	1	3	2	4	0
Wolves	W	W	3	2	0	1	1	2	1	1
Blackburn	W	D	3	2	1	0	1	2	1	2
Nottm Forest	D	W	5	3	1	1	2	3	2	2
Reading	W	D	4	3	1	0	3	1	3	1
Bristol City	D	W	4	3	1	0	3	1	3	1
Huddersfield	W	W	3	3	0	0	1	2	1	2
Fulham	D	L	3	2	1	0	1	2	2	1
Rotherham	D	L	2	0	2	0	1	1	1	1
Wigan			1	1	0	0	0	1	0	1
Burton			-	-	-	-	-	-	-	-
Barnsley			3	1	2	0	2	1	3	0

Season	Division	Pos	P	W	D	L	F	A	GD	Pts
2015-16	Championship	8	46	17	17	12	56	51	+5	68
2014-15	Championship	11	46	16	14	16	57	61	-4	62
2013-14	Premier League	20	38	7	9	22	32	74	-42	30

Over/Under 43%/57% 12th   **Both score** 54%/46% 9th

DERBY

Nickname: The Rams
Colours: White and black
Ground: Pride Park Stadium (33,502)
Tel: 0871-472-1884   www.dcfc.co.uk

Derby supporters suffered promotion heartbreak for a third-successive season.

This time their team didn't choke horribly and were not robbed in a playoff final. They occupied a top-six berth for much of the season – bizarrely sacking Paul Clement in that position – before failing to show up in the first leg of their playoff semi-final and losing 3-0 at home to Hull. Nigel Pearson's arrival in the dugout suggests the Derby rollercoaster isn't ready to come to a halt just yet.

Longest run without win/loss: 8/10
High/low league position: 2/11
Clean sheets: 19 **Yellows:** 67 **Reds:** 0
Avg attendance: 24,013 **Players used:** 25
Leading scorer: C Martin 15 (5,13)
Key stat: Fifth-placed Derby had the fifth-best defence, the joint fifth-best attack and the fifth-best goal difference

	2015-16		Last six seasons at home							
	H	A	P	W	D	L	OV	UN	BS	CS
Newcastle			-	-	-	-	-	-	-	-
Norwich			2	0	1	1	2	0	2	0
Aston Villa			-	-	-	-	-	-	-	-
Brighton	D	D	5	2	2	1	2	3	1	3
Derby										
Sheffield Weds	D	D	4	2	2	0	3	1	3	1
Ipswich	L	W	6	0	3	3	2	4	3	1
Cardiff	W	L	5	1	2	2	3	2	3	1
Brentford	W	W	2	1	1	0	0	2	1	1
Birmingham	L	W	5	2	2	1	4	1	4	0
Preston	D	W	2	1	1	0	1	1	0	2
QPR	W	L	3	2	1	0	1	2	1	2
Leeds	L	D	6	5	0	1	4	2	4	2
Wolves	W	L	3	2	1	0	2	1	1	2
Blackburn	W	D	4	2	2	0	0	4	2	2
Nottm Forest	W	L	6	3	1	2	2	4	2	3
Reading	D	W	5	0	1	4	3	2	3	0
Bristol City	D	W	4	3	0	1	3	1	1	2
Huddersfield	W	W	4	4	0	0	3	1	2	2
Fulham	W	D	2	2	0	0	1	1	1	1
Rotherham	W	D	2	2	0	0	1	1	0	2
Wigan			2	0	0	2	1	1	1	0
Burton			-	-	-	-	-	-	-	-
Barnsley			4	2	2	0	1	3	2	2

Season	Division	Pos	P	W	D	L	F	A	GD	Pts
2015-16	Championship	5	46	21	15	10	66	43	+23	78
2014-15	Championship	8	46	21	14	11	85	56	+29	77
2013-14	Championship	3	46	25	10	11	84	52	+32	85

Over/Under 39%/61% 18th   **Both score** 46%/54% 18th

FULHAM

Nickname: The Cottagers
Colours: White and black
Ground: Craven Cottage (25,700)
Tel: 0870-442-1222   www.fulhamfc.com

A club with the Championship's second-highest wage bill and two of the division's best strikers should be doing far better than bumping around near the bottom.

Kit Symons' time at the Cottage proved an unhappy introduction to management but the club was at least stable in mid-table when he was fired. Replacement Slavisa Jokanovic arrived after Fulham had dropped to 18th, but they continued to slide under him and were just a point off the bottom three going into April.

Longest run without win/loss: 9/5
High/low league position: 11/21
Clean sheets: 4 **Yellows:** 81 **Reds:** 4
Avg attendance: 17,485 **Players used:** 33
Leading scorer: R McCormack 21 (6,20)
Key stat: Kit Symons' points-per-game ratio was 1.25 in his 16 games in charge, but that dropped to 1.17 under Slavisa Jokanovic

	2015-16 H	A	Last six seasons at home P	W	D	L	OV	UN	BS	CS
Newcastle			4	4	0	0	2	2	2	2
Norwich			4	4	0	0	2	2	1	3
Aston Villa			4	2	2	0	0	4	1	3
Brighton	L	L	2	0	0	2	1	1	1	0
Derby	D	L	2	1	1	0	0	2	1	1
Sheffield Weds	L	L	2	1	0	1	1	1	0	1
Ipswich	L	D	2	0	0	2	2	0	2	0
Cardiff	W	D	3	1	1	1	2	1	3	0
Brentford	D	L	2	0	1	1	2	0	2	0
Birmingham	L	D	3	0	2	1	1	2	3	0
Preston	D	W	1	0	1	0	0	1	1	0
QPR	W	W	3	3	0	0	3	0	1	2
Leeds	D	D	2	0	1	1	1	1	1	0
Wolves	L	L	4	2	0	2	3	1	1	1
Blackburn	W	L	4	2	1	1	2	2	3	0
Nottm Forest	L	L	2	1	0	1	2	0	2	0
Reading	W	D	3	2	0	1	3	0	3	0
Bristol City	L	W	1	0	0	1	0	1	0	0
Huddersfield	D	D	2	1	1	0	1	1	2	0
Fulham										
Rotherham	W	W	2	1	1	0	1	1	2	0
Wigan			4	2	2	0	2	2	3	1
Burton			-	-	-	-	-	-	-	-
Barnsley			-	-	-	-	-	-	-	-

Season	Division	Pos	P	W	D	L	F	A	GD	Pts
2015-16	Championship	20	46	12	15	19	66	79	-13	51
2014-15	Championship	17	46	14	10	22	62	83	-21	52
2013-14	Premier League	19	38	9	5	24	40	85	-45	32

Over/Under 65%/35% 1st   **Both score** 72%/28% 1st

HUDDERSFIELD

Nickname: The Terriers
Colours: Blue and white
Ground: John Smith's Stadium (24,554)
Tel: 01484-484-100   www.htafc.com

Huddersfield took their foot off the gas after securing safety and conceded nine goals in their final two games of 2015-16. But until then they had defended like a mid-table side and only eight second-tier teams could better their 59 goals scored.

Former Borussia Dortmund reserve-team coach David Wagner can take plenty of credit after improving the side upon his appointment in November and his bold early moves in the transfer market offer plenty of encouragement.

Longest run without win/loss: 6/5
High/low league position: 13/22
Clean sheets: 9 **Yellows:** 82 **Reds:** 3
Avg attendance: 15,203 **Players used:** 34
Leading scorer: N Wells 17 (8,16)
Key stat: After a slow start to the season, Nahki Wells scored 12 goals in 23 league games in the second half of the campaign

	2015-16 H	A	Last six seasons at home P	W	D	L	OV	UN	BS	CS
Newcastle			-	-	-	-	-	-	-	-
Norwich			1	0	1	0	1	0	1	0
Aston Villa			-	-	-	-	-	-	-	-
Brighton	D	L	5	1	3	1	2	3	5	0
Derby	L	L	4	1	2	1	2	2	3	1
Sheffield Weds	L	L	6	1	2	3	0	6	0	3
Ipswich	L	D	4	1	1	2	1	3	1	1
Cardiff	L	L	3	0	2	1	1	2	1	2
Brentford	L	L	4	2	1	1	4	0	4	0
Birmingham	D	W	4	0	2	2	1	3	3	0
Preston	W	L	2	2	0	0	2	0	2	0
QPR	L	D	2	0	1	1	0	2	1	0
Leeds	L	W	4	1	0	3	4	0	3	0
Wolves	W	L	3	2	0	1	2	1	2	1
Blackburn	D	W	4	0	3	1	3	1	4	0
Nottm Forest	D	W	4	1	2	1	2	2	2	1
Reading	D	W	3	2	0	1	2	1	1	1
Bristol City	L	L	2	1	0	1	1	1	1	1
Huddersfield										
Fulham	D	D	2	0	1	1	0	2	1	0
Rotherham	W	D	2	1	0	1	0	2	0	1
Wigan			2	1	1	0	0	2	0	2
Burton			-	-	-	-	-	-	-	-
Barnsley			2	1	1	0	2	0	1	1

Season	Division	Pos	P	W	D	L	F	A	GD	Pts
2015-16	Championship	19	46	13	12	21	59	70	-11	51
2014-15	Championship	16	46	13	16	17	58	75	-17	55
2013-14	Championship	17	46	14	11	21	58	65	-7	53

Over/Under 48%/52% 10th   **Both score** 57%/43% 6th

IPSWICH

Nickname: Town/Tractor Boys
Colours: Blue and white
Ground: Portman Road (30,311)
Tel: 01473-400-500   www.itfc.co.uk

The Tractor Boys flirted with the playoff places during the Christmas period but a run of four defeats in five going into February undid much of their good work and their season fizzled out thereafter.

A fair slice of misfortune, particularly with injuries, played a part. But while Mick McCarthy remains one of the best managers in the division, he has arguably been overachieving with a squad that cannot be faulted for its commitment but probably lacks genuine top-six quality.

Longest run without win/loss: 7/6
High/low league position: 5/13
Clean sheets: 16 **Yellows:** 64 **Reds:** 2
Avg attendance: 18,416 **Players used:** 31
Leading scorer: B Pitman 10 (3,10)
D Murphy 10 (3,6)
Key stat: Only eight teams scored fewer goals than seventh-placed Ipswich

	2015-16 H	A	P	W	D	L	OV	UN	BS	CS
Newcastle			-	-	-	-	-	-	-	-
Norwich			2	0	0	2	1	1	1	0
Aston Villa			-	-	-	-	-	-	-	-
Brighton	L	W	5	3	0	2	3	2	2	2
Derby	L	W	6	2	0	4	2	4	2	1
Sheffield Weds	W	D	4	3	0	1	4	0	3	0
Ipswich										
Cardiff	D	L	5	3	1	1	3	2	2	3
Brentford	L	D	2	0	1	1	1	1	2	0
Birmingham	D	L	5	3	2	0	2	3	4	1
Preston	D	W	2	1	1	0	1	1	2	0
QPR	W	L	3	1	0	2	3	0	2	0
Leeds	W	W	6	5	0	1	6	0	5	1
Wolves	D	D	3	1	1	1	2	1	2	0
Blackburn	W	L	4	2	2	0	1	3	3	1
Nottm Forest	W	D	6	3	1	2	3	3	4	1
Reading	W	L	5	2	0	3	3	2	3	1
Bristol City	D	L	4	2	2	0	2	2	2	2
Huddersfield	D	W	4	1	3	0	3	1	3	1
Fulham	D	W	2	1	1	0	1	1	2	0
Rotherham	L	W	2	1	0	1	0	2	0	1
Wigan			2	0	1	1	1	1	1	1
Burton			-	-	-	-	-	-	-	-
Barnsley			4	1	2	1	1	3	3	1

Season	Division	Pos	P	W	D	L	F	A	GD	Pts
2015-16	Championship	7	46	18	15	13	53	51	+2	69
2014-15	Championship	6	46	22	12	12	72	54	+18	78
2013-14	Championship	9	46	18	14	14	60	54	+6	68

Over/Under 41%/59% 16th   **Both score** 46%/54% 18th

LEEDS

Nickname: United
Colours: White
Ground: Elland Road (37,914)
Tel: 0113-367-6000   www.leedsunited.com

Not a single eyebrow was raised when Uwe Rosler survived just 12 games in the Elland Road dugout, and it's hard to know what chairman Massimo Cellino expects to achieve by keeping the club in a constant state of uncertainty.

Steve Evans took over with United in 18th and led them to 13th place, which is only just below par given Leeds' wage expenditure. Needless to say that wasn't enough for Cellino, who sacked Evans and replaced him with Garry Monk.

Longest run without win/loss: 6/7
High/low league position: 11/18
Clean sheets: 8 **Yellows:** 94 **Reds:** 3
Avg attendance: 21,368 **Players used:** 26
Leading scorer: C Wood 13 (6,12)
Key stat: Leeds scored just 23 goals at Elland Road last season – only Preston and MK Dons were less prolific on home soil

	2015-16 H	A	P	W	D	L	OV	UN	BS	CS
Newcastle			-	-	-	-	-	-	-	-
Norwich			2	0	1	1	1	1	1	0
Aston Villa			-	-	-	-	-	-	-	-
Brighton	L	L	5	1	0	4	4	1	4	0
Derby	D	W	6	1	2	3	3	3	4	1
Sheffield Weds	D	L	4	1	3	0	1	3	4	0
Ipswich	L	L	6	3	2	1	2	4	3	2
Cardiff	W	W	5	1	1	3	2	3	2	1
Brentford	D	D	2	0	1	1	0	2	1	0
Birmingham	L	W	5	1	1	3	2	3	2	1
Preston	W	D	2	1	0	1	1	1	1	1
QPR	D	L	3	1	1	1	0	3	1	1
Leeds										
Wolves	W	W	3	2	0	1	2	1	2	1
Blackburn	L	W	4	0	1	3	3	1	2	0
Nottm Forest	L	D	6	2	1	3	3	3	3	1
Reading	W	D	5	1	2	2	2	3	2	2
Bristol City	W	D	4	4	0	0	2	2	2	2
Huddersfield	L	W	4	2	0	2	4	0	3	1
Fulham	D	D	2	0	1	1	0	2	1	0
Rotherham	L	L	2	0	1	1	0	2	0	1
Wigan			2	1	0	1	0	2	0	1
Burton			-	-	-	-	-	-	-	-
Barnsley			4	1	2	1	2	2	2	2

Season	Division	Pos	P	W	D	L	F	A	GD	Pts
2015-16	Championship	13	46	14	17	15	50	58	-8	59
2014-15	Championship	15	46	15	11	20	50	61	-11	56
2013-14	Championship	15	46	15	9	21	59	61	-8	57

Over/Under 43%/57% 12th   **Both score** 61%/39% 2nd

NEWCASTLE

Nickname: The Magpies
Colours: Black and white
Ground: St James' Park (52,405)
Tel: 0191-201-8400   www.nufc.co.uk

Newcastle's relegation felt entirely avoidable and fans were again let down by poor decision-making at the club.

It clearly wasn't working out for Steve McClaren so to leave it so late to replace him was madness, as was proved by the upturn in results under Rafa Benitez.

However, getting Benitez to extend his deal was a real coup for Mike Ashley and everything looks to be in place for Newcastle to repeat their 2009-10 bounceback campaign.

Longest run without win/loss: 8/6
High/low league position: 15/20
Clean sheets: 8 **Yellows:** 61 **Reds:** 5
Avg attendance: 42,886 **Players used:** 31
Leading scorer: G Wijnaldum 11 (2,7)
Key stat: Benitez raised Newcastle's points-per-game ratio from 0.86 to 1.3 – enough for a mid-table finish in the Premier League

	2015-16 H	2015-16 A	Last six seasons at home P	W	D	L	OV	UN	BS	CS
Newcastle										
Norwich	W	L	4	4	0	0	2	2	2	2
Aston Villa	D	D	6	4	2	0	2	4	3	3
Brighton	-	-	-	-	-	-	-	-	-	-
Derby	-	-	-	-	-	-	-	-	-	-
Sheffield Weds	-	-	-	-	-	-	-	-	-	-
Ipswich	-	-	-	-	-	-	-	-	-	-
Cardiff	-	-	1	1	0	0	1	0	0	1
Brentford	-	-	-	-	-	-	-	-	-	-
Birmingham	-	-	1	1	0	0	1	0	1	0
Preston	-	-	-	-	-	-	-	-	-	-
QPR	-	-	3	3	0	0	0	3	0	3
Leeds	-	-	-	-	-	-	-	-	-	-
Wolves	-	-	2	1	1	0	2	0	2	0
Blackburn	-	-	2	1	0	1	2	0	2	0
Nottm Forest	-	-	-	-	-	-	-	-	-	-
Reading	-	-	1	0	0	1	1	0	1	0
Bristol City	-	-	-	-	-	-	-	-	-	-
Huddersfield	-	-	-	-	-	-	-	-	-	-
Fulham	-	-	4	3	1	0	1	3	1	3
Rotherham	-	-	-	-	-	-	-	-	-	-
Wigan	-	-	3	2	1	0	2	1	1	2
Burton	-	-	-	-	-	-	-	-	-	-
Barnsley	-	-	-	-	-	-	-	-	-	-

Season	Division	Pos	P	W	D	L	F	A	GD	Pts
2015-16	Premier League	18	38	9	10	19	44	65	-21	37
2014-15	Premier League	15	38	10	9	19	40	63	-23	39
2013-14	Premier League	10	38	15	4	19	43	59	-16	49

Over/Under 53%/47% 7th   **Both score** 50%/50% 11th

NORWICH

Nickname: The Canaries
Colours: Yellow and green
Ground: Carrow Road (27,224)
Tel: 01603-760-760   www.canaries.co.uk

Norwich were the only promoted side who failed to stay in the Premier League last season, and they kick off in a new league for the seventh time in nine years.

Alex Neil has rightly earned plenty of praise in his time as Norwich manager and he maintains support from the stands, but his squad needs investment.

The spirit, tactics and shape of the team were fine, but they just about deserved to go down because many of the players lack the quality required in the top flight.

Longest run without win/loss: 10/3
High/low league position: 13/19
Clean sheets: 5 **Yellows:** 62 **Reds:** 3
Avg attendance: 31,732 **Players used:** 28
Leading scorer: Dieumerci Mbokani 7 (0,6)
Key stat: Norwich lost nine of their final ten league away games last season, failing to score in eight of those matches

	2015-16 H	2015-16 A	Last six seasons at home P	W	D	L	OV	UN	BS	CS
Newcastle	W	L	4	2	2	0	2	2	2	2
Norwich										
Aston Villa	W	L	4	2	0	2	1	3	1	2
Brighton			1	0	1	0	1	0	1	0
Derby			2	1	1	0	1	1	2	0
Sheffield Weds			1	1	0	0	0	1	0	1
Ipswich			2	2	0	0	1	1	1	1
Cardiff			3	1	2	0	1	2	2	1
Brentford			1	0	0	1	1	0	1	0
Birmingham			1	0	1	0	1	0	1	0
Preston			1	0	1	0	0	1	1	0
QPR			3	2	1	0	1	2	2	1
Leeds			2	0	2	0	0	2	2	0
Wolves			2	2	0	0	1	1	1	1
Blackburn			2	1	1	0	2	0	2	0
Nottm Forest			2	2	0	0	2	0	2	0
Reading			3	2	0	1	3	0	3	0
Bristol City			1	1	0	0	1	0	1	0
Huddersfield			1	1	0	0	1	0	0	1
Fulham			4	1	2	1	2	2	3	1
Rotherham			1	0	1	0	0	1	1	0
Wigan			3	1	1	1	1	2	2	0
Burton			-	-	-	-	-	-	-	-
Barnsley			1	1	0	0	1	0	1	0

Season	Division	Pos	P	W	D	L	F	A	GD	Pts
2015-16	Premier League	19	38	9	7	22	39	67	-28	34
2014-15	Championship	3	46	25	11	10	88	48	+40	86
2013-14	Premier League	18	38	8	9	21	28	62	-34	33

Over/Under 53%/47% 7th   **Both score** 47%/53% 14th

NOTTINGHAM FOREST

Nickname: Forest
Colours: Red and white
Ground: City Ground (30,540)
Tel: 0115-982-4444   nottinghamforest.co.uk

Fawaz Al-Hasawi sacked yet another Forest manager but Dougie Freedman's 13-month reign outlasted many of his predecessors and his 33.3 per cent win ratio was bettered by only two of the last nine Forest managers and caretakers.

There are high hopes for former Real Sociedad and Rennes head coach Philippe Montanier, but if he is to adapt to the English game and make a success of his stay with Forest he will need financial backing and, most importantly, time.

Longest run without win/loss: 8/13
High/low league position: 8/20
Clean sheets: 11 **Yellows:** 88 **Reds:** 6
Avg attendance: 19,962 **Players used:** 34
Leading scorer: Nelson Oliveira 9 (6,8)
Key stat: Forest have finished between eighth and 19th in each of their last five seasons, with an average finishing place of 14th

	2015-16 H	A	Last six seasons at home P	W	D	L	OV	UN	BS	CS
Newcastle			-	-	-	-	-	-	-	-
Norwich			2	1	1	0	1	1	2	0
Aston Villa			-	-	-	-	-	-	-	-
Brighton	L	L	5	0	3	2	3	2	4	1
Derby	W	L	6	3	1	2	2	4	3	2
Sheffield Weds	L	L	4	1	1	2	2	2	1	1
Ipswich	D	L	6	3	3	0	2	4	3	3
Cardiff	L	D	5	2	0	3	4	1	4	0
Brentford	L	L	2	0	0	2	2	0	1	0
Birmingham	D	W	5	1	2	2	3	2	4	1
Preston	W	L	2	1	1	0	1	1	1	1
QPR	D	W	3	1	2	0	0	3	0	3
Leeds	D	W	6	2	3	1	3	3	5	0
Wolves	D	D	3	1	1	1	2	1	3	0
Blackburn	D	D	4	1	2	1	2	2	3	1
Nottm Forest										
Reading	W	L	5	3	0	2	4	1	3	2
Bristol City	L	L	4	2	0	2	1	3	1	2
Huddersfield	L	D	4	2	0	2	1	3	1	1
Fulham	W	W	2	2	0	0	2	0	1	1
Rotherham	W	D	2	2	0	0	1	1	1	1
Wigan			2	1	0	1	2	0	1	1
Burton			-	-	-	-	-	-	-	-
Barnsley			4	1	3	0	2	2	2	2

Season	Division	Pos	P	W	D	L	F	A	GD	Pts
2015-16	Championship	16	46	13	16	17	43	47	-4	55
2014-15	Championship	14	46	15	14	17	71	69	+2	59
2013-14	Championship	11	46	16	17	13	67	64	+3	65

Over/Under 35%/65% 22nd   **Both score** 52%/48% 12th

PRESTON

Nickname: Lilywhites/North End
Colours: White and navy blue
Ground: Deepdale (23,404)
Tel: 0870-442-1964   www.pnefc.co.uk

Operating on one of the tightest budgets in a hugely competitive division, Preston can be extremely proud of finishing 11th on their return to the Championship.

Many clubs can use the feelgood factor of promotion to propel them to safety, but Preston had to do it the hard way after a poor start left them second-bottom after ten games. That they finished closer to the top six than the relegation places says plenty about the value of having a steady hand like Simon Grayson in the dugout.

Longest run without win/loss: 9/6
High/low league position: 9/23
Clean sheets: 15 **Yellows:** 93 **Reds:** 5
Avg attendance: 15,294 **Players used:** 29
Leading scorer: D Johnson 8 (3,8)
Key stat: Preston had only the 20th-strongest attack in the Championship, but the sixth-best defence

	2015-16 H	A	Last six seasons at home P	W	D	L	OV	UN	BS	CS
Newcastle			-	-	-	-	-	-	-	-
Norwich			1	0	0	1	0	1	0	0
Aston Villa			-	-	-	-	-	-	-	-
Brighton	D	D	1	0	1	0	0	1	0	1
Derby	L	D	2	0	0	2	2	0	2	0
Sheffield Weds	W	L	2	1	0	1	0	2	0	1
Ipswich	L	D	2	1	0	1	1	1	1	1
Cardiff	D	L	2	0	1	1	0	2	0	1
Brentford	L	L	4	0	1	3	3	1	3	0
Birmingham	D	W	1	0	1	0	0	1	1	0
Preston										
QPR	D	D	2	0	2	0	0	2	2	0
Leeds	D	L	2	0	1	1	1	1	2	0
Wolves	D	W	2	0	2	0	0	2	1	1
Blackburn	L	W	1	0	0	1	0	1	0	0
Nottm Forest	W	L	2	1	0	1	1	1	1	1
Reading	W	W	2	1	1	0	0	2	1	1
Bristol City	D	W	4	1	2	1	1	3	2	1
Huddersfield	W	L	2	2	0	0	1	1	1	1
Fulham	L	D	1	0	0	1	1	0	1	0
Rotherham	W	D	2	1	1	0	2	0	2	0
Wigan			-	-	-	-	-	-	-	-
Burton			-	-	-	-	-	-	-	-
Barnsley			2	1	0	1	1	1	1	1

Season	Division	Pos	P	W	D	L	F	A	GD	Pts
2015-16	Championship	11	46	15	17	14	45	45	0	62
2014-15	League 1	3	46	25	14	7	79	40	+39	89
2013-14	League 1	5	46	23	16	7	72	46	+26	85

Over/Under 41%/59% 16th   **Both score** 57%/43% 6th

QPR

Nickname: The R's
Colours: Blue and white
Ground: Loftus Road (18,439)
Tel: 020-8743-0262   www.qpr.co.uk

Supporters are growing tired of the empty rhetoric coming from the owners, but QPR do seem to have got one thing right in appointing Jimmy Floyd Hasselbaink.

There was little justification for the club showing so much loyalty to Chris Ramsay as they were sliding rapidly under the relative rookie. Hasselbaink may not have worked miracles, but he inherited a bloated and unbalanced squad which will take plenty of fixing. Given a summer to work with it, he will hope to kick on.

Longest run without win/loss: 7/5
High/low league position: 9/17
Clean sheets: 15 **Yellows:** 69 **Reds:** 3
Avg attendance: 16,958 **Players used:** 32
Leading scorers: T Chery 10 (4,9)
C Austin 10 (3,8)
Key stat: QPR had the fifth-best home attack but the fourth-worst attack away from home

	2015-16 H	A	Last six seasons at home P	W	D	L	OV	UN	BS	CS
Newcastle			3	1	1	1	2	1	2	1
Norwich			3	0	2	1	1	2	1	2
Aston Villa			3	1	2	0	0	3	2	1
Brighton	D	L	2	0	2	0	1	1	1	1
Derby	W	L	3	2	1	0	1	2	1	2
Sheffield Weds	D	D	2	1	1	0	1	1	1	1
Ipswich	W	L	3	3	0	0	0	3	0	3
Cardiff	D	D	2	1	1	0	2	0	2	0
Brentford	W	L	1	1	0	0	1	0	0	1
Birmingham	W	L	2	2	0	0	0	2	0	2
Preston	D	D	2	1	1	0	1	1	1	1
QPR										
Leeds	W	D	3	1	1	1	1	2	2	1
Wolves	D	W	2	0	1	1	1	1	2	0
Blackburn	D	D	3	0	3	0	1	2	2	1
Nottm Forest	L		3	1	1	1	2	1	3	0
Reading	D	W	4	1	2	1	2	2	4	0
Bristol City	W	D	2	1	1	0	1	1	1	1
Huddersfield	D	W	2	1	1	0	1	1	2	0
Fulham	L	L	3	1	0	2	2	1	2	0
Rotherham	W	W	1	1	0	0	1	0	1	0
Wigan			3	2	1	0	1	2	2	1
Burton			-	-	-	-	-	-	-	-
Barnsley			2	2	0	0	1	1	0	2

Season	Division	Pos	P	W	D	L	F	A	GD	Pts
2015-16	Championship	12	46	14	18	14	54	54	0	60
2014-15	Premier League	20	38	8	6	24	42	73	-31	30
2013-14	Championship	4	46	23	11	12	60	44	+16	80

Over/Under 39%/61% 18th   **Both score** 50%/50% 14th

READING

Nickname: The Royals
Colours: Blue and white
Ground: Madejski Stadium (24,197)
Tel: 0118 968-1100   www.readingfc.co.uk

Having finished no lower than ninth in the second tier for 12 years up to 2014 – including two Premier League excursions – Reading have now spent two years in the bottom eight of the Championship.

There was no threat of relegation last term as six of the Royals' 20 defeats came in the last seven games when they were safe, but it was another wasted year for a club who should be in the promotion mix.

The appointment of untested manager Jaap Stam looks like guesswork, too.

Longest run without win/loss: 7/5
High/low league position: 3/17
Clean sheets: 11 **Yellows:** 71 **Reds:** 2
Avg attendance: 17,112 **Players used:** 30
Leading scorer: N Blackman 11 (6,10)
Key stat: Reading scored more goals away from home (27) than at the Madejski (25) but also conceded far more – 39 away, 20 at home

	2015-16 H	A	Last six seasons at home P	W	D	L	OV	UN	BS	CS
Newcastle			1	0	1	0	1	0	1	0
Norwich			3	1	2	0	1	2	1	2
Aston Villa			1	0	0	1	1	0	1	0
Brighton	D	L	4	2	2	0	2	2	2	2
Derby	L	D	5	1	2	2	3	2	2	1
Sheffield Weds	D		3	1	1	0	3	1	1	1
Ipswich	W	L	5	5	0	0	2	3	2	3
Cardiff	D	L	4	0	3	1	1	3	4	0
Brentford	L	W	2	0	0	2	1	1	1	0
Birmingham	L	L	4	2	0	2	0	4	0	2
Preston	L	L	2	1	0	1	2	0	2	0
QPR	L	D	4	0	2	2	0	4	1	1
Leeds	D	L	5	2	2	1	0	5	0	4
Wolves	D	L	2	0	2	0	1	1	1	1
Blackburn	W	L	3	1	1	1	0	3	0	2
Nottm Forest	W	L	5	2	2	1	2	3	3	1
Reading										
Bristol City	W	W	3	3	0	0	1	2	1	2
Huddersfield	D	L	3	0	2	1	2	1	3	0
Fulham	W	L	3	1	2	0	3	0	2	1
Rotherham	W	D	2	2	0	0	1	1	0	2
Wigan			3	0	0	3	2	1	1	0
Burton			-	-	-	-	-	-	-	-
Barnsley			3	1	0	2	3	0	2	1

Season	Division	Pos	P	W	D	L	F	A	GD	Pts
2015-16	Championship	17	46	13	13	20	52	59	-7	52
2014-15	Championship	19	46	13	11	22	48	69	-21	50
2013-14	Championship	7	46	19	14	13	70	56	+14	71

Over/Under 43%/57% 12th   **Both score** 59%/41% 4th

ROTHERHAM

Nickname: The Millers
Colours: Red and white
Ground: New York Stadium (12,009)
Tel: 08444-140-733   www.themillers.co.uk

The Millers finished one place above the drop for a second successive season and it was a bit more of a nail-biter this time.

They were in the bottom three for more than half of the campaign but brought in Neil Warnock in February to perform a rescue mission and he delivered in style.

Having lost 19 of 30 games before he arrived, Warnock led Rotherham on a stunning 11-match unbeaten run to finish nine points clear of relegation. Job done, he stepped aside for Alan Stubbs.

Longest run without win/loss: 7/11
High/low league position: 19/24
Clean sheets: 14 **Yellows:** 68 **Reds:** 5
Avg attendance: 13,854 **Players used:** 39
Leading scorer: M Derbyshire 8 (5,8)
Key stat: Erratic Rotherham lost to each of the other bottom six teams but also beat five of the top seven in the Championship

	2015-16		Last six seasons at home							
	H	A	P	W	D	L	OV	UN	BS	CS
Newcastle	-	-	-	-	-	-	-	-	-	-
Norwich			1	0	1	0	0	1	1	0
Aston Villa	-	-	-	-	-	-	-	-	-	-
Brighton	W	L	2	2	0	0	0	2	0	2
Derby	D	L	2	0	2	0	2	0	2	0
Sheffield Weds	L	W	2	0	0	2	2	0	2	0
Ipswich	L	W	2	1	0	1	1	1	1	1
Cardiff	W	D	2	1	0	1	2	0	2	0
Brentford	W	L	3	2	0	1	2	1	1	1
Birmingham	D	W	2	0	1	1	0	2	0	1
Preston	D	L	2	0	2	0	2	0	2	0
QPR	L	L	1	0	0	1	1	0	0	0
Leeds	W	W	2	2	0	0	2	0	2	0
Wolves	L	D	3	1	1	1	2	1	2	1
Blackburn	L	L	2	1	0	1	0	2	0	1
Nottm Forest	D	L	2	0	2	0	2	0	2	0
Reading	D	L	2	1	1	0	1	1	2	0
Bristol City	W	D	2	2	0	0	2	0	1	1
Huddersfield	D	L	2	0	2	0	1	1	2	0
Fulham	L	L	2	0	1	1	2	0	2	0
Rotherham										
Wigan			1	0	0	1	1	0	1	0
Burton			3	1	1	1	2	1	1	1
Barnsley	-	-	-	-	-	-	-	-	-	-

Season	Division	Pos	P	W	D	L	F	A	GD	Pts
2015-16	Championship	21	46	13	10	23	53	71	-18	49
2014-15	Championship	21	46	11	16	19	46	67	-21	46
2013-14	League 1	4	46	24	14	8	86	58	+28	86

Over/Under 54%/46% 4th   **Both score** 52%/48% 12th

SHEFFIELD WED

Nickname: The Owls
Colours: Blue and white
Ground: Hillsborough (39,732)
Tel: 0870-999-1867   www.swfc.co.uk

Upon taking over the club last summer, Dejphon Chansiri said he intended to do whatever was needed to get the club back in the top flight by 2017 – and he nearly delivered a year ahead of schedule.

The Owls were well beaten in the playoff final but a sixth-place finish maintained their upward trajectory and everything at the club is pointing in the right direction – ambitious owner, settled manager, good football and happy fans. At this rate, they're heading only one way.

Longest run without win/loss: 6/9
High/low league position: 5/18
Clean sheets: 17 **Yellows:** 81 **Reds:** 5
Avg attendance: 20,268 **Players used:** 29
Leading scorer: F Forestieri 15 (8,13)
Key stat: Sheffield Wednesday have improved their league position in each of the last six seasons

	2015-16		Last six seasons at home							
	H	A	P	W	D	L	OV	UN	BS	CS
Newcastle	-	-	-	-	-	-	-	-	-	-
Norwich			1	0	1	0	0	1	0	1
Aston Villa	-	-	-	-	-	-	-	-	-	-
Brighton	D	D	5	3	2	0	1	4	1	4
Derby	D	D	4	0	3	1	1	3	1	2
Sheffield Wed										
Ipswich	D	L	4	0	4	0	0	4	4	0
Cardiff	W	D	3	1	1	1	1	2	1	1
Brentford	W	W	4	2	1	1	2	2	1	3
Birmingham	W	W	4	3	1	0	3	1	2	2
Preston	W	L	2	2	0	0	1	1	1	1
QPR	D	D	2	1	1	0	1	1	1	1
Leeds	W	D	4	2	1	1	2	2	2	2
Wolves	W	L	3	1	1	1	2	1	1	1
Blackburn	W	D	4	2	1	1	4	0	4	0
Nottm Forest	W	W	4	1	0	3	0	4	0	1
Reading	D	D	3	2	1	0	1	2	2	1
Bristol City	W	L	2	1	0	1	1	1	1	1
Huddersfield	W	W	6	1	2	3	4	2	5	0
Fulham	W	W	2	1	1	0	1	1	2	0
Rotherham	L	W	2	0	1	1	0	2	0	1
Wigan			2	1	0	1	2	0	1	0
Burton	-	-	-	-	-	-	-	-	-	-
Barnsley			2	2	0	0	1	1	1	1

Season	Division	Pos	P	W	D	L	F	A	GD	Pts
2015-16	Championship	6	46	19	17	10	66	45	+21	74
2014-15	Championship	13	46	14	18	14	43	49	-6	60
2013-14	Championship	16	46	13	14	19	63	65	-2	53

Over/Under 50%/50% 8th   **Both score** 57%/43% 6th

WIGAN

Nickname: The Latics
Colours: Blue and white
Ground: DW Stadium (25,133)
Tel: 01942-774-000   www.wiganlatics.co.uk

The Latics landed awkwardly in League One, winning just four of their first 12 league games and falling at the first hurdle in the FA Cup and League Cup.

But rookie boss Gary Caldwell soon got his team back on track and from October there were only a couple of minor blips in a steady rise to the top of the division.

The undoubted star of the show was Will Grigg who really was on fire for the second half of the season, scoring 20 goals in the final 21 games.

Longest run without win/loss: 4/20
High/low league position: 1/10
Clean sheets: 19 **Yellows:** 68 **Reds:** 6
Avg attendance: 8,606 **Players used:** 36
Leading scorer: W Grigg 25 (10,18)
Key stat: Oxford United were the only team across the top four divisions to score more goals than Wigan last season

	2015-16		Last six seasons at home							
	H	A	P	W	D	L	OV	UN	BS	CS
Newcastle			3	2	0	1	2	1	1	1
Norwich			3	1	1	1	0	3	1	1
Aston Villa			3	0	2	1	2	1	2	1
Brighton			2	1	0	1	1	1	1	0
Derby			2	0	0	2	1	1	1	0
Sheffield Weds			2	1	0	1	0	2	0	1
Ipswich			2	1	0	1	1	1	1	1
Cardiff			1	0	0	1	0	1	0	0
Brentford			1	0	1	0	0	1	0	1
Birmingham			3	2	1	0	2	1	1	2
Preston			-	-	-	-	-	-	-	-
QPR			3	1	2	0	1	2	1	2
Leeds			2	1	0	1	0	2	0	1
Wolves			3	2	0	1	1	2	1	1
Blackburn			4	2	2	0	3	1	4	0
Nottm Forest			2	1	1	0	1	1	1	1
Reading			3	2	1	0	3	0	2	1
Bristol City			-	-	-	-	-	-	-	-
Huddersfield			2	1	0	1	1	1	1	0
Fulham			4	0	2	2	2	2	3	0
Rotherham			1	0	0	1	1	0	1	0
Wigan										
Burton	L	D	1	0	0	1	0	1	0	0
Barnsley	L	W	2	1	0	1	1	1	1	1

Season	Division	Pos	P	W	D	L	F	A	GD	Pts
2015-16	League 1	1	46	24	15	7	82	45	+37	87
2014-15	Championship	23	46	9	12	25	39	64	-25	39
2013-14	Championship	5	46	21	10	15	61	48	+13	73

Over/Under 48%/52% 14th   **Both score** 50%/50% 13th

WOLVES

Nickname: Wolves
Colours: Gold and black
Ground: Molineux Stadium (30,852)
Tel: 0871-880-8442   www.wolves.co.uk

Wolves fans were hoping to push on after a year of consolidation in the second tier but their playoff tilt failed to ignite.

Indeed a lack of spark dogged them all season, which was no surprise given the three men to reach double-figure tallies in 2014-15 – Bakary Sako, Benik Afobe and Nouha Dicko – either left the club or were out injured. The attack needs rebuilding but it's unlikely the current owners will splash out given a takeover of the club is looming on the horizon.

Longest run without win/loss: 7/6
High/low league position: 9/18
Clean sheets: 14 **Yellows:** 49 **Reds:** 1
Avg attendance: 19,512 **Players used:** 33
Leading scorer: B Afobe 9 (4,8)
Key stat: Seven of Wolves's 23 home games ended 0-0

	2015-16		Last six seasons at home							
	H	A	P	W	D	L	OV	UN	BS	CS
Newcastle			2	0	1	1	1	1	2	0
Norwich			2	1	1	0	1	1	1	1
Aston Villa			2	0	0	2	2	0	2	0
Brighton	D	W	3	0	3	0	1	2	2	1
Derby	W	L	3	2	1	0	1	2	2	1
Sheffield Weds	W	L	3	3	0	0	2	1	1	2
Ipswich	D	D	3	0	2	1	0	3	1	1
Cardiff	L	L	3	1	0	2	2	1	2	1
Brentford	L	L	3	1	1	1	1	2	1	1
Birmingham	D	D	4	2	2	0	0	4	0	4
Preston	L	D	2	1	0	1	1	1	1	1
QPR	L	D	2	0	0	2	2	0	1	0
Leeds	L	L	3	1	1	1	3	0	3	0
Wolves										
Blackburn	D	W	5	1	2	2	2	3	3	1
Nottm Forest	D	D	3	0	1	2	2	1	2	0
Reading	W	D	2	1	0	1	1	1	1	1
Bristol City	W	L	3	3	0	0	3	0	3	0
Huddersfield	W	L	3	1	0	2	3	0	2	1
Fulham	W	W	4	3	1	0	2	2	2	2
Rotherham	D	W	3	2	1	0	2	1	1	2
Wigan			3	1	1	1	3	0	3	0
Burton			-	-	-	-	-	-	-	-
Barnsley			1	1	0	0	1	0	1	0

Season	Division	Pos	P	W	D	L	F	A	GD	Pts
2015-16	Championship	14	46	14	16	16	53	58	-5	58
2014-15	Championship	7	46	22	12	12	70	56	+14	78
2013-14	League 1	1	46	31	10	5	89	31	+58	103

Over/Under 52%/48% 7th   **Both score** 59%/41% 4th

Championship stats 2015-16

Key Points in all tables (except the league table) do not include any deductions imposed by the league.
POS H A Overall league position, rank from home games only, rank from away games only **Sup** Average match supremacy **GFA** Goals For Average **GAA** Goals Against Average **PGA** Points Gained Average

Pos	H	A	Championship 2015-16	Home P	W	D	L	F	A	Away W	D	L	F	A	GD	Pts
1	3	1	Burnley (P)	46	15	6	2	38	14	11	9	3	34	21	+37	93
2	1	3	Middlesbrough (P)	46	16	5	2	34	8	10	6	7	29	23	+32	89
3	4	2	Brighton	46	15	5	3	40	18	9	12	2	32	24	+30	89
4	2	9	Hull (P)	46	15	7	1	47	12	9	4	10	22	23	+34	83
5	7	4	Derby	46	12	7	4	37	16	9	8	6	29	27	+23	78
6	5	11	Sheff Wed	46	13	8	2	42	17	6	9	8	24	28	+21	74
7	9	5	Ipswich	46	9	8	6	28	24	9	7	7	25	27	+2	69
8	6	17	Cardiff	46	12	9	2	33	20	5	8	10	23	31	+5	68
9	10	7	Brentford	46	10	4	9	33	30	9	4	10	39	37	+5	65
10	13	6	Birmingham	46	9	5	9	27	27	7	10	6	26	22	+4	63
11	15	8	Preston	46	7	10	6	21	21	8	7	8	24	24	0	62
12	8	19	QPR	46	10	9	4	37	25	4	9	10	17	29	0	60
13	19	10	Leeds	46	7	8	8	23	28	7	9	7	27	30	-8	59
14	14	12	Wolves	46	7	10	6	26	26	7	6	10	27	32	-5	58
15	12	16	Blackburn	46	8	8	7	29	23	5	8	10	17	23	0	55
16	18	13	Nottm Forest	46	7	8	8	25	26	6	8	9	18	21	-4	55
17	11	20	Reading	46	8	9	6	25	20	5	4	14	27	39	-7	52
18	20	15	Bristol City	46	7	7	9	34	34	6	6	11	20	37	-17	52
19	21	14	Huddersfield	46	7	6	10	33	33	6	6	11	26	37	-11	51
20	17	18	Fulham	46	8	5	10	36	36	4	10	9	30	43	-13	51
21	16	21	Rotherham	46	8	6	9	31	34	5	4	14	22	37	-18	49
22	24	22	Charlton (R)	46	5	8	10	23	35	4	5	14	17	45	-40	40
23	23	23	MK Dons (R)	46	7	3	13	21	37	2	9	12	18	32	-30	39
24	22	24	Bolton (R)	46	5	11	7	24	26	0	4	19	17	55	-40	30

Best attack

		GF	GFA
1	Burnley	72	1.57
2	Brighton	72	1.57
3	Brentford	72	1.57
4	Hull	69	1.5
5	Sheff Wed	66	1.43
6	Fulham	66	1.43
7	Derby	66	1.43
8	Middlesbro	63	1.37
9	Huddersfield	59	1.28
10	Cardiff	56	1.22
11	QPR	54	1.17
12	Bristol City	54	1.17
13	Wolves	53	1.15
14	Rotherham	53	1.15
15	Ipswich	53	1.15
16	Birmingham	53	1.15
17	Reading	52	1.13
18	Leeds	50	1.09
19	Blackburn	46	1
20	Preston	45	0.98
21	Nottm Forest	43	0.93
22	Bolton	41	0.89
23	Charlton	40	0.87
24	MK Dons	39	0.85

Best defence

		GA	GAA
1	Middlesbro	31	0.67
2	Burnley	35	0.76
3	Hull	35	0.76
4	Brighton	42	0.91
5	Derby	43	0.93
6	Sheff Wed	45	0.98
7	Preston	45	0.98
8	Blackburn	46	1
9	Nottm Forest	47	1.02
10	Birmingham	49	1.07
11	Ipswich	51	1.11
12	Cardiff	51	1.11
13	QPR	54	1.17
14	Leeds	58	1.26
15	Wolves	58	1.26
16	Reading	59	1.28
17	Brentford	67	1.46
18	MK Dons	69	1.5
19	Huddersfield	70	1.52
20	Bristol City	71	1.54
21	Rotherham	71	1.54
22	Fulham	79	1.72
23	Charlton	80	1.74
24	Bolton	81	1.76

Top scorers

	Team	Goals scored
A Gray	Burnley	25
R McCormack	Fulham	21
A Hernandez	Hull	20
J Kodjia	Bristol City	19
T Hemed	Brighton	17
N Wells	Huddersfield	17

Over 2.5 goals

	H	A	%
Fulham	15	15	65%
Brentford	14	16	65%
Charlton	12	15	59%
Bolton	10	15	54%
Brighton	13	12	54%

Under 2.5 goals

	H	A	%
Blackburn	13	18	67%
Hull	13	17	65%
Nottm Forest	12	18	65%
Birmingham	12	17	63%
Middlesbro	15	14	63%

Both to score

	H	A	%
Fulham	16	17	72
Brentford	14	14	61
Leeds	14	14	61
Reading	11	16	59
Wolves	13	14	59

Both not to score

	H	A	%
Middlesbrough	6	10	65%
Hull	9	8	63%
Blackburn	11	9	57%
Birmingham, Derby, Charlton, Ipswich			54%

SOCCERBASE.COM

Championship results 2015-16

	Birmingham	Blackburn	Bolton	Brentford	Brighton	Bristol City	Burnley	Cardiff	Charlton	Derby	Fulham	Huddersfield	Hull	Ipswich	Leeds	Middlesbrough	MK Dons	Nottm Forest	Preston	QPR	Reading	Rotherham	Sheffield Wed	Wolves
Birmingham		0-0	1-0	2-1	1-2	4-2	1-2	1-0	0-1	1-1	1-1	0-2	1-0	3-0	1-2	2-2	1-0	0-1	2-2	2-1	2-1	0-2	1-2	0-2
Blackburn	2-0		0-0	1-1	0-1	2-2	0-1	1-1	3-0	0-0	3-0	0-2	0-2	2-0	1-2	2-1	3-2	0-0	1-2	1-1	3-1	1-0	2-2	1-2
Bolton	0-1	1-0		1-1	2-2	0-0	1-2	2-3	0-0	0-0	2-2	0-2	1-0	2-2	1-1	1-2	3-1	1-1	1-2	1-1	0-1	2-1	0-0	2-1
Brentford	0-2	0-1	3-1		0-0	1-1	1-3	2-1	1-2	1-3	3-0	4-2	0-2	2-2	1-1	0-1	2-0	2-1	2-1	1-0	1-3	2-1	1-2	3-0
Brighton	2-1	1-0	3-2	3-0		2-1	2-2	1-1	3-2	1-1	5-0	2-1	1-0	0-1	4-0	0-3	2-1	1-0	0-0	4-0	1-0	2-1	0-0	0-1
Bristol City	0-0	0-2	6-0	2-4	0-4		1-2	0-2	1-1	2-3	1-4	4-0	1-1	2-1	2-2	1-0	1-1	2-0	1-2	1-1	0-2	1-1	4-1	1-0
Burnley	2-2	1-0	2-0	1-0	1-1	4-0		0-0	4-0	4-1	3-1	2-1	1-0	0-0	1-0	1-1	2-1	1-0	0-2	1-0	1-2	2-0	3-1	1-1
Cardiff	1-1	1-0	2-1	3-2	4-1	0-0	2-2		2-1	2-1	1-1	2-0	0-2	1-0	0-2	1-0	0-0	1-1	2-1	0-0	2-0	2-2	2-2	2-0
Charlton	2-1	1-1	2-2	0-3	1-3	0-1	0-3	0-0		0-1	2-2	1-2	2-1	0-3	0-0	2-0	0-0	1-1	0-3	2-0	3-4	1-1	3-1	0-2
Derby	0-3	1-0	4-1	2-0	2-2	4-0	0-0	0-0	1-1		2-0	2-0	4-0	1-2	1-1	0-1	1-0	0-0	1-0	1-1	3-0	1-1	3-0	4-2
Fulham	2-5	2-1	1-0	2-2	1-2	1-2	2-3	2-1	3-0	1-1		1-1	0-1	1-2	1-0	0-2	2-1	1-3	1-1	4-0	4-2	4-1	0-1	0-3
Huddersfield	1-1	1-1	4-1	1-5	1-1	1-2	1-3	2-3	5-0	1-2	1-1		2-2	0-1	0-3	0-2	2-0	1-1	3-1	0-1	3-1	2-0	0-1	1-0
Hull	2-0	1-1	1-0	2-0	0-0	4-0	3-0	2-0	6-0	0-2	2-1	2-0		3-0	2-2	3-0	1-1	1-1	2-0	1-1	2-1	5-1	0-0	2-1
Ipswich	1-1	2-0	2-0	1-3	2-3	2-2	2-0	0-0	0-0	0-1	1-1	0-0	0-1		2-1	0-2	3-2	1-0	1-1	2-1	2-1	0-1	2-1	2-2
Leeds	0-2	0-2	2-1	1-1	1-2	1-0	1-1	1-0	1-2	2-2	1-1	1-4	2-1	0-1		0-0	1-1	0-1	1-0	1-1	3-2	0-1	1-1	2-1
Middlesbrough	0-0	1-1	3-0	3-1	1-1	0-1	1-0	3-1	3-0	2-0	0-0	3-0	1-0	0-0	3-0		2-0	0-1	1-0	1-1	2-1	1-0	1-0	2-1
MK Dons	0-2	3-0	1-0	1-4	1-2	0-2	0-5	2-1	1-0	1-3	1-1	1-0	0-2	0-1	1-2	1-1		1-2	0-1	2-0	1-0	0-4	2-1	1-1
Nottm Forest	1-1	1-1	3-0	0-3	1-2	1-2	1-1	1-2	0-0	1-0	3-0	0-2	0-1	1-1	1-1	1-2	2-1		1-0	0-0	3-1	2-1	0-3	1-1
Preston	1-1	1-2	0-0	1-3	0-0	1-1	0-1	0-0	2-1	1-2	1-2	1-1	1-0	0-1	1-0	1-0	1-1	1-0		1-1	1-0	2-1	1-0	1-1
QPR	2-0	2-2	4-3	3-0	2-2	1-0	0-0	2-2	2-1	2-0	1-3	1-1	1-2	1-0	1-0	2-3	3-0	1-2	0-0		1-1	4-2	0-0	1-1
Reading	0-2	1-0	2-1	1-2	1-1	1-0	0-0	1-1	1-0	0-1	2-2	2-2	1-2	5-1	0-0	2-0	0-0	2-1	1-2	0-1		1-0	1-1	0-0
Rotherham	0-0	0-1	4-0	2-1	2-0	3-0	1-2	2-1	1-4	3-3	1-3	1-1	2-0	2-5	2-1	1-0	1-4	0-0	0-0	0-3	1-1		1-2	1-2
Sheffield Wed	3-0	2-1	3-2	4-0	0-0	2-0	1-1	3-0	3-0	0-0	3-2	3-1	1-1	1-1	2-0	1-3	0-0	1-0	3-1	1-1	1-1	0-1		4-1
Wolves	0-0	0-0	2-2	0-2	0-0	2-1	0-0	1-3	2-1	2-1	3-2	3-0	1-1	0-0	2-3	1-3	0-0	1-1	1-2	2-3	1-0	0-0	2-1	

Record when first to score

		P	W	D	L	F	A	Sup	PGA	Pts
1	Burnley	27	25	2	0	55	13	+1.56	2.9	77
2	Middlesbrough	26	23	3	0	50	11	+1.50	2.8	72
3	Hull	23	21	2	0	47	5	+1.83	2.8	65
4	Derby	24	20	4	0	52	20	+1.33	2.7	64
5	Brighton	28	21	7	0	61	25	+1.29	2.5	70
6	Ipswich	20	15	5	0	38	16	+1.10	2.5	50
7	Brentford	22	16	5	1	50	21	+1.32	2.4	53
8	Sheff Wed	21	15	5	1	44	20	+1.14	2.4	50
9	Cardiff	22	15	5	2	42	24	+0.82	2.3	50
10	Rotherham	19	13	3	3	33	16	+0.89	2.2	42
11	Leeds	19	12	5	2	30	20	+0.53	2.2	41
12	Blackburn	18	12	4	2	30	13	+0.94	2.2	40
13	Preston	18	11	6	1	24	14	+0.56	2.2	39
14	Bristol City	17	11	4	2	30	14	+0.94	2.2	37
15	Huddersfield	17	11	4	2	32	14	+1.06	2.2	37
16	Wolves	19	12	3	4	34	24	+0.53	2.1	39
17	Birmingham	26	15	8	3	46	23	+0.88	2	53
18	Reading	20	12	3	5	35	24	+0.55	2	39
19	QPR	24	12	9	3	37	19	+0.75	1.9	45
20	Fulham	21	10	10	1	41	23	+0.86	1.9	40
21	Nottm Forest	20	10	8	2	28	17	+0.55	1.9	38
22	MK Dons	17	9	5	3	25	15	+0.59	1.9	32
23	Charlton	14	8	3	3	26	16	+0.71	1.9	27
24	Bolton	13	5	2	6	19	21	-0.15	1.3	17

Record when keeping a clean sheet

		P	W	D	F	Sup	PGA	Pts
1	Hull	20	18	2	41	+2.05	2.8	56
2	Huddersfield	9	8	1	18	+2	2.8	25
3	Brentford	8	7	1	17	+2.13	2.8	22
4	Middlesbrough	22	17	5	32	+1.45	2.5	56
5	Derby	19	14	5	27	+1.42	2.5	47
6	Bristol City	11	8	3	18	+1.64	2.5	27
7	Fulham	4	3	1	8	+2	2.5	10
8	Burnley	20	14	6	28	+1.4	2.4	48
9	Birmingham	16	11	5	19	+1.19	2.4	38
10	Rotherham	14	10	4	21	+1.5	2.4	34
11	Ipswich	16	10	6	15	+0.94	2.3	36
12	QPR	15	10	5	18	+1.2	2.3	35
13	Blackburn	14	9	5	17	+1.21	2.3	32
14	Reading	11	7	4	9	+0.82	2.3	25
15	Nottm Forest	11	7	4	11	+1	2.3	25
16	Leeds	8	5	3	8	+1	2.3	18
17	Brighton	17	10	7	25	+1.47	2.2	37
18	Sheff Wed	17	10	7	23	+1.35	2.2	37
19	MK Dons	11	6	5	9	+0.82	2.1	23
20	Cardiff	14	7	7	11	+0.79	2	28
21	Preston	15	7	8	10	+0.67	1.9	29
22	Wolves	14	6	8	12	+0.86	1.9	26
23	Charlton	9	3	6	5	+0.56	1.7	15
24	Bolton	8	2	6	2	+0.25	1.5	12

Neil Harris's Lions look the likeliest to tame the most dangerous of divisions

Millwall can use the heartbreak of missing out on promotion to the Championship last season by taking a wide-open League One this term, writes Mark Langdon. The Lions, beaten by Barnsley in the playoff final, had a number of younger players in their squad last season who should improve for a full campaign under their belt and the same is also true of manager Neil Harris.

The Lions were flying at the finish and lost just four league games in 2016, and Millwall used home advantage well to win seven league games in a row and six of those to nil.

Harris has been promised a top-six budget but it is not a team that needs major work. There should be more to come from the likes of Mahlon Romeo, Ben Thompson and Jordan Archer, and they will hope to keep the front two of Lee Gregory and Steve Morison together.

There are many with chances but Sheffield United have repeatedly let their backers down and they face a major rebuilding job under Chris Wilder after he quite rightly decided to ditch most of the dead wood left behind by Nigel Adkins.

Bradford, beaten by Millwall in the playoff semi-finals, look a live danger but two of last term's best players – Reece Burke and Lee Evans – were on loan deals and will need replacing, as will manager Phil Parkinson who went to Bolton.

However, Bolton, like the other relegated clubs, all have plenty to prove.

Charlton have made a good managerial appointment in Russell Slade, and striker Nicky Ajose's signing bodes well. But there are still issues behind the scenes which makes them a risky betting proposition.

MK Dons were unable to take the title the last time they were in at this level despite possessing the talents of Benik Afobe, Dele Alli and Will Grigg, while Bolton need to prove they are stable off the pitch before taking a chance on the Trotters.

Peterborough must improve their dodgy defence if they are to become challengers but are making the right moves in the transfer market. And a couple of new sides to the section will fancy their chances of repeating the feat achieved by Burton last term by gaining successive promotions straight through the third tier.

Northampton won League Two last term but Wilder's departure leaves a question mark, although replacement Rob Page did a very respectable job at Port Vale.

Bristol Rovers' ambition has been shown by boss Darrell Clarke's decision to turn down Leeds in favour of staying with a club aiming for a third straight promotion, while for many Oxford were actually the best team in League Two last season.

However, United are getting full respect from bookmakers and in a fascinating division there are many runners. But Walsall may have missed their chance to go up last term and Coventry reportedly have some off-field issues to solve.

Scunthorpe are one to consider at a bigger price. The Iron finished last season in excellent fashion and only missed out on the playoffs on goal difference to Barnsley.

Lee Gregory and Steve Morison (right) scored 33 of Millwall's 73 League One goals last term

AFC WIMBLEDON

Nickname: The Dons
Colours: Blue and yellow
Ground: Cherry Red Records Stadium (5,339)
Tel: 0208-547-3528   www.afcwimbledon.co.uk

In 14 years, Wimbledon have risen from the ashes to the third tier and manager Neil Ardley can be proud of how he led the Wombles to a playoff final victory after finishing seventh in League Two.

Wimbledon were 14th at Christmas but finished brilliantly with six wins in eight and Wembley hero Lyle Taylor was instrumental to the success with 20 league goals. However, he has previously struggled in League One with both Sheffield United and Scunthorpe.

Longest run without win/loss: 7/6
High/low league position: 5/16
Clean sheets: 13 **Yellows:** 65 **Reds:** 5
Avg attendance: 4,480 **Players used:** 29
Leading scorer: L Taylor 20 (6,15)
Key stat: Wimbledon conceded two goals in their last nine matches in all competitions

	2015-16		Last six seasons at home							
	H	A	P	W	D	L	OV	UN	BS	CS
Charlton			-	-	-	-	-	-	-	-
MK Dons			-	-	-	-	-	-	-	-
Bolton			-	-	-	-	-	-	-	-
Walsall			-	-	-	-	-	-	-	
Millwall			-	-	-	-	-	-	-	
Bradford			2	2	0	0	2	0	2	0
Scunthorpe			1	1	0	0	1	0	1	0
Coventry			-	-	-	-	-	-	-	
Gillingham			2	1	0	1	1	1	1	0
Rochdale			2	0	0	2	2	0	1	0
Sheffield United			-	-	-	-	-	-		
Port Vale			2	1	1	0	2	0	2	0
Peterborough			-	-	-	-	-	-		
Bury			2	1	0	1	1	1	1	0
Southend			4	0	1	3	2	2	1	1
Swindon			1	0	1	0	0	1	1	0
Oldham			-	-	-	-	-	-		
Chesterfield			2	1	1	0	0	2	1	1
Fleetwood Town			3	3	0	0	1	2	1	2
Shrewsbury			2	1	1	0	2	0	2	0
Northampton	D	D	5	0	3	2	2	3	3	0
Oxford	L	L	5	0	1	4	2	3	1	1
Bristol Rovers	D	L	4	1	2	1	2	2	2	2
AFC Wimbledon										

Season	Division	Pos	P	W	D	L	F	A	GD	Pts
2015-16	League 2	7	46	21	12	13	64	50	+14	75
2014-15	League 2	15	46	14	16	16	54	60	-6	58
2013-14	League 2	20	46	14	14	18	49	57	-8	53

Over/Under 43%/57% 18th   **Both score** 59%/41% 5th

BOLTON

Nickname: The Trotters
Colours: White and blue
Ground: The Reebok Stadium (28,100)
Tel: 01204-673-673   www.bwfc.co.uk

They are sure to be a big club at this level but last season was a disaster for Bolton, who finished bottom of the Championship and were terrible in both boxes with only 41 goals scored and 81 conceded.

Neil Lennon was sacked as the cash-strapped Trotters failed to win away from home all season and much will depend on how the club is able to rebuild after a Dean Holdsworth-led consortium took control of the club. Phil Parkinson joins as manager from Bradford.

Longest run without win/loss: 17/4
High/low league position: 17/24
Clean sheets: 8 **Yellows:** 71 **Reds:** 8
Avg attendance: 16,255 **Players used:** 34
Leading scorer: Z Clough 7 (2,6)
Key stat: Bolton lost 19 of their 23 away league matches in the Championship last season

	2015-16		Last six seasons at home							
	H	A	P	W	D	L	OV	UN	BS	CS
Charlton	D	D	4	1	3	0	0	4	2	2
MK Dons	W	L	1	1	0	0	1	0	1	0
Bolton										
Walsall			-	-	-	-	-	-	-	
Millwall			3	2	1	0	1	2	2	1
Bradford			-	-	-	-	-	-		
Scunthorpe			-	-	-	-	-	-		
Coventry			-	-	-	-	-	-		
Gillingham			-	-	-	-	-	-		
Rochdale			-	-	-	-	-	-		
Sheffield United			-	-	-	-	-	-		
Port Vale			-	-	-	-	-	-		
Peterborough			1	1	0	0	0	1	0	1
Bury			-	-	-	-	-	-		
Southend			-	-	-	-	-	-		
Swindon			-	-	-	-	-	-		
Oldham			-	-	-	-	-	-		
Chesterfield			-	-	-	-	-	-		
Fleetwood Town			-	-	-	-	-	-		
Shrewsbury			-	-	-	-	-	-		
Northampton			-	-	-	-	-	-		
Oxford			-	-	-	-	-	-		
Bristol Rovers			-	-	-	-	-	-		
AFC Wimbledon			-	-	-	-	-	-		

Season	Division	Pos	P	W	D	L	F	A	GD	Pts
2015-16	Championship	24	46	5	15	26	41	81	-40	30
2014-15	Championship	18	46	13	12	21	54	57	-13	51
2013-14	Championship	14	46	14	17	15	59	60	-1	59

Over/Under 54%/46% 4th   **Both score** 54%/46% 9th

BRADFORD

Nickname: The Bantams
Colours: Claret and amber
Ground: Coral Windows Stadium (25,136)
Tel: 01274-773-355   www.bradfordcityfc.co.uk

Bradford finished fifth to continue their record of reaching a higher position in every campaign under Phil Parkinson, but their promotion dream ended in the playoff semi-finals and Parkinson left for Bolton in the summer.

Parkinson departs the club having laid excellent defensive foundations but key to that last term was West Ham's on-loan Reece Burke who needs replacing.

That task should be helped by the fact that new owners bought the club in May.

Longest run without win/loss: 4/9
High/low league position: 4/19
Clean sheets: 22 **Yellows:** 63 **Reds:** 3
Avg attendance: 11,445 **Players used:** 30
Leading scorer: J Hanson 11 (3,8)
Key stat: Bradford kept 22 clean sheets in League One last season

	2015-16 H	2015-16 A	Last six seasons at home P	W	D	L	OV	UN	BS	CS
Charlton			-	-	-	-	-	-	-	-
MK Dons			2	2	0	0	1	1	1	1
Bolton			-	-	-	-	-	-	-	-
Walsall	W	L	3	1	1	1	1	2	1	1
Millwall	W	D	1	1	0	0	0	1	0	1
Bradford										
Scunthorpe	W	W	2	1	1	0	0	2	1	1
Coventry	D	L	3	1	2	0	2	1	2	1
Gillingham	L	L	6	1	3	2	2	4	4	1
Rochdale	D	W	3	0	1	2	3	0	3	0
Sheffield United	D	L	3	1	1	1	1	2	1	1
Port Vale	W	D	6	2	2	2	0	6	2	2
Peterborough	L	W	3	1	0	2	0	3	0	1
Bury	W	D	2	2	0	0	1	1	1	1
Southend	W	W	4	2	1	1	1	3	1	2
Swindon	W	L	4	1	2	1	1	3	2	2
Oldham	W	W	3	2	0	1	2	1	2	2
Chesterfield	W	W	4	1	1	2	0	4	0	2
Fleetwood Town	W	D	3	2	1	0	2	1	2	1
Shrewsbury	D	D	4	2	1	1	3	1	4	0
Northampton			3	2	1	0	1	2	2	1
Oxford			3	2	0	1	3	0	2	1
Bristol Rovers			2	1	1	0	2	0	2	0
AFC Wimbledon			2	1	1	0	2	0	2	0

Season	Division	Pos	P	W	D	L	F	A	GD	Pts
2015-16	League 1	5	46	23	11	12	55	40	+15	80
2014-15	League 1	7	46	17	14	15	55	55	0	65
2013-14	League 1	11	46	14	17	15	57	54	+3	59

Over/Under 35%/65% 22nd   **Both score** 39%/61% 22nd

BRISTOL ROVERS

Nickname: The Pirates/The Gas
Colours: Blue and white
Ground: Memorial Stadium (11,626)
Tel: 01179-096-648   www.bristolrovers.co.uk

The Pirates completed successive promotions last term, leapfrogging Accrington on the final day to finish third.

Rovers won 11 of their last 14 matches and seem to be making a habit of improving as the season goes on because that is exactly what happened the season before in the Conference.

There was nothing lucky about Rovers' success, although they did win only one match against a fellow-top six rival which is a concern going up another level.

Longest run without win/loss: 5/7
High/low league position: 3/14
Clean sheets: 14 **Yellows:** 59 **Reds:** 2
Avg attendance: 6,788 **Players used:** 30
Leading scorer: M Taylor 27 (6,21)
Key stat: Forward Matty Taylor won the League Two Golden Boot with a 27-goal tally

	2015-16 H	2015-16 A	Last six seasons at home P	W	D	L	OV	UN	BS	CS
Charlton			1	0	1	0	1	0	1	0
MK Dons			1	0	0	1	1	0	1	0
Bolton			-	-	-	-	-	-	-	-
Walsall			1	0	1	0	1	0	1	0
Millwall			-	-	-	-	-	-	-	-
Bradford			2	1	1	0	2	0	2	0
Scunthorpe			1	0	1	0	0	1	0	1
Coventry			-	-	-	-	-	-	-	-
Gillingham			2	0	1	1	1	1	1	0
Rochdale			3	2	0	1	3	0	3	0
Sheffield United			-	-	-	-	-	-	-	-
Port Vale			2	1	0	1	1	1	0	1
Peterborough			1	0	1	0	1	0	1	0
Bury			1	0	1	0	1	0	1	0
Southend			3	1	1	1	1	2	1	2
Swindon			2	1	1	0	1	1	2	0
Oldham			1	1	0	0	0	1	0	1
Chesterfield			2	1	1	0	1	1	1	1
Fleetwood Town			2	0	1	1	1	1	1	1
Shrewsbury			1	1	0	0	0	1	0	1
Northampton	L	D	4	3	0	1	2	2	2	1
Oxford	L	W	4	0	2	2	0	4	1	1
Bristol Rovers										
AFC Wimbledon	W	D	4	4	0	0	2	2	1	3

Season	Division	Pos	P	W	D	L	F	A	GD	Pts
2015-16	League 2	3	46	26	7	13	77	46	+31	85
2014-15	Conference	2	46	25	16	5	73	34	+39	91
2013-14	League 2	23	46	12	14	20	43	54	-11	50

Over/Under 59%/41% 3rd   **Both score** 54%/46% 14th

BURY

Nickname: The Shakers
Colours: White and blue
Ground: Gigg Lane (11,313)
Tel: 0161-764-4881   www.buryfc.co.uk

Few League One clubs can match Bury's training facilities after the Shakers moved into Man City's old complex and 14th spot was about par last term under David Flitcroft, particularly as the squad was hit by serious injury problems.

More was expected of six-goal striker Tom Pope but fellow new arrival Leon Clarke scored 15 times. Flitcroft will be looking for an improvement on the road after Bury recorded six wins and 13 away defeats.

Longest run without win/loss: 6/10
High/low league position: 3/16
Clean sheets: 13 **Yellows:** 89 **Reds:** 2
Avg attendance: 5,447 **Players used:** 40
Leading scorer: L Clarke 15 (9,13)
Key stat: Bury conceded 44 goals away from home in League One last season – only relegated Colchester shipped more

	2015-16		Last six seasons at home							
	H	A	P	W	D	L	OV	UN	BS	CS
Charlton			1	0	0	1	1	0	1	0
MK Dons			2	0	1	1	1	1	1	1
Bolton			-	-	-	-	-	-	-	-
Walsall	L	W	3	1	1	1	2	1	3	0
Millwall	L	L	1	0	0	1	1	0	1	0
Bradford	D	L	2	0	1	1	0	2	0	1
Scunthorpe	L	L	4	1	2	1	3	1	3	1
Coventry	W	L	2	1	0	1	1	1	1	0
Gillingham	L	L	2	1	0	1	1	1	1	0
Rochdale	D	L	3	0	2	1	1	2	1	2
Sheffield United	W	W	3	1	0	2	1	2	0	1
Port Vale	W	L	2	1	0	1	0	2	0	1
Peterborough	W	W	1	1	0	0	1	0	1	0
Bury										
Southend	W	L	4	2	1	1	1	3	2	1
Swindon	D	W	2	0	1	1	1	1	1	0
Oldham	D	W	3	0	2	1	0	3	1	1
Chesterfield	W	L	4	1	2	1	0	4	2	1
Fleetwood Town	L	L	2	0	1	1	2	0	2	0
Shrewsbury	D	L	4	2	2	0	2	2	2	2
Northampton			3	1	2	0	1	2	3	0
Oxford			3	1	1	1	1	2	1	1
Bristol Rovers			1	1	0	0	1	0	1	0
AFC Wimbledon			2	1	1	0	0	2	1	1

Season	Division	Pos	P	W	D	L	F	A	GD	Pts
2015-16	League 1	14	46	16	12	18	56	73	-17	60
2014-15	League 2	3	46	26	7	13	60	40	+20	85
2013-14	League 2	12	46	13	20	13	59	51	+8	59

Over/Under 52%/48% 10th   **Both score** 50%/50% 13th

CHARLTON

Nickname: Addicks
Colours: Red and white
Ground: The Valley (27,111)
Tel: 020-8333-4000   www.cafc.co.uk

For many Charlton are a club in complete crisis after last season's relegation was compounded by a supporter revolt against the club's owners, who have made numerous poor managerial choices.

Chris Wilder turned down the chance to sit in the Valley hotseat and there is a negative vibe around the Addicks, who got progressively worse despite opening up with eight points from their first four games. A 5-0 loss at Huddersfield and 6-0 defeat at Hull were particular low points.

Longest run without win/loss: 11/4
High/low league position: 12/24
Clean sheets: 9 **Yellows:** 84 **Reds:** 6
Avg attendance: 16,698 **Players used:** 37
Leading scorer: J Gudmundsson 6 (2,6)
Key stat: Charlton had the worst home statistics in the Championship last season with a record of W5 D8 L10

	2015-16		Last six seasons at home							
	H	A	P	W	D	L	OV	UN	BS	CS
Charlton										
MK Dons	D	L	3	2	1	0	1	2	1	2
Bolton	D	D	4	2	2	0	3	1	3	1
Walsall			2	1	0	1	0	2	0	1
Millwall			3	0	1	2	0	3	0	1
Bradford			-	-	-	-	-	-	-	-
Scunthorpe			1	0	1	0	1	0	1	0
Coventry			-	-	-	-	-	-	-	-
Gillingham			-	-	-	-	-	-	-	-
Rochdale			2	1	1	0	1	1	2	0
Sheffield United			1	1	0	0	0	1	0	1
Port Vale			-	-	-	-	-	-	-	-
Peterborough			2	2	0	0	1	1	1	1
Bury			1	0	1	0	0	1	1	0
Southend			-	-	-	-	-	-	-	-
Swindon			1	0	0	1	1	0	1	0
Oldham			2	0	2	0	0	2	2	0
Chesterfield			1	1	0	0	1	0	1	0
Fleetwood Town			-	-	-	-	-	-	-	-
Shrewsbury			-	-	-	-	-	-	-	-
Northampton			-	-	-	-	-	-	-	-
Oxford			-	-	-	-	-	-	-	-
Bristol Rovers			1	0	1	0	0	1	1	0
AFC Wimbledon			-	-	-	-	-	-	-	-

Season	Division	Pos	P	W	D	L	F	A	GD	Pts
2015-16	Championship	22	46	9	13	24	40	80	-40	40
2014-15	Championship	12	46	14	18	14	54	60	-6	60
2013-14	Championship	18	46	13	12	21	41	61	-20	51

Over/Under 59%/41% 3rd   **Both score** 46%/54% 18th

CHESTERFIELD

Nickname: Spireites
Colours: Blue and white
Ground: The Proact Stadium (10,300)
Tel: 01246-209-765 www.chesterfield-fc.co.uk

Going from a playoff side to one that finished 18th looks a woeful drop, but last season always looked set to be difficult for Chesterfield after they lost several key players as well as manager Paul Cook.

Replacement Dean Saunders had a shocker – as his record suggested he probably would – but Chesterfield steadied the ship under experienced head Danny Wilson and never once went into the relegation zone thanks to on-loan Lee Novak's 14 goals.

Longest run without win/loss: 8/5
High/low league position: 7/20
Clean sheets: 7 **Yellows:** 73 **Reds:** 9
Avg attendance: 7,064 **Players used:** 32
Leading scorer: L Novak 14 (4,12)
Key stat: Sixteen of Chesterfield's 23 home league matches had over 2.5 goals and there were 75 goals scored in total in those games

	2015-16 H	A	P	W	D	L	OV	UN	BS	CS
Charlton			1	0	0	1	1	0	0	0
MK Dons			2	0	1	1	0	2	1	0
Bolton			-	-	-	-	-	-	-	-
Walsall	L	W	3	1	1	1	1	2	2	1
Millwall	L	W	1	0	0	1	1	0	1	0
Bradford	L	L	4	0	2	2	2	2	2	0
Scunthorpe	L	D	4	1	1	2	3	1	3	0
Coventry	D	L	2	0	1	1	1	1	2	0
Gillingham	L	W	4	2	0	2	3	1	2	1
Rochdale	D	W	5	2	3	0	3	2	4	1
Sheffield United	L	L	3	1	0	2	2	1	1	0
Port Vale	W	L	4	3	1	0	3	1	2	2
Peterborough	L	L	2	1	0	1	1	1	1	0
Bury	W	L	4	3	0	1	3	1	1	3
Southend	W	W	4	3	0	1	3	1	2	1
Swindon	L	L	2	0	0	2	2	0	0	0
Oldham	L	L	3	0	2	1	1	2	3	0
Chesterfield										
Fleetwood Town	D	W	4	2	1	1	3	1	2	2
Shrewsbury	W	W	2	2	0	0	2	0	2	0
Northampton			3	2	1	0	2	1	1	2
Oxford			3	2	0	1	3	0	2	1
Bristol Rovers			2	2	0	0	1	1	1	1
AFC Wimbledon			2	2	0	0	2	0	2	0

Season	Division	Pos	P	W	D	L	F	A	GD	Pts
2015-16	League 1	18	46	15	8	23	58	70	-12	53
2014-15	League 1	6	46	19	12	15	68	55	+13	69
2013-14	League 2	1	46	23	15	8	71	40	+31	84

Over/Under 54%/46% 8th   **Both score** 52%/48% 10th

COVENTRY

Nickname: The Sky Blues
Colours: Sky blue
Ground: Ricoh Arena (32,604)
Tel: 0870-421-1987   www.ccfc.co.uk

Not much was expected of Coventry in pre-season but expectations rose after Tony Mowbray's men made it to the top of the division going into December.

However, they had dropped to seventh by March and at one stage it looked as if Coventry would finish in the bottom half, but four wins in their final five fixtures saw the Sky Blues to eighth. Mowbray has said he is not interested in having as many loan players for this season after his squad was packed with them last term.

Longest run without win/loss: 5/11
High/low league position: 1/13
Clean sheets: 16 **Yellows:** 50 **Reds:** 2
Avg attendance: 9,242 **Players used:** 36
Leading scorer: A Armstrong 20 (6,12)
Key stat: On-loan Adam Armstrong scored 20 goals for Coventry last season, nobody else was in double figures

	2015-16 H	A	P	W	D	L	OV	UN	BS	CS
Charlton			-	-	-	-	-	-	-	-
MK Dons			3	1	1	1	2	1	3	0
Bolton			-	-	-	-	-	-	-	-
Walsall	D	L	4	2	2	0	2	2	3	1
Millwall	W	W	3	2	0	1	2	1	2	0
Bradford	W	D	3	1	2	0	0	3	1	2
Scunthorpe	L	L	4	0	2	2	2	2	4	0
Coventry										
Gillingham	W	D	3	3	0	0	2	1	2	1
Rochdale	L	D	2	0	1	1	1	1	1	0
Sheffield United	W	L	5	3	2	0	2	3	3	2
Port Vale	W	D	3	1	1	1	2	1	2	1
Peterborough	W	L	4	3	1	0	4	0	4	0
Bury	W	L	2	1	0	0	2	0	1	0
Southend	D	L	1	0	1	0	1	0	1	0
Swindon	D	D	4	0	1	3	3	1	2	1
Oldham	D	D	4	1	3	0	1	3	4	0
Chesterfield	W	D	2	1	0	0	2	0	2	0
Fleetwood Town	L	W	2	0	1	1	1	2	2	0
Shrewsbury	W	L	3	1	1	1	1	2	0	2
Northampton			-	-	-	-	-	-	-	-
Oxford			-	-	-	-	-	-	-	-
Bristol Rovers			-	-	-	-	-	-	-	-
AFC Wimbledon			-	-	-	-	-	-	-	-

Season	Division	Pos	P	W	D	L	F	A	GD	Pts
2015-16	League 1	8	46	19	12	15	67	49	+18	69
2014-15	League 1	17	46	13	16	17	60	60	-11	55
2013-14	League 1	18	46	16	13	17	74	77	-3	51

Over/Under 48%/52% 14th   **Both score** 46%/54% 19th

FLEETWOOD TOWN

Nickname: The Cod Army
Colours: Red and white
Ground: Highbury Stadium (5,092)
Tel: 01253 770702   fleetwoodtownfc.com

Fleetwood were not mathematically safe on the final day of the season but finished five points clear of the drop zone following a frustrating campaign.

They lacked efficiency in both boxes and their shot statistics were reasonably good despite the final league position with a shot ratio (share of match shots) figure of 0.53, which was above average.

Fleetwood didn't make enough of their chances created with ten-goal Bobby Grant topping the club's scoring charts.

Longest run without win/loss: 8/5
High/low league position: 13/23
Clean sheets: 11 **Yellows:** 69 **Reds:** 3
Avg attendance: 5,128 **Players used:** 35
Leading scorer: R Grant 10 (4,9)
Key stat: Only Oldham (18) drew more matches than Fleetwood (15) in League One last season

	2015-16 H	A	Last six seasons at home P	W	D	L	OV	UN	BS	CS
Charlton			-	-	-	-	-	-	-	-
MK Dons			1	0	0	1	1	0	0	0
Bolton			-	-	-	-	-	-	-	-
Walsall	L	L	2	0	0	2	0	2	0	0
Millwall	W	L	1	1	0	0	1	0	1	0
Bradford	D	L	3	0	2	1	1	2	2	0
Scunthorpe	W	L	3	1	1	1	2	1	2	0
Coventry	L	W	2	0	0	2	0	2	0	0
Gillingham	W	L	3	2	1	0	2	1	2	1
Rochdale	D	L	4	1	2	1	1	3	1	2
Sheffield United	D	L	2	0	2	0	1	1	2	0
Port Vale	L	D	3	1	0	2	2	1	2	1
Peterborough	W	L	2	1	1	0	0	2	1	1
Bury	W	W	2	2	0	0	1	1	1	1
Southend	D	D	3	0	3	0	0	3	2	1
Swindon	W	D	2	1	1	0	2	0	2	0
Oldham	D	L	2	0	1	1	0	2	1	0
Chesterfield	L	D	4	0	2	2	1	3	2	1
Fleetwood Town										
Shrewsbury	D	D	1	0	1	0	0	1	0	1
Northampton			2	2	0	0	0	2	0	2
Oxford			2	1	1	0	1	1	1	1
Bristol Rovers			2	1	0	1	2	0	1	0
AFC Wimbledon			3	0	3	0	0	3	2	1

Season	Division	Pos	P	W	D	L	F	A	GD	Pts
2015-16	League 1	19	46	12	15	19	52	56	-4	51
2014-15	League 1	10	46	17	12	17	49	52	-3	63
2013-14	League 2	4	46	22	10	14	66	52	+14	76

Over/Under 41%/59% 19th   **Both score** 52%/48% 10th

GILLINGHAM

Nickname: The Gills
Colours: Blue and white
Ground: Priestfield Stadium (11,440)
Tel: 01634-300-000   gillinghamfootballclub.com

It was a season of heartbreak for the Gills, even though not many had fancied Justin Edinburgh's squad to challenge for promotion before a ball was kicked.

The Kent team are not the prettiest to watch but Gillingham's direct approach worked as they occupied a top-six place from matchday one right through until the 43rd set of fixtures. However, an injury to star man Bradley Dack ruined their chances with only one point gained from the last 18 available.

Longest run without win/loss: 8/7
High/low league position: 1/9
Clean sheets: 14 **Yellows:** 93 **Reds:** 2
Avg attendance: 6,645 **Players used:** 26
Leading scorer: B Dack 13 (4,12)
Key stat: No top-half League One team scored more home goals than Gillingham's tally of 41

	2015-16 H	A	Last six seasons at home P	W	D	L	OV	UN	BS	CS
Charlton			-	-	-	-	-	-	-	-
MK Dons			2	2	0	0	2	0	2	0
Bolton			-	-	-	-	-	-	-	-
Walsall	L	L	3	0	2	1	2	1	2	1
Millwall	L	W	1	0	0	1	1	0	1	0
Bradford	W	W	6	4	1	1	2	4	1	4
Scunthorpe	W	D	2	1	0	1	2	0	1	0
Coventry	D	L	3	2	1	0	2	1	2	1
Gillingham										
Rochdale	W	D	3	2	0	1	1	2	1	2
Sheffield United	W	D	3	2	0	1	1	2	0	2
Port Vale	L	D	6	2	2	2	4	2	4	1
Peterborough	W	D	3	2	1	0	3	0	3	0
Bury	W	W	2	1	1	0	1	1	2	0
Southend	D	D	4	1	2	1	1	3	2	2
Swindon	W	W	4	2	2	0	2	2	2	2
Oldham	D	L	3	1	1	1	2	1	2	0
Chesterfield	L	W	4	0	1	3	2	2	3	0
Fleetwood Town	W	L	3	1	1	1	2	1	2	0
Shrewsbury	L	D	4	1	1	2	1	3	2	1
Northampton			3	3	0	0	1	2	1	2
Oxford			3	1	1	0	0	3	0	2
Bristol Rovers			2	2	0	0	2	0	1	1
AFC Wimbledon			2	0	1	1	2	0	2	0

Season	Division	Pos	P	W	D	L	F	A	GD	Pts
2015-16	League 1	9	46	19	12	15	71	56	+15	69
2014-15	League 1	12	46	16	14	16	65	66	-1	62
2013-14	League 1	17	46	15	8	23	60	79	-19	53

Over/Under 61%/39% 3rd   **Both score** 61%/39% 4th

MILLWALL

Nickname: The Lions
Colours: Blue and white
Ground: The Den (19,734)
Tel: 020-7232-1222   www.millwallfc.co.uk

Millwall's fans hit the headlines for the wrong reasons in the League One playoff final defeat to Barnsley but it should not overly detract from a decent season for Millwall, who eventually went down 3-1 at Wembley.

The Lions improved as the season went on and the deadly duo of Lee Gregory and Steve Morison combined for 33 league goals to bring back memories of when Teddy Sheringham and Tony Cascarino and were running riot at The Den.

Longest run without win/loss: 4/6
High/low league position: 4/17
Clean sheets: 17 **Yellows:** 89 **Reds:** 5
Avg attendance: 8,172 **Players used:** 29
Leading scorer: L Gregory 18 (8,16)
Key stat: Millwall won their last seven home league games by an aggregate score of 16-1

	2015-16 H	A	Last six seasons at home P	W	D	L	OV	UN	BS	CS
Charlton			3	1	2	0	1	2	1	2
MK Dons			-	-	-	-	-	-	-	-
Bolton			3	1	1	1	1	2	2	0
Walsall	L	W	1	0	0	1	0	1	0	0
Millwall										
Bradford	D	L	1	0	1	0	0	1	0	1
Scunthorpe	L	D	2	1	0	1	1	1	0	1
Coventry	L	L	3	2	0	1	3	0	1	1
Gillingham	L	W	1	0	0	1	0	0	1	0
Rochdale	W	W	1	1	0	0	1	0	1	0
Sheffield United	W	W	2	1	0	1	0	2	0	1
Port Vale	W	W	1	1	0	0	1	0	1	0
Peterborough	W	L	3	1	1	1	3	0	2	1
Bury	W	W	1	1	0	0	1	0	1	0
Southend	L	W	1	0	0	1	0	1	0	0
Swindon	W	D	1	1	0	0	0	1	0	1
Oldham	W	W	1	1	0	0	1	0	0	1
Chesterfield	L	W	1	0	0	1	0	1	0	0
Fleetwood Town	W	L	1	1	0	0	0	1	0	1
Shrewsbury	W	W	1	1	0	0	1	0	1	0
Northampton			-	-	-	-	-	-	-	-
Oxford			-	-	-	-	-	-	-	-
Bristol Rovers			-	-	-	-	-	-	-	-
AFC Wimbledon			-	-	-	-	-	-	-	-

Season	Division	Pos	P	W	D	L	F	A	GD	Pts
2015-16	League 1	4	46	24	9	13	73	49	+24	81
2014-15	Championship	22	46	9	14	23	42	76	-34	41
2013-14	Championship	19	46	11	15	20	46	74	-28	48

Over/Under 57%/43% 5th   **Both score** 48%/52% 16th

MK DONS

Nickname: The Dons
Colours: White
Ground: stadium:mk (22,233)
Tel: 01908-622-922   www.mkdons.co.uk

Losing Dele Alli and Will Grigg among others meant MK Dons actually had a poorer side in the Championship than the one which had gained promotion from League One the season before and it always looked a tough ask for Karl Robinson to keep them in the second tier.

That said, Robinson must be disappointed with the collapse of his side, with the Dons winning only one of their last 15 matches and just three times in the whole of 2016.

Longest run without win/loss: 11/3
High/low league position: 15/23
Clean sheets: 11 **Yellows:** 85 **Reds:** 4
Avg attendance: 15,062 **Players used:** 33
Leading scorer: N Maynard 6 (2,6)
Key stat: MK Dons scored just 39 goals in last season's Championship

	2015-16 H	A	Last six seasons at home P	W	D	L	OV	UN	BS	CS
Charlton	W	D	3	2	1	0	0	3	1	2
MK Dons										
Bolton	W	L	1	1	0	0	0	1	0	1
Walsall			5	1	1	3	2	3	2	1
Millwall			-	-	-	-	-	-	-	-
Bradford			2	0	0	2	2	0	2	0
Scunthorpe			3	1	1	1	0	3	0	2
Coventry			3	0	1	2	2	1	2	1
Gillingham			2	1	0	1	1	1	1	0
Rochdale			3	1	2	0	2	1	3	0
Sheffield United			4	3	0	1	0	4	0	3
Port Vale			2	2	0	0	1	1	0	2
Peterborough			3	2	0	1	1	2	0	2
Bury			2	1	1	0	1	1	2	0
Southend			-	-	-	-	-	-	-	-
Swindon			4	3	1	0	2	2	3	1
Oldham			5	4	1	0	3	2	1	4
Chesterfield			2	1	0	1	2	0	2	0
Fleetwood Town			1	1	0	0	1	0	1	0
Shrewsbury			2	1	0	1	2	0	2	0
Northampton			-	-	-	-	-	-	-	-
Oxford			-	-	-	-	-	-	-	-
Bristol Rovers			1	1	0	0	0	1	0	1
AFC Wimbledon			-	-	-	-	-	-	-	-

Season	Division	Pos	P	W	D	L	F	A	GD	Pts
2015-16	Championship	23	46	9	12	25	39	69	-30	39
2014-15	League 1	2	46	27	10	9	101	44	+57	91
2013-14	League 1	10	46	17	9	20	63	65	-2	60

Over/Under 43%/57% 12th   **Both score** 50%/50% 14th

NORTHAMPTON

Nickname: The Cobblers
Colours: Claret and white
Ground: Sixfields Stadium (7,300)
Tel: 01604-683-700   www.ntfc.co.uk

Northampton fell just one short of 100 points but it was still a sensational season of success from the League Two champions, who finished 13 points clear of the chasing pack despite nearly entering administration at one stage.

Unfortunately for them that attracted interest in manager Chris Wilder, who left for Sheffield United. Rob Page arrives as his replacement with the club unbeaten since Christmas and with solid foundations at boardroom level.

Longest run without win/loss: 4/24
High/low league position: 1/11
Clean sheets: 15 **Yellows:** 71 **Reds:** 5
Avg attendance: 4,982 **Players used:** 28
Leading scorer: M Richards 15 (6,15)
Key stat: Twenty of Northampton's 29 league wins last season were by a one-goal margin

	2015-16 H	A	Last six seasons at home P	W	D	L	OV	UN	BS	CS
Charlton			-	-	-	-	-	-	-	-
MK Dons			-	-	-	-	-	-	-	-
Bolton			-	-	-	-	-	-	-	-
Walsall			-	-	-	-	-	-	-	-
Millwall			-	-	-	-	-	-	-	-
Bradford			3	1	0	2	1	2	1	1
Scunthorpe			1	0	1	0	0	1	1	0
Coventry			-	-	-	-	-	-	-	-
Gillingham			3	1	1	1	2	1	3	0
Rochdale			2	1	0	1	2	0	1	0
Sheffield United			-	-	-	-	-	-	-	-
Port Vale			3	1	1	1	1	2	1	2
Peterborough			-	-	-	-	-	-	-	-
Bury			3	0	0	3	3	0	2	0
Southend			5	2	2	1	4	1	5	0
Swindon			1	0	0	1	1	0	1	0
Oldham			-	-	-	-	-	-	-	-
Chesterfield			3	0	1	2	2	1	2	1
Fleetwood Town			2	2	0	0	1	1	1	1
Shrewsbury			3	0	1	2	2	1	3	0
Northampton										
Oxford	W	W	6	5	0	1	4	2	4	2
Bristol Rovers	D	W	4	2	2	0	2	2	2	2
AFC Wimbledon	D	D	5	3	2	0	1	4	2	3

Season	Division	Pos	P	W	D	L	F	A	GD	Pts
2015-16	League 2	1	46	29	12	5	82	46	+36	99
2014-15	League 2	12	46	18	7	21	67	62	+5	61
2013-14	League 2	21	46	13	14	19	42	57	-15	53

Over/Under 57%/43% 6th   **Both score** 63%/37% 3rd

OLDHAM

Nickname: The Latics
Colours: Blue
Ground: Boundary Park (10,850)
Tel: 08712-262-235   oldhamathletic.co.uk

The League One draw specialists looked in real danger of relegation after winning just three of their first 26 games. They struggled for home results, with the poor playing surface at Boundary Park put up as one reason for Oldham collecting more points on their travels (28) compared to in front of their own supporters (26).

Appointing John Sheridan proved a shrewd move but the club was rocked this summer when he dropped down a level to manage Notts County in League Two.

Longest run without win/loss: 11/7
High/low league position: 17/23
Clean sheets: 13 **Yellows:** 69 **Reds:** 3
Avg attendance: 5,773 **Players used:** 39
Leading scorer: L Kelly 6 (2,6)
Key stat: Oldham drew 18 League One matches last season and a whopping 13 of those came on the road

	2015-16 H	A	Last six seasons at home P	W	D	L	OV	UN	BS	CS
Charlton			2	0	1	1	0	2	0	1
MK Dons			5	2	0	3	5	0	5	0
Bolton			-	-	-	-	-	-	-	-
Walsall	W	D	6	3	2	1	2	4	4	1
Millwall	L	L	1	0	0	1	1	0	1	0
Bradford	L	L	3	1	1	1	2	1	3	0
Scunthorpe	L	D	4	1	1	2	3	1	4	0
Coventry	L	D	4	1	1	2	1	3	1	1
Gillingham	W	D	3	2	1	0	1	2	1	2
Rochdale	L	D	4	2	0	2	3	1	2	2
Sheffield United	D	L	5	0	3	2	1	4	3	0
Port Vale	D	D	3	1	2	0	1	2	3	0
Peterborough	L	W	4	1	1	2	3	1	3	0
Bury	L	D	3	0	0	3	1	2	1	0
Southend	L	W	1	0	0	1	1	0	1	0
Swindon	W	W	5	4	0	1	2	3	2	2
Oldham										
Chesterfield	W	W	3	2	1	0	1	2	1	2
Fleetwood Town	W	D	2	2	0	0	0	2	0	2
Shrewsbury	D	W	3	1	1	1	2	2	2	1
Northampton			-	-	-	-	-	-	-	-
Oxford			-	-	-	-	-	-	-	-
Bristol Rovers			1	0	1	0	0	1	1	0
AFC Wimbledon			-	-	-	-	-	-	-	-

Season	Division	Pos	P	W	D	L	F	A	GD	Pts
2015-16	League 1	17	46	12	18	16	44	58	-14	54
2014-15	League 1	15	46	14	15	17	54	67	-13	57
2013-14	League 1	15	46	14	14	18	50	59	-9	56

Over/Under 35%/65% 22nd   **Both score** 57%/43% 6th

OXFORD UNITED

Nickname: The U's
Colours: Yellow
Ground: The Kassam Stadium (12,500)
Tel: 01865-337533   www.oufc.co.uk

Oxford arguably became the most talked about club in League Two last season after they reached the FA Cup fourth round, beating Swansea en route, and also made the Football League Trophy final.

Those cup runs possibly hindered their league form at various times, but to many observers Michael Appleton's men played the best football in the division and United came through to finish second with the most goals scored in the division as well as the fewest conceded.

Longest run without win/loss: 3/7
High/low league position: 1/8
Clean sheets: 18 **Yellows:** 65 **Reds:** 3
Avg attendance: 5,867 **Players used:** 28
Leading scorer: K Roofe 18 (8,16)
Key stat: Oxford's goal difference of plus 42 was the best tally in League Two last season

	2015-16 H	A	Last six seasons at home P	W	D	L	OV	UN	BS	CS
Charlton			-	-	-	-	-	-	2	0
MK Dons			-	-	-	-	-	-	-	-
Bolton			-	-	-	-	-	-	-	-
Walsall			-	-	-	-	-	-	-	-
Millwall			-	-	-	-	-	-	-	-
Bradford			3	1	1	1	1	2	2	0
Scunthorpe			1	0	0	1	0	1	0	0
Coventry			-	-	-	-	-	-	-	-
Gillingham			3	0	2	1	0	3	0	2
Rochdale			2	1	1	0	1	1	1	1
Sheffield United			-	-	-	-	-	-	-	-
Port Vale			3	3	0	0	3	0	3	0
Peterborough			-	-	-	-	-	-	-	-
Bury			3	2	0	1	3	0	3	0
Southend			5	1	0	4	1	4	1	1
Swindon			1	1	0	0	0	1	0	1
Oldham			-	-	-	-	-	-	-	-
Chesterfield			3	0	1	2	0	3	0	1
Fleetwood Town			2	0	0	2	1	1	1	0
Shrewsbury			3	2	0	1	2	1	1	0
Northampton	L	L	6	4	1	1	2	4	3	2
Oxford										
Bristol Rovers	L	W	4	1	0	3	2	2	1	1
AFC Wimbledon	W	W	5	4	1	0	2	3	2	3

Season	Division	Pos	P	W	D	L	F	A	GD	Pts
2015-16	League 2	2	46	24	14	8	84	41	+43	86
2014-15	League 2	13	46	15	16	15	50	49	+1	61
2013-14	League 2	8	46	16	14	16	53	50	+3	62

Over/Under 50%/50% 13th   **Both score** 54%/46% 14th

PETERBOROUGH

Nickname: The Posh
Colours: Blue
Ground: London Road (11,494)
Tel: 01733-563 947   www.theposh.com

A topsy-turvy season saw Peterborough finish 13th, which was a disappointment for chairman Darragh MacAnthony who had demanded promotion and was on to a third manager by the end of the season.

Dave Robertson was quickly replaced by Graham Westley and that initially did the trick. But Posh, who scored the most goals in the division, totally lost their way after star striker Conor Washington was sold to QPR. Grant McCann is the new manager after replacing Westley.

Longest run without win/loss: 7/5
High/low league position: 5/18
Clean sheets: 7 **Yellows:** 110 **Reds:** 7
Avg attendance: 6,480 **Players used:** 41
Leading scorer: J Taylor 11 (4,8) L Angol 11 (4,9) M Maddison 11 (1,5)
Key stat: Peterborough's League One matches produced 155 goals last season

	2015-16 H	A	Last six seasons at home P	W	D	L	OV	UN	BS	CS
Charlton			2	0	1	1	2	0	2	0
MK Dons			3	3	0	0	3	0	3	0
Bolton			1	1	0	0	1	0	1	0
Walsall	D	L	4	1	3	0	1	3	2	2
Millwall	W	L	3	1	0	2	3	0	2	0
Bradford	L	W	3	2	0	1	2	1	1	1
Scunthorpe	L	W	2	0	0	2	1	1	1	0
Coventry	W	L	4	3	0	1	1	3	1	2
Gillingham	D	L	3	1	1	1	1	2	2	1
Rochdale	L	L	3	2	0	1	3	0	3	0
Sheffield United	L	W	3	0	1	2	2	1	2	1
Port Vale	L	D	3	1	1	1	2	1	2	1
Peterborough										
Bury	L	L	1	0	0	1	0	1	0	1
Southend	D	L	1	0	1	0	0	1	0	1
Swindon	L	W	4	2	0	2	3	1	3	1
Oldham	L	W	4	2	1	1	4	0	4	0
Chesterfield	W	W	2	2	0	0	0	2	0	2
Fleetwood Town	W	L	2	2	0	0	1	1	1	1
Shrewsbury	D	W	2	1	1	0	0	2	1	1
Northampton			-	-	-	-	-	-	-	-
Oxford			-	-	-	-	-	-	-	-
Bristol Rovers			1	1	0	0	1	0	0	1
AFC Wimbledon			-	-	-	-	-	-	-	-

Season	Division	Pos	P	W	D	L	F	A	GD	Pts
2015-16	League 1	13	46	19	6	21	82	73	+9	63
2014-15	League 1	9	46	19	9	18	53	56	-3	63
2013-14	League 1	6	46	23	5	18	72	58	+14	74

Over/Under 65%/35% 2nd   **Both score** 65%/35% 1st

PORT VALE

Nickname: The Valiants
Colours: White and black
Ground: Vale Park (19,148)
Tel: 01782-655-800   www.port-vale.co.uk

Having been on a tight budget and among the relegation favourites, Port Vale surpassed expectations to finish 12th – enough to scoop the each-way money on the ante-post seasonal handicap.

The wage bill has been slashed again and manager Rob Page has departed for Northampton so another tricky season lies ahead. But there was nothing wrong with the Valiants' efforts last season, even though AJ Leitch-Smith was their top scorer with just ten goals.

Longest run without win/loss: 4/4
High/low league position: 8/16
Clean sheets: 11 **Yellows:** 74 **Reds:** 3
Avg attendance: 6,148 **Players used:** 27
Leading scorer: A Leitch-Smith 10 (7,9)
Key stat: Port Vale lost nine of their 11 away games to teams who finished above them last season

	2015-16 H	A	Last six seasons at home P	W	D	L	OV	UN	BS	CS
Charlton	-	-	-	-	-	-	-	-	-	-
MK Dons			2	1	1	0	0	2	0	2
Bolton			-	-	-	-	-	-	-	-
Walsall	L	L	3	1	1	1	1	2	1	1
Millwall	L	L	1	0	0	1	0	1	0	0
Bradford	D	L	6	3	3	0	4	2	5	1
Scunthorpe	D	L	2	0	2	0	1	1	2	0
Coventry	D	L	3	1	1	1	2	1	2	0
Gillingham	D	W	6	3	2	1	3	3	4	1
Rochdale	W	L	3	2	1	0	2	1	2	1
Sheffield United	W	L	3	2	0	1	3	0	3	0
Port Vale										
Peterborough	D	W	3	1	1	1	1	2	2	0
Bury	W	L	2	1	1	0	0	2	0	2
Southend	W	L	4	1	1	2	3	1	4	0
Swindon	W	D	4	1	0	3	1	3	1	1
Oldham	D	D	3	1	1	1	0	3	1	1
Chesterfield	W	L	4	1	1	2	2	2	3	0
Fleetwood Town	D	W	3	0	1	2	1	2	1	1
Shrewsbury	W	D	4	3	0	1	2	2	2	2
Northampton			3	1	2	0	2	1	2	1
Oxford			3	2	0	1	3	0	1	2
Bristol Rovers			2	2	0	0	1	1	0	2
AFC Wimbledon			2	1	0	1	2	0	1	1

Season	Division	Pos	P	W	D	L	F	A	GD	Pts
2015-16	League 1	12	46	18	11	17	56	58	-2	65
2014-15	League 1	18	46	15	9	22	55	65	-10	54
2013-14	League 1	9	46	18	7	21	59	73	-14	61

Over/Under 41%/59% 19th   **Both score** 48%/52% 16th

ROCHDALE

Nickname: The Dale
Colours: Blue and black
Ground: Spotland Stadium (10,037)
Tel: 0870-822-1907   www.rochdaleafc.co.uk

Magic man Keith Hill did it again. There are many clubs in League One with better players, bigger budgets and superior facilities, but Hill thrives on the underdog spirit and led Rochdale to tenth place.

That was a fine effort, although at one stage it looked as if Rochdale could even force their way into the playoff reckoning.

Home is where the heart is for dependable Dale, who won 12 times at Spotland and scored an impressive 41 goals in the process.

Longest run without win/loss: 7/4
High/low league position: 5/17
Clean sheets: 14 **Yellows:** 83 **Reds:** 3
Avg attendance: 4,993 **Players used:** 28
Leading scorer: I Henderson 13 (4,12)
Key stat: Rochdale's goal difference of plus ten was the worst of teams who finished in the top ten

	2015-16 H	A	Last six seasons at home P	W	D	L	OV	UN	BS	CS
Charlton			2	1	0	1	1	1	1	1
MK Dons			3	0	0	3	3	0	3	0
Bolton			-	-	-	-	-	-	-	-
Walsall	L	W	4	2	1	1	4	0	3	1
Millwall	L	L	1	0	0	1	0	1	0	0
Bradford	L	D	3	0	1	2	1	2	1	1
Scunthorpe	W	D	4	3	0	1	3	1	2	1
Coventry	D	W	2	1	1	0	0	2	0	2
Gillingham	D	L	3	0	3	0	0	3	3	0
Rochdale										
Sheffield United	W	L	3	1	0	2	2	1	2	1
Port Vale	W	L	3	2	1	0	2	1	2	1
Peterborough	W	W	3	1	1	1	1	2	1	1
Bury	W	D	3	3	0	0	2	1	0	3
Southend	W	D	3	2	0	1	3	0	2	0
Swindon	D	L	3	0	2	1	3	0	3	0
Oldham	D	W	4	1	2	1	2	2	2	1
Chesterfield	L	D	5	1	3	1	2	3	4	1
Fleetwood Town	W	D	4	1	1	2	1	3	1	2
Shrewsbury	W	L	1	1	0	0	1	0	1	0
Northampton			2	1	1	0	1	1	1	1
Oxford			2	2	0	0	1	0	2	2
Bristol Rovers			3	3	0	0	2	1	2	1
AFC Wimbledon			2	0	0	2	1	1	1	0

Season	Division	Pos	P	W	D	L	F	A	GD	Pts
2015-16	League 1	10	46	19	12	15	68	61	+7	69
2014-15	League 1	8	46	19	6	21	72	66	+6	63
2013-14	League 2	3	46	24	9	13	69	48	+21	81

Over/Under 57%/43% 5th   **Both score** 54%/46% 8th

LEAGUE ONE

SCUNTHORPE

Nickname: The Iron
Colours: Claret and blue
Ground: Glanford Park (9,144)
Tel: 01724-848 077   scunthorpe-united.co.uk

It was a season of fine margins for Scunthorpe, who had a nice payday from their FA Cup defeat at Chelsea and very nearly sneaked into the playoffs.

The Iron eventually had to settle for seventh, missing out to Barnsley on goal difference, so it must have been galling for United to watch as the Tykes then ran riot in the playoffs to secure promotion.

Scunny can still be proud of their efforts, particularly after winning just two of their opening ten matches.

Longest run without win/loss: 4/8
High/low league position: 7/21
Clean sheets: 19 **Yellows:** 69 **Reds:** 1
Avg attendance: 5,279 **Players used:** 30
Leading scorer: P Madden 20 (9,17)
Key stat: Scunthorpe lost just two of their last 20 matches after sacking manager Mark Robins

	2015-16		Last six seasons at home							
	H	A	P	W	D	L	OV	UN	BS	CS
Charlton			1	0	1	0	0	1	1	0
MK Dons			3	0	1	2	2	1	1	0
Bolton			-	-	-	-	-	-	-	-
Walsall	L	D	4	1	1	2	1	3	2	0
Millwall	D	W	2	0	1	1	1	1	1	1
Bradford	L	L	2	0	1	1	0	2	1	0
Scunthorpe										
Coventry	W	W	4	2	0	2	2	2	2	1
Gillingham	D	L	2	1	1	0	1	1	1	1
Rochdale	D	L	4	3	0	0	2	2	2	2
Sheffield United	L	W	5	1	3	1	1	4	4	0
Port Vale	W	D	2	1	1	0	0	2	1	1
Peterborough	L	W	2	1	0	1	1	1	0	1
Bury	W	W	4	1	1	2	4	0	4	0
Southend	W	L	2	1	1	0	1	1	1	1
Swindon	W	L	3	3	0	0	3	0	2	1
Oldham	D	W	4	0	2	2	2	2	3	0
Chesterfield	D	W	4	1	3	0	1	3	3	1
Fleetwood Town	W	L	3	1	1	1	0	3	0	2
Shrewsbury	W	D	2	1	1	0	1	1	1	1
Northampton			1	0	0	0	0	1	1	0
Oxford			1	1	0	0	0	1	0	1
Bristol Rovers			1	0	1	0	0	1	1	0
AFC Wimbledon			1	0	1	0	0	1	0	1

Season	Division	Pos	P	W	D	L	F	A	GD	Pts
2015-16	League 1	7	46	21	11	14	60	47	+13	74
2014-15	League 1	16	46	14	14	18	62	75	-13	56
2013-14	League 2	2	46	20	21	5	68	44	+24	81

Over/Under 43%/57% 18th   **Both score** 41%/59% 21st

SHEFFIELD UNITED

Nickname: The Blades
Colours: Red and white
Ground: Bramall Lane (32,609)
Tel: 0871-222-1899   www.sufc.co.uk

The perennial League One ante-post favourites again made a total mess of it and those who backed United knew their fate early on as the Blades were battered 4-0 on the opening day at Gillingham.

Things rarely improved in terms of performances, despite the best efforts of Billy Sharp and Che Adams. And after a season that saw Sheffield United finish a woeful 11th, it was no surprise to see manager Nigel Adkins replaced by Chris Wilder in the summer.

Longest run without win/loss: 6/5
High/low league position: 5/13
Clean sheets: 15 **Yellows:** 75 **Reds:** 0
Avg attendance: 13,656 **Players used:** 35
Leading scorer: B Sharp 21 (8,21)
Key stat: Sheffield United lost as many matches at home (eight) as they did away last season

	2015-16		Last six seasons at home							
	H	A	P	W	D	L	OV	UN	BS	CS
Charlton			1	0	0	1	0	1	0	0
MK Dons			4	1	1	2	1	3	1	1
Bolton			-	-	-	-	-	-	-	-
Walsall	W	D	5	3	2	0	1	4	3	2
Millwall	L	L	2	0	1	1	1	1	2	0
Bradford	W	D	3	1	2	0	2	1	3	0
Scunthorpe	L	W	5	3	0	2	4	1	1	2
Coventry	W	L	5	2	1	2	3	2	3	1
Gillingham	D	L	3	1	1	1	2	1	2	1
Rochdale	W	L	3	3	0	0	2	1	1	2
Sheffield United										
Port Vale	W	L	3	3	0	0	1	2	1	2
Peterborough	L	W	3	1	0	2	2	1	2	1
Bury	L	L	3	1	1	1	2	1	2	1
Southend	D	L	1	0	1	0	1	0	1	0
Swindon	D	L	4	3	1	0	0	4	1	3
Oldham	W	D	5	1	3	1	2	3	4	1
Chesterfield	W	W	3	2	1	0	1	2	2	1
Fleetwood Town	W	D	2	1	0	1	2	0	1	1
Shrewsbury	L	D	3	2	0	1	1	2	1	2
Northampton			-	-	-	-	-	-	-	-
Oxford			-	-	-	-	-	-	-	-
Bristol Rovers			-	-	-	-	-	-	-	-
AFC Wimbledon			-	-	-	-	-	-	-	-

Season	Division	Pos	P	W	D	L	F	A	GD	Pts
2015-16	League 1	11	46	18	12	16	64	59	+5	66
2014-15	League 1	5	46	19	14	13	66	53	+13	71
2013-14	League 1	7	46	18	13	15	48	46	+2	67

Over/Under 50%/50% 11th   **Both score** 50%/50% 13th

SHREWSBURY

Nickname: The Shrews
Colours: Blue and amber
Ground: New Meadow (9,875)
Tel: 0871-811-8800   shrewsburytown.com

Thankfully for Shrewsbury there are no pictures on scorecards and the record books will say they remain a League One club. But it was a close-run thing with some heavy defeats along the way, such as a crushing 7-1 defeat at Chesterfield and a 5-1 hammering at home to Wigan.

Micky Mellon has rung the changes over the summer with a virtually new squad set to play at the New Meadow as the club looks to seriously improve on last season's narrow escape.

Longest run without win/loss: 7/9
High/low league position: 15/21
Clean sheets: 7 **Yellows:** 85 **Reds:** 6
Avg attendance: 6,120 **Players used:** 36
Leading scorer: S Kaikai 12 (6,10)
Key stat: Shrewsbury lost 13 home matches last season – the most in the division

	2015-16 H	2015-16 A	P	W	D	L	OV	UN	BS	CS
Charlton	-	-	-	-	-	-	-	-	-	-
MK Dons			2	0	2	0	1	1	1	1
Bolton	-	-	-	-	-	-	-	-	-	-
Walsall	L	L	3	1	0	2	1	2	1	1
Millwall	L	L	1	0	0	1	1	0	1	0
Bradford	D	D	4	3	1	0	2	2	3	1
Scunthorpe	D	L	2	0	1	1	1	1	1	0
Coventry	W	L	3	2	1	0	2	1	3	0
Gillingham	D	W	4	2	2	0	1	3	1	3
Rochdale	W	L	1	1	0	0	0	1	0	1
Sheffield United	L	W	3	1	0	2	2	1	2	1
Port Vale	D	L	4	1	3	0	1	3	2	2
Peterborough	L	D	2	0	0	2	2	0	2	0
Bury	W	D	4	2	1	1	2	2	0	3
Southend	L	W	4	1	2	1	2	2	4	0
Swindon	L	L	4	2	0	2	1	3	1	1
Oldham	L	D	3	1	0	2	1	2	1	1
Chesterfield	L	L	2	0	1	1	1	1	1	1
Fleetwood Town	D	D	1	0	1	0	0	1	1	0
Shrewsbury										
Northampton			3	1	1	1	2	1	3	0
Oxford			3	2	1	0	2	1	1	2
Bristol Rovers			1	1	0	0	0	1	0	1
AFC Wimbledon			2	1	1	0	0	2	0	2

Season	Division	Pos	P	W	D	L	F	A	GD	Pts
2015-16	League 1	20	46	13	11	22	58	79	-21	50
2014-15	League 2	2	46	27	8	11	67	31	+36	89
2013-14	League 1	23	46	9	15	22	44	65	-21	42

Over/Under 59%/41% 4th   **Both score** 65%/35% 1st

SOUTHEND

Nickname: The Shrimpers
Colours: Blue
Ground: Roots Hall (11,927)
Tel: 01702-304-050   southendunited.co.uk

Southend briefly flirted with the playoffs but a poor finish saw their top-six hopes fade and the Shrimpers eventually finished down in 15th, much to the disappointment of manager Phil Brown.

That still isn't a bad effort considering the Essex club had only been promoted via the League Two playoffs the season before, but Brown needs a goalscorer as nobody reached double figures. And it's been a tricky summer with most of his best players out of contract.

Longest run without win/loss: 7/8
High/low league position: 7/21
Clean sheets: 10 **Yellows:** 97 **Reds:** 2
Avg attendance: 7,096 **Players used:** 32
Leading scorer: J Payne 9 (4,9)
Key stat: Southend won only one of their last ten matches and lost all of their last five

	2015-16 H	2015-16 A	P	W	D	L	OV	UN	BS	CS
Charlton	-	-	-	-	-	-	-	-	-	-
MK Dons	-	-	-	-	-	-	-	-	-	-
Bolton	-	-	-	-	-	-	-	-	-	-
Walsall	L	L	1	0	0	1	0	1	0	0
Millwall	L	W	1	0	0	1	1	0	0	0
Bradford	L	L	4	1	1	2	2	2	1	1
Scunthorpe	W	L	2	1	0	1	1	0	0	1
Coventry	W	D	1	1	0	0	1	0	0	1
Gillingham	D	D	4	1	2	1	1	3	2	1
Rochdale	D	L	3	1	2	0	2	1	3	0
Sheffield United	W	D	1	1	0	0	1	0	1	0
Port Vale	W	L	4	2	1	1	2	2	1	3
Peterborough	W	L	1	1	0	0	1	0	1	0
Bury	W	L	4	1	3	0	1	3	3	1
Southend										
Swindon	L	L	2	0	0	2	1	1	1	0
Oldham	L	W	1	0	0	1	0	1	0	0
Chesterfield	L	L	4	2	0	2	3	1	1	2
Fleetwood Town	D	D	3	1	2	0	1	2	2	1
Shrewsbury	L	W	4	2	0	2	1	3	0	2
Northampton			5	2	2	1	2	3	3	2
Oxford			5	4	1	0	3	2	3	2
Bristol Rovers			3	0	3	0	0	3	2	1
AFC Wimbledon			4	1	0	3	1	3	1	1

Season	Division	Pos	P	W	D	L	F	A	GD	Pts
2015-16	League 1	15	46	16	11	19	58	64	-6	59
2014-15	League 2	5	46	24	12	10	54	38	+16	84
2013-14	League 2	5	46	19	15	12	56	39	+17	72

Over/Under 50%/50% 11th   **Both score** 48%/52% 16th

SWINDON

Nickname: The Robins
Colours: Red and white
Ground: County Ground (14,983)
Tel: 0871-423-6433   swindontownfc.co.uk

Swindon won only three of their first 16 matches last term and it was no surprise to see Mark Cooper depart the dugout, although it is debatable as to whether he was solely to blame for the club going backwards as the Robins had lost some of their best players.

Departed striker Nicky Ajose stepped up well to fill his boots and rookie manager Luke Williams will need to shape the side to his liking now that he has had a summer to work with the squad.

Longest run without win/loss: 10/7
High/low league position: 8/23
Clean sheets: 8 **Yellows:** 82 **Reds:** 4
Avg attendance: 7,254 **Players used:** 39
Leading scorer: N Ajose 24 (6,17)
Key stat: Nicky Ajose scored 24 goals in League One last season

| | 2015-16 | | Last six seasons at home | | | | | | | |
	H	A	P	W	D	L	OV	UN	BS	CS
Charlton			1	0	0	1	1	0	0	0
MK Dons			4	1	0	3	2	2	1	1
Bolton			-	-	-	-	-	-	-	-
Walsall	W	D	5	1	3	1	4	1	4	1
Millwall	D	L	1	0	1	0	1	0	1	0
Bradford	W	L	4	3	1	0	2	2	2	2
Scunthorpe	W	L	3	2	1	0	2	1	3	0
Coventry	D	D	4	1	3	0	3	1	4	0
Gillingham	L	D	4	1	1	2	3	1	2	1
Rochdale	W	D	3	1	1	1	2	1	3	0
Sheffield United	L	D	4	2	1	1	2	2	2	1
Port Vale	D	L	4	3	1	0	3	1	2	2
Peterborough	L	W	4	2	1	1	2	2	3	1
Bury	L	D	2	0	0	2	0	2	0	0
Southend	W	W	2	2	0	0	1	1	1	1
Swindon										
Oldham	L	L	5	0	2	3	2	3	3	0
Chesterfield	W	W	2	2	0	0	1	1	1	1
Fleetwood Town	D	L	2	1	1	0	0	2	1	1
Shrewsbury	W	W	4	4	0	0	3	1	2	2
Northampton			1	1	0	0	0	1	0	1
Oxford			1	0	0	1	0	1	0	0
Bristol Rovers			2	1	1	0	1	1	1	1
AFC Wimbledon			1	1	0	0	0	1	0	1

Season	Division	Pos	P	W	D	L	F	A	GD	Pts
2015-16	League 1	16	46	16	11	19	64	71	-7	59
2014-15	League 1	4	46	23	10	13	76	57	+19	79
2013-14	League 1	8	46	19	9	18	63	59	+4	66

Over/Under 57%/43% 5th   **Both score** 57%/43% 6th

WALSALL

Nickname: The Saddlers
Colours: Red and white
Ground: Banks's Stadium (10,989)
Tel: 0871-221-0442   www.saddlers.co.uk

How Walsall must be cursing the decision of the excellent Dean Smith to leave the club to lead second-tier outfit Brentford.

It totally destabilised the surprise promotion chasers and their misery was compounded by the poor results under Sean O'Driscoll, who briefly came in to replace Smith. Jon Whitney steadied the ship but Walsall slipped to third and were outclassed by Barnsley in the playoffs.

It felt like a huge missed opportunity that may not come around again.

Longest run without win/loss: 6/6
High/low league position: 1/4
Clean sheets: 15 **Yellows:** 48 **Reds:** 0
Avg attendance: 5,950 **Players used:** 24
Leading scorer: T Bradshaw 17 (8,16)
Key stat: Walsall won 13 of their away matches in League One last season

| | 2015-16 | | Last six seasons at home | | | | | | | |
	H	A	P	W	D	L	OV	UN	BS	CS
Charlton			2	1	1	0	0	2	1	1
MK Dons			5	1	1	3	2	3	2	1
Bolton			-	-	-	-	-	-	-	-
Walsall										
Millwall	L	W	1	0	0	1	1	0	0	0
Bradford	W	L	3	1	1	1	1	2	1	1
Scunthorpe	D	W	4	0	2	2	3	1	3	1
Coventry	W	D	4	2	0	2	2	1	1	1
Gillingham	W	W	3	1	2	0	1	2	3	0
Rochdale	L	W	4	1	2	1	2	2	1	2
Sheffield United	D	L	5	2	3	0	2	3	5	0
Port Vale	W	W	3	1	0	2	0	3	0	1
Peterborough	W	D	4	2	1	1	1	3	1	3
Bury	L	W	3	0	1	2	1	2	2	0
Southend	W	W	1	1	0	0	0	1	0	1
Swindon	D	L	5	0	2	3	2	3	4	0
Oldham	D	L	6	3	2	1	1	5	3	2
Chesterfield	L	W	3	2	0	1	2	1	2	1
Fleetwood Town	W	W	2	2	0	0	1	1	1	1
Shrewsbury	W	W	3	3	0	0	2	1	2	1
Northampton			-	-	-	-	-	-	-	-
Oxford			-	-	-	-	-	-	-	-
Bristol Rovers			1	1	0	0	1	0	1	0
AFC Wimbledon			-	-	-	-	-	-	-	-

Season	Division	Pos	P	W	D	L	F	A	GD	Pts
2015-16	League 1	3	46	24	12	10	71	49	+22	84
2014-15	League 1	14	46	14	17	15	50	54	-4	59
2013-14	League 1	13	46	14	16	16	49	49	0	59

Over/Under 48%/52% 14th   **Both score** 54%/46% 8th

League One stats 2015-16

Key Points in all tables (except the league table) do not include any deductions imposed by the league.
POS H A Overall league position, rank from home games only, rank from away games only **Sup** Average
match supremacy **GFA** Goals For Average **GAA** Goals Against Average **PGA** Points Gained Average

			League One 2015-16	Home					Away						
Pos	H	A		P	W	D	L	F	A	W	D	L	F	A	GD	Pts
1	1	2	Wigan (P)	46	14	6	3	39	17	10	9	4	43	28	+37	87
2	3	4	Burton (P)	46	13	8	2	32	16	12	2	9	25	21	+20	85
3	10	1	Walsall	46	11	6	6	31	26	13	6	4	40	23	+22	84
4	9	3	Millwall	46	13	3	7	34	22	11	6	6	39	27	+24	81
5	2	6	Bradford	46	14	5	4	32	16	9	6	8	23	24	+15	80
6	12	5	Barnsley (P)	46	11	4	8	35	24	11	4	8	35	30	+16	74
7	8	8	Scunthorpe	46	12	6	5	28	15	9	5	9	32	32	+13	74
8	6	13	Coventry	46	12	6	5	41	24	7	6	10	26	25	+18	69
9	4	15	Gillingham	46	13	4	6	41	24	6	8	9	30	32	+15	69
10	7	14	Rochdale	46	12	6	5	41	25	7	6	10	27	36	+7	69
11	13	10	Sheff Utd	46	11	4	8	37	29	7	8	8	27	30	+5	66
12	5	18	Port Vale	46	12	7	4	35	25	6	4	13	21	33	-2	65
13	17	7	Peterborough	46	9	4	10	42	37	10	2	11	40	36	+9	63
14	11	19	Bury	46	10	8	5	36	29	6	4	13	20	44	-17	60
15	15	17	Southend	46	10	5	8	30	26	6	6	11	28	38	-6	59
16	16	16	Swindon	46	10	4	9	39	36	6	7	10	25	35	-7	59
17	20	12	Oldham	46	7	5	11	25	35	5	13	5	19	23	-14	54
18	21	11	Chesterfield	46	6	6	11	36	39	9	2	12	22	31	-12	53
19	14	23	Fleetwood	46	9	8	6	33	20	3	7	13	19	36	-4	51
20	23	9	Shrewsbury	46	5	5	13	29	39	8	6	9	29	40	-21	50
21	19	21	Doncaster (R)	46	7	7	9	27	24	4	6	13	21	40	-16	46
22	18	22	Blackpool (R)	46	8	5	10	22	24	4	5	14	18	39	-23	46
23	22	20	Colchester (R)	46	4	9	10	32	43	5	4	14	25	56	-42	40
24	24	24	Crewe (R)	46	4	7	12	25	40	3	6	14	21	43	-37	34

Best attack

		GF	GFA
1	Wigan	82	1.78
2	Peterborough	82	1.78
3	Millwall	73	1.59
4	Walsall	71	1.54
5	Gillingham	71	1.54
6	Barnsley	70	1.52
7	Rochdale	68	1.48
8	Coventry	67	1.46
9	Sheff Utd	64	1.39
10	Swindon	64	1.39
11	Scunthorpe	60	1.3
12	Southend	58	1.26
13	Chesterfield	58	1.26
14	Shrewsbury	58	1.26
15	Burton	57	1.24
16	Colchester	57	1.24
17	Port Vale	56	1.22
18	Bury	56	1.22
19	Bradford	55	1.2
20	Fleetwood	52	1.13
21	Doncaster	48	1.04
22	Crewe	46	1
23	Oldham	44	0.96
24	Blackpool	40	0.87

Best defence

		GA	GAA
1	Burton	37	0.8
2	Bradford	40	0.87
3	Wigan	45	0.98
4	Scunthorpe	47	1.02
5	Walsall	49	1.07
6	Millwall	49	1.07
7	Coventry	49	1.07
8	Barnsley	54	1.17
9	Gillingham	56	1.22
10	Fleetwood	56	1.22
11	Port Vale	58	1.26
12	Oldham	58	1.26
13	Sheff Utd	59	1.28
14	Rochdale	61	1.33
15	Blackpool	63	1.37
16	Southend	64	1.39
17	Doncaster	64	1.39
18	Chesterfield	70	1.52
19	Swindon	71	1.54
20	Peterborough	73	1.59
21	Bury	73	1.59
22	Shrewsbury	79	1.72
23	Crewe	83	1.8
24	Colchester	99	2.15

Top scorers

	Team	Goals scored
W Grigg	Wigan	25 |||||||||||||||||||||||||
N Ajose	Swindon	24 ||||||||||||||||||||||||
B Sharp	Sheff Utd	21 |||||||||||||||||||||
S Winnall	Barnsley	21 |||||||||||||||||||||
A Armstrong	Coventry	20 ||||||||||||||||||||
P Madden	Scunthorpe	20 ||||||||||||||||||||

Over 2.5 goals

	H	A	%
Colchester	15	16	67%
Peterborough	16	14	65%
Gillingham	15	13	61%
Shrewsbury	13	14	59%
Swindon, Millwall			
Rochdale			57%

Under 2.5 goals

	H	A	%
Blackpool	18	14	70%
Oldham	14	16	65%
Bradford	15	15	65%
Burton	13	15	61%
Port Vale	14	13	59%
Fleetwood	14	13	59%

Both to score

	H	A	%
Colchester	16	14	65%
Peterborough	16	14	65%
Shrewsbury	15	15	65%
Gillingham	12	16	61%
Crewe	16	11	59%

Both not to score

	H	A	%
Blackpool	5	9	70%
Burton	12	5	63%
Bradford	9	9	61%
Scunthorpe	6	13	59%
Coventry, Doncaster			54%

SOCCERBASE.COM

League One results 2015-16

	Barnsley	Blackpool	Bradford	Burton	Bury	Chesterfield	Colchester	Coventry	Crewe	Doncaster	Fleetwood	Gillingham	Millwall	Oldham	Peterborough	Port Vale	Rochdale	Scunthorpe	Sheffield United	Shrewsbury	Southend	Swindon	Walsall	Wigan
Barnsley		4-2	0-0	1-0	3-0	1-2	2-2	2-0	1-2	1-0	0-1	2-0	2-1	2-1	1-0	1-2	6-1	0-0	1-1	1-2	0-2	4-1	0-2	0-2
Blackpool	1-1		0-1	1-2	1-1	2-0	0-1	0-1	2-0	0-2	1-0	1-0	1-1	0-0	2-0	0-1	0-2	5-0	0-0	2-3	2-0	1-0	0-4	0-4
Bradford	0-1	1-0		2-0	2-1	2-0	1-2	0-0	2-0	2-1	2-1	1-2	1-0	1-0	0-2	1-0	2-2	1-0	2-2	1-1	2-0	1-0	4-0	1-1
Burton	0-0	1-0	3-1		1-1	1-0	5-1	1-2	0-0	3-3	2-1	2-1	2-1	0-0	2-1	2-0	1-0	2-1	0-0	1-2	1-0	1-0	0-0	1-1
Bury	0-0	4-3	0-0	1-0		1-0	5-2	2-1	0-0	1-0	3-4	0-1	1-3	1-1	3-1	1-0	0-0	1-2	1-0	2-2	3-2	2-2	2-3	2-2
Chesterfield	3-1	1-1	0-1	1-2	3-0		3-3	1-1	3-1	1-1	0-0	1-3	1-2	1-2	0-1	4-2	0-0	0-3	0-3	7-1	3-0	0-4	1-4	2-3
Colchester	2-3	2-2	2-0	0-3	0-1	1-1		1-3	2-3	4-1	1-1	2-1	0-0	0-0	1-4	2-1	1-2	2-2	1-2	0-0	0-2	1-4	4-4	3-3
Coventry	4-3	0-0	1-0	0-2	6-0	1-0	0-1		3-2	2-2	1-2	4-1	2-1	1-1	3-2	1-0	0-1	1-2	3-1	3-0	2-2	0-0	1-1	2-0
Crewe	1-2	1-2	0-1	1-1	3-3	1-2	1-1	0-5		3-1	1-1	0-1	1-3	1-0	1-5	0-0	2-0	2-3	1-0	1-2	1-2	1-3	1-1	1-1
Doncaster	2-1	0-1	0-1	0-0	1-1	3-0	2-0	2-0	3-2		2-0	2-2	1-1	1-1	1-2	1-2	0-2	0-1	0-1	0-1	0-0	2-2	1-2	3-1
Fleetwood	0-2	0-0	1-1	4-0	2-0	0-1	4-0	0-1	2-0	0-0		2-1	2-1	1-1	2-0	1-2	1-1	2-2	0-0	1-1	5-1	0-1	1-3	
Gillingham	2-1	2-1	3-0	3-1	1-2	1-0	0-0	3-0	1-0	5-1		1-2	3-3	2-1	0-2	2-1	4-0	2-3	1-1	0-0	1-2	2-0		
Millwall	2-3	3-0	0-0	2-0	1-0	0-2	4-1	0-4	1-1	2-0	1-0	0-3		3-0	3-0	3-1	3-1	0-2	1-0	3-1	0-2	2-0	0-1	1-0
Oldham	1-2	1-0	1-2	0-1	0-1	1-0	1-1	0-2	1-0	1-2	1-0	2-1	1-2		1-5	1-1	2-3	2-4	1-1	1-1	2-5	2-0	1-0	1-1
Peterborough	3-2	5-1	0-4	0-1	2-3	2-0	2-1	3-1	3-0	4-0	2-1	1-1	5-3	1-2		2-3	1-2	0-2	1-3	1-1	0-0	1-2	1-1	2-3
Port Vale	0-1	2-0	1-1	0-4	1-0	3-2	2-0	1-1	3-0	3-0	0-0	1-1	0-2	1-1	1-1		4-1	1-1	2-1	2-0	3-1	1-0	0-5	3-2
Rochdale	3-0	3-0	1-3	2-1	3-0	2-3	3-1	0-0	2-2	2-2	1-0	1-1	0-1	0-0	2-0	2-1		2-1	2-0	3-2	4-1	2-2	1-2	0-2
Scunthorpe	2-0	0-1	0-2	1-0	2-1	1-1	3-0	1-0	2-0	2-0	1-0	0-0	0-0	1-1	0-4	1-0	1-1		0-1	2-1	1-0	6-0	0-1	1-1
Sheffield United	0-0	2-0	3-1	0-1	1-3	2-0	2-3	1-0	3-2	3-1	3-0	0-0	1-2	3-0	2-3	1-0	3-2	0-2		2-4	2-2	1-1	2-0	0-2
Shrewsbury	0-3	2-0	1-1	0-1	2-0	1-2	4-2	2-1	0-1	1-2	1-2	1-2	0-1	3-4	1-1	2-0	2-2	1-2		1-2	0-1	1-3	1-5	
Southend	2-1	1-0	0-1	3-1	4-1	0-1	3-0	3-0	1-1	0-3	2-2	1-1	0-4	0-1	2-1	1-0	2-2	2-1	3-1	0-1		0-1	0-2	0-0
Swindon	0-1	3-2	4-1	0-1	0-1	1-0	1-2	2-2	4-3	2-0	1-1	1-3	2-2	1-2	1-2	2-2	2-1	2-1	0-2	3-0	4-2		2-1	1-4
Walsall	1-3	1-1	2-1	2-0	0-1	1-2	2-1	2-1	1-1	2-0	3-1	3-2	0-3	1-1	2-0	2-0	0-3	0-0	1-1	2-1	1-0	1-1		1-2
Wigan	1-4	0-1	1-0	0-1	3-0	3-1	5-0	1-0	1-0	0-0	2-1	3-2	2-2	0-0	1-1	3-0	1-0	3-0	3-3	1-0	4-1	1-0	0-0	

Record when first to score

		P	W	D	L	F	A	Sup	PGA	Pts
1	Burton	24	22	0	2	38	8	+1.25	2.8	66
2	Sheff Utd	22	18	3	1	44	15	+1.32	2.6	57
3	Barnsley	21	18	1	2	45	16	+1.38	2.6	55
4	Bradford	28	22	3	3	45	16	+1.04	2.5	69
5	Walsall	27	20	7	0	54	18	+1.33	2.5	67
6	Millwall	26	21	3	2	57	17	+1.54	2.5	66
7	Scunthorpe	25	19	4	2	45	14	+1.24	2.4	61
8	Port Vale	22	16	4	2	43	19	+1.09	2.4	52
9	Rochdale	21	15	6	0	42	15	+1.29	2.4	51
10	Wigan	31	21	8	2	66	28	+1.23	2.3	71
11	Coventry	22	15	6	1	52	19	+1.50	2.3	51
12	Peterborough	21	16	1	4	59	29	+1.43	2.3	49
13	Bury	20	14	4	2	36	24	+0.60	2.3	46
14	Southend	21	14	4	3	46	26	+0.95	2.2	46
15	Blackpool	18	12	3	3	28	15	+0.72	2.2	39
16	Swindon	17	11	4	2	35	22	+0.76	2.2	37
17	Gillingham	20	13	4	3	42	20	+1.10	2.1	43
18	Oldham	17	10	6	1	21	11	+0.59	2.1	36
19	Chesterfield	20	13	2	5	42	22	+1.00	2	41
20	Fleetwood	19	11	5	3	34	25	+0.47	2	38
21	Doncaster	16	9	4	3	29	18	+0.69	1.9	31
22	Shrewsbury	18	9	4	5	32	28	+0.22	1.7	31
23	Crewe	14	5	5	4	20	19	+0.07	1.4	20
24	Colchester	19	7	4	8	27	33	-0.32	1.3	25

Record when keeping a clean sheet

		P	W	D	F	Sup	PGA	Pts
1	Peterborough	7	6	1	16	+2.29	2.7	19
2	Bradford	22	18	4	29	+1.32	2.6	58
3	Scunthorpe	19	15	4	30	+1.58	2.6	49
4	Walsall	15	12	3	25	+1.67	2.6	39
5	Port Vale	11	9	2	17	+1.55	2.6	29
6	Burton	22	16	6	25	+1.14	2.5	54
7	Wigan	19	14	5	30	+1.58	2.5	47
8	Millwall	17	13	4	28	+1.65	2.5	43
9	Blackpool	15	11	4	19	+1.27	2.5	37
10	Sheff Utd	15	11	4	21	+1.4	2.5	37
11	Swindon	8	6	2	12	+1.5	2.5	20
12	Barnsley	16	11	5	18	+1.13	2.4	38
13	Coventry	16	11	5	27	+1.69	2.4	38
14	Rochdale	14	10	4	22	+1.57	2.4	34
15	Gillingham	14	10	4	21	+1.5	2.4	34
16	Bury	13	9	4	9	+0.69	2.4	31
17	Southend	10	7	3	14	+1.4	2.4	24
18	Shrewsbury	7	5	2	8	+1.14	2.4	17
19	Chesterfield	7	5	2	10	+1.43	2.4	17
20	Oldham	13	8	5	9	+0.69	2.2	29
21	Doncaster	10	6	4	14	+1.4	2.2	22
22	Fleetwood	11	6	5	15	+1.36	2.1	23
23	Crewe	7	4	3	5	+0.71	2.1	15
24	Colchester	6	3	3	4	+0.67	2	12

Pilgrims and Stanley can put last season's playoff heartbreak behind them

T here are some big teams with some big budgets in League Two and the market will revolve around whether Portsmouth can finally win the title having been favourites for each of their failed campaigns in the basement section, writes Mark Langdon. Pompey were 13th in 2014, 16th in 2015 and sixth last term, but it feels a case of sooner rather than later that a club of their size will move up the Football League.

However, at the prices they are by no means the perfect punting proposition as Paul Cook still needs to find a proper solution to their goalscoring woes. Classy playmaker Gary Roberts turns 33 this season too, and there is better value elsewhere.

Doncaster are another club who will believe they are too big for this level but they were horrendous in the second half of last season and it will take a big summer to turn around the losing mentality which comes with relegation.

Luton are respected after improving as last season went on under Nathan Jones and likewise Cambridge under Shaun Derry, while Leyton Orient have the financial backing to make a splash. But the same was true last season when the east London outfit failed to make the playoffs.

Newly-promoted Cheltenham and Grimsby should give a solid account of themselves and Notts County have made an excellent managerial appointment in John Sheridan, so expect the Magpies to leave last season's woes behind them.

County are now out of the transfer embargo so keep an eye on them as the summer progresses, but for now a much safer bet comes in the shape of Plymouth, beaten playoff finalists at Wembley in May.

Argyle were top and seen as good things for promotion in the first half of last season but just missed out under Derek Adams, who was getting his first taste of English football.

Adams will now have gained a greater understanding of the division and players of the calibre of Graham Carey have already signed on for next season, so the ambition is clearly there.

Plymouth have been top seven for two seasons in a row and should be bankers for at least that again, while a chance should also be taken on beaten playoff semi-finalists Accrington.

Stanley have lost two of their best players after Rangers signed Matt Crooks and Josh Windass and they are a side with one of the smallest attendances and budgets in the division.

However, local owner Andy Holt is putting money into the club and a number of influential performers from last season, including Billy Kee, have signed up for another crack at promotion.

Accrington were hampered by a number of postponements that saw them having to fit matches in at the end of a packed schedule, but they were still just seconds away from gaining automatic promotion before losing in extra-time of the playoff semi-final to eventual winners Wimbledon. That demonstrated that they were one of the best sides in the division.

After last season's near-miss, there should smiles all round again for Plymouth this term

ACCRINGTON

Nickname: Stanley
Colours: Red
Ground: Crown Ground (5,070)
Tel: 01254-356-950   accringtonstanley.co.uk

Considering many had tipped them for relegation, it turned into a fine campaign for Accrington – at least until the final day of the season when they missed out on a surprise automatic promotion slot by failing to beat Stevenage at home.

John Coleman was unable to rally the troops in the playoffs as Stanley suffered a semi-final defeat at the hands of Wimbledon, so all the hard work to finish fourth and all the enterprising football that came with it was ultimately wasted.

Longest run without win/loss: 4/12
High/low league position: 2/10
Clean sheets: 14 **Yellows:** 77 **Reds:** 5
Avg attendance: 3,061 **Players used:** 28
Leading scorer: B Kee 17 (6,15)
Key stat: Accrington scored the most home goals (43) in League Two last season

	2015-16 H	A	Last six seasons at home P	W	D	L	OV	UN	BS	CS
Doncaster			-	-	-	-	-	-	-	-
Blackpool			-	-	-	-	-	-	-	-
Colchester			-	-	-	-	-	-	-	-
Crewe			2	1	0	1	1	1	1	0
Accrington										
Plymouth	W	L	5	2	2	1	2	3	3	1
Portsmouth	L	D	3	0	2	1	2	1	3	0
Leyton Orient	W	W	1	1	0	0	0	1	0	1
Cambridge U	D	W	2	1	1	0	1	1	2	0
Carlisle	D	L	2	1	1	0	1	1	2	0
Luton	D	W	2	0	2	0	1	1	2	0
Mansfield	W	W	3	2	1	0	1	2	2	1
Wycombe	D	W	5	0	4	1	0	5	4	0
Exeter	W	L	4	1	0	3	4	0	3	0
Barnet	D	W	4	2	1	1	4	0	3	0
Hartlepool	W	W	3	2	1	0	2	1	2	1
Notts County	W	D	1	1	0	0	1	0	1	0
Stevenage	D	D	3	1	2	0	1	2	1	2
Yeovil	W	L	1	1	0	0	1	0	1	0
Crawley Town	W	W	2	1	0	1	1	1	1	0
Morecambe	D	L	6	3	3	0	3	3	5	1
Newport County	D	W	3	0	2	1	2	1	2	0
Cheltenham			5	0	2	3	2	3	3	0
Grimsby			-	-	-	-	-	-	-	-

Season	Division	Pos	P	W	D	L	F	A	GD	Pts
2015-16	League 2	4	46	24	13	9	74	48	+26	85
2014-15	League 2	17	46	15	11	20	58	77	-19	56
2013-14	League 2	15	46	14	15	17	54	56	-2	57

Over/Under 48%/52% 15th   **Both score** 59%/41% 5th

BARNET

Nickname: The Bees
Colours: Amber and black
Ground: Underhill Stadium (6,023)
Tel: 020-8441-6932   www.barnetfc.com

Many opponents were stung at the Hive last season as Barnet turned their new home into a fortress – their 13 home-wins tally was three superior to second-placed Oxford and more than any side other than Northampton and Bristol Rovers.

John Akinde bagged 24 goals but nobody else hit double figures for the Bees, who finished 15th but did improve their awful away record as the season went on with just one defeat in their last ten on the road.

Longest run without win/loss: 5/4
High/low league position: 15/23
Clean sheets: 14 **Yellows:** 71 **Reds:** 3
Avg attendance: 3,478 **Players used:** 39
Leading scorer: J Akinde 24 (7,18)
Key stat: Thirteen of Barnet's 17 victories last season came at home

	2015-16 H	A	Last six seasons at home P	W	D	L	OV	UN	BS	CS
Doncaster			-	-	-	-	-	-	-	-
Blackpool			-	-	-	-	-	-	-	-
Colchester			-	-	-	-	-	-	-	-
Crewe			2	2	0	0	1	1	1	1
Accrington	L	D	4	1	2	1	1	3	2	2
Plymouth	W	L	3	2	0	1	1	2	1	2
Portsmouth	W	L	1	1	0	0	0	1	0	1
Leyton Orient	W	L	1	1	0	0	1	0	0	1
Cambridge U	D	L	2	0	2	0	1	1	1	1
Carlisle	D	L	1	0	1	0	0	1	0	1
Luton	W	L	2	1	0	1	2	0	2	0
Mansfield	L	D	1	0	0	1	1	0	1	0
Wycombe	D	D	3	1	0	2	0	3	0	1
Exeter	W	D	2	1	0	1	1	1	1	1
Barnet										
Hartlepool	L	D	1	0	0	1	1	0	1	0
Notts County	W	L	1	1	0	0	1	0	1	0
Stevenage	W	D	2	1	0	1	2	0	1	0
Yeovil	L	D	1	0	0	1	1	0	1	0
Crawley Town	W	L	2	1	0	1	2	0	2	0
Morecambe	D	L	4	1	1	2	2	2	2	1
Newport County	W	W	1	1	0	0	1	0	1	0
Cheltenham			3	1	2	0	2	1	2	1
Grimsby			2	1	0	1	2	0	2	0

Season	Division	Pos	P	W	D	L	F	A	GD	Pts
2015-16	League 2	15	46	17	11	18	67	68	-1	62
2014-15	Conference	1	46	28	8	10	94	46	+48	92
2013-14	Conference	8	46	19	13	14	58	53	+5	70

Over/Under 57%/43% 6th   **Both score** 57%/43% 10th

LEAGUE TWO

BLACKPOOL

Nickname: Seasiders/Tangerines
Colours: Tangerine and white
Ground: Bloomfield Road (16,007)
Tel: 0870-443-1953   www.blackpoolfc.co.uk

A statement from the Blackpool board took full responsibility for the consecutive relegations, admitting "mistakes have been made in the last few years" but the club remains in a mess.

Neil McDonald, who has since been replaced by Gary Bowyer, led Blackpool to 22nd in League One with a dismal run-in sealing their fate. One goal scored and one point taken from the last five games – with a 5-1 defeat at Peterborough on the last day – summed up the final stretch.

Longest run without win/loss: 8/5
High/low league position: 17/24
Clean sheets: 15 **Yellows:** 70 **Reds:** 4
Avg attendance: 7,046 **Players used:** 32
Leading scorer: M Cullen 9 (6,8)
Key stat: Blackpool lost 19 league games to nil last season

	2015-16		Last six seasons at home							
	H	A	P	W	D	L	OV	UN	BS	CS
Doncaster	L	W	3	1	1	1	1	2	2	0
Blackpool										
Colchester	L	D	1	0	0	1	0	1	0	0
Crewe	W	W	1	1	0	0	0	1	0	1
Accrington			-	-	-	-	-	-	-	-
Plymouth			-	-	-	-	-	-	-	-
Portsmouth			1	0	1	0	0	1	1	0
Leyton Orient			-	-	-	-	-	-	-	-
Cambridge U			-	-	-	-	-	-	-	-
Carlisle			-	-	-	-	-	-	-	-
Luton			-	-	-	-	-	-	-	-
Mansfield			-	-	-	-	-	-	-	-
Wycombe			-	-	-	-	-	-	-	-
Exeter			-	-	-	-	-	-	-	-
Barnet			-	-	-	-	-	-	-	-
Hartlepool			-	-	-	-	-	-	-	-
Notts County			-	-	-	-	-	-	-	-
Stevenage			-	-	-	-	-	-	-	-
Yeovil			1	0	0	1	1	0	1	0
Crawley Town			-	-	-	-	-	-	-	-
Morecambe			-	-	-	-	-	-	-	-
Newport County			-	-	-	-	-	-	-	-
Cheltenham			-	-	-	-	-	-	-	-
Grimsby			-	-	-	-	-	-	-	-

Season	Division	Pos	P	W	D	L	F	A	GD	Pts
2015-16	League 1	22	46	12	10	24	40	63	-23	46
2014-15	Championship	24	46	4	14	28	36	91	-55	26
2013-14	Championship	20	46	11	13	22	38	66	-28	46

Over/Under 30%/70% 24th   **Both score** 30%/70% 24th

CAMBRIDGE UNITED

Nickname: The U's
Colours: Yellow and black
Ground: Abbey Stadium (9,617)
Tel: 01223-566500   cambridge-united.co.uk

It was a season of two parts for Cambridge, who were considered lively dark horses for the League Two title but started terribly under Richard Money.

Money was given the boot in November with United stuck in 18th spot but the U's finished brilliantly and were only seven points off the playoff spots as Shaun Derry led the club to ninth. Cambridge lost just one of their last 11 matches and hammered Morecambe 7-0 in April, suggesting more is to come this season.

Longest run without win/loss: 5/8
High/low league position: 8/17
Clean sheets: 14 **Yellows:** 65 **Reds:** 3
Avg attendance: 4,998 **Players used:** 41
Leading scorer: B Corr 12 (4,10)
L Berry 12 (3,11) B Williamson 12 (3,3)
Key stat: Cambridge lost just two home league games since the start of December

	2015-16		Last six seasons at home							
	H	A	P	W	D	L	OV	UN	BS	CS
Doncaster			-	-	-	-	-	-	-	-
Blackpool			-	-	-	-	-	-	-	-
Colchester			-	-	-	-	-	-	-	-
Crewe			-	-	-	-	-	-	-	-
Accrington	L	D	2	0	1	1	2	0	2	0
Plymouth	D	W	2	1	1	0	1	1	1	1
Portsmouth	L	L	2	0	0	2	2	0	2	0
Leyton Orient	D	W	1	0	1	0	0	1	1	0
Cambridge U										
Carlisle	D	D	2	1	1	0	1	1	0	2
Luton	L	D	6	0	4	2	2	4	4	1
Mansfield	D	D	5	2	1	2	4	1	5	0
Wycombe	W	L	2	1	0	1	0	2	0	1
Exeter	L	L	2	0	0	2	1	1	1	0
Barnet	W	D	2	1	1	0	1	1	2	0
Hartlepool	D	D	2	1	1	0	1	1	2	0
Notts County	W	W	1	1	0	0	1	0	1	0
Stevenage	W	L	2	1	1	0	0	2	1	1
Yeovil	W	W	1	1	0	0	1	0	0	1
Crawley Town	L	L	2	0	1	1	2	0	1	0
Morecambe	W	W	2	1	0	1	2	0	1	1
Newport County	W	W	5	2	2	1	2	3	1	3
Cheltenham			1	0	0	1	0	1	0	0
Grimsby			4	0	2	2	1	3	2	1

Season	Division	Pos	P	W	D	L	F	A	GD	Pts
2015-16	League 2	9	46	18	14	14	66	55	+11	68
2014-15	League 2	19	46	13	12	21	61	66	-5	51
2013-14	Conference	2	46	23	13	10	72	35	+37	82

Over/Under 54%/46% 9th   **Both score** 52%/48% 17th

CARLISLE

Nickname: Cumbrians/The Blues
Colours: Blue
Ground: Brunton Park (16,683)
Tel: 01228-526-237   www.carlisleunited.co.uk

Carlisle were great entertainers early in the season, with both teams scoring in 11 of their first 12 games, and going gung-ho worked for Keith Curle's men who were in the promotion race at Christmas.

However, the Cumbrians always looked as if they were punching above their weight given their modest budget, and Carlisle eventually finished tenth after a difficult winter which included taking games on the road as their Brunton Park ground was flooded.

Longest run without win/loss: 6/5
High/low league position: 5/14
Clean sheets: 12 **Yellows:** 62 **Reds:** 6
Avg attendance: 4,574 **Players used:** 29
Leading scorer: J Ibehre 15 (1,10)
Key stat: Both teams scored in nine of Carlisle's first ten league matches last season

	2015-16 H	A	P	W	D	L	OV	UN	BS	CS
Doncaster			1	0	0	1	1	0	1	0
Blackpool			-	-	-	-	-	-	-	-
Colchester			4	2	0	2	2	2	2	1
Crewe			2	1	1	0	1	1	1	1
Accrington	W	D	2	2	0	0	0	2	0	2
Plymouth	L	L	3	1	1	1	0	3	1	1
Portsmouth	D	L	3	1	2	0	3	0	3	0
Leyton Orient	D	W	5	1	1	3	4	1	4	0
Cambridge U	D	D	2	0	1	1	1	1	1	0
Carlisle										
Luton	L	W	2	0	0	2	1	1	1	0
Mansfield	L	D	2	1	0	1	2	0	2	0
Wycombe	D	D	3	0	2	1	2	1	3	0
Exeter	W	D	4	2	1	1	3	1	3	1
Barnet	W	D	1	1	0	0	1	0	1	0
Hartlepool	W	W	5	3	1	1	3	2	2	3
Notts County	W	W	5	3	0	2	4	1	1	2
Stevenage	W	W	5	4	1	0	2	3	1	4
Yeovil	W	D	4	2	1	1	3	1	3	0
Crawley Town	W	W	3	1	1	1	1	2	2	0
Morecambe	L	W	2	0	1	1	1	1	2	0
Newport County	L	L	2	0	0	2	1	1	1	0
Cheltenham			1	1	0	0	0	1	0	1
Grimsby			-	-	-	-	-	-	-	-

Season	Division	Pos	P	W	D	L	F	A	GD	Pts
2015-16	League 2	10	46	17	16	13	67	62	+5	67
2014-15	League 2	20	46	14	8	24	56	74	-18	50
2013-14	League 1	22	46	11	12	23	43	76	-33	45

Over/Under 48%/52% 15th   **Both score** 59%/41% 5th

CHELTENHAM

Nickname: The Robins
Colours: Red and white
Ground: The Abbey Business Stadium (7,133)
Tel: 01242-573-558   www.ctfc.com

Cheltenham bounced back to the Football League at the first attempt, romping away with the National League Premier title in fine fashion. The rampant Robins gained 101 points and possessed the best attack and best defence in the division.

The Whaddon Road outfit lost just one home game and are unbeaten in front of their own fans since late September.

Dan Holman was a brilliant signing with 16 goals in 18 games, while Danny Wright helped himself to 22 in 43 fixtures.

Longest run without win/loss: 3/22
High/low league position: 1/6
Clean sheets: 20 **Yellows:** 61 **Reds:** 2
Avg attendance: 2,394 **Players used:** 27
Leading scorer: D Wright 22 (9,9)
Key stat: Cheltenham's goal difference of plus 57 was 20 better than anyone else in the National League

	2015-16 H	A	P	W	D	L	OV	UN	BS	CS
Doncaster			-	-	-	-	-	-	-	-
Blackpool			-	-	-	-	-	-	-	-
Colchester			-	-	-	-	-	-	-	-
Crewe			2	1	0	1	1	1	1	0
Accrington			5	2	0	3	5	0	4	0
Plymouth			4	2	0	2	4	0	3	0
Portsmouth			2	0	2	0	1	1	2	0
Leyton Orient			-	-	-	-	-	-	-	-
Cambridge U			1	1	0	0	1	0	1	0
Carlisle			1	0	1	0	0	1	0	1
Luton			1	0	1	0	0	1	1	0
Mansfield			2	0	1	1	1	1	2	0
Wycombe			4	1	1	2	3	1	3	1
Exeter			3	2	0	1	2	1	1	2
Barnet			3	2	1	0	0	3	1	2
Hartlepool			2	1	1	0	1	1	1	1
Notts County			-	-	-	-	-	-	-	-
Stevenage			2	1	0	1	0	2	0	1
Yeovil			-	-	-	-	-	-	-	-
Crawley Town			1	1	0	0	1	0	1	0
Morecambe			5	2	2	1	2	3	3	2
Newport County			2	0	1	1	0	2	0	1
Cheltenham										
Grimsby	W	W	1	1	0	0	1	0	1	0

Season	Division	Pos	P	W	D	L	F	A	GD	Pts
2015-16	Conference	1	46	30	11	5	87	30	+57	101
2014-15	League 2	23	46	9	14	23	40	67	-27	41
2013-14	League 2	17	46	13	16	17	53	63	-10	55

Over/Under 46%/54% 22nd   **Both score** 50%/50% 16th

COLCHESTER

Nickname: The U's
Colours: Blue and white
Ground: Weston Homes Community Stadium (10,105)
Tel: 01206-508-800 www.cu-fc.com

Colchester needed a great escape to survive in 2015 but there was no repeat in 2016 and there was no case for the defence with United shipping 99 League One goals.

A 0-0 draw with Oldham in mid-August did not hint at defensive issues but that was to be Colchester's only shutout until late February by which time the U's were in deep trouble. Kevin Keen replaced Tony Humes as manager in December, but he couldn't improve the side drastically.

Longest run without win/loss: 19/6
High/low league position: 8/24
Clean sheets: 6 **Yellows:** 58 **Reds:** 4
Avg attendance: 5,367 **Players used:** 34
Leading scorer: G Moncur 12 (4,11)
Key stat: Colchester went on a 19-match winless run during the season

	2015-16		Last six seasons at home							
	H	A	P	W	D	L	OV	UN	BS	CS
Doncaster	W	L	3	1	0	2	2	1	2	0
Blackpool	D	W	1	0	1	0	1	0	1	0
Colchester										
Crewe	L	D	4	0	0	4	4	0	4	0
Accrington			-	-	-	-	-	-	-	-
Plymouth			1	0	1	0	0	1	1	0
Portsmouth			1	0	1	0	1	0	1	0
Leyton Orient			5	3	1	1	3	2	4	1
Cambridge U			-	-	-	-	-	-	-	-
Carlisle			4	1	3	0	0	4	3	1
Luton			-	-	-	-	-	-	-	-
Mansfield			-	-	-	-	-	-	-	-
Wycombe			1	0	1	0	0	1	1	0
Exeter			2	2	0	0	1	1	1	1
Barnet			-	-	-	-	-	-	-	-
Hartlepool			3	2	1	0	2	1	3	0
Notts County			5	2	0	3	3	2	2	0
Stevenage			3	2	0	1	2	1	1	2
Yeovil			4	2	2	0	1	3	1	3
Crawley Town			3	0	2	1	1	2	3	0
Morecambe			-	-	-	-	-	-	-	-
Newport County			-	-	-	-	-	-	-	-
Cheltenham			-	-	-	-	-	-	-	-
Grimsby			-	-	-	-	-	-	-	-

Season	Division	Pos	P	W	D	L	F	A	GD	Pts
2015-16	League 1	23	46	9	13	24	57	99	-42	40
2014-15	League 1	19	46	14	10	22	58	77	-19	52
2013-14	League 1	16	46	13	14	19	53	61	-8	53

Over/Under 67%/33% 1st **Both score** 65%/35% 1st

CRAWLEY

Nickname: The Red Devils
Colours: Red and white
Ground: Broadfield Stadium (5,973)
Tel: 01293-410002 www.crawleytownfc.com

It would be entirely understandable if Crawley supporters were nervous going into this season after a shambolic finish to 2015-16 saw them lose eight straight matches with the Red Devils scoring just twice during that sorry finale.

Thankfully for Crawley they had enough points in the bank to finish 20th, but Mark Yates was sacked just before the climax with Dermot Drummy coming in for the 3-0 defeats to Dagenham and Barnet – which do not bode well.

Longest run without win/loss: 10/5
High/low league position: 13/22
Clean sheets: 10 **Yellows:** 74 **Reds:** 5
Avg attendance: 3,486 **Players used:** 37
Leading scorer: R Murphy 9 (2,7)
Key stat: Crawley lost 15 of their 23 away matches last season

	2015-16		Last six seasons at home							
	H	A	P	W	D	L	OV	UN	BS	CS
Doncaster			2	0	1	1	1	1	1	0
Blackpool			-	-	-	-	-	-	-	-
Colchester			3	2	1	0	1	2	0	3
Crewe			4	1	2	1	1	3	3	1
Accrington	L	L	2	0	1	1	1	1	1	0
Plymouth	D	L	2	1	1	0	0	2	1	1
Portsmouth	D	L	2	0	1	1	1	1	0	1
Leyton Orient	W	L	4	4	0	0	2	2	2	2
Cambridge U	W	W	2	2	0	0	1	1	0	2
Carlisle	L	L	3	0	2	1	0	3	1	1
Luton	W	W	2	1	1	0	1	1	2	0
Mansfield	L	L	2	1	0	1	0	2	0	1
Wycombe	D	L	1	0	1	0	0	1	0	1
Exeter	L	D	1	0	0	1	0	1	0	0
Barnet	L	L	2	1	0	1	1	1	0	1
Hartlepool	D	D	2	0	2	0	1	1	1	1
Notts County		L	4	2	1	1	0	4	0	3
Stevenage	W	W	3	1	2	0	1	2	3	0
Yeovil	L	L	3	1	0	2	1	3	0	1
Crawley Town										
Morecambe	D	L	2	0	2	0	0	2	2	0
Newport County	W		2	1	0	1	1	1	1	1
Cheltenham			1	1	0	0	1	0	1	0
Grimsby			1	0	0	1	0	1	0	0

Season	Division	Pos	P	W	D	L	F	A	GD	Pts
2015-16	League 2	20	46	13	8	25	45	78	-33	47
2014-15	League 1	22	46	13	11	22	51	77	-26	50
2013-14	League 1	14	46	14	15	17	48	54	-6	57

Over/Under 59%/41% 3rd **Both score** 48%/52% 22nd

CREWE

Nickname: The Railwaymen
Colours: Red and white
Ground: Gresty Road (10,109)
Tel: 01270-213-014   www.crewealex.net

The once-famous Crewe academy is not churning out quite the same calibre of player these days and their reliance on their youngsters to pay the bills came back to bite with Alex finishing a distant last in League One with only 34 points – a whopping 16 adrift of safety.

Young Ryan Colclough did his best with seven goals in 27 fixtures but was sold to eventual champions Wigan. Their misery was complete when local rivals Port Vale sent Crewe down in early April.

Longest run without win/loss: 15/6
High/low league position: 22/24
Clean sheets: 7 **Yellows:** 50 **Reds:** 0
Avg attendance: 5,665 **Players used:** 31
Leading scorer: B Inman 10 (1,9)
Key stat: Crewe won just seven matches all season

	2015-16		Last six seasons at home							
	H	A	P	W	D	L	OV	UN	BS	CS
Doncaster	W	L	3	1	1	1	2	1	3	0
Blackpool	L	L	1	0	0	1	1	0	1	0
Colchester	D	W	4	1	2	1	2	2	2	1
Crewe										
Accrington			2	1	1	0	0	2	0	2
Plymouth			1	1	0	0	1	0	1	0
Portsmouth			1	0	0	1	1	0	1	0
Leyton Orient			3	0	2	1	1	2	3	0
Cambridge U			-	-	-	-	-	-	-	-
Carlisle			2	2	0	0	1	1	1	1
Luton			-	-	-	-	-	-	-	-
Mansfield			-	-	-	-	-	-	-	-
Wycombe			1	1	0	0	1	0	0	1
Exeter			-	-	-	-	-	-	-	-
Barnet			2	2	0	0	2	0	1	1
Hartlepool			1	1	0	0	1	0	1	0
Notts County			3	0	0	3	3	0	2	0
Stevenage			3	0	0	3	2	1	1	0
Yeovil			2	1	0	1	0	2	0	1
Crawley Town			4	2	2	0	0	4	1	3
Morecambe			2	1	0	1	1	1	1	0
Newport County			-	-	-	-	-	-	-	-
Cheltenham			2	2	0	0	1	1	1	1
Grimsby			-	-	-	-	-	-	-	-

Season	Division	Pos	P	W	D	L	F	A	GD	Pts
2015-16	League 1	24	46	7	13	26	46	83	-37	34
2014-15	League 1	20	46	14	10	22	43	75	-32	52
2013-14	League 1	19	46	13	12	21	54	80	-26	51

Over/Under 50%/50% 11th   **Both score** 59%/41% 5th

DONCASTER

Nickname: Rovers
Colours: Red and white
Ground: Keepmoat Stadium (15,231)
Tel: 01302-764-664   doncasterroversfc.co.uk

One of the major surprises of the Football League season was seeing Doncaster nosedive out of League One considering they started the season with serious hope of pushing for the Championship.

Andy Williams notched 12 times – double the amount of anyone else – and the decision to replace Paul Dickov with Darren Ferguson in October could hardly have gone worse even though Rovers actually started brilliantly for their new boss and were still mid-table in January.

Longest run without win/loss: 16/4
High/low league position: 12/22
Clean sheets: 10 **Yellows:** 49 **Reds:** 3
Avg attendance: 6,881 **Players used:** 36
Leading scorer: A Williams 12 (4,11)
Key stat: Doncaster won three matches in 2016

	2015-16		Last six seasons at home							
	H	A	P	W	D	L	OV	UN	BS	CS
Doncaster										
Blackpool	L	W	3	0	0	3	2	1	2	0
Colchester	W	L	3	3	0	0	0	3	0	3
Crewe	W	L	3	2	0	1	2	1	2	0
Accrington			-	-	-	-	-	-	-	-
Plymouth			-	-	-	-	-	-	-	-
Portsmouth			3	0	1	2	1	2	2	0
Leyton Orient			2	1	0	1	0	2	0	1
Cambridge U			-	-	-	-	-	-	-	-
Carlisle			1	0	0	1	0	1	0	0
Luton			-	-	-	-	-	-	-	-
Mansfield			-	-	-	-	-	-	-	-
Wycombe			-	-	-	-	-	-	-	-
Exeter			-	-	-	-	-	-	-	-
Barnet			-	-	-	-	-	-	-	-
Hartlepool			1	1	0	0	1	0	0	1
Notts County			2	0	1	1	0	2	0	1
Stevenage			1	0	1	0	0	1	1	0
Yeovil			3	2	1	0	2	1	2	1
Crawley Town			2	0	1	1	0	2	0	1
Morecambe			-	-	-	-	-	-	-	-
Newport County			-	-	-	-	-	-	-	-
Cheltenham			-	-	-	-	-	-	-	-
Grimsby			-	-	-	-	-	-	-	-

Season	Division	Pos	P	W	D	L	F	A	GD	Pts
2015-16	League 1	21	46	11	13	22	48	64	-16	46
2014-15	League 1	13	46	16	13	17	58	62	-4	61
2013-14	Championship	22	46	11	11	24	39	70	-31	44

Over/Under 46%/54% 17th   **Both score** 46%/54% 19th

EXETER

Nickname: The Grecians
Colours: Black and white
Ground: St James' Park (8,830)
Tel: 0871-855-1904 www.exetercityfc.co.uk

Reaching the FA Cup third round was the highlight of Exeter's season. After holding Liverpool to a draw at home they took the Reds back to Anfield, and even though they were outclassed the second time around it provided a bumper payday.

Paul Tisdale's team finished 14th in League Two but it was a congested section with only seven points separating eighth from 15th. But losing 12-goal top scorer Tom Nichols to Peterborough was a big blow at the wrong time of the season.

Longest run without win/loss: 6/10
High/low league position: 6/16
Clean sheets: 11 **Yellows:** 56 **Reds:** 0
Avg attendance: 4,416 **Players used:** 26
Leading scorer: J Stockley 10 (4,8)
T Nichols 10 (4,9)
Key stat: Exeter drew just two away matches last season

GRIMSBY

Nickname: The Mariners
Colours: Black and white
Ground: (0)
Tel: 01472-605-050 grimsby-townfc.co.uk

If at first you don't succeed then try and try again. Or in Grimsby's case try, try, try and try again, with the Mariners winning the National League playoffs at the fourth attempt.

Grimsby had run into some decent sides in previous years but last season's playoffs was nowhere near as strong. They saw off Braintree in a tight semi-final before beating managerless Forest Green at Wembley despite finishing below both teams in the regular campaign.

Longest run without win/loss: 4/11
High/low league position: 3/11
Clean sheets: 15 **Yellows:** 58 **Reds:** 1
Avg attendance: 3,124 **Players used:** 31
Leading scorer: P Amond 30 (9,20)
Key stat: Padraig Almond scored 30 league goals last season

Exeter — 2015-16 and last six seasons at home

	2015-16 H	2015-16 A	P	W	D	L	OV	UN	BS	CS
Doncaster			-	-	-	-	-	-	-	-
Blackpool			-	-	-	-	-	-	-	-
Colchester			2	0	2	0	1	1	2	0
Crewe			-	-	-	-	-	-	-	-
Accrington	W	L	4	2	0	2	2	2	2	1
Plymouth	W	W	5	3	1	1	3	2	4	1
Portsmouth	D	W	3	0	3	0	0	3	3	0
Leyton Orient	W	W	3	3	0	0	3	0	1	2
Cambridge U	W	W	2	1	1	0	1	1	1	1
Carlisle	D	L	4	2	2	0	2	2	2	2
Luton	L	L	2	0	1	1	1	1	2	0
Mansfield	L	W	3	0	0	3	2	1	2	0
Wycombe	L	L	5	2	0	3	3	2	3	0
Exeter										
Barnet	D	L	2	0	2	0	1	1	2	0
Hartlepool	W	W	5	1	1	3	3	2	2	2
Notts County	D	W	3	1	2	0	1	2	3	0
Stevenage	D	W	3	0	3	0	1	2	2	1
Yeovil	W	W	3	1	1	1	2	1	3	0
Crawley Town	D	W	1	0	1	0	1	0	1	0
Morecambe	D	D	4	0	3	1	1	3	3	0
Newport County	D	D	3	1	1	1	0	3	1	1
Cheltenham			3	1	1	1	0	3	1	1
Grimsby			-	-	-	-	-	-	-	-

Season	Division	Pos	P	W	D	L	F	A	GD	Pts
2015-16	League 2	14	46	17	13	16	63	65	-2	64
2014-15	League 2	10	46	17	13	16	61	65	-4	64
2013-14	League 2	16	46	14	13	19	54	57	-3	55

Over/Under 48%/52% 15th **Both score** 59%/41% 5th

Grimsby — 2015-16 and last six seasons at home

	2015-16 H	2015-16 A	P	W	D	L	OV	UN	BS	CS
Doncaster			-	-	-	-	-	-	-	-
Blackpool			-	-	-	-	-	-	-	-
Colchester			-	-	-	-	-	-	-	-
Crewe			-	-	-	-	-	-	-	-
Accrington			-	-	-	-	-	-	-	-
Plymouth			-	-	-	-	-	-	-	-
Portsmouth			-	-	-	-	-	-	-	-
Leyton Orient			-	-	-	-	-	-	-	-
Cambridge U			4	1	1	2	1	3	2	0
Carlisle			-	-	-	-	-	-	-	-
Luton			4	2	0	2	2	2	2	1
Mansfield			3	2	1	0	2	1	2	1
Wycombe			-	-	-	-	-	-	-	-
Exeter			-	-	-	-	-	-	-	-
Barnet			2	2	0	0	2	0	2	0
Hartlepool			-	-	-	-	-	-	-	-
Notts County			-	-	-	-	-	-	-	-
Stevenage			-	-	-	-	-	-	-	-
Yeovil			-	-	-	-	-	-	-	-
Crawley Town			1	0	1	0	0	1	0	1
Morecambe			-	-	-	-	-	-	-	-
Newport County			3	2	1	0	2	1	1	2
Cheltenham	L	L	1	0	0	1	0	1	0	0
Grimsby										

Season	Division	Pos	P	W	D	L	F	A	GD	Pts
2015-16	Conference	4	46	22	14	10	82	45	+37	80
2014-15	Conference	3	46	25	11	10	74	40	+34	86
2013-14	Conference	4	46	22	12	12	65	46	+19	78

Over/Under 50%/50% 11th **Both score** 57%/43% 9th

HARTLEPOOL

Nickname: Pools
Colours: White and blue
Ground: Victoria Park (7,856)
Tel: 01429-272-584   hartlepoolunited.co.uk

Some managerial appointments work out better than others but Hartlepool will be glad they made their change in February – Craig Hignett replaced Ronnie Moore and guided Pools away from danger to finish a respectable 16th.

It could have been even better for Hignett but Hartlepool eased up once survival had been secured. United lost their last four games, but they were extremely tough fixtures against Oxford, Accrington, Portsmouth and Plymouth.

Longest run without win/loss: 5/7
High/low league position: 15/22
Clean sheets: 10 **Yellows:** 68 **Reds:** 2
Avg attendance: 4,196 **Players used:** 36
Leading scorer: B Paynter 14 (6,13)
Key stat: Craig Hignett won eight of his 20 matches in charge

	2015-16 H	A	Last six seasons at home P	W	D	L	OV	UN	BS	CS
Doncaster			1	0	1	0	0	1	1	0
Blackpool			-	-	-	-	-	-	-	-
Colchester			3	1	1	1	0	3	0	2
Crewe			1	1	0	0	1	0	0	1
Accrington	L	L	3	1	1	1	2	1	3	0
Plymouth	L	L	4	3	0	1	2	2	2	2
Portsmouth	L	L	4	0	3	1	0	4	0	3
Leyton Orient	W	W	4	3	0	1	3	1	3	0
Cambridge U	D	D	2	1	1	0	1	1	1	1
Carlisle	L	L	5	1	0	4	5	0	2	1
Luton	L	L	2	0	0	2	2	0	2	0
Mansfield	W	L	3	2	0	1	2	1	2	1
Wycombe	W	L	4	1	0	3	3	1	3	1
Exeter	L	L	5	2	0	3	2	3	2	1
Barnet	D	W	1	0	1	0	0	1	1	0
Hartlepool										
Notts County	L	L	4	2	1	1	3	1	3	1
Stevenage	L	L	4	0	1	3	2	2	2	1
Yeovil	W	W	4	2	1	1	2	2	2	1
Crawley Town	L	D	2	0	0	2	1	1	1	0
Morecambe	W	W	3	2	0	1	1	2	1	1
Newport County	W	D	3	2	1	0	2	1	1	2
Cheltenham			2	1	0	1	0	2	0	1
Grimsby			-	-	-	-	-	-	-	-

Season	Division	Pos	P	W	D	L	F	A	GD	Pts
2015-16	League 2	16	46	15	6	25	49	72	-23	51
2014-15	League 2	22	46	12	9	25	39	70	-31	45
2013-14	League 2	19	46	14	11	21	50	56	-6	53

Over/Under 54%/46% 9th   **Both score** 52%/48% 17th

LEYTON ORIENT

Nickname: The O's
Colours: Red
Ground: Matchroom Stadium (9,311)
Tel: 0871-310-1881   www.leytonorient.com

At the end of August Leyton Orient looked as if they were going to run their League Two opponents ragged, racking up five straight victories with a budget in place to launch a sustained promotion push.

However, there were issues behind the scenes and Ian Hendon's managerial reign eventually ended in January.

There was still enough time to finish in the playoffs but Orient could never regain the early-season consistency even though Jay Simpson scored 25 goals.

Longest run without win/loss: 5/6
High/low league position: 1/14
Clean sheets: 13 **Yellows:** 58 **Reds:** 4
Avg attendance: 5,161 **Players used:** 35
Leading scorer: J Simpson 25 (10,21)
Key stat: Five of Leyton Orient's 19 League Two wins came in August

	2015-16 H	A	Last six seasons at home P	W	D	L	OV	UN	BS	CS
Doncaster			2	0	0	2	0	2	0	0
Blackpool			-	-	-	-	-	-	-	-
Colchester			5	2	0	3	2	3	2	0
Crewe			3	2	1	0	1	2	2	1
Accrington	L	L	1	0	0	1	0	1	0	0
Plymouth	L	D	2	1	0	1	1	1	1	1
Portsmouth	W	W	2	2	0	0	1	1	1	1
Leyton Orient										
Cambridge U	L	D	1	0	0	1	1	0	1	0
Carlisle	L	D	5	2	1	2	4	1	3	2
Luton	L	D	1	0	0	1	0	1	0	0
Mansfield	W	D	1	1	0	0	0	1	0	1
Wycombe	D	W	2	0	1	1	1	1	2	0
Exeter	L	L	3	2	0	1	3	0	1	2
Barnet	W	L	1	1	0	0	0	1	0	1
Hartlepool	L	L	4	2	1	1	0	4	1	2
Notts County	W	W	6	4	0	2	4	2	3	1
Stevenage	W	D	4	2	1	1	1	3	0	3
Yeovil	D	W	5	2	2	1	4	1	4	1
Crawley Town	W	L	4	2	0	2	2	2	2	1
Morecambe	W	W	1	1	0	0	0	1	0	1
Newport County	W	W	1	1	0	0	0	1	0	1
Cheltenham			-	-	-	-	-	-	-	-
Grimsby			-	-	-	-	-	-	-	-

Season	Division	Pos	P	W	D	L	F	A	GD	Pts
2015-16	League 2	8	46	19	12	15	60	61	-1	69
2014-15	League 1	23	46	12	13	21	59	69	-10	49
2013-14	League 1	3	46	25	11	10	85	45	+40	86

Over/Under 43%/57% 18th   **Both score** 54%/46% 14th

LUTON

Nickname: The Hatters
Colours: Orange, navy and white
Ground: Kenilworth Road (10,356)
Tel: 01582-411-622   www.lutontown.co.uk

Plenty of punters had their fingers burnt by backing Luton last season with the Hatters the division's plunge team after a summer of big spending by John Still.

However, Still never looked at ease working on a bigger budget – he previously preferred lower-profile performers – and it was no surprise when he was sacked in December after four straight defeats.

Replacement Nathan Jones finally got Luton going and they produced a few eye-catching performances to finish 11th.

Longest run without win/loss: 5/5
High/low league position: 10/20
Clean sheets: 13 **Yellows:** 73 **Reds:** 3
Avg attendance: 6,950 **Players used:** 34
Leading scorer: J Marriott 14 (7,11)
Key stat: Luton lost ten home matches last season – the most in the top half

	2015-16 H	A	Last six seasons at home P	W	D	L	OV	UN	BS	CS
Doncaster			-	-	-	-	-	-	-	-
Blackpool			-	-	-	-	-	-	-	-
Colchester			-	-	-	-	-	-	-	-
Crewe			-	-	-	-	-	-	-	-
Accrington	L	D	2	1	0	1	0	2	0	1
Plymouth	L	W	2	0	0	2	1	1	1	0
Portsmouth	L	D	2	0	1	1	1	1	2	0
Leyton Orient	D	W	1	0	1	0	0	1	1	0
Cambridge U	D	W	6	3	2	1	2	4	2	3
Carlisle	L	W	2	1	0	1	1	1	1	1
Luton										
Mansfield	W	W	5	3	1	1	2	3	1	4
Wycombe	L	W	2	0	0	2	1	1	1	0
Exeter	W	W	2	1	0	1	2	0	2	0
Barnet	W	L	2	2	0	0	1	1	1	1
Hartlepool	W	W	2	2	0	0	2	0	1	1
Notts County	L	L	1	0	0	1	0	1	0	0
Stevenage	L	D	2	1	0	1	0	2	0	1
Yeovil	D	L	1	0	1	0	0	1	1	0
Crawley Town	L	L	2	0	0	2	1	1	1	0
Morecambe	L	W	2	1	0	1	1	1	1	1
Newport County	D	L	5	2	3	0	2	3	3	2
Cheltenham			1	1	0	0	0	1	0	1
Grimsby			4	1	3	0	0	4	2	2

Season	Division	Pos	P	W	D	L	F	A	GD	Pts
2015-16	League 2	11	46	19	9	18	63	61	+2	66
2014-15	League 2	8	46	19	11	16	54	44	+10	68
2013-14	Conference	1	46	30	11	5	102	35	+67	101

Over/Under 43%/57% 18th   **Both score** 52%/48% 17th

MANSFIELD

Nickname: The Stags
Colours: Yellow and blue
Ground: Field Mill (8,186)
Tel: 01623-482 482   www.mansfieldtown.net

Finishing 12th may have been considered unlucky by manager Adam Murray but Stags fans should have been partying at that placing considering many had them down as relegation candidates.

Mansfield were excellent early on and went as high as fourth in October following a superb goalless draw at Portsmouth, but they predictably fell away. Matt Green grabbed 16 goals on his return to the club but nobody else notched more than five.

Longest run without win/loss: 7/4
High/low league position: 4/13
Clean sheets: 10 **Yellows:** 86 **Reds:** 7
Avg attendance: 3,922 **Players used:** 26
Leading scorer: M Green 16 (6,12)
Key stat: Mansfield kept two clean sheet in their last 17 matches

	2015-16 H	A	Last six seasons at home P	W	D	L	OV	UN	BS	CS
Doncaster			-	-	-	-	-	-	-	-
Blackpool			-	-	-	-	-	-	-	-
Colchester			-	-	-	-	-	-	-	-
Crewe			-	-	-	-	-	-	-	-
Accrington	L	L	3	0	0	3	2	1	2	0
Plymouth	D	L	3	1	1	1	0	3	0	2
Portsmouth	D	D	3	0	2	1	2	1	3	0
Leyton Orient	D	L	1	0	1	0	0	1	1	0
Cambridge U	D	D	5	2	2	1	2	3	2	3
Carlisle	D	W	2	1	1	0	1	1	2	0
Luton	L	L	5	1	3	1	1	4	2	2
Mansfield										
Wycombe	L	L	3	0	2	1	1	2	1	1
Exeter	L	W	3	0	1	2	1	2	1	1
Barnet	D	W	1	0	1	0	0	1	1	0
Hartlepool	W	L	3	1	1	1	2	1	3	0
Notts County	W	W	1	1	0	0	1	0	0	1
Stevenage	W	W	2	2	0	0	1	1	1	1
Yeovil	L	W	1	0	0	1	0	0	1	0
Crawley Town	W	W	2	1	0	1	2	0	1	1
Morecambe	W	W	3	2	0	1	2	1	2	1
Newport County	W	L	6	4	1	1	5	1	3	3
Cheltenham			2	0	1	1	0	2	1	0
Grimsby			3	2	0	1	1	2	1	1

Season	Division	Pos	P	W	D	L	F	A	GD	Pts
2015-16	League 2	12	46	17	13	16	61	53	+8	64
2014-15	League 2	21	46	13	9	24	38	62	-24	48
2013-14	League 2	11	46	15	15	16	49	58	-9	60

Over/Under 43%/57% 18th   **Both score** 52%/48% 17th

MORECAMBE

Nickname: The Shrimps
Colours: Red and white
Ground: The Globe Arena (6,400)
Tel: 01524-411-797   www.morecambefc.com

Morecambe will be relieved there were two really poor clubs in League Two last season in relegated York and Dagenham, otherwise they may also have fallen through the relegation trapdoor.

The Shrimps were hopeless in the second half of the season and won only two of their last 21 matches, suffering some horrendous results along the way.

Their 7-0 loss at Cambridge and a 5-2 defeat to Hartlepool hint at trouble ahead for one of the smaller clubs at this level.

Longest run without win/loss: 10/4
High/low league position: 5/21
Clean sheets: 5 **Yellows:** 77 **Reds:** 5
Avg attendance: 3,110 **Players used:** 27
Leading scorer: S Miller 15 (5,12)
Key stat: Morecambe's League Two matches produced 160 goals

	2015-16 H	A	P	W	D	L	OV	UN	BS	CS
Doncaster			-	-	-	-	-	-	-	-
Blackpool			-	-	-	-	-	-	-	-
Colchester			-	-	-	-	-	-	-	-
Crewe			2	0	0	2	2	0	2	0
Accrington	W	D	6	1	2	3	3	3	4	2
Plymouth	L	L	5	2	1	2	4	1	4	0
Portsmouth	D	D	3	1	2	0	2	1	3	0
Leyton Orient	L	L	1	0	0	1	0	1	0	0
Cambridge U	L	L	2	0	0	2	1	1	1	0
Carlisle	L	W	2	0	0	2	1	1	1	0
Luton	L	L	2	1	0	1	2	0	1	1
Mansfield	L	L	3	1	0	2	2	1	2	0
Wycombe	L	W	5	0	1	4	2	3	2	0
Exeter	D	D	4	1	1	2	1	3	1	1
Barnet	W	D	4	2	1	1	3	1	3	0
Hartlepool	L	L	3	0	0	3	2	1	2	0
Notts County	W	D	1	1	0	0	1	0	1	0
Stevenage	L	L	3	0	2	1	1	2	1	2
Yeovil	W	W	1	1	0	0	1	0	1	0
Crawley Town	W	D	2	2	0	0	2	0	1	1
Morecambe										
Newport County	L	W	3	2	0	1	3	0	3	0
Cheltenham			5	1	3	1	1	4	2	2
Grimsby			-	-	-	-	-	-	-	-

Season	Division	Pos	P	W	D	L	F	A	GD	Pts
2015-16	League 2	21	46	12	10	24	69	91	-22	46
2014-15	League 2	11	46	17	12	17	53	52	+1	63
2013-14	League 2	18	46	13	15	18	52	64	-12	54

Over/Under 63%/37% 2nd   **Both score** 72%/28% 1st

NEWPORT COUNTY

Nickname: The Exiles
Colours: Yellow and black
Ground: Rodney Parade (5,511)
Tel: 01633-670-690   newport-county.co.uk

Like Morecambe, Newport will have been relieved that there were two worse teams than them in League Two last season. County finished 22nd and started and finished the season in terrible form.

Terry Butcher was sacked in October after only one win before John Sheridan turned things around. But when he left for Oldham, replacement Warren Feeney struggled. Newport picked up three points in their last 11 matches and failed to score in seven of those.

Longest run without win/loss: 11/7
High/low league position: 17/24
Clean sheets: 11 **Yellows:** 64 **Reds:** 3
Avg attendance: 3,729 **Players used:** 40
Leading scorer: S Boden 13 (5,12)
Key stat: Newport won four home matches last season

	2015-16 H	A	P	W	D	L	OV	UN	BS	CS
Doncaster			-	-	-	-	-	-	-	-
Blackpool			-	-	-	-	-	-	-	-
Colchester			-	-	-	-	-	-	-	-
Crewe			-	-	-	-	-	-	-	-
Accrington	L	D	3	1	1	1	1	2	2	0
Plymouth	L	L	3	1	0	2	2	1	2	1
Portsmouth	L	W	3	1	0	2	1	2	1	1
Leyton Orient	L	L	1	0	0	1	1	0	1	0
Cambridge U	L	L	5	1	2	2	1	4	3	0
Carlisle	W	W	2	2	0	0	1	1	1	1
Luton	W	D	5	3	1	1	2	3	2	2
Mansfield	W	L	6	4	1	1	0	6	1	4
Wycombe	W	W	3	2	0	1	0	3	0	2
Exeter	D	D	3	0	3	0	1	2	3	0
Barnet	L	L	1	0	0	1	0	0	1	0
Hartlepool	D	L	3	1	2	0	2	1	2	2
Notts County	L	L	1	0	0	1	0	1	0	0
Stevenage	D	W	2	1	1	0	1	1	1	1
Yeovil	D	L	1	0	1	0	0	1	0	1
Crawley Town	L	L	2	0	0	2	1	1	0	0
Morecambe	L	W	3	0	0	3	2	1	2	0
Newport County										
Cheltenham			2	0	1	1	0	2	1	0
Grimsby			3	1	2	0	1	2	1	2

Season	Division	Pos	P	W	D	L	F	A	GD	Pts
2015-16	League 2	22	46	10	13	23	43	64	-21	43
2014-15	League 2	9	46	18	11	17	51	54	-3	65
2013-14	League 2	14	46	14	16	16	54	59	-3	58

Over/Under 43%/57% 18th   **Both score** 39%/61% 25th

LEAGUE TWO

NOTTS COUNTY

Nickname: The Magpies
Colours: Black and white
Ground: Meadow Lane (20,280)
Tel: 0115-952-9000 www.nottscountyfc.co.uk

Appointing Ricardo Moniz, a former skills coach at Tottenham, always looked risky and he was sacked in December after some wildly inconsistent performances. Moniz was more than partly to blame as he used a heavy rotation policy to make best use of County's oversized squad.

However, replacement Jamie Fullarton was even worse, so Mark Cooper took over until the end of the season. There is chaos behind the scenes and the Magpies finished a bitterly disappointing 17th.

Longest run without win/loss: 10/4
High/low league position: 13/20
Clean sheets: 11 **Yellows:** 84 **Reds:** 4
Avg attendance: 4,780 **Players used:** 36
Leading scorer: J Stead 11 (4,10)
Key stat: Notts County conceded three goals or more on seven occasions in 2016

	2015-16 H	A	Last six seasons at home P	W	D	L	OV	UN	BS	CS
Doncaster			2	1	0	1	1	1	1	0
Blackpool			-	-	-	-	-	-	-	-
Colchester			5	5	0	0	3	2	3	2
Crewe			3	2	1	0	2	1	2	1
Accrington	D	L	1	0	1	0	0	1	1	0
Plymouth	L	L	2	1	0	1	0	2	0	1
Portsmouth	W	L	2	2	0	0	2	0	1	1
Leyton Orient	L	L	6	1	3	2	2	4	4	1
Cambridge U	L	L	1	0	0	1	1	0	1	0
Carlisle	L	L	5	3	0	2	2	3	1	2
Luton	W	W	1	1	0	0	1	0	1	0
Mansfield	L	L	1	0	0	1	0	1	0	0
Wycombe	D	D	2	0	2	0	0	2	1	1
Exeter	L	D	3	1	0	2	2	1	2	0
Barnet	W	L	1	1	0	0	1	0	1	0
Hartlepool	W	W	4	4	0	0	2	2	0	4
Notts County										
Stevenage	W	W	4	2	0	2	1	3	1	2
Yeovil	W	L	5	3	0	2	4	1	3	2
Crawley Town	W	W	4	3	1	0	2	2	3	1
Morecambe	D	L	1	0	1	0	1	0	1	0
Newport County	W	W	1	1	0	0	1	0	1	0
Cheltenham			-	-	-	-	-	-	-	-
Grimsby			-	-	-	-	-	-	-	-

Season	Division	Pos	P	W	D	L	F	A	GD	Pts
2015-16	League 2	17	46	14	9	23	54	83	-29	51
2014-15	League 1	21	46	12	14	20	45	63	-18	50
2013-14	League 1	20	46	15	5	26	64	77	-13	50

Over/Under 54%/46% 9th **Both score** 52%/48% 17th

PLYMOUTH

Nickname: The Pilgrims
Colours: Green and white
Ground: Home Park (16,388)
Tel: 01752-562 561 www.pafc.co.uk

Plymouth will have felt they had promotion in the bag on a couple of occasions but ultimately fell short when the pressure was on and must now face a sixth-straight season in League Two.

Argyle were producing the best results in the division for the first few months of the season, were still top heading towards the end of January and were in the top three until April. However, they eventually finished fifth and then lost the playoff final to Wimbledon.

Longest run without win/loss: 4/7
High/low league position: 1/6
Clean sheets: 14 **Yellows:** 73 **Reds:** 1
Avg attendance: 6,637 **Players used:** 29
Leading scorer: G Carey 11 (4,11)
J Jervis 11 (4,9)
Key stat: Plymouth failed to score in only six League Two matches last season

	2015-16 H	A	Last six seasons at home P	W	D	L	OV	UN	BS	CS
Doncaster			-	-	-	-	-	-	-	-
Blackpool			-	-	-	-	-	-	-	-
Colchester			1	1	0	0	1	0	1	0
Crewe			1	0	0	1	0	1	0	0
Accrington	W	L	5	2	3	0	1	4	1	4
Plymouth										
Portsmouth	L	W	3	1	1	1	2	1	2	1
Leyton Orient	D	W	2	0	1	1	1	1	2	0
Cambridge U	L	D	2	1	0	1	1	1	1	1
Carlisle	W	W	3	2	1	0	1	2	2	1
Luton	L	W	2	0	0	2	0	2	0	0
Mansfield	W	D	3	2	1	0	2	1	2	1
Wycombe	L	W	4	0	0	4	1	3	0	0
Exeter	L	L	5	3	0	2	3	2	2	3
Barnet	W	L	3	2	1	0	2	1	2	1
Hartlepool	W	W	4	2	1	1	1	3	1	2
Notts County	W	W	2	1	1	0	0	2	1	1
Stevenage	W	L	2	1	1	0	1	1	2	0
Yeovil	W	D	2	1	1	0	0	2	0	2
Crawley Town	W	D	2	1	1	0	1	1	2	0
Morecambe	W	W	5	3	2	0	2	3	3	2
Newport County	W		3	1	2	0	0	3	0	3
Cheltenham			4	2	1	1	2	2	2	2
Grimsby			-	-	-	-	-	-	-	-

Season	Division	Pos	P	W	D	L	F	A	GD	Pts
2015-16	League 2	5	46	24	9	13	72	46	+26	81
2014-15	League 2	7	46	20	11	15	55	57	+18	71
2013-14	League 2	10	46	16	12	18	51	58	-7	60

Over/Under 54%/46% 9th **Both score** 61%/39% 4th

PORTSMOUTH

Nickname: Pompey
Colours: Blue and white
Ground: Fratton Park (21,178)
Tel: 02392-731-204   www.portsmouthfc.co.uk

The ante-post League Two favourites once again let down their backers, and Portsmouth's supporters must pick themselves up for another attempt at getting out of the basement.

Paul Cook's men underachieved in the regular season, finishing only sixth, and then lost a tight semi-final playoff to Plymouth. A lot of their attractive football was pleasing on the eye but no player scored more than ten league goals which wasn't good enough.

Longest run without win/loss: 5/9
High/low league position: 2/8
Clean sheets: 16 **Yellows:** 59 **Reds:** 7
Avg attendance: 10,476 **Players used:** 32
Leading scorer: G Evans 10 (5,10)
M McNulty 10 (2,8)
Key stat: Portsmouth were held to five 0-0 home draws last season

	2015-16		Last six seasons at home							
	H	A	P	W	D	L	OV	UN	BS	CS
Doncaster			3	1	0	2	2	1	2	0
Blackpool			1	1	0	0	0	1	0	1
Colchester			1	0	0	1	1	0	1	0
Crewe			1	1	0	0	0	1	0	1
Accrington	D	W	3	1	1	1	1	2	1	2
Plymouth	L	W	3	1	1	1	3	0	3	0
Portsmouth										
Leyton Orient	L	L	2	0	0	2	1	1	1	0
Cambridge U	W	W	2	2	0	0	2	0	2	0
Carlisle	W	D	3	2	1	0	1	2	1	2
Luton	D	W	2	1	1	0	0	2	0	2
Mansfield	D	D	3	0	3	0	0	3	2	1
Wycombe	W	D	3	1	2	0	2	1	3	0
Exeter	L	D	3	2	0	1	2	1	2	1
Barnet	W	L	1	1	0	0	1	0	1	0
Hartlepool	W	W	4	3	0	1	2	2	1	3
Notts County	W	L	2	1	0	1	1	1	0	1
Stevenage	D	W	3	1	2	0	2	2	2	1
Yeovil	D	D	2	0	1	1	1	1	1	1
Crawley Town	W	D	2	1	0	1	2	0	1	1
Morecambe	D	D	3	2	1	0	3	0	1	2
Newport County	L	W	3	0	0	3	1	2	0	0
Cheltenham			2	0	2	0	1	1	1	1
Grimsby			-	-	-	-	-	-	-	-

Season	Division	Pos	P	W	D	L	F	A	GD	Pts
2015-16	League 2	6	46	21	15	10	75	44	+31	78
2014-15	League 2	16	46	14	15	17	52	54	-2	57
2013-14	League 2	13	46	14	17	15	56	66	-10	59

Over/Under 57%/43% 6th   **Both score** 57%/43% 10th

STEVENAGE

Nickname: The Boro
Colours: White and red
Ground: Lamex Stadium (6,722)
Tel: 01438-223223   www.stevenagefc.com

Stevenage picked up plenty of column inches last summer when they decided to appoint former England star Teddy Sheringham as their manager, but it always looked a bad fit for both parties.

Sheringham was sacked in early February after a run of three points in eight games but, in fairness to him, it was a spell in which the treatment room was packed. Stevenage finished 18th which was 12 places worse than the campaign before under Graham Westley.

Longest run without win/loss: 9/6
High/low league position: 16/22
Clean sheets: 9 **Yellows:** 80 **Reds:** 4
Avg attendance: 3,883 **Players used:** 47
Leading scorer: C Whelpdale 8 (0,6)
Key stat: Stevenage drew 0-0 in four of their last nine matches

	2015-16		Last six seasons at home							
	H	A	P	W	D	L	OV	UN	BS	CS
Doncaster			1	0	0	1	1	0	1	0
Blackpool			-	-	-	-	-	-	-	-
Colchester			3	0	1	2	1	2	1	1
Crewe			3	1	2	0	1	2	2	1
Accrington	D	D	3	1	2	0	2	1	3	0
Plymouth	W	L	2	2	0	0	1	1	1	1
Portsmouth	L	D	3	2	0	1	1	2	1	1
Leyton Orient	D	L	4	0	1	3	1	3	1	0
Cambridge U	W	L	2	2	0	0	1	1	1	1
Carlisle	L	L	5	2	1	2	1	4	2	2
Luton	D	W	2	0	1	1	1	1	1	1
Mansfield	L	L	2	1	0	1	1	1	0	1
Wycombe	L	L	4	1	1	2	2	2	3	0
Exeter	L	L	3	1	1	1	0	3	0	2
Barnet	L	L	2	1	1	0	1	1	1	1
Hartlepool	W	W	4	3	1	0	1	3	1	3
Notts County	L	L	4	1	0	3	0	4	0	1
Stevenage										
Yeovil	D	D	3	0	2	1	0	3	0	2
Crawley Town	L	L	3	1	0	2	1	2	1	1
Morecambe	W	W	3	2	1	0	1	2	2	1
Newport County	W	D	2	2	0	0	2	0	2	0
Cheltenham			2	2	0	0	2	0	1	1
Grimsby			-	-	-	-	-	-	-	-

Season	Division	Pos	P	W	D	L	F	A	GD	Pts
2015-16	League 2	18	46	11	15	20	52	67	-15	48
2014-15	League 2	6	46	20	12	14	62	54	+8	72
2013-14	League 1	24	46	11	9	26	46	72	-26	42

Over/Under 50%/50% 13th   **Both score** 57%/43% 10th

WYCOMBE

Nickname: The Chairboys
Colours: Sky and navy blue
Ground: Adams Park (10,000)
Tel: 01494-472-100   www.wwfc.com

Gareth Ainsworth is a charismatic character and his energy rubs off on his team, even if Wycombe were unable to match their playoff run in 2014-15.

But their 13th-place finish looks harsh given Wanderers were just five points behind Leyton Orient in eighth, but Ainsworth's small squad was pushed to the limit in the latter stages of the season. They won just once in the last 11 games, with defeats to Portsmouth, Accrington and Oxford ending any playoff hopes.

Longest run without win/loss: 8/6
High/low league position: 1/13
Clean sheets: 17 **Yellows:** 65 **Reds:** 3
Avg attendance: 4,435 **Players used:** 29
Leading scorer: G Thompson 7 (3,6)
M Harriman 7 (4,6)
Key stat: Wycombe scored more than one goal just once in 2016

	2015-16		Last six seasons at home							
	H	A	P	W	D	L	OV	UN	BS	CS
Doncaster			-	-	-	-	-	-	-	-
Blackpool			-	-	-	-	-	-	-	-
Colchester			1	0	1	0	0	1	0	1
Crewe			1	1	0	0	0	1	0	1
Accrington	L	D	5	0	2	3	2	3	2	1
Plymouth	L	W	4	0	1	3	1	3	2	0
Portsmouth	D	L	3	0	2	1	1	2	1	1
Leyton Orient	L	D	2	1	0	1	1	1	1	0
Cambridge U	W	L	2	2	0	0	0	2	0	2
Carlisle	D	D	3	1	2	0	1	2	3	0
Luton	L	W	2	0	1	1	0	2	1	0
Mansfield	W	W	3	2	0	1	2	1	1	1
Wycombe										
Exeter	W	W	5	3	1	1	2	3	3	1
Barnet	D	W	3	1	2	0	1	2	2	1
Hartlepool	W	L	4	4	0	0	3	1	2	2
Notts County	D	W	2	0	1	1	2	0	2	0
Stevenage	W	L	4	1	1	2	1	3	1	1
Yeovil	D	W	2	0	1	1	1	1	1	1
Crawley Town	W	D	1	1	0	0	0	1	0	1
Morecambe	L	W	5	2	1	2	1	4	1	2
Newport County	L	L	3	0	0	3	1	2	1	0
Cheltenham			4	2	1	1	3	1	4	0
Grimsby			-	-	-	-	-	-	-	-

Season	Division	Pos	P	W	D	L	F	A	GD	Pts
2015-16	League 2	13	46	17	13	16	45	44	+1	64
2014-15	League 2	4	46	23	15	8	67	45	+22	84
2013-14	League 2	22	46	12	14	20	46	54	-8	50

Over/Under 28%/72% 26th   **Both score** 39%/61% 25th

YEOVIL

Nickname: The Glovers
Colours: Green and white
Ground: Huish Park (9,565)
Tel: 01935-423-662   www.ytfc.net

The most unwanted of hat-tricks looked on the cards before Yeovil eventually battled back to avoid a third straight relegation, which had seemed inevitable until Darren Way replaced Paul Sturrock as manager.

In fairness to Sturrock, he sometimes had seven or eight men missing through injury, but they were on the back foot from the moment they started with three straight defeats. However, Way guided them out of the drop zone and to safety.

Longest run without win/loss: 16/6
High/low league position: 18/24
Clean sheets: 14 **Yellows:** 58 **Reds:** 4
Avg attendance: 4,470 **Players used:** 36
Leading scorer: R Bird 8 (3,7)
Key stat: Darren Way won ten and lost only eight of his matches in charge

	2015-16		Last six seasons at home							
	H	A	P	W	D	L	OV	UN	BS	CS
Doncaster			3	2	0	1	2	1	1	1
Blackpool			1	1	0	0	0	1	0	1
Colchester			4	3	0	1	3	1	3	0
Crewe			2	1	1	0	0	2	1	1
Accrington	W	L	1	1	0	0	0	1	0	1
Plymouth	D	L	2	1	1	0	0	2	0	2
Portsmouth	D	D	2	0	1	1	1	2	1	0
Leyton Orient	L	D	5	2	1	2	4	1	2	1
Cambridge U	L	L	1	0	0	1	1	0	1	0
Carlisle	D	L	4	1	1	2	2	2	1	2
Luton	W	D	1	1	0	0	1	0	1	0
Mansfield	L	W	1	0	0	1	0	1	0	0
Wycombe	L	D	2	1	0	1	0	2	0	1
Exeter	L	L	3	0	1	2	2	1	2	0
Barnet	D	W	1	0	1	0	1	0	1	0
Hartlepool	L	L	4	1	0	3	1	3	1	1
Notts County	W	L	5	3	2	0	1	4	2	3
Stevenage	D	D	3	0	1	2	3	0	2	0
Yeovil										
Crawley Town	W	W	3	2	1	0	3	0	3	0
Morecambe	L	L	1	0	0	1	1	0	1	0
Newport County	W	D	1	1	0	0	0	1	0	1
Cheltenham			-	-	-	-	-	-	-	-
Grimsby			-	-	-	-	-	-	-	-

Season	Division	Pos	P	W	D	L	F	A	GD	Pts
2015-16	League 2	19	46	11	15	20	43	59	-16	48
2014-15	League 1	24	46	10	10	26	36	75	-39	40
2013-14	Championship	24	46	8	13	25	44	75	-31	37

Over/Under 37%/63% 25th   **Both score** 46%/54% 23rd

League Two stats 2015-16

Key Points in all tables (except the league table) do not include any deductions imposed by the league.
POS H A Overall league position, rank from home games only, rank from away games only **Sup** Average match supremacy **GFA** Goals For Average **GAA** Goals Against Average **PGA** Points Gained Average

LEAGUE TWO

Pos	H	A	League Two 2015-16	P	Home					Away					GD	Pts
					W	D	L	F	A	W	D	L	F	A		
1	1	2	Northampton (P)	46	15	5	3	38	19	14	7	2	44	27	+36	99
2	7	1	Oxford Utd (P)	46	10	7	6	37	20	14	7	2	47	21	+43	86
3	2	7	Bristol Rovers (P)	46	15	2	6	41	21	11	5	7	36	25	+31	85
4	3	3	Accrington	46	11	9	3	43	30	13	4	6	31	18	+26	85
5	5	4	Plymouth	46	12	3	8	39	26	12	6	5	33	20	+26	81
6	6	5	Portsmouth	46	10	7	6	38	19	11	8	4	37	25	+31	78
7	8	8	AFC Wimbledon (P)	46	11	4	8	30	25	10	8	5	34	25	+14	75
8	9	12	Leyton Orient	46	11	4	8	33	31	8	8	7	27	30	-1	69
9	10	11	Cambridge Utd	46	10	6	7	37	28	8	8	7	29	27	+11	68
10	11	13	Carlisle	46	10	6	7	38	35	7	10	6	29	27	+5	67
11	18	6	Luton	46	7	6	10	27	29	12	3	8	36	32	+2	66
12	13	10	Mansfield	46	7	10	6	34	26	10	3	10	27	27	+8	64
13	12	14	Wycombe	46	9	6	8	25	24	8	7	8	20	20	+1	64
14	16	9	Exeter	46	6	11	6	32	33	11	2	10	31	32	-2	64
15	4	20	Barnet	46	13	3	7	37	27	4	8	11	30	41	-1	62
16	15	19	Hartlepool	46	9	3	11	27	32	6	3	14	22	40	-23	51
17	14	22	Notts County	46	9	4	10	30	38	5	5	13	24	45	-29	51
18	20	16	Stevenage	46	6	8	9	23	32	5	7	11	29	35	-15	48
19	19	18	Yeovil	46	6	9	8	23	27	5	6	12	20	32	-16	48
20	17	23	Crawley	46	8	5	10	21	30	5	3	15	24	48	-33	47
21	22	17	Morecambe	46	7	3	13	36	47	5	7	11	33	44	-22	46
22	23	15	Newport County	46	4	8	11	21	35	6	5	12	22	29	-21	43
23	24	21	Dagenham & R (R)	46	3	5	15	17	37	5	5	13	29	44	-35	34
24	21	24	York (R)	46	6	7	10	33	41	1	6	16	18	46	-36	34

Best attack

		GF	GFA
1	Oxford Utd	84	1.83
2	Northampton	82	1.78
3	Bristol Rovers	77	1.67
4	Portsmouth	75	1.63
5	Accrington	74	1.61
6	Plymouth	72	1.57
7	Morecambe	69	1.5
8	Carlisle	67	1.46
9	Barnet	67	1.46
10	Cambridge U	66	1.43
11	Wimbledon	64	1.39
12	Luton	63	1.37
13	Exeter	63	1.37
14	Mansfield	61	1.33
15	Leyton Orient	60	1.3
16	Notts County	54	1.17
17	Stevenage	52	1.13
18	York	51	1.11
19	Hartlepool	49	1.07
20	Dag & Red	46	1
21	Wycombe	45	0.98
22	Crawley	45	0.98
23	Yeovil	43	0.93
24	Newport Co	43	0.93

Best defence

		GA	GAA
1	Oxford Utd	41	0.89
2	Portsmouth	44	0.96
3	Wycombe	44	0.96
4	Northampton	46	1
5	Bristol Rovers	46	1
6	Plymouth	46	1
7	Accrington	48	1.04
8	Wimbledon	50	1.09
9	Mansfield	53	1.15
10	Cambridge U	55	1.2
11	Yeovil	59	1.28
12	Leyton Orient	61	1.33
13	Luton	61	1.33
14	Carlisle	62	1.35
15	Newport Co	64	1.39
16	Exeter	65	1.41
17	Stevenage	67	1.46
18	Barnet	68	1.48
19	Hartlepool	72	1.57
20	Crawley	78	1.7
21	Dag & Red	81	1.76
22	Notts County	83	1.8
23	York	87	1.89
24	Morecambe	91	1.98

Top scorers

	Team	Goals scored
M Taylor	Bristol Rovers	27
J Simpson	Leyton	25
J Akinde	Barnet	23
L Taylor	Wimbledon	20
K Roofe	Oxford	18
B Kee	Accrington	17
M Green	Mansfield	16

Over 2.5 goals

	H	A	%
York	17	13	65%
Morecambe	15	14	63%
Crawley	10	17	59%
Bristol Rovers	15	12	59%
Dag & Red	10	17	59%

Under 2.5 goals

	H	A	%
Wycombe	15	18	72%
Yeovil	15	14	63%
Luton	16	10	57%
Mansfield	13	13	57%
Newport Co	11	15	57%
Wimbledon	13	13	57%
Leyton Orient	12	14	57%

Both to score

	H	A	%
Morecambe	18	15	72%
York	20	12	70%
Northampton	12	17	63%
Plymouth	14	14	61%
Exeter, Accrington			
Carlisle, Wimbledon			59%

Both not to score

	H	A	%
Newport	10	8	61%
Wycombe	10	8	61%
Yeovil	11	10	54%
Crawley	10	12	52%
Cambridge, Hartlepool, Luton,			
Mansfield, Notts County			48%

League Two results 2015-16

	Accrington	AFC Wimbledon	Barnet	Bristol Rovers	Cambridge Utd	Carlisle	Crawley Town	Dag & Red	Exeter	Hartlepool	Leyton Orient	Luton	Mansfield	Morecambe	Newport County	Northampton	Notts County	Oxford	Plymouth	Portsmouth	Stevenage	Wycombe	Yeovil	York
Accrington		3-4	2-2	1-0	1-1	1-1	4-1	3-1	4-2	3-1	1-0	1-1	1-0	2-2	2-2	1-1	3-2	1-3	2-1	1-3	0-0	1-1	2-1	3-0
AFC Wimbledon	0-0		2-0	0-0	1-2	1-0	1-0	0-1	2-1	2-0	1-0	4-1	3-1	2-5	1-0	1-1	2-1	1-2	0-2	0-1	1-2	1-1	2-3	2-1
Barnet	1-2	1-2		1-0	0-0	0-0	4-2	3-1	2-0	1-3	3-0	2-1	1-3	0-0	2-0	2-0	3-1	0-3	1-0	1-0	3-2	0-2	3-4	3-1
Bristol Rovers	0-1	3-1	3-1		3-0	2-0	0-3	2-1	3-1	4-1	2-1	2-0	1-0	2-1	1-4	0-1	0-0	0-1	1-1	1-2	1-2	3-0	2-1	2-1
Cambridge Utd	2-3	1-4	2-1	1-2		0-0	0-3	1-0	0-1	1-1	1-1	1-3	1-1	7-0	3-0	2-1	3-1	0-0	2-2	1-3	1-0	1-0	3-0	3-1
Carlisle	2-0	1-1	3-2	3-2	4-4		3-1	2-1	1-0	1-0	2-2	1-2	1-2	2-3	0-1	1-4	3-0	0-2	0-2	2-2	1-0	1-1	3-2	1-1
Crawley Town	0-3	1-2	0-3	2-1	1-0	0-1		3-2	0-2	0-0	3-2	2-1	0-1	1-1	2-0	1-2	0-1	1-5	1-1	0-0	2-1	0-0	0-1	1-0
Dag & Red	0-1	0-2	0-2	0-3	0-3	0-0	3-0		1-2	0-1	1-3	0-2	3-4	2-1	0-0	1-2	1-1	0-1	1-1	1-4	1-1	1-2	0-1	1-0
Exeter	2-1	0-2	1-1	1-1	1-0	2-2	2-2	1-2		1-0	4-0	2-3	2-3	1-1	1-1	0-0	1-1	1-4	2-1	1-1	3-3	0-2	3-2	0-0
Hartlepool	1-2	1-0	1-1	0-3	0-0	2-3	1-2	3-1	0-2		3-1	1-4	2-1	2-0	1-0	0-0	2-3	0-1	1-2	0-2	1-2	1-0	2-1	2-1
Leyton Orient	0-1	1-1	2-0	2-0	1-3	1-2	2-0	3-2	1-3	0-2		0-1	1-0	1-0	1-0	0-4	3-1	2-2	1-3	3-2	3-0	1-1	1-1	3-2
Luton	0-2	2-0	2-0	0-1	0-0	3-4	0-1	1-0	4-1	2-1	1-1		1-0	1-0	1-1	3-4	0-2	2-2	1-2	1-1	0-2	2-1	1-1	1-1
Mansfield	2-3	1-1	1-1	1-2	0-0	1-0	4-0	3-2	0-2	3-1	1-1	0-2		2-1	3-0	2-2	5-0	1-1	0-0	1-1	2-1	0-2	0-1	1-1
Morecambe	1-0	2-1	4-2	3-4	2-4	1-2	3-1	1-0	1-1	2-5	0-1	1-3	1-2		1-2	2-4	4-1	2-4	0-2	1-1	1-4	0-1	2-1	1-1
Newport County	0-2	2-2	0-3	1-4	0-1	1-0	0-3	2-2	1-1	0-0	2-3	3-0	1-0	1-2		2-2	0-1	1-1	1-2	0-1	2-2	1-0	0-0	0-3
Northampton	1-0	1-1	3-0	2-2	1-1	3-2	2-1	1-2	3-0	2-1	1-1	2-0	1-0	3-1	1-0		2-2	1-0	0-2	1-2	2-1	1-0	2-0	2-0
Notts County	1-1	0-2	4-2	0-2	1-2	0-5	4-1	0-0	1-4	1-0	0-1	3-2	0-2	2-2	4-3	1-2		2-4	0-2	2-1	1-0	0-0	2-0	1-0
Oxford	1-2	1-0	2-3	1-2	1-0	1-1	1-1	4-0	3-0	2-0	0-1	2-3	2-2	0-0	1-1	0-1	3-1		1-0	1-1	1-1	3-0	2-0	4-0
Plymouth	1-0	1-2	2-1	1-1	1-2	4-1	2-1	2-3	1-2	5-0	1-1	0-1	3-0	2-0	1-0	1-2	0-0	2-2		1-2	3-2	0-1	1-0	3-2
Portsmouth	0-0	0-0	3-1	3-1	2-1	1-0	3-0	3-0	1-2	4-0	0-1	0-0	0-0	3-3	0-3	1-2	4-0	0-1	1-2		1-1	2-1	0-0	6-0
Stevenage	1-1	0-0	0-0	0-0	2-0	0-1	0-1	1-3	0-2	2-0	2-2	0-0	0-2	4-3	2-1	2-3	0-2	1-5	2-1	0-2		2-1	0-0	2-2
Wycombe	0-1	1-2	1-1	1-0	1-0	1-1	2-0	1-1	1-0	2-1	0-2	0-1	1-0	0-2	0-2	2-3	2-2	2-1	1-2	2-2	1-0		0-0	3-0
Yeovil	1-0	1-1	2-2	0-1	2-3	0-0	2-1	2-2	0-2	1-2	0-1	3-2	0-1	2-4	1-0	1-1	1-0	0-0	0-0	1-1	2-2	0-1		1-0
York	1-5	1-3	1-1	1-4	2-2	2-2	2-2	2-2	2-0	1-2	1-1	2-3	1-2	2-1	0-1	1-2	2-1	1-2	1-2	3-1	2-1	1-1	1-0	

Record when first to score

		P	W	D	L	F	A	Sup	PGA	Pts
1	Bristol Rovers	22	20	2	0	54	17	+1.68	2.8	62
2	Plymouth	26	21	3	2	55	21	+1.31	2.5	66
3	Accrington	26	21	3	2	53	21	+1.23	2.5	66
4	Hartlepool	15	12	2	1	28	12	+1.07	2.5	38
5	Northampton	32	23	7	2	58	24	+1.06	2.4	76
6	Wycombe	23	17	5	1	35	15	+0.87	2.4	56
7	Oxford Utd	32	22	6	4	66	25	+1.28	2.3	72
8	Leyton Orient	26	18	5	3	46	25	+0.81	2.3	59
9	Luton	25	18	3	4	52	33	+0.76	2.3	57
10	Portsmouth	23	17	3	3	49	16	+1.43	2.3	54
11	Exeter	21	14	7	0	41	19	+1.05	2.3	49
12	Cambridge Utd	21	15	3	3	48	23	+1.19	2.3	48
13	Mansfield	20	13	6	1	44	20	+1.20	2.3	45
14	Wimbledon	23	16	3	4	38	21	+0.74	2.2	51
15	Barnet	21	14	2	5	44	24	+0.81	2.1	44
16	Carlisle	20	12	6	2	39	21	+0.90	2.1	42
17	Newport County	16	10	3	3	23	18	+0.31	2.1	33
18	Stevenage	14	9	2	3	27	19	+0.57	2.1	29
19	Crawley	18	11	3	4	27	24	+0.17	2	36
20	Notts County	18	11	3	4	27	21	+0.33	2	36
21	Yeovil	17	8	6	3	21	17	+0.24	1.8	30
22	Morecambe	18	8	5	5	33	28	+0.28	1.6	29
23	York	20	7	9	4	31	24	+0.35	1.5	30
24	Dag & Red	17	7	5	5	28	25	+0.18	1.5	26

Record when keeping a clean sheet

		P	W	D	F	Sup	PGA	Pts
1	Leyton Orient	13	13	0	19	+1.46	3	39
2	Oxford Utd	18	15	3	30	+1.67	2.7	48
3	Northampton	15	13	2	23	+1.53	2.7	41
4	Plymouth	14	12	2	24	+1.71	2.7	38
5	Wycombe	17	14	3	21	+1.24	2.6	45
6	Bristol Rovers	14	11	3	24	+1.71	2.6	36
7	Accrington	14	11	3	17	+1.21	2.6	36
8	Exeter	11	9	2	17	+1.55	2.6	29
9	Luton	13	10	3	14	+1.08	2.5	33
10	Notts County	11	8	3	11	+1	2.5	27
11	Newport County	11	8	3	13	+1.18	2.5	27
12	York	4	3	1	6	+1.5	2.5	10
13	Barnet	14	10	4	20	+1.43	2.4	34
14	Wimbledon	13	9	4	14	+1.08	2.4	31
15	Crawley	10	7	3	12	+1.2	2.4	24
16	Mansfield	10	7	3	18	+1.8	2.4	24
17	Portsmouth	16	10	6	27	+1.69	2.3	36
18	Carlisle	12	8	4	15	+1.25	2.3	28
19	Hartlepool	10	6	4	8	+0.8	2.2	22
20	Morecambe	5	3	2	4	+0.8	2.2	11
21	Cambridge Utd	14	8	6	20	+1.43	2.1	30
22	Yeovil	14	7	7	7	+0.5	2	28
23	Dag & Red	6	3	3	5	+0.83	2	12
24	Stevenage	9	3	6	5	+0.56	1.7	15

Canny Cooper the man to plot Forest Green's path into the Football League

None of the 24 sides contesting this season's National League have spent as long in non-league's top tier as Forest Green but that could all be about to change, writes Danny Hayes. Rovers have been competing at this level since 1998 but since green energy tycoon Dale Vince took over in 2010 Rovers have made steady progression, culminating in playoff defeats for the past two seasons.

However, the ante-post favourites should have no need for the playoffs this time in a league where they look comfortably the best outfit, with quotes of 5-1 looking generous.

They have kept the nucleus of the squad which won their opening ten games last season before injuries begun to take their toll and, importantly, they have freshened up the side and added depth.

Striker Christian Doidge has joined from Dagenham & Redbridge, where he did well in a struggling team, while fellow new boys Liam Noble and Drissa Traore are dropping down into non-league football to make the Green Army look an even stronger outfit.

Perhaps Forest Green's most important signing was the luring of manager Mark Cooper. Cooper has enjoyed recent success in charge of Swindon and Notts County, and could have stayed with County but took the decision to drop back into non-league and build something special with Forest Green. With his league contacts there is every chance Rovers will bring in more quality signings before the season commences.

The biggest dangers, in both the ante-post markets and strength of their squads, are Tranmere and Eastleigh.

Tranmere have had a year to acclimatise to life at this level and experienced manager Gary Brabin did a good job in steadying the ship last term.

They have strengthened their squad over the summer and the signings of Andy Cook and Conner Jennings should address their lack of goal threat, so they should improve on last season's sixth-place finish.

Eastleigh also finished outside the playoffs last season but paid the price for inconsistency and the distraction of a run to the FA Cup third round. They look strong enough for another playoff push without being good enough to touch Forest Green.

The two teams dropping down from League Two – Dagenham and York – might take heart from the instant returns that Bristol Rovers and Cheltenham have made in the past two seasons, but they both face tough tasks and the playoffs could be the best either can hope for.

Dover and Braintree, both defeated in the playoffs last season, overachieved and may struggle to match those exploits. Braintree have lost manager Danny Cowley to league rivals Lincoln and while his replacement Jamie Day has plenty of experience at this level, the loss of Cowley is a big blow.

Ambitious Barrow and Aldershot, who have re-appointed Gary Waddock – the man who led them to the title in 2008 – look the pick of the outsiders.

At the other end of the table, Boreham Wood face a battle to survive another season. They won their final three games last term

Forest Green's Anthony Jeffrey skips a challenge during last season's playoff final defeat

to stay up but their small squad may be stretched to far this time around.

North Ferriby, Guiseley and Southport may struggle, but Sutton have the advantage of playing on a 3G pitch – which might unsettle visitors – and Solihull Moors, who romped to the National League North title, should have enough about them to survive.

In the National League South, Ebbsfleet again dominate the market. But they fluffed their lines badly last season after achieving a dominate position and a chance is taken on

Maidenhead at a much bigger price.

Led by experienced manager Alan Devonshire, Maidenhead finished a respectable seventh back at this level last season. With Devonshire at the helm further improvement is likely.

Halifax Town look the strongest outfit in the National League North. Relegated from the National League last season, they have persuaded Neil Young to leave promoted North Ferriby and have been quick to bolster their squad.

National League 2015-16				P	Home					Away					GD	Pts
Pos	H	A			W	D	L	F	A	W	D	L	F	A		
1	1	1	Cheltenham (P)	46	17	5	1	49	13	13	6	4	38	17	+57	101
2	2	2	Forest Green	46	15	3	5	37	17	11	8	4	32	25	+27	89
3	4	4	Braintree	46	13	6	4	24	12	10	6	7	32	26	+18	81
4	3	7	Grimsby (P)	46	13	6	4	44	17	9	8	6	38	28	+37	80
5	5	5	Dover	46	13	5	5	43	22	10	6	7	32	31	+22	80
6	9	3	Tranmere	46	12	2	9	31	23	10	10	3	30	21	+17	78
7	6	9	Eastleigh	46	13	5	5	32	23	8	7	8	32	30	+11	75
8	7	14	Wrexham	46	13	4	6	48	27	7	5	11	23	29	+15	69
9	17	6	Gateshead	46	9	4	10	33	39	10	6	7	26	31	-11	67
10	13	8	Macclesfield	46	10	5	8	28	21	9	4	10	32	27	+12	66
11	8	17	Barrow	46	11	8	4	38	26	6	6	11	26	45	-7	65
12	14	13	Woking	46	9	7	7	36	29	8	3	12	35	39	+3	61
13	11	16	Lincoln	46	10	7	6	37	25	6	6	11	32	43	+1	61
14	10	18	Bromley	46	11	4	8	38	26	6	5	12	29	46	-5	60
15	20	10	Aldershot	46	7	4	12	23	31	9	4	10	31	41	-18	56
16	21	11	Southport	46	6	7	10	34	44	8	6	9	18	21	-13	55
17	12	20	Chester	46	9	8	6	43	29	5	4	14	24	42	-4	54
18	19	15	Torquay	46	7	5	11	26	33	6	7	10	28	43	-22	51
19	22	12	Boreham W	46	5	7	11	18	24	7	7	9	26	25	-5	50
20	16	22	Guiseley	46	8	7	8	33	38	3	9	11	14	32	-23	49
21	18	19	Halifax (R)	46	6	10	7	35	43	6	2	15	20	39	-27	48
22	15	24	Altrincham (R)	46	8	9	6	34	30	2	5	16	14	43	-25	44
23	23	21	Kidderminster (R)	46	5	7	11	21	29	4	6	13	28	42	-22	40
24	24	23	Welling (R)	46	5	6	12	21	33	3	5	15	14	40	-38	35

National League results

	Aldershot	Altrincham	Barrow	Boreham W	Braintree	Bromley	Cheltenham	Chester	Dover	Eastleigh	Forest Green	Gateshead	Grimsby	Guiseley	Halifax	Kidderminster	Lincoln	Macclesfield	Southport	Torquay	Tranmere	Welling	Woking	Wrexham
Aldershot		2-0	0-1	1-2	2-1	1-1	0-2	3-1	1-1	1-2	0-3	1-2	3-4	1-0	3-2	1-0	1-2	0-3	1-2	0-0	0-0	1-0	0-1	0-1
Altrincham	4-0		1-0	1-0	0-4	0-0	2-1	0-3	1-2	1-1	0-1	2-3	2-1	1-1	1-3	2-2	3-3	0-0	1-1	1-1	2-1	5-0	3-1	1-1
Barrow	1-3	3-2		0-0	2-0	1-1	1-2	3-2	2-1	1-0	2-2	0-0	1-3	1-1	4-1	1-1	1-0	1-1	1-0	4-0	3-4	1-1	2-1	2-0
Boreham Wood	0-1	0-1	0-2		1-0	2-3	0-0	0-0	3-0	1-1	0-1	2-3	1-3	1-0	3-1	0-2	1-1	0-0	0-2	0-1	0-0	2-0	1-1	0-1
Braintree	1-2	3-0	1-1	0-2		1-0	1-0	2-0	1-0	2-0	1-1	0-0	0-0	0-1	2-0	2-1	1-3	1-0	1-0	0-0	0-0	1-0	2-1	1-0
Bromley	1-3	1-3	5-0	1-2	1-2		1-2	3-0	1-1	2-2	2-2	3-0	1-2	2-0	1-0	3-2	2-0	1-0	0-0	0-2	2-1	2-0	2-1	3-1
Cheltenham	0-0	1-0	2-1	4-1	1-1	4-1		3-1	3-2	1-1	1-1	0-0	3-1	5-0	2-0	2-0	3-1	2-0	3-0	1-0	0-1	2-0	4-0	2-1
Chester	8-2	1-1	1-2	2-2	1-0	1-1	1-1		1-1	1-0	1-2	4-2	1-1	1-1	2-1	3-1	2-3	0-2	0-0	4-1	0-1	4-0	1-2	3-2
Dover	5-2	2-1	3-1	2-1	0-0	2-3	1-2	0-0		1-2	0-1	4-0	1-0	3-2	4-1	2-1	1-2	5-0	0-0	2-1	2-0	2-1		
Eastleigh	1-1	2-0	3-1	1-0	0-2	2-0	1-0	1-0	2-5		3-2	1-2	0-1	1-1	2-1	3-1	1-1	1-0	1-0	3-2	0-1	0-0	2-1	1-1
Forest Green	0-0	2-0	4-0	1-0	1-0	2-1	2-2	2-1	3-1	2-1		0-1	0-1	3-0	0-1	3-0	3-1	2-1	2-1	3-1	0-2	1-0	1-2	0-0
Gateshead	3-2	2-2	1-1	2-1	2-3	3-1	1-1	1-0	2-3	2-1	0-1		1-0	3-0	1-4	1-1	2-0	0-3	0-1	1-2	1-4	1-2	1-5	2-1
Grimsby	4-1	5-0	4-1	0-0	0-1	4-1	0-1	1-2	1-0	0-0	1-1	2-1		1-1	7-0	1-0	2-0	0-2	1-0	2-2	1-1	3-1	3-1	1-0
Guiseley	0-4	1-0	3-1	1-1	1-1	2-0	0-2	3-3	0-1	1-4	0-1	0-2	2-2		2-1	1-0	0-3	1-1	4-3	2-2	2-0	4-4	3-1	
Halifax	0-2	1-0	3-1	3-2	3-6	2-2	1-7	0-1	4-2	0-0	0-2	1-1	4-2	1-1		1-1	2-2	1-1	2-2	2-3	1-1	1-1	0-3	2-0
Kidderminster	2-0	1-1	0-0	1-1	0-1	1-0	1-2	2-1	1-1	3-2	0-2	0-1	2-2	0-1	1-0		0-2	3-1	0-1	2-2	0-2	0-1	1-0	1-3
Lincoln	2-0	1-1	2-2	3-1	2-0	0-1	1-1	2-1	2-3	3-0	0-1	1-1	1-0	0-1	1-2			5-3	3-1	2-0	1-0	1-1	2-3	1-1
Macclesfield	0-2	3-0	1-2	0-0	3-1	2-0	0-1	1-2	0-0	1-2	4-1	1-0	2-1	1-0	0-1	2-1	1-1		0-0	1-2	1-2	2-1	2-1	0-0
Southport	1-1	3-0	2-1	0-3	1-1	5-3	0-4	1-2	0-0	0-4	0-1	1-2	0-4	2-0	0-1	3-4	2-2	3-1		0-1	2-2	3-3	2-2	3-2
Torquay	0-2	2-0	2-2	1-2	0-0	3-7	0-3	2-0	2-3	0-1	4-1	0-2	1-1	1-1	0-0	3-2	1-3	1-0	1-0		0-1	2-0	0-1	0-1
Tranmere	3-1	1-0	0-1	0-2	1-2	4-0	0-1	2-0	0-1	1-2	1-1	3-1	1-0	2-1	1-0	2-2	3-2	0-1	1-0	2-1		1-2	1-0	1-2
Welling	0-1	1-1	1-2	0-3	1-2	1-2	1-1	2-1	1-2	2-2	1-1	0-1	0-4	1-0	2-1	1-1	0-1	0-1	1-1	1-1			2-1	0-2
Woking	2-1	1-2	0-0	2-2	0-0	1-1	2-0	0-1	5-2	0-1	2-1	2-1	1-1	1-3	0-1	1-1	3-1	2-5	1-2	2-2	4-1	2-0		0-1
Wrexham	3-0	3-1	4-1	1-0	2-3	2-0	2-1	3-0	0-1	2-3	2-2	4-0	0-0	3-3	3-1	2-0	3-1	2-3	0-1	3-1	2-2	1-0	1-3	

Cheltenham Town wasted no time in bouncing back to the Football League

National League North 2015-16

Pos	H	A		P	Home					Away					GD	Pts
					W	D	L	F	A	W	D	L	F	A		
1	2	1	Solihull Moors (P)	42	14	1	6	39	21	11	9	1	45	27	+36	85
2	1	7	North Ferriby (P)	42	13	5	3	41	14	9	5	7	41	35	+33	76
3	6	3	AFC Fylde	42	11	4	6	41	26	11	5	5	35	27	+23	75
4	3	6	Harrogate Town	42	11	6	4	43	21	10	3	8	31	25	+28	72
5	4	8	Boston Utd	42	12	3	6	37	27	10	2	9	36	33	+13	71
6	9	2	Nuneaton*	42	8	9	4	28	17	12	4	5	44	29	+26	70
7	5	10	Chorley	42	11	5	5	36	21	7	4	10	29	34	+10	63
8	7	9	Tamworth	42	9	9	3	28	18	7	6	8	27	27	+10	63
9	19	5	Stockport	42	6	7	8	24	28	9	7	5	26	21	+1	59
10	20	4	Alfreton	42	6	6	9	26	29	9	7	5	32	25	+4	58
11	10	13	Curzon Ashton	42	9	6	6	30	27	5	9	7	26	27	+2	57
12	16	11	Stalybridge	42	7	7	7	35	38	7	4	10	27	37	-13	53
13	15	12	FC United	42	8	4	9	38	37	7	4	10	22	39	-16	53
14	8	22	Bradford Park Av	42	10	6	5	37	28	3	5	13	16	31	-6	50
15	18	14	Gloucester	42	7	5	9	20	23	5	9	7	20	27	-10	50
16	13	15	Gainsborough	42	8	6	7	24	27	6	2	13	22	35	-16	50
17	14	16	Worcester	42	7	7	7	34	27	5	5	11	21	34	-6	48
18	11	20	Telford	42	9	4	8	28	29	4	4	13	19	33	-15	47
19	17	17	Brackley	42	7	6	8	27	28	4	7	10	18	27	-10	46
20	12	21	Lowestoft T (R)	42	8	6	7	28	27	4	4	13	20	42	-21	46
21	21	18	Hednesford (R)	42	5	6	10	26	38	3	8	10	24	40	-28	38
22	22	19	Corby (R)	42	4	3	14	27	51	3	8	10	21	42	-45	32

*Nuneaton deducted 3pts

National League North results

	AFC Fylde	Alfreton	Boston Utd	Brackley	Bradford PA	Chorley	Corby	Curzon Ashton	FC United	Gainsborough	Gloucester	Harrogate T	Hednesford	Lowestoft T	North Ferriby	Nuneaton	Solihull Moors	Stalybridge	Stockport	Tamworth	Telford	Worcester
AFC Fylde		0-1	5-2	2-2	1-0	1-0	2-1	1-2	4-0	2-2	1-0	2-1	2-0	1-0	2-3	2-2	1-2	5-0	2-3	2-2	1-0	2-3
Alfreton	1-2		1-2	1-1	0-1	1-0	1-1	2-2	0-1	1-0	1-1	3-2	4-0	0-1	0-1	2-2	2-2	1-3	0-3	1-0	2-3	2-1
Boston Utd	0-3	2-1		1-2	3-0	1-2	2-0	2-1	3-1	1-0	1-0	3-3	3-1	4-1	1-2	2-1	1-4	0-3	4-0	1-1	1-0	1-1
Brackley	0-0	1-4	1-3		0-0	1-2	1-2	2-0	4-0	3-2	1-0	1-0	1-1	2-2	2-4	2-3	0-1	1-0	0-0	0-2	1-0	3-1
Bradford PA	1-2	2-2	1-2	1-0		1-0	1-0	4-2	3-1	1-4	1-0	3-1	1-1	3-0	4-4	2-3	1-1	3-1	0-0	0-2	1-0	3-1
Chorley	3-2	1-2	2-0	1-0	2-2		3-0	2-0	3-0	3-1	0-1	0-1	2-2	2-0	2-3	2-3	2-2	0-0	1-0	1-1	2-1	2-0
Corby	1-2	2-3	2-3	1-1	2-0	2-2		0-4	2-3	1-2	3-1	0-3	0-0	3-5	1-4	1-3	1-3	0-3	0-4	2-0	3-2	0-3
Curzon Ashton	0-2	0-2	0-2	1-1	2-1	4-2	2-3		0-0	3-0	2-2	1-2	3-2	4-1	0-3	1-0	1-3	0-0	0-0	2-0	1-0	3-1
FC United	1-2	1-3	1-2	3-2	2-1	2-0	1-0	3-3		1-2	1-2	4-3	1-1	6-1	3-2	3-2	2-2	0-1	1-2	1-1	1-3	0-2
Gainsborough	0-2	1-1	1-0	1-0	0-1	2-1	1-1	0-2	0-1		3-3	2-1	3-1	1-1	2-0	1-0	1-6	3-1	0-1	0-2	1-1	1-1
Gloucester	1-3	1-1	1-0	0-0	1-3	1-1	1-0	3-1	1-0	0-2		0-1	2-2	0-1	3-2	0-0	1-2	0-0	2-3	0-0	1-2	1-0
Harrogate T	2-2	1-2	0-0	1-0	2-1	2-4	5-0	1-1	5-0	3-1	0-0		3-1	4-0	3-3	0-3	6-0	2-1	2-1	0-0	0-1	1-0
Hednesford	0-1	3-3	3-2	0-2	0-0	1-3	3-3	0-3	0-3	0-2	2-2	2-3		2-1	1-1	2-4	0-0	2-1	1-2	2-1	2-0	0-1
Lowestoft T	3-1	1-0	3-0	1-2	3-0	2-0	2-2	0-0	1-4	1-0	1-1	1-2	0-0		0-3	0-1	2-2	0-2	2-2	0-4	3-0	2-1
North Ferriby	3-0	0-1	4-3	2-1	1-0	4-0	5-0	0-0	1-0	4-0	3-0	0-1	1-1	0-0		1-2	1-1	1-0	2-0	3-1	2-0	3-3
Nuneaton	1-1	2-0	1-3	1-0	1-0	2-2	0-0	0-1	3-2	2-0	0-1	0-0	3-0	1-0	3-1		0-1	3-3	1-1	3-0	0-0	1-1
Solihull Moors	3-0	2-1	0-1	3-0	2-1	0-2	4-1	2-0	1-2	3-2	0-0	1-0	1-2	2-1	1-3	3-1		4-1	1-0	1-2	2-1	3-0
Stalybridge	1-1	1-1	0-5	3-1	1-1	0-1	2-3	1-1	1-0	0-0	1-0	0-1	4-2	3-1	2-0	2-5	1-3		1-1	3-5	5-5	3-1
Stockport	0-4	1-0	2-1	1-1	2-0	1-3	2-2	0-0	1-2	2-0	3-0	1-2	3-0	0-2	1-1	1-1	2-4	0-3		1-1	0-1	0-0
Tamworth	3-1	1-2	1-2	1-2	0-0	2-1	0-0	2-1	1-1	2-2	1-0	1-0	1-1	1-1	1-1	1-1	1-1	1-1	1-1		2-1	3-0
Telford	1-2	1-1	2-2	2-0	3-3	2-0	3-0	0-0	5-1	0-2	0-1	0-4	1-3	1-0	1-1	1-5	0-3	2-0	0-1	1-0		2-0
Worcester	2-2	1-1	2-1	0-0	3-1	2-3	1-2	2-2	0-0	2-0	1-2	0-0	1-4	2-1	2-0	0-1	2-2	5-0	2-3	1-2	3-0	

National League South 2015-16

Pos	H	A		P	W	D	L	F	A	W	D	L	F	A	GD	Pts
					Home					Away						
1	1	1	Sutton Utd (P)	42	11	8	2	42	19	15	4	2	41	13	+51	90
2	3	2	Ebbsfleet	42	11	6	4	40	22	13	6	2	33	14	+37	84
3	4	3	Maidstone (P)	42	12	2	7	29	22	12	3	6	26	18	+15	77
4	6	7	Truro City	42	10	4	7	35	32	7	10	4	28	23	+8	65
5	10	4	Whitehawk	42	9	3	9	32	23	9	7	5	43	39	+13	64
6	16	5	Hemel	42	7	7	7	33	30	9	6	6	39	36	+6	61
7	2	19	Maidenhead	42	11	7	3	36	21	5	4	12	30	42	+3	59
8	9	9	Dartford	42	8	7	6	36	27	8	4	9	23	29	+3	59
9	11	11	Gosport Borough	42	8	6	7	33	34	7	5	9	22	29	-8	56
10	21	6	Concord Rangers	42	6	4	11	29	32	9	6	6	37	36	-2	55
11	8	16	Bishop's Stortford	42	10	2	9	30	26	5	8	8	26	37	-7	55
12	17	10	Oxford City	42	6	9	6	36	30	7	6	8	34	30	+10	54
13	15	12	Wealdstone	42	6	10	5	38	32	6	7	8	26	33	-1	53
14	14	14	Bath City	42	8	5	8	25	26	6	6	9	25	36	-12	53
15	12	15	Chelmsford	42	9	2	10	42	35	6	5	10	24	29	+2	52
16	18	13	Weston-s-Mare	42	8	3	10	31	38	6	6	9	33	40	-14	51
17	13	18	Eastbourne	42	7	8	6	32	25	6	3	12	28	40	-5	50
18	7	20	St Albans	42	9	5	7	41	26	4	5	12	17	39	-7	49
19	19	17	Margate	42	7	4	10	25	34	6	4	11	26	39	-22	47
20	5	22	Havant & W (R)	42	10	4	7	30	25	2	7	12	22	50	-23	47
21	22	8	Hayes & Y (R)	42	3	9	9	26	45	8	4	9	26	31	-24	46
22	20	21	Basingstoke (R)	42	6	6	9	24	27	3	5	13	22	42	-23	38

National League South results

	Basingstoke	Bath City	Bishop's St.	Chelmsford	Concord R	Dartford	Eastbourne	Ebbsfleet	Gosport Bor	Havant & W	Hayes & Y	Hemel	Maidenhead	Maidstone	Margate	Oxford City	St Albans	Sutton Utd	Truro City	Wealdstone	Weston-s-M	Whitehawk
Basingstoke		1-2	1-1	1-2	0-2	0-1	1-5	1-2	0-1	1-1	1-0	2-0	2-1	0-1	0-0	2-0	2-2	1-2	2-0	1-1	2-2	3-1
Bath City	0-0		2-2	2-0	0-1	0-0	1-0	1-1	0-1	5-0	2-3	1-1	2-1	0-2	2-0	1-3	1-0	1-3	0-3	2-1	2-1	0-3
Bishop's Stortford	1-2	3-2		1-2	3-2	1-2	1-1	1-2	2-0	3-0	0-0	1-0	0-2	0-1	4-1	3-0	2-1	0-2	0-3	2-1	0-1	2-1
Chelmsford	0-2	3-1	4-1		5-2	0-1	0-3	0-0	6-1	2-2	4-0	0-1	4-1	3-0	2-3	0-4	2-1	0-1	2-2	1-2	0-2	2-3 4-3
Concord Rangers	5-0	1-2	2-2	1-0		2-3	4-1	0-0	0-0	0-3	0-3	2-0	1-2	2-1	0-2	1-2	0-3	1-2	0-3	1-2	2-2	4-1 1-2
Dartford	0-0	5-1	3-1	1-1	1-2		1-0	0-1	2-3	4-2	2-0	2-2	2-0	1-1	1-1	2-2	2-0	2-2	0-1	1-2	2-1	2-4
Eastbourne	1-2	5-2	0-1	2-0	0-0	1-1		1-2	3-0	2-2	2-0	2-3	1-2	1-0	1-4	1-1	1-0	1-1	0-0	3-0	3-3	1-1
Ebbsfleet	1-0	0-1	4-2	3-1	4-2	1-1	4-2		2-0	2-2	0-0	6-0	3-1	0-1	1-2	1-1	1-0	1-0	0-0	2-3	2-1	2-2
Gosport Borough	3-2	3-1	0-0	2-1	2-3	1-3	-	1-2		2-1	2-5	2-6	2-1	0-0	1-2	0-0	0-0	0-2	3-1	1-1	1-0	2-2
Havant & W	1-0	1-1	2-1	0-1	2-1	2-0	4-0	1-4	1-3		1-0	1-2	3-1	2-1	2-0	2-1	1-1	0-2	0-0	1-2	1-1	2-3
Hayes & Yeading	3-0	0-3	0-2	0-5	2-2	2-2	4-4	0-5	0-0	0-0		1-1	3-5	1-0	0-2	2-1	1-3	1-3	2-2	0-0	1-1	3-4
Hemel	2-2	1-1	1-2	1-1	1-2	1-0	1-0	0-1	2-2	4-0		0-1	0-1	1-2	2-2	2-2	2-1	2-2	5-5	0-3		
Maidenhead	4-3	3-1	4-1	1-0	2-2	1-2	2-0	0-0	0-0	2-2	2-1	2-3		0-2	3-1	2-1	0-1	1-1	0-0	1-1	2-0	3-0
Maidstone	3-1	1-0	1-1	0-1	2-2	1-2	2-1	0-2	2-1	1-0	3-1	2-1	1-2		2-1	0-1	1-0	1-2	2-1	1-0	3-1	0-1
Margate	2-1	1-1	1-1	4-1	0-1	0-2	0-1	0-2	1-0	4-1	1-2	4-3	3-2	1-0		0-2	0-1	0-4	1-1	0-0	0-2	2-6
Oxford City	2-2	1-1	3-1	2-2	5-1	2-1	2-2	1-1	1-2	1-3	2-2	0-2	0-0	2-3	1-1		4-1	0-1	1-2	3-2	3-0	0-0
St Albans	3-0	0-1	1-1	1-1	2-2	4-0	3-1	0-2	1-3	6-0	1-1	2-2	3-2	1-2	3-0	1-3		0-3	0-1	1-0	2-1	6-0
Sutton Utd	2-0	1-1	2-0	2-0	2-2	2-0	2-1	2-0	1-0	3-0	0-1	2-2	2-2	0-2	4-1	1-1	5-0		2-2	-	0-0	2-2
Truro City	2-0	3-1	0-1	1-0	2-1	3-0	1-0	1-1	2-2	3-0	0-2	4-2	4-4	1-3	2-1	0-6	2-0	0-2		1-2	2-3	1-1
Wealdstone	4-4	2-0	3-1	0-0	1-2	2-1	0-1	1-2	1-1	3-2	3-0	0-0	0-0	2-2	4-1	2-2	1-0	2-4	4-4		3-4	2-2
Weston-s-Mare	2-1	1-1	1-1	0-3	0-3	2-1	1-2	2-1	0-4	3-2	0-2	2-4	2-0	1-2	1-0	5-2	4-1	0-2	2-2	1-2		1-2
Whitehawk	1-0	0-1	2-3	4-2	0-2	0-1	1-2	0-1	3-0	1-1	1-3	0-1	3-2	1-0	2-2	2-0	6-0	2-0	0-0	3-0	0-2	

A welcome return of Old Firm rivalries but still too soon for Gers to challenge

A fter four years of an Old Firm-free top flight, Rangers are back to resume hostilities with bitter foe Celtic and the other Premiership contenders, writes Steve Davies. Reborn perhaps, but Rangers' rivalry with Celtic will be as strong as ever, while the smaller clubs cannot wait for their showdowns with the Light Blues and all the revenue possibilities those high-profile clashes bring.

From a point of pure competition it would be nice to think the Gers could mount a title challenge. In their extended absence from the Premiership, Celtic have landed the spoils by 16, 29, 17 and 15 points respectively.

However, Celtic, who seemed to stagnate under Ronnie Deila, ought to have little difficulty making it six titles in a row under Brendan Rodgers. And there is no guarantee Rangers are good things for second, either.

Their run to the Scottish Cup final and runaway success in the second tier suggests Gers should flourish, and Mark Warburton continues to improve the squad dramatically with the likes of Clint Hill, Joey Barton and Niko Krancjar bringing the nous and class, while Jordan Rossiter, Matt Crooks and Josh Windass arrive with youthful exuberance.

But they still must upstage Hearts – third last term on their return to the top flight – and Aberdeen, who continue to improve. The Dons, runners-up for the past two seasons, could very well split the Glasgow giants.

At the other end, it was a real struggle for Hamilton last season under Martin Canning and you can only envisage another campaign of toil. They got away with it last time, limping home in eighth, but this could be their time to return to the Championship.

In the Championship it was Falkirk who made a mess of the popular Rangers-Hibs forecast, splitting the big two before losing

to Kilmarnock in the playoffs. Can they, or anyone else for that matter, repeat the feat, this time to Hibs and Dundee United?

Certainly Dundee United don't come with any guarantees of a major challenge after they dropped down in pitiful fashion.

Hibs were hugely disappointed to finish third but can surely only improve with Neil Lennon at the helm. The Edinburgh side merit favouritism but there is a case for finding an alternative each-way shot to the Tangerines.

St Mirren should improve on last season's sixth place and they finished the campaign quite nicely with just three losses in the last nine and good draws against Hibs and Rangers. They could be a value alternative.

In League One, Livingston can bounce straight back. The Lions, who have remained full-time despite the drop, have made plenty of new signings under David Hopkin, who has enjoyed a first full summer with his troops after replacing Mark Burchill in December.

You can throw a blanket over half a dozen sides in League Two, where Clyde go off favourites for a second-successive season. There has also been early money for Arbroath with Dick Campbell on a massive recruitment drive over the summer.

But you could do worse than an each-way punt on Stirling, who have added Berwick's top scorer Blair Henderson to their roster.

*Celtic's Erik Sviachenko
celebrates last season's
Scottish Cup semi-final
leveller against Rangers*

ABERDEEN

Nickname: The Dons
Colours: Red
Ground: Pittodrie (21,421)
Tel: 01224 650-400   www.afc.co.uk

The Dons were once again Celtic's nearest challengers and there were points in the season when it looked as though they could finally depose the Hoops.

Eight straight wins to start the campaign set the tone, confirming Derek McInnes' men as title rivals once more. By March 12 they were just a point adrift.

McInnes felt a lack of physicality was their undoing so has sought to sign some strapping players, among them Callum Morris and Jayden Stockley.

Longest run without win/loss: 5/12
High/low league position: 1/9
Clean sheets: 13 **Yellows:** 47 **Reds:** 3
Avg attendance: 11,949 **Players used:** 31
Leading scorer: A Rooney 20 (9,18)
Key stat: Aberdeen ran out of steam at the back end of 2015-16, losing six of their last eight league matches

	2015-16 H	A	Last six seasons at home P	W	D	L	OV	UN	BS	CS
Celtic	W W	L L	10	3	1	6	5	5	5	0
Aberdeen										
Hearts	W L	W L	9	2	4	3	1	8	2	5
St Johnstone	L D	W L	12	3	5	4	1	11	3	6
Motherwell	D W	W L	10	3	3	4	5	5	6	2
Ross County	W L	L W	7	4	1	2	4	3	1	4
Inverness CT	D	L L	10	5	1	4	5	5	5	3
Dundee	W W	W	5	4	1	0	1	4	1	4
Partick	D	W W	4	2	2	0	1	3	0	4
Hamilton	W W	D	5	5	0	0	3	2	0	5
Kilmarnock	W W	W	11	7	2	2	5	6	4	5
Rangers			3	0	0	3	2	1	2	0

Season	Division	Pos	P	W	D	L	F	A	GD	Pts
2015-16	Premiership	2	38	22	5	11	62	48	+14	71
2014-15	Premiership	2	38	23	6	9	57	33	+24	75
2013-14	Premiership	3	38	20	8	10	53	38	+15	68

Over/Under 58%/42% 5th   **Both score** 55%/45% 6th

League scorers	P	G		Y	R
A Rooney	22 (5)	20		-	-
N McGinn	33 (3)	10		-	-
S Church	13	6		1	-
K McLean	38	6		4	-
J Hayes	35	5		2	1
S Logan	35 (2)	4		9	-
A Taylor	36 (1)	4		6	-
A Considine	26 (6)	2		3	-
D Goodwillie	7 (10)	2		1	-
P Pawlett, P Quinn, G Shinnie – 1 goal					

CELTIC

Nickname: The Bhoys
Colours: Green and white
Ground: Celtic Park (60,355)
Tel: 0871-226-1888   www.celticfc.net

After a fifth straight title, former Liverpool boss Brendan Rodgers has replaced Ronnie Deila in the dugout.

He inherited a squad which the Northern Irishman said was "bloated" though even after he slims it down it will still be odds-on to be champions.

The resumption of Old Firm rivalries adds spice, but Rodgers' main focus will be on Europe after the Bhoys suffered a second successive Champions League qualifying playoff round exit last term.

Longest run without win/loss: 2/12
High/low league position: 1/5
Clean sheets: 15 **Yellows:** 55 **Reds:** 3
Avg attendance: 26,795 **Players used:** 36
Leading scorer: L Griffiths 31 (14,24)
Key stat: Free-scoring Celtic had a goal difference of plus 62 last season, 43 goals better than next best Hearts

	2015-16 H	A	Last six seasons at home P	W	D	L	OV	UN	BS	CS
Celtic										
Aberdeen	W W	L L	11	11	0	0	9	2	7	4
Hearts	D W	D W	9	8	1	0	5	4	2	7
St Johnstone	W W	W L	11	8	1	2	5	6	4	5
Motherwell	L W	W W	11	9	1	1	6	5	2	9
Ross County	W W D	W	7	4	3	0	2	5	3	4
Inverness CT	W W	W	12	9	2	1	8	4	4	7
Dundee	W D	D	6	5	1	0	4	2	1	5
Partick	W	W W	4	4	0	0	0	4	0	4
Hamilton	W	W D	5	4	0	1	3	2	2	2
Kilmarnock	D	D W	8	5	2	1	4	4	4	3
Rangers			4	3	0	1	3	1	1	3

Season	Division	Pos	P	W	D	L	F	A	GD	Pts
2015-16	Premiership	1	38	26	8	4	93	31	+62	86
2014-15	Premiership	1	38	29	5	4	84	17	+67	92
2013-14	Premiership	1	38	31	6	1	102	25	+77	99

Over/Under 68%/32% 1st   **Both score** 61%/39% 3rd

Top league scorers	P	G		Y	R
L Griffiths	32 (2)	31		6	-
T Rogic	24 (6)	8		2	-
P Roberts	9 (2)	6		-	-
N Biton	28 (2)	5		6	1
S Armstrong	19 (6)	4		3	-
D Boyata	25 (1)	4		1	1
N Ciftci	5 (6)	4		2	1
K Commons	16 (5)	4		-	-
M Lustig	29 (1)	4		3	-
G Mackay-Steven	15 (10)	4		1	-
C McGregor	15 (12)	4		1	-

SCOTTISH PREMIERSHIP

DUNDEE

Nickname: The Dark Blues
Colours: Blue and white
Ground: Dens Park (11,506)
Tel: 01382-889966   www.dundeefc.co.uk

Manager Paul Hartley said defensive failings proved costly for a side who never managed to string three successive wins together over the course of the season. Hammerings by Celtic, Ross, Inverness and, in the Scottish Cup, by Rangers, confirmed Hartley's conclusion that he needs a stronger back line this term.

Only four wins in their first 18 games ensured a bottom-half finish, but Dundee were only denied a place in the top six by a 2-1 defeat at Hamilton in match 33.

Longest run without win/loss: 8/5
High/low league position: 4/36
Clean sheets: 7 **Yellows:** 66 **Reds:** 2
Avg attendance: 8,355 **Players used:** 30
Leading scorer: K Hemmings 21 (8,15)
Key stat: Dundee have won only four of their last 27 away matches – going back to February 2015 – in all competitions

HAMILTON

Nickname: The Accies
Colours: Red and white
Ground: New Douglas Park (6,018)
Tel: 01698-368-652   www.acciesfc.co.uk

Having fallen to pieces at the end of 2014-15, the Accies started last term brightly with five wins in their first nine. They only managed another six over the rest of the campaign but were never in danger of going down.

The pressure was on Martin Canning though – the low point coming in January when a 4-1 Scottish Cup thrashing at Annan was followed by an 8-1 mauling at Celtic – and a club that tends to operate via loans and frees should struggle again.

Longest run without win/loss: 8/3
High/low league position: 3/48
Clean sheets: 10 **Yellows:** 10 **Reds:** 5
Avg attendance: 5,568 **Players used:** 29
Leading scorer: C Morris 8 (4,7)
Key stat: After beating Motherwell on September 19, Hamilton had to wait almost seven months for the next home win

	2015-16		Last six seasons at home							
	H	A	P	W	D	L	OV	UN	BS	CS
Celtic	D L D	L D	4	0	2	2	1	3	2	1
Aberdeen	L	L L	6	0	3	3	2	4	5	0
Hearts	L L	D	4	2	0	2	1	3	1	2
St Johnstone	W W	D	6	2	2	2	3	3	4	1
Motherwell	W D	L	5	2	1	2	5	0	4	0
Ross County	D W	L	9	2	4	3	3	6	5	2
Inverness CT	D D	D L	6	0	3	3	2	4	5	0
Dundee										
Partick	D	W W W	7	3	2	2	3	4	4	1
Hamilton	W L	D L	8	3	3	2	6	2	4	
Kilmarnock	L D	W D	6	1	3	2	2	4	4	2
Rangers			-	-	-	-	-	-	-	-

Season	Division	Pos	P	W	D	L	F	A	GD	Pts
2015-16	Premiership	8	38	11	15	12	53	57	-4	48
2014-15	Premiership	6	38	11	12	15	46	57	-11	45
2013-14	Championship	1	36	21	6	9	54	26	+28	69

Over/Under 53%/47% 8th   **Both score** 63%/37% 2nd

League scorers	P	G		Y	R
K Hemmings	34 (3)	21		1	-
R Loy	21 (8)	9		1	-
G Stewart	36 (1)	9		10	-
G Harkins	22 (8)	4		6	1
K Holt	34	2		5	-
J McPake	16	2		4	-
C Wighton	7 (6)	2		-	-
K Gadzhalov	8 (6)	1		1	-
R Healey	4 (3)	1		-	-
P McGowan	27 (3)	1		4	-
N Ross	36 (1)	1		4	-

	2015-16		Last six seasons at home							
	H	A	P	W	D	L	OV	UN	BS	CS
Celtic	L D	L	4	0	2	2	1	3	3	0
Aberdeen	D	L L	5	1	2	3	2	3	2	1
Hearts	W D	L	4	1	1	2	2	2	1	1
St Johnstone	L	L D	5	1	2	2	2	3	3	2
Motherwell	W L	D	5	3	1	1	1	4	0	4
Ross County	L	L L	5	2	1	2	4	1	3	1
Inverness CT	L L	W W	6	0	0	6	3	3	3	0
Dundee	D W	L W	7	3	2	2	5	2	6	0
Partick	D L	D D	8	2	4	2	3	5	4	3
Hamilton										
Kilmarnock	L L	W W	6	0	4	2	2	4	2	2
Rangers			2	0	0	2	1	1	1	0

Season	Division	Pos	P	W	D	L	F	A	GD	Pts
2015-16	Premiership	10	38	11	10	17	42	63	-21	43
2014-15	Premiership	7	38	15	8	15	50	53	-3	45
2013-14	Championship	2	36	19	10	7	68	41	+27	67

Over/Under 50%/50% 9th   **Both score** 50%/50% 9th

League scorers	P	G		Y	R
C Morris	27 (5)	8		11	1
D Imrie	34 (1)	6		14	-
A Crawford	32 (1)	5		5	-
J Tena	20 (3)	4		7	1
G Kurtaj	28 (6)	3		5	-
L Tagliapietra	34	3		7	1
Z Gordon	38	2		5	-
C Nade	4 (13)	2		2	-
G Docherty, G Gillespie, L Longridge, D MacKinnon – 1 goal					

HEARTS

Nickname: Jambos
Colours: Claret and white
Ground: Tynecastle (17,590)
Tel: 0871-663-1874   www.heartsfc.co.uk

Hearts made the transition from the Championship appear fairly routine last term. Robbie Neilson's men won their first five league games and were a model of consistency from then on, suffering just seven defeats before the split.

Nine-goal Osman Sow's exit in January left them short of firepower right at the end of term, when the Jambos managed just two wins in their last nine. Connor Sammon's arrival from Derby should see the frontline beefed up.

Longest run without win/loss: 5/8
High/low league position: 2/17
Clean sheets: 17 **Yellows:** 78 **Reds:** 9
Avg attendance: 13,385 **Players used:** 30
Leading scorer: Juanma 12 (4,9)
Key stat: Slow starters Hearts scored only seven first-half goals in 19 away league fixtures last season

	2015-16		Last six seasons at home							
	H	A	P	W	D	L	OV	UN	BS	CS
Celtic	D L	D L	9	2	1	6	6	3	3	2
Aberdeen	L W	L W	8	6	1	1	6	2	4	4
Hearts										
St Johnstone	W L	D D	10	5	2	3	4	6	4	4
Motherwell	W W	D L	10	4	2	4	3	7	2	5
Ross County	W D	W W	6	3	3	0	3	3	4	2
Inverness CT	W	L D	6	2	2	2	3	3	4	1
Dundee	D	W W	3	1	1	1	0	3	1	1
Partick	W W	W	4	2	0	2	2		1	2
Hamilton	W	L D	2	2	0	0	0	2	0	2
Kilmarnock	D W	D	9	2	1	6	5	4	2	2
Rangers			6	2	1	3	3	3	2	2

Season Division	Pos	P	W	D	L	F	A	GD	Pts
2015-16 Premiership	3	38	18	11	9	59	40	+19	65
2014-15 Championship	1	36	29	4	3	96	26	+70	91
2013-14 Premiership	12	38	10	8	20	45	65	-20	23

Over/Under 50%/50% 9th   **Both score** 45%/55% 11th

Top league scorers	P	G		Y	R
Juanma	28 (5)	12		8	1
O Sow	22 (1)	9		-	-
J Walker	20 (2)	7		3	-
Arnaud Djoum	24 (4)	5		3	-
A Dauda	7 (6)	5		-	1
C Paterson	27 (2)	5		7	-
G Reilly	11 (17)	4		-	1
S Nicholson	28 (8)	3		2	-
P Buaben	33 (3)	2		9	-
B King	7 (8)	2		-	-
I Rossi	28 (1)	2		7	1

INVERNESS CT

Nickname: Caley
Colours: Blue and red
Ground: Caledonian Stadium (7,750)
Tel: 01463-222-880   www.ictfc.com

Caley suffered a hangover after their cup success of 2014-15, failing to win any of their first six league games and exiting the Europa League at the first hurdle.

Their run of three successive top-six finishes thus ended with Caley finishing in the bottom half and John Hughes called it a day – having been named manager of the month in April – to be replaced by Richie Foran, whose last act as a player was to score the final goal of the season in a 4-0 hammering of Dundee.

Longest run without win/loss: 6/5
High/low league position: 6/32
Clean sheets: 9 **Yellows:** 74 **Reds:** 4
Avg attendance: 6,516 **Players used:** 25
Leading scorer: M Storey 11 (6,11)
Key stat: Ten of Thistle's first 11 games last season – in Europe as well as the league – produced two goals or less

	2015-16		Last six seasons at home							
	H	A	P	W	D	L	OV	UN	BS	CS
Celtic	L	L L	9	2	1	6	4	5	5	1
Aberdeen	W W	D	12	5	2	5	6	6	6	3
Hearts	W D		9	3	5	1	1	8	4	5
St Johnstone	L	D L	10	5	3	2	1	9	3	5
Motherwell	L L	W	10	4	0	6	8	2	7	2
Ross County	W	W W	6	3	2	1	3	3	5	1
Inverness CT										
Dundee	D W	D D	5	2	3	0	2	3	3	2
Partick	D D	L W	5	1	2	2	2	3	1	3
Hamilton	L L	W W	5	1	1	3	1	4	2	0
Kilmarnock	W W	L L	10	5	4	1	6	4	9	1
Rangers			3	0	1	2	1	2	2	0

Season Division	Pos	P	W	D	L	F	A	GD	Pts
2015-16 Premiership	7	38	14	10	14	54	48	+6	52
2014-15 Premiership	3	38	19	8	11	52	42	+10	65
2013-14 Premiership	5	38	16	9	13	44	44	0	52

Over/Under 50%/50% 9th   **Both score** 55%/45% 6th

Top league scorers	P	G		Y	R
M Storey	29 (1)	11		3	-
G Tansey	37	8		8	-
L Polworth	33 (3)	6		2	-
I Vigurs	24 (6)	6		12	-
R Draper	31 (1)	5		8	-
R Christie	12 (1)	3		2	1
D Devine	37	2		8	-
J Meekings	21	2		1	-
J Roberts	8 (1)	2		3	-
C Tremarco	28 (4)	2		8	-
J Vincent	14 (2)	2		-	-

KILMARNOCK

Nickname: Killie
Colours: Blue and white
Ground: Rugby Park (18,128)
Tel: 01563 545-300   www.kilmarnockfc.co.uk

It was another desperate season for Killie, the gloom only lifted at the end by a 4-0 playoff success over Falkirk which secured top-flight status for another year.

The season began badly, with no wins in their first six games, and manager Gary Locke quit at the end of January having won just 11 of his 43 matches in charge.

Player Lee McCulloch took interim control before Lee Clark's appointment. The Geordie's first task once survival was attained was to get rid of 14 players.

Longest run without win/loss: 7/3
High/low league position: 8/53
Clean sheets: 8 **Yellows:** 77 **Reds:** 3
Avg attendance: 6,203 **Players used:** 34
Leading scorer: J Magennis 10 (1,10)
Key stat: Killie have won just three of 14 games under former Birmingham manager Lee Clark, who was appointed in February

	2015-16 H	A	Last six seasons at home P	W	D	L	OV	UN	BS	CS
Celtic	D L	D	11	0	2	9	8	3	5	0
Aberdeen	L	L L	9	2	2	5	3	6	4	2
Hearts	D	D L	9	3	4	2	4	5	5	3
St Johnstone	W W	L	9	2	3	4	5	4	5	3
Motherwell	L	L W	10	4	1	5	3	7	3	4
Ross County	L L	L	7	2	1	4	5	2	2	2
Inverness CT	W W	L L	10	4	1	5	7	3	8	2
Dundee	L D	W D	5	0	2	3	3	2	2	2
Partick	L L	D D	6	2	1	3	5	1	4	1
Hamilton	L	W W	5	2	0	3	3	2	2	2
Kilmarnock										
Rangers			3	1	0	2	2	1	2	1

Season	Division	Pos	P	W	D	L	F	A	GD	Pts
2015-16	Premiership	11	38	9	9	20	41	64	-23	36
2014-15	Premiership	10	38	11	8	19	44	59	-15	41
2013-14	Premiership	9	38	11	6	21	45	66	-21	39

Over/Under 55%/45% 6th   **Both score** 50%/50% 9th

League scorers	P	G		Y	R
J Magennis	32 (2)	10		9	-
G Kiltie	30 (5)	6		3	-
K Boyd	15 (14)	5		1	-
K Higginbotham	23 (4)	5		5	-
C Balatoni	30	3		5	-
T Obadeyi	15 (15)	3		2	-
M Connolly	10	2		4	-
C Slater	23 (3)	2		2	-
S Smith	21 (1)	2		7	-
K McHattie, R McKenzie – 1 goal					

MOTHERWELL

Nickname: The Well/The Steelmen
Colours: Amber and claret
Ground: Fir Park (13,677)
Tel: 01698-333-333   www.motherwellfc.co.uk

Few predicted how the Steelmen's season would end based on how it started.

Still reeling from an 11th-place finish in 2014-15, the Well lost seven of their first 11 and lost to Morton in the League Cup. Ian Baraclough was sacked in September and, after a dismal 2-0 home loss to Kilmarnock in February, they were again occupying 11th spot. But six wins in seven not only ended any lingering relegation fears but saw Mark McGhee's side finish the season in the top half.

Longest run without win/loss: 6/5
High/low league position: 4/31
Clean sheets: 7 **Yellows:** 63 **Reds:** 4
Avg attendance: 7,161 **Players used:** 27
Leading scorer: L Moult 15 (6,13)
Key stat: Motherwell finished fifth in the top flight last season, despite a goal difference of minus 16

	2015-16 H	A	Last six seasons at home P	W	D	L	OV	UN	BS	CS
Celtic	L L	W L	12	3	1	8	7	5	5	1
Aberdeen	L W	D L	10	5	2	3	6	4	7	2
Hearts	D W	L L	8	5	2	1	5	3	4	4
St Johnstone	W L	L L	12	7	2	3	8	4	7	3
Motherwell										
Ross County	D L	L W	8	4	3	1	5	3	7	1
Inverness CT	L	W W	10	6	1	3	6	4	4	4
Dundee	W	L D	4	1	1	2	2	2	3	0
Partick	W W	L	6	5	1	0	3	3	3	3
Hamilton	D	L W	5	2	1	2	3	2	1	2
Kilmarnock	W L	W	10	3	4	3	4	6	6	2
Rangers			4	0	0	4	4	0	2	0

Season	Division	Pos	P	W	D	L	F	A	GD	Pts
2015-16	Premiership	5	38	15	5	18	47	63	-16	50
2014-15	Premiership	11	38	10	6	22	38	63	-25	36
2013-14	Premiership	2	38	22	4	12	64	60	+4	70

Over/Under 63%/37% 3rd   **Both score** 58%/42% 4th

League scorers	P	G		Y	R
L Moult	34 (4)	15		4	-
S McDonald	34 (3)	10		5	-
S Pearson	25 (1)	7		8	-
M Johnson	34 (4)	5		1	-
L Ainsworth	17 (12)	2		1	-
C Cadden	16 (4)	2		2	-
W Fletcher	5 (9)	1		-	-
B Hall	16 (2)	1		1	-
L Laing	13 (2)	1		2	-
K Lasley	30	1		5	2
S McManus	37	1		6	1

PARTICK

Nickname: The Jags
Colours: Yellow and red
Ground: Firhill Stadium (10,915)
Tel: 0141-579-1971   www.ptfc.co.uk

Bottom at the end of September having failed to win any of their first nine matches, Thistle would doubtless have settled for the ninth place they eventually claimed. That ultimately was little more than most Jags' fans had anticipated.

One point from a possible 27 against the division's big three demonstrated something of an inferiority complex so it was their ability to beat the teams around them that saw Partick reach 46 points – the same tally they achieved in 2014-15.

Longest run without win/loss: 9/6
High/low league position: 7/45
Clean sheets: 12 **Yellows:** 74 **Reds:** 5
Avg attendance: 6,112 **Players used:** 29
Leading scorer: K Doohlan 14 (6,12)
Key stat: Partick suffered the worst possible start last term, failing to score in seven of their first eight league matches

	2015-16		Last six seasons at home							
	H	A	P	W	D	L	OV	UN	BS	CS
Celtic	L L	L	5	0	0	5	4	1	3	0
Aberdeen	L L	D	5	1	0	4	3	2	2	0
Hearts	L	L L	3	0	1	2	2	1	2	0
St Johnstone	W	W W	4	2	1	1	1	3	0	3
Motherwell	W	L L	4	3	0	1	2	2	2	2
Ross County	W	L L	9	2	3	4	4	5	5	2
Inverness CT	W L	D D	5	3	1	1	3	2	3	2
Dundee	L L L	D	8	1	3	4	2	6	3	3
Partick										
Hamilton	D D	D W	8	4	3	1	4	4	4	4
Kilmarnock	D D	W W	6	0	5	1	2	4	5	1
Rangers	-	-	-	-	-	-	-	-	-	-

Season	Division	Pos	P	W	D	L	F	A	GD	Pts
2015-16	Premiership	9	38	12	10	16	41	50	-9	46
2014-15	Premiership	8	38	12	10	16	48	44	+4	46
2013-14	Premiership	10	38	8	14	16	46	65	-19	38

Over/Under 47%/53% 12th   **Both score** 45%/55% 11th

League scorers	P	G		Y	R
K Doohlan	24 (12)	14		-	-
D Amoo	27 (10)	5		2	-
S Lawless	36 (1)	5		3	-
C Booth	34	2		6	-
R Edwards	10 (7)	2		2	-
R Muirhead	4 (4)	2		2	-
M Pogba	13 (15)	2		2	-

S Bannigan, M Dumbuya, F Frans, G Fraser,
L Lindsay, G Miller, R Stevenson, S Welsh – 1 goal

RANGERS

Nickname: The Gers
Colours: Blue
Ground: Ibrox Stadium (51,082)
Tel: 0871-702-1972   www.rangers.co.uk

Playoff defeat by Motherwell at the end of 2014-15 might have suggested Rangers were not ready for the step up, but they made no mistake last season.

Twenty-goal Martyn Waghorn led the title romp which went hand in hand with a run to the Scottish Cup final, beating Kilmarnock, Dundee and Celtic en route.

Back in the top flight for the first time since 2012, Mark Warburton is thinking big again based on signings of the calibre of Niko Kranjcar and Joey Barton.

Longest run without win/loss: 4/11
High/low league position: 1/1
Clean sheets: 15 **Yellows:** 41 **Reds:** 2
Avg attendance: 22,842 **Players used:** 25
Leading scorer: M Waghorn 20 (3,13)
Key stat: Rangers went through the entire Championship campaign unbeaten at Ibrox and scored in all 18 home games

	2015-16		Last six seasons at home							
	H	A	P	W	D	L	OV	UN	BS	CS
Celtic			4	2	1	1	2	2	2	1
Aberdeen			3	2	1	0	0	3	1	2
Hearts			6	3	1	2	4	2	4	2
St Johnstone			3	2	1	0	2	1	1	2
Motherwell			4	3	1	0	3	1	1	3
Ross County			-	-	-	-	-	-	-	-
Inverness CT			3	2	1	0	1	2	2	1
Dundee			-	-	-	-	-	-	-	-
Partick			-	-	-	-	-	-	-	-
Hamilton			1	1	0	0	1	0	0	1
Kilmarnock			4	3	0	1	2	2	2	1
Rangers										

Season	Division	Pos	P	W	D	L	F	A	GD	Pts
2015-16	Championship	1	36	25	6	5	88	34	+54	81
2014-15	Championship	3	36	19	10	7	69	39	+30	67
2013-14	League One	1	36	33	3	0	106	18	+88	102

Over/Under 64%/36% 1st   **Both score** 56%/44% 3rd

Top league scorers	P	G		Y	R
M Waghorn	25	20		3	-
K Miller	22 (10)	14		2	-
J Holt	31 (1)	10		1	-
J Tavernier	36	10		3	-
L Wallace	36	7		5	-
B McKay	33 (1)	6		1	-
A Halliday	35	5		6	2
H Forrester	6 (5)	4		-	-
M O'Halloran	9 (3)	3		1	-
N Clark	5 (17)	2		-	-
D Shiels	5 (26)	2		1	-

ROSS COUNTY

Nickname: County
Colours: Blue, red and white
Ground: Victoria Park (6,541)
Tel: 01349-860860   rosscountyfootballclub.co.uk

Jim McIntyre, many people's idea of manager of the season, worked wonders once again in Dingwall, the highlights being defeats of Inverness, Celtic and then Hibernian to land the League Cup – the first major trophy in the club's history.

Maybe it was a reaction to that cup win that they managed to win just two of their last nine league games. But a top-six finish was another fine achievement and signing off with a 4-0 win at Aberdeen capped a near-perfect campaign.

Longest run without win/loss: 4/5
High/low league position: 4/46
Clean sheets: 8 **Yellows:** 63 **Reds:** 2
Avg attendance: 6,577 **Players used:** 26
Leading scorer: L Boyce 15 (4,12)
Key stat: There has not been a single draw in any of Ross County's last 41 home league matches

ST JOHNSTONE

Nickname: The Saints
Colours: Blue and white
Ground: McDiarmid Park (10,673)
Tel: 01738-459090   perthstjohnstonefc.co.uk

Those who thought St Johnstone's fourth-place finish in 2014-15 was a flash in the pan were proved very wrong as 12 months later Saints came in fourth again – a feat which earned Tommy Wright manager of the season accolades.

A run of nine wins in 13 matches going into December kept the Perth club dreaming of a top-three finish but, such are the fine lines, they then went seven without a win, failing to score in four games in a row.

Longest run without win/loss: 7/6
High/low league position: 4/25
Clean sheets: 7 **Yellows:** 66 **Reds:** 3
Avg attendance: 6,675 **Players used:** 28
Leading scorer: S MacLean 14 (1,10)
Key stat: There was no shortage of goalmouth action in early Saints' games with both teams scoring in 16 of their first 17 matches

Ross County

	2015-16		Last six seasons at home							
	H	A	P	W	D	L	OV	UN	BS	CS
Celtic	L L	L L D	7	1	2	4	4	3	5	0
Aberdeen	W L	L W	6	3	1	2	2	4	3	2
Hearts	L L	L D	5	1	1	3	5	0	4	0
St Johnstone	L L	D D	7	3	0	4	3	4	3	3
Motherwell	W L	D W	7	3	1	3	6	1	4	3
Ross County										
Inverness CT	L L	L	7	1	1	5	5	2	3	2
Dundee	W	D L	8	4	2	2	4	4	4	2
Partick	W W	W	10	4	3	3	4	6	4	5
Hamilton	W W	W	6	5	0	1	3	3	3	2
Kilmarnock	W	W W	7	3	1	3	5	2	5	1
Rangers	-	-	-	-	-	-	-	-	-	-

Season	Division	Pos	P	W	D	L	F	A	GD	Pts
2015-16	Premiership	6	38	14	6	18	55	61	-6	48
2014-15	Premiership	9	38	12	8	18	46	63	-17	44
2013-14	Premiership	7	38	11	7	20	44	62	-18	40

Over/Under 55%/45% 6th   **Both score** 53%/47% 8th

Top league scorers	P	G	Y	R
L Boyce	29 (6)	15	2	-
C Curran	15 (4)	7	4	-
B Graham	10 (13)	6	1	-
M Gardyne	34 (1)	5	2	-
A Schalk	14 (4)	5	2	-
A Davies	31	3	6	1
I McShane	16 (2)	3	-	-
T Dingwall	5 (7)	2	2	-
J Irvine	34 (2)	2	6	-
S Murdoch	14 (15)	2	4	-

St Johnstone

	2015-16		Last six seasons at home							
	H	A	P	W	D	L	OV	UN	BS	CS
Celtic	L W	L L	12	2	3	7	7	5	5	1
Aberdeen	L W	W D	10	3	2	5	5	5	5	3
Hearts	D L	W D	7	3	3	1	3	4	3	3
St Johnstone										
Motherwell	W W	L W	10	7	0	3	6	4	4	4
Ross County	D D	W W	7	2	4	1	3	4	5	1
Inverness CT	D W	W	12	6	4	2	2	10	2	8
Dundee	D	L L	4	2	1	1	0	4	1	2
Partick	L L	L	5	1	2	2	2	3	4	1
Hamilton	W D	W	5	3	1	1	1	4	1	3
Kilmarnock	W L	L L	9	5	2	2	5	4	4	4
Rangers			4	0	4	0	2	2	1	0

Season	Division	Pos	P	W	D	L	F	A	GD	Pts
2015-16	Premiership	4	38	16	8	14	58	55	+3	56
2014-15	Premiership	4	38	16	9	13	34	34	0	57
2013-14	Premiership	6	38	15	8	15	48	42	+6	53

Over/Under 63%/37% 3rd   **Both score** 66%/34% 1st

Top league scorers	P	G	Y	R
S MacLean	29 (4)	14	3	-
D Wotherspoon	32 (3)	9	8	-
G Cummins	23 (9)	8	1	-
L Craig	24 (11)	6	8	1
C Kane	10 (19)	4	2	-
M Davidson	30	3	7	-
S Lappin	14 (9)	2	2	-
M O'Halloran	19 (1)	2	3	-
T Scobbie	28 (2)	2	4	-

Scottish Premiership stats 2015-16
Key Points in all tables (except the league table) do not include any deductions imposed by the league.
POS H A Overall league position, rank from home games only, rank from away games only **Sup** Average match supremacy **GFA** Goals For Average **GAA** Goals Against Average **PGA** Points Gained Average

Scottish Premiership 2015-16				Home					Away						
Pos	H	A		P	W	D	L	F	A	W	D	L	F	A	GD	Pts
1	1	1	Celtic (CL)	38	14	4	1	55	12	12	4	3	38	19	+62	86
2	2	2	Aberdeen (EL)	38	12	4	3	30	19	10	1	8	32	29	+14	71
3	3	3	Hearts (EL)	38	11	5	3	37	22	7	6	6	22	18	+19	65
4	4	5	St Johnstone	38	8	6	5	27	22	8	2	9	31	33	+3	56
5	6	8	Motherwell	38	8	3	8	27	27	7	2	10	20	36	-16	50
6	7	9	Ross County	38	9	0	10	29	33	5	6	8	26	28	-6	48
7	8	4	Inverness CT	38	7	5	7	25	20	7	5	7	29	28	+6	52
8	5	11	Dundee	38	7	7	5	30	23	4	8	7	23	34	-4	48
9	9	7	Partick	38	6	4	9	21	29	6	6	7	20	21	-9	46
10	10	6	Hamilton	38	4	6	9	21	28	7	4	8	21	35	-21	43
11	11	10	Kilmarnock	38	4	4	11	19	37	5	5	9	22	27	-23	36
12	12	12	Dundee Utd* (R)	38	3	4	12	22	35	5	3	11	23	35	-25	28

*Dundee Utd deducted 3pts

SCOTTISH PREMIERSHIP

Best attack

		GF	GFA
1	Celtic	93	2.45
2	Aberdeen	62	1.63
3	Hearts	59	1.55
4	St Johnstone	58	1.53
5	Ross County	55	1.45
6	Inverness CT	54	1.42
7	Dundee	53	1.39
8	Motherwell	47	1.24
9	Dundee Utd	45	1.18
10	Hamilton	42	1.11
11	Partick	41	1.08
12	Kilmarnock	41	1.08

Best defence

		GA	GAA
1	Celtic	31	0.82
2	Hearts	40	1.05
3	Aberdeen	48	1.26
4	Inverness CT	48	1.26
5	Partick	50	1.32
6	St Johnstone	55	1.45
7	Dundee	57	1.5
8	Ross County	61	1.61
9	Motherwell	63	1.66
10	Hamilton	63	1.66
11	Kilmarnock	64	1.68
12	Dundee Utd	70	1.84

Top scorers

		Team	Goals scored	
L Griffiths	Celtic	31	|||||||||||||||||||||||||||||||
K Hemmings	Dundee	21	|||||||||||||||||||||
A Rooney	Aberdeen	20	||||||||||||||||||||
L Moult	Motherwell	15	|||||||||||||||
L Boyce	Ross County	15	|||||||||||||||
K Doolan	Partick	14	||||||||||||||
S MacLean	St Johnstone	14	||||||||||||||
B Mckay	Dundee Utd	12	||||||||||||
Juanma	Hearts	12	||||||||||||

SOCCERBASE.COM

Record when first to score

		P	W	D	L	F	A	Sup	PGA	Pts
1	Hearts	19	15	3	1	36	10	+1.37	2.5	48
2	Celtic	30	23	4	3	87	27	+2.00	2.4	73
3	Inverness CT	17	12	4	1	37	15	+1.29	2.4	40
4	Aberdeen	23	17	3	3	43	17	+1.13	2.3	54
5	Ross County	17	12	3	2	36	20	+0.94	2.3	39
6	Hamilton	12	9	0	3	21	11	+0.83	2.3	27
7	Partick	16	10	5	1	30	17	+0.81	2.2	35
8	St Johnstone	13	9	2	2	29	11	+1.38	2.2	29
9	Motherwell	19	12	3	4	32	21	+0.58	2.1	39
10	Dundee	16	9	5	2	35	20	+0.94	2	32
11	Kilmarnock	13	8	2	3	24	13	+0.85	2	26
12	Dundee Utd	18	8	3	7	32	26	+0.33	1.5	27

Record when keeping a clean sheet

		P	W	D	F	Sup	PGA	Pts
1	Ross County	8	8	0	19	+2.38	3	24
2	Motherwell	7	7	0	10	+1.43	3	21
3	Aberdeen	13	12	1	22	+1.69	2.8	37
4	Dundee Utd	5	4	1	7	+1.4	2.6	13
5	Hearts	17	13	4	29	+1.71	2.5	43
6	Celtic	15	11	4	33	+2.2	2.5	37
7	St Johnstone	7	5	2	9	+1.29	2.4	17
8	Inverness CT	9	6	3	14	+1.56	2.3	21
9	Kilmarnock	8	5	3	12	+1.5	2.3	18
10	Partick	12	7	5	11	+0.92	2.2	26
11	Hamilton	10	6	4	10	+1	2.2	22
12	Dundee	7	4	3	11	+1.57	2.1	15

Over 2.5 goals

	H	A	%
Celtic	12	14	68%
Dundee Utd	12	13	66%
Motherwell	12	12	63%
St Johnstone	11	13	63%
Aberdeen	9	13	58%

Under 2.5 goals

	H	A	%
Partick	9	11	53%
Hearts	9	10	50%
Hamilton	10	9	50%
Inverness CT	10	9	50%
Dundee	9	9	47%

Both to score

	H	A	%
St Johnstone	13	12	66%
Dundee	13	11	63%
Celtic	9	14	61%
Dundee United	12	10	58%
Motherwell	13	9	58%

Both not to score

	H	A	%
Hearts	10	7	55%
Partick	9	8	55%
Hamilton	10	9	50%
Kilmarnock	8	11	50%
Ross County	10	10	47%

Scottish Premiership results 2015-16

	Aberdeen	Celtic	Dundee	Dundee United	Hamilton	Hearts	Inverness CT	Kilmarnock	Motherwell	Partick	Ross County	St Johnstone
Aberdeen		2-1/2-1	2-0/1-0	2-0	1-0/3-0	1-0/0-1	2-2	2-0/2-1	1-1/4-1	0-0	3-1/0-4	1-5/1-1
Celtic	3-1/3-2		6-0/0-0	5-0	8-1	0-0/3-1	4-2/3-0	0-0	1-2/7-0	1-0	2-0/2-0/1-1	3-1/3-1
Dundee	0-2	0-0		2-1/2-1	4-0/0-1	1-2/0-1	1-1/1-1	1-2/1-1	2-1/2-2	1-1	3-3/5-2	2-1/2-0
Dundee United	0-1/0-1	1-3/1-4	2-2/2-2		1-2/1-3	0-1/2-1	1-1/0-2	1-2/5-1	0-3	0-1/3-3	1-0	1-2
Hamilton	1-1	1-2/1-1	1-1/2-1	4-0/0-0		3-2/0-0	3-4/0-1	0-1/0-4	1-0/0-1	0-0/1-2	1-3	2-4
Hearts	1-3/2-1	2-2/1-3	1-1	3-2	2-0		2-0	1-1/1-0	2-0/6-0	3-0/1-0	2-0/1-1	4-3/0-3/2-2
Inverness CT	2-1/3-1	1-3	1-1/4-0	2-2/2-3	0-2/0-1	2-0/0-0		2-1/3-1	0-1/1-2	0-0/0-0	2-0	0-1
Kilmarnock	0-4	2-2/0-1	0-4/0-0	1-1/2-4	1-2/0-1	2-2	2-0/2-1		0-1	2-5/0-2	0-4/0-2	2-1/3-0
Motherwell	1-2/2-1	0-1/1-2	3-1	0-2/2-1	3-3	2-2/1-0	1-3	1-0/0-2		2-1/3-1	1-1/1-2	2-0/1-2
Partick	0-2/1-2	0-2/1-2	0-1/2-4/1-2	3-0/1-0	1-1/2-2	0-4	2-1/1-4	2-2/0-0	1-0		1-0	2-0
Ross County	2-0/2-3	1-4	5-2	2-1/0-3	2-0/2-1	1-2/0-3	1-2/0-3	3-2	3-0/1-3	1-0/1-0		2-3/0-1
St Johnstone	3-4/3-0	0-3/2-1	1-1	2-1/0-1	4-1/0-0	0-0	1-1/1-0	2-1	2-1/2-1	1-2/1-2	1-1/1-1	

*Patrick Roberts looks
a star in the making
on loan at Celtic Park*

AYR

Nickname: The Honest Men **Ground:** Somerset Park
Web: www.ayrunitedfc.co.uk

Ian McCall capped a fine turnaround from relegation scrappers in 2014-15 to League One runners-up 12 months later.

They won the playoff final on penalties, but on the last two occasions the part-timers went up they were relegated straight away.

	2015-16 H A	Last six seasons at home P W D L OV UN BS CS
Dundee United	- -	- - - - - - - -
Falkirk	2 1	1 0 1 1 1 1
Hibernian	- -	- - - - - - - -
Raith	2 1	1 0 1 1 2 0
Morton	4 1	2 1 0 4 1 2
St Mirren	- -	- - - - - - - -
Queen of Sth	4 1	1 2 2 2 3 1
Dumbarton	2 2	0 0 0 2 0 2
Dunfermline **L L W L**	6 0	1 5 2 4 3 0
Ayr		

Season	Division	Pos	P	W	D	L	F	A	GD	Pts
2015-16	League One	2	36	19	4	13	65	47	+18	61
2014-15	League One	8	36	9	7	20	45	60	-15	34
2013-14	League One	4	36	14	7	15	65	66	-1	49

Over/Under 69%/31% 1st **Both score** 56%/44% 6th

DUMBARTON

Nickname: The Sons **Ground:** Bet Butler Stadium
Web: www.dumbartonfootballclub.com

Eighth place was the height of Dumbarton's ambitions last term and they pulled it off.

Stevie Aitken's men took some hidings – hit for six by both Rangers and Queen of the South – but 14 points off the two teams below them kept the part-timers afloat.

	2015-16 H A	Last six seasons at home P W D L OV UN BS CS
Dundee United	- -	- - - - - - - -
Falkirk **L D L L**	8 2	2 4 3 5 3 1
Hibernian **W W L L**	4 2	0 2 4 0 4 0
Raith **D L L D**	8 2	3 3 8 0 8 0
Morton **L D D L**	6 2	1 3 4 2 3 2
St Mirren **W W W L**	2 2	0 0 1 1 1 1
Queen of Sth **L W L L**	6 1	1 4 3 3 1 1
Dumbarton		
Dunfermline	2 0	0 2 0 2 0 0
Ayr	2 1	0 1 2 0 2 0

Season	Division	Pos	P	W	D	L	F	A	GD	Pts
2015-16	Championship	8	36	10	7	19	35	66	-31	37
2014-15	Championship	7	36	9	7	20	36	79	-43	34
2013-14	Championship	5	36	15	6	15	65	64	+1	51

Over/Under 50%/50% 4th **Both score** 44%/56% 8th

DUNDEE UNITED

Nickname: The Terrors **Ground:** Tannadice Park
Web: www.dundeeunitedfc.co.uk

Despite having the third-highest budget in the top tier, United managed just eight wins.

Ray McKinnon became the club's third manager of the season when he replaced Mixu Paatelainen, and seven points from the final three games at least hinted at hope.

	2015-16 H A	Last six seasons at home P W D L OV UN BS CS
Dundee United	- -	- - - - - - - -
Falkirk	- -	- - - - - - - -
Hibernian	6 4	2 0 5 1 3 3
Raith	- -	- - - - - - - -
Morton	- -	- - - - - - - -
St Mirren	7 3	2 2 5 2 4 3
Queen of Sth	- -	- - - - - - - -
Dumbarton	- -	- - - - - - - -
Dunfermline	2 1	0 1 1 1 0 1
Ayr	- -	- - - - - - - -

Season	Division	Pos	P	W	D	L	F	A	GD	Pts
2015-16	Premiership	12	38	8	7	23	45	70	-25	28
2014-15	Premiership	5	38	17	5	16	58	56	+2	56
2013-14	Premiership	4	38	16	10	12	65	50	+15	58

Over/Under 66%/34% 2nd **Both score** 58%/42% 4th

DUNFERMLINE

Nickname: The Pars **Ground:** East End Park
Web: www.dafc.co.uk

Allan Johnston's reign at the Pars began with a 6-1 win at Brechin and a 7-1 hammering of Cowdenbeath, and they never let up.

They beat Dundee in the League Cup, lost just five league games all season and romped to League One glory by 18 points.

	2015-16 H A	Last six seasons at home P W D L OV UN BS CS
Dundee United	1 0	0 1 1 0 1 0
Falkirk	4 1	1 2 1 3 1 1
Hibernian	2 0	1 1 2 0 2 0
Raith	4 3	1 0 3 1 3 1
Morton	6 1	1 4 5 1 4 1
St Mirren	2 0	2 0 0 2 1 1
Queen of Sth	2 2	0 0 1 1 1 1
Dumbarton	2 1	0 1 2 0 1 1
Dunfermline		
Ayr **L W W W**	6 5	0 1 5 1 4 1

Season	Division	Pos	P	W	D	L	F	A	GD	Pts
2015-16	League One	1	36	24	7	5	83	30	+53	79
2014-15	League One	7	36	13	9	14	46	48	-2	48
2013-14	League One	2	36	19	6	11	68	54	+14	63

Over/Under 61%/39% 4th **Both score** 47%/53% 10th

FALKIRK

Nickname: The Bairns   **Ground:** Falkirk Stadium
Web: www.falkirkfc.co.uk

Falkirk surprised many by finishing between Rangers and Hibernian. Peter Houston's men lost only four league games – three of them to Gers and Hibs – and beat Hibernian in the playoffs. However, their promotion dreams died in the final against Kilmarnock.

	2015-16 H	A	Last six seasons at home P	W	D	L	OV	UN	BS	CS
Dundee United			-	-	-	-	-	-	-	-
Falkirk										
Hibernian	L D	D D	4	1	1	2	1	3	1	1
Raith	W D	W D	12	6	3	3	5	7	6	4
Morton	W W	D W	10	7	1	2	3	7	4	4
St Mirren	W W	W D	2	2	0	0	2	0	1	1
Queen of Sth	D W	D D	10	6	3	1	5	5	5	4
Dumbarton	W W	W D	8	3	2	3	5	3	6	2
Dunfermline			4	1	1	2	2	2	2	1
Ayr			2	1	1	0	1	1	1	1

Season	Division	Pos	P	W	D	L	F	A	GD	Pts
2015-16	Championship	2	36	19	13	4	61	34	+27	70
2014-15	Championship	5	36	14	11	11	48	48	0	53
2013-14	Championship	3	36	19	9	8	59	33	+26	66

Over/Under 50%/50% 4th   **Both score** 58%/42% 2nd

HIBERNIAN

Nickname: The Hibees   **Ground:** Easter Road
Web: www.hibernianfc.co.uk

Hibs blew promotion, finishing adrift of Rangers then losing to Falkirk in the playoffs.

But there was joy in the Scottish Cup and they beat Hearts, Inverness, Dundee United and Rangers en route to glory. Alan Stubbs left so Neil Lennon takes them into Europe.

	2015-16 H	A	Last six seasons at home P	W	D	L	OV	UN	BS	CS
Dundee United			6	1	3	2	4	2	5	0
Falkirk	D D	W D	4	0	3	1	2	2	3	0
Hibernian										
Raith	W W	W L	4	2	2	0	0	4	2	2
Morton	W L	W D	2	1	0	1	1	1	0	1
St Mirren	D W	W D	10	4	4	2	5	5	7	3
Queen of Sth	W W	W L	4	2	1	1	0	4	0	3
Dumbarton	W W	L L	4	3	1	0	3	1	1	3
Dunfermline			2	1	0	1	1	1	0	1
Ayr			-	-	-	-	-	-	-	-

Season	Division	Pos	P	W	D	L	F	A	GD	Pts
2015-16	Championship	3	36	21	7	8	59	34	+25	70
2014-15	Championship	2	36	21	7	8	70	32	+38	70
2013-14	Premiership	11	38	12	11	15	31	51	-20	35

Over/Under 53%/47% 2nd   **Both score** 47%/53% 5th

MORTON

Nickname: The Ton   **Ground:** Cappielow Park
Web: www.gmfc.net

Morton's return to the Championship started brightly with just one defeat in the first seven and a League Cup win over Motherwell.

But they won just five more games from mid-November, drifting into fifth without ever looking like challenging the top four.

	2015-16 H	A	Last six seasons at home P	W	D	L	OV	UN	BS	CS
Dundee United			-	-	-	-	-	-	-	-
Falkirk	D L	L W	10	2	5	3	3	7	5	3
Hibernian	L D	L W	2	0	1	1	0	2	0	1
Raith	L L	L L	10	2	4	4	2	8	4	4
Morton										
St Mirren	D L	D L	2	0	1	1	0	2	0	1
Queen of Sth	W W	D L	8	3	3	2	4	4	4	2
Dumbarton	D W	W D	8	3	3	0	5	3	3	3
Dunfermline			6	4	0	2	3	3	3	1
Ayr			4	3	0	1	3	1	3	0

Season	Division	Pos	P	W	D	L	F	A	GD	Pts
2015-16	Championship	5	36	11	10	15	39	42	-3	43
2014-15	League One	1	36	22	3	11	65	40	+25	69
2013-14	Championship	10	36	6	8	22	32	71	-39	26

Over/Under 42%/58% 9th   **Both score** 42%/58% 9th

QUEEN OF THE SOUTH

Nickname: Doonhamers **Ground:** Palmerston Park
Web: www.qosfc.com

After making the playoffs in 2014-15, last season was a major disappointment with the Doonhamers finishing seventh.

James Fowler was sacked in April as the side bowed out on a run of nine losses in 14. Gavin Skelton replaced him full-time in May.

	2015-16 H	A	Last six seasons at home P	W	D	L	OV	UN	BS	CS
Dundee United			-	-	-	-	-	-	-	-
Falkirk	D D	D L	10	3	3	4	6	4	5	4
Hibernian	L W	L L	4	2	0	2	1	3	0	2
Raith	D L	L L	10	4	1	5	4	6	5	3
Morton	D W	L L	8	6	1	1	5	3	4	4
St Mirren	L W	L L	2	1	0	1	0	2	0	1
Queen of Sth										
Dumbarton	W W	W L	6	5	0	1	5	1	3	3
Dunfermline			2	1	0	1	1	1	1	1
Ayr			4	4	0	0	2	2	2	2

Season	Division	Pos	P	W	D	L	F	A	GD	Pts
2015-16	Championship	7	36	12	6	18	46	56	-10	42
2014-15	Championship	4	36	17	9	10	58	41	+17	60
2013-14	Championship	4	36	16	7	13	53	39	+14	55

Over/Under 50%/50% 4th   **Both score** 47%/53% 5th

RAITH

Nickname: The Rovers **Ground:** Stark's Park
Web: www.raithrovers.net

No side finished stronger than Raith, who lost just one of their last 14 in the league.

But that failed to take them past Hibs and into the playoffs. Ray McKinnon, Raith's popular and successful boss, headed for Dundee United to be replaced by Gary Locke.

	2015-16 H	A	Last six seasons at home P	W	D	L	OV	UN	BS	CS
Dundee United			-	-	-	-	-	-	-	-
Falkirk	L D	L D	12	3	6	3	8	4	9	3
Hibernian	L W	L L	4	2	0	2	4	0	4	0
Raith										
Morton	W W	W W	10	7	3	0	8	2	8	2
St Mirren	D W	W W	2	1	1	0	1	1	2	0
Queen of Sth	W W	D W	10	6	0	4	5	5	4	3
Dumbarton	W D	D W	8	5	2	1	6	2	6	2
Dunfermline			4	2	1	1	2	2	3	1
Ayr			2	0	1	1	1	1	1	0

Season	Division	Pos	P	W	D	L	F	A	GD	Pts
2015-16	Championship	4	36	18	8	10	52	46	+6	62
2014-15	Championship	6	36	12	7	17	42	65	-23	43
2013-14	Championship	7	36	11	9	16	48	61	-13	42

Over/Under 53%/47% 2nd **Both score** 50%/50% 4th

ST MIRREN

Nickname: The Saints **Ground:** St Mirren Park
Web: www.saintmirren.net

The Buddies followed relegation from the top flight with a shocking start, winning just two of their first 16 league matches.

Ian Murray quit with his team in eighth place and was replaced by Alex Rae, who eventually hoisted St Mirren up to sixth.

	2015-16 H	A	Last six seasons at home P	W	D	L	OV	UN	BS	CS
Dundee United			8	1	5	2	3	5	5	1
Falkirk	L D	L L	2	0	1	1	1	1	1	1
Hibernian	L D	D L	10	3	2	5	4	6	4	4
Raith	L L	D L	2	0	0	2	2	0	2	0
Morton	D W	D W	2	1	1	0	1	1	2	0
St Mirren										
Queen of Sth	W W	W L	2	2	0	0	1	1	1	1
Dumbarton	L W	L L	2	1	0	1	1	1	1	1
Dunfermline			2	1	1	0	2	0	2	0
Ayr			-	-	-	-	-	-	-	-

Season	Division	Pos	P	W	D	L	F	A	GD	Pts
2015-16	Championship	6	36	11	9	16	44	53	-9	42
2014-15	Premiership	12	38	9	3	26	30	66	-36	30
2013-14	Premiership	8	38	10	9	19	39	58	-19	39

Over/Under 50%/50% 4th **Both score** 61%/39% 1st

Mark Warburton did the business in his first season at Ibrox

Scottish Championship results 2015-16

	Alloa	Dumbarton	Falkirk	Hibernian	Livingston	Morton	Queen of Sth	Raith	Rangers	St Mirren
Alloa		0-2/1-1	1-1/0-1	0-1/1-0	0-3/1-3	0-1/2-2	1-2/2-2	0-1/1-1	1-5/1-1	0-2/0-1
Dumbarton	0-2/3-1		0-5/1-1	2-1/3-2	2-1/1-0	1-2/0-0	0-2/4-2	3-3/2-3	1-2/0-6	1-0/2-1
Falkirk	5-0/2-0	2-1/1-0		0-1/1-1	2-0/1-2	1-0/1-0	0-0/3-1	1-0/2-2	2-1/3-2	3-0/3-2
Hibernian	3-0/3-0	4-2/4-0	1-1/2-2		2-1/2-1	1-0/0-3	1-0/2-0	2-0/1-0	2-1/3-2	1-1/3-1
Livingston	0-1/0-0	1-1/2-0	1-2/1-1	0-1/0-0		2-4/0-0	0-1/0-2	3-0/0-1	1-1/1-0	0-1/2-3
Morton	1-0/4-1	0-0/2-0	1-1/0-1	0-1/0-0	1-0/2-1		2-0/3-2	1-2/0-1	0-4/0-2	0-0/0-1
Queen of Sth	3-1/1-0	1-0/6-0	2-2/2-2	0-3/1-0	1-4/3-1	2-2/1-0		1-1/1-2	1-5/0-1	0-2/1-0
Raith	3-0/0-1	1-0/0-0	1-2/2-2	1-2/2-1	3-0/2-0	2-1/3-2	1-0/2-0		0-1/3-3	1-1/4-3
Rangers	4-0/1-1	4-0/1-0	3-1/1-0	1-0/4-2	3-0/4-1	2-2/3-1	2-1/4-3	5-0/2-0		3-1/1-0
St Mirren	1-1/3-1	1-2/1-0	2-3/0-0	1-4/2-2	1-1/1-4	1-1/3-1	1-0/2-1	1-2/1-2	0-1/2-2	

Scottish Championship 2015-16

Pos	H	A		P	Home W	Home D	Home L	Home F	Home A	Away W	Away D	Away L	Away F	Away A	GD	Pts
1	1	1	Rangers (P)	36	16	2	0	48	13	9	4	5	40	21	+54	81
2	3	2	Falkirk	36	13	3	2	33	13	6	10	2	28	21	+27	70
3	2	4	Hibernian	36	14	3	1	37	15	7	4	7	22	19	+25	70
4	4	3	Raith	36	10	4	4	31	19	8	4	6	21	27	+6	62
5	7	6	Morton	36	7	4	7	17	17	4	6	8	22	25	-3	43
6	8	5	St Mirren	36	5	6	7	24	28	6	3	9	20	25	-9	42
7	5	8	Queen of Sth	36	8	4	6	27	26	4	2	12	19	30	-10	42
8	6	10	Dumbarton	36	8	3	7	26	34	2	4	12	9	32	-31	37
9	9	7	Livingston (R)	36	3	6	9	14	19	5	1	12	23	32	-14	31
10	10	9	Alloa (R)	36	1	6	11	12	30	3	3	12	10	37	-45	21

Best attack

		GF	GFA
1	Rangers	88	2.44
2	Falkirk	61	1.69
3	Hibernian	59	1.64
4	Raith	52	1.44
5	Queen of Sth	46	1.28
6	St Mirren	44	1.22
7	Morton	39	1.08
8	Livingston	37	1.03
9	Dumbarton	35	0.97
10	Alloa	22	0.61

Best defence

		GA	GAA
1	Rangers	34	0.94
2	Falkirk	34	0.94
3	Hibernian	34	0.94
4	Morton	42	1.17
5	Raith	46	1.28
6	Livingston	51	1.42
7	St Mirren	53	1.47
8	Queen of Sth	56	1.56
9	Dumbarton	66	1.83
10	Alloa	67	1.86

Top scorers

	Team	Goals scored	
M Waghorn	Rangers	20	▌▌▌▌▌▌▌▌▌▌▌▌▌▌▌▌▌▌▌▌
J Cummings	Hibernian	18	▌▌▌▌▌▌▌▌▌▌▌▌▌▌▌▌▌▌
J Baird	Falkirk	17	▌▌▌▌▌▌▌▌▌▌▌▌▌▌▌▌▌
D Johnstone	Morton	14	▌▌▌▌▌▌▌▌▌▌▌▌▌▌
K Miller	Rangers	14	▌▌▌▌▌▌▌▌▌▌▌▌▌▌
D Lyle	Queen of Sth	13	▌▌▌▌▌▌▌▌▌▌▌▌▌

Key Points in all tables (except the league table) do not include any deductions imposed by the league. **POS H A** Position, home/away rank **Sup** Average supremacy **GFA/GAA** Goals For/ Against Average **PGA** Pts Gained Average

Record when first to score

		P	W	D	L	F	A	Sup	PGA	Pts
1	Rangers	25	22	2	1	68	15	+2.12	2.7	68
2	Dumbarton	10	9	0	1	22	11	+1.10	2.7	27
3	Hibernian	23	19	2	2	47	18	+1.26	2.6	59
4	Raith	21	15	5	1	40	20	+0.95	2.4	50
5	Falkirk	24	15	9	0	44	17	+1.13	2.3	54
6	Morton	14	10	2	2	27	13	+1.00	2.3	32
7	Queen of Sth	13	10	0	3	25	13	+0.92	2.3	30
8	Livingston	11	7	1	3	22	11	+1.00	2	22
9	St Mirren	18	10	5	3	27	19	+0.44	1.9	35
10	Alloa	11	4	5	2	13	11	+0.18	1.5	17

Record when keeping a clean sheet

		P	W	D	F	Sup	PGA	Pts
1	Rangers	15	15	0	37	+2.47	3	45
2	Raith	10	9	1	15	+1.5	2.8	28
3	Queen of Sth	10	9	1	16	+1.6	2.8	28
4	Hibernian	15	13	2	24	+1.6	2.7	41
5	Falkirk	13	11	2	23	+1.77	2.7	35
6	St Mirren	9	7	2	9	+1	2.6	23
7	Alloa	5	4	1	5	+1	2.6	13
8	Morton	11	6	5	10	+0.91	2.1	23
9	Livingston	7	4	3	9	+1.29	2.1	15
10	Dumbarton	6	3	3	4	+0.67	2	12

Over 2.5 goals

	H	A	%
Rangers	12	11	64%
Raith	10	9	53%
Hibernian	11	8	53%

Under 2.5 goals

	H	A	%
Alloa	12	9	58%
Morton	13	8	58%
Livingston	14	5	53%

Both to score

	H	A	%
St Mirren	14	8	61%
Falkirk	8	13	58%
Rangers	9	11	56%

Both not to score

	H	A	%
Alloa	9	6	58%
Morton	5	10	58%
Dumbarton	11	5	56%

AIRDRIEONIANS

Nickname: The Diamonds **Ground:** Excelsior Stadium
Web: www.airdriefc.com

The Diamonds' last year as a part-time club was traumatic. The promotion challenge never happened and manager Eddie Wolecki Black, appointed in September, suffered a stroke in March. Kevin McBride assumes control with the club going full-time.

	2015-16 H A	Last six seasons at home P W D L OV UN BS CS
Livingston		4 0 0 4 2 2 2 0
Alloa		2 0 0 2 0 2 0 0
Peterhead	W L L L	6 2 1 3 3 3 3 2
Stranraer	L D W L	6 1 4 1 2 4 5 0
Airdrieonians		
Albion	D D W W	4 2 2 0 1 3 2 2
Brechin	W L W D	10 5 3 2 6 4 7 2
Stenhousemuir	L D L L	10 4 3 3 4 6 5 2
East Fife		6 2 2 2 4 2 5 1
Queen's Park		- - - - - - - -

Season	Division	Pos	P	W	D	L	F	A	GD	Pts
2015-16	League One	5	36	14	7	15	48	50	-2	49
2014-15	League One	5	36	16	10	10	53	39	+14	58
2013-14	League One	6	36	12	9	15	47	57	-10	45

Over/Under 47%/53% 9th   **Both score** 50%/50% 9th

ALBION

Nickname: The Wee Rovers   **Ground:** Cliftonhill
Web: www.albionroversfc.com

In the playoff places at the end of February despite having been favourites to finish bottom, an eight-game winless streak saw Albion fall away. A lack of goals was the undoing of Darren Young's side – they were the division's lowest scorers with 40 goals.

	2015-16 H A	Last six seasons at home P W D L OV UN BS CS
Livingston		- - - - - - - -
Alloa		2 0 0 2 2 0 1 0
Peterhead	W D D L	4 1 2 1 1 3 2 2
Stranraer	L L W D	6 2 0 4 3 3 3 1
Airdrieonians	L L D D	4 1 0 3 3 1 3 0
Albion		
Brechin	W W W L	6 3 0 3 5 1 5 0
Stenhousemuir	W D W W	6 3 3 0 2 4 4 2
East Fife		6 1 2 3 3 3 3 1
Queen's Park		6 5 0 1 4 2 4 2

Season	Division	Pos	P	W	D	L	F	A	GD	Pts
2015-16	League One	6	36	13	10	13	40	44	-4	49
2014-15	League Two	1	36	22	5	9	61	33	+28	71
2013-14	League Two	7	36	12	8	16	41	54	-13	44

Over/Under 39%/61% 11th   **Both score** 53%/47% 8th

Almondvale hosts League One football for the first time since 2011

ALLOA

Nickname: The Wasps **Ground:** Recreation Park
Web: www.alloaathletic.co.uk

Relegated from the Championship with just four wins, one of which came against Hibs.

A terrible start saw Danny Lennon resign with Jack Ross overseeing the inevitable fall. Ross stays in charge of the Wasps, who finished a grim campaign unbeaten in five.

	2015-16 H A	P	W	D	L	OV	UN	BS	CS
Livingston	L L W D	8	2	2	4	6	2	4	2
Alloa									
Peterhead		4	2	2	0	3	1	3	1
Stranraer		4	4	0	0	3	1	2	2
Airdrieonians		2	1	0	1	1	1	1	1
Albion		2	2	0	0	2	0	2	0
Brechin		4	0	3	1	3	1	3	0
Stenhousemuir		4	2	0	2	1	3	1	2
East Fife		4	1	2	1	2	2	4	0
Queen's Park		2	2	0	0	1	1	0	2

Season	Division	Pos	P	W	D	L	F	A	GD	Pts
2015-16	Championship	10	36	4	9	23	22	67	-45	21
2014-15	Championship	9	36	6	9	21	34	56	-22	27
2013-14	Championship	8	36	11	7	18	34	51	-17	40

Over/Under 42%/58% 9th   **Both score** 42%/58% 9th

BRECHIN

Nickname: The City **Ground:** Glebe Park
Web: www.brechincity.com

Darren Dods' first term as a manager looked destined to end in relegation, with his team bottom of the section at the end of February.

Then came the great escape – eight wins in ten which earned Dods manager of the month plaudits and survival for his team.

	2015-16 H A	P	W	D	L	OV	UN	BS	CS
Livingston		2	1	0	1	1	1	1	1
Alloa		4	3	0	1	4	0	4	0
Peterhead	D W W L	6	3	3	0	4	2	6	0
Stranraer	W W L L	8	3	2	3	5	3	5	3
Airdrieonians	L D L W	10	2	6	2	5	5	9	1
Albion	L W L L	6	4	0	2	3	3	3	2
Brechin									
Stenhousemuir	L W D D	12	7	1	4	6	6	6	5
East Fife		8	4	0	4	6	2	4	3
Queen's Park		-	-	-	-	-	-	-	-

Season	Division	Pos	P	W	D	L	F	A	GD	Pts
2015-16	League One	7	36	12	6	18	47	59	-12	42
2014-15	League One	4	36	15	14	7	58	46	+12	59
2013-14	League One	8	36	12	6	18	57	71	-14	42

Over/Under 58%/42% 5th   **Both score** 58%/42% 2nd

EAST FIFE

Nickname: The Fifers **Ground:** Bayview Stadium
Web: www.eastfifefc.info

Sixth in League Two at Christmas after an unspectacular first half of the season, the Fifers came to life in the New Year.

Twelve wins in 16 matches from Boxing Day saw Gary Naysmith's men storm clear at the top and ensure a return to League One.

	2015-16 H A	P	W	D	L	OV	UN	BS	CS
Livingston		2	0	0	2	2	0	2	0
Alloa		4	3	0	1	3	1	3	0
Peterhead		2	2	0	0	2	0	2	0
Stranraer		4	0	2	2	1	3	3	0
Airdrieonians		6	3	2	1	1	5	1	4
Albion		6	3	1	2	2	4	2	4
Brechin		8	0	4	4	6	2	6	1
Stenhousemuir		8	3	2	3	5	3	6	2
East Fife									
Queen's Park	L D W L	4	0	3	1	1	3	2	1

Season	Division	Pos	P	W	D	L	F	A	GD	Pts
2015-16	League Two	1	36	18	8	10	62	41	+21	62
2014-15	League Two	4	36	15	8	13	56	48	+8	53
2013-14	League One	9	36	9	5	22	31	69	-38	32

Over/Under 42%/58% 9th   **Both score** 47%/53% 7th

LIVINGSTON

Nickname: Livi Lions **Ground:** Almondvale Stadium
Web: www.livingstonfc.co.uk

After five years in the second tier, Livingston dropped back down following an 8-6 aggregate defeat by Stranraer in the playoffs.

David Hopkin, who replaced Mark Burchill as head coach in December, couldn't save Livi, who are staying full-time this season.

	2015-16 H A	P	W	D	L	OV	UN	BS	CS
Livingston									
Alloa	L D W W	8	4	3	1	4	4	2	5
Peterhead		2	2	0	0	1	1	1	1
Stranraer		-	-	-	-	-	-	-	-
Airdrieonians		4	3	0	1	2	2	2	1
Albion		-	-	-	-	-	-	-	-
Brechin		2	1	1	0	0	2	0	2
Stenhousemuir		2	2	0	0	2	0	2	0
East Fife		2	1	1	0	1	1	2	0
Queen's Park		-	-	-	-	-	-	-	-

Season	Division	Pos	P	W	D	L	F	A	GD	Pts
2015-16	Championship	9	36	8	7	21	37	51	-14	31
2014-15	Championship	8	36	8	8	20	41	53	-12	32
2013-14	Championship	6	36	13	7	16	51	56	-5	46

Over/Under 47%/53% 8th   **Both score** 47%/53% 5th

PETERHEAD

Nickname: The Blue Toon   **Ground:** Balmoor Stadium
Web: www.peterheadfc.com

The manager of the month curse certainly struck Peterhead. Jim McInally won back-to-back prizes in January and February as a 19-match league unbeaten run unfolded.

But they ended with eight straight defeats, including a 6-2 playoff drubbing against Ayr.

	2015-16 H	A	Last six seasons at home P	W	D	L	OV	UN	BS	CS
Livingston	2	1	1	0	1	1	0	2		
Alloa	4	2	1	1	1	3	2	1		
Peterhead										
Stranraer	D D W W	6	0	3	3	3	3	5	1		
Airdrieonians	W W L W	6	3	1	2	2	4	3	2		
Albion	D W L D	4	2	2	0	1	3	3	1		
Brechin	L W D L	6	2	2	2	4	2	4	1		
Stenhousemuir	D W L W	6	3	2	1	4	2	3	2		
East Fife	2	0	1	1	1	1	1	0		
Queen's Park	6	4	1	1	2	4	3	2		

Season	Division	Pos	P	W	D	L	F	A	GD	Pts
2015-16	League One	3	36	16	11	9	72	47	+25	59
2014-15	League One	6	36	14	9	13	51	54	-3	51
2013-14	League One	1	36	23	7	6	74	38	+36	76

Over/Under 56%/44% 8th   **Both score** 58%/42% 2nd

QUEEN'S PARK

Nickname: The Spiders   **Ground:** Hampden Park
Web: www.queensparkfc.co.uk

After seven years in the basement, the Spiders went up the hard way – Gus McPherson's lads pinched the final playoff place on the final day before beating Cowdenbeath and Clyde in the playoffs. Twenty-three of their 36 league games produced two goals or less.

	2015-16 H	A	Last six seasons at home P	W	D	L	OV	UN	BS	CS
Livingston	-	-	-	-	-	-	-	-		
Alloa	2	0	0	2	2	0	2	0		
Peterhead	6	0	2	4	2	4	1	1		
Stranraer	4	2	1	1	3	1	3	1		
Airdrieonians	-	-	-	-	-	-	-	-		
Albion	6	2	1	3	2	4	2	1		
Brechin	-	-	-	-	-	-	-	-		
Stenhousemuir	-	-	-	-	-	-	-	-		
East Fife	L W W D	4	3	0	1	2	2	0	3		
Queen's Park										

Season	Division	Pos	P	W	D	L	F	A	GD	Pts
2015-16	League Two	4	36	15	11	10	46	32	+14	56
2014-15	League Two	2	36	17	10	9	51	34	+17	61
2013-14	League Two	10	36	5	9	22	36	68	-32	24

Over/Under 36%/64% 10th   **Both score** 47%/53% 7th

STENHOUSEMUIR

Nickname: Warriors   **Ground:** Ochilview Park
Web: www.stenhousemuirfc.com

The Warriors survived another flirtation with relegation, winning 3-1 at Cowdenbeath on the penultimate weekend to see them safe.

Brown Ferguson's side kept just four clean sheets all season and shipped 80 goals, the worst record in the section.

	2015-16 H	A	Last six seasons at home P	W	D	L	OV	UN	BS	CS
Livingston	2	0	0	2	2	0	1	0		
Alloa	4	0	1	3	1	3	2	0		
Peterhead	W L D L	6	4	0	2	6	0	6	0		
Stranraer	W L W L	8	3	3	2	3	5	4	4		
Airdrieonians	W W W D	10	4	2	4	5	5	6	2		
Albion	L L L D	6	2	0	4	3	3	2	2		
Brechin	D D W L	12	4	6	2	8	4	9	2		
Stenhousemuir										
East Fife	8	4	3	1	3	5	5	2		
Queen's Park	-	-	-	-	-	-	-	-		

Season	Division	Pos	P	W	D	L	F	A	GD	Pts
2015-16	League One	8	36	11	7	18	46	80	-34	40
2014-15	League One	9	36	8	5	23	42	63	-21	29
2013-14	League One	5	36	12	12	12	57	66	-9	48

Over/Under 69%/31% 1st   **Both score** 64%/36% 1st

STRANRAER

Nickname: The Blues   **Ground:** Stair Park
Web: www.stranraerfc.org

The 5-1 second favourites for promotion failed to score in six of their first 11 games and were bottom at Christmas.

Brian Reid's men eventually came fourth and pipped Livingston in extra-time of their playoff semi, only to lose to Ayr on penalties.

	2015-16 H	A	Last six seasons at home P	W	D	L	OV	UN	BS	CS
Livingston	-	-	-	-	-	-	-	-		
Alloa	4	1	0	3	4	0	3	0		
Peterhead	L L D D	6	3	0	3	5	1	2	2		
Stranraer										
Airdrieonians	L W W D	6	4	1	1	3	3	3	3		
Albion	L D W W	6	2	2	2	3	3	4	1		
Brechin	W W L L	8	4	1	3	4	4	3	3		
Stenhousemuir	L W L W	8	3	3	2	3	5	6	1		
East Fife	4	3	0	1	2	2	2	2		
Queen's Park	4	2	0	2	3	1	3	1		

Season	Division	Pos	P	W	D	L	F	A	GD	Pts
2015-16	League One	4	36	15	6	15	43	49	-6	51
2014-15	League One	2	36	20	7	9	59	38	+21	67
2013-14	League One	3	36	14	9	13	57	57	0	51

Over/Under 47%/53% 9th   **Both score** 44%/56% 11th

Scottish League One results 2015-16

	Airdrieonians	Albion	Ayr	Brechin	Cowdenbeath	Dunfermline	Forfar	Peterhead	Stenhousemuir	Stranraer
Airdrieonians		1-1/1-1	1-2/0-1	1-0/0-2	3-2/2-0	0-2/3-0	0-1/1-1	1-0/3-4	0-1/1-1	0-1/1-1
Albion	1-3/1-2		3-0/1-3	3-1/4-1	2-1/0-0	1-1/0-1	1-1/3-2	1-0/1-1	2-0/1-1	0-2/0-1
Ayr	3-0/0-3	1-0/0-1		2-1/2-1	5-0/4-1	1-2/0-2	2-2/2-1	1-1/1-2	5-2/4-1	3-1/2-1
Brechin	1-2/3-3	0-1/2-1	1-1/1-0		2-0/2-2	1-6/1-2	0-2/4-0	1-1/5-1	1-2/1-0	2-0/1-0
Cowdenbeath	3-0/1-3	1-0/1-2	4-2/1-0	3-0/2-1		0-0/0-1	2-1/1-4	2-2/2-3	2-2/1-3	1-2/0-2
Dunfermline	1-1/0-1	3-0/1-1	0-2/3-2	3-1/3-1	7-1/2-1		4-0/2-2	0-0/1-0	1-0/5-0	3-1/6-1
Forfar	2-3/0-2	4-0/1-0	2-2/3-1	0-1/1-2	0-1/1-1	0-4/2-4		0-2/2-0	4-1/0-1	1-2/1-1
Peterhead	2-0/1-0	1-1/5-1	3-0/0-4	2-3/4-1	7-0/0-1	2-1/0-0	2-2/3-2		2-2/4-1	1-1/0-0
Stenhousemuir	2-1/3-2	0-1/1-3	0-1/0-4	2-2/0-0	4-2/2-3	0-5/0-3	2-2/2-1	4-3/1-4		1-0/1-5
Stranraer	1-3/4-0	0-1/0-0	1-2/1-0	1-0/2-0	0-3/1-0	0-3/4-1	0-0/1-0	0-4/1-5	1-2/3-1	

Scottish League One 2015-16

Pos	H	A		P	Home W	D	L	F	A	Away W	D	L	F	A	GD	Pts
1	1	1	Dunfermline (P)	36	12	4	2	45	15	12	3	3	38	15	+53	79
2	2	4	Ayr (P)	36	11	2	5	38	22	8	2	8	27	25	+18	61
3	3	3	Peterhead	36	9	6	3	39	20	7	5	6	33	27	+25	59
4	6	5	Stranraer	36	8	2	8	21	25	7	4	7	22	24	-6	51
5	9	2	Airdrieonians	36	5	5	8	19	21	9	2	7	29	29	-2	49
6	5	6	Albion	36	7	5	6	25	21	6	5	7	15	23	-4	49
7	4	10	Brechin	36	8	4	6	29	24	4	2	12	18	35	-12	42
8	8	7	Stenhousemuir	36	6	3	9	25	42	5	4	9	21	38	-34	40
9	7	9	Cowdenbeath (R)	36	7	3	8	27	28	4	3	11	19	44	-26	39
10	10	8	Forfar (R)	36	5	3	10	24	28	3	7	8	24	32	-12	34

Best attack

		GF	GFA
1	Dunfermline	83	2.31
2	Peterhead	72	2
3	Ayr	65	1.81
4	Airdrieonians	48	1.33
5	Forfar	48	1.33
6	Brechin	47	1.31
7	Stenhousemuir	46	1.28
8	Cowdenbeath	46	1.28
9	Stranraer	43	1.19
10	Albion	40	1.11

Best defence

		GA	GAA
1	Dunfermline	30	0.83
2	Albion	44	1.22
3	Ayr	47	1.31
4	Peterhead	47	1.31
5	Stranraer	49	1.36
6	Airdrieonians	50	1.39
7	Brechin	59	1.64
8	Forfar	60	1.67
9	Cowdenbeath	72	2
10	Stenhousemuir	80	2.22

Top scorers

	Team	Goals scored	
F El Bakhtaoui	Dunfermline	22	IIIIIIIIIIIIIIIIIIIIIII
R McAllister	Peterhead	22	IIIIIIIIIIIIIIIIIIIIIII
G Spence	Cowdenbeath	17	IIIIIIIIIIIIIIIII
R Thomson	Brechin	15	IIIIIIIIIIIIIII
J Cardle	Dunfermline	14	IIIIIIIIIIIIII
C Moore	Ayr	14	IIIIIIIIIIIIII

Key POS H A Overall league position, rank from home games, rank from away games **Sup** Avg match supremacy **GFA** Goals For Avg **GAA** Goals Against Avg **PGA** Points Gained Avg

Record when first to score

		P	W	D	L	F	A	Sup	PGA	Pts
1	Brechin	11	11	0	0	24	4	+1.82	3	33
2	Dunfermline	26	23	2	1	76	17	+2.27	2.7	71
3	Stranraer	16	13	3	0	26	6	+1.25	2.6	42
4	Ayr	22	18	2	2	56	21	+1.59	2.5	56
5	Peterhead	19	14	4	1	55	20	+1.84	2.4	46
6	Albion	16	11	2	3	27	15	+0.75	2.2	35
7	Stenhousemuir	13	8	4	1	22	17	+0.38	2.2	28
8	Airdrieonians	20	13	4	3	42	23	+0.95	2.1	43
9	Cowdenbeath	15	10	2	3	26	17	+0.60	2.1	32
10	Forfar	14	7	6	1	29	15	+1.00	1.9	27

Record when keeping a clean sheet

		P	W	D	F	Sup	PGA	Pts
1	Ayr	8	8	0	21	+2.63	3	24
2	Airdrieonians	7	7	0	13	+1.86	3	21
3	Brechin	9	8	1	14	+1.56	2.8	25
4	Forfar	6	5	1	10	+1.67	2.7	16
5	Dunfermline	16	13	3	35	+2.19	2.6	42
6	Albion	9	7	2	10	+1.11	2.6	23
7	Cowdenbeath	9	7	2	13	+1.44	2.6	23
8	Stranraer	13	10	3	16	+1.23	2.5	33
9	Stenhousemuir	4	3	1	3	+0.75	2.5	10
10	Peterhead	9	6	3	19	+2.11	2.3	21

Over 2.5 goals

	H	A	%
Ayr	14	11	69%
Stenhousemuir	14	11	69%
Cowdenbeath	13	11	67%

Under 2.5 goals

	H	A	%
Albion		10	12	61%
Stranraer	8	11	53%
Airdrieonians	14	5	53%

Both to score

	H	A	%
Stenhousemuir	11	12	64%
Brechin, Forfar,			
Peterhead			58%

Both not to score

	H	A	%
Stranraer	6	10	56%
Dunfermline	10	7	53%
Airdrieonians	8	10	50%

ANNAN

Nickname: Galabankies   **Ground:** Galabank
Web: www.annanathleticfc.com

Games involving the League Two top scorers averaged 3.5 goals and they didn't feature in a single 0-0 draw. Thumping Hamilton 4-1 in the cup was a highlight, but they needed to beat Queen's Park by two goals on the last day to make the playoffs and won only 1-0.

	2015-16 H	A	P	W	D	L	OV	UN	BS	CS
			Last six seasons at home							
Cowdenbeath			-	-	-	-	-	-	-	-
Forfar			-	-	-	-	-	-	-	-
Elgin	D W	L D	12	4	6	2	6	6	9	2
Clyde	L D	L L	12	4	1	7	5	7	5	3
Annan										
Berwick	W W	W L	12	7	4	1	7	5	8	4
Stirling	D D	L L	6	1	3	2	4	2	5	0
Montrose	W D	D W	12	7	4	1	10	2	11	1
Arbroath	D W	W L	6	3	1	2	4	2	3	2
Edinburgh City										

Season	Division	Pos	P	W	D	L	F	A	GD	Pts
2015-16	League Two	5	36	16	8	12	69	57	+12	56
2014-15	League Two	5	36	14	8	14	56	56	0	50
2013-14	League Two	2	36	19	6	11	69	49	+20	63

Over/Under 64%/36% 2nd   **Both score** 69%/31% 1st

ARBROATH

Nickname: The Red Lichties   **Ground:** Gayfield Park
Web: www.arbroathfc.co.uk

Just four points off the playoffs at the end of January, the season quickly deteriorated.

A run of five matches without scoring cost Todd Lumsden his job, with Dick Campbell replacing him. Arbroath won just two of their final 15 matches to finish ninth.

	2015-16 H	A	P	W	D	L	OV	UN	BS	CS
			Last six seasons at home							
Cowdenbeath			2	0	2	0	0	2	2	0
Forfar			6	3	1	2	4	2	4	1
Elgin	L L	L L	6	2	1	3	4	2	3	2
Clyde	L L	W W	6	4	0	2	3	3	2	2
Annan	L W	D L	6	3	1	2	3	3	4	0
Berwick	W L	D L	6	5	0	1	5	1	4	2
Stirling	W D	L L	4	3	1	0	1	3	2	2
Montrose	W D	L W	6	4	2	0	5	1	4	2
Arbroath										
Edinburgh City										

Season	Division	Pos	P	W	D	L	F	A	GD	Pts
2015-16	League Two	9	36	11	6	19	42	51	-9	39
2014-15	League Two	3	36	16	8	12	65	46	+19	56
2013-14	League One	10	36	9	4	23	52	75	-23	31

Over/Under 56%/44% 4th   **Both score** 44%/56% 10th

BERWICK

Nickname: The Borderers   **Ground:** Shielfield Park
Web: www.berwickrangersfc.co.uk

The season began poorly and, after back-to-back 4-1 hidings at Annan and Montrose in October, Colin Cameron was fired. John Coughlin struggled to arrest the slide and they were soon bottom. Finished strongly with just two losses in 12 to finish sixth.

	2015-16 H	A	P	W	D	L	OV	UN	BS	CS
			Last six seasons at home							
Cowdenbeath			-	-	-	-	-	-	-	-
Forfar			-	-	-	-	-	-	-	-
Elgin	L W	L L	12	4	4	4	7	5	8	3
Clyde	L W	D L	12	6	3	3	8	4	4	5
Annan	L W	L L	12	4	2	6	8	4	8	1
Berwick										
Stirling	L W	W L	6	4	1	1	3	3	3	3
Montrose	W W	L L	12	5	4	3	8	4	7	4
Arbroath	D W	L W	6	3	1	2	6	0	4	1
Edinburgh City										

Season	Division	Pos	P	W	D	L	F	A	GD	Pts
2015-16	League Two	6	36	14	7	15	45	50	-5	49
2014-15	League Two	8	36	11	10	15	60	57	+3	43
2013-14	League Two	6	36	15	7	14	63	49	+14	52

Over/Under 53%/47% 5th   **Both score** 47%/53% 7th

CLYDE

Nickname: The Bully Wee   **Ground:** Broadwood
Web: www.clydefc.co.uk

Barry Ferguson's 3-1 pre-season favourites made hard work of things and were seventh at the end of February, but a run of seven wins in nine nudged them into the top four.

They beat Elgin in the semis but suffered a 3-2 two-legged playoff loss to Queen's Park.

	2015-16 H	A	P	W	D	L	OV	UN	BS	CS
			Last six seasons at home							
Cowdenbeath			-	-	-	-	-	-	-	-
Forfar			-	-	-	-	-	-	-	-
Elgin	W W	D L	12	5	4	3	7	5	8	2
Clyde										
Annan	W W	W D	12	5	3	4	6	6	7	2
Berwick	D W	W L	12	5	4	3	9	3	9	2
Stirling	L W	W W	6	4	0	2	4	2	4	1
Montrose	W D	L L	12	5	3	4	6	6	7	4
Arbroath	L L	W W	6	0	2	4	3	3	4	0
Edinburgh City										

Season	Division	Pos	P	W	D	L	F	A	GD	Pts
2015-16	League Two	3	36	17	6	13	56	45	+11	57
2014-15	League Two	6	36	13	8	15	40	50	-10	47
2013-14	League Two	3	36	17	6	13	50	48	+2	57

Over/Under 50%/50% 6th   **Both score** 50%/50% 5th

COWDENBEATH

Nickname: The Blue Brazil **Ground:** Central Park
Web: www.cowdenbeathfc.com

The wheels came off in the second half of the season as just one win in Cowdenbeath's first 11 games of 2016 saw them slip towards a playoff which they lost against Queen's Park.

Back-to-back relegations saw Colin Nish axed and Liam Fox arrive.

	2015-16 H A	Last six seasons at home P W D L OV UN BS CS
Cowdenbeath		
Forfar	W L W D	4 3 0 1 3 1 3 1
Elgin		- - - - - - - -
Clyde		- - - - - - - -
Annan		- - - - - - - -
Berwick		- - - - - - - -
Stirling		4 4 0 0 2 2 2 2
Montrose		- - - - - - - -
Arbroath		2 0 1 1 1 1 1 1
Edinburgh City		

Season	Division	Pos	P	W	D	L	F	A	GD	Pts
2015-16	League One	9	36	11	6	19	46	72	-26	39
2014-15	Championship	10	36	7	4	25	31	86	-55	25
2013-14	Championship	9	36	11	7	18	50	72	-22	40

Over/Under 67%/33% 3rd   **Both score** 56%/44% 6th

EDINBURGH CITY

Nickname: City **Ground:** Meadowbank Stadium
Web: www.edinburghcityfc.com

Twelve months after losing to Brora in the playoffs, Edinburgh got it right last term.

After a near-faultless Lowland League season – won by 15 points – Gary Jardine's side beat Cove Rangers and then East Stirling to earn their spot in League Two.

	2015-16 H A	Last six seasons at home P W D L OV UN BS CS
Cowdenbeath		- - - - - - - -
Forfar		- - - - - - - -
Elgin		- - - - - - - -
Clyde		- - - - - - - -
Annan		- - - - - - - -
Berwick		- - - - - - - -
Stirling		- - - - - - - -
Montrose		- - - - - - - -
Arbroath		- - - - - - - -
Edinburgh City		

Season	Division	Pos	P	W	D	L	F	A	GD	Pts
2015-16	Lowland Lg	1	28	24	1	3	74	28	46	73
2014-15	Lowland Lg	1	26	22	3	1	65	14	51	69
2013-14	Lowland Lg	5	22	12	1	9	49	32	17	37

Over/Under 82%/18%   **Both score** 64%/36%

ELGIN

Nickname: Black & Whites **Ground:** Borough Briggs
Web: www.elgincity.com

Elgin were dreaming of a first-ever league promotion when they hit the top in March.

However, two points from their next six matches saw them drop back into the pack and eventually finish second. Jim Weir's men were beaten by Clyde in the playoffs.

	2015-16 H A	Last six seasons at home P W D L OV UN BS CS
Cowdenbeath		- - - - - - - -
Forfar		- - - - - - - -
Elgin		
Clyde	D W L L	12 7 2 3 4 8 5 4
Annan	W D D L	12 4 3 5 10 2 9 3
Berwick	W W W L	12 8 1 3 10 2 9 3
Stirling	W W L D	6 4 0 2 5 1 4 2
Montrose	W D L L	12 8 2 2 8 4 8 3
Arbroath	W W W W	6 4 1 1 4 2 5 1
Edinburgh City		

Season	Division	Pos	P	W	D	L	F	A	GD	Pts
2015-16	League Two	2	36	17	8	11	59	46	+13	59
2014-15	League Two	7	36	12	9	15	55	58	-3	45
2013-14	League Two	9	36	9	9	18	62	73	-11	36

Over/Under 50%/50% 6th   **Both score** 53%/47% 4th

FORFAR

Nickname: The Loons **Ground:** Station Park
Web: www.forfarathletic.co.uk

In the League One promotion playoffs in 2014-15, Forfar began where they left off, winning their first three games of the season.

But that was as good as it got for Gary Bollan's men, who won only five more games all season and finished bottom of the table.

	2015-16 H A	Last six seasons at home P W D L OV UN BS CS
Cowdenbeath	L D L W	4 1 2 1 1 3 2 1
Forfar		
Elgin		- - - - - - - -
Clyde		- - - - - - - -
Annan		- - - - - - - -
Berwick		- - - - - - - -
Stirling		4 3 1 0 4 0 3 1
Montrose		- - - - - - - -
Arbroath		6 0 3 3 2 4 5 0
Edinburgh City		

Season	Division	Pos	P	W	D	L	F	A	GD	Pts
2015-16	League One	10	36	8	10	18	48	60	-12	34
2014-15	League One	3	36	20	6	10	59	41	+18	66
2013-14	League One	7	36	12	7	17	55	62	-7	43

Over/Under 58%/42% 5th   **Both score** 58%/42% 2nd

MONTROSE

Nickname: The Gable Endies   **Ground:** Links Park
Web: www.montrosefc.co.uk

Having finished bottom by ten points a year earlier, many had tipped Montrose to fall.

But six wins in their first ten gave Paul Hegarty's side a platform and despite the odd blip – hit for six by Queen's Park and seven by Stirling – they survived comfortably.

	2015-16		Last six seasons at home							
	H	A	P	W	D	L	OV	UN	BS	CS
Cowdenbeath	-	-	-	-	-	-	-	-		
Forfar	-	-	-	-	-	-	-	-		
Elgin	W W	L D	12	6	2	4	9	3	7	3
Clyde	W W	L D	12	6	1	5	7	5	5	3
Annan	D L	L D	12	4	4	4	5	7	7	2
Berwick	W W	L L	12	4	5	3	5	7	9	2
Stirling	L D	L L	6	1	3	2	4	2	5	1
Montrose										
Arbroath	W L	L D	6	3	0	3	5	1	1	3
Edinburgh City										

Season	Division	Pos	P	W	D	L	F	A	GD	Pts
2015-16	League Two	8	36	11	10	15	50	70	-20	43
2014-15	League Two	10	36	9	6	21	42	78	-36	33
2013-14	League Two	6	36	12	10	14	44	56	-12	46

Over/Under 58%/42% 3rd   **Both score** 64%/36% 2nd

STIRLING

Nickname: The Binos **Ground:** Forthbank Stadium
Web: www.stirlingalbionfc.co.uk

Looking to bounce back after relegation, the Binos knew it would be tough after winning just two of their first nine matches.

Five wins in six before Christmas got them back in touch but Stuart McLaren's men lacked consistency and finished in seventh.

	2015-16		Last six seasons at home							
	H	A	P	W	D	L	OV	UN	BS	CS
Cowdenbeath			4	0	1	3	2	2	3	0
Forfar			4	0	2	2	3	1	3	0
Elgin	W D	L L	6	1	4	1	3	3	5	1
Clyde	L L	W L	6	2	1	3	2	4	3	1
Annan	W W	D D	6	4	1	1	3	3	4	1
Berwick	L W	W L	6	5	0	1	5	1	5	1
Stirling										
Montrose	W W	W D	6	4	1	1	5	1	4	2
Arbroath	W W	L D	4	2	1	1	1	3	2	1
Edinburgh City										

Season	Division	Pos	P	W	D	L	F	A	GD	Pts
2015-16	League Two	7	36	13	9	14	47	46	+1	48
2014-15	League One	10	36	4	8	24	35	84	-49	20
2013-14	League Two	3	36	16	10	10	60	50	+10	58

Over/Under 50%/50% 6th   **Both score** 56%/44% 3rd

East Fife's Bayview welcomes League One football in 2016-17

Scottish League Two results 2015-16

	Annan	Arbroath	Berwick	Clyde	East Fife	East Stirling	Elgin	Montrose	Queens Park	Stirling
Annan		2-2/4-1	1-0/1-0	2-3/3-3	2-0/2-4	3-1/1-3	1-1/4-2	3-2/3-3	3-1/1-0	1-1/2-2
Arbroath	0-2/2-1		3-1/1-2	0-1/0-1	1-1/0-1	0-0/3-0	0-3/2-3	3-1/0-0	1-2/0-1	2-0/1-1
Berwick	0-2/3-2	2-2/3-0		0-5/3-0	1-1/2-0	2-1/2-2	2-3/2-0	2-1/1-0	1-0/1-1	1-2/1-0
Clyde	4-2/2-1	0-2/1-2	1-1/2-1		2-0/0-0	3-1/0-1	4-2/1-0	3-1/3-3	0-2/0-1	0-1/3-1
East Fife	0-1/4-2	0-1/2-1	5-0/1-0	1-0/2-0		5-3/1-1	2-1/0-2	1-1/3-0	0-2/1-1	1-1/1-0
East Stirling	3-1/0-1	0-4/0-3	0-4/0-0	0-3/2-4	1-0/1-3		2-0/0-3	3-1/2-4	2-1/0-3	2-3/3-2
Elgin	3-2/2-2	2-0/4-1	4-1/1-0	1-1/1-0	4-2/1-3	4-0/2-0		2-0/1-1	0-0/1-1	1-0/2-1
Montrose	1-1/0-5	3-0/0-2	4-1/1-0	2-0/2-1	1-4/2-2	2-1/3-2	2-0/3-1		1-6/1-1	1-3/1-1
Queens Park	0-1/1-3	1-0/2-1	0-1/0-0	1-1/2-1	0-2/3-0	5-1/0-3	3-1/0-0	0-1/1-1		1-0/1-1
Stirling	1-0/2-1	3-1/1-0	1-3/2-1	0-1/1-2	1-3/0-6	0-0/3-0	3-1/0-0	1-0/7-0	1-2/0-0	

Scottish League Two 2015-16

Pos	H	A		P	W	D	L	F	A	W	D	L	F	A	GD	Pts
					Home					Away						
1	2	2	East Fife (P)	36	10	4	4	30	17	8	4	6	32	24	+21	62
2	1	7	Elgin City	36	12	5	1	36	15	5	3	10	23	31	+13	59
3	6	3	Clyde	36	9	3	6	29	22	8	3	7	27	23	+11	57
4	8	1	Queen's Park (P)	36	7	5	6	21	18	8	6	4	25	14	+14	56
5	4	4	Annan	36	9	6	3	39	29	7	2	9	30	28	+12	56
6	3	8	Berwick	36	10	4	4	29	22	4	3	11	16	28	-5	49
7	7	6	Stirling	36	9	3	6	27	21	4	6	8	20	25	+1	48
8	5	10	Montrose	36	9	4	5	30	31	2	6	10	20	39	-20	43
9	9	5	Arbroath	36	5	4	9	19	21	6	2	10	23	30	-9	39
10	10	9	East Stirling (R)	36	6	1	11	21	40	3	4	11	20	39	-38	32

Best attack

		GF	GFA
1	Annan	69	1.92
2	East Fife	62	1.72
3	Elgin City	59	1.64
4	Clyde	56	1.56
5	Montrose	50	1.39
6	Stirling	47	1.31
7	Queen's Park	46	1.28
8	Berwick	45	1.25
9	Arbroath	42	1.17
10	East Stirling	41	1.14

Best defence

		GA	GAA
1	Queen's Park	32	0.89
2	East Fife	41	1.14
3	Clyde	45	1.25
4	Elgin City	46	1.28
5	Stirling	46	1.28
6	Berwick	50	1.39
7	Arbroath	51	1.42
8	Annan	57	1.58
9	Montrose	70	1.94
10	East Stirling	79	2.19

Top scorers

	Team	Goals scored	
N Austin	East Fife	22	‖‖‖‖‖‖‖‖‖‖‖‖‖‖‖‖‖‖‖‖‖‖
C Gunn	Elgin	21	‖‖‖‖‖‖‖‖‖‖‖‖‖‖‖‖‖‖‖‖‖
G Fraser	Montrose	19	‖‖‖‖‖‖‖‖‖‖‖‖‖‖‖‖‖‖‖
B Henderson	Berwick	17	‖‖‖‖‖‖‖‖‖‖‖‖‖‖‖‖‖
P Weatherson	Annan	15	‖‖‖‖‖‖‖‖‖‖‖‖‖‖‖
J Todd	Annan	13	‖‖‖‖‖‖‖‖‖‖‖‖‖

Key POS H A Overall league position, rank from home games, rank from away games **Sup** Avg match supremacy **GFA** Goals For Avg **GAA** Goals Against Avg **PGA** Points Gained Avg

Record when first to score

		P	W	D	L	F	A	Sup	PGA	Pts
1	Queen's Park	17	14	3	0	33	9	+1.41	2.6	45
2	Elgin City	20	16	3	1	45	15	+1.50	2.5	51
3	East Fife	20	15	0	5	54	18	+1.80	2.5	50
4	Clyde	19	15	2	2	41	17	+1.26	2.5	47
5	Stirling	12	10	0	2	26	10	+1.33	2.5	30
6	Annan	24	16	7	1	50	23	+1.13	2.3	55
7	Arbroath	12	9	1	2	25	9	+1.33	2.3	28
8	Berwick	18	12	3	3	32	16	+0.89	2.2	39
9	Montrose	15	9	4	2	32	23	+0.60	2.1	31
10	East Stirling	13	8	1	4	24	15	+0.69	1.9	25

Record when keeping a clean sheet

		P	W	D	F	Sup	PGA	Pts
1	Annan	10	10	0	17	+1.7	3	30
2	East Fife	10	9	1	22	+2.2	2.8	28
3	Clyde	8	7	1	14	+1.75	2.8	22
4	Montrose	6	5	1	9	+1.5	2.7	16
5	Berwick	11	9	2	18	+1.64	2.6	29
6	Arbroath	9	7	2	17	+1.89	2.6	23
7	Elgin City	13	10	3	21	+1.62	2.5	33
8	Queen's Park	12	8	4	14	+1.17	2.3	28
9	Stirling	9	6	3	14	+1.56	2.3	21
10	East Stirling	7	4	3	7	+1	2.1	15

Over 2.5 goals

	H	A	%
East Stirling	14	13	75%
Annan	12	11	64%
Montrose	11	10	58%

Under 2.5 goals

	H	A	%
Queen's Park	11	12	64%
East Fife	12	9	58%
Clyde, Stirling, Elgin			50%

Both to score

	H	A	%
Annan	14	11	69%
Montrose	12	11	64%
Stirling	8	12	56%

Both not to score

	H	A	%
Arbroath	8	8	56%
Berwick, East Fife,			
Queens Park			53%

A world of ever-decreasing margins still offers up a wealth of profitable punts

The factors that determine a market are diverse, writes Alex Deacon. Consequently, as those factors become more complex to determine, the accuracy of the odds swing wildly between being impressively accurate and totally ill-considered. But in this rapidly maturing area we have seen how the ever-growing range of match-related markets are compiled from established, well-oiled and highly profitable algorithms.

The price differences that we would have seen on a coupon ten to 20 years ago are now replaced with computerised uniformity, and any price ricks are inevitably small and largely insignificant. This is dismal from a value betting perspective and depressing for the vast majority of punters.

Thankfully there remains fertile betting territory in the outright markets. It is these markets that I am taking to task and profiting from every week throughout the season and not least when the outright markets are as unpredictable as they have been over the past few seasons.

There can be no logic behind the fact that immediately after Leicester romped to the 2015-16 title by little short of a country mile, the prices for them to repeat the feat in 2016-17 saw them considered as three times less likely to do so than Arsenal, the team they beat into second place. That's not to say that Leicester are my tip for this season's title more an observation that it is patently absurd that, on the basis of zero change in the real life situation, Leicester should be taken so lightly in the current markets.

For me, the interesting question is not whether Leicester can put up a fight this term, it is a wider question as to whether we can expect the division to continue opening up as it has been for the past couple of seasons or whether it will revert to the closed

shop of the previous decade or so.

On the evidence available there is no sign of the latter occurring – in fact, quite the opposite is true.

Putting Leicester to one side for a moment to consider the division as a whole, I believe the competitiveness of the league is going to continue on its current trajectory with an increasingly competitive English top flight. The sheer amount of cash sloshing around renders the previous advantages of club size and scale increasingly irrelevant given the sums involved. Any club can, in theory, afford pretty much any player. And the idea of the big club is, for the moment at least, largely meaningless.

Therefore, for a trader such as myself, it's a joy to see an absurd situation arise whereby Arsenal, Man City, Man United and Chelsea are all priced shorter than 4-6 for a top-four finish in the Premier League. Given the obvious competitiveness of England's top tier, these prices are clearly out of kilter with any sensible view of the market.

Shrewd bettors should look forward to another season of opposing – and profiting from – what increasingly looks a redundant view of the current footballing landscape.

You can follow me and my unique outright market forecasts throughout the season on Twitter at @rfoindex

About the Outlook Index

Our unique ratings provide an objective view of every club. Each team has a rating, roughly on a scale of 0 to 1,000, which goes up or down with league results and takes into account the relative strength of the opposition. The tables show each team's overall rating, plus ratings for home and away form (a separate ratings system) and a Trend rating (-20 to +20). The Last 40 column shows the change, in graphical form, over the last 40 league matches – approximately a season's worth of games running chronologically from left to right, with the scale relative to each individual team's highest and lowest ratings during that time – while the red and blue bars show the Trend value, based on the last 60 matches but weighted towards more recent games, to help identify the teams in form. Red is hot, blue is not. The tables show final ratings for 2015-16.

Premier League

	Current	Last 40	H	A	Trend	
Leicester	953		936	915		3
Arsenal	939		956	931		-2
Man Utd	936		960	903		4
Man City	930		969	918		-4
Tottenham	930		933	934		-6
Southampton	929		928	899		12
Chelsea	926		960	930		0
Liverpool	924		940	914		0
West Ham	922		919	887		4
Swansea	906		908	876		10
Stoke	896		910	876		-5
Sunderland	895		886	875		11
Everton	889		897	884		-5
West Brom	888		880	870		-3
Watford	880		871	861		-4
Bournemouth	879		866	874		-8
Crystal Palace	877		868	876		-5
Newcastle	876		904	830		7
Norwich	861		878	840		-4
Aston Villa	833		850	834		-7

Championship

	Current	Last 40	H	A	Trend	
Burnley	887		882	867		8
Middlesbrough	875		890	832		3
Brighton	872		861	855		8
Hull	853		889	823		-3
Derby	852		854	837		2
Sheff Wed	849		853	830		-3
Ipswich	838		849	836		0
QPR	838		859	805		-1
Brentford	836		826	827		9
Leeds	836		817	827		4
Preston	834		826	818		-4
Cardiff	831		859	812		-6
Birmingham	830		819	820		0
Wolves	826		832	817		-2
Nottm Forest	826		810	824		1
Blackburn	826		823	816		2
Bristol City	818		816	806		1
Fulham	817		814	818		3
Rotherham	814		815	790		2
Huddersfield	812		814	809		-4
Reading	800		819	790		-9
Charlton	800		804	799		1
MK Dons	783		788	776		-10
Bolton	781		804	751		-5

Southampton finished 2015-16 as the Premier League's form team with a Trend value of +12

Wigan are back in the second tier, but their Index and Trend values suggest 2016-17 may be tricky

League One

	Current	Last 40	H	A	Trend
Wigan	800		807	794	-1
Millwall	800		806	785	7
Scunthorpe	794		788	758	13
Bradford	794		794	766	8
Burton	788		793	759	-1
Walsall	787		765	790	4
Barnsley	784		776	785	5
Rochdale	769		775	744	3
Sheff Utd	765		772	757	0
Coventry	762		764	747	4
Swindon	759		774	747	1
Port Vale	758		768	733	-2
Oldham	753		742	763	3
Fleetwood	752		760	728	2
Bury	751		765	727	-1
Peterborough	750		755	758	1
Gillingham	747		774	747	-13
Chesterfield	742		743	750	0
Shrewsbury	740		733	748	-5
Southend	739		748	731	-15
Blackpool	732		755	730	-6
Doncaster	731		745	730	-2
Colchester	730		733	726	0
Crewe	715		732	710	-8

League Two

	Current	Last 40	H	A	Trend
Northampton	769		761	743	2
Bristol Rovers	755		762	720	9
Accrington	749		731	734	8
Oxford Utd	743		718	758	3
Wimbledon	730		728	722	2
Plymouth	727		726	726	-2
Portsmouth	726		723	725	3
Luton	719		701	726	5
Carlisle	718		723	715	-1
Cambridge	718		721	714	3
Exeter	716		705	720	-1
Yeovil	716		723	709	3
Leyton Orient	714		727	730	-2
Mansfield	712		714	694	5
Barnet	712		728	686	1
Stevenage	703		714	696	7
Wycombe	700		711	713	-11
Hartlepool	690		703	674	-2
Notts Co	684		714	695	-6
Newport Co	680		689	693	-10
Morecambe	675		682	691	-6
York	671		699	669	-2
Dag & Red	671		670	684	0
Crawley	670		718	674	-16

National League

	Current	Last 40	H	A	Trend
Cheltenham	718		718	697	4
Braintree	692		689	669	7
Tranmere	689		683	698	8
Forest Green	689		690	692	-9
Dover	683		684	672	1
Grimsby	680		690	686	-12
Eastleigh	677		684	666	-4
Macclesfield	674		671	668	3
Barrow	673		673	647	8
Wrexham	668		682	652	-4
Torquay	657		651	653	7
Woking	656		670	658	2
Halifax	653		671	629	2
Boreham Wood	652		640	656	4
Southport	648		634	660	-2
Kidderminster	647		644	630	13
Gateshead	644		651	668	-9
Bromley	644		663	641	-7
Chester	643		660	632	3
Guiseley	640		652	626	1
Aldershot	639		634	656	-2
Lincoln	637		670	639	-8
Altrincham	628		652	606	-4
Welling	608		624	609	-7

Scottish Premiership

	Current	Last 40	H	A	Trend
Celtic	908		950	884	-1
Aberdeen	852		858	839	-13
St Johnstone	846		835	825	9
Hearts	846		849	820	-2
Inverness CT	833		822	826	5
Motherwell	828		826	796	5
Ross County	813		794	808	0
Dundee	812		810	788	-4
Hamilton	810		782	797	2
Partick	808		794	806	-6
Dundee Utd	796		794	787	6
Kilmarnock	789		775	791	-2

Scottish Championship

	Current	Last 40	H	A	Trend
Rangers	810		912	792	-13
Hibernian	790		811	770	-5
Raith	785		764	751	18
Falkirk	785		801	766	-2
St Mirren	754		764	751	3
Queen Of Sth	737		776	704	-8
Morton	733		741	709	-1
Dumbarton	728		748	700	2
Livingston	724		721	718	1
Alloa	703		702	686	7

Scottish League One

	Current	Last 40	H	A	Trend	
Dunfermline	726		726	716		0
Stranraer	696		697	680		8
Peterhead	690		703	679		-11
Brechin	688		699	661		13
Airdrieonians	680		680	697		2
Ayr	678		692	669		-4
Albion	676		668	666		7
Cowdenbeath	659		681	672		-6
Forfar	652		671	654		-5
Stenhousemuir	648		652	653		-4

Scottish League Two

	Current	Last 40	H	A	Trend	
East Fife	639		656	640		3
Elgin	630		652	604		1
Clyde	626		630	634		1
Queen's Park	620		624	643		-1
Berwick	619		648	596		9
Annan	617		651	609		-2
Stirling	612		643	615		-3
Montrose	606		629	584		5
Arbroath	589		612	612		-10
East Stirling	576		584	591		-4

Italian Serie A

	Current	Last 40	H	A	Trend	
Juventus	988		1033	980		0
Roma	964		988	960		11
Napoli	949		1004	930		0
Inter	918		948	916		-4
Sassuolo	916		920	913		7
Fiorentina	915		946	923		-6
Lazio	905		935	916		1
Milan	901		947	908		-6
Chievo	898		916	898		0
Genoa	893		926	878		-1
Carpi	892		896	897		4
Atalanta	888		914	878		3
Torino	885		902	904		-3
Palermo	884		899	881		6
Empoli	881		906	879		-5
Udinese	876		902	885		-3
Bologna	876		877	896		-3
Sampdoria	875		905	883		-3
Verona	868		890	871		0
Frosinone	844		867	805		-2

German Bundesliga

	Current	Last 40	H	A	Trend	
B Munich	1003		1010	996		2
Dortmund	973		983	944		1
Leverkusen	949		960	932		7
B M'gladbach	938		978	890		1
Schalke	922		950	900		1
Wolfsburg	915		964	894		-6
H Berlin	911		910	889		-7
Cologne	910		891	906		4
Mainz	910		920	902		-5
Augsburg	908		898	911		1
W Bremen	908		906	887		8
Hoffenheim	902		922	878		0
Hamburg	901		890	890		1
Frankfurt	901		919	864		5
Darmstadt	901		874	913		1
Ingolstadt	892		903	884		-5
Stuttgart	880		886	882		-13
Hannover	864		874	872		1

Spanish Primera Liga

	Current	Last 40	H	A	Trend	
Real Madrid	1027		1048	1016		8
Barcelona	1019		1057	1012		-5
Atl Madrid	1009		1026	990		1
Ath Bilbao	965		974	944		3
Celta Vigo	952		953	932		0
Villarreal	947		980	937		-10
Real Sociedad	936		946	931		4
Seville	934		996	902		-17
Malaga	931		945	913		0
Valencia	930		968	928		-7
Granada	928		918	909		8
Las Palmas	927		945	890		1
Real Betis	926		924	912		4
Espanyol	924		950	898		5
Elche	921		920	920		0
Rayo Vallecano	921		927	904		3
Sporting Gijon	918		925	891		7
Deportivo	914		904	926		-4
Getafe	911		917	882		1
Levante	906		932	872		1

French Ligue 1

	Current	Last 40	H	A	Trend	
Paris St-G	958		982	952		-2
Lyon	906		936	886		6
Lille	903		931	894		12
Monaco	901		920	910		-2
Nice	895		906	876		9
St Etienne	882		914	882		-3
Bastia	870		902	836		3
Rennes	870		866	882		-6
Bordeaux	870		924	864		-2
Toulouse	870		870	843		9
Marseille	869		881	892		-5
Caen	869		876	866		2
Montpellier	868		874	877		6
Nantes	861		880	857		-4
Lorient	857		874	856		-4
Guingamp	851		857	858		-2
Angers	850		855	820		-6
Gazelec	846		847	838		-5
Reims	842		871	831		-4
Troyes	809		837	804		-5

Portuguese Primeira Liga

	Current	Last 40	H	A	Trend	
Benfica	966		974	948		6
Sporting	963		948	938		5
Porto	926		959	918		-6
Arouca	882		859	857		5
Braga	881		911	851		-4
Rio Ave	868		850	860		4
Estoril	867		881	848		3
Pacos Ferreira	862		867	858		1
Belenenses	857		849	857		0
V Guimaraes	856		869	847		-4
Nacional	848		886	826		-3
Tondela	848		832	847		15
Moreirense	847		831	859		-1
Boavista	847		846	826		8
Maritimo	835		862	826		-7
Acad. Coimbra	826		841	806		-6
Uniao	825		848	812		-10
Vitoria Setubal	823		834	809		-9

Pools draws chart 2015-16   **X score-draw, 0 goalless draw**

Pools No.	Aug				Sep				Oct					Nov				Dec				Jan					Feb				Mar				Apr					May		X	0
	8	15	22	29	5	12	19	26	3	10	17	24	31	7	14	21	28	5	12	19	26	2	9	16	23	30	6	13	20	27	5	12	19	26	2	9	16	23	30	7	14	X	0
1	-	-	-	X	-	-	-	-	-	-	-	-	-	X	-	-	-	-	-	-	X	-	-	X	-	-	-	-	0	-	X	-	X	-	-	-	X	-	-	0	-	7	2
2	-	-	-	X	-	-	-	-	-	X	-	-	0	0	-	-	-	X	-	-	-	0	-	-	-	-	-	-	-	-	-	-	-	-	X	-	X	-	-	-	X X	7	3
3	X	-	-	-	-	-	X	-	X	-	-	-	-	-	-	-	-	-	-	-	-	X	X	-	X	-	-	X	-	-	-	-	-	-	-	-	-	-	X	-	-	8	0
4	X	-	X	-	-	-	-	-	-	-	-	-	X	-	X	0	-	X	-	0	0	-	-	-	X	-	-	-	-	-	-	-	-	X	-	X	-	-			8	3
5	-	-	0	-	X	-	-	-	-	-	X	0	-	-	-	-	X	-	-	-	-	-	-	-	-	0	-	-	X	0	X	-	X	-	-	-						6	4
6	-	-	X	-	-	0	-	X	X	-	X	0	-	-	-	X	-	X	-	-	-	-	-	X	-	-	-	-	-	X	0	-	-	-	-	-	X	-				9	3
7	X	-	X	-	-	-	X	-	-	-	-	-	-	-	-	-	X	-	X	-	-	-	-	-	X	-	-	-	-	-	-	-	-	X	X	-	-	-				8	0
8	-	X	0	-	0	-	0	X	-	-	-	-	-	-	-	-	-	-	X	-	-	-	0	-	-	-	X	-	-	X	-	-	-	X	-	0	-	-	X			7	5
9	-	0	-	-	-	-	-	-	X	-	-	-	-	-	-	-	-	0	-	-	-	0	0	-	X	-	X	-	-	-	-	0	X	-	-	-	-	X				5	5
10	-	-	-	0	-	-	-	-	X	-	-	X	X	-	X	X	0	X	-	-	X	-	X	-	-	-	-	-	-	-	-	-	X	X	-	-	-	X				11	2
11	-	-	-	-	-	-	-	-	X	-	X	-	X	X	-	-	-	-	-	-	-	0	-	-	-	-	X	-	-	-	-	0	-	-	-							5	2
12	-	X	X	-	-	X	-	-	X	-	-	0	-	0	-	-	-	X	0	-	-	-	-	-	-	-	-	-	-	X	-											6	3
13	0	X	-	-	-	-	X	X	-	0	-	-	X	X	X	-	0	-	X	-	X	-	-	-	-	-	-	X	X	-	-	-										10	3
14	X	-	-	-	-	X	-	X	X	-	-	0	-	-	-	X	-	X	-	-	0	-	-	-	-	0	-	-	-	X	X	-	X	-	-	-						9	3
15	-	-	-	-	X	X	-	0	-	-	-	X	X	-	X	-	-	X	X	X	X	0	-	-	-	-	-	-	X	0	-	-	-									11	3
16	X	-	-	-	-	-	X	-	-	-	-	-	X	-	-	X	-	-	X	-	-	X	-	0	-	-	0	-	-													6	2
17	-	-	X	-	X	-	-	0	-	-	-	-	-	X	-	-	-	X	-	-	-	0	-	-	-	-																4	2
18	-	-	X	-	-	-	-	0	-	-	-	0	X	-	X	-	-	-	X	-	-	-	-	-	X	-																5	2
19	X	-	-	-	-	0	-	-	0	0	-	X	0	-	0	-	-	X	-	-	X	X	0	-	0	-	X	-	X	-	X	-	X	-								8	7
20	0	X	-	-	-	X	X	-	-	0	-	-	-	X	-	X	-	-	X	-	-	0	-	X	-	X	-	-	-	0	0	-	X	-								9	5
21	-	0	-	-	0	-	X	-	-	-	X	0	0	-	-	-	0	X	-	-	-	X	-	-	0	-	X	-	-	-	X	-	-	-								6	6
22	-	X	0	-	X	-	X	-	-	-	-	-	0	-	0	-	-	-	X	-	0	-	0	0	-	-	0	0	0	0	-	-	-	0								4	11
23	-	-	0	-	-	-	-	-	X	X	-	-	-	-	-	-	-	-	-	X	X	-	-	-	X	-	-															5	1
24	-	-	-	-	-	X	-	-	-	-	X	-	-	-	-	-	-	-	X	-	0	X	-	-	-																	4	1
25	X	X	0	X	-	X	-	-	X	X	-	-	-	-	-	-	X	-	-																							7	1
26	-	X	X	X	-	-	-	X	-	0	-	0	-	-	X	-	-	-	X	-	X	-	X	-	X	-	-	0	-													9	3
27	0	-	-	-	X	X	X	-	0	-	-	-	-	0	-	X	-	-	X	0	-	-	-	X	-	-																6	5
28	X	-	-	-	-	-	-	-	-	-	X	-	-	-	0	X	-	0	-	X	X	-																				5	3
29	X	-	X	-	-	-	-	X	-	-	X	X	0	-	X	-	0	-	0	0	-	-	X	-	0	-																7	5
30	-	X	-	X	-	-	-	-	0	X	X	-	X	-	X	-	X	0	X	X	0	-	-	X	-																	11	3
31	-	-	0	-	X	-	-	-	-	X	-	0	X	-	X	-	-	X	-	X	-	X	-	X	-																	9	2
32	-	-	-	X	-	-	0	X	-	X	-	-	0	-	X	X	-	X	-	X	X	-	-	X	X	-	-	0	-	X												11	3
33	-	-	-	-	-	-	X	-	X	-	-	-	0	-	X	X	-	-	X	-	-																					5	1
34	X	0	-	-	0	-	-	X	-	-	-	X	-	-	0	-	-	X	-	X	-																					6	3
35	-	X	-	0	-	-	0	-	X	0	-	X	-	-	-	0	-	-	X	-	X	-																				7	4
36	X	X	-	X	X	-	0	X	-	X	-	-	0	X	-	-	X	-	X	0	-																					10	3
37	-	-	X	0	-	0	-	-	X	X	-	-	X	-	-	X	-	-	0	-	0																					6	4
38	-	-	0	0	-	X	0	-	0	-	X	-	X	-	-	X	-	X	-	-	0	-																				6	5
39	-	X	X	X	-	X	-	X	-	X	-	-	0	-	0	-	X	-																								7	2
40	-	-	-	-	0	-	X	-	0	0	-	0	-	0	-	X	-	0																								3	6
41	-	X	-	-	X	X	X	0	-	X	-	0	-	X	-	X	-	X																								9	3
42	X	-	X	-	X	X	-	X	0	X	-	X	-	X	X	-																										10	1
43	X	-	X	-	X	-	-	X	-	0																																5	1
44	-	-	X	-	X	-	X	-	0	X	X	-	0																													5	2
45	-	X	-	X	-	X	X	X	-	X	X																															8	0
46	-	-	X	X	0	X	X	X	-	0	-	0	-	X	X	-																										7	3
47	X	X	-	0	-	X	X	-	X	X	X	-																														7	2
48	-	X	-	X	X	-	X	-	X	-	0																															7	1
49	X	-	-	X	X	-	X	X	X																																	7	0
X	13	13	13	8	6	10	12	9	11	6	8	11	4	6	6	8	14	8	10	12	7	7	9	5	14	6	7	2	6	5	10	10	12	7	10	6	10	7	7	7	6	**348**	
0	3	3	7	3	3	1	4	2	2	2	5	4	5	5	3	3	5	6	4	0	4	3	2	5	3	2	7	6	2	4	6	2	2	3	4	2	5	5	1	4	2	**144**	

British weekend results only. European and international games used in some weeks. May 10 featured British results for matches 1-10 only

FA CUP

First round

Friday November 6, 2015
Salford City ...(0) 2-0 (0) Notts County

Saturday November 7, 2015
AFC W'bledon(1)1-2 (1).Forest Green
Accrington ....(2) 3-2 (1)..............York
Altrincham....(0) 1-0 (0)....... Barnsley
Barnet...........(2) 2-0 (0)..... Blackpool
Barwell.........(0) 0-2 (1)....... Welling
Burton ....(0) 0-3 (1)Peterborough
Bury..............(3) 4-0 (0).......... Wigan
Cambridge U (1) 1-0 (0)..Basingstoke
Coventry........(1) 1-2 (2)Northampton
Crawley ....(0) 1-2 (0)........... Luton
Crewe...........(0) 0-1 (0)...... Eastleigh
Dag & Red ....(0) 0-0 (0)..Morecambe
Doncaster .....(1) 2-0 (0)...Stalybridge
Dover ....(1) 1-2 (1).. Stourbridge
Grimsby........(2) 5-1 (0)......St Albans
Hartlepool.....(1) 1-0 (0)..Cheltenham
Leyton Orient(4) 6-1 (1)......... Staines
Mansfield .....(0) 0-0 (0)........ Oldham
Millwall ....(0) 3-1 (0).....AFC Fylde
Northwich.....(1) 1-1 (1)..Boreham W
Plymouth ......(0) 0-2 (2).......... Carlisle
Portsmouth ...(2) 2-1 (1). Macclesfield
Rochdale ......(1) 3-1 (0)......Swindon
Scunthorpe ...(1) 2-1 (1)......Southend
Sheff Utd ......(1) 3-0 (0)..... Worcester
Stevenage.....(2) 3-0 (0)... Gillingham
Walsall ....(1) 2-0 (0)....Fleetwood
Wealdstone ..(2) 2-6 (2).... Colchester

Sunday November 8, 2015
Aldershot......(0) 0-0 (0).......Bradford
Brackley........(0) 2-2 (2)..Newport Co
Braintree.......(0) 1-1 (1).......... Oxford
Bristol Rovers(0) 0-1 (0)...... Chesham
Didcot Town .(0) 0-3 (0)..........Exeter
Gainsborough(0)0-1 (0).. Shrewsbury
Halifax..........(0) 0-4 (1)..... Wycombe

Maidstone ....(0) 0-1 (0).......... Yeovil
Port Vale ....(1) 1-1 (0).Maidenhead
Whitehawk...(2) 5-3 (1)......... Lincoln

Monday November 9, 2015
FC United......(0) 1-4 (2)..Chesterfield

First-round replays

Monday November 16, 2015
Boreham W ..(0) 1-2 (1).... Northwich

Tuesday November 17, 2015
Morecambe ..(2) 2-4 (2)...Dag & Red
Newport Co ..(2) 4-1 (1)...... Brackley
Oldham ....(0) 2-0 (0)..... Mansfield
Oxford ....(1) 3-1 (1)...... Braintree

Wednesday November 18, 2015
Bradford ....(0) 2-0 (0)..... Aldershot

Thursday November 19, 2015
Maidenhead .(1) 1-3 (1)......Port Vale

Second round

Friday December 4, 2015
Salford City ...(1) 1-1 (1).... Hartlepool

Saturday December 5, 2015
Barnet...........(0) 0-1 (0)..Newport Co
Chesterfield ..(0) 1-1 (1)........ Walsall
Leyton Orient(0) 0-0 (0)...Scunthorpe
Millwall ....(0) 1-2 (0).....Wycombe
Northampton(0) 3-2 (1).... Northwich
Portsmouth ...(1) 1-0 (0)..Accrington
Sheff Utd ......(0) 1-0 (0)........ Oldham
Stourbridge...(0) 0-2 (0)...... Eastleigh
Yeovil............(0) 1-0 (0).... Stevenage

Sunday December 6, 2015
Bradford ....(2) 4-0 (0)...... Chesham
Cambridge U (1) 1-3 (0).....Doncaster
Colchester.....(1) 3-2 (1)....Altrincham
Dag & Red ....(1) 1-1 (0)...Whitehawk
Exeter ....(1) 2-0 (0).......Port Vale
Oxford ....(0) 1-0 (0).Forest Green
Peterborough(1) 2-0 (0)........... Luton
Rochdale ......(0) 0-1 (1)............. Bury

Welling ....(0) 0-5 (2)........ Carlisle

Monday December 7, 2015
Grimsby........(0) 0-0 (0).. Shrewsbury

Second-round replays

Tuesday December 15, 2015
Hartlepool.....(0) 2-0 (0)...Salford City
AET – 0-0 after 90 mins
Scunthorpe ...(0) 3-0 (0)Leyton Orient
Shrewsbury ..(0) 1-0 (0).......Grimsby
Walsall ....(0) 0-0 (0)..Chesterfield
AET – Walsall won 5-3 on penalties

Wednesday December 16, 2015
Whitehawk...(0) 2-3 (1)....Dag & Red
AET – 2-2 after 90 mins

Third round

Friday January 8, 2016
Exeter ....(2) 2-2 (1)...... Liverpool

Saturday January 9, 2016
Arsenal ....(1) 3-1 (1)...Sunderland
Birmingham ..(1) 1-2 (1)Bournemouth
Brentford ......(0) 0-1 (1)......... Walsall
Bury...............(0) 0-0 (0)......Bradford
Colchester.....(2) 2-1 (0)....... Charlton
Doncaster .....(1) 1-2 (1)...........Stoke
Eastleigh.......(0) 1-1 (0).......... Bolton
Everton.........(1) 2-0 (0)....Dag & Red
Hartlepool.....(0) 1-2 (0)........ Derby
Huddersfield .(0) 2-2 (0).......Reading
Hull ....(1) 1-0 (0)...... Brighton
Ipswich..........(0) 2-2 (0)...Portsmouth
Leeds............(1) 2-0 (0)... Rotherham
Man Utd ....(0) 1-0 (0)...... Sheff Utd
Middlesbro ...(1) 1-2 (1).........Burnley
Northampton(0) 2-2 (1)..... MK Dons
Norwich........(0) 0-3 (2)..... Man City
Nottm Forest.(1) 1-0 (0)..............QPR
Peterborough(1) 2-0 (0).........Preston
Sheff Wed.....(1) 2-1 (1)........Fulham
Southampton(0) 1-2 (1)...... C Palace
Watford ....(1) 1-0 (0).... Newcastle

Eighth-tier Northwich made it all the way to the second round

West Brom....(0) 2-2 (0)....Bristol City
West Ham.....(0) 1-0 (0).........Wolves
Wycombe .....(0) 1-1 (1)....Aston Villa

Sunday January 10, 2016
Cardiff ....(0) 0-1 (0).. Shrewsbury
Carlisle ....(1) 2-2 (0)...........Yeovil
Chelsea.........(1) 2-0 (0)...Scunthorpe
Oxford ....(1) 3-2 (1).....Swansea
Tottenham ....(1) 2-2 (1).......Leicester

Monday January 18, 2016
Newport Co ..(1) 1-2 (1).....Blackburn

Third-round replays
Tuesday January 19, 2016
Aston Villa ....(0) 2-0 (0).....Wycombe
Bolton...........(2) 3-2 (2)......Eastleigh
Bradford ....(0) 0-0 (0)............Bury
AET – Bury won 4-2 on penalties
Bristol City ....(0) 0-1 (0)... West Brom
MK Dons.......(0) 3-0 (0)Northampton
Portsmouth...(2) 2-1 (0)........Ipswich
Reading........(1) 5-2 (2).Huddersfield
Yeovil............(1) 1-1 (0).........Carlisle
AET – 1-1 after 90, Carlisle won 5-4 on pens

Wednesday January 20, 2016
Leicester ....(0) 0-2 (1)....Tottenham
Liverpool ......(1) 3-0 (0)...........Exeter

Fourth round
Friday January 29, 2016
Derby ....(1) 1-3 (1).......Man Utd

Saturday January 30, 2016
Arsenal.........(1) 2-1 (1).........Burnley
Aston Villa ....(0) 0-4 (2)...... Man City
Bolton...........(0) 1-2 (2)..........Leeds
Bury..............(0) 1-3 (1).............. Hull
C Palace........(1) 1-0 (0)...........Stoke
Colchester.....(0) 1-4 (1)....Tottenham
Liverpool ......(0) 0-0 (0).... West Ham
Nottm Forest.(0) 0-1 (0)........Watford
Oxford ....(0) 0-3 (2).....Blackburn
Portsmouth...(1) 1-2 (0)Bournemouth
Reading........(2) 4-0 (0)........Walsall
Shrewsbury ..(0) 3-2 (1).... Sheff Wed
West Brom....(1) 2-2 (0)Peterborough

Sunday January 31, 2016
Carlisle ....(0) 0-3 (2)........ Everton
MK Dons.......(1) 1-5 (3)........ Chelsea

Fourth-round replays
Tuesday February 9, 2016
West Ham.....(1) 2-1 (0)......Liverpool
AET – 1-1 after 90 mins

Wednesday February 10, 2016
Peterborough(0) 1-1 (0)... West Brom
AET – 1-1 after 90, WBA won 4-3 on pens

Fifth round
Saturday February 20, 2016
Arsenal ....(0) 0-0 (0).............. Hull
Bournemouth(0) 0-2 (0)........ Everton
Reading........(0) 3-1 (0)... West Brom
Watford ....(0) 1-0 (0)...........Leeds

Sunday February 21, 2016
Blackburn .....(1) 1-5 (2).... West Ham
Chelsea.........(1) 5-1 (1)...... Man City
Tottenham ....(0) 0-1 (1)....... C Palace

Monday February 22, 2016
Shrewsbury ..(0) 0-3 (2).......Man Utd

Fifth-round replay
Tuesday March 8, 2016
Hull ....(0) 0-4 (1).........Arsenal

Quarter-finals
Friday March 11, 2016
Reading........(0) 0-2 (0)....... C Palace

Saturday March 12, 2016
Everton.........(0) 2-0 (0)........ Chelsea

Sunday March 13, 2016
Arsenal ....(0) 1-2 (0).......Watford
Man Utd ....(0) 1-1 (0).... West Ham

Quarter-final replay
Wednesday April 13, 2016
West Ham.....(0) 1-2 (0).......Man Utd

Semi-finals
Saturday April 23, 2016
Everton..........(0) 1-2 (1).......Man Utd

Sunday April 24, 2016
C Palace........(1) 2-1 (0)........Watford

Final
Saturday May 21, 2016
C Palace........(0) 1-2 (0).......Man Utd
AET – 1-1 after 90 minutes

FA TROPHY

First round
Saturday December 12, 2015
Aldershot......(0) 0-1 (0)...... Eastleigh
Boreham W ..(1) 1-2 (0)........ Woking
Burscough ....(0) 2-2 (1)........ Guiseley
Bury Town ....(0) 1-2 (1).... Dulwich H
Cheltenham ..(1) 3-1 (1)...Chelmsford
Corinthian C..(1) 1-2 (1)Hungerford T
E Thurrock ....(1) 1-4 (1).Maidenhead
Eastbourne ...(3) 7-4 (0)........ Hemel
Grimsby........(0) 1-1 (1)Solihull Moors
Havant & W..(0) 2-0 (0).Forest Green
Maidstone ....(0) 0-1 (1) Bognor Regis
Nantwich T....(1) 2-0 (0)........Matlock
Oxford City ...(1) 3-1 (1)...... Ebbsfleet
Stourbridge...(0) 2-1 (0)Kidderminster
Sutton Cold...(0) 0-1 (0)......... Barrow

Wayne Rooney finally gets his hands on the FA Cup trophy. Well, most of it...

Truro City ......(0) 2-2 (0). Macclesfield
Woking ....(0) 6-1 (1).Maidenhead
Tuesday January 19, 2016
Bognor Regis (0) 2-1 (0)....Altrincham
Halifax ....(0) 1-0 (0) .... Barrow
Wednesday January 20, 2016
Bradford PA ..(0) 1-1 (0)...Nantwich T
Second-round replays
Tuesday January 19, 2016
Macclesfield..(1) 2-0 (0) ......Truro City
Tuesday January 26, 2016
Cheltenham ..(0) 0-3 (1)...Oxford City
Nantwich T ...(1) 5-0 (0).. Bradford PA

Third round
Saturday February 6, 2016
Dover ....(0) 2-2 (1)...... Guiseley
Gateshead ....(0) 1-0 (0)..... AFC Fylde
Grimsby ....(0) 3-0 (0)..Havant & W
Sutton Utd ....(0) 0-0 (0) Bognor Regis
Woking ....(1) 1-0 (0)... Oxford City
Tuesday February 9, 2016
Torquay ....(1) 3-3 (0). Macclesfield
Wednesday February 10, 2016
Halifax ....(1) 1-0 (0).........Chester
Tuesday February 16, 2016
Nantwich T ...(0) 1-0 (0).. Stourbridge
Third-round replays
Tuesday February 9, 2016
Bognor Regis (1) 2-1 (1)....Sutton Utd
AET – 1-1 after 90 mins
Tuesday February 16, 2016
Guiseley........(0) 0-3 (1)........... Dover
Macclesfield..(0) 0-1 (0)........Torquay

Quarter-finals
Saturday February 27, 2016
Bognor Regis (0) 1-0 (0).......Torquay
Grimsby........(2) 2-0 (0)........ Woking
Halifax ....(0) 0-0 (0)....Gateshead
Nantwich T ...(0) 2-1 (0)........... Dover
Quarter-final replay
Wednesday March 2, 2016
Gateshead ....(1) 3-3 (1).........Halifax
AET – 2-2 after 90, Halifax won 5-4 on pens
Semi-finals
Saturday March 12, 2016
Bognor Regis (0) 0-1 (0)........Grimsby
Nantwich T ...(1) 2-4 (2).........Halifax
Second legs
Saturday March 19, 2015
Grimsby........(1) 2-1 (1) Bognor Regis
Grimsby won 3-1 on aggregate
Halifax ....(1) 2-2 (2)...Nantwich T
Halifax won 6-4 on aggregate
Final
Sunday May 22, 2016
Halifax ....(0) 1-0 (0)........Grimsby

Telford ....(0) 0-2 (0).........Chester
Tilbury ....(0) 3-4 (3)........ Welling
Tranmere ......(1) 2-4 (2)......Wrexham
Truro City ......(2) 2-2 (0)... Cirencester
Whitehawk...(0) 1-3 (0)........... Dover
Sunday December 13, 2015
Torquay ....(0) 0-0 (0) ......Chesham
Monday December 14, 2015
Curzon Ashton(3)3-1 (0).....Nuneaton
Tuesday December 15, 2015
AFC Fylde .....(2) 4-4 (0) Skelmersdale
Altrincham....(0) 1-1 (0)..Leamington
Gateshead ....(1) 4-1 (1).Stocksbridge
Halifax ....(2) 5-0 (0).....Tamworth
Southport .....(0) 0-0 (0).....Worcester
Monday December 21, 2015
Bradford PA ..(1) 2-1 (0)......... Lincoln
Tuesday December 22, 2015
Braintree........(0) 1-0 (0)......Bromley
Macclesfield..(3) 4-0 (0)....Ashton Utd
Monday January 4, 2016
Sutton Utd ....(2) 3-1 (1)..Lowestoft T
Wednesday January 13, 2016
Weston-s-M..(2) 3-2 (1)..Wealdstone

First-round replays
Tuesday December 15, 2015
Chesham ......(0) 0-2 (2)........Torquay
Cirencester....(0) 0-1 (0)......Truro City
Guiseley........(3) 3-2 (1)....Burscough
Tuesday December 22, 2015
Solihull Moors(0)2-3 (0)........Grimsby
Worcester .....(1) 2-3 (1).....Southport
Wednesday January 13, 2016
Skelmersdale (0) 0-4 (1).....AFC Fylde
Saturday January 16, 2016
Leamington ..(0) 1-2 (1)....Altrincham
AET – 1-1 after 90 mins

Second round
Saturday January 16, 2016
Braintree.......(0) 0-1 (0).. Stourbridge
Chester ....(0) 4-0 (0)Hungerford T
Dover ....(1) 2-1 (0).....Southport
Dulwich H.....(1) 1-2 (2)....... Guiseley
Eastbourne ...(1) 1-4 (1)..... AFC Fylde
Eastleigh.......(1) 1-2 (0)....Gateshead
Grimsby........(2) 3-1 (1)..Weston-s-M
Havant & W..(1) 2-1 (1)........ Welling
Oxford City ...(0) 2-2 (0)..Cheltenham
Sutton Utd ....(1) 1-0 (0)Curzon Ashton
Torquay ....(0) 1-0 (0).....Wrexham

First round

Tuesday August 11, 2015

Accrington ....(0) 2-2 (0) .... Hull
AET – 0-0 after 90 mins, Hull won 4-3 on pens
Blackburn .....(1) 1-2 (2).. Shrewsbury
Bolton...........(0) 0-1 (0) .... Burton
Brentford ......(0) 0-4 (3)..........Oxford
Bristol Rovers (0) 1-2 (0). Birmingham
Cardiff ....(1) 1-0 (0).. Wimbledon
Carlisle ....(0) 3-1 (0)..Chesterfield
AET – 1-1 after 90 mins
Charlton ....(2) 4-1 (0)....Dag & Red
Colchester.....(0) 0-1 (0).......Reading
AET – 0-0 after 90 mins
Fleetwood ....(0) 0-1 (0).... Hartlepool
Huddersfield .(1) 1-2 (1) Notts County
Ipswich.........(0) 2-1 (1).... Stevenage
Luton............(1) 3-1 (0)....Bristol City
MK Dons........(0) 2-1 (1)Leyton Orient
Millwall ....(0) 1-2 (1).......... Barnet
AET – 1-1 after 90 mins
Morecambe ..(0) 0-1 (0)......Sheff Utd
Northampton(3) 3-0 (0)..... Blackpool
Nottm Forest.(1) 3-4 (2)........ Walsall
Peterborough(1) 2-0 (0)........Crawley
Plymouth ......(0) 1-2 (0)... Gillingham
Port Vale ......(0) 1-0 (0)........Burnley
Rochdale ......(1) 1-1 (0)...... Coventry
AET – 1-1 after 90 mins, Rochdale won 5-3 pens
Rotherham....(1) 1-0 (0) Cambridge U
Scunthorpe ...(0) 1-1 (0)....... Barnsley
AET – 1-1 after 90 mins, Barnsley 7-6 on pens
Sheff Wed.....(2) 4-1 (1).....Mansfield
Southend ......(0) 0-1 (0)........ Brighton
Swindon ....(0) 1-2 (2)..........Exeter
Wigan...........(0) 1-2 (0)............ Bury
Wolves ....(1) 2-1 (1)..Newport Co
Wycombe .....(0) 0-1 (0).........Fulham
Yeovil...........(0) 0-3 (2)............QPR
York..............(0) 2-2 (1)......Bradford
AET – 2-2 after 90 mins, York won 4-2 pens

Wednesday August 12, 2015

Crewe...........(1) 1-3 (2)........Preston
Oldham ....(0) 1-3 (2)...Middlesbro
Portsmouth...(0) 2-1 (0).......... Derby

Thursday August 13, 2015

Doncaster .....(1) 1-1 (1).......... Leeds
AET – 1-1 after 90 mins, Doncaster won 4-2 pens

Second round

Tuesday August 25, 2015

Aston Villa ....(1) 5-3 (2) Notts County
AET – 3-3 after 90 mins
Birmingham..(1) 2-0 (0)... Gillingham
Burton ....(1) 1-2 (0)...Middlesbro
AET – 1-1 after 90 mins
Bury..............(0) 1-4 (2)......Leicester
C Palace........(1) 4-1 (1).. Shrewsbury
AET – 1-1 after 90 mins
Doncaster .....(1) 1-4 (2)........ Ipswich
AET – 1-1 after 90 mins

Fulham ....(0) 3-0 (0)..... Sheff Utd
Hartlepool.....(0) 0-4 (3)Bournemouth
Hull ....(1) 1-0 (0)..... Rochdale
Luton............(0) 1-1 (0)...........Stoke
AET – 1-1 after 90 mins, Stoke won 8-7 pens
MK Dons........(0) 2-1 (0)........ Cardiff
AET – 1-1 after 90 mins
Newcastle.....(2) 4-1 (1)Northampton
Peterborough(0) 1-4 (1).......Charlton
Portsmouth...(1) 1-2 (0).......Reading
Preston ....(1) 1-0 (0).......Watford
QPR...............(1) 1-2 (1).......Carlisle
Rotherham....(0) 1-2 (1).......Norwich
Sheff Wed.....(0) 1-0 (0).........Oxford
Sunderland ...(3) 6-3 (3)..........Exeter
Swansea.......(1) 3-0 (0).............York
Walsall ....(0) 2-1 (1)....... Brighton
West Brom....(0) 0-0 (0)......Port Vale
AET – 0-0 after 90 mins, WBA won 5-3 pens
Wolves ....(1) 2-1 (0).......... Barnet

Wednesday August 26, 2015

Barnsley........(2) 3-5 (0)........ Everton
AET – 3-3 after 90 mins

Third round

Tuesday September 22, 2015

Aston Villa ....(0) 1-0 (0). Birmingham
Fulham ....(0) 0-1 (1)...........Stoke
Hull ....(1) 1-0 (0)...... Swansea

Leicester ....(1) 2-1 (1).... West Ham
AET – 1-1 after 90 mins
Middlesbro ...(1) 3-0 (0)........Wolves
Preston ....(0) 2-2 (1)Bournemouth
AET – 1-1 after 90, Bournemouth 3-2 pens
Reading.........(1) 1-2 (0)....... Everton
Sunderland ...(0) 1-4 (4)..... Man City

Wednesday September 23, 2015

C Palace........(0) 4-1 (0).......Charlton
Liverpool ......(1) 1-1 (1).........Carlisle
AET – 1-1 after 90 mins, Liverpool won 3-2 pens
MK Dons........(0) 0-6 (3)Southampton
Man Utd ....(1) 3-0 (0)........ Ipswich
Newcastle.....(0) 0-1 (0).... Sheff Wed
Norwich........(0) 3-0 (0)... West Brom
Tottenham ....(0) 1-2 (1)........Arsenal
Walsall ....(1) 1-4 (2)........ Chelsea

Fourth round

Tuesday October 27, 2015

Everton..........(0) 1-1 (0)...... Norwich
AET – 1-1 after 90 mins, Everton 4-3 pens
Hull ....(0) 1-1 (0)......Leicester
AET – 0-0 after 90 mins, Hull 5-4 on pens
Sheff Wed.....(2) 3-0 (0)........Arsenal
Stoke ....(0) 1-1 (0)........ Chelsea
AET – 1-1 after 90 mins, Stoke won 5-4 on pens

Wednesday October 28, 2015

Liverpool ......(1) 1-0 (0)Bournemouth
Man City.......(2) 5-1 (0)....... C Palace

Willy Caballero earns cult hero status with three saves in the League Cup final shootout

Man Utd ......(0) 0-0 (0) ...Middlesbro
AET – 0-0 after 90, Middlesbro won 3-1 pens
Southampton(0) 2-1 (0) ....Aston Villa

Quarter-finals
Tuesday December 1, 2015
Man City.......(1) 4-1 (0) .... Hull
Middlesbro ...(0) 0-2 (2) .... Everton
Stoke ....(1) 2-0 (0) .... Sheff Wed

Wednesday December 2, 2015
Southampton(1) 1-6 (3) ...... Liverpool

Semi-final, first legs
Tuesday January 5, 2016
Stoke ....(0) 0-1 (1) ...... Liverpool

Wednesday January 6, 2016
Everton ....(1) 2-1 (0) ...... Man City

Semi-final, second legs
Tuesday January 26, 2016
Liverpool ......(0) 0-1 (1) ....Stoke
AET – 1-1 on agg, Liverpool won 6-5 pens

Wednesday January 27, 2016
Man City.......(1) 3-1 (1) .... Everton
Man City won 4-3 on aggregate

Final
Sunday February 28, 2016
Liverpool ......(0) 1-1 (0) ...... Man City
AET – 1-1 after 90 mins, Man City won 3-1 pens

FOOTBALL LEAGUE TROPHY

First round
Tuesday September 1, 2015
Accrington ....(0) 1-2 (0) .... Bury
Cambridge U (0) 0-2 (2) ....Dag & Red
Doncaster .....(0) 0-0 (0) .... Burton
Doncaster won 5-3 on penalties
Exeter ....(0) 2-0 (0) ...Portsmouth
Hartlepool.....(0) 1-1 (1) ..... Sheff Utd
Sheff Utd won 4-3 on penalties
Luton ....(1) 2-1 (0)Leyton Orient
Millwall ....(0) 1-0 (0)Peterborough
Morecambe ..(0) 2-0 (0) .... Walsall
Newport Co ..(0) 1-1 (1) ......Swindon
Swindon won 7-6 on penalties
Northampton(1) 3-2 (1).... Colchester
Notts County (0) 3-1 (0) ..... Mansfield
Port Vale ....(0) 1-0 (0) .... Carlisle
Scunthorpe ...(0) 1-2 (0) ...... Barnsley
Shrewsbury ..(1) 2-0 (0) .... Oldham
Yeovil............(1) 1-0 (0) .... Barnet
Wimbledon...(2) 2-3 (1) ......Plymouth

Second round
Tuesday October 6, 2015
Bristol Rovers (2) 2-0 (0) ..... Wycombe
Bury..............(0) 0-1 (0) .. Morecambe
Crawley ....(0) 0-3 (2) .....Southend
Crewe...........(2) 2-3 (1) .... Wigan

Fleetwood ....(0) 2-1 (1) .. Shrewsbury
Gillingham ....(0) 2-1 (1) .... Luton
Millwall ....(0) 2-0 (0)Northampton
Oxford ....(1) 2-0 (0) ....Swindon
Plymouth ......(1) 2-0 (0) ....Exeter
Port Vale ....(0) 1-2 (1) ..... Blackpool
Rochdale ......(1) 2-1 (0) .. Chesterfield
Sheff Utd ......(3) 5-1 (0) Notts County
Yeovil............(0) 0-0 (0) ...... Coventry
Yeovil won 4-3 on penalties
York ....(1) 2-0 (0) .....Doncaster

Wednesday October 7, 2015
Stevenage.....(0) 1-2 (0) ....Dag & Red

Tuesday October 13, 2015
Bradford ....(1) 1-2 (1) ...... Barnsley

Area quarter-finals
Northern section
Tuesday November 10, 2015
Barnsley........(0) 2-1 (1) ....York
Fleetwood ....(0) 0-0 (0) ...... Sheff Utd
Fleetwood won 4-1 on penalties
Rochdale ......(0) 0-1 (1) .. Morecambe
Wigan...........(1) 4-0 (0) ..... Blackpool

Southern section
Tuesday November 10, 2015
Gillingham ....(1) 1-1 (1) .... Yeovil
Yeovil won 5-4 on penalties
Plymouth ......(1) 3-5 (2) .... Millwall

Wednesday November 11, 2015
Dag & Red ....(0) 0-2 (1) ....Oxford
Southend ......(1) 1-0 (0) Bristol Rovers

Area semi-finals
Northern section
Saturday December 5, 2015
Wigan...........(0) 2-2 (1) ...... Barnsley
Barnsley won 4-2 on penalties

Tuesday December 8, 2015
Fleetwood ....(0) 2-0 (0) .. Morecambe

Southern section
Tuesday December 8, 2015
Oxford ....(2) 3-2 (1) .... Yeovil
Southend ......(0) 0-2 (1) .... Millwall

Northern area final
Saturday January 9, 2016
Barnsley........(0) 1-1 (0) .... Fleetwood

Second leg
Thursday February 4, 2016
Fleetwood ....(0) 1-1 (0) ...... Barnsley
2-2 on aggregate, Barnsley won 4-2 on pens

Southern area final
Thursday January 14, 2016
Millwall ....(0) 0-2 (2) ....Oxford

Second leg
Tuesday February 2, 2016
Oxford ....(0) 0-1 (0) .... Millwall
Oxford won 2-1 on aggregate

Final
Sunday April 3, 2016
Barnsley........(0) 3-2 (1) ....Oxford

SCOTTISH CUP

First round

Saturday September 26, 2015
BSC Glasgow (0) 2-2 (0)....Auchinleck
Banks O'Dee .(0) 2-3 (0)Cove Rangers
Buckie Thistle(0) 7-0 (0)..........Rothes
Deveronvale .(0) 0-5 (0) Clachnacuddin
Formartine Utd(0) 3-1 (0).Gretna 2008
Fraserburgh ..(0) 3-2 (0)..Dalbeattie S
Gala Fairydean(0) 0-2 (0)....Linlithgow
Hawick Royal(0) 0-3 (0).......... Huntly
Keith.............(0) 1-5 (0)....Inverurie L
Lossiemouth .(0) 1-4 (0). Forres Mech
Lothian T ......(0) 3-0 (0)..Kelty Hearts
Nairn County (0) 5-1 (0).......... Selkirk
Preston Ath...(0) 2-3 (0)..Fort William
Spartans ....(0) 5-1 (0)...Coldstream
Strathspey T..(0) 1-2 (0).Edinburgh U
Threave Rovers(0) 1-3 (0). Stirling Univ
Wick Academy (0) 2-2 (0).. Whitehill W

Sunday September 27, 2015
Cumbernauld(0) 3-0 (0) Glasgow Uni

First-round replays

Saturday October 3, 2015
Auchinleck....(0) 5-0 (0) BSC Glasgow
Whitehill W ..(0) 2-3 (0) Wick Academy

Second round

Saturday October 24, 2015
Annan...........(0) 4-1 (1)........ Berwick
Brora Rangers .(0) 1-2 (1).......Arbroath
Clachnacuddin (1) 1-3 (1).Linlithgow R
Cumbernauld(0) 2-0 (0)....Auchinleck
East Fife........(0) 0-0 (0)......... Stirling
East Kilbride..(0) 1-1 (0). Forres Mech
Edinburgh C..(1) 1-2 (0)Buckie Thistle
Elgin City ......(0) 1-0 (0).......Spartans
Formartine U..(1) 2-0 (0)............Clyde
Huntly...........(2) 2-1 (0).. East Stirling
Inverurie L ....(1) 2-1 (1). Edinburgh U
Lothian T ......(1) 1-1 (1).... Montrose
Nairn County (1) 2-2 (1) Wick Academy
Stirling Univ..(0) 0-2 (1) Queen's Park

Saturday October 31, 2015
Turriff U ....(1) 2-3 (1)..Fraserburgh

Monday November 2, 2015
Fort William ..(0) 0-4 (3)Cove Rangers

Second-round replays

Saturday October 31, 2015
Wick Academy (3) 5-1 (1) Nairn County
Forres Mech..(1) 2-3 (2). East Kilbride

Tuesday November 3, 2015
Montrose......(1) 1-2 (1)......Lothian T
AET – 1-1 after 90 mins
Stirling.........(1) 1-0 (0)....... East Fife

Third round

Saturday November 28, 2015
Airdrieonians (2) 3-1 (1)........Brechin
Albion...........(0) 0-2 (1).........Morton
Ayr ....(0) 0-1 (1). Dunfermline

Cowdenbeath(0) 1-1 (0).......Arbroath
Elgin City ......(0) 1-2 (1)............ Raith
Falkirk...........(1) 4-1 (0)..Fraserburgh
Formartine U.(1) 1-1 (0)Cove Rangers
Huntly...........(1) 1-1 (0)....Lothian T
Inverurie Locos(1) 4-4 (1).......... Annan
Peterhead .....(0) 1-3 (2).... Livingston
Queen's Park.(1) 1-1 (0)..........Forfar
Stenh'semuir.(0) 2-2 (1). East Kilbride
Stranraer.......(1) 3-1 (0)Buckie Thistle

Tuesday December 1, 2015
Stirling.........(2) 6-0 (0)Cumbernauld

Tuesday December 8, 2015
Dumbarton ...(2) 5-0 (0)............ Alloa

Wednesday December 16, 2015
Wick Academy (1) 2-2 (1).Linlithgow R

Third-round replays

Saturday December 5, 2015
Cove Rangers(2) 4-1 (0) Formartine U
East Kilbride..(1) 2-1 (1) Stenh'semuir
AET – 1-1 after 90 mins
Forfar ....(1) 2-1 (0) Queen's Park

Monday December 7, 2015
Arbroath.......(1) 2-4 (4)Cowdenbeath
Lothian T ......(1) 3-0 (0).......... Huntly

Tuesday December 8, 2015
Annan...........(1) 1-0 (0)....Inverurie L

Tuesday December 22, 2015
Linlithgow R .(3) 5-1 (1) Wick Academy

Fourth round

Friday January 8, 2016
St Mirren .....(0) 1-2 (0).......... Partick

Saturday January 9, 2016
Airdrieonians (0) 0-1 (0)..Dundee Utd
Annan...........(1) 4-1 (0)...... Hamilton
Dumbarton...(1) 2-1 (0) Queen of Sth
Dunfermline..(1) 2-2 (2). Ross County
Hearts...........(1) 1-0 (0)..... Aberdeen
Linlithgow R .(1) 3-3 (1)..........Forfar
Livingston.....(0) 0-1 (0).........Morton
Motherwell...(4) 5-0 (0)Cove Rangers
Raith.............(0) 0-2 (0)..... Hibernian
St Johnstone .(0) 0-1 (1)... Kilmarnock
Stirling.........(0) 0-0 (0).Inverness CT

Sunday January 10, 2016
Rangers ....(2) 5-1 (1)Cowdenbeath
Stranraer.......(0) 0-3 (2)............Celtic

Wednesday January 20, 2016
East Kilbride..(1) 2-0 (0)......Lothian T

Tuesday January 26, 2016
Dundee.........(1) 3-1 (1).......... Falkirk

Fourth-round replays

Tuesday January 12, 2016
Ross County..(0) 1-0 (0). Dunfermline

Tuesday January 19, 2016
Inverness CT .(1) 2-0 (0)......... Stirling

Tuesday January 26, 2016
Forfar ....(0) 0-1 (0).Linlithgow R
AET – 0-0 after 90 mins

Fifth round

Saturday February 6, 2016
Annan...........(0) 1-4 (2)..........Morton
Dumbarton ...(0) 0-0 (0)........ Dundee
Dundee Utd ..(0) 1-0 (0).......... Partick
Motherwell...(0) 1-2 (1).Inverness CT
Rangers ....(0) 0-0 (0)... Kilmarnock
Ross County..(1) 4-2 (1).Linlithgow R

Anthony Stokes celebrates his third-minute opener for Hibs in the Scottish Cup final

Sunday February 7, 2016
East Kilbride..(0) 0-2 (1)............Celtic
Hearts...........(2) 2-2 (0)..... Hibernian

Fifth-round replays
Tuesday February 16, 2016
Hibernian......(1) 1-0 (0).......... Hearts
Kilmarnock....(1) 1-2 (1)........Rangers
Tuesday February 23, 2016
Dundee.........(2) 5-0 (0)...Dumbarton

Quarter-finals
Saturday March 5, 2016
Rangers........(1) 4-0 (0)........ Dundee
Ross County..(1) 2-3 (0)..Dundee Utd
Sunday March 6, 2016
Celtic ....(3) 3-0 (0).........Morton
Hibernian......(0) 1-1 (0).Inverness CT
Quarter-final replay
Wednesday March 16, 2016
Inverness CT .(0) 1-2 (2)..... Hibernian

Semi-finals
Saturday April 16, 2016
Hibernian......(0) 0-0 (0)..Dundee Utd
AET. Hibernian won 4-2 on penalties
Sunday April 17, 2016
Rangers........(1) 2-2 (0)............Celtic
AET – 1-1 after 90, Rangers won 5-4 on pens

Final
Saturday May 21, 2016
Rangers........(1) 2-3 (1)..... Hibernian

SCOTTISH LEAGUE CUP
First round
Thursday July 30, 2015
Hearts...........(0) 4-2 (1).......Arbroath

Friday July 31, 2015
Falkirk..........(1) 5-0 (0).. East Stirling
Saturday August 1, 2015
Annan..........(0) 3-4 (1) Queen of Sth
AET – 3-3 after 90 mins
Ayr ....(1) 2-0 (0).........Brechin
Berwick ....(0) 3-2 (2)............ Alloa
AET – 2-2 after 90 mins
Dunfermline..(0) 5-1 (0)Cowdenbeath
East Fife........(0) 1-1 (0)...Dumbarton
AET – 1-1 after 90 mins, E Fife won 4-3 on pens
Hibernian......(1) 3-0 (0)..... Montrose
Livingston.....(0) 1-0 (0)............Clyde
AET – 0-0 after 90 mins
Morton ....(0) 5-0 (0).....Elgin City
Queen's Park.(0) 0-2 (2)..........Forfar
Raith.............(2) 3-0 (0)........... Albion
Stirling ....(0) 0-1 (1) Airdrieonians
Stranraer.......(1) 2-0 (0) Stenh'semuir
Sunday August 2, 2015
Rangers ....(1) 3-0 (0).....Peterhead

Second round
Tuesday August 25, 2015
Dunfermline..(1) 3-1 (0)........ Dundee
East Fife........(0) 1-3 (0).. Motherwell
AET – 1-1 after 90 mins
Forfar ....(0) 1-2 (0).......... Hearts
AET – 1-1 after 90 mins
Kilmarnock....(1) 4-1 (0)....... Berwick
Partick ....(0) 0-1 (1).......... Falkirk
Queen of Sth.(0) 0-1 (0).........Morton
Raith.............(1) 2-1 (0)...... Hamilton
Ross County..(1) 2-0 (0)............. Ayr
St Mirren ......(2) 2-3 (2).... Livingston

Wednesday August 26, 2015
Airdrieonians (0) 0-5 (3).......Rangers
Hibernian......(0) 1-0 (0)..... Stranraer

Third round
Tuesday September 22, 2015
Dundee Utd ..(1) 3-1 (1). Dunfermline
AET – 1-1 after 90 mins
Livingston.....(0) 0-2 (2).Inverness CT
Morton ....(1) 3-2 (0).. Motherwell
AET – 1-1 after 90 mins
Rangers ....(0) 1-3 (2).St Johnstone
Ross County..(3) 7-0 (0).......... Falkirk

Wednesday September 23, 2015
Celtic ....(1) 2-0 (0)............ Raith
Hibernian......(0) 2-0 (0)..... Aberdeen
Kilmarnock....(1) 2-3 (0).......... Hearts

Quarter-finals
Tuesday October 27, 2015
Inverness CT .(0) 1-2 (1). Ross County
Morton ....(0) 1-3 (0).St Johnstone

Wednesday October 28, 2015
Hearts...........(0) 1-2 (0)............Celtic

Wednesday November 4, 2015
Hibernian......(1) 3-0 (0)..Dundee Utd

Semi-finals
Saturday January 30, 2016
Hibernian......(1) 2-1 (1).St Johnstone
Sunday January 31, 2016
Ross County..(1) 3-1 (1)............Celtic

Final
Sunday March 13, 2016
Hibernian......(1) 1-2 (1). Ross County

SCOTTISH CHALLENGE CUP
First round
Saturday July 25, 2015
Annan...........(0) 3-1 (1) Airdrieonians
Arbroath ....(0) 1-4 (3). Dunfermline
Ayr ....(1) 3-1 (0)......... Albion
Brechin ....(0) 0-3 (0)....Peterhead
Brora Rangers .(0) 0-1 (0)............ Alloa
Cowdenbeath(0) 0-1 (1)............ Raith
East Stirling ..(1) 2-3 (2) Stenh'semuir
Edinburgh C..(0) 0-0 (0) Queen's Park
AET – Queen's Park won 3-1 on pens
Elgin City ......(1) 3-2 (1)........ Stirling
Falkirk...........(1) 3-1 (1)...... East Fife
Forfar ....(0) 1-0 (0)..... Montrose
Hibernian......(1) 2-6 (2).......Rangers
Livingston.....(2) 2-1 (1)............Clyde
Morton ....(0) 2-3 (2)...Dumbarton
Queen of Sth.(1) 2-0 (0)..... Stranraer
St Mirren ......(1) 3-1 (1)....... Berwick

Second round
Tuesday August 18, 2015
Annan...........(1) 1-2 (0)...... St Mirren
Falkirk...........(0) 3-5 (0)....Peterhead
Forfar ....(0) 0-3 (2). Dunfermline
Queen of Sth.(0) 0-1 (0).... Livingston
AET – 0-0 after 90 mins
Queen's Park.(0) 1-0 (0)...Dumbarton
AET – 0-0 after 90 mins
Stenh'semuir.(0) 2-0 (0)............ Raith

Wednesday August 19, 2015
Alloa.............(0) 0-2 (0)......Elgin City
AET – 0-0 after 90 mins
Ayr ....(0) 0-2 (2).......Rangers

Quarter-finals
Saturday October 10, 2015
Peterhead .....(3) 3-0 (0) Stenh'semuir
Queen's Park.(2) 2-1 (0)......Elgin City
St Mirren ......(3) 4-0 (0). Dunfermline
Tuesday October 20, 2015
Rangers ....(0) 1-0 (0).... Livingston

Semi-finals
Saturday November 14, 2015
Queen's Park.(1) 1-2 (1).....Peterhead
Saturday November 28, 2015
Rangers ....(1) 4-0 (0)...... St Mirren

Final
Sunday April 10, 2016
Rangers ....(2) 4-0 (0).....Peterhead

Continental giants show no sign of releasing their domestic strangleholds

The 2015-16 Premier League campaign featured arguably the greatest upset in sporting history but across the continent the status quo was very much maintained, writes Joe Champion. Barcelona, Bayern Munich, Juventus and Paris Saint-Germain all justified favouritism to retain their domestic titles in Spain, Germany, Italy and France.

Some had to work harder than others. Barcelona, pursued all the way by the Madrid clubs, would have to wait until the final day of the season to start their celebrations but PSG looked nailed on for the Ligue 1 title for months, even if they had to wait until March before their success was confirmed.

Juve started slowly but their run of 15 consecutive Serie A wins in the middle of the season put them firmly on track for the title. They finished up nine points clear of a Napoli side who had dared to dream of a first Scudetto since the days of Diego Maradona.

Bayern gave the departing Pep Guardiola a third-successive Bundesliga title, but failure to win the Champions League during his time in Bavaria will go down as one of the only major failures of his managerial career.

Despite Barcelona securing another league and cup double, plenty of the plaudits in Spain went to Real Madrid as they claimed a second Champions League crown in three seasons.

It was a strange campaign for Real, who sacked Rafa Benitez at the beginning of 2016. The subsequent appointment of Zinedine Zidane has already paid off and the French legend will be looking to build on his European success in his first full season in the Bernabeu hotseat.

Barcelona remain a brilliant side, of course. Luis Suarez's 40 goals wrestled the Pichichi away from Cristiano Ronaldo but he was fresh after missing the 2015 edition of the Copa America. Lionel Messi – embroiled in a draining tax-evasion trail – is again on international duty this summer with Argentina while Neymar will contest the Olympics for Brazil.

Atletico Madrid – beaten finalists in the Champions League – seem likely to hold on to manager Diego Simeone for another season and they can't be fully discounted. But at 13-10 their city rivals look worth backing to win a first domestic title in five years.

Deportivo Alaves will return to Spain's top-flight for the first time since relegation at the end of the 2005-06 season.

El Glorioso, best known to Premier League fans as the team who lost 5-4 to Liverpool in the 2001 Uefa Cup final, had been crippled by debt problems and yo-yoed between the second and third tiers before winning the Segunda. They will be joined by tiny Madrid-based outfit Leganes – who will make their Primera debut – and playoff winners Osasuna.

Unsurprisingly, Juventus are odds-on favourites as they chase a sixth-straight Serie A title, but it is difficult to see who will rival Max Allegri's men.

Napoli were the Old Lady's closest challengers last term but their success was fuelled by the goals of record-breaking striker Gonzalo Higuain and there is a possibility that the Argentinian might not be at the Stadio San Paolo next season.

Even if Juventus lose Paul Pogba, they still have a watertight defence and Paulo Dybala – who should improve further – is a potentially world-class goalscorer.

Roma might be the team to chase them home. Last season was not easy season for the Wolves but they finished strongly under Luciano Spalletti and could figure in the title race this time around.

Frosinone and Carpi were both relegated to Serie B alongside one-time Italian champions Verona and will be replaced by Cagliari, who return after a year in the second tier, minnows Crotone, who will make their top-flight debut, and playoff winners Pescara.

Borussia Dortmund bounced back from their season in the doldrums and new coach Thomas Tuchel helped them push Bayern hard in the Bundesliga. However, the departures of Mats Hummels, Ilkay Gundogan and, potentially, African Footballer of the Year Pierre-Emerick Aubameyang this summer will make it difficult for BVB to build on a fine campaign.

The signing of highly rated Rennes youngster Ousmane Dembele looks like a step in the right direction but it is not easy to replace three world-class players in one transfer window.

Bayern are long odds-on to retain their title and Carlo Ancelotti is a safe appointment.

One team to watch may be Hoffenheim, who had a terrific second half of the season under Julian Nagelsmann.

Nagelsmann – the youngest manager in Bundesliga history at just 28 – took over in February with the club staring relegation in the face. He led them to seven wins from 13 games, avoiding the drop by a point.

They will have to do without star winger Kevin Volland, who moves to Leverkusen, but have at least managed to sign Andrej Kramaric on a permanent deal from Leicester.

It is fanciful to suggest that Hoffenheim can replicate the success of the Foxes but Nagelsmann has made a fine start to his managerial career at the club and they should not be expected to flirt with relegation this season.

One side who might struggle to survive in the top flight is Ingolstadt. Despite finishing in mid-table, Die Schanzer scored just 33 goals last term and the manner in which they scored those goals was remarkable. Just 13 of their goals came from open play, with the other 20 coming from set-pieces – including nine from the penalty spot. Solid centre-half Benjamin Hubner has left for Hoffenheim, so Ingolstadt could be set for a long season.

Paris Saint-Germain are 1-12 to retain their Ligue 1 title and should do so with minimal fuss. But they will have to do it without the 38 goals contributed by Zlatan Ibrahimovic after the colossal Swede departed the French capital for Manchester United.

It might be possible for the also-rans to get closer to the Parisian giants this term, but a 31-point gap will still be extremely difficult to bridge.

Lyon finished the season strongly and are in pole position to challenge. They look a good thing in the 'without PSG' market providing they keep hold of star striker Alexandre Lacazette, who overcame a tough start to net 21 goals, including 11 in his last ten games. Lacazette has been linked with a move to the Premier League but his absence from France's Euro 2016 squad may have helped to cool speculation.

Gareth Bale's Real will be on the hunt for domestic silverware

ATALANTA
Ground: Stadio Atleti Azzurri d'Italia   atalanta.it

	2015-16 H	2015-16 A	P	W	D	L	OV	UN	BS	CS
Juventus	L	L	5	0	0	5	2	3	1	0
Napoli	L	L	5	2	2	1	2	3	3	2
Roma	D	W	5	1	2	2	4	1	5	0
Inter	D	L	5	1	3	1	2	3	5	0
Fiorentina	L	L	5	1	0	4	1	4	1	1
Sassuolo	D	D	4	2	1	1	1	3	2	1
Milan	W	D	5	2	0	3	3	2	3	0
Lazio	W	L	5	2	1	2	2	3	3	0
Chievo	W	L	5	3	2	0	2	3	3	2
Empoli	D	W	3	0	2	1	2	1	2	1
Genoa	L	W	5	1	1	3	1	4	2	1
Torino	L	L	5	2	0	3	3	2	3	1
Atalanta										
Bologna	W	L	4	3	1	0	1	3	2	2
Sampdoria	W	D	4	2	1	1	3	1	2	2
Palermo	W	D	4	3	1	0	2	2	1	3
Udinese	D	L	5	1	4	0	0	5	2	3
Cagliari			4	3	1	0	1	3	2	2
Crotone			1	1	0	0	0	1	0	1
Pescara			2	2	0	0	1	1	1	1

Season	Division	Pos	P	W	D	L	F	A	GD	Pts
2015-16	Serie A	13	38	11	12	15	41	47	-6	45
2014-15	Serie A	17	38	7	16	15	38	57	-19	37
2013-14	Serie A	11	38	15	5	18	43	51	-8	50

Over/Under 45%/55% 13th   Both score 47%/53% 12th

BOLOGNA
Ground: Stadio Renato Dall'Ara   www.bolognafc.it

	2015-16 H	2015-16 A	P	W	D	L	OV	UN	BS	CS
Juventus	D	L	5	0	3	2	0	5	1	2
Napoli	W	L	5	2	1	2	3	2	2	1
Roma	D	D	5	0	2	3	2	3	2	0
Inter	L	L	5	0	2	3	2	3	3	1
Fiorentina	D	L	5	2	2	1	2	3	3	0
Sassuolo	L	W	2	0	1	1	0	2	0	1
Milan	L	W	5	0	2	3	4	1	3	0
Lazio	D	L	5	1	3	1	2	3	2	2
Chievo	L	D	5	2	2	1	3	2	2	2
Empoli	L	D	1	0	0	1	1	0	1	0
Genoa	W	W	5	3	2	0	1	4	2	3
Torino	L	L	3	0	1	2	2	1	2	0
Atalanta	W	L	4	3	0	1	3	1	2	1
Bologna										
Sampdoria	W	L	4	1	3	0	2	2	4	0
Palermo	L	D	4	2	0	2	2	2	1	2
Udinese	L	W	5	1	1	3	3	2	4	0
Cagliari			4	3	1	0	2	2	1	3
Crotone			1	0	0	1	0	1	0	0
Pescara			2	0	2	0	0	2	1	1

Season	Division	Pos	P	W	D	L	F	A	GD	Pts
2015-16	Serie A	14	38	11	9	18	33	45	-12	42
2014-15	Serie B	4	42	17	17	8	49	35	+14	68
2013-14	Serie A	19	38	5	14	19	28	58	-30	29

Over/Under 32%/68% 21st   Both score 32%/68% 21st

CAGLIARI
Ground: Stadio Sant'Elia   www.cagliaricalcio.net

	2015-16 H	2015-16 A	P	W	D	L	OV	UN	BS	CS
Juventus			5	0	0	5	4	1	4	0
Napoli			5	0	2	3	1	4	1	1
Roma			5	2	0	3	5	0	4	0
Inter			5	1	2	2	2	3	3	1
Fiorentina			5	2	1	2	3	2	2	2
Sassuolo			2	1	1	0	2	0	2	0
Milan			5	0	2	3	1	4	3	0
Lazio			5	2	0	3	2	3	1	2
Chievo			5	1	1	3	1	4	1	1
Empoli			1	0	1	0	0	1	1	0
Genoa			5	3	1	1	3	2	3	1
Torino			3	2	0	1	3	0	3	0
Atalanta			4	2	1	1	2	2	3	1
Bologna			4	2	1	1	1	3	1	2
Sampdoria			4	1	3	0	3	1	3	1
Palermo			4	2	1	1	2	2	3	0
Udinese			5	2	1	2	3	2	1	2
Cagliari										
Crotone	W	L	1	1	0	0	1	0	0	1
Pescara	W	L	2	1	0	1	2	0	2	0

Season	Division	Pos	P	W	D	L	F	A	GD	Pts
2015-16	Serie B	1	42	25	8	9	78	41	+37	83
2014-15	Serie A	18	38	8	10	20	48	68	-20	34
2013-14	Serie A	15	38	9	12	17	34	53	-19	39

Over/Under 62%/38% 2nd   Both score 55%/45% 9th

CHIEVO
Ground: Marc'Antonio Bentegodi   chievoverona.tv

	2015-16 H	2015-16 A	P	W	D	L	OV	UN	BS	CS
Juventus	L	D	6	0	2	4	3	3	3	1
Napoli	L	L	6	3	0	3	2	4	2	3
Roma	D	L	6	1	4	1	2	4	2	3
Inter	L	L	6	2	0	4	2	4	2	0
Fiorentina	D	L	6	1	2	3	2	4	3	2
Sassuolo	D	D	3	0	2	1	0	3	1	1
Milan	D	L	6	0	3	3	1	5	1	3
Lazio	W	L	6	1	1	4	3	3	1	2
Chievo										
Empoli	D	W	2	0	2	0	0	2	2	0
Genoa	W	L	6	3	1	2	3	3	3	2
Torino	W	W	4	1	2	1	0	4	1	2
Atalanta	W	L	5	2	2	1	0	5	1	3
Bologna	D	W	5	3	1	1	1	4	0	4
Sampdoria	D	W	5	2	2	1	2	3	3	1
Palermo	W	L	5	3	2	0	1	4	2	3
Udinese	L	D	6	1	3	2	3	3	4	1
Cagliari			5	2	3	0	0	5	0	5
Crotone			-	-	-	-	-	-	-	-
Pescara			1	1	0	0	0	1	0	1

Season	Division	Pos	P	W	D	L	F	A	GD	Pts
2015-16	Serie A	9	38	13	11	14	43	45	-2	50
2014-15	Serie A	14	38	10	13	15	28	41	-13	43
2013-14	Serie A	16	38	10	6	22	34	54	-20	36

Over/Under 37%/63% 20th   Both score 45%/55% 15th

ITALIAN SERIE A

CROTONE

Ground: Stadio Ezio Scida www.fccrotone.it

	2015-16 H	A	Last six seasons at home P	W	D	L	OV	UN	BS	CS
Juventus			-	-	-	-	-	-	-	-
Napoli			-	-	-	-	-	-	-	-
Roma			-	-	-	-	-	-	-	-
Inter			-	-	-	-	-	-	-	-
Fiorentina			-	-	-	-	-	-	-	-
Sassuolo			3	2	1	0	1	2	2	1
Milan			-	-	-	-	-	-	-	-
Lazio			-	-	-	-	-	-	-	-
Chievo			-	-	-	-	-	-	-	-
Empoli			4	3	1	0	3	1	4	0
Genoa			-	-	-	-	-	-	-	-
Torino			2	0	2	0	0	2	1	1
Atalanta			1	0	1	0	1	0	1	0
Bologna			1	0	0	1	0	1	0	0
Sampdoria			1	1	0	0	0	1	0	1
Palermo			1	0	0	1	1	0	1	0
Udinese			-	-	-	-	-	-	-	-
Cagliari	W	L	1	1	0	0	1	0	1	0
Crotone										
Pescara	W	L	5	2	0	3	4	1	3	1

Season	Division	Pos	P	W	D	L	F	A	GD	Pts
2015-16	Serie B	2	42	23	13	6	61	36	+25	82
2014-15	Serie B	17	42	12	12	18	42	52	-10	48
2013-14	Serie B	6	42	17	12	13	56	52	+4	63

Over/Under 43%/57% 16th **Both score** 43%/57% 24th

EMPOLI

Ground: Stadio Carlo Castellani empolicalcio.it

	2015-16 H	A	Last six seasons at home P	W	D	L	OV	UN	BS	CS
Juventus	L	L	2	0	0	2	1	1	1	0
Napoli	D	L	2	1	1	0	2	0	2	0
Roma	L	L	2	0	0	2	1	1	1	0
Inter	L	L	2	0	1	1	0	2	0	1
Fiorentina	W	D	2	1	0	1	1	1	1	1
Sassuolo	W	L	5	2	1	2	2	3	2	1
Milan	D	L	2	0	2	0	2	0	2	0
Lazio	W	L	2	2	0	0	1	1	1	1
Chievo	L	D	2	1	0	1	2	0	1	1
Empoli										
Genoa	W	L	2	1	1	0	0	2	1	1
Torino	W	W	4	2	2	0	1	3	2	2
Atalanta	L	D	3	1	1	1	1	2	0	2
Bologna	D	W	1	0	1	0	0	1	0	1
Sampdoria	D	D	3	0	2	1	1	2	3	0
Palermo	D	D	3	1	2	0	1	2	1	2
Udinese	D	W	2	0	1	1	1	1	2	0
Cagliari			1	0	0	1	1	0	0	0
Crotone			4	1	3	0	1	3	2	2
Pescara			3	1	1	1	0	3	0	2

Season	Division	Pos	P	W	D	L	F	A	GD	Pts
2015-16	Serie A	10	38	12	10	16	40	49	-9	46
2014-15	Serie A	15	38	8	18	12	46	52	-6	42
2013-14	Serie B	2	42	20	12	10	59	35	+24	72

Over/Under 42%/58% 14th **Both score** 50%/50% 11th

FIORENTINA

Ground: Stadio Artemio Franchi violachannel.tv

	2015-16 H	A	Last six seasons at home P	W	D	L	OV	UN	BS	CS
Juventus	L	L	6	1	3	2	3	3	2	3
Napoli	D	L	6	0	3	3	2	4	4	0
Roma	L	L	6	1	2	3	3	3	3	1
Inter	W	W	6	3	1	2	5	1	4	2
Fiorentina										
Sassuolo	W	D	3	1	1	1	2	1	2	1
Milan	W	L	6	2	2	2	3	3	3	2
Lazio	L	W	6	1	0	5	3	3	3	1
Chievo	W	D	6	5	0	1	4	2	3	3
Empoli	D	L	2	0	2	0	1	1	2	0
Genoa	W	D	6	4	0	2	4	2	4	1
Torino	W	L	4	2	2	0	2	2	3	1
Atalanta	W	W	5	4	1	0	4	1	3	2
Bologna	W	W	5	4	1	0	1	4	1	4
Sampdoria	D	W	5	2	3	0	2	3	3	2
Palermo	D	W	5	2	2	1	2	3	2	3
Udinese	W	L	6	6	0	0	6	0	4	2
Cagliari			5	2	2	1	2	3	3	2
Crotone			-	-	-	-	-	-	-	-
Pescara			1	0	0	1	0	1	0	0

Season	Division	Pos	P	W	D	L	F	A	GD	Pts
2015-16	Serie A	5	38	18	10	10	60	42	+18	64
2014-15	Serie A	4	38	18	10	10	61	46	+15	64
2013-14	Serie A	4	38	19	8	11	65	44	+21	65

Over/Under 50%/50% 6th **Both score** 58%/42% 4th

GENOA

Ground: Stadio Luigi Ferraris www.genoafc.it

	2015-16 H	A	Last six seasons at home P	W	D	L	OV	UN	BS	CS
Juventus	L	L	6	1	1	4	1	5	1	2
Napoli	D	L	6	1	1	4	3	3	3	1
Roma	L	L	6	3	0	3	4	2	4	1
Inter	L	L	6	3	1	2	1	5	1	3
Fiorentina	D	L	6	0	4	2	2	4	4	1
Sassuolo	W	L	3	2	1	0	2	1	2	1
Milan	W	L	6	2	1	3	1	5	2	2
Lazio	D	L	6	4	2	0	2	4	2	4
Chievo	D	L	6	2	0	4	4	2	4	0
Empoli	W	L	2	1	1	0	0	2	1	1
Genoa										
Torino	W	D	4	2	2	0	2	2	4	0
Atalanta	L	W	5	0	4	1	3	2	5	0
Bologna	L	W	5	3	1	1	1	4	1	3
Sampdoria	L	W	5	1	3	2	3	3	3	0
Palermo	L	W	5	3	2	0	1	4	3	0
Udinese	W	D	6	3	2	1	4	2	5	1
Cagliari			5	3	0	2	2	3	2	2
Crotone			-	-	-	-	-	-	-	-
Pescara			1	1	0	0	1	0	1	0

Season	Division	Pos	P	W	D	L	F	A	GD	Pts
2015-16	Serie A	11	38	13	7	18	45	48	-3	46
2014-15	Serie A	6	38	16	11	11	62	47	+15	59
2013-14	Serie A	14	38	11	11	16	41	50	-9	44

Over/Under 42%/58% 14th **Both score** 39%/61% 19th

INTER

Ground: San Siro www.inter.it

	2015-16 H	A	P	W	D	L	OV	UN	BS	CS
Juventus	D	L	6	0	3	3	3	3	4	2
Napoli	W	L	6	3	2	1	4	2	3	2
Roma	W	D	6	3	1	2	4	2	3	2
Inter										
Fiorentina	L	L	6	4	0	2	4	2	4	1
Sassuolo	L	L	3	2	0	1	1	2	0	2
Milan	W	L	6	3	2	1	1	5	2	3
Lazio	L	L	6	3	1	2	6	0	6	0
Chievo	W	W	6	4	2	0	1	5	2	4
Empoli	W	W	2	2	0	0	2	0	2	0
Genoa	W	L	6	5	1	0	3	3	4	2
Torino	L	W	4	1	1	2	2	2	2	1
Atalanta	W	D	5	2	1	2	2	3	2	3
Bologna	W	W	5	2	1	2	4	1	3	0
Sampdoria	W	D	5	3	2	0	2	3	4	1
Palermo	W	D	5	4	1	0	4	1	3	2
Udinese	W	W	6	2	1	3	4	2	4	1
Cagliari			5	2	2	1	3	2	4	1
Crotone			-	-	-	-	-	-	-	-
Pescara			1	1	0	0	0	1	0	1

Season	Division	Pos	P	W	D	L	F	A	GD	Pts
2015-16	Serie A	4	38	20	7	11	50	38	+12	67
2014-15	Serie A	8	38	14	13	11	59	48	+11	55
2013-14	Serie A	5	38	15	15	8	62	39	+23	60

Over/Under 42%/58% 14th **Both score** 47%/53% 12th

JUVENTUS

Ground: Juventus Stadium www.juventus.com

	2015-16 H	A	P	W	D	L	OV	UN	BS	CS
Juventus										
Napoli	W	L	6	5	1	0	4	2	2	4
Roma	W	L	6	5	1	0	4	2	3	3
Inter	W	D	6	4	1	1	2	4	3	3
Fiorentina	W	W	6	5	1	0	3	3	4	2
Sassuolo	W	L	3	3	0	0	1	2	0	3
Milan	W	W	6	5	0	1	2	4	2	3
Lazio	W	W	6	5	1	0	4	2	3	3
Chievo	D	W	6	3	3	0	2	4	4	2
Empoli	W	W	2	2	0	0	2	0	2	0
Genoa	W	W	6	4	2	0	2	4	3	3
Torino	W	W	4	4	0	0	3	1	2	2
Atalanta	W	W	5	3	0	0	3	2	2	3
Bologna	W	D	5	3	1	1	2	3	3	1
Sampdoria	W	W	5	2	2	1	4	1	4	1
Palermo	W	W	5	4	0	1	3	2	1	4
Udinese	L	W	6	4	0	2	3	3	2	3
Cagliari			5	2	3	0	2	3	4	1
Crotone			-	-	-	-	-	-	-	-
Pescara			1	1	0	0	1	0	1	0

Season	Division	Pos	P	W	D	L	F	A	GD	Pts
2015-16	Serie A	1	38	29	4	5	75	20	+55	91
2014-15	Serie A	1	38	26	9	3	72	24	+48	87
2013-14	Serie A	1	38	33	3	2	80	23	+57	102

Over/Under 50%/50% 6th **Both score** 37%/63% 20th

LAZIO

Ground: Stadio Olimpico www.sslazio.it

	2015-16 H	A	P	W	D	L	OV	UN	BS	CS
Juventus	L	L	6	0	1	5	1	5	1	0
Napoli	L	L	6	2	1	3	2	4	3	1
Roma	L	L	6	2	1	3	2	4	2	1
Inter	W	W	6	5	0	1	3	3	3	3
Fiorentina	L	W	6	3	1	2	2	4	1	4
Sassuolo	L	L	3	2	0	1	2	1	2	0
Milan	L	D	6	3	2	1	3	3	5	1
Lazio										
Chievo	W	L	6	2	3	1	2	4	3	2
Empoli	W	L	2	2	0	0	1	1	0	2
Genoa	W	D	6	2	0	4	2	4	2	1
Torino	W	D	4	2	2	0	3	1	3	1
Atalanta	W	L	5	4	0	1	1	4	0	4
Bologna	W	D	5	4	0	1	4	1	3	2
Sampdoria	D	L	5	4	1	0	4	1	4	4
Palermo	D	W	5	3	2	0	3	2	3	2
Udinese	W	D	6	4	1	1	4	2	3	2
Cagliari			5	5	0	0	3	2	3	2
Crotone			-	-	-	-	-	-	-	-
Pescara			1	1	0	0	0	1	0	1

Season	Division	Pos	P	W	D	L	F	A	GD	Pts
2015-16	Serie A	8	38	15	9	14	52	52	0	54
2014-15	Serie A	3	38	21	6	11	71	38	+33	69
2013-14	Serie A	9	38	16	11	12	54	54	0	56

Over/Under 50%/50% 6th **Both score** 47%/53% 12th

MILAN

Ground: San Siro www.acmilan.com

	2015-16 H	A	P	W	D	L	OV	UN	BS	CS
Juventus	L	L	6	1	1	4	2	4	3	1
Napoli	L	D	6	2	2	2	3	3	2	3
Roma	L	D	6	2	2	2	4	2	4	1
Inter	W	L	6	3	1	2	2	4	1	3
Fiorentina	W	L	6	2	1	3	2	4	3	2
Sassuolo	W	L	3	2	0	1	3	0	3	0
Milan										
Lazio	D	W	6	2	4	0	3	3	4	2
Chievo	W	D	6	6	0	0	4	2	2	4
Empoli	W	D	2	1	1	0	1	1	2	0
Genoa	W	L	6	4	1	1	2	4	3	3
Torino	W	D	4	3	1	0	1	3	1	3
Atalanta	D	L	5	2	1	2	1	4	0	3
Bologna	L	W	5	3	1	1	1	4	2	2
Sampdoria	W	W	5	3	1	1	2	3	2	2
Palermo	W	W	5	4	0	1	3	2	2	2
Udinese	D	W	6	3	3	0	2	4	4	2
Cagliari			5	5	0	0	4	1	3	2
Crotone			-	-	-	-	-	-	-	-
Pescara			1	1	0	0	1	0	1	0

Season	Division	Pos	P	W	D	L	F	A	GD	Pts
2015-16	Serie A	7	38	15	12	11	49	43	+6	57
2014-15	Serie A	10	38	13	13	12	56	50	+6	52
2013-14	Serie A	8	38	16	9	13	57	49	+8	57

Over/Under 42%/58% 14th **Both score** 53%/47% 9th

ITALIAN SERIE A

NAPOLI

Ground: Stadio San Paolo — www.ssnapoli.it

	2015-16 H	A	Last six seasons at home P	W	D	L	OV	UN	BS	CS
Juventus	W	L	6	3	2	1	4	2	4	2
Napoli										
Roma	D	L	6	4	1	1	2	4	2	4
Inter	W	L	6	4	2	0	4	2	5	1
Fiorentina	W	D	6	3	2	1	3	3	2	3
Sassuolo	W	L	3	2	1	0	1	2	2	1
Milan	D	W	6	3	2	1	5	1	5	1
Lazio	W	W	6	4	1	1	5	1	3	3
Chievo	W	W	6	3	1	2	2	4	3	2
Empoli	W	D	2	1	1	0	2	0	2	0
Genoa	W	D	6	5	1	0	3	3	4	2
Torino	W	W	4	3	1	0	2	2	3	1
Atalanta	W	W	5	3	1	1	3	2	4	1
Bologna	W	L	5	3	1	1	4	1	3	2
Sampdoria	D	W	5	3	2	0	3	2	2	3
Palermo	W	W	5	4	1	0	2	3	1	4
Udinese	W	L	6	4	1	1	4	2	4	2
Cagliari			5	4	1	0	5	0	4	1
Crotone			-	-	-	-	-	-	-	-
Pescara			1	1	0	0	1	0	1	0

Season	Division	Pos	P	W	D	L	F	A	GD	Pts
2015-16	Serie A	2	38	25	7	6	80	32	+48	82
2014-15	Serie A	5	38	18	9	11	70	54	+16	63
2013-14	Serie A	3	38	23	9	6	77	39	+38	78

Over/Under 61%/39% 1st   **Both score** 53%/47% 9th

PALERMO

Ground: Stadio Renzo Barbera — palermocalcio.it

	2015-16 H	A	Last six seasons at home P	W	D	L	OV	UN	BS	CS
Juventus	L	L	5	1	0	4	2	3	1	0
Napoli	L	L	5	2	0	3	4	1	3	0
Roma	L	L	5	2	1	2	2	3	3	1
Inter	D	L	5	2	2	1	2	3	4	1
Fiorentina	L	D	5	1	0	4	4	1	3	1
Sassuolo	L	D	2	1	0	1	1	1	1	0
Milan	L	L	5	1	1	3	3	2	2	1
Lazio	L	L	5	1	1	3	4	1	2	0
Chievo	W	L	5	3	1	1	3	2	3	2
Empoli	L	D	3	0	1	2	1	2	1	1
Genoa	W	L	5	4	1	0	2	3	2	3
Torino	L	L	3	0	2	1	2	1	2	1
Atalanta	D	L	4	1	1	2	4	0	4	0
Bologna	D	W	4	2	2	0	2	2	3	1
Sampdoria	W	L	4	3	1	0	1	3	1	3
Palermo										
Udinese	W	W	5	1	2	2	3	2	4	0
Cagliari			4	2	2	0	2	2	2	2
Crotone			1	0	1	0	0	1	0	1
Pescara			2	1	1	0	2	0	1	0

Season	Division	Pos	P	W	D	L	F	A	GD	Pts
2015-16	Serie A	16	38	10	9	19	38	65	-27	39
2014-15	Serie A	11	38	12	13	13	53	55	-2	49
2013-14	Serie B	1	42	25	11	6	62	28	+34	86

Over/Under 50%/50% 6th   **Both score** 42%/58% 18th

PESCARA

Ground: Adriatico-Giovanni Cornacchia — pescaracalcio.com

	2015-16 H	A	Last six seasons at home P	W	D	L	OV	UN	BS	CS
Juventus			1	0	0	1	1	0	1	0
Napoli			1	0	0	1	1	0	1	0
Roma			1	0	0	1	0	1	0	0
Inter			1	0	0	1	1	0	0	0
Fiorentina			1	0	0	1	1	0	1	0
Sassuolo			2	2	0	0	1	1	1	1
Milan			1	0	0	1	1	0	0	0
Lazio			1	0	0	1	1	0	0	0
Chievo			1	0	0	1	0	1	0	0
Empoli			3	2	0	1	2	1	2	1
Genoa			1	1	0	0	0	1	0	1
Torino			3	2	0	1	0	3	0	2
Atalanta			2	0	1	1	0	2	0	1
Bologna			2	0	0	2	2	0	2	0
Sampdoria			2	1	0	1	1	1	1	1
Palermo			2	1	0	1	1	1	1	1
Udinese			1	0	0	1	0	1	0	0
Cagliari	W	L	2	1	0	1	0	2	0	1
Crotone	W	L	5	4	1	0	3	2	3	2
Pescara										

Season	Division	Pos	P	W	D	L	F	A	GD	Pts
2015-16	Serie B	4	42	21	9	12	69	52	+17	72
2014-15	Serie B	7	42	16	13	13	69	55	+14	61
2013-14	Serie B	15	42	13	13	16	50	53	-3	52

Over/Under 60%/40% 3rd   **Both score** 57%/43% 6th

ROMA

Ground: Stadio Olimpico — www.asroma.it

	2015-16 H	A	Last six seasons at home P	W	D	L	OV	UN	BS	CS
Juventus	W	W	6	2	2	2	1	5	3	1
Napoli	W	D	6	4	1	1	2	4	2	3
Roma										
Inter	D	L	6	3	3	0	2	4	3	3
Fiorentina	W	W	6	5	0	1	5	1	5	1
Sassuolo	D	W	3	0	0	3	0	5	3	0
Milan	D	W	6	2	3	1	2	4	3	3
Lazio	W	W	6	3	2	1	2	4	3	3
Chievo	W	W	6	5	0	1	2	4	0	5
Empoli	W	W	2	1	1	0	1	1	2	0
Genoa	W	W	6	6	0	0	3	3	2	4
Torino	W	W	4	4	0	0	3	1	2	2
Atalanta	L	L	5	3	1	1	2	3	3	1
Bologna	D	D	5	1	3	1	2	4	3	1
Sampdoria	W	W	5	3	1	1	3	2	3	1
Palermo	W	W	5	3	0	2	4	1	3	2
Udinese	W	W	6	5	0	1	5	1	5	1
Cagliari			5	2	1	2	3	2	2	3
Crotone			-	-	-	-	-	-	-	-
Pescara			1	0	1	0	0	1	1	0

Season	Division	Pos	P	W	D	L	F	A	GD	Pts
2015-16	Serie A	3	38	23	11	4	83	41	+42	80
2014-15	Serie A	2	38	24	13	1	54	31	+23	70
2013-14	Serie A	2	38	26	7	5	72	25	+47	85

Over/Under 61%/39% 1st   **Both score** 71%/29% 1st

SAMPDORIA

Ground: Stadio Luigi Ferraris   www.sampdoria.it

	2015-16 H	A	Last six seasons at home P	W	D	L	OV	UN	BS	CS
Juventus	L	L	5	1	1	3	2	3	2	1
Napoli	L	D	5	0	1	4	3	2	4	0
Roma	W	L	5	3	1	1	3	2	3	1
Inter	D	L	5	1	1	3	1	4	1	1
Fiorentina	L	D	5	2	1	2	3	2	2	1
Sassuolo	L	D	4	0	2	2	2	2	4	0
Milan	L	L	5	0	3	2	1	4	2	1
Lazio	W	D	5	2	1	2	1	4	2	1
Chievo	L	D	5	3	1	1	2	3	2	2
Empoli	D	D	3	2	1	0	0	3	1	2
Genoa	L	W	5	1	1	3	3	2	2	0
Torino	D	L	5	1	3	1	3	2	4	1
Atalanta	D	L	4	2	1	1	1	3	1	3
Bologna	W	L	4	3	1	0	1	3	2	2
Sampdoria										
Palermo	W	L	4	1	1	2	2	2	3	1
Udinese	W	L	5	2	2	1	2	3	1	3
Cagliari			4	2	0	2	0	4	0	2
Crotone			1	1	0	0	0	1	0	1
Pescara			2	1	0	1	2	0	1	1

Season	Division	Pos	P	W	D	L	F	A	GD	Pts
2015-16	Serie A	15	38	10	10	18	48	61	-13	40
2014-15	Serie A	7	38	13	17	8	48	42	+6	56
2013-14	Serie A	12	38	12	9	17	48	62	-14	45

Over/Under 50%/50% 6th   **Both score** 58%/42% 4th

SASSUOLO

Ground: Stadio Citta del Tricolore   sassuolocalcio.it

	2015-16 H	A	Last six seasons at home P	W	D	L	OV	UN	BS	CS
Juventus	W	L	3	1	1	1	1	2	2	1
Napoli	W	L	3	1	0	2	1	2	1	0
Roma	L	D	3	0	0	3	1	2	0	0
Inter	W	W	3	2	0	1	3	0	2	0
Fiorentina	D	L	3	0	1	2	1	2	2	0
Sassuolo										
Milan	W	L	3	3	0	0	2	1	2	1
Lazio	W	W	3	1	1	1	3	0	2	0
Chievo	D	D	3	1	1	1	0	3	1	1
Empoli	W	L	5	4	1	0	2	3	3	2
Genoa	L	L	3	2	0	1	2	1	2	0
Torino	D	W	5	0	3	2	1	4	3	1
Atalanta	D	D	4	1	2	1	3	1	3	2
Bologna	L	W	2	1	0	1	1	1	1	0
Sampdoria	D	D	4	0	3	1	1	3	1	3
Palermo	D	D	2	0	2	0	1	1	1	1
Udinese	D	D	3	0	2	1	1	2	3	0
Cagliari			2	0	2	0	0	2	2	0
Crotone			3	3	0	0	1	2	1	2
Pescara			2	1	1	0	0	2	1	1

Season	Division	Pos	P	W	D	L	F	A	GD	Pts
2015-16	Serie A	6	38	16	13	9	49	40	+9	61
2014-15	Serie A	12	38	12	13	13	49	57	-8	49
2013-14	Serie A	17	38	9	7	22	43	72	-29	34

Over/Under 39%/61% 19th   **Both score** 58%/42% 4th

TORINO

Ground: Stadio Olimpico Grande Torino   torino.it

	2015-16 H	A	Last six seasons at home P	W	D	L	OV	UN	BS	CS
Juventus	L	L	4	1	0	3	2	2	2	0
Napoli	L	L	4	1	0	3	2	2	2	1
Roma	D	L	4	0	3	1	1	3	4	0
Inter	L	W	4	0	2	2	1	3	1	1
Fiorentina	W	L	4	1	3	0	2	2	3	1
Sassuolo	L	D	5	2	0	3	3	2	2	2
Milan	D	L	4	0	3	1	2	2	4	0
Lazio	D	L	4	2	1	1	0	4	1	2
Chievo	L	L	4	3	0	1	2	2	2	2
Empoli	L	L	4	2	0	2	2	2	0	0
Genoa	D	L	4	2	2	0	3	1	3	1
Torino										
Atalanta	W	W	5	3	1	1	3	2	3	2
Bologna	W	W	3	2	0	1	1	2	1	2
Sampdoria	W	D	5	3	1	1	2	3	2	2
Palermo	W	W	3	1	2	0	2	1	2	1
Udinese	L	W	4	2	1	1	0	4	0	3
Cagliari			3	1	1	1	1	2	2	0
Crotone			2	1	0	1	1	1	2	0
Pescara			3	3	0	0	3	0	2	1

Season	Division	Pos	P	W	D	L	F	A	GD	Pts
2015-16	Serie A	12	38	12	9	17	52	55	-3	45
2014-15	Serie A	9	38	14	12	12	48	45	+3	54
2013-14	Serie A	7	38	15	12	11	58	48	+10	57

Over/Under 58%/42% 3rd   **Both score** 66%/34% 2nd

UDINESE

Ground: Stadio Friuli   www.udinese.it

	2015-16 H	A	Last six seasons at home P	W	D	L	OV	UN	BS	CS
Juventus	L	W	6	0	2	4	3	3	1	2
Napoli	W	W	6	3	3	0	3	3	4	2
Roma	L	L	6	1	1	4	2	4	3	1
Inter	L	L	6	2	0	4	6	0	3	1
Fiorentina	W	L	6	5	1	0	4	2	4	2
Sassuolo	D	D	3	1	1	1	0	3	0	2
Milan	L	D	6	3	1	2	4	2	4	2
Lazio	D	L	6	3	1	2	2	4	2	3
Chievo	D	W	6	4	2	0	3	3	3	3
Empoli	L	L	2	1	0	1	1	1	1	1
Genoa	D	L	6	2	2	2	5	1	2	3
Torino	L	L	4	2	0	2	2	2	2	1
Atalanta	W	D	5	3	2	0	2	3	3	2
Bologna	L	W	5	1	3	1	0	5	2	2
Sampdoria	W	L	5	3	1	1	3	2	3	2
Palermo	L	L	5	2	1	2	2	3	3	1
Udinese										
Cagliari			5	2	3	0	2	3	3	2
Crotone			-	-	-	-	-	-	-	-
Pescara			1	1	0	0	0	1	0	1

Season	Division	Pos	P	W	D	L	F	A	GD	Pts
2015-16	Serie A	17	38	10	9	19	35	60	-25	39
2014-15	Serie A	16	38	10	11	17	43	53	-10	41
2013-14	Serie A	13	38	12	8	18	46	57	-11	44

Over/Under 47%/53% 12th   **Both score** 55%/45% 8th

ITALIAN SERIE A

Serie A 2015-16

Pos	H	A		P	Home					Away					GD	Pts
					W	D	L	F	A	W	D	L	F	A		
1	2	1	Juventus (CL)	38	16	2	1	37	6	13	2	4	38	14	+55	91
2	1	3	Napoli (CL)	38	16	3	0	49	12	9	4	6	31	20	+48	82
3	3	2	Roma (CL)	38	13	5	1	44	17	10	6	3	39	24	+42	80
4	4	6	Inter (EL)	38	13	2	4	29	15	7	5	7	21	23	+12	67
5	5	5	Fiorentina (EL)	38	11	5	3	34	16	7	5	7	26	26	+18	64
6	9	4	Sassuolo (EL)	38	8	8	3	25	20	8	5	6	24	20	+9	61
7	8	7	Milan	38	9	6	4	28	22	6	6	7	21	21	+6	57
8	7	10	Lazio	38	10	3	6	32	23	5	6	8	20	29	0	54
9	11	11	Chievo	38	7	8	4	25	18	6	3	10	18	27	-2	50
10	13	12	Empoli	38	7	6	6	22	20	5	4	10	18	29	-9	46
11	6	17	Genoa	38	10	3	6	29	19	3	4	12	16	29	-3	46
12	14	9	Torino	38	6	6	7	25	25	6	3	10	27	30	-3	45
13	10	15	Atalanta	38	8	6	5	27	21	3	6	10	14	26	-6	45
14	19	8	Bologna	38	5	5	9	20	21	6	4	9	13	24	-12	42
15	12	18	Sampdoria	38	8	4	7	29	25	2	6	11	19	36	-13	40
16	16	14	Palermo	38	6	4	9	24	30	4	5	10	14	35	-27	39
17	18	13	Udinese	38	6	4	9	18	28	4	5	10	17	32	-25	39
18	15	16	Carpi (R)	38	6	5	8	23	26	3	6	10	14	31	-20	38
19	17	20	Frosinone (R)	38	6	4	9	18	26	2	3	14	17	50	-41	31
20	20	19	Verona (R)	38	4	6	9	21	30	1	7	11	13	33	-29	28

Serie A results 2015-16

	Atalanta	Bologna	Carpi	Chievo	Empoli	Fiorentina	Frosinone	Genoa	Hellas Verona	Inter	Juventus	Lazio	Milan	Napoli	Palermo	Roma	Sampdoria	Sassuolo	Torino	Udinese
Atalanta		2-0	3-0	1-0	0-0	2-3	2-0	0-2	1-1	1-1	0-2	2-1	2-1	1-3	3-0	3-3	2-1	1-1	0-1	1-1
Bologna	3-0		0-0	0-1	2-3	1-1	1-0	2-0	0-1	0-0	2-2	0-1	3-2	0-1	2-2	3-2	0-1	0-1	1-2	
Carpi	1-1	1-2		1-2	1-0	0-1	2-1	4-1	0-0	1-2	2-3	1-3	0-0	0-0	1-1	1-3	2-1	1-3	2-1	2-1
Chievo	1-0	0-0	1-0		1-1	0-0	5-1	1-0	1-1	0-1	0-4	4-0	0-0	0-1	3-1	3-3	1-1	1-1	1-0	2-3
Empoli	0-1	0-0	3-0	1-3		2-0	1-2	2-0	1-0	0-1	1-3	1-0	2-2	2-2	0-0	1-3	1-1	1-0	2-1	1-1
Fiorentina	3-0	2-0	2-1	2-0	2-2		4-1	1-0	1-1	2-1	1-2	1-3	2-0	1-1	0-0	1-2	1-1	3-1	2-0	3-0
Frosinone	0-0	1-0	2-1	0-2	2-0	0-0		2-2	3-2	0-1	0-2	0-0	2-4	1-5	0-2	0-2	2-0	0-1	1-2	2-0
Genoa	1-2	0-1	1-2	3-2	1-0	0-0	4-0		2-0	1-0	0-2	0-0	1-0	0-0	4-0	2-3	2-3	2-1	3-2	2-1
Hellas Verona	2-1	0-2	1-2	3-1	0-1	0-2	1-2	1-1		3-3	2-1	1-2	2-1	0-2	0-1	1-1	0-3	1-1	2-2	1-1
Inter	1-0	2-1	1-1	1-0	2-1	1-4	4-0	1-0	1-0		0-0	1-2	1-0	2-0	3-1	1-0	3-1	0-1	1-2	3-1
Juventus	2-0	3-1	2-0	1-1	3-1	1-1	1-0	3-0	2-0	3-0		2-0	3-0	1-0	1-0	4-0	5-0	1-0	2-1	0-1
Lazio	2-0	2-1	0-0	4-1	2-0	2-4	2-0	2-0	5-2	2-0	0-2		1-3	0-2	1-1	1-4	1-1	0-2	3-0	2-0
Milan	0-0	0-1	0-0	1-0	2-1	2-0	3-3	2-1	1-1	3-0	1-2	1-1		0-4	3-2	1-3	4-1	2-1	1-0	1-1
Napoli	2-1	6-0	1-0	3-1	5-1	2-1	4-0	3-1	3-0	2-1	2-1	5-0	1-1		2-0	0-0	2-2	3-1	2-1	1-0
Palermo	2-2	0-0	2-2	1-0	0-1	1-3	4-1	1-0	3-2	1-1	0-3	0-3	0-2	0-1		2-4	2-0	0-1	1-3	4-1
Roma	0-2	1-1	5-1	3-0	3-1	4-1	3-1	2-0	1-1	1-1	2-1	2-0	1-1	1-0	5-0		2-1	2-2	3-2	3-1
Sampdoria	0-0	2-0	5-2	0-1	1-1	0-2	2-0	0-3	4-1	1-1	1-2	2-1	0-1	2-4	2-0	2-1		1-3	2-2	2-0
Sassuolo	2-2	0-2	1-0	1-1	3-2	1-1	2-1	0-1	3-1	1-0	2-1	2-0	2-1	2-2	2-0	0-0			1-1	1-1
Torino	2-1	2-0	0-0	1-2	0-1	3-1	4-2	3-3	0-0	0-1	1-4	1-1	1-1	2-1	1-1	2-1	1-1	2-0		0-1
Udinese	2-1	0-1	1-2	0-0	1-2	2-1	1-0	1-1	2-0	0-4	0-4	0-0	2-3	3-1	0-1	1-2	0-1	0-0	1-5	

Top scorers

	Team	Goals scored
G Higuain	Napoli	36
P Dybala	Juventus	19
C Bacca	Milan	18
M Icardi	Inter	16
L Pavoletti	Genoa	14
M Salah	Roma	14

Over 2.5 goals top ten

	H	A	%
Roma	11	12	61%
Napoli	14	9	61%
Carpi	12	10	58%
Torino	9	13	58%
Lazio, Palermo, Sampdoria, Juve, Fior, Frosinone			50%

Both to score top five

	H	A	%
Roma	13	14	71%
Torino	12	13	66%
Carpi	14	9	61%
Fiorentina, Sassuolo, Hellas Verona, Sampdoria,			58%

AUGSBURG

Ground: SGL arena   www.fcaugsburg.de

	2015-16 H	A	Last six seasons at home P	W	D	L	OV	UN	BS	CS
Bayern Munich	L	L	5	1	0	4	3	2	2	1
Dortmund	L	L	5	0	1	4	4	1	3	1
Leverkusen	D	D	5	0	2	3	5	0	5	0
M'gladbach	D	L	5	2	3	0	3	2	4	1
Schalke	W	D	5	1	3	1	2	3	3	2
Mainz	D	L	5	2	2	1	3	2	4	0
Hertha	L	L	5	2	2	1	1	4	1	3
Wolfsburg	D	W	5	2	2	1	1	4	1	4
Cologne	D	W	3	1	2	0	1	2	1	2
Hamburg	L	W	5	3	0	2	3	2	3	1
Ingolstadt	L	L	2	1	0	1	0	2	0	1
Augsburg										
Werder Bremen	L	W	5	3	1	1	4	1	5	0
Darmstadt	L	D	1	0	0	1	0	1	0	0
Hoffenheim	L	L	5	3	0	2	3	2	3	1
Ein Frankfurt	D	D	4	2	2	0	2	2	2	2
Freiburg			4	2	2	0	2	2	3	1
RB Leipzig			-	-	-	-	-	-	-	-

Season	Division	Pos	P	W	D	L	F	A	GD	Pts
2015-16	Bundesliga	12	34	9	11	14	42	52	-10	38
2014-15	Bundesliga	5	34	15	4	15	43	43	0	49
2013-14	Bundesliga	8	34	15	7	12	47	47	0	52

Over/Under 53%/47% 10th   **Both score** 59%/41% 5th

BAYERN MUNICH

Ground: Allianz Arena   www.fcbayern.de

	2015-16 H	A	Last six seasons at home P	W	D	L	OV	UN	BS	CS
Bayern Munich										
Dortmund	W	D	6	2	1	3	4	2	4	0
Leverkusen	W	D	6	5	0	1	5	1	3	3
M'gladbach	D	L	6	2	2	2	1	5	3	1
Schalke	W	W	6	5	1	0	4	2	3	3
Mainz	L	W	6	3	1	2	4	2	4	2
Hertha	W	W	4	4	0	0	2	2	1	3
Wolfsburg	W	W	6	6	0	0	4	2	3	3
Cologne	W	W	4	3	1	0	3	1	1	3
Hamburg	W	W	6	6	0	0	6	0	2	4
Ingolstadt	W	W	1	1	0	0	1	0	1	0
Augsburg	W	W	5	4	0	1	4	1	2	2
Werder Bremen	W	W	6	5	1	0	5	1	3	3
Darmstadt	W	W	1	1	0	0	1	0	1	0
Hoffenheim	W	W	6	5	1	0	4	2	2	4
Ein Frankfurt	W	D	5	5	0	0	3	2	1	4
Freiburg			5	5	0	0	3	2	1	4
RB Leipzig			-	-	-	-	-	-	-	-

Season	Division	Pos	P	W	D	L	F	A	GD	Pts
2015-16	Bundesliga	1	34	28	4	2	80	17	+63	88
2014-15	Bundesliga	1	34	25	4	5	80	18	+62	79
2013-14	Bundesliga	1	34	29	3	2	94	23	+71	90

Over/Under 62%/38% 6th   **Both score** 41%/59% 17th

COLOGNE

Ground: RheinEnergieStadion   www.fc-koeln.de

	2015-16 H	A	Last six seasons at home P	W	D	L	OV	UN	BS	CS
Bayern Munich	L	L	4	1	0	3	2	2	2	0
Dortmund	W	D	4	2	0	2	4	0	4	0
Leverkusen	L	W	4	1	1	2	0	4	1	1
M'gladbach	W	L	4	1	1	2	2	2	0	2
Schalke	L	W	4	2	0	2	3	1	3	1
Mainz	D	W	4	1	3	0	1	3	2	2
Hertha	L	L	4	1	0	3	2	2	2	1
Wolfsburg	W	L	4	0	3	1	2	2	3	0
Cologne										
Hamburg	W	D	4	2	1	1	2	2	2	1
Ingolstadt	D	D	3	1	1	1	0	3	1	1
Augsburg	L	D	3	1	0	2	2	1	1	1
Werder Bremen	D	D	4	1	3	0	1	3	2	2
Darmstadt	W	D	1	1	0	0	1	0	1	0
Hoffenheim	D	D	4	2	2	0	1	3	2	2
Ein Frankfurt	W	L	3	3	0	0	2	1	2	1
Freiburg			3	2	0	1	1	2	0	2
RB Leipzig			-	-	-	-	-	-	-	-

Season	Division	Pos	P	W	D	L	F	A	GD	Pts
2015-16	Bundesliga	9	34	10	13	11	38	42	-4	43
2014-15	Bundesliga	12	34	9	13	12	34	41	-7	40
2013-14	2.Bundesliga	1	34	19	11	4	53	20	+33	68

Over/Under 38%/62% 17th   **Both score** 53%/47% 9th

GERMAN BUNDESLIGA

DARMSTADT

Ground: Merck-Stadion am Bollenfalltor   www.sv98.de

	2015-16 H	A	P	W	D	L	OV	UN	BS	CS
Bayern Munich	L	L	1	0	0	1	1	0	0	0
Dortmund	L	D	1	0	0	1	0	1	0	0
Leverkusen	L	W	1	0	0	1	1	0	1	0
M'gladbach	L	L	1	0	0	1	0	1	0	0
Schalke	L	D	1	0	0	1	0	1	0	0
Mainz	L	D	1	0	0	1	1	0	1	0
Hertha	L	W	1	0	0	1	1	0	1	0
Wolfsburg	L	D	1	0	0	1	0	1	0	0
Cologne	D	L	1	0	1	0	0	1	0	1
Hamburg	D	W	1	0	1	0	0	1	1	0
Ingolstadt	W	L	2	1	1	0	1	1	1	1
Augsburg	D	W	1	0	1	0	0	1	0	0
Werder Bremen	W	D	1	1	0	0	1	0	1	0
Darmstadt										
Hoffenheim	D	W	1	0	1	0	0	1	0	1
Ein Frankfurt	L	W	1	0	0	1	1	0	1	0
Freiburg			-	-	-	-	-	-	-	-
RB Leipzig			1	1	0	0	0	1	0	1

Season	Division	Pos	P	W	D	L	F	A	GD	Pts
2015-16	Bundesliga	14	34	9	11	14	38	53	-15	38
2014-15	2.Bundesliga	2	34	15	14	5	44	26+18		59
2013-14	3.Liga	3	38	21	9	8	58	29+29		72

Over/Under 53%/47% 10th   **Both score** 56%/44% 8th

DORTMUND

Ground: Westfalenstadion   www.bvb.de

	2015-16 H	A	P	W	D	L	OV	UN	BS	CS
Bayern Munich	D	L	6	2	2	2	1	5	1	3
Dortmund										
Leverkusen	W	W	6	3	0	3	2	4	0	3
M'gladbach	W	W	6	5	0	1	4	2	2	4
Schalke	W	D	6	3	2	1	3	3	2	4
Mainz	W	W	6	5	1	0	3	3	4	2
Hertha	W	D	4	2	0	2	3	1	3	1
Wolfsburg	W	W	6	4	1	1	5	1	5	1
Cologne	W	L	4	2	2	0	2	2	1	3
Hamburg	W	L	6	4	0	2	4	2	3	2
Ingolstadt	W	W	1	1	0	0	1	0	1	0
Augsburg	W	W	5	3	1	1	4	1	3	1
Werder Bremen	W	W	6	6	0	0	3	3	3	3
Darmstadt	D		1	0	1	0	1	0	1	0
Hoffenheim	W	D	6	4	1	1	4	2	5	1
Ein Frankfurt	W		5	5	0	0	4	1	2	3
Freiburg			5	5	0	0	5	0	2	3
RB Leipzig			-	-	-	-	-	-	-	-

Season	Division	Pos	P	W	D	L	F	A	GD	Pts
2015-16	Bundesliga	2	34	24	6	4	82	34+48		78
2014-15	Bundesliga	7	34	13	7	14	47	42	+5	46
2013-14	Bundesliga	2	34	22	5	7	80	38+42		71

Over/Under 71%/29% 3rd   **Both score** 59%/41% 5th

Pep Guardiola made a splash at Bayern

EINTRACHT FRANKFURT

Ground: Commerzbank-Arena   www.eintracht.de

	2015-16 H	A	P	W	D	L	OV	UN	BS	CS
Bayern Munich	D	L	5	0	2	3	1	4	1	1
Dortmund	W	L	5	3	1	1	2	3	2	3
Leverkusen	L	L	5	2	0	3	4	1	3	0
M'gladbach	L	L	5	1	1	3	1	4	1	2
Schalke	D	L	5	2	3	0	1	4	1	4
Mainz	W	L	5	3	1	1	4	1	4	1
Hertha	D	L	3	1	2	0	1	2	2	1
Wolfsburg	W	L	5	2	2	1	4	1	5	0
Cologne	W	D	3	2	0	1	2	1	2	0
Hamburg	D	D	5	2	2	1	4	1	4	1
Ingolstadt	D		2	0	2	0	0	2	2	0
Augsburg	D	D	4	1	2	1	1	3	3	0
Werder Bremen	W	L	5	3	2	0	3	4	1	3
Darmstadt	L	W	1	0	0	1	0	1	0	0
Hoffenheim	L	D	5	2	0	3	4	1	3	0
Ein Frankfurt										
Freiburg			4	2	0	2	2	2	2	1
RB Leipzig			-	-	-	-	-	-	-	-

Season	Division	Pos	P	W	D	L	F	A	GD	Pts
2015-16	Bundesliga	16	34	9	9	16	34	52	-18	36
2014-15	Bundesliga	9	34	11	10	13	56	62	-6	43
2013-14	Bundesliga	13	34	9	9	16	40	57	-17	36

Over/Under 47%/53% 14th   **Both score** 50%/50% 13th

FREIBURG

Ground: Dreisamstadion www.scfreiburg.com

	2015-16		Last six seasons at home							
	H	A	P	W	D	L	OV	UN	BS	CS
Bayern Munich			5	1	2	2	2	3	3	1
Dortmund			5	0	0	5	3	2	2	0
Leverkusen			5	1	2	2	1	4	1	2
M'gladbach			5	4	1	0	2	3	1	4
Schalke			5	2	0	3	3	2	3	1
Mainz			5	1	1	3	3	2	4	1
Hertha			3	0	3	0	2	1	3	0
Wolfsburg			5	2	0	3	5	0	3	1
Cologne			3	3	0	0	2	1	2	1
Hamburg			5	1	2	2	2	3	1	3
Ingolstadt			-	-	-	-	-	-	-	-
Augsburg			4	3	0	1	1	3	1	3
Werder Bremen			5	1	1	3	4	1	4	0
Darmstadt			-	-	-	-	-	-	-	-
Hoffenheim			5	2	3	0	2	3	4	1
Ein Frankfurt			4	1	3	0	1	3	2	2
Freiburg										
RB Leipzig	W	D	1	1	0	0	1	0	1	0

Season	Division	Pos	P	W	D	L	F	A	GD	Pts
2015-16	2.Bundesliga	1	34	22	6	6	75	39	+36	72
2014-15	Bundesliga	17	34	7	13	14	36	47	-11	34
2013-14	Bundesliga	14	34	9	9	16	43	61	-18	36

Over/Under 65%/35% 2nd **Both score** 65%/35% 1st

HAMBURG

Ground: Volksparkstadion www.hsv.de

	2015-16		Last six seasons at home							
	H	A	P	W	D	L	OV	UN	BS	CS
Bayern Munich	L	L	6	0	3	3	3	3	3	2
Dortmund	W	L	6	3	2	1	4	2	4	2
Leverkusen	D	L	6	2	2	2	2	4	3	2
M'gladbach	W	W	6	2	2	2	1	5	3	1
Schalke	L	L	6	3	0	3	4	2	3	1
Mainz	L	D	6	2	1	3	4	2	4	2
Hertha	W	L	4	1	1	2	2	2	1	1
Wolfsburg	L	D	6	0	2	4	2	4	4	0
Cologne	D	L	4	1	1	2	2	2	3	0
Hamburg										
Ingolstadt	D	W	1	0	1	0	0	1	1	0
Augsburg	L	W	5	1	1	3	1	4	2	0
Werder Bremen	W	W	6	4	0	2	4	2	3	2
Darmstadt	L	D	1	0	0	1	1	0	1	0
Hoffenheim	L	W	6	3	1	2	3	3	4	2
Ein Frankfurt	D	D	5	1	2	2	1	4	2	2
Freiburg			5	0	2	3	1	4	3	0
RB Leipzig			-	-	-	-	-	-	-	-

Season	Division	Pos	P	W	D	L	F	A	GD	Pts
2015-16	Bundesliga	10	34	11	8	15	40	46	-6	41
2014-15	Bundesliga	16	34	9	8	17	25	50	-25	35
2013-14	Bundesliga	16	34	7	6	21	51	75	-24	27

Over/Under 56%/44% 9th **Both score** 53%/47% 9th

HERTHA BERLIN

Ground: Olympiastadion www.herthabsc.de

	2015-16		Last six seasons at home							
	H	A	P	W	D	L	OV	UN	BS	CS
Bayern Munich	L	L	4	0	0	4	2	2	1	0
Dortmund	D	L	4	1	1	2	1	3	0	2
Leverkusen	W	L	4	1	1	2	2	2	2	0
M'gladbach	L	L	4	1	0	3	3	1	3	1
Schalke	W	L	4	1	1	2	2	2	2	1
Mainz	W	D	4	2	1	1	2	2	2	2
Hertha										
Wolfsburg	D	L	4	1	1	2	2	2	3	1
Cologne	W	W	4	2	2	0	1	3	1	3
Hamburg	W	L	4	3	0	1	3	1	1	3
Ingolstadt	W	W	3	2	1	0	2	1	2	1
Augsburg	D	W	5	2	3	0	2	3	2	3
Werder Bremen	D	D	4	2	2	0	2	2	3	1
Darmstadt	L	W	1	0	0	1	1	0	1	0
Hoffenheim	W	L	4	2	1	1	2	2	2	1
Ein Frankfurt	W	D	3	2	1	0	1	2	1	2
Freiburg			3	0	1	2	1	2	1	1
RB Leipzig										

Season	Division	Pos	P	W	D	L	F	A	GD	Pts
2015-16	Bundesliga	7	34	14	8	12	42	42	0	50
2014-15	Bundesliga	15	34	9	8	17	36	52	-16	35
2013-14	Bundesliga	11	34	11	8	15	40	48	-8	41

Over/Under 44%/56% 16th **Both score** 44%/56% 16th

HOFFENHEIM

Ground: Rhein-Neckar Arena www.achtzehn99.de

	2015-16		Last six seasons at home							
	H	A	P	W	D	L	OV	UN	BS	CS
Bayern Munich	L	L	6	0	1	5	3	3	3	1
Dortmund	D	L	6	2	3	1	2	4	4	2
Leverkusen	D	L	6	0	2	4	3	4	3	0
M'gladbach	D	L	6	3	2	1	4	2	4	2
Schalke	L	L	6	3	2	1	4	2	5	1
Mainz	L	L	6	2	2	2	3	3	4	2
Hertha	W	L	4	2	1	1	3	1	4	0
Wolfsburg	W	L	6	3	1	2	4	2	5	1
Cologne	D	D	4	0	3	1	1	3	4	0
Hamburg	L	W	6	3	1	2	4	2	1	4
Ingolstadt	D	D	1	1	0	0	1	0	1	0
Augsburg	W	D	5	3	2	0	2	3	2	3
Werder Bremen	L	D	6	1	1	4	6	0	6	0
Darmstadt	L	D	1	0	0	1	0	1	0	0
Hoffenheim										
Ein Frankfurt	D	W	5	2	2	1	2	3	1	3
Freiburg			5	1	3	1	3	2	4	0
RB Leipzig										

Season	Division	Pos	P	W	D	L	F	A	GD	Pts
2015-16	Bundesliga	15	34	9	10	15	39	54	-15	37
2014-15	Bundesliga	8	34	12	8	14	49	55	-6	44
2013-14	Bundesliga	9	34	11	11	12	72	70	+2	44

Over/Under 50%/50% 13th **Both score** 65%/35% 3rd

GERMAN BUNDESLIGA

INGOLSTADT

Ground: Audi-Sportpark   www.fcingolstadt.de

	2015-16 H	A	Last six seasons at home P	W	D	L	OV	UN	BS	CS
Bayern Munich	L	L	1	0	0	1	1	0	1	0
Dortmund	L	L	1	0	0	1	1	0	0	0
Leverkusen	L	L	1	0	0	1	0	1	0	0
M'gladbach	W	D	1	1	0	0	0	1	0	1
Schalke	W	D	1	1	0	0	1	0	0	1
Mainz	W	W	1	1	0	0	0	1	0	1
Hertha	L	L	3	0	2	1	0	3	2	0
Wolfsburg	D	L	1	0	1	0	0	1	0	1
Cologne	D	D	3	0	2	1	1	2	2	0
Hamburg	L	D	1	0	0	1	0	1	0	0
Ingolstadt										
Augsburg	W	W	2	1	0	1	2	0	2	0
Werder Bremen	W	W	1	1	0	0	0	1	0	1
Darmstadt	W	L	2	1	1	0	2	0	2	0
Hoffenheim	D	L	1	0	1	0	0	1	1	0
Ein Frankfurt	W	D	2	1	1	0	0	2	1	1
Freiburg			-	-	-	-	-	-	-	-
RB Leipzig			1	1	0	0	1	0	1	0

Season	Division	Pos	P	W	D	L	F	A	GD	Pts
2015-16	Bundesliga	11	34	10	10	14	33	42	-9	40
2014-15	2.Bundesliga	1	34	17	13	4	53	32	+21	64
2013-14	2.Bundesliga	10	34	11	11	12	34	33	+1	44

Over/Under 32%/68% 18th   **Both score** 41%/59% 17th

LEVERKUSEN

Ground: BayArena   www.bayer04.de

	2015-16 H	A	Last six seasons at home P	W	D	L	OV	UN	BS	CS
Bayern Munich	D	L	6	2	3	1	1	5	3	3
Dortmund	L	L	6	0	3	3	3	3	3	2
Leverkusen										
M'gladbach	W	L	6	2	2	2	4	2	5	1
Schalke	D	W	6	3	1	2	1	5	2	3
Mainz	W	L	6	2	2	2	2	4	2	2
Hertha	L	L	4	3	1	0	4	0	4	0
Wolfsburg	W	L	6	4	1	1	5	1	4	2
Cologne	L	W	4	2	0	2	4	0	4	0
Hamburg	W	D	6	4	2	0	4	2	3	3
Ingolstadt	W	W	1	1	0	0	1	0	1	0
Augsburg	D	D	5	4	1	0	3	2	4	1
Werder Bremen	L	W	6	3	2	1	4	2	4	2
Darmstadt	L		1	0	0	1	0	1	0	0
Hoffenheim	W	D	6	5	0	1	4	2	3	3
Ein Frankfurt	W	W	5	3	1	1	3	2	3	1
Freiburg			5	3	1	1	2	3	2	2
RB Leipzig			-	-	-	-	-	-	-	-

Season	Division	Pos	P	W	D	L	F	A	GD	Pts
2015-16	Bundesliga	3	34	18	6	10	56	40	+16	60
2014-15	Bundesliga	4	34	17	10	7	62	37	+25	61
2013-14	Bundesliga	4	34	19	4	11	60	41	+19	61

Over/Under 62%/38% 6th   **Both score** 50%/50% 13th

MAINZ

Ground: Coface Arena   www.mainz05.de

	2015-16 H	A	Last six seasons at home P	W	D	L	OV	UN	BS	CS
Bayern Munich	L	W	6	1	0	5	5	1	3	0
Dortmund	L	L	6	1	0	5	3	3	3	1
Leverkusen	W	W	6	3	0	3	3	3	3	2
M'gladbach	W	W	6	2	2	3	3	3	2	3
Schalke	W	L	6	2	1	3	3	3	3	1
Mainz										
Hertha	D	L	4	0	2	2	1	3	2	1
Wolfsburg	W	D	6	2	3	1	0	6	2	3
Cologne	L	D	4	3	0	1	2	2	1	3
Hamburg	D	W	6	1	2	3	3	3	3	2
Ingolstadt	L	L	1	0	0	1	0	1	0	0
Augsburg	W	D	5	4	0	1	3	2	2	2
Werder Bremen	L	D	6	1	2	3	4	2	5	1
Darmstadt	D	W	1	0	1	0	0	1	0	1
Hoffenheim	W	L	6	3	2	1	5	1	3	2
Ein Frankfurt	W	L	5	4	1	0	3	2	2	3
Freiburg			5	2	3	0	2	3	3	2
RB Leipzig			-	-	-	-	-	-	-	-

Season	Division	Pos	P	W	D	L	F	A	GD	Pts
2015-16	Bundesliga	6	34	14	8	12	46	42	+4	50
2014-15	Bundesliga	11	34	9	13	12	45	47	-2	40
2013-14	Bundesliga	7	34	16	5	13	52	54	-2	53

Over/Under 53%/47% 10th   **Both score** 53%/47% 9th

MONCHENGLADBACH

Ground: Borussia-Park   www.borussia.de

	2015-16 H	A	Last six seasons at home P	W	D	L	OV	UN	BS	CS
Bayern Munich	W	D	6	2	2	2	4	2	4	1
Dortmund	L	L	6	3	2	1	2	4	4	2
Leverkusen	W	L	6	2	2	2	5	1	4	1
M'gladbach										
Schalke	W	L	6	5	0	1	5	1	4	1
Mainz	L	L	6	3	1	2	3	3	4	2
Hertha	W	L	4	3	1	0	3	1	1	3
Wolfsburg	W	L	6	4	0	2	4	3	3	3
Cologne	W	L	4	4	0	0	2	2	1	3
Hamburg	L	L	6	2	2	2	4	2	4	1
Ingolstadt	D	L	1	0	1	0	0	1	0	1
Augsburg	W	D	5	2	1	2	3	2	3	2
Werder Bremen	W	L	6	4	1	1	5	1	5	1
Darmstadt	W	L	1	1	0	0	1	0	1	0
Hoffenheim	W	D	6	4	1	1	5	1	5	1
Ein Frankfurt	W	L	5	3	0	2	4	1	2	2
Freiburg			5	3	2	0	0	5	1	4
RB Leipzig			-	-	-	-	-	-	-	-

Season	Division	Pos	P	W	D	L	F	A	GD	Pts
2015-16	Bundesliga	4	34	17	4	13	67	50	+17	55
2014-15	Bundesliga	3	34	19	9	6	53	26	+27	66
2013-14	Bundesliga	6	34	16	7	11	59	43	+16	55

Over/Under 74%/26% 1st   **Both score** 59%/41% 5th

RED BULL LEIPZIG

Ground: Red Bull Arena www.dierotenbullen.com

	2015-16 H	A	Last six seasons at home P	W	D	L	OV	UN	BS	CS
Bayern Munich			-	-	-	-	-	-	-	-
Dortmund			-	-	-	-	-	-	-	-
Leverkusen			-	-	-	-	-	-	-	-
M'gladbach			-	-	-	-	-	-	-	-
Schalke			-	-	-	-	-	-	-	-
Mainz			-	-	-	-	-	-	-	-
Hertha			-	-	-	-	-	-	-	-
Wolfsburg			-	-	-	-	-	-	-	-
Cologne			-	-	-	-	-	-	-	-
Hamburg			-	-	-	-	-	-	-	-
Ingolstadt			1	0	0	1	0	1	0	0
Augsburg			-	-	-	-	-	-	-	-
Werder Bremen			-	-	-	-	-	-	-	-
Darmstadt			1	1	0	0	1	0	1	0
Hoffenheim			-	-	-	-	-	-	-	-
Ein Frankfurt			-	-	-	-	-	-	-	-
Freiburg	D	L	1	0	1	0	0	1	1	0
RB Leipzig										

Season	Division	Pos	P	W	D	L	F	A	GD	Pts
2015-16	2.Bundesliga	2	34	20	7	7	54	32	+22	67
2014-15	2.Bundesliga	5	34	13	11	10	39	31	+8	50
2013-14	3.Liga	2	38	24	7	7	65	34	+31	79

Over/Under 44%/56% 12th **Both score** 56%/44% 7th

SCHALKE

Ground: Veltins-Arena www.schalke04.de

	2015-16 H	A	Last six seasons at home P	W	D	L	OV	UN	BS	CS
Bayern Munich	L	L	6	1	1	4	2	4	2	1
Dortmund	D	L	6	2	1	3	6	0	6	0
Leverkusen	L	D	6	2	1	3	2	4	2	2
M'gladbach	W	L	6	3	2	1	2	4	3	2
Schalke										
Mainz	W	L	6	3	2	1	4	2	4	2
Hertha	W	L	4	4	0	0	2	2	1	3
Wolfsburg	W	L	6	6	0	0	5	1	2	4
Cologne	L	W	4	2	0	2	4	0	2	1
Hamburg	W	W	6	3	2	1	4	2	4	1
Ingolstadt	D	L	1	0	1	0	0	1	1	0
Augsburg	D	L	5	4	1	0	3	2	4	1
Werder Bremen	L	W	6	4	1	1	5	1	4	2
Darmstadt	D	W	1	0	1	0	0	1	1	0
Hoffenheim	W	W	6	5	0	1	4	2	2	3
Ein Frankfurt	W	D	5	3	2	0	2	3	3	2
Freiburg			5	3	1	1	2	3	2	3
RB Leipzig			-	-	-	-	-	-	-	-

Season	Division	Pos	P	W	D	L	F	A	GD	Pts
2015-16	Bundesliga	5	34	15	7	12	51	49	+2	52
2014-15	Bundesliga	6	34	13	9	12	42	40	+2	48
2013-14	Bundesliga	3	34	19	7	8	63	43	+20	64

Over/Under 65%/35% 5th **Both score** 62%/38% 4th

WERDER BREMEN

Ground: Weserstadion www.werder.de

	2015-16 H	A	Last six seasons at home P	W	D	L	OV	UN	BS	CS
Bayern Munich	L	L	6	0	0	6	4	2	2	0
Dortmund	L	L	6	2	0	4	4	2	3	1
Leverkusen	L	W	6	2	2	2	4	2	4	1
M'gladbach	W	L	6	2	3	1	3	3	4	1
Schalke	L	W	6	0	2	4	3	3	3	0
Mainz	D	W	6	1	2	3	3	3	3	1
Hertha	D	D	4	3	1	0	2	2	2	2
Wolfsburg	W	L	6	2	0	4	5	1	4	0
Cologne	D	D	4	2	1	1	2	2	3	0
Hamburg	L	L	6	5	0	1	2	4	2	4
Ingolstadt	L	L	1	0	0	1	0	1	0	0
Augsburg	L	W	5	2	1	2	2	3	3	1
Werder Bremen										
Darmstadt	D	L	1	0	1	0	1	0	1	0
Hoffenheim	D	W	6	2	4	0	3	3	6	0
Ein Frankfurt	W	L	5	2	2	1	1	4	1	3
Freiburg			5	2	2	1	3	2	4	1
RB Leipzig			-	-	-	-	-	-	-	-

Season	Division	Pos	P	W	D	L	F	A	GD	Pts
2015-16	Bundesliga	13	34	10	8	16	50	65	-15	38
2014-15	Bundesliga	10	34	11	10	13	50	65	-15	43
2013-14	Bundesliga	12	34	10	9	15	42	66	-24	39

Over/Under 68%/32% 4th **Both score** 71%/29% 1st

WOLFSBURG

Ground: Volkswagen Arena www.vfl-wolfsburg.de

	2015-16 H	A	Last six seasons at home P	W	D	L	OV	UN	BS	CS
Bayern Munich	L	L	6	1	1	4	2	4	3	0
Dortmund	L	L	6	2	1	3	6	0	5	0
Leverkusen	W	L	6	5	0	1	6	0	6	0
M'gladbach	W	L	6	5	0	1	6	0	4	2
Schalke	W	L	6	3	2	1	5	1	4	2
Mainz	W	L	6	2	2	2	4	2	3	2
Hertha	W	D	4	3	0	1	2	2	2	2
Wolfsburg										
Cologne	D	D	4	3	1	0	2	2	3	1
Hamburg	W	W	6	2	3	1	1	5	4	1
Ingolstadt	W	D	1	1	0	0	0	1	0	1
Augsburg	L	D	5	1	2	2	1	4	3	1
Werder Bremen	W	W	6	4	2	0	4	2	3	3
Darmstadt	D	W	1	0	1	0	0	1	1	0
Hoffenheim	W	W	6	3	2	1	6	0	5	1
Ein Frankfurt	W	L	5	2	2	1	3	2	4	0
Freiburg			5	3	1	1	4	1	3	1
RB Leipzig			-	-	-	-	-	-	-	-

Season	Division	Pos	P	W	D	L	F	A	GD	Pts
2015-16	Bundesliga	8	34	12	9	13	47	49	-2	45
2014-15	Bundesliga	2	34	20	9	5	73	38	+35	69
2013-14	Bundesliga	5	34	18	6	10	63	50	+13	60

Over/Under 47%/53% 14th **Both score** 53%/47% 9th

Bundesliga 2015-16

Pos	H	A		P	W	D	L	F	A	W	D	L	F	A	GD	Pts
					Home					**Away**						
1	1	1	Bayern Munich (CL)	34	15	1	1	51	8	13	3	1	29	9	+63	88
2	2	2	B Dortmund (CL)	34	14	3	0	49	14	10	3	4	33	20	+48	78
3	4	3	B Leverkusen (CL)	34	10	3	4	31	17	8	3	6	25	23	+16	60
4	3	12	B M'gladbach (CL)	34	13	1	3	42	18	4	3	10	25	32	+17	55
5	7	6	Schalke (EL)	34	8	5	4	28	24	7	2	8	23	25	+2	52
6	8	8	Mainz (EL)	34	8	4	5	23	18	6	4	7	23	24	+4	50
7	6	10	Hertha Berlin (EL)	34	9	5	3	24	15	5	3	9	18	27	0	50
8	5	17	Wolfsburg	34	9	5	3	32	17	3	4	10	15	32	-2	45
9	12	7	Cologne	34	5	5	7	16	18	5	8	4	22	24	-4	43
10	14	9	Hamburg	34	5	4	8	20	23	6	4	7	20	23	-6	41
11	9	13	Ingolstadt	34	7	5	5	22	18	3	5	9	11	24	-9	40
12	10	18	E Frankfurt	36	6	7	5	23	25	4	3	11	13	28	-17	40
13	16	5	Augsburg	34	3	6	8	18	27	6	5	6	24	25	-10	38
14	13	11	Werder Bremen	34	5	5	7	27	30	5	3	9	23	35	-15	38
15	17	4	Darmstadt	34	2	6	9	15	29	7	5	5	23	24	-15	38
16	11	15	Hoffenheim	34	6	6	5	22	25	3	4	10	17	29	-15	37
17	15	14	Stuttgart (R)	34	6	1	10	22	32	3	5	9	28	43	-25	33
18	18	16	Hannover (R)	34	4	0	13	15	30	3	4	10	16	32	-31	25

Bundesliga results 2015-16

	Augsburg	Bayern Munich	Cologne	Darmstadt	Dortmund	E Frankfurt	Hamburg	Hannover	Hertha	Hoffenheim	Ingolstadt	Leverkusen	Mainz	B M'gladbach	Schalke	Stuttgart	Werder Bremen	Wolfsburg
Augsburg		1-3	0-0	0-2	1-3	0-0	1-3	2-0	0-1	1-3	0-1	3-3	3-3	2-2	2-1	1-0	1-2	0-0
Bayern Munich	2-1		4-0	3-1	5-1	1-0	5-0	3-1	2-0	2-0	2-0	3-0	1-2	1-1	3-0	4-0	5-0	5-1
Cologne	0-1	0-1		4-1	2-1	3-1	2-1	0-1	0-1	0-0	1-1	0-2	0-0	1-0	1-3	1-3	0-0	1-1
Darmstadt	2-2	0-3	0-0		0-2	1-2	1-1	2-2	0-4	0-0	2-0	1-2	2-3	0-2	0-2	2-2	2-1	0-1
Dortmund	5-1	0-0	2-2	2-2		4-1	3-0	1-0	3-1	3-1	2-0	3-0	2-0	4-0	3-2	4-1	3-2	5-1
Eintract Frankfurt	1-1	0-0	6-2	0-1	1-0		0-0	1-0	1-1	0-2	1-1	1-3	2-1	1-5	0-0	2-4	2-1	3-2
Hamburg	0-1	1-2	1-1	1-2	3-1	0-0		1-2	2-0	1-3	1-1	0-0	1-3	3-2	0-1	3-2	2-1	0-1
Hannover	0-1	0-1	0-2	1-2	2-4	1-2	0-3		1-3	1-0	4-0	0-1	0-1	2-0	1-3	1-3	1-0	0-4
Hertha	0-0	0-2	2-0	1-2	0-0	2-0	3-0	2-2		1-0	2-1	2-1	2-0	1-4	2-0	2-1	1-1	1-1
Hoffenheim	2-1	1-2	1-1	0-2	1-1	0-0	0-1	1-0	2-1		2-1	1-1	3-2	3-3	1-4	2-2	1-3	1-0
Ingolstadt	2-1	1-2	1-1	3-1	0-4	2-0	0-1	2-2	0-1	1-1		0-1	1-0	1-0	3-0	3-3	2-0	0-0
Leverkusen	1-1	0-0	1-2	0-1	0-1	3-0	1-0	3-0	2-1	2-1	3-2		1-0	5-0	1-1	4-3	1-4	3-0
Mainz	4-2	0-3	2-3	0-0	0-2	2-1	0-0	3-0	0-0	3-1	0-1	3-1		1-0	2-1	0-0	1-3	2-0
B M'gladbach	4-2	3-1	1-0	3-2	1-3	3-0	0-3	2-1	5-0	3-1	0-0	2-1	1-2		3-1	4-0	5-1	2-0
Schalke	1-1	1-3	0-3	1-1	2-2	2-0	3-2	3-1	2-1	1-0	1-1	2-3	2-1	2-1		1-1	1-3	3-0
Stuttgart	0-4	1-3	1-3	2-0	0-3	1-4	2-1	1-2	2-0	5-1	1-0	0-2	1-3	1-3	0-1		1-1	3-1
Werder Bremen	1-2	0-1	1-1	2-2	1-3	1-0	1-3	4-1	3-3	1-1	0-1	0-3	1-1	2-1	0-3	6-2		3-2
Wolfsburg	0-2	0-2	1-1	1-1	1-2	2-1	1-1	1-1	2-0	4-2	2-0	2-1	2-1	2-1	3-0	3-1	6-0	

Top scorers

	Team	Goals scored
R Lewandowski	B Munich	30
P Aubameyang	Dortmund	25
T Muller	B Munich	20
J Hernandez	Leverkusen	17
A Modeste	Cologne	15

Over 2.5 goals top five

	H	A	%
Stuttgart	11	14	74%
B M'gladbach	14	11	74%
B Dortmund	13	11	71%
W Bremen	11	12	68%
Schalke	11	11	65%

Both to score top seven

	H	A	%
Werder	12	12	71%
Stuttgart	10	13	68%
Hoffenheim	12	10	65%
Schalke	13	8	62%
Augsburg, Dortmund,			
B M'gladbach			59%

VORSPRUNG DURCH TECHNIK

SOCCERBASE.COM

ALAVES

Estadio Mendizorrotza   www.deportivoalaves.com

	2015-16 H	A	Last six seasons at home P	W	D	L	OV	UN	BS	CS
Barcelona	-	-	-	-	-	-	-	-	-	-
Real Madrid	-	-	-	-	-	-	-	-	-	-
Atl Madrid	-	-	-	-	-	-	-	-	-	-
Villarreal	-	-	-	-	-	-	-	-	-	-
Ath Bilbao	-	-	-	-	-	-	-	-	-	-
Celta	-	-	-	-	-	-	-	-	-	-
Sevilla	-	-	-	-	-	-	-	-	-	-
Malaga	-	-	-	-	-	-	-	-	-	-
Sociedad	-	-	-	-	-	-	-	-	-	-
Betis		1	0	0	1	1	0	1	0
Las Palmas		2	0	2	0	0	2	2	0
Valencia	-	-	-	-	-	-	-	-	-	-
Espanyol	-	-	-	-	-	-	-	-	-	-
Eibar		1	0	0	1	0	1	0	0
Deportivo		1	0	1	0	0	1	1	0
Granada	-	-	-	-	-	-	-	-	-	-
Sp Gijon		2	1	1	0	1	1	0	2
Alaves									
Leganes	D	L	2	1	1	0	0	2	0	2
Osasuna	W	L	2	2	0	0	2	0	0	2

Season	Division	Pos	P	W	D	L	F	A	GD	Pts
2015-16	Liga Segunda	1	42	21	12	9	49	35	+14	75
2014-15	Liga Segunda	12	42	14	11	17	49	53	-4	53
2013-14	Liga Segunda	18	42	13	12	17	57	57	0	51

Over/Under 31%/69% 28th   **Both score** 36%/64% 27th

ATHLETIC BILBAO

San Mames   www.athletic-club.net

	2015-16 H	A	Last six seasons at home P	W	D	L	OV	UN	BS	CS
Barcelona	L	L	6	1	2	3	4	2	4	1
Real Madrid	L	L	6	1	1	4	4	2	2	1
Atl Madrid	L	L	6	2	0	4	5	1	3	2
Villarreal	D	L	5	2	2	1	1	4	1	3
Ath Bilbao										
Celta	W	W	4	3	1	0	2	2	3	1
Sevilla	W	L	6	6	0	0	3	3	3	3
Malaga	D	W	6	2	4	0	2	4	2	4
Sociedad	L	D	6	2	2	2	2	4	4	1
Betis	W	W	4	2	0	2	4	0	4	0
Las Palmas	D	D	1	0	1	0	1	0	1	0
Valencia	W	W	6	2	2	2	3	3	4	1
Espanyol	W	L	6	3	1	2	6	0	5	0
Eibar	W	L	2	1	1	0	1	1	1	1
Deportivo	W	D	4	1	2	1	2	2	4	0
Granada	D	L	5	2	1	2	1	4	1	2
Sp Gijon	W	W	3	2	1	0	2	1	1	2
Alaves			-	-	-	-	-	-	-	-
Leganes			-	-	-	-	-	-	-	-
Osasuna			4	4	0	0	1	3	1	3

Season	Division	Pos	P	W	D	L	F	A	GD	Pts
2015-16	Primera Liga	5	38	18	8	12	58	45	+13	62
2014-15	Primera Liga	7	38	15	10	13	42	41	+1	55
2013-14	Primera Liga	4	38	20	10	8	66	39	+27	70

Over/Under 55%/45% 7th   **Both score** 47%/53% 13th

ATLETICO MADRID

Vicente Calderon   www.clubatleticodemadrid.com

	2015-16 H	A	Last six seasons at home P	W	D	L	OV	UN	BS	CS
Barcelona	L	L	6	0	1	5	4	2	4	1
Real Madrid	D	W	6	1	2	3	5	1	5	1
Atl Madrid										
Villarreal	D	L	5	3	1	1	2	3	1	3
Ath Bilbao	W	W	6	4	1	1	3	3	2	3
Celta	W	W	4	3	1	0	2	2	2	2
Sevilla	D	W	6	2	4	0	3	3	2	4
Malaga	W	L	6	4	1	1	4	2	4	1
Sociedad	W	W	6	4	1	1	3	3	1	4
Betis	W	W	4	3	0	1	2	2	1	2
Las Palmas	W	W	1	1	0	0	0	1	0	1
Valencia	W	W	6	2	3	1	3	3	4	2
Espanyol	W	W	6	5	0	1	2	4	2	4
Eibar	W	W	2	2	0	0	2	0	2	0
Deportivo	W	D	4	4	0	0	2	2	0	4
Granada	W	W	5	5	0	0	2	3	0	5
Sp Gijon	W	L	3	3	0	0	2	1	0	3
Alaves			-	-	-	-	-	-	-	-
Leganes			-	-	-	-	-	-	-	-
Osasuna			4	3	1	0	3	1	2	2

Season	Division	Pos	P	W	D	L	F	A	GD	Pts
2015-16	Primera Liga	3	38	28	4	6	63	18	+45	88
2014-15	Primera Liga	3	38	23	9	6	67	29	+38	78
2013-14	Primera Liga	1	38	28	6	4	77	26	+51	90

Over/Under 39%/61% 17th   **Both score** 32%/68% 20th

BARCELONA

Camp Nou   www.fcbarcelona.cat

	2015-16 H	A	Last six seasons at home P	W	D	L	OV	UN	BS	CS
Barcelona										
Real Madrid	L	W	6	3	1	2	6	0	5	1
Atl Madrid	W	W	6	5	1	0	5	1	4	2
Villarreal	W	D	5	5	0	0	5	0	3	2
Ath Bilbao	W	W	6	6	0	0	4	2	3	3
Celta	W	L	4	3	0	1	3	1	2	1
Sevilla	W	W	6	5	1	0	5	1	4	2
Malaga	W	W	6	5	0	1	4	2	3	2
Sociedad	W	L	6	6	0	0	5	1	3	3
Betis	W	W	4	4	0	0	4	0	3	1
Las Palmas	W	W	1	1	0	0	1	0	1	0
Valencia	L	D	6	4	0	2	4	2	4	2
Espanyol	W	W	6	6	0	0	4	2	1	5
Eibar	W	W	2	2	0	0	2	0	1	1
Deportivo	D	W	4	1	3	0	2	2	2	2
Granada	W	W	5	5	0	0	4	1	1	4
Sp Gijon	W	W	3	3	0	0	2	1	1	2
Alaves			-	-	-	-	-	-	-	-
Leganes			-	-	-	-	-	-	-	-
Osasuna			4	4	0	0	3	1	1	3

Season	Division	Pos	P	W	D	L	F	A	GD	Pts
2015-16	Primera Liga	1	38	29	4	5	112	29	+83	91
2014-15	Primera Liga	1	38	30	4	4	110	21	+89	94
2013-14	Primera Liga	2	38	27	6	5	100	33	+67	87

Over/Under 79%/21% 1st   **Both score** 50%/50% 11th

BETIS

Benito Villamarin — www.realbetisbalompie.es

	2015-16 H	A	Last six seasons at home P	W	D	L	OV	UN	BS	CS
Barcelona	L	L	4	0	1	3	3	1	3	0
Real Madrid	D	L	4	1	1	2	2	2	2	1
Atl Madrid	L	L	4	0	1	3	2	2	2	0
Villarreal	D	L	3	2	1	0	1	2	2	1
Ath Bilbao	L	L	4	1	1	2	2	2	3	0
Celta	D	D	4	1	2	1	1	3	3	1
Sevilla	D	L	4	0	3	1	1	3	2	1
Malaga	L	L	4	1	1	2	2	2	1	2
Sociedad	W	L	4	2	0	2	1	3	1	2
Betis										
Las Palmas	W	L	3	2	1	0	1	2	1	2
Valencia	W	W	4	4	0	0	2	2	2	2
Espanyol	L	W	4	2	1	1	1	3	2	2
Eibar	L	D	1	0	0	1	1	0	0	0
Deportivo	L	D	2	0	1	1	1	1	2	0
Granada	W	D	5	2	1	2	3	2	3	2
Sp Gijon	D	W	3	1	1	1	1	2	1	1
Alaves			1	0	0	1	1	0	1	0
Leganes			1	0	0	1	1	0	1	0
Osasuna			4	3	0	1	3	1	2	2

Season	Division	Pos	P	W	D	L	F	A	GD	Pts
2015-16	Primera Liga	10	38	11	12	15	34	52	-18	45
2014-15	Liga Segunda	1	42	25	9	8	73	40	+33	84
2013-14	Primera Liga	20	38	6	7	25	36	78	-42	25

Over/Under 37%/63% 19th Both score 45%/55% 14th

CELTA VIGO

Balaidos — www.celtavigo.net

	2015-16 H	A	Last six seasons at home P	W	D	L	OV	UN	BS	CS
Barcelona	W	L	4	1	1	2	3	1	2	0
Real Madrid	L	L	4	1	0	3	3	1	3	1
Atl Madrid	L	L	4	1	0	3	1	3	1	1
Villarreal	D	W	3	0	2	1	1	2	1	2
Ath Bilbao	L	L	4	0	2	2	1	3	2	1
Celta										
Sevilla	D	W	4	2	2	0	0	4	2	2
Malaga	W	W	4	2	0	2	0	4	0	2
Sociedad	W	W	4	1	3	0	2	2	3	1
Betis	D	D	4	1	2	1	1	3	3	0
Las Palmas	D	L	3	1	1	1	2	1	2	1
Valencia	L	W	4	1	1	2	2	2	3	0
Espanyol	W	D	4	3	1	0	2	2	2	2
Eibar	W	D	2	1	0	1	1	1	1	0
Deportivo	D	L	4	1	2	1	2	2	4	0
Granada	W	W	5	2	3	0	2	3	4	1
Sp Gijon	W	W	1	1	0	0	1	0	1	0
Alaves			-	-	-	-	-	-	-	-
Leganes			-	-	-	-	-	-	-	-
Osasuna			2	1	1	0	0	2	1	1

Season	Division	Pos	P	W	D	L	F	A	GD	Pts
2015-16	Primera Liga	6	38	17	9	12	51	59	-8	60
2014-15	Primera Liga	8	38	13	12	13	47	44	+3	51
2013-14	Primera Liga	9	38	14	7	17	49	54	-5	49

Over/Under 47%/53% 11th Both score 58%/42% 4th

DEPORTIVO LA CORUNA

Estadio Municipal de Riazor — canaldeportivo.com

	2015-16 H	A	Last six seasons at home P	W	D	L	OV	UN	BS	CS
Barcelona	L	D	4	0	0	4	4	0	1	0
Real Madrid	L	L	4	0	1	3	2	2	2	1
Atl Madrid	D	L	4	0	2	2	1	3	2	1
Villarreal	L	W	3	1	1	1	1	2	2	1
Ath Bilbao	D	L	4	2	2	0	2	2	3	1
Celta	W	D	4	3	0	1	2	2	1	2
Sevilla	D	D	4	0	2	2	2	2	3	0
Malaga	D	L	4	2	1	1	2	2	1	2
Sociedad	D	D	4	1	2	1	1	3	1	2
Betis	W	L	2	0	1	1	2	0	2	0
Las Palmas	L	W	3	1	0	2	3	0	3	0
Valencia	D	D	4	1	1	2	2	2	2	1
Espanyol	W	L	4	3	1	0	2	2	0	4
Eibar	W	D	3	2	1	0	0	3	1	2
Deportivo										
Granada	L	D	3	0	1	2	2	1	1	0
Sp Gijon	L	D	3	0	2	1	1	2	3	0
Alaves			1	1	0	0	1	0	1	0
Leganes			-	-	-	-	-	-	-	-
Osasuna			2	1	1	0	0	2	0	2

Season	Division	Pos	P	W	D	L	F	A	GD	Pts
2015-16	Primera Liga	15	38	8	18	12	45	61	-16	42
2014-15	Liga Segunda	2	42	19	12	11	48	36	+12	69
2013-14	Liga Segunda	2	42	19	12	11	48	36	+12	69

Over/Under 42%/58% 16th Both score 61%/39% 2nd

EIBAR

Estadio Municipal de Ipurua — www.sdeibar.com

	2015-16 H	A	Last six seasons at home P	W	D	L	OV	UN	BS	CS
Barcelona	L	L	2	0	0	2	1	1	0	0
Real Madrid	L	L	2	0	0	2	1	1	1	0
Atl Madrid	L	L	2	0	0	2	1	1	1	0
Villarreal	D	L	2	0	1	1	1	1	2	0
Ath Bilbao	W	L	2	1	0	1	0	2	0	1
Celta	D	D	2	0	1	1	1	1	2	0
Sevilla	D	W	2	0	1	1	1	1	2	0
Malaga	L	D	2	1	0	1	1	1	1	1
Sociedad	W	L	2	2	0	0	1	1	1	1
Betis	D	W	1	0	1	0	0	1	0	0
Las Palmas	L	W	2	1	0	1	0	2	0	1
Valencia	D	D	2	0	1	1	0	2	1	0
Espanyol	W	L	2	1	0	1	1	1	1	0
Eibar										
Deportivo	D	L	3	1	1	1	1	2	2	0
Granada	W	W	2	1	1	0	1	1	2	0
Sp Gijon	W	L	2	2	0	0	1	0	2	2
Alaves			1	1	0	0	1	0	1	0
Leganes			-	-	-	-	-	-	-	-
Osasuna			-	-	-	-	-	-	-	-

Season	Division	Pos	P	W	D	L	F	A	GD	Pts
2015-16	Primera Liga	14	38	11	10	17	49	61	-12	43
2014-15	Primera Liga	18	38	13	14	17	35	60	-25	35
2013-14	Liga Segunda	1	42	19	14	9	49	28	+21	71

Over/Under 47%/53% 11th Both score 58%/42% 4th

ESPANYOL

Cornella-El Prat — www.rcdespanyol.com

2015-16	H	A	P	W	D	L	OV	UN	BS	CS
			Last six seasons at home							
Barcelona	D	L	6	0	2	4	1	5	2	1
Real Madrid	L	L	6	0	1	5	3	3	2	0
Atl Madrid	L	L	6	2	2	2	3	3	3	2
Villarreal	D	L	5	0	3	2	2	3	3	1
Ath Bilbao	W	L	6	5	1	0	5	1	5	1
Celta	D	L	4	3	1	0	0	4	1	3
Sevilla	W	L	6	1	2	3	4	2	5	1
Malaga	W	D	6	2	3	1	2	4	2	4
Sociedad	L	W	6	2	2	2	5	1	4	1
Betis	L	W	4	2	1	1	1	3	0	3
Las Palmas	W	L	1	1	0	0	0	1	0	1
Valencia	W	L	6	3	2	1	5	1	4	2
Espanyol										
Eibar	W	L	2	1	0	1	2	0	2	0
Deportivo	W	L	4	3	1	0	0	4	0	4
Granada	D	D	5	3	1	1	2	3	2	2
Sp Gijon	L	W	3	1	0	2	2	1	1	1
Alaves			-	-	-	-	-	-	-	-
Leganes			-	-	-	-	-	-	-	-
Osasuna			4	1	1	2	2	2	1	1

Season	Division	Pos	P	W	D	L	F	A	GD	Pts
2015-16	Primera Liga	13	38	12	7	19	40	74	-34	43
2014-15	Primera Liga	10	38	13	10	15	47	51	-4	49
2013-14	Primera Liga	14	38	11	9	18	41	51	-10	42

Over/Under 61%/39% 4th   Both score 53%/47% 8th

GRANADA

Nuevo Los Carmenes — www.granadacf.es

2015-16	H	A	P	W	D	L	OV	UN	BS	CS
			Last six seasons at home							
Barcelona	L	L	5	1	0	4	3	2	2	1
Real Madrid	L	L	5	1	0	4	3	2	2	1
Atl Madrid	L	L	5	0	2	3	1	4	1	2
Villarreal	L	L	4	2	1	1	1	3	1	3
Ath Bilbao	W	D	5	2	2	1	2	3	2	3
Celta	L	L	5	1	2	2	2	3	4	0
Sevilla	W	W	5	1	2	2	3	2	4	0
Malaga	D	D	5	4	1	0	2	3	2	3
Sociedad	L	L	5	1	2	2	3	2	3	1
Betis	D	L	5	2	1	2	2	3	2	2
Las Palmas	W	L	2	2	0	0	2	0	2	0
Valencia	L	L	5	0	1	4	2	3	3	0
Espanyol	D	D	5	1	2	2	3	2	3	1
Eibar	L	L	2	0	1	1	1	1	1	1
Deportivo	D	W	3	1	2	0	1	2	3	0
Granada										
Sp Gijon	W	D	2	2	0	0	1	1	1	1
Alaves			-	-	-	-	-	-	-	-
Leganes			-	-	-	-	-	-	-	-
Osasuna			3	1	2	0	1	2	1	2

Season	Division	Pos	P	W	D	L	F	A	GD	Pts
2015-16	Primera Liga	16	38	10	9	19	46	69	-23	39
2014-15	Primera Liga	17	38	7	14	17	29	64	-35	35
2013-14	Primera Liga	15	38	12	5	21	32	56	-24	41

Over/Under 61%/39% 4th   Both score 61%/39% 2nd

LAS PALMAS

Estadio Gran Canaria — www.udlaspalmas.es

2015-16	H	A	P	W	D	L	OV	UN	BS	CS
			Last six seasons at home							
Barcelona	L	L	1	0	0	1	1	0	1	0
Real Madrid	L	L	1	0	0	1	1	0	1	0
Atl Madrid	L	L	1	0	0	1	1	0	0	0
Villarreal	D	W	2	0	2	0	1	1	1	1
Ath Bilbao	D	D	1	0	1	0	0	1	0	1
Celta	W	D	3	2	1	0	2	1	3	0
Sevilla	W	L	1	1	0	0	0	1	0	1
Malaga	D	L	1	0	1	0	0	1	1	0
Sociedad	W	W	1	1	0	0	0	1	0	1
Betis	W	L	3	1	1	2	1	1	1	1
Las Palmas										
Valencia	W	D	1	1	0	0	1	0	1	0
Espanyol	W	L	1	1	0	0	1	0	0	1
Eibar	L	W	2	0	1	1	0	2	1	0
Deportivo	L	W	3	0	0	3	0	3	0	0
Granada	W	L	2	1	1	0	1	1	2	0
Sp Gijon	D	L	4	2	2	0	2	2	4	0
Alaves			2	1	0	1	1	1	1	0
Leganes			1	1	0	0	0	1	0	1
Osasuna			1	0	0	1	1	0	1	0

Season	Division	Pos	P	W	D	L	F	A	GD	Pts
2015-16	Primera Liga	11	38	12	8	18	45	53	-8	44
2014-15	Liga Segunda	4	42	22	12	8	73	47	+26	78
2013-14	Liga Segunda	6	42	18	9	15	51	50	+1	63

Over/Under 47%/53% 11th   Both score 45%/55% 14th

LEGANES

Estadio Municipal Butarque — deportivoleganes.com

2015-16	H	A	P	W	D	L	OV	UN	BS	CS
			Last six seasons at home							
Barcelona			-	-	-	-	-	-	-	-
Real Madrid			-	-	-	-	-	-	-	-
Atl Madrid			-	-	-	-	-	-	-	-
Villarreal			-	-	-	-	-	-	-	-
Ath Bilbao			-	-	-	-	-	-	-	-
Celta			-	-	-	-	-	-	-	-
Sevilla			-	-	-	-	-	-	-	-
Malaga			-	-	-	-	-	-	-	-
Sociedad			-	-	-	-	-	-	-	-
Betis			1	1	0	0	0	1	0	1
Las Palmas			1	1	0	0	1	0	1	0
Valencia			-	-	-	-	-	-	-	-
Espanyol			-	-	-	-	-	-	-	-
Eibar			-	-	-	-	-	-	-	-
Deportivo			-	-	-	-	-	-	-	-
Granada			-	-	-	-	-	-	-	-
Sp Gijon			1	0	0	1	0	1	0	0
Alaves	W	D	2	1	1	0	0	2	1	1
Leganes										
Osasuna	W	L	2	1	1	0	0	2	1	1

Season	Division	Pos	P	W	D	L	F	A	GD	Pts
2015-16	Liga Segunda	2	42	20	14	8	59	34	+25	74
2014-15	Liga Segunda	2	42	15	11	16	48	42	+6	56
2013-14	Segunda B	2	38	20	10	8	53	24	+29	70

Over/Under 43%/57% 6th   Both score 40%/60% 23rd

MALAGA

La Rosaleda — www.malagacf.es

2015-16		Last six seasons at home							
	H A	P	W	D	L	OV	UN	BS	CS
Barcelona	L L	6	0	1	5	4	2	4	1
Real Madrid	D D	6	1	1	4	4	2	4	0
Atl Madrid	W W	6	1	3	2	2	4	1	3
Villarreal	L L	5	2	1	2	2	3	3	1
Ath Bilbao	L D	6	3	1	2	1	5	2	3
Celta	W L	4	2	1	1	1	3	1	2
Sevilla	D L	6	2	2	2	4	2	4	2
Malaga									
Sociedad	W D	6	1	2	3	3	3	5	0
Betis	L W	4	2	0	2	2	2	1	1
Las Palmas	W D	1	1	0	0	1	0	1	0
Valencia	L L	6	3	1	2	3	3	2	4
Espanyol	D L	6	2	1	3	2	4	3	1
Eibar	D W	2	1	1	0	1	1	1	1
Deportivo	W D	4	2	2	0	1	3	2	2
Granada	D D	5	4	1	0	5	0	3	2
Sp Gijon	W L	3	3	0	0	0	3	0	3
Alaves		-	-	-	-	-	-	-	-
Leganes		-	-	-	-	-	-	-	-
Osasuna		4	1	1	2	0	4	1	1

Season	Division	Pos	P	W	D	L	F	A	GD	Pts
2015-16	Primera Liga	8	38	12	12	14	38	35	+3	48
2014-15	Primera Liga	9	38	14	8	16	42	48	-6	50
2013-14	Primera Liga	11	38	12	9	17	39	46	-7	45

Over/Under 32%/68% 20th Both score 39%/61% 18th

OSASUNA

El Sadar — www.osasuna.es

2015-16		Last six seasons at home							
	H A	P	W	D	L	OV	UN	BS	CS
Barcelona		4	1	1	2	3	1	2	1
Real Madrid		4	1	2	1	2	2	2	2
Atl Madrid		4	1	0	3	2	2	1	1
Villarreal		3	2	0	1	2	1	1	1
Ath Bilbao		4	1	0	3	3	1	3	0
Celta		2	1	0	1	0	2	0	1
Sevilla		4	2	1	1	3	1	3	1
Malaga		4	1	2	1	1	3	1	2
Sociedad		4	2	2	0	1	3	2	2
Betis		4	3	1	0	3	1	3	1
Las Palmas		1	0	0	1	1	0	1	0
Valencia		4	1	2	1	0	4	2	1
Espanyol		4	3	0	1	1	3	0	3
Eibar		-	-	-	-	-	-	-	-
Deportivo		2	1	1	0	1	1	1	1
Granada		3	1	0	2	3	0	3	0
Sp Gijon		3	2	1	0	1	2	1	2
Alaves	W L	2	1	0	1	2	0	2	0
Leganes	W L	2	2	0	0	2	0	2	0
Osasuna									

Season	Division	Pos	P	W	D	L	F	A	GD	Pts
2015-16	Liga Segunda	6	42	17	13	12	47	40	+7	64
2014-15	Liga Segunda	18	42	11	12	19	41	60	-19	45
2013-14	Primera Liga	18	38	10	9	19	32	62	-30	39

Over/Under 40%/60% 12th Both score 36%/64% 27th

REAL MADRID

Santiago Bernabeu — www.realmadrid.com

2015-16		Last six seasons at home							
	H A	P	W	D	L	OV	UN	BS	CS
Barcelona	L W	6	2	1	3	5	1	5	0
Real Madrid									
Atl Madrid	L D	6	3	0	3	2	4	2	2
Villarreal	W L	5	4	1	0	4	1	3	2
Ath Bilbao	W W	6	6	0	0	6	0	5	1
Celta	W W	4	4	0	0	3	1	1	3
Sevilla	W L	6	6	0	0	5	1	3	3
Malaga	D D	6	4	2	0	3	3	3	3
Sociedad	W W	6	6	0	0	6	0	6	0
Betis	W D	4	4	0	0	4	0	3	1
Las Palmas	W W	1	1	0	0	1	0	1	0
Valencia	W D	6	2	4	0	3	3	4	2
Espanyol	W W	6	5	1	0	6	0	2	4
Eibar	W W	2	2	0	0	2	0	2	2
Deportivo	W W	4	4	0	0	3	1	2	2
Granada	W W	5	5	0	0	3	2	2	3
Sp Gijon	W D	3	2	0	1	2	1	2	0
Alaves		-	-	-	-	-	-	-	-
Leganes		-	-	-	-	-	-	-	-
Osasuna		4	4	0	0	3	1	2	2

Season	Division	Pos	P	W	D	L	F	A	GD	Pts
2015-16	Primera Liga	2	38	28	6	4	110	34	+76	90
2014-15	Primera Liga	2	38	30	2	6	118	38	+80	92
2013-14	Primera Liga	3	38	27	6	5	104	38	+66	87

Over/Under 71%/29% 2nd Both score 55%/45% 7th

SEVILLA

Ramón Sanchez Pizjuan — www.sevillafc.es

2015-16		Last six seasons at home							
	H A	P	W	D	L	OV	UN	BS	CS
Barcelona	W L	6	1	2	3	4	2	5	0
Real Madrid	W L	6	3	0	3	5	1	5	1
Atl Madrid	L D	6	1	2	3	3	3	3	1
Villarreal	W L	5	3	1	1	4	1	4	1
Ath Bilbao	W W	6	4	1	1	3	3	4	2
Celta	L D	4	2	0	2	2	2	2	1
Sevilla									
Malaga	W D	6	3	2	1	3	3	3	2
Sociedad	L W	6	4	0	2	3	3	3	3
Betis	W D	4	3	0	1	3	1	2	2
Las Palmas	W L	1	1	0	0	0	1	0	1
Valencia	W L	6	4	2	0	1	5	2	4
Espanyol	W L	6	4	1	1	4	2	3	3
Eibar	W L	2	1	1	0	0	2	0	2
Deportivo	D D	4	2	2	0	2	2	3	1
Granada	L L	5	3	0	2	5	0	3	2
Sp Gijon	W L	3	3	0	0	2	1	1	2
Alaves		-	-	-	-	-	-	-	-
Leganes		-	-	-	-	-	-	-	-
Osasuna		4	4	0	0	1	3	1	3

Season	Division	Pos	P	W	D	L	F	A	GD	Pts
2015-16	Primera Liga	7	38	14	10	14	51	50	+1	52
2014-15	Primera Liga	5	38	23	8	7	71	45	+26	76
2013-14	Primera Liga	5	38	18	9	11	69	52	+17	63

Over/Under 50%/50% 8th Both score 58%/42% 4th

SOCIEDAD

Anoeta www.realsociedad.com

	2015-16 H	A	P	W	D	L	OV	UN	BS	CS
Barcelona	W	L	6	5	1	0	4	2	4	2
Real Madrid	L	L	6	1	1	4	4	2	3	0
Atl Madrid	L	L	6	1	0	5	4	2	3	0
Villarreal	L	D	5	1	2	2	1	4	2	2
Ath Bilbao	D	W	6	3	2	1	1	5	2	4
Celta	L	L	4	2	1	1	3	1	4	0
Sevilla	W	W	6	4	1	1	3	3	4	2
Malaga	D	L	6	2	2	2	2	4	3	1
Sociedad										
Betis	W	L	4	2	2	0	3	1	4	0
Las Palmas	L	L	1	0	0	1	0	1	0	0
Valencia	W	W	6	4	1	1	2	4	3	3
Espanyol	L	W	6	3	1	2	2	4	2	3
Eibar	W	L	2	2	0	0	1	1	1	1
Deportivo	D	D	4	1	3	0	2	2	3	1
Granada	W	W	5	2	2	1	3	2	2	2
Sp Gijon	D	L	3	2	1	0	2	1	2	1
Alaves			-	-	-	-	-	-	-	-
Leganes			-	-	-	-	-	-	-	-
Osasuna			4	2	2	0	1	3	0	4

Season	Division	Pos	P	W	D	L	F	A	GD	Pts
2015-16	Primera Liga	9	38	13	9	16	45	48	-3	48
2014-15	Primera Liga	12	38	11	13	14	44	51	-7	46
2013-14	Primera Liga	7	38	16	11	11	62	55	+7	59

Over/Under 47%/53% 11th **Both score** 42%/58% 17th

SPORTING GIJON

El Molinon .com

	2015-16 H	A	P	W	D	L	OV	UN	BS	CS
Barcelona	L	L	3	0	1	2	1	2	2	0
Real Madrid	D	L	3	0	1	2	1	2	0	1
Atl Madrid	W	L	3	2	1	0	1	2	2	1
Villarreal	W	L	4	2	1	1	1	3	2	2
Ath Bilbao	L	L	3	0	2	1	1	2	2	0
Celta	L	L	1	0	0	1	0	1	0	0
Sevilla	W	W	3	3	0	0	1	2	1	2
Malaga	W	L	3	2	0	1	2	1	2	1
Sociedad	W	D	3	1	0	2	3	0	3	0
Betis	L	D	3	1	0	2	3	0	3	0
Las Palmas	W	D	4	1	2	1	2	2	4	0
Valencia	L	W	3	0	0	3	0	3	0	0
Espanyol	L	W	3	1	0	2	2	1	2	1
Eibar	W	L	2	2	0	0	1	1	1	1
Deportivo	D	L	3	1	2	0	1	2	2	1
Granada	D	L	2	1	1	0	1	1	1	1
Sp Gijon										
Alaves			2	2	0	0	0	2	0	2
Leganes			1	1	0	0	1	0	1	0
Osasuna			3	2	1	0	0	3	2	0

Season	Division	Pos	P	W	D	L	F	A	GD	Pts
2015-16	Primera Liga	17	38	10	9	19	40	62	-22	39
2014-15	Liga Segunda	2	42	21	19	2	57	27	+30	82
2013-14	Liga Segunda	5	42	16	16	10	63	51	+12	64

Over/Under 47%/53% 11th **Both score** 50%/50% 11th

VALENCIA

Mestalla www.valenciafc.com

	2015-16 H	A	P	W	D	L	OV	UN	BS	CS
Barcelona	D	W	6	0	3	3	2	4	4	0
Real Madrid	D	W	6	1	1	4	6	0	5	0
Atl Madrid	L	L	6	3	1	2	2	4	3	2
Villarreal	L	L	5	3	1	1	2	3	1	3
Ath Bilbao	L	L	6	2	3	1	3	3	4	1
Celta	L	W	4	2	1	1	2	2	1	0
Sevilla	W	L	6	4	0	2	4	2	4	1
Malaga	W	W	6	6	0	0	4	2	2	4
Sociedad	L	L	6	2	0	4	3	3	2	2
Betis	D	L	4	3	1	0	3	1	0	4
Las Palmas	D	L	1	0	1	0	0	1	1	0
Valencia										
Espanyol	W	L	6	5	1	0	6	0	6	0
Eibar	W	L	2	2	0	0	2	0	1	1
Deportivo	D	D	4	2	2	0	1	3	2	2
Granada	W	W	5	5	0	0	2	3	1	4
Sp Gijon	L	W	3	1	1	1	1	2	0	2
Alaves			-	-	-	-	-	-	-	-
Leganes			-	-	-	-	-	-	-	-
Osasuna			4	3	1	0	4	0	1	3

Season	Division	Pos	P	W	D	L	F	A	GD	Pts
2015-16	Primera Liga	12	38	11	11	16	46	48	-2	44
2014-15	Primera Liga	4	38	22	11	5	70	32	+38	77
2013-14	Primera Liga	8	38	13	10	15	51	53	-2	49

Over/Under 50%/50% 8th **Both score** 53%/47% 8th

VILLARREAL

El Madrigal www.villarrealcf.es

	2015-16 H	A	P	W	D	L	OV	UN	BS	CS
Barcelona	D	L	5	0	2	3	2	3	2	1
Real Madrid	W	D	5	1	2	2	3	3	3	1
Atl Madrid	W	D	5	2	1	2	0	5	1	2
Villarreal										
Ath Bilbao	W	D	5	3	2	0	2	3	2	4
Celta	L	W	3	1	0	2	2	1	2	0
Sevilla	W	L	5	2	1	2	3	2	3	1
Malaga	W	L	5	3	2	0	2	3	4	1
Sociedad	D	W	5	3	2	0	3	2	3	2
Betis	D	L	3	1	2	0	0	3	1	2
Las Palmas	L	D	2	0	1	1	0	2	1	0
Valencia	W	D	5	2	2	1	3	2	4	1
Espanyol	W	D	5	3	1	1	4	1	2	2
Eibar	D	L	2	1	1	0	0	2	1	1
Deportivo	L	W	3	2	0	1	1	2	0	2
Granada	W	W	4	4	0	0	2	2	1	3
Sp Gijon	W	L	4	3	1	0	2	2	2	2
Alaves			-	-	-	-	-	-	-	-
Leganes			-	-	-	-	-	-	-	-
Osasuna			3	2	1	0	2	1	3	0

Season	Division	Pos	P	W	D	L	F	A	GD	Pts
2015-16	Primera Liga	4	38	18	10	10	44	35	+9	64
2014-15	Primera Liga	6	38	16	12	10	48	37	+11	60
2013-14	Primera Liga	6	38	17	8	13	60	44	+16	64

Over/Under 39%/61% 17th **Both score** 37%/63% 19th

Primera Liga 2015-16

Pos	H	A		P	W	D	L	F	A	W	D	L	F	A	GD	Pts
					Home					Away						
1	2	1	Barcelona (CL)	38	16	1	2	67	14	13	3	3	45	15	+83	91
2	1	2	Real Madrid (CL)	38	16	1	2	70	16	12	5	2	40	18	+76	90
3	3	3	Atl Madrid (CL)	38	15	3	1	33	7	13	1	5	30	11	+45	88
4	5	6	Villarreal (CL)	38	12	4	3	26	12	6	6	7	18	23	+9	64
5	6	5	Ath Bilbao (EL)	38	11	4	4	35	17	7	4	8	23	28	+13	62
6	7	4	Celta Vigo (EL)	38	9	6	4	29	25	8	3	8	22	34	-8	60
7	4	19	Seville (CL)	38	14	1	4	38	21	0	9	10	13	29	+1	52
8	9	11	Malaga	38	8	6	5	26	15	4	6	9	12	20	+3	48
9	13	7	Sociedad	38	7	5	7	22	20	6	4	9	23	28	-3	48
10	18	9	Real Betis	38	6	6	7	17	23	5	6	8	17	29	-18	45
11	10	13	Las Palmas	38	8	5	6	25	17	4	3	12	20	36	-8	44
12	16	10	Valencia	38	6	7	6	25	23	5	4	10	21	25	-2	44
13	8	16	Espanyol	38	9	5	5	22	28	3	2	14	18	46	-34	43
14	11	14	Eibar	38	8	5	6	26	22	3	5	11	23	39	-12	43
15	20	8	Deportivo	38	4	8	7	25	34	4	10	5	20	27	-16	42
16	19	12	Granada	38	6	5	8	26	31	4	4	11	20	38	-23	39
17	17	15	Sporting Gijon	38	7	4	8	28	28	3	5	11	12	34	-22	39
18	12	18	Rayo Vallecano (R)	38	8	4	7	29	29	1	7	11	23	44	-21	38
19	15	17	Getafe (R)	38	6	7	6	23	20	3	2	14	14	47	-30	36
20	14	20	Levante (R)	38	7	5	7	23	26	1	3	15	14	44	-33	32

Primera Liga results 2015-16

	Ath Bilbao	Atl Madrid	Barcelona	Betis	Celta	Deportivo	Eibar	Espanyol	Getafe	Granada	Las Palmas	Levante	Malaga	Real Madrid	Seville	Sociedad	Sp Gijon	Valencia	Vallecano	Villarreal
Athletic Bilbao		0-1	0-1	3-1	2-1	4-1	5-2	2-1	3-1	1-1	2-2	2-0	0-0	1-2	3-1	0-1	3-0	3-1	1-0	0-0
Atletico Madrid	2-1		1-2	5-1	2-0	3-0	3-1	1-0	2-0	3-0	1-0	1-0	1-1	0-0	3-0	1-0	2-1	1-0	0-0	
Barcelona	6-0	2-1		4-0	6-1	2-2	3-1	5-0	6-0	4-0	2-1	4-1	1-0	1-2	2-1	4-0	6-0	1-2	5-2	3-0
Betis	1-3	0-1	0-2		1-1	1-2	0-4	1-3	2-1	2-0	1-0	1-0	0-1	1-1	0-0	1-0	1-1	1-0	2-2	1-1
Celta	0-1	0-2	4-1	1-1		1-1	3-2	1-0	0-0	2-1	3-3	4-3	1-0	1-3	1-1	1-0	2-1	1-5	3-0	0-0
Deportivo	2-2	1-1	0-8	2-2	2-0		2-0	3-0	0-2	0-1	1-3	2-1	3-3	0-2	1-1	0-0	2-3	1-1	2-2	1-2
Eibar	2-0	0-2	0-4	1-1	1-1	1-1		2-1	3-1	5-1	0-1	2-0	1-2	0-2	1-1	2-1	2-0	1-1	1-0	1-2
Espanyol	2-1	1-3	0-0	0-3	1-1	1-0	4-2		1-0	1-1	1-0	1-1	2-0	0-6	1-0	0-5	1-2	1-0	2-1	2-2
Getafe	0-1	0-1	0-2	1-0	0-1	0-0	1-1	3-1		1-2	4-0	3-0	1-0	1-5	1-1	1-1	1-1	2-2	1-1	2-0
Granada	2-0	0-2	0-3	1-1	0-2	1-1	1-3	1-1	3-2		3-2	5-1	0-0	1-2	2-1	0-3	2-0	1-2	2-2	1-3
Las Palmas	0-0	0-3	1-2	1-0	2-1	0-2	0-2	4-0	4-0	4-1		0-0	1-1	1-2	2-0	2-0	1-1	2-1	0-1	0-0
Levante	2-2	2-1	0-2	0-1	1-2	1-1	2-2	2-1	3-0	1-2	3-2		0-1	1-3	1-1	0-4	0-0	1-0	2-1	1-0
Malaga	0-1	1-0	1-2	0-1	2-0	2-0	0-0	1-1	3-0	2-2	4-1	3-1		1-1	0-0	3-1	1-0	1-2	1-1	0-1
Real Madrid	4-2	0-1	0-4	5-0	7-1	5-0	4-0	6-0	4-1	1-0	3-1	3-0	0-0		4-0	3-1	5-1	3-2	10-2	3-0
Seville	2-0	0-3	2-1	2-0	1-2	1-1	1-0	2-0	5-0	1-4	2-0	3-1	2-1	3-2		1-2	2-0	1-0	3-2	4-2
Sociedad	0-0	0-2	1-0	2-1	2-3	1-1	2-1	2-3	1-2	3-0	0-1	1-1	1-1	0-1	2-0		0-0	2-0	2-1	0-2
Sporting Gijon	0-2	2-1	1-3	1-2	0-1	1-1	2-0	2-4	1-2	3-3	3-1	0-3	1-0	0-0	2-1	5-1		0-1	2-2	2-0
Valencia	0-3	1-3	1-1	0-0	0-2	1-1	4-0	2-1	2-2	1-0	1-1	3-0	3-0	2-2	2-1	0-1	0-1		2-2	0-2
Vallecano	0-3	0-2	1-5	0-2	3-0	1-3	1-1	3-0	2-0	2-1	2-0	3-1	1-2	2-3	2-2	2-2	2-1	0-0		2-1
Villarreal	3-1	1-0	2-2	0-0	1-2	0-2	1-1	3-1	2-0	1-0	0-1	3-0	1-0	1-0	0-0	2-0	1-0	2-1		

Top scorers

	Team	Goals scored
L Suarez	Barca	40
C Ronaldo	R Madrid	35
L Messi	Barca	26
K Benzema	R Madrid	24
Neymar	Barca	24
A Griezmann	Atl Madrid	22

Over 2.5 goals top six

	H	A	%
Barcelona	18	12	79%
Real Madrid	16	11	71%
Rayo Vallecano	13	13	68%
Granada	11	12	61%
Levante	11	12	61%
Espanyol	9	14	61%

Both to score top six

	H	A	%
Vallecano	11	14	66%
Deportivo	11	12	61%
Granada	12	11	61%
Celta	11	11	58%
Eibar	11	11	58%
Sevilla	10	12	58%

ANGERS

Ground: Stade Jean Bouin   www.angers-sco.fr

	2015-16		Last six seasons at home							
	H	A	P	W	D	L	OV	UN	BS	CS
Paris SG	D	L	1	0	1	0	0	1	0	1
Lyon	L	W	1	0	0	1	1	0	0	0
Monaco	W	L	3	1	0	2	3	0	2	1
Nice	D	L	1	0	1	0	0	1	1	0
Lille	W	D	1	1	0	0	0	1	0	1
St Etienne	D	L	1	0	1	0	0	1	0	1
Caen	W	D	3	1	1	1	1	2	2	1
Rennes	L	L	1	0	0	1	0	1	0	0
Angers										
Bastia	W	L	2	1	1	0	0	2	1	1
Bordeaux	D	W	1	0	1	0	0	1	1	0
Montpellier	L	W	1	0	0	1	1	0	1	0
Marseille	L	W	1	0	0	1	0	1	0	0
Nantes	D	L	4	2	2	0	0	4	1	3
Lorient	W	L	1	1	0	0	1	0	1	0
Guingamp	D	D	3	1	1	1	1	2	1	2
Toulouse	L	W	1	0	0	1	0	1	0	0
Nancy			2	1	1	0	1	1	2	0
Dijon			4	2	2	0	1	3	1	3
Metz			3	1	2	0	1	2	1	2

Season	Division	Pos	P	W	D	L	F	A	GD	Pts
2015-16	Ligue 1	9	38	13	11	14	40	38	+2	50
2014-15	Ligue 2	3	38	18	10	10	47	30	+17	64
2013-14	Ligue 2	9	38	14	13	11	46	45	+1	55

Over/Under 34%/66% 16th **Both score** 34%/66% 19th

BASTIA

Ground: Stade Armand Cesari   www.sc-bastia.net

	2015-16		Last six seasons at home							
	H	A	P	W	D	L	OV	UN	BS	CS
Paris SG	L	L	4	1	0	3	3	1	1	0
Lyon	W	L	4	2	1	1	2	2	2	2
Monaco	L	L	4	0	1	3	2	2	3	0
Nice	L	W	4	2	0	2	2	2	2	1
Lille	L	L	4	1	1	2	3	1	4	0
St Etienne	L	L	4	1	0	3	1	3	0	1
Caen	W	D	2	1	1	0	0	2	1	1
Rennes	W	W	4	3	0	1	1	3	1	2
Angers	W	L	2	2	0	0	1	1	1	1
Bastia										
Bordeaux	W	D	4	3	1	0	1	3	1	3
Montpellier	W	L	4	3	1	0	1	3	1	3
Marseille	W	L	4	1	2	1	3	1	3	1
Nantes	D	D	4	1	3	0	1	3	1	3
Lorient	D	D	4	2	1	1	2	2	2	1
Guingamp	W	L	4	3	1	0	3	1	2	2
Toulouse	W	L	4	3	1	0	2	2	1	3
Nancy			1	1	0	0	1	0	1	0
Dijon			-	-	-	-	-	-	-	-
Metz			2	2	0	0	1	1	0	2

Season	Division	Pos	P	W	D	L	F	A	GD	Pts
2015-16	Ligue 1	10	38	14	8	16	36	42	-6	50
2014-15	Ligue 1	12	38	12	11	15	37	46	-9	47
2013-14	Ligue 1	10	38	13	10	15	42	56	-14	49

Over/Under 34%/66% 16th **Both score** 37%/63% 16th

BORDEAUX

Ground: Matmut Atlantique   girondins.com

	2015-16		Last six seasons at home							
	H	A	P	W	D	L	OV	UN	BS	CS
Paris SG	D	D	6	2	2	2	1	5	3	1
Lyon	W	W	6	3	0	3	4	2	2	2
Monaco	W	W	4	2	0	2	2	2	2	0
Nice	D	L	6	1	3	2	2	4	4	2
Lille	W	D	6	3	3	0	0	6	3	3
St Etienne	L	L	6	3	1	2	2	4	2	4
Caen	L	L	4	1	1	2	2	2	3	1
Rennes	W	D	6	4	2	0	3	3	2	4
Angers	L	L	1	0	0	1	1	0	1	0
Bastia	D	L	4	2	2	0	0	4	2	2
Bordeaux										
Montpellier	D	W	6	4	2	0	3	3	3	3
Marseille	D	D	6	3	3	0	1	5	4	2
Nantes	D	L	3	2	0	1	2	1	1	1
Lorient	W	L	6	5	1	0	3	3	3	3
Guingamp	W	W	3	2	1	0	1	2	2	1
Toulouse	D	L	6	3	1	2	2	4	3	2
Nancy			3	3	0	0	2	1	2	1
Dijon			1	0	1	0	0	1	1	0
Metz			1	0	1	0	0	1	1	0

Season	Division	Pos	P	W	D	L	F	A	GD	Pts
2015-16	Ligue 1	11	38	12	14	12	50	57	-7	50
2014-15	Ligue 1	6	38	17	12	9	47	44	+3	63
2013-14	Ligue 1	7	38	13	14	11	49	43	+6	53

Over/Under 50%/50% 4th **Both score** 58%/42% 4th

CAEN

Ground: Stade Michel D'Ornano   www.smcaen.fr

	2015-16		Last six seasons at home							
	H	A	P	W	D	L	OV	UN	BS	CS
Paris SG	L	L	4	0	1	3	3	1	2	0
Lyon	L	L	4	3	0	1	3	1	1	2
Monaco	D	D	4	1	2	1	3	1	1	2
Nice	W	L	4	1	2	1	1	3	2	2
Lille	L	L	4	0	0	4	3	1	3	0
St Etienne	W	L	4	3	0	1	1	3	1	3
Caen										
Rennes	W	D	4	2	0	2	0	4	0	2
Angers	D	L	3	1	2	0	0	3	1	2
Bastia	D	L	2	0	2	0	0	2	1	1
Bordeaux	W	W	4	2	1	1	3	1	3	3
Montpellier	W	W	4	2	1	1	2	2	3	1
Marseille	W	W	4	0	1	3	4	0	4	0
Nantes	L	W	3	0	0	3	1	2	1	0
Lorient	L	L	4	2	0	2	2	2	2	1
Guingamp	W	D	3	1	0	2	2	1	2	0
Toulouse	W	L	4	2	1	1	0	4	1	2
Nancy			3	0	0	3	3	0	3	0
Dijon			3	2	1	0	2	0	2	0
Metz			2	0	1	1	0	2	0	1

Season	Division	Pos	P	W	D	L	F	A	GD	Pts
2015-16	Ligue 1	7	38	16	6	16	39	52	-13	54
2014-15	Ligue 1	13	38	12	10	16	54	55	-1	46
2013-14	Ligue 2	3	38	18	10	10	65	44	+21	64

Over/Under 45%/55% 12th **Both score** 45%/55% 12th

DIJON

Ground: Stade Gaston Gerard   www.dfco.fr

	2015-16 H	A	Last six seasons at home P	W	D	L	OV	UN	BS	CS
Paris SG	1	0	0	1	1	0	1	0
Lyon	1	0	0	1	1	0	1	0
Monaco	1	0	1	0	1	0	1	0	0
Nice	1	1	0	0	1	0	0	1
Lille	1	0	0	1	0	1	0	0
St Etienne	1	0	0	1	1	0	1	0
Caen	3	2	1	0	1	2	1	2
Rennes	1	0	0	1	1	0	1	0
Angers	4	0	3	1	1	3	2	2
Bastia	-	-	-	-	-	-	-	-
Bordeaux	1	1	0	0	0	1	0	1
Montpellier	1	0	1	0	1	0	1	0
Marseille	1	0	0	1	1	0	1	0
Nantes	2	1	1	0	1	1	1	1
Lorient	1	1	0	0	0	1	0	1
Guingamp	1	1	0	0	0	1	0	1
Toulouse	1	0	1	0	0	1	1	0
Nancy	D	L	4	2	1	1	1	3	1	2
Dijon								
Metz	L	W	3	1	1	1	3	0	2	0

Season	Division	Pos	P	W	D	L	F	A	GD	Pts
2015-16	Ligue 2	2	38	20	10	8	62	36	+26	70
2014-15	Ligue 2	4	38	17	10	11	44	34	+10	61
2013-14	Ligue 2	6	38	14	15	9	53	42	+11	57

Over/Under 55%/45% 4th   Both score 45%/55% 15th

GUINGAMP

Ground: Stade du Roudourou   eaguingamp.com

	2015-16 H	A	Last six seasons at home P	W	D	L	OV	UN	BS	CS
Paris SG	L	L	3	1	1	1	0	3	1	1
Lyon	L	L	3	0	0	3	1	2	1	0
Monaco	D	L	5	2	1	2	3	2	2	2
Nice	L	W	3	1	0	2	2	1	2	1
Lille	D	D	3	0	2	1	0	3	1	1
St Etienne	W	L	3	1	1	1	0	3	0	2
Caen	D	L	3	2	1	0	1	2	2	1
Rennes	L	W	3	1	0	2	0	3	0	1
Angers	D	D	3	2	1	0	2	1	2	1
Bastia	W	L	4	2	2	0	0	4	2	2
Bordeaux	L	L	3	1	0	2	2	1	2	0
Montpellier	D	L	3	0	1	2	2	1	2	0
Marseille	W	D	3	1	0	2	1	2	1	1
Nantes	D	L	5	3	1	1	2	3	2	2
Lorient	D	L	3	2	1	0	2	1	2	1
Guingamp								
Toulouse	W	W	3	3	0	0	1	2	1	2
Nancy			-	-	-	-	-	-	-	-
Dijon			1	1	0	0	0	1	0	1
Metz			2	0	2	0	2	0	0

Season	Division	Pos	P	W	D	L	F	A	GD	Pts
2015-16	Ligue 1	16	38	11	11	16	47	56	-9	44
2014-15	Ligue 1	10	38	15	4	19	41	55	-14	49
2013-14	Ligue 1	16	38	11	9	18	34	42	-8	42

Over/Under 53%/47% 3rd   Both score 45%/55% 12th

LILLE

Ground: Stade Pierre-Mauroy   www.losc.fr

	2015-16 H	A	Last six seasons at home P	W	D	L	OV	UN	BS	CS
Paris SG	L	D	6	1	2	3	3	4	1
Lyon	W	D	6	3	3	0	2	4	4	2
Monaco	W	D	4	3	0	1	2	2	2	1
Nice	D	D	6	0	4	2	1	5	3	1
Lille								
St Etienne	W	W	6	3	3	0	1	5	3	3
Caen	W	W	4	4	0	0	2	2	1	3
Rennes	D	D	6	4	2	0	2	4	3	3
Angers	D	L	1	0	1	0	0	1	0
Bastia	D	W	4	2	2	0	1	3	2	2
Bordeaux	D	L	6	3	2	1	3	3	4	2
Montpellier	W	L	6	4	1	1	2	4	2	3
Marseille	L	D	6	2	1	3	4	2	3	2
Nantes	L	W	3	1	1	1	0	3	0	2
Lorient	W	W	6	5	1	0	3	3	2	4
Guingamp	D	D	3	1	1	1	1	2	1	2
Toulouse	W	D	6	6	0	0	2	4	1	5
Nancy			3	2	1	0	2	1	2	1
Dijon			1	1	0	0	0	1	0	1
Metz			1	0	1	0	0	1	0	1

Season	Division	Pos	P	W	D	L	F	A	GD	Pts
2015-16	Ligue 1	5	38	15	15	8	39	27	+12	60
2014-15	Ligue 1	8	38	16	8	14	43	42	+1	56
2013-14	Ligue 1	3	38	20	11	7	46	26	+20	71

Over/Under 24%/76% 20th   Both score 37%/63% 16th

LORIENT

Ground: Stade du Moustoir   www.fclweb.fr

	2015-16 H	A	Last six seasons at home P	W	D	L	OV	UN	BS	CS
Paris SG	L	D	6	0	1	5	4	2	5	0
Lyon	L	D	6	1	3	2	4	2	4	1
Monaco	L	W	4	1	1	2	2	2	2	0
Nice	D	L	6	2	3	1	2	4	2	4
Lille	L	L	6	2	1	3	1	5	2	2
St Etienne	L	L	6	3	1	2	4	1	4	3
Caen	W	W	4	2	1	1	3	1	2
Rennes	D	D	6	2	2	2	4	2	2
Angers	W	L	1	1	0	0	1	0	1	0
Bastia	D	D	4	2	2	0	1	3	3	1
Bordeaux	W	W	6	2	3	1	4	2	4	1
Montpellier	D	D	6	2	4	0	3	3	4	2
Marseille	D	D	6	1	3	2	2	4	4	0
Nantes	D	L	3	1	1	1	2	1	2	1
Lorient								
Guingamp	W	D	3	3	0	0	2	1	1	2
Toulouse	D	W	6	1	3	2	1	5	2	3
Nancy			3	2	1	0	2	1	2	1
Dijon			1	0	1	0	0	1	0	1
Metz			1	1	0	0	1	0	1	0

Season	Division	Pos	P	W	D	L	F	A	GD	Pts
2015-16	Ligue 1	15	38	11	13	14	47	58	-11	46
2014-15	Ligue 1	8	38	12	7	19	44	50	-6	43
2013-14	Ligue 1	8	38	13	10	15	48	53	-5	49

Over/Under 50%/50% 4th   Both score 63%/37% 2nd

LYON

Ground: Parc Olympique Lyonnais   www.olweb.fr

	2015-16 H	A	Last six seasons at home P	W	D	L	OV	UN	BS	CS
Paris SG	W	L	6	2	3	1	3	3	4	1
Lyon										
Monaco	W	D	4	2	1	1	3	1	3	1
Nice	D	L	6	3	1	2	4	2	3	3
Lille	D	L	6	3	2	1	4	2	3	3
St Etienne	W	L	6	2	2	2	3	3	3	2
Caen	W	W	4	2	1	1	3	1	2	2
Rennes	L	W	6	2	2	2	2	4	3	3
Angers	L	W	1	0	0	1	0	1	0	0
Bastia	W	L	4	4	0	0	2	2	2	2
Bordeaux	W	L	6	2	3	1	2	4	3	2
Montpellier	L	W	6	4	1	1	4	2	4	2
Marseille	D	D	6	3	3	0	2	4	3	3
Nantes	W	D	3	3	0	0	1	2	1	2
Lorient	D	W	6	4	1	1	4	2	2	3
Guingamp	W	W	3	3	0	0	2	1	2	1
Toulouse	W	W	6	5	1	0	4	2	3	3
Nancy			3	2	1	0	2	1	2	1
Dijon			1	1	0	0	1	0	1	0
Metz			1	1	0	0	0	1	0	1

Season	Division	Pos	P	W	D	L	F	A	GD	Pts
2015-16	Ligue 1	2	38	19	8	11	67	43	+24	65
2014-15	Ligue 1	2	38	22	9	7	72	33	+39	75
2013-14	Ligue 1	5	38	17	10	11	56	44	+12	61

Over/Under 55%/45% 2nd   **Both score** 50%/50% 9th

MARSEILLE

Ground: Stade Velodrome   www.om.net

	2015-16 H	A	Last six seasons at home P	W	D	L	OV	UN	BS	CS
Paris SG	L	L	6	2	1	3	6	0	5	1
Lyon	D	D	6	1	4	1	3	3	5	1
Monaco	D	L	4	1	2	1	4	0	4	0
Nice	L	D	6	3	1	2	4	2	2	0
Lille	D	W	6	3	2	1	2	4	3	3
St Etienne	D	W	6	4	2	0	3	3	4	2
Caen	L	W	4	0	1	3	2	2	3	0
Rennes	L	W	6	2	1	3	3	3	2	2
Angers	L	W	1	0	0	1	1	0	1	0
Bastia	W	L	4	4	0	0	4	0	2	2
Bordeaux	D	D	6	3	3	0	3	3	3	3
Montpellier	D	D	6	3	1	2	4	2	3	2
Marseille										
Nantes	D	W	3	1	1	1	0	3	1	1
Lorient	D	D	6	3	1	2	3	3	3	2
Guingamp	D	L	3	2	1	0	1	2	1	2
Toulouse	D	D	6	2	3	1	3	3	4	1
Nancy			3	2	0	1	0	3	0	2
Dijon			1	0	0	1	1	0	1	0
Metz			1	1	0	0	1	0	1	0

Season	Division	Pos	P	W	D	L	F	A	GD	Pts
2015-16	Ligue 1	13	38	10	18	10	48	42	+6	48
2014-15	Ligue 1	4	38	21	6	11	76	42	+34	69
2013-14	Ligue 1	6	38	16	12	10	53	40	+13	60

Over/Under 32%/68% 18th   **Both score** 66%/34% 1st

METZ

Ground: Stade Saint-Symphorien   fcmetz.com

	2015-16 H	A	Last six seasons at home P	W	D	L	OV	UN	BS	CS
Paris SG			1	0	0	1	1	0	1	0
Lyon			1	1	0	0	1	0	1	0
Monaco			2	0	0	2	0	2	0	0
Nice			1	0	1	0	0	1	0	1
Lille			1	0	0	1	1	0	1	0
St Etienne			1	0	0	1	1	0	1	0
Caen			2	2	0	0	2	0	2	0
Rennes			1	0	1	0	0	1	0	1
Angers			3	1	2	0	0	3	2	1
Bastia			2	1	0	1	1	1	1	0
Bordeaux			1	0	1	0	0	1	0	1
Montpellier			1	0	0	1	1	0	1	0
Marseille			1	0	0	1	1	0	1	0
Nantes			3	0	2	1	1	2	3	0
Lorient			1	0	0	1	1	0	0	0
Guingamp			2	0	0	2	1	1	1	0
Toulouse			1	1	0	0	1	0	0	0
Nancy	D	D	2	1	1	0	1	1	0	2
Dijon	L	W	3	2	0	1	2	1	2	1
Metz										

Season	Division	Pos	P	W	D	L	F	A	GD	Pts
2015-16	Ligue 2	3	38	19	8	11	54	39	+15	65
2014-15	Ligue 1	19	38	7	9	22	31	61	-30	30
2013-14	Ligue 2	1	38	22	10	6	55	28	+27	76

Over/Under 53%/47% 6th   **Both score** 50%/50% 10th

MONACO

Ground: Stade Louis II   www.asm-fc.com

	2015-16 H	A	Last six seasons at home P	W	D	L	OV	UN	BS	CS
Paris SG	L	W	4	0	3	1	1	3	2	1
Lyon	D	L	4	1	2	1	1	3	2	1
Monaco										
Nice	W	W	4	2	1	1	0	4	1	2
Lille	D	W	4	1	3	0	0	4	2	2
St Etienne	W	D	4	2	1	1	1	3	2	1
Caen	D	D	4	0	3	1	2	2	3	0
Rennes	D	D	4	2	2	0	0	4	2	2
Angers	W	L	3	1	1	1	2	1	2	1
Bastia	W	W	4	3	0	1	2	2	0	3
Bordeaux	L	L	4	0	3	1	2	2	3	1
Montpellier	W	W	4	2	2	0	1	3	1	3
Marseille	W	D	4	3	1	0	1	3	1	3
Nantes	W	W	5	4	0	1	2	3	2	3
Lorient	L	W	4	2	0	2	3	1	3	1
Guingamp	W	D	5	3	2	0	2	3	3	2
Toulouse	W	D	4	2	2	0	2	2	1	3
Nancy			1	0	0	1	0	1	0	0
Dijon			1	0	1	0	0	1	1	0
Metz			2	1	0	1	0	2	0	1

Season	Division	Pos	P	W	D	L	F	A	GD	Pts
2015-16	Ligue 1	3	38	17	14	7	57	50	+7	65
2014-15	Ligue 1	3	38	20	11	7	51	26	+25	71
2013-14	Ligue 1	2	38	23	11	4	63	31	+32	80

Over/Under 50%/50% 4th   **Both score** 58%/42% 4th

MONTPELLIER

Ground: Stade de la Mosson   www.mhscfoot.com

	2015-16 H	2015-16 A	Last six seasons at home P	W	D	L	OV	UN	BS	CS
Paris SG	L	D	6	0	3	3	2	4	4	0
Lyon	L	W	6	2	0	4	4	2	4	1
Monaco	L	L	4	0	1	3	1	3	2	0
Nice	L	L	6	4	1	1	3	3	4	1
Lille	W	L	6	3	1	2	2	4	1	4
St Etienne	L	L	6	1	1	4	2	4	3	1
Caen	L	L	4	2	1	1	2	2	1	3
Rennes	W	L	6	3	2	1	1	5	0	5
Angers	L	W	1	0	0	1	0	1	0	0
Bastia	W	L	4	3	0	1	2	2	1	2
Bordeaux	L	D	6	3	1	2	0	6	1	3
Montpellier										
Marseille	L	D	6	2	0	4	3	3	3	1
Nantes	W	W	3	2	1	0	2	1	2	1
Lorient	W	D	6	5	0	1	3	3	2	3
Guingamp	W	D	3	2	1	0	2	1	3	0
Toulouse	W	D	6	4	2	0	1	5	3	3
Nancy			3	2	0	1	1	2	1	2
Dijon			1	1	0	0	1	0	1	0
Metz			1	1	0	0	0	1	0	1

Season	Division	Pos	P	W	D	L	F	A	GD	Pts
2015-16	Ligue 1	12	38	14	7	17	49	47	+2	49
2014-15	Ligue 1	7	38	16	8	14	46	39	+7	56
2013-14	Ligue 1	15	38	8	18	12	45	53	-8	42

Over/Under 45%/55% 12th   Both score 42%/58% 14th

NANCY

Ground: Stade Marcel Picot   www.asnl.net

	2015-16 H	2015-16 A	Last six seasons at home P	W	D	L	OV	UN	BS	CS
Paris SG			3	2	0	1	1	2	1	1
Lyon			3	1	0	2	2	1	1	1
Monaco			1	0	0	1	1	0	0	0
Nice			3	3	0	0	1	2	0	3
Lille			3	0	2	1	1	2	2	0
St Etienne			3	1	1	1	2	1	2	0
Caen			3	1	2	0	0	3	2	1
Rennes			3	0	1	2	2	1	1	1
Angers			2	1	1	0	1	1	1	1
Bastia			1	0	0	1	1	0	1	0
Bordeaux			3	0	3	0	1	2	2	1
Montpellier			3	1	0	2	1	2	1	1
Marseille			3	0	0	3	2	1	2	0
Nantes			-	-	-	-	-	-	-	-
Lorient			3	2	1	0	2	1	2	1
Guingamp			-	-	-	-	-	-	-	-
Toulouse			3	0	0	3	1	2	0	0
Nancy										
Dijon	W	D	4	2	1	1	3	1	4	0
Metz	D	D	2	0	1	1	1	1	1	0

Season	Division	Pos	P	W	D	L	F	A	GD	Pts
2015-16	Ligue 2	1	38	21	11	6	60	32	+28	74
2014-15	Ligue 2	5	38	15	13	10	53	39	+14	58
2013-14	Ligue 2	4	38	16	13	9	47	37	+10	61

Over/Under 45%/55% 9th   Both score 45%/55% 15th

NANTES

Ground: Beaujoire-Louis Fonteneau   fcnantes.com

	2015-16 H	2015-16 A	Last six seasons at home P	W	D	L	OV	UN	BS	CS
Paris SG	L	L	3	0	0	3	2	1	2	0
Lyon	D	L	3	0	2	1	1	2	2	1
Monaco	D	L	5	1	2	2	1	4	1	2
Nice	W	W	3	3	0	0	1	2	1	2
Lille	L	L	3	0	1	2	1	2	1	0
St Etienne	W	L	3	1	1	1	2	1	2	1
Caen	L	W	3	1	0	2	3	0	3	0
Rennes	L	L	3	0	1	2	1	2	1	0
Angers	W	D	4	4	0	0	1	3	1	3
Bastia	D	D	4	1	1	2	0	4	0	2
Bordeaux	D	L	3	1	2	0	2	1	2	1
Montpellier	L	L	3	2	0	1	1	2	1	1
Marseille	L	D	3	1	1	1	0	3	1	1
Nantes										
Lorient	W	D	3	2	1	0	1	2	2	1
Guingamp	W	D	5	4	1	0	1	4	1	4
Toulouse	D	D	3	0	1	2	2	1	3	0
Nancy			-	-	-	-	-	-	-	-
Dijon			2	1	1	0	0	2	1	1
Metz			3	0	3	0	0	3	0	3

Season	Division	Pos	P	W	D	L	F	A	GD	Pts
2015-16	Ligue 1	14	38	12	12	14	33	44	-11	48
2014-15	Ligue 1	14	38	11	12	15	29	40	-11	45
2013-14	Ligue 1	13	38	12	10	16	38	43	-5	46

Over/Under 37%/63% 15th   Both score 37%/63% 16th

NICE

Ground: Allianz Riviera   www.ogcnice.com

	2015-16 H	2015-16 A	Last six seasons at home P	W	D	L	OV	UN	BS	CS
Paris SG	L	L	6	1	1	4	4	2	2	1
Lyon	W	D	6	1	2	3	4	2	4	1
Monaco	L	L	4	1	0	3	3	1	2	0
Nice										
Lille	D	D	6	2	2	2	1	5	1	3
St Etienne	W	W	6	2	2	2	1	5	2	2
Caen	W	L	4	2	1	1	2	2	2	1
Rennes	W	W	6	4	0	2	4	2	3	3
Angers	W	D	1	1	0	0	1	0	1	0
Bastia	L	W	4	1	1	2	1	3	1	1
Bordeaux	W	D	6	3	0	3	5	1	4	1
Montpellier	W	W	6	2	2	2	1	5	2	2
Marseille	D	W	6	3	2	1	1	5	3	2
Nantes	L	L	3	0	2	1	1	2	1	2
Lorient	W	D	6	4	1	1	3	3	4	2
Guingamp	L	W	3	1	0	2	1	2	1	1
Toulouse	W	L	6	4	1	1	5	1	2	3
Nancy			3	1	2	0	1	2	3	0
Dijon			1	0	1	0	0	1	0	1
Metz			1	1	0	0	0	1	0	1

Season	Division	Pos	P	W	D	L	F	A	GD	Pts
2015-16	Ligue 1	4	38	18	9	11	58	41	+17	63
2014-15	Ligue 1	11	38	13	9	16	41	48	-7	48
2013-14	Ligue 1	17	38	12	6	20	30	44	-14	42

Over/Under 47%/53% 9th   Both score 50%/50% 9th

PARIS SAINT-GERMAIN
Ground: Parc des Princes www.psg.fr

RENNES
Ground: Stade Route de Lorient staderennais.com

PARIS SAINT-GERMAIN

	2015-16 H	A	Last six seasons at home P	W	D	L	OV	UN	BS	CS
Paris SG										
Lyon	W	L	6	5	1	0	2	4	2	4
Monaco	L	W	4	0	3	1	1	3	3	0
Nice	W	W	6	5	1	0	4	2	3	3
Lille	D	W	6	2	4	0	3	3	3	3
St Etienne	W	W	6	5	0	1	4	2	3	3
Caen	W	W	4	3	1	0	4	0	3	1
Rennes	W	W	6	3	1	2	4	2	2	4
Angers	W	D	1	1	0	0	1	0	1	0
Bastia	W	W	4	4	0	0	2	2	1	3
Bordeaux	D	D	6	2	3	1	3	3	3	3
Montpellier	D	W	6	2	4	0	3	3	2	4
Marseille	W	W	6	6	0	0	3	3	3	3
Nantes	W	W	3	3	0	0	3	0	1	2
Lorient	W	W	6	3	2	1	4	2	3	2
Guingamp	W	W	3	3	0	0	2	1	0	3
Toulouse	W	W	6	6	0	0	4	2	3	3
Nancy			3	1	1	1	2	1	2	0
Dijon			1	1	0	0	0	1	0	1
Metz			1	1	0	0	0	1	0	1

Season	Division	Pos	P	W	D	L	F	A	GD	Pts
2015-16	Ligue 1	1	38	30	6	2	102	19	+83	96
2014-15	Ligue 1	1	38	24	11	3	83	36	+47	83
2013-14	Ligue 1	1	38	27	8	3	84	23	+61	89

Over/Under 61%/39% 1st Both score 39%/61% 15th

RENNES

	2015-16 H	A	Last six seasons at home P	W	D	L	OV	UN	BS	CS
Paris SG	L	L	6	1	2	3	1	5	3	1
Lyon	D	W	6	1	3	2	1	5	3	1
Monaco	D	D	4	2	1	1	0	4	1	2
Nice	L	L	6	3	1	2	4	2	3	2
Lille	D	D	6	2	4	0	0	6	3	3
St Etienne	L	D	6	1	4	1	2	4	3	2
Caen	D	L	4	1	2	1	2	2	4	0
Rennes										
Angers	W	W	1	1	0	0	0	1	0	1
Bastia	L	L	4	2	0	2	3	1	2	1
Bordeaux	D	L	6	1	4	1	1	5	3	2
Montpellier	W	L	6	2	1	3	3	3	2	1
Marseille	L	W	6	0	3	3	2	4	4	0
Nantes	W	W	3	1	1	1	2	1	2	1
Lorient	D	D	6	2	2	2	3	3	4	2
Guingamp	L	W	3	1	0	2	1	2	0	1
Toulouse	W	D	6	3	0	3	4	2	3	1
Nancy			3	0	1	2	0	3	1	0
Dijon			1	1	0	0	1	0	0	1
Metz			1	1	0	0	1	0	0	1

Season	Division	Pos	P	W	D	L	F	A	GD	Pts
2015-16	Ligue 1	8	38	13	13	12	52	54	-2	52
2014-15	Ligue 1	9	38	13	11	14	35	42	-7	50
2013-14	Ligue 1	12	38	11	13	14	47	45	+2	46

Over/Under 47%/53% 9th Both score 61%/39% 3rd

ST ETIENNE
Ground: Stade Geoffroy-Guichard www.asse.fr

TOULOUSE
Ground: Stadium Municipal www.tfc.info

ST ETIENNE

	2015-16 H	A	Last six seasons at home P	W	D	L	OV	UN	BS	CS
Paris SG	L	L	6	0	3	3	2	4	3	0
Lyon	W	L	6	2	0	4	3	3	2	2
Monaco	D	L	4	1	3	0	0	4	3	1
Nice	L	L	6	2	1	3	4	2	3	2
Lille	L	L	6	2	0	4	3	3	3	2
St Etienne										
Caen	L	L	4	2	1	1	1	3	2	2
Rennes	D	W	6	2	3	1	2	4	2	4
Angers	W	D	1	1	0	0	0	1	0	1
Bastia	W	W	4	3	1	0	1	3	1	2
Bordeaux	D	W	6	1	4	1	3	3	5	1
Montpellier	W	W	6	5	1	0	3	3	2	4
Marseille	L	D	6	1	4	1	1	5	3	2
Nantes	W	W	3	3	0	0	3	0	0	3
Lorient	W	W	6	4	0	2	3	3	3	2
Guingamp	W	L	3	3	0	0	2	1	1	2
Toulouse	D	L	6	1	3	2	3	3	4	1
Nancy			3	3	0	0	2	1	1	2
Dijon			1	1	0	0	0	1	0	1
Metz			1	1	0	0	0	1	0	1

Season	Division	Pos	P	W	D	L	F	A	GD	Pts
2015-16	Ligue 1	6	38	17	7	14	42	37	+5	58
2014-15	Ligue 1	5	38	19	12	7	51	30	+21	69
2013-14	Ligue 1	4	38	20	9	9	56	34	+22	69

Over/Under 32%/68% 18th Both score 34%/66% 19th

TOULOUSE

	2015-16 H	A	Last six seasons at home P	W	D	L	OV	UN	BS	CS
Paris SG	L	L	6	0	1	5	3	3	3	0
Lyon	L	L	6	4	1	1	2	4	2	4
Monaco	D	L	4	1	1	2	0	4	1	1
Nice	W	L	6	2	2	2	4	3	3	3
Lille	D	L	6	2	3	1	3	3	5	1
St Etienne	W	D	6	2	2	2	4	3	3	1
Caen	W	L	4	3	1	0	1	3	1	3
Rennes	L	L	6	2	1	3	5	1	4	1
Angers	L	W	1	0	0	1	1	0	1	0
Bastia	W	D	4	1	2	1	2	2	2	2
Bordeaux	W	D	6	4	2	0	3	3	3	3
Montpellier	D	L	6	2	2	2	0	6	2	2
Marseille	D	D	6	0	3	3	1	5	3	1
Nantes	D	D	3	0	3	0	0	3	2	1
Lorient	L	D	6	2	1	3	3	3	3	2
Guingamp	L	L	3	0	2	1	1	2	2	1
Toulouse										
Nancy			3	3	0	0	1	2	1	2
Dijon			1	1	0	0	0	1	0	1
Metz			1	1	0	0	0	1	0	1

Season	Division	Pos	P	W	D	L	F	A	GD	Pts
2015-16	Ligue 1	17	38	9	13	16	45	55	-10	40
2014-15	Ligue 1	17	38	12	6	20	33	51	-18	42
2013-14	Ligue 1	9	38	12	13	13	46	53	-7	49

Over/Under 47%/53% 9th Both score 53%/47% 7th

FRENCH LIGUE 1

Ligue 1 2015-16

Pos	H	A		P	W	D	L	F	A	W	D	L	F	A	GD	Pts
					Home					**Away**						
1	1	1	Paris St-G (CL)	38	15	3	1	59	12	15	3	1	43	7	+83	96
2	2	7	Lyon (CL)	38	12	4	3	42	16	7	4	8	25	27	+24	65
3	4	2	Monaco (CL)	38	10	6	3	30	19	7	8	4	27	31	+7	65
4	3	6	Nice (EL)	38	12	2	5	32	16	6	7	6	26	25	+17	63
5	7	4	Lille (EL)	38	9	6	4	21	11	6	9	4	18	16	+12	60
6	6	9	St-Etienne (EL)	38	10	4	5	25	15	7	3	9	17	22	+5	58
7	9	10	Caen	38	9	3	7	19	23	7	3	9	20	29	-13	54
8	17	5	Rennes	38	6	7	6	25	25	7	6	6	27	29	-2	52
9	14	8	Angers	38	6	8	5	20	15	7	3	9	20	23	+2	50
10	5	17	Bastia	38	11	2	6	23	14	3	6	10	13	28	-6	50
11	8	14	Bordeaux	38	8	7	4	27	20	4	7	8	23	37	-7	50
12	12	11	Montpellier	38	9	0	10	26	23	5	7	7	23	24	+2	49
13	19	3	Marseille	38	3	11	5	27	24	7	7	5	21	18	+6	48
14	10	12	Nantes	38	8	5	6	20	20	4	7	8	13	24	-11	48
15	11	15	Lorient	38	7	7	5	26	21	4	6	9	21	37	-11	46
16	16	13	Guingamp	38	6	7	6	31	28	5	4	10	16	28	-9	44
17	15	18	Toulouse	38	6	7	6	29	21	3	6	10	16	34	-10	40
18	13	19	Reims (R)	38	7	5	7	28	23	3	4	12	16	34	-13	39
19	18	16	GFC Ajaccio (R)	38	5	7	7	23	32	3	6	10	14	26	-21	37
20	20	20	Troyes (R)	38	1	7	11	13	36	2	2	15	15	47	-55	18

Ligue 1 results 2015-16

	Angers	Bastia	Bordeaux	Caen	GFC Ajaccio	Guingamp	Lille	Lorient	Lyon	Marseille	Monaco	Montpellier	Nantes	Nice	Paris SG	Reims	Rennes	St Etienne	Toulouse	Troyes
Angers		1-0	1-1	2-0	0-0	0-0	2-0	5-1	0-3	0-1	3-0	2-3	0-0	1-1	0-0	0-0	0-2	0-0	2-3	1-0
Bastia	1-0		1-0	1-0	1-2	3-0	1-2	0-0	1-0	2-1	1-2	1-0	0-0	1-3	0-2	2-0	2-1	0-1	3-0	2-0
Bordeaux	1-3	1-1		1-4	1-1	1-0	1-0	3-0	3-1	1-1	3-1	0-0	2-0	0-0	1-1	1-2	4-0	1-4	1-1	1-0
Caen	0-0	0-0	1-0		2-0	2-1	1-2	1-2	0-4	1-3	2-2	2-1	0-2	2-0	0-3	0-2	1-0	1-0	1-0	2-1
GFC Ajaccio	0-2	3-2	2-0	1-0		0-0	2-4	1-1	2-1	1-1	0-1	0-4	1-1	3-1	0-4	2-2	1-1	0-2	2-2	2-3
Guingamp	2-2	1-0	2-4	1-1	2-1		1-1	2-2	0-1	2-0	3-3	2-2	2-2	2-3	0-2	1-2	0-2	2-0	2-0	4-0
Lille	0-0	1-1	0-0	1-0	1-0	0-0		3-0	1-0	1-2	4-1	2-0	0-1	1-1	0-1	2-0	1-1	1-0	1-0	1-3
Lorient	3-1	1-1	3-2	2-0	1-0	4-3	0-1		1-3	1-1	0-2	1-1	0-0	0-0	1-2	2-0	1-1	0-1	1-1	4-1
Lyon	0-2	2-0	3-0	4-1	2-1	5-1	0-0	0-0		1-1	6-1	2-4	2-0	1-1	2-1	1-0	1-2	3-0	3-0	4-1
Marseille	1-2	4-1	0-0	1-1	0-0	1-1	1-1	1-0	1-1		3-3	2-2	1-1	0-1	1-2	1-0	2-5	1-1	1-1	6-0
Monaco	1-0	2-0	1-2	1-1	2-2	3-2	0-0	2-3	1-1	2-1		2-0	1-0	0-0	0-3	2-0	1-1	1-0	4-0	3-1
Montpellier	0-2	2-0	0-1	1-2	0-2	2-1	3-0	2-1	0-2	0-1	2-3		2-1	0-2	0-1	3-1	2-0	1-2	2-0	4-1
Nantes	2-0	0-0	2-2	1-2	3-1	1-0	0-3	2-1	0-0	0-1	0-0	0-2		1-0	1-4	0-2	2-1	1-1	3-0	
Nice	2-1	0-2	6-1	2-1	3-0	0-1	0-0	2-1	3-0	1-1	1-2	1-0	1-2		0-3	2-0	3-0	2-0	1-0	2-1
Paris St-Germain	5-1	2-0	2-2	6-0	2-0	3-0	0-0	3-1	5-1	2-1	0-2	0-0	4-0	4-1		4-1	4-0	4-1	5-0	4-1
Reims	2-1	0-1	4-1	0-1	1-2	0-1	1-0	4-1	4-1	1-0	0-1	2-3	2-1	1-1	1-1		2-2	1-1	1-3	1-1
Rennes	1-0	1-2	2-2	1-1	1-0	0-3	1-1	2-2	2-2	0-1	1-1	1-0	4-1	1-4	0-1	3-1		0-1	3-1	1-1
St Etienne	1-0	2-1	1-1	1-2	2-0	3-0	0-1	2-0	1-0	0-2	1-1	3-0	2-0	0-2	3-0	1-1	0-1		0-0	1-0
Toulouse	1-2	4-0	4-0	2-0	1-1	1-2	1-1	2-3	2-3	1-1	1-1	1-1	0-0	2-0	0-1	2-2	1-2	2-1		1-0
Troyes	0-1	1-1	2-4	1-3	0-0	0-1	1-1	0-1	0-1	1-1	0-0	0-0	0-1	3-3	0-9	2-1	2-4	0-3		

Top scorers

	Team	Goals scored	
Z Ibrahimovic	PSG	38	▐▐▐▐▐▐▐▐▐▐▐▐▐▐▐▐▐▐▐▐▐▐▐▐
A Lacazette	Lyon	21	▐▐▐▐▐▐▐▐▐▐▐▐▐
E Cavani	PSG	19	▐▐▐▐▐▐▐▐▐▐▐▐
M Batshuayi	Marseille	17	▐▐▐▐▐▐▐▐▐▐▐
H Ben Arfa	Nice	17	▐▐▐▐▐▐▐▐▐▐▐
W Ben Yedder	Toulouse	17	▐▐▐▐▐▐▐▐▐▐▐

Over 2.5 goals top eight

	H	A	%
Paris St-G	14	9	61%
Lyon	11	10	55%
Guingamp	10	10	53%
Reims, Monaco,			
Troyes, Lorient,			
Bordeaux			50%

Both to score top five

	H	A	%
Marseille	13	12	66%
Lorient	11	13	63%
Rennes	12	11	61%
Bordeaux	11	11	58%
Monaco	10	12	58%
Reims	13	9	58%

Uefa Association Coefficients 2015-16

Pos	Change	Country	11-12	12-13	13-14	14-15	15-16	Pts	Change
1	=	Spain	20.857	17.714	23	20.214	23.928	**105.713**	6.29
2	1	Germany	15.25	17.928	14.714	15.857	16.428	**80.177**	0.76
3	-1	England	15.25	16.428	16.785	13.571	14.25	**76.284**	-4.11
4	=	Italy	11.357	14.416	14.166	19	11.5	**70.439**	-0.07
5	=	Portugal	11.833	11.75	9.916	9.083	10.5	**53.082**	-8.30
6	=	France	10.5	11.75	8.5	10.916	11.083	**52.749**	0.33
7	=	Russia	9.75	9.75	10.416	9.666	11.5	**51.082**	0.58
8	=	Ukraine	7.75	9.5	7.833	10	9.8	**44.883**	-0.28
9	1	Belgium	10.1	6.5	6.4	9.6	7.4	**40**	2.80
10	-1	Holland	13.6	4.214	5.916	6.083	5.75	**35.563**	-5.42
11	1	Turkey	5.1	10.2	6.7	6	6.6	**34.6**	2.00
12	-1	Switzerland	6	8.375	7.2	6.9	5.3	**33.775**	-0.60
13	1	Czech Republic	5.25	8.5	8	3.875	7.3	**32.925**	3.80
14	-1	Greece	7.6	4.4	6.1	6.2	5.4	**29.7**	-2.20
15	=	Romania	4.333	6.8	6.875	5.125	2.25	**25.383**	-0.92
16	=	Austria	7.125	2.25	7.8	4.125	3.8	**25.1**	-0.57
17	=	Croatia	3.75	4.375	4.375	6.875	4.5	**23.875**	0.38
18	1	Poland	6.625	2.5	3.125	4.75	5.5	**22.5**	1.00
19	-1	Cyprus	9.125	4	2.75	3.3	3	**22.175**	-0.13
20	1	Belarus	3.125	4.5	1.75	5.5	5.125	**20**	-0.75
21	3	Sweden	2.9	5.125	3.2	3.9	4.75	**19.875**	2.15
22	4	Norway	2.3	4.9	2.6	2.2	7.25	**19.25**	4.88
23	-3	Israel	6	3.25	5.75	1.375	2.25	**18.625**	-2.38
24	-2	Denmark	3.1	3.3	3.8	2.9	5.5	**18.6**	-1.20
25	-2	Scotland	2.75	4.3	3.25	4	3	**17.3**	-0.60
26	3	Azerbaijan	1.375	3	2.5	3.625	4.375	**14.875**	2.38
27	=	Serbia	2.125	3	2.5	2.75	4.25	**14.625**	0.75
28	4	Kazakhstan	1.625	1.375	3.125	3.375	4.625	**14.125**	3.75
29	-4	Bulgaria	1.5	0.75	5.625	4.25	1	**13.125**	-3.63
30	-2	Slovenia	2.25	3.25	2.625	4	1	**13.125**	-0.50
31	-1	Slovakia	2.375	1.5	1.625	2.75	3.75	**12**	0.75
32	6	Liechtenstein	2	0	1	2.5	5	**10.5**	4.50
33	-2	Hungary	2.25	3	0.875	2.125	1.625	**9.875**	-1.13
34	-1	Moldova	0.5	2.25	3.375	1.75	1.25	**9.125**	-0.88
35	1	Iceland	1.375	1.25	2.5	2.5	1.125	**8.75**	0.75
36	-2	Georgia	2.875	1.5	1.875	1.25	0.625	**8.125**	-1.25
37	-2	Finland	1.5	2	0.5	2.4	1	**7.4**	-0.80
38	-1	Bosnia-Hz	1.125	1.25	1.5	1.75	1.5	**7.125**	-0.38
39	3	Albania	0.875	0.75	2	0.875	2.125	**6.625**	1.25
40	-1	Macedonia	1.625	1.25	0.5	1.125	1.5	**6**	0.13
41	-1	Ireland	1.5	1	0.25	2	0.7	**5.45**	-0.30
42	4	Latvia	0.625	1.25	1.625	0.25	1.625	**5.375**	1.13
43	=	Luxembourg	1.125	1.375	1.5	0.5	0.75	**5.25**	0.13
44	-3	Montenegro	0.5	1.375	1.25	0.75	1	**4.875**	-0.75
45	=	Lithuania	1	1.125	1.25	0.5	0.75	**4.625**	0.13
46	-2	Northern Ireland	0.5	1	0.875	1.375	0.75	**4.5**	-0.38
47	1	Estonia	0.375	0.375	1	1.5	1	**4.25**	0.75
48	3	Armenia	0.125	0.875	1.125	0.375	1.625	**4.125**	1.38
49	=	Faroe Islands	0.5	0.5	0.875	1.375	0.375	**3.625**	0.13
50	-3	Malta	0.833	0.875	0.875	0.125	0.875	**3.583**	-0.63
51	-1	Wales	0.625	0.5	0.75	0.125	1.5	**3.5**	0.63
52	2	Gibraltar	0	0	0	0.25	0.75	**1**	0.75
53	-1	Andorra	0	0	0.333	0.5	0.166	**0.999**	0.17
54	-1	San Marino	0	0	0.333	0	0	**0.333**	-0.17
55	=	Kosovo	0	0	0	0	0	**0**	0.00

Uefa's country coefficients are calculated from performances of each FA's clubs in the last five Europa League and Champions League seasons. They are used to allocate places in Uefa's club competitions and determine seedings with the top 12, shown on the facing page, receiving at least one place in the Champions League group stage.

Two points are awarded for a win and one for a draw, and half that in qualifying matches. An extra point is awarded for every round from the last 16 of the Champions League and the quarter-finals of the Europa League. Four extra points are given for reaching the group stage of the Champions League and four more for the knockout rounds.

The country coefficient is the sum of the average points for each nation in each of the last five seasons. England's clubs have averaged 15.25, 16.428, 16.785, 13.571 and 14.25 over the last five campaigns – add them together and you get 76.284, England's country coefficient.

Portugal

		P	W	D	L	F	A	GD	Pts
1	Benfica	34	29	1	4	88	22	+66	88
2	Sporting	34	27	5	2	79	21	+58	86
3	Porto	34	23	4	7	67	30	+37	73
4	Braga	34	16	10	8	54	35	+19	58
5	Arouca	34	13	15	6	47	38	+9	54
6	Rio Ave	34	14	8	12	44	44	+0	50
7	Pacos Ferreira	34	13	10	11	43	42	+1	49
8	Estoril	34	13	8	13	40	41	-1	47
9	Belenenses	34	10	11	13	44	66	-22	41
10	Vit Guimaraes	34	9	13	12	45	53	-8	40
11	Nacional	34	10	8	16	40	56	-16	38
12	Moreirense	34	9	9	16	38	54	-16	36
13	Maritimo	34	10	5	19	45	63	-18	35
14	Boavista	34	8	9	17	24	41	-17	33
15	Vitoria Setubal	34	6	12	16	40	61	-21	30
16	Tondela	34	8	6	20	34	54	-20	30
17	Uniao Madeira	34	7	8	19	27	50	-23	29
18	Academica	34	5	10	19	32	60	-28	25

Russia

		P	W	D	L	F	A	GD	Pts
1	CSKA Moscow	30	20	5	5	51	25	+26	65
2	Rostov	30	19	6	5	41	20	+21	63
3	Zenit	30	17	8	5	61	32	+29	59
4	Krasnodar	30	16	8	6	54	25	+29	56
5	Spartak Moscow	30	15	5	10	48	39	+9	50
6	Lok Moscow	30	14	8	8	43	33	+10	50
7	Terek Grozny	30	11	11	8	35	30	+5	44
8	Ural	30	10	9	11	39	46	-7	39
9	Krylya Sovetov	30	9	8	13	19	31	-12	35
10	Rubin Kazan	30	9	6	15	33	39	-6	33
11	Amkar Perm	30	7	10	13	22	33	-11	31
12	Ufa	30	6	9	15	25	44	-19	27
13	Anzhi	30	6	8	16	28	50	-22	26
14	Kuban	30	5	11	14	34	44	-10	26
15	Din Moscow	30	5	10	15	25	47	-22	25
16	Mordovia	30	4	12	14	30	50	-20	24

Ukraine

		P	W	D	L	F	A	GD	Pts
1	Dynamo Kiev	26	23	1	2	54	11	+43	70
2	Shakhtar Donetsk	26	20	3	3	76	25	+51	63
3	Dnipro	26	16	5	5	50	22	+28	53
4	Zorya	26	14	6	6	51	26	+25	48
5	Vorskla	26	11	9	6	32	26	+6	42
6	Oleksandria	26	10	8	8	30	29	+1	38
7	Karpaty	26	8	6	12	26	37	-11	30
8	Dniprodzerzhynsk	26	7	8	11	22	31	-9	29
9	Olimpik Donetsk	26	6	7	13	22	35	-13	25
10	Met Kharkiv*	26	5	9	12	19	46	-27	24
11	Chornomorets	26	4	10	12	20	39	-19	22
12	Volyn	26	10	8	8	36	36	+0	20
13	Hoverla*	26	3	7	16	13	45	-32	7
14	Met Zaporizhya*	26	0	3	23	7	50	-43	3

Metalist Kharkiv, Hoverla and Zaporizhya all disqualified from league

THE SMARTER WAY
TO BET ON FOOTBALL
SOCCERBASE.COM

Belgium (Championship playoff)

		P	W	D	L	F	A	GD	Pts
1	Club Brugge	10	7	1	2	25	9	+16	54
2	Anderlecht	10	6	1	3	15	16	-1	47
3	Gent	10	3	3	4	10	15	-5	42
4	Genk	10	5	1	4	20	13	+7	40
5	KV Oostende	10	3	2	5	14	19	-5	36
6	Zulte-Waregem	10	1	2	7	11	23	-12	27

Points from regular season are halved, rounded up and carried over into round-robin championship playoff

Holland

		P	W	D	L	F	A	GD	Pts
1	PSV	34	26	6	2	88	32	+56	84
2	Ajax	34	25	7	2	81	21	+60	82
3	Feyenoord	34	19	6	9	62	40	+22	63
4	AZ	34	18	5	11	70	53	+17	59
5	Utrecht	34	15	8	11	57	48	+9	53
6	Heracles	34	14	9	11	47	49	-2	51
7	Groningen	34	14	8	12	41	48	-7	50
8	PEC Zwolle	34	14	6	14	56	52	+4	48
9	Vitesse	34	12	10	12	55	38	+17	46
10	NEC	34	13	7	14	37	42	-5	46
11	ADO Den Haag	34	10	13	11	48	49	-1	43
12	Heerenveen	34	11	9	14	46	61	-15	42
13	Twente	34	12	7	15	49	64	-15	40
14	Roda JC	34	8	10	16	34	55	-21	34
15	Excelsior	34	7	9	18	34	60	-26	30
16	Willem II	34	6	11	17	35	53	-18	29
17	De Graafschap	34	5	8	21	39	66	-27	23
18	Cambuur	34	3	9	22	33	79	-46	18

Turkey

		P	W	D	L	F	A	GD	Pts
1	Besiktas	34	25	4	5	75	35	+40	79
2	Fenerbahce	34	22	8	4	60	27	+33	74
3	Konyaspor	34	19	9	6	44	33	+11	66
4	Basaksehir	34	16	11	7	54	36	+18	59
5	Osmanlispor	34	14	10	10	52	36	+16	52
6	Galatasaray	34	13	12	9	69	49	+20	51
7	Kasimpasa	34	14	8	12	50	40	+10	50
8	Akhisar Belediye	34	11	13	10	42	41	+1	46
9	Antalyaspor	34	12	9	13	53	52	+1	45
10	Genclerbirligi	34	13	6	15	42	42	+0	45
11	Bursaspor	34	13	5	16	47	55	-8	44
12	Trabzonspor	34	12	4	18	40	59	-19	40
13	Rizespor	34	9	10	15	39	48	-9	37
14	Gaziantepspor	34	9	9	16	31	50	-19	36
15	Kayserispor	34	7	13	14	25	41	-16	34
16	Sivasspor	34	6	13	15	34	48	-14	31
17	Eskisehirspor	34	8	6	20	39	64	-25	30
18	Mersin	34	5	6	23	31	71	-40	21

Switzerland

		P	W	D	L	F	A	GD	Pts
1	Basel	36	26	5	5	88	38	+50	83
2	Young Boys	36	20	9	7	78	47	+31	69
3	Luzern	36	15	9	12	59	50	+9	54
4	Grasshopper	36	15	8	13	65	56	+9	53
5	Sion	36	14	8	14	52	49	+3	50
6	Thun	36	10	11	15	45	54	-9	41
7	St Gallen	36	10	8	18	41	66	-25	38
8	Vaduz	36	7	15	14	44	60	-16	36
9	Lugano	36	9	8	19	46	75	-29	35
10	Zurich	36	7	13	16	48	71	-23	34

EUROPA LEAGUE

First qualifying round
Tuesday June 30, 2015

Balzan .... (0) 0-2 (2) ...... Zeljeznicar
P Niedercorn... (0) 0-0 (0) .....Shamrock R
Renova .... (0) 0-1 (1) .... Dacia

Thursday July 2, 2015

Airbus UK .... (1) 1-3 (0) ...Loko. Zagreb
Aktobe............ (0) 0-1 (0) ..Nomme Kalju
Alashkert .... (0) 1-0 (0) ... St Johnstone
Atlantas.......... (0) 0-2 (0) ..... Beroe Stara
Birkirkara .... (0) 0-0 (0) .... FC Ulisses
Botosani .... (1) 1-1 (0) ....Tskhinvali
Brondby.......... (6) 9-0 (0) .... Juvenes
Buducnost P. ... (1) 1-3 (2) .....Sp Jurmala
College Europa(0) 0-6 (5) ....Sl Bratislava
Cork City........ (1) 1-1 (1) ... KR Reykjavik
Crvena Zvezda (0) 0-2 (1) ..Kairat Almaty
Debrecen .... (1) 3-0 (0) .... Sutjeska
Differdange..... (3) 3-1 (1) ....Bala Town
D Batumi .... (1) 1-0 (0) .... Omonia
Dinamo Tbilisi.(0) 2-1 (0) ....Qabala
Domzale .... (0) 0-1 (1) ....Cukaricki
FC Lahti .... (1) 2-2 (1) .... Elfsborg
FC Sheriff........ (0) 0-3 (3). Odd Grenland
FK Trakai .... (1) 3-0 (0) ....HB Torshavn
Flora Tallinn .... (0) 1-0 (0) .....Rabotnicki
Glenavon........ (0) 1-2 (2)........ Shakhtyor
Glentoran .... (0) 1-4 (2) .... Zilina
Go Ahead E .... (1) 1-1 (1) .... Ferencvaros

Jelgava .... (0) 1-1 (0) .... Litex
KF Laci .... (1) 1-1 (0) ....Inter Baku
Kalev Sillamae (1) 1-1 (1) .... Hajduk Split
Kruoja............ (0) 0-1 (0) ...... Jagiellonia
Kukesi............. (1) 2-0 (0) ..... Torpedo Zh
La Fiorita .... (0) 0-5 (3) .... Vaduz
Linfield .... (0) 2-0 (0) .... NSI Runavik
MTK............... (0) 0-0 (0) .... Vojvodina
NK Celje.......... (0) 0-1 (1) Slask Wroclaw
Neftchi Baku... (1) 2-2 (1) .. Mladost Pod.
Newtown .... (1) 2-1 (0) .... Valletta
Ol Sarajevo ..... (1) 1-1 (0) .....Sp Trnava
Ordabasy........ (0) 0-0 (0) ..Beitar J'salem
SJK................. (0) 0-1 (0) ..Hafnarfjordur
Saxan Ceadir... (0) 0-2 (1) .... Ap Limassol
Shirak Gumri... (1) 2-0 (0) Zrinjski Mostar
Shkendija........ (0) 1-1 (0) ....Aberdeen
Skonto Riga .... (1) 2-1 (1)..... St Patrick's
Stromsgodset..(1) 3-1 (0) Partizan Tirana
UCD................ (1) 1-0 (0)F91 Dudelange
UE Sant Julia... (0) 0-1 (1) ..Randers Freja
VPS Vaasa....... (1) 2-2 (0) ...... AIK Solna
Vikingur (FIs).. (0) 0-2 (0) ...... Rosenborg
Vikingur (Ice) .. (0) 0-1 (0) .... Koper
West Ham....... (2) 3-0 (0) ..... FC Lusitans

Second legs
Tuesday July 7, 2015

Shamrock R..... (2) 3-0 (0) ...P Niedercorn
Aggregate: 3-0

Thursday July 9, 2015

AIK Solna........ (1) 4-0 (0) ......VPS Vaasa
Aggregate: 6-2

Aberdeen........ (0) 0-0 (0) ....Shkendija
Agg: 1-1. Aberdeen won on away goals
Ap Limassol .... (1) 2-0 (0) ...Saxan Ceadir
Aggregate: 4-0
Bala Town....... (0) 2-1 (0) ....Differdange
Aggregate: 3-4
Beitar J'salem.. (1) 2-1 (0) ....Ordabasy
Aggregate: 2-1
Beroe Stara ..... (2) 3-1 (0) ....Atlantas
Aggregate: 5-1
Cukaricki........ (0) 0-0 (0) .... Domzale
Aggregate: 1-0
Dacia .... (1) 4-1 (1) .... Renova
Aggregate: 5-1
Elfsborg .... (3) 5-0 (0) .... FC Lahti
Aggregate: 7-2
F91 Dudelange(2) 2-1 (1)...............UCD
Agg: 2-2. UCD won on away goals
FC Lusitans ..... (0) 0-1 (1) ......West Ham
Aggregate: 0-4
FC Ulisses .... (0) 1-3 (2) .... Birkirkara
Aggregate: 1-3
Ferencvaros .... (3) 4-1 (0) .... Go Ahead E
Aggregate: 5-2
HB Torshavn.... (0) 1-4 (2) ....FK Trakai
Aggregate: 1-7
Hafnarfjordur.. (0) 1-0 (0) ....SJK
Aggregate: 2-0
Hajduk Split .... (2) 6-2 (2) Kalev Sillamae
Aggregate: 7-3
Inter Baku........ (0) 0-0 (0) ....KF Laci
Agg: 1-1. Inter Baku won on away goals
Jagiellonia ...... (4) 8-0 (0) ....Kruoja
Aggregate: 9-0

St Johnstone, Inverness and Aberdeen all failed to navigate the Europa League qualifying rounds

Juvenes .... (0) 0-2 (0) ....Brondby
Aggregate: 0-11
KR Reykjavik ... (0) 2-1 (1) ....Cork City
AET. 1-1 after 90 mins. Agg: 3-2
Kairat Almaty.. (1) 2-1 (0) Crvena Zvezda
Aggregate: 4-1
Koper............. (1) 2-2 (0) ....Vikingur
Aggregate: 3-2
Litex .... (1) 2-2 (1) ....Jelgava
Agg: 3-3. Jelgava won on away goals
Loko. Zagreb... (0) 2-2 (0) ...... Airbus UK
Aggregate: 5-3
Mladost Pod. .. (0) 1-1 (0) ...Neftchi Baku
Agg: 3-3. Mladost won on away goals
NSI Runavik .... (3) 4-3 (2) .... Linfield
Aggregate: 4-5
Nomme Kalju.. (0) 0-0 (0) ....Aktobe
Aggregate: 1-0
Odd Grenland . (0) 0-0 (0) ...... FC Sheriff
Aggregate: 3-0
Omonia Nicosia(0) 2-0 (0) .... D Batumi
Aggregate: 2-1
Partizan Tirana (0) 0-1 (0) ..Stromsgodset
Aggregate: 1-4
Qabala........... (0) 2-0 (0) .Dinamo Tbilisi
Aggregate: 3-2
Rabotnicki....... (0) 2-0 (0) .... Flora Tallinn
Aggregate: 2-1
Randers Freja.. (1) 3-0 (0)..UE Sant Julia
Aggregate: 4-0
Rosenborg ...... (0) 0-0 (0) ....Vikingur
Aggregate: 2-0
Sl Bratislava .... (2) 3-0 (0)College Europa
Aggregate: 9-0
Shakhtyor .... (1) 3-0 (0) ......Glenavon
Aggregate: 5-1
Slask Wroclaw (0) 3-1 (0) ....NK Celje
Aggregate: 4-1
Spartak Trnava (0) 0-0 (0) ..... Ol Sarajevo
Agg: 1-1. Spartak won on away goals
Sp Jurmala...... (0) 0-0 (0) ....Buducnost P
Aggregate: 3-1
St Johnstone ... (1) 2-1 (0) .... Alashkert
Agg: 2-2. Alashkert won on away goals
St Patrick's ..... (0) 0-2 (1) ..... Skonto Riga
Aggregate: 1-4
Sutjeska .... (0) 2-0 (0) .... Debrecen
Aggregate: 2-3
Torpedo Zh ..... (0) 0-0 (0) ....Kukesi
Aggregate: 0-2
Tskhinvali....... (0) 1-3 (1) .... Botosani
Aggregate: 2-4
Vaduz .... (3) 5-1 (0) .... La Fiorita
Aggregate: 10-1
Valletta .... (0) 1-2 (1) .... Newtown
Aggregate: 2-4
Vojvodina ...... (2) 3-1 (1) ....MTK
Aggregate: 3-1
Zeljeznicar ...... (0) 1-0 (0) .... Balzan
Aggregate: 3-0
Zilina .... (1) 3-0 (0) .... Glentoran
Aggregate: 7-1
Zrinjski Mostar (0) 2-1 (0) ...Shirak Gumri
Aggregate: 2-3

Second qualifying round
Thursday July 16, 2015
AIK Solna........ (1) 2-0 (0) ...Shirak Gumri

Ap Limassol .... (1) 4-0 (0) ....FK Trakai
Beroe Stara ..... (0) 0-1 (0) ....Brondby
Charleroi......... (1) 5-1 (1) ..Beitar J'salem
Cherno More .. (1) 1-1 (0) Dinamo Minsk
Cukaricki........ (0) 1-0 (0) ....Qabala
Dacia .... (0) 1-2 (0) .... Zilina
Copenhagen ... (1) 2-0 (0) ...... Newtown
Ferencvaros .... (0) 0-1 (0) ..... Zeljeznicar
H. Beer Sheva . (1) 1-1 (0) ....Thun
Hafnarfjordur.. (1) 1-2 (0) ......Inter Baku
Inverness CT ... (0) 0-1 (1) .. Astra Giurgiu
Jagiellonia ...... (0) 0-0 (0) .... Omonia
Jelgava .... (0) 1-0 (0) ......Rabotnicki
KR Reykjavik ... (0) 1-0 (0) ...... Rosenborg
Kairat Almaty.. (1) 3-0 (0) ...... Alashkert
Koper............. (3) 3-2 (1) .... Hajduk Split
Kukesi............. (0) 0-1 (0) ... Mladost Pod
Legia Warsaw . (0) 1-0 (0) .... Botosani
Loko. Zagreb... (2) 2-1 (0) PAOK Salonika
Mlada Boleslav(1) 1-2 (1) ..Stromsgodset
Randers Freja.. (0) 0-0 (0) ...... Elfsborg
Rijeka .... (0) 0-3 (1) ....Aberdeen
Sl Bratislava .... (0) 1-0 (0) ....UCD
Shakhtyor .... (0) 0-1 (0) .... Wolfsberger
Shamrock R..... (0) 0-2 (0) .Odd Grenland
Skonto Riga .... (1) 2-2 (1) .... Debrecen
Slask Wroclaw (0) 0-0 (0) . IFK Goth'burg
Spartak Trnava (2) 2-1 (1) .... Linfield
Trabzonspor.... (1) 1-0 (0) .....Differdange
Vaduz .... (1) 3-1 (0) ..Nomme Kalju
Vojvodina ...... (2) 3-0 (0) ......Sp Jurmala
West Ham....... (0) 1-0 (0) .... Birkirkara

Second legs
Tuesday July 21, 2015
Elfsborg .... (0) 1-0 (0)..Randers Freja
AET. 0-0 after 90 mins. Agg: 1-0
Thursday July 23, 2015
Aberdeen........ (0) 2-2 (0) .... Rijeka
Aggregate: 5-2
Alashkert .... (1) 2-1 (1)..Kairat Almaty
Aggregate: 2-4
Astra Giurgiu .. (0) 0-0 (0)... Inverness CT
Aggregate: 1-0
Beitar J'salem.. (1) 1-4 (1) ....Charleroi
Aggregate: 2-9
Birkirkara .... (1) 1-0 (0) ......West Ham
AET. 1-0 after 90 mins. Agg: 1-1.
West Ham won 5-3 on penalties
Botosani .... (0) 0-3 (2) .Legia Warsaw
Aggregate: 0-4
Brondby......... (0) 0-0 (0) ..... Beroe Stara
Aggregate: 1-0
Debrecen .... (5) 9-2 (0) ..... Skonto Riga
Aggregate: 11-4
Differdange..... (0) 1-2 (1) ....Trabzonspor
Aggregate: 1-3
Dinamo Minsk (1) 4-0 (0).. Cherno More
Aggregate: 5-1
FK Trakai........ (0) 0-0 (0) .... Ap Limassol
Aggregate: 0-4
Hajduk Split .... (2) 4-1 (1) ....Koper
Aggregate: 6-4
IFK Goth'burg . (0) 2-0 (0) Slask Wroclaw
Aggregate: 2-0

Inter Baku....... (1) 2-2 (0) ..Hafnarfjordur
AET. 1-2 after 90 mins. Agg: 4-3
Linfield .... (1) 1-3 (0) ....Sp Trnava
Aggregate: 2-5
Mladost Pod. .. (0) 2-4 (3) ....Kukesi
Aggregate: 3-4
Newtown .... (0) 1-3 (2) ... Copenhagen
Aggregate: 1-5
Nomme Kalju.. (0) 0-2 (0) .... Vaduz
Aggregate: 1-5
Odd Grenland . (0) 2-1 (0) .....Shamrock R
Aggregate: 4-1
Omonia Nicosia(1) 1-0 (0) ...... Jagiellonia
Aggregate: 1-0
PAOK Salonika (4) 6-0 (0) ...Loko. Zagreb
Aggregate: 7-2
Qabala........... (1) 2-0 (0) ....Cukaricki
Aggregate: 2-1
Rabotnicki....... (2) 2-0 (0) .... Jelgava
Aggregate: 2-1
Rosenborg ..... (3) 3-0 (0) ... KR Reykjavik
Aggregate: 4-0
Shirak Gumri ... (0) 0-2 (2) ....AIK Solna
Aggregate: 0-4
Sp Jurmala ...... (0) 1-1 (0) ...... Vojvodina
Aggregate: 1-4
Stromsgodset.. (0) 0-1 (1)Mlada Boleslav
Agg: 2-2. Stromsgodset won on away goals
Thun.............. (1) 2-1 (1) . H. Beer Sheva
Aggregate: 3-2
UCD............... (0) 1-5 (1) ...S. Bratislava
Aggregate: 1-6
Wolfsberger.... (1) 2-0 (0) ...... Shakhtyor
Aggregate: 3-0
Zeljeznicar ...... (1) 2-0 (0) .... Ferencvaros
Aggregate: 3-0
Zilina .... (1) 4-2 (0) .... Dacia
Aggregate: 6-3

Third qualifying round
Wednesday July 29, 2015
Jablonec .... (0) 0-1 (0) ... Copenhagen
Thursday July 30, 2015
AIK Solna........ (0) 1-3 (0) .... Atromitos
AZ Alkmaar..... (1) 2-0 (0) Istanbul Buyuk
Altach............. (1) 2-1 (0) ...V Guimaraes
Ap Limassol .... (1) 1-1 (0) ....Qabala
Ath Bilbao ...... (1) 2-0 (0) ......Inter Baku
Belenenses ..... (2) 2-1 (0) . IFK Goth'burg
Bordeaux........ (0) 3-0 (0) ...AEK Larnaca
Brondby.......... (0) 0-0 (0) .... Omonia
Charleroi......... (0) 0-2 (0) ....Zorya
Debrecen .... (1) 2-3 (0) ...... Rosenborg
Elfsborg .... (1) 2-1 (1) . Odd Grenland
FC Zurich .... (0) 0-1 (0) Dinamo Minsk
Krasnodar .... (1) 2-0 (0) ...S. Bratislava
Hajduk Split .... (0) 2-0 (0) ..Stromsgodset
Kairat Almaty.. (2) 2-1 (0) ....Aberdeen
Kukesi............. (0) 0-3 (0) .Legia Warsaw
Match forfeited due to crowd trouble
PAOK Salonika (0) 1-0 (0) Spartak Trnava
Rabotnicki....... (1) 1-0 (0) ...Trabzonspor
Sampdoria ...... (0) 0-4 (1) ...... Vojvodina
Slovan Liberec (1) 2-1 (0) ...Ironi Kiryat S
Southampton.. (2) 3-0 (0) ... Vitesse Arn.
Standard Liege (2) 2-1 (0) ...... Zeljeznicar

Sturm Graz......(1) 2-3 (2).............Rubin
Targu Mures....(0) 0-3 (1).......St-Etienne
Thun.............(0) 0-0 (0)............Vaduz
West Ham.......(1) 2-2 (0).. Astra Giurgiu
Wolfsberger....(0) 0-1 (1)....B Dortmund
Zilina.............(1) 2-0 (0)..........Poltava

West Ham boss Slaven Bilic contemplates an early European exit

Second legs

Thursday August 6, 2015

AEK Larnaca....(0) 0-1 (1).......Bordeaux
Aggregate: 0-4
Aberdeen........(0) 1-1 (0)..Kairat Almaty
Aggregate: 2-3
Astra Giurgiu ..(2) 2-1 (1)......West Ham
Aggregate: 4-3
Atromitos ....(0) 1-0 (0).......AIK Solna
Aggregate: 4-1
B Dortmund....(0) 5-0 (0)....Wolfsberger
Aggregate: 6-0
Dinamo Minsk (0) 1-1 (1)........FC Zurich
AET. 0-1 after 90 mins. Agg: 2-1
Copenhagen...(0) 2-3 (1).........Jablonec
Agg: 3-3. Jablonec won on away goals
IFK Goth'burg .(0) 0-0 (0).....Belenenses
Aggregate: 1-2
Inter Baku.......(0) 0-0 (0)......Ath Bilbao
Aggregate: 0-2
Ironi Kiryat S...(0) 0-3 (2) Slovan Liberec
Aggregate: 1-5
Istanbul Buyuk (1) 1-2 (1).....AZ Alkmaar
Aggregate: 1-4
Legia Warsaw.(0) 1-0 (0)............Kukesi
Aggregate: 4-0
Odd Grenland.(1) 2-0 (0)..........Elfsborg
Aggregate: 3-2
Omonia Nicosia(2) 2-2 (2).........Brondby
Agg: 2-2. Brondby won on away goals
Poltava ....(0) 3-1 (0)..............Zilina
AET. 2-0 after 90 mins. Agg: 3-3.
Zilina won on away goals
Qabala...........(0) 1-0 (0)....Ap Limassol
Aggregate: 2-1
Rosenborg ......(2) 3-1 (1)........Debrecen
Aggregate: 6-3
Rubin.............(0) 1-1 (0)......Sturm Graz
Aggregate: 4-3
Sl Bratislava...(0) 3-3 (2)......Krasnodar
Aggregate: 3-5
Spartak Trnava (1) 1-1 (0) PAOK Salonika
Aggregate: 1-2
St-Etienne.......(0) 1-2 (1)....Targu Mures
Aggregate: 4-2
Stromsgodset..(0) 0-2 (0)....Hajduk Split
Aggregate: 0-4
Trabzonspor....(0) 1-1 (0)......Rabotnicki
AET. 1-0 after 90 mins. Agg: 1-2
V Guimaraes...(0) 1-4 (1)..........Altach
Aggregate: 2-6
Vaduz ....(2) 2-2 (1)...............Thun
Agg: 2-2. Thun won on away goals
Vitesse Arnhem(0) 0-2 (1)..Southampton
Aggregate: 0-5

Vojvodina ....(0) 0-2 (1).....Sampdoria
Aggregate: 4-2
Zeljeznicar ......(0) 0-1 (0)Standard Liege
Aggregate: 1-3
Zorya.............(0) 3-0 (0).........Charleroi
Aggregate: 5-0

Playoff round

Thursday August 20, 2015

Ajax...............(0) 1-0 (0).........Jablonec
Altach.............(0) 0-1 (1).....Belenenses
Astra Giurgiu ..(3) 3-2 (2).....AZ Alkmaar
Atromitos ....(0) 0-1 (0)....Fenerbahce
Bordeaux........(1) 1-0 (0)..Kairat Almaty
Dinamo Minsk (0) 2-0 (0)....RB Salzburg
Krasnodar.......(2) 5-1 (1)....HJK Helsinki
Lech Poznan....(1) 3-0 (0).........Videoton
Milsami Orhei.(0) 1-1 (1).......St-Etienne
Molde............(2) 2-0 (0)Standard Liege
Odd Grenland.(3) 3-4 (1)....B Dortmund
PAOK Salonika (2) 5-0 (0).........Brondby
Qabala...........(0) 0-0 (0).Panathinaikos
Rabotnicki......(0) 1-1 (0).............Rubin
Slovan Liberec (0) 1-0 (0)....Hajduk Split
Southampton..(0) 1-1 (1).... Midtjylland
Sparta Prague.(2) 3-1 (1)...............Thun
Steaua ....(0) 0-3 (0).....Rosenborg
Viktoria Plzen..(1) 3-0 (0).......Vojvodina
Young Boys.....(0) 0-1 (0).....FK Qarabag
Zilina ....(0) 3-2 (2)......Ath Bilbao
Zorya.............(0) 0-1 (0).Legia Warsaw

Second legs

Thursday August 27, 2015

AZ Alkmaar.....(0) 2-0 (0).. Astra Giurgiu
Aggregate: 4-3
Ath Bilbao ......(1) 1-0 (0)............Zilina
Agg: 3-3. Ath Bilbao won on away goals

B Dortmund....(4) 7-2 (1).Odd Grenland
Aggregate: 11-5
Belenenses .....(0) 0-0 (0)............Altach
Aggregate: 1-0
Brondby..........(1) 1-1 (1) PAOK Salonika
Aggregate: 1-6
FK Qarabag.....(2) 3-0 (0).....Young Boys
Aggregate: 4-0
Fenerbahce.....(1) 3-0 (0).......Atromitos
Aggregate: 4-0
HJK Helsinki....(0) 0-0 (0).......Krasnodar
Aggregate: 1-5
Hajduk Split....(0) 0-1 (1) Slovan Liberec
Aggregate: 0-2
Jablonec.........(0) 0-0 (0)...............Ajax
Aggregate: 0-1
Kairat Almaty..(1) 2-1 (0)........Bordeaux
Agg: 2-2. Bordeaux won on away goals
Legia Warsaw.(1) 3-2 (1)............Zorya
Aggregate: 4-2
Midtjylland .....(1) 1-0 (0)..Southampton
Aggregate: 2-1
Panathinaikos .(1) 2-2 (1)...........Qabala
Agg: 2-2. Qabala won on away goals
RB Salzburg ....(0) 2-0 (0)...Dinamo Minsk
AET. 2-0 after 90 mins. Agg: 2-2.
Dinamo Minsk won 3-2 on penalties
Rosenborg ......(0) 0-1 (0)............Steaua
Aggregate: 3-1
Rubin.............(1) 1-0 (0)........Rabotnicki
Aggregate: 2-1
St-Etienne.......(1) 1-0 (0).Milsami Orhei
Standard Liege (1) 3-1 (1)............Molde
Agg: 3-3. Molde won on away goals
Thun.............(1) 3-3 (2).Sparta Prague
Aggregate: 4-6
Videoton........(0) 0-1 (0)....Lech Poznan
Aggregate: 0-4
Vojvodina ....(0) 0-2 (1)..Viktoria Plzen
Aggregate: 0-5

Group stage

Group A

	P	W	D	L	F	A	GD	Pts
Molde	6	3	2	1	10	7	3	11
Fenerbahce	6	2	3	1	7	6	1	9
Ajax	6	1	4	1	6	6	0	7
Celtic	6	0	3	3	8	12	-4	3

Thursday September 17, 2015
Ajax .... (1) 2-2 (2) .... Celtic
Fenerbahce ..... (1) 1-3 (1) .... Molde
Thursday October 1, 2015
Celtic .... (2) 2-2 (1) ..... Fenerbahce
Molde .... (1) 1-1 (1) .... Ajax
Thursday October 22, 2015
Fenerbahce ..... (0) 1-0 (0) .... Ajax
Molde .... (2) 3-1 (0) .... Celtic
Thursday November 5, 2015
Ajax .... (0) 0-0 (0) .... Fenerbahce
Celtic .... (1) 1-2 (2) .... Molde
Thursday November 26, 2015
Celtic .... (1) 1-2 (1) .... Ajax
Molde .... (0) 0-2 (0) ..... Fenerbahce
Thursday December 10, 2015
Ajax .... (1) 1-1 (1) .... Molde
Fenerbahce ..... (1) 1-1 (0) .... Celtic

Group B

	P	W	D	L	F	A	GD	Pts
Liverpool	6	2	4	0	6	4	2	10
FC Sion	6	2	3	1	5	5	0	9
Rubin Kazan	6	1	3	2	6	6	0	6
Bordeaux	6	0	4	2	5	7	-2	4

Thursday September 17, 2015
Bordeaux .... (0) 1-1 (0) .... Liverpool
FC Sion .... (2) 2-1 (0) .... Rubin
Thursday October 1, 2015
Liverpool .... (1) 1-1 (1) .... FC Sion
Rubin............. (0) 0-0 (0) .... Bordeaux
Thursday October 22, 2015
Bordeaux .... (0) 0-1 (1) .... FC Sion
Liverpool .... (1) 1-1 (1) .... Rubin
Thursday November 5, 2015
FC Sion .... (0) 1-1 (0) .... Bordeaux
Rubin............. (0) 0-1 (0) .... Liverpool
Thursday November 26, 2015
Rubin............. (0) 2-0 (0) .... FC Sion
Liverpool .... (2) 2-1 (1) .... Bordeaux
Thursday December 10, 2015
Bordeaux .... (0) 2-2 (1) .... Rubin
FC Sion .... (0) 0-0 (0) .... Liverpool

Group C

	P	W	D	L	F	A	GD	Pts
Krasnodar	6	4	1	1	9	4	5	13
B Dortmund	6	3	1	2	10	5	5	10
PAOK	6	1	4	1	3	3	0	7
Qabala	6	0	2	4	2	12	-10	2

Thursday September 17, 2015
B Dortmund .... (1) 2-1 (1) ...... Krasnodar
Qabala .... (0) 0-0 (0) PAOK Salonika

Thursday October 1, 2015
Krasnodar ...... (1) 2-1 (0) ....Qabala
PAOK Salonika (1) 1-1 (0) .... B Dortmund
Thursday October 22, 2015
PAOK Salonika (0) 0-0 (0) ...... Krasnodar
Qabala .... (0) 1-3 (2) .... B Dortmund
Thursday November 5, 2015
B Dortmund .... (2) 4-0 (0) ....Qabala
Krasnodar ...... (1) 2-1 (0) PAOK Salonika
Thursday November 26, 2015
Krasnodar ...... (1) 1-0 (0) .... B Dortmund
PAOK Salonika (0) 0-0 (0) ....Qabala
Thursday December 10, 2015
B Dortmund .... (0) 0-1 (1) PAOK Salonika
Qabala .... (0) 0-3 (2) ...... Krasnodar

Group D

	P	W	D	L	F	A	GD	Pts
Napoli	6	6	0	0	22	3	19	18
Midtjylland	6	2	1	3	6	12	-6	7
FC Bruges	6	1	2	3	4	11	-7	5
Legia Warsaw	6	1	1	4	4	10	-6	4

Thursday September 17, 2015
Napoli .... (3) 5-0 (0) ...... FC Bruges
Midtjylland ..... (0) 1-0 (0). Legia Warsaw
Thursday October 1, 2015
FC Bruges .... (0) 1-3 (0) ..... Midtjylland
Legia Warsaw. (0) 0-2 (0) .... Napoli
Thursday October 22, 2015
Legia Warsaw. (0) 1-1 (1) ...... FC Bruges
Midtjylland ..... (1) 1-4 (3) .... Napoli
Thursday November 5, 2015
FC Bruges .... (1) 1-0 (0). Legia Warsaw
Napoli .... (3) 5-0 (0) ..... Midtjylland
Thursday November 26, 2015
FC Bruges .... (0) 0-1 (1) .... Napoli
Legia Warsaw. (1) 1-0 (0) ..... Midtjylland

Group E

Thursday December 10, 2015
Midtjylland ..... (1) 1-1 (0) ...... FC Bruges
Napoli .... (2) 5-2 (0). Legia Warsaw

	P	W	D	L	F	A	GD	Pts
Rapid Vienna	6	5	0	1	10	6	4	15
Villarreal	6	4	1	1	12	6	6	13
Viktoria Plzen	6	1	1	4	8	10	-2	4
Dinamo Minsk	6	1	0	5	3	11	-8	3

Thursday September 17, 2015
Rapid Vienna .. (0) 2-1 (1) .... Villarreal
Viktoria Plzen.. (1) 2-0 (0) Dinamo Minsk
Thursday October 1, 2015
Dinamo Minsk (0) 0-1 (0) .. Rapid Vienna
Villarreal .... (0) 1-0 (0) ..Viktoria Plzen
Thursday October 22, 2015
Rapid Vienna .. (1) 3-2 (1) ..Viktoria Plzen
Villarreal .... (2) 4-0 (0) Dinamo Minsk
Thursday November 5, 2015
Dinamo Minsk (0) 1-2 (0) .... Villarreal
Viktoria Plzen.. (0) 1-2 (1) .. Rapid Vienna
Thursday November 26, 2015
Dinamo Minsk (0) 1-0 (0) ..Viktoria Plzen
Villarreal .... (0) 1-0 (0) .. Rapid Vienna
Thursday December 10, 2015
Rapid Vienna .. (1) 2-1 (0) Dinamo Minsk
Viktoria Plzen.. (1) 3-3 (1) .... Villarreal

Group F

	P	W	D	L	F	A	GD	Pts
Braga	6	4	1	1	7	4	3	13
Marseille	6	4	0	2	12	7	5	12
Slovan Liberec	6	2	1	3	6	8	-2	7
Groningen	6	0	2	4	2	8	-6	2

Dejan Lovren completes Liverpool's stunning comeback against Dortmund

Thursday September 17, 2015
Groningen......(0) 0-3 (2)........Marseille
Slovan Liberec (0) 0-1 (0)............Braga
Thursday October 1, 2015
Braga............(1) 1-0 (0)...... Groningen
Marseille........(0) 0-1 (0) Slovan Liberec
Thursday October 22, 2015
Braga............(0) 3-2 (0)........Marseille
Slovan Liberec (0) 1-1 (0)...... Groningen
Thursday November 5, 2015
Groningen......(0) 0-1 (0) Slovan Liberec
Marseille........(1) 1-0 (0)............Braga
Thursday November 26, 2015
Braga............(1) 2-1 (1) Slovan Liberec
Marseille........(1) 2-1 (0)...... Groningen
Thursday December 10, 2015
Groningen......(0) 0-0 (0)............Braga
Slovan Liberec (0) 2-4 (2)........Marseille

Group G

	P	W	D	L	F	A	GD	Pts
Lazio	6	4	2	0	13	6	7	14
St-Etienne	6	2	3	1	10	7	3	9
Dnipro	6	2	1	3	6	8	-2	7
Rosenborg	6	0	2	4	4	12	-8	2

Thursday September 17, 2015
Dnipro...........(0) 1-1 (1)..............Lazio
St-Etienne.......(1) 2-2 (1)...... Rosenborg
Thursday October 1, 2015
Lazio.............(1) 3-2 (1)......St-Etienne
Rosenborg......(0) 0-1 (1).......... Dnipro
Thursday October 22, 2015
Dnipro...........(0) 0-1 (1)......St-Etienne
Lazio.............(1) 3-1 (0)...... Rosenborg
Thursday November 5, 2015
Rosenborg......(0) 0-2 (2)............Lazio
St-Etienne.......(1) 3-0 (0)...........Dnipro
Thursday November 26, 2015
Lazio.............(1) 3-1 (0)......... Dnipro
Rosenborg......(1) 1-1 (0).......St-Etienne
Thursday December 10, 2015
Dnipro...........(1) 3-0 (0)...... Rosenborg
St-Etienne.......(0) 1-1 (0)..............Lazio

Group H

	P	W	D	L	F	A	GD	Pts
Lok. Moscow	6	3	2	1	12	7	5	11
Sp. Lisbon	6	3	1	2	14	11	3	10
Besiktas	6	2	3	1	7	6	1	9
Skenderbeu	6	1	0	5	4	13	-9	3

Thursday September 17, 2015
Skenderbeu....(0) 0-1 (1).........Besiktas
Sp. Lisbon.......(0) 1-3 (1).. Lok. Moscow
Thursday October 1, 2015
Besiktas.........(0) 1-1 (1).......Sp. Lisbon
Lok. Moscow ..(1) 2-0 (0)..... Skenderbeu
Thursday October 22, 2015
Lok. Moscow ..(0) 1-1 (0).........Besiktas
Sp. Lisbon.......(2) 5-1 (0).... Skenderbeu
Thursday November 5, 2015
Besiktas.........(0) 1-1 (0).. Lok. Moscow
Skenderbeu....(2) 3-0 (0).......Sp. Lisbon

Thursday November 26, 2015
Besiktas.........(1) 2-0 (0).... Skenderbeu
Lok. Moscow ..(1) 2-4 (3)......Sp. Lisbon
Thursday December 10, 2015
Skenderbeu....(0) 0-3 (1).. Lok. Moscow
Sp. Lisbon.......(0) 3-1 (0).........Besiktas

Group I

	P	W	D	L	F	A	GD	Pts
Basel	6	4	1	1	10	5	5	13
Fiorentina	6	3	1	2	11	6	5	10
Lech Poznan	6	1	2	3	2	6	-4	5
Belenenses	6	1	2	3	2	8	-6	5

Thursday September 17, 2015
Fiorentina......(1) 1-2 (0)............. Basel
Lech Poznan....(0) 0-0 (0)..... Belenenses
Thursday October 1, 2015
Basel ....(0) 2-0 (0)....Lech Poznan
Belenenses .....(0) 0-4 (2).... Fiorentina
Thursday October 22, 2015
Basel ....(1) 1-2 (2)..... Belenenses
Fiorentina......(0) 1-2 (0)....Lech Poznan
Thursday November 5, 2015
Belenenses .....(0) 0-2 (1)............. Basel
Lech Poznan....(0) 0-2 (1)..... Fiorentina
Thursday November 26, 2015
Basel ....(1) 2-2 (2)...... Fiorentina
Belenenses .....(0) 0-0 (0)....Lech Poznan
Thursday December 10, 2015
Fiorentina......(0) 1-0 (0)..... Belenenses
Lech Poznan....(0) 0-1 (0)..... Basel

Group J

	P	W	D	L	F	A	GD	Pts
Tottenham	6	4	1	1	12	6	6	13
Anderlecht	6	3	1	2	8	6	2	10
Monaco	6	1	3	2	5	9	-4	6
FK Qarabag	6	1	1	4	4	8	-4	4

Thursday September 17, 2015
Anderlecht......(1) 1-1 (0).........Monaco
Tottenham ......(2) 3-1 (1).....FK Qarabag
Thursday October 1, 2015
FK Qarabag.....(1) 1-0 (0).....Anderlecht
Monaco ....(0) 1-1 (1).....Tottenham
Thursday October 22, 2015
Anderlecht......(1) 2-1 (1)..... Tottenham
Monaco ....(0) 1-0 (0).....FK Qarabag
Thursday November 5, 2015
FK Qarabag.....(1) 1-1 (0)..........Monaco
Tottenham ......(1) 2-1 (0).....Anderlecht
Thursday November 26, 2015
FK Qarabag.....(0) 0-1 (0)...... Tottenham
Monaco ....(0) 0-2 (1).....Anderlecht
Thursday December 10, 2015
Anderlecht......(2) 2-1 (1).....FK Qarabag
Tottenham ......(3) 4-1 (0)..........Monaco

Group K

	P	W	D	L	F	A	GD	Pts
Schalke	6	4	2	0	15	3	12	14
Sparta Prague	6	3	3	0	10	5	5	12
Asteras	6	1	1	4	4	12	-8	4
Apoel Nicosia	6	1	0	5	3	12	-9	3

Thursday September 17, 2015
Apoel Nicosia .(0) 0-3 (2).........Schalke
Asteras T........(1) 1-1 (0). Sparta Prague
Thursday October 1, 2015
Schalke..........(3) 4-0 (0).......Asteras T.
Sparta Prague.(1) 2-0 (0). Apoel Nicosia
Thursday October 22, 2015
Apoel Nicosia .(1) 2-1 (1)....... Asteras T.
Schalke..........(1) 2-2 (0). Sparta Prague
Thursday November 5, 2015
Asteras T........(2) 2-0 (0). Apoel Nicosia
Sparta Prague.(1) 1-1 (1)..........Schalke
Thursday November 26, 2015
Schalke..........(0) 1-0 (0). Apoel Nicosia
Sparta Prague.(1) 1-0 (0).......Asteras T.
Thursday December 10, 2015
Apoel Nicosia .(1) 1-3 (0). Sparta Prague
Asteras T........(0) 0-4 (2)..........Schalke

Group L

	P	W	D	L	F	A	GD	Pts
Ath Bilbao	6	4	1	1	16	8	8	13
Augsburg	6	3	0	3	12	11	1	9
Partizan	6	3	0	3	10	14	-4	9
AZ Alkmaar	6	1	1	4	8	13	-5	4

Thursday September 17, 2015
Ath Bilbao ......(0) 3-1 (1).....Augsburg
Partizan ....(2) 3-2 (1).....AZ Alkmaar
Thursday October 1, 2015
Augsburg........(0) 1-3 (1)......... Partizan
AZ Alkmaar.....(0) 2-1 (1)...... Ath Bilbao
Thursday October 22, 2015
AZ Alkmaar.....(0) 0-1 (1)......Augsburg
Partizan ....(0) 0-2 (1)..... Ath Bilbao
Thursday November 5, 2015
Ath Bilbao ......(3) 5-1 (1)........ Partizan
Augsburg........(2) 4-1 (1).....AZ Alkmaar
Thursday November 26, 2015
Augsburg........(1) 2-3 (1)..... Ath Bilbao
AZ Alkmaar.....(0) 1-2 (0)........ Partizan
Thursday December 10, 2015
Ath Bilbao ......(1) 2-2 (1).....AZ Alkmaar
Partizan ....(1) 1-3 (1).....Augsburg

Round of 32

Tuesday February 16, 2016
Fenerbahce.....(1) 2-0 (0).. Lok. Moscow
Thursday February 18, 2016
Anderlecht......(0) 1-0 (0)....Olympiakos
Augsburg........(0) 0-0 (0)...... Liverpool
B Dortmund....(1) 2-0 (0)..............Porto
FC Sion ....(0) 1-2 (1)............Braga
Fiorentina......(0) 1-1 (1).... Tottenham
Galatasaray ....(1) 1-1 (1)..............Lazio
Marseille........(0) 0-1 (0)... Ath Bilbao
Midtjylland .....(1) 2-1 (1).... Man United
Seville............(1) 3-0 (0)..........Molde
Shakhtar........(0) 0-0 (0)..........Schalke
Sp. Lisbon.......(0) 0-1 (1).. B Leverkusen
Sparta Prague.(0) 1-0 (0)... Krasnodar
St-Etienne.......(2) 3-2 (1)............. Basel
Valencia.........(5) 6-0 (0).. Rapid Vienna
Villarreal........(0) 1-0 (0)............ Napoli

Seville celebrate a third consecutive Europa League title

Second legs

Wednesday February 24, 2016

Braga.............(1) 2-2 (2)...........FC Sion
        Aggregate: 4-3

Thursday February 25, 2016

Ath Bilbao ......(0) 1-1 (1).........Marseille
        Aggregate: 2-1

B Leverkusen ..(1) 3-1 (1).......Sp. Lisbon
        Aggregate: 4-1

Basel ....(1) 2-1 (0).......St-Etienne
    Agg: 4-4. Basel won on away goals

Krasnodar.......(0) 0-3 (0).Sparta Prague
        Aggregate: 0-4

Lazio..............(0) 3-1 (0)....Galatasaray
        Aggregate: 4-2

Liverpool ....(1) 1-0 (0).........Augsburg
        Aggregate: 1-0

Lok. Moscow ..(1) 1-1 (0).....Fenerbahce
        Aggregate: 1-3

Man United ....(1) 5-1 (1).....Midtjylland
        Aggregate: 6-3

Molde.............(1) 1-0 (0).............Seville
        Aggregate: 1-3

Napoli ....(1) 1-1 (0).........Villarreal
        Aggregate: 1-2

Olympiakos.....(1) 1-2 (0)......Anderlecht
    AET. 1-0 after 90 mins. Agg: 1-3

Porto..............(0) 0-1 (1)....B Dortmund
        Aggregate: 0-3

Rapid Vienna ..(0) 0-4 (0)..........Valencia
        Aggregate: 0-10

Schalke ....(0) 0-3 (1).........Shakhtar
        Aggregate: 0-3

Tottenham ......(1) 3-0 (0).......Fiorentina
        Aggregate: 4-1

Round of 16

Thursday March 10, 2016

Ath Bilbao ......(1) 1-0 (0).........Valencia

B Dortmund ....(1) 3-0 (0).....Tottenham

Basel ....(0) 0-0 (0).........Seville

Fenerbahce......(0) 1-0 (0).............Braga

Liverpool ....(1) 2-0 (0)....Man United

Shakhtar.........(2) 3-1 (0)......Anderlecht

Sparta Prague . (1) 1-1 (1)...............Lazio

Villarreal ....(1) 2-0 (0)..B Leverkusen

Second legs

Thursday March 17, 2016

Anderlecht ......(0) 0-1 (0).........Shakhtar
        Aggregate: 1-4

B Leverkusen ..(0) 0-0 (0).........Villarreal
        Aggregate: 0-2

Braga.............(1) 4-1 (1).....Fenerbahce
        Aggregate: 4-2

Lazio..............(0) 0-3 (3).Sparta Prague
        Aggregate: 1-4

Man United ....(1) 1-1 (1).........Liverpool
        Aggregate: 1-3

Seville.............(3) 3-0 (0)..............Basel
        Aggregate: 3-0

Tottenham ......(0) 1-2 (1)....B Dortmund
        Aggregate: 1-5

Valencia..........(2) 2-1 (0)......Ath Bilbao
  Agg: 2-2. Ath Bilbao won on away goals

Quarter-finals

Thursday April 7, 2016

Ath Bilbao ......(0) 1-2 (0)............Seville

B Dortmund....(0) 1-1 (1)........Liverpool

Braga.............(0) 1-2 (1)........Shakhtar

Villarreal ....(1) 2-1 (1).Sparta Prague

Second legs

Thursday April 14, 2016

Liverpool ....(0) 4-3 (2)....B Dortmund
        Aggregate: 5-4

Seville.............(0) 1-2 (0)......Ath Bilbao
    AET. 1-2 after 90 mins. Agg: 3-3.
    Seville won 5-4 on penalties

Shakhtar.........(2) 4-0 (0)..............Braga
        Aggregate: 6-1

Sparta Prague . (0) 2-4 (3).........Villarreal
        Aggregate: 3-6

Semi-finals

Thursday April 28, 2016

Shakhtar.........(2) 2-2 (1)............Seville

Villarreal ....(0) 1-0 (0)........Liverpool

Second legs

Thursday May 5, 2016

Liverpool ....(1) 3-0 (0).........Villarreal
        Aggregate: 3-1

Seville.............(1) 3-1 (1).........Shakhtar
        Aggregate: 5-3

Final

Wednesday May 18, 2016

Liverpool ....(1) 1-3 (0).............Seville

First qualifying round

Tuesday June 30, 2015
Crusaders .... (0) 0-0 (0) Levadia Tallinn
Lincoln Red Imps(0) 0-0 (0)FC Santa Coloma
Pyunik Yerevan(1) 2-1 (0)Folgore/Falciano

Wednesday July 1, 2015
B36 Torshavn .. (1) 1-2 (1)The New Saints

Second legs

Tuesday July 7, 2015
FC Santa Coloma(1) 1-2 (0)Lincoln Red Imps
    Aggregate: 1-2
Folgore/Falciano(0) 1-2 (2)Pyunik Yerevan
    Aggregate: 2-4
Levadia Tallinn (1) 1-1 (1) ...... Crusaders
    Agg: 1-1. Crusaders won on away goals
The New Saints(2) 4-1 (0) ..B36 Torshavn
    Aggregate: 6-2

Second qualifying round

Tuesday July 14, 2015
Apoel Nicosia . (0) 0-0 (0) . Vardar Skopje
Dukla Trencin .. (0) 0-2 (0) .... Steaua
Hibernians ...... (0) 2-1 (1) ......M. Tel Aviv
Ludogorets ..... (0) 0-1 (1) . Milsami Orhei
Midtjylland ..... (1) 1-0 (0)Lincoln Red Imps
Molde .... (2) 5-0 (0)Pyunik Yerevan
NK Maribor..... (1) 1-0 (0) .... Astana
Partizan .... (0) 1-0 (0) ....Dila
Sarajevo .... (0) 0-2 (1) ....Lech Poznan
Skenderbeu .... (2) 4-1 (0) .... Crusaders
The New Saints(0) 0-1 (0) .... Videoton
Ventspils........ (0) 1-3 (0) .... HJK Helsinki

Wednesday July 15, 2015
Bate Borisov ... (2) 2-1 (1) .... Dundalk
Celtic .... (1) 2-0 (0) .... Stjarnan

Din Zagreb...... (1) 1-1 (1) .... Fola Esch
FK Qarabag..... (0) 0-0 (0) ..Rudar Pljevlja
Malmo .... (0) 0-0 (0) Zalgiris Vilnius

Second legs

Tuesday July 21, 2015
Crusaders ...... (0) 3-2 (0) .... Skenderbeu
    Aggregate: 4-6
Dila................ (0) 0-2 (1) .... Partizan
    Aggregate: 0-3
HJK Helsinki .... (0) 1-0 (0) .... Ventspils
    Aggregate: 4-1
Lincoln Red Imps(0) 0-2 (1) ..... Midtjylland
    Aggregate: 0-3
M. Tel Aviv...... (1) 5-1 (0) ...... Hibernians
    Aggregate: 6-3
Milsami Orhei . (1) 2-1 (1) ..... Ludogorets
    Aggregate: 3-1
Pyunik Yerevan(0) 1-0 (0) ....Molde
    Aggregate: 1-5
Vardar Skopje . (0) 1-1 (0) . Apoel Nicosia
    Agg: 1-1. Apoel won on away goals
Zalgiris Vilnius (0) 0-1 (0) ....Malmo
    Aggregate: 0-1

Wednesday July 22, 2015
Astana .... (2) 3-1 (1) .....NK Maribor
    Aggregate: 3-2
Dundalk.......... (0) 0-0 (0) ... Bate Borisov
    Aggregate: 1-2
Fola Esch .... (0) 0-3 (2) ......Din Zagreb
    Aggregate: 1-4
Lech Poznan.... (1) 1-0 (0) .... Sarajevo
    Aggregate: 3-0
Rudar Pljevlja.. (0) 0-1 (0) .....FK Qarabag
    Aggregate: 0-1
Steaua .... (0) 2-3 (2) ..Dukla Trencin
    Aggregate: 4-3
Stjarnan.......... (1) 1-4 (1) .... Celtic
    Aggregate: 1-6
Videoton......... (0) 1-1 (0)The New Saints
    AET. 0-1 after 90 mins. Agg: 2-1

Third qualifying round

Tuesday July 28, 2015
CSKA Moscow (1) 2-2 (1) . Sparta Prague
Din Zagreb...... (1) 1-1 (1) ....Molde
Fenerbahce..... (0) 0-0 (0) .... Shakhtar
M. Tel Aviv...... (0) 1-2 (2) ..Viktoria Plzen
Midtjylland ..... (0) 1-2 (2) . Apoel Nicosia
Milsami Orhei . (0) 0-2 (0) .... Skenderbeu
Panathinaikos . (1) 2-1 (1) ..... FC Bruges
Videoton......... (0) 1-1 (0) ... Bate Borisov
Young Boys..... (0) 1-3 (0) .... Monaco

Wednesday July 29, 2015
Celtic .... (0) 1-0 (0) .....FK Qarabag
HJK Helsinki .... (0) 0-0 (0) ....Astana
Lech Poznan.... (1) 1-3 (1) .... Basel
RB Salzburg .... (0) 2-0 (0) ....Malmo
Rapid Vienna .. (0) 2-2 (2) ....Ajax
Steaua .... (0) 1-1 (0) .... Partizan

Second legs

Tuesday August 4, 2015
Ajax................ (0) 2-3 (2) .. Rapid Vienna
    Aggregate: 4-5
Apoel Nicosia . (0) 0-1 (1) ..... Midtjylland
    Agg: 2-2. Apoel won on away goals
Molde............. (1) 3-3 (3) ......Din Zagreb
    Agg: 4-4. Din Zagreb won on away goals
Monaco .... (0) 4-0 (0) .....Young Boys
    Aggregate: 7-1

Wednesday August 5, 2015
Astana .... (1) 4-3 (2) ....HJK Helsinki
    Aggregate: 4-3
Basel .... (0) 1-0 (0) ....Lech Poznan
    Aggregate: 4-1
Bate Borisov ... (0) 1-0 (0) .... Videoton
    Aggregate: 2-1
FC Bruges .... (0) 3-0 (0) . Panathinaikos
    Aggregate: 4-2
FK Qarabag..... (0) 0-0 (0) .... Celtic
    Aggregate: 0-1
Malmo............ (3) 3-0 (0) ... RB Salzburg
    Aggregate: 3-2
Partizan .... (1) 4-2 (2) .... Steaua
    Aggregate: 5-3
Shakhtar......... (1) 3-0 (0) .....Fenerbahce
    Aggregate: 3-0
Skenderbeu .... (1) 2-0 (0) . Milsami Orhei
    Aggregate: 4-0
Sparta Prague . (2) 2-3 (2) . CSKA Moscow
    Aggregate: 4-5
Viktoria Plzen.. (0) 0-2 (0) ......M. Tel Aviv
    Aggregate: 2-3

Playoff round

Tuesday August 18, 2015
Astana .... (1) 1-0 (0) . Apoel Nicosia
Bate Borisov ... (0) 1-0 (0) .... Partizan
Lazio.............. (0) 1-0 (0) .. B Leverkusen
Man United .... (2) 3-1 (1) .... FC Bruges
Sp. Lisbon....... (1) 2-1 (1) CSKA Moscow

Wednesday August 19, 2015
Basel .... (1) 2-2 (1) ......M. Tel Aviv
Celtic .... (2) 3-2 (0) ....Malmo
Rapid Vienna .. (0) 0-1 (1) .... Shakhtar
Skenderbeu .... (1) 1-2 (0) ......Din Zagreb
Valencia.......... (1) 3-1 (0) .... Monaco

Celtic found Malmo
too hot to handle

2015/2016 STATS

SOFIANE FEGHOULI
VALENCIA ▶ WEST HAM UNITED

NATIONALITY	Algerian
POSITION	Midfield
AGE	26
HEIGHT	5'8"
APPS	31
GOALS	4

	W	D	L	WIN%
MATCHES WITH SUB APPEARANCES NOT INCLUDED				
	9	2	8	**47%**
MATCHES WITHOUT				
	12	11	14	**25%**

FEGHOULI WHO?

GET SET FOR THE NEW SEASON WITH OUR
IN-DEPTH DATABASE OF PLAYER, TEAM
AND COMPETITION STATS, PLUS EXPERT
ADVICE FROM THE BETTING BOFFINS AT
RACING POST SPORT

Second legs

Tuesday August 25, 2015

Din Zagreb...... (2) 4-1 (1) .... Skenderbeu
Aggregate: 6-2

M. Tel Aviv...... (1) 1-1 (1) .... Basel
Agg: 3-3. M. Tel Aviv won on away goals

Malmo............ (1) 2-0 (0) .... Celtic
Aggregate: 4-3

Monaco .... (1) 2-1 (1) .... Valencia
Aggregate: 3-4

Shakhtar .... (2) 2-2 (2) .. Rapid Vienna
Aggregate: 3-2

Wednesday August 26, 2015

Apoel Nicosia . (0) 1-1 (0) .... Astana
Aggregate: 1-2

B Leverkusen .. (1) 3-0 (0) .... Lazio
Aggregate: 3-1

CSKA Moscow (0) 3-1 (1) .... Sp. Lisbon
Aggregate: 4-3

FC Bruges .... (0) 0-4 (1) .... Man United
Aggregate: 1-7

Partizan .... (0) 2-1 (1) ... Bate Borisov
Agg: 2-2. Bate won on away goals

Group A

	P	W	D	L	F	A	GD	Pts
Real Madrid	6	5	1	0	19	3	16	16
Paris St-G	6	4	1	1	12	1	11	13
Shakhtar	6	1	0	5	7	14	-7	3
Malmo	6	1	0	5	1	21	-20	3

Tuesday September 15, 2015

Real Madrid.... (1) 4-0 (0) .... Shakhtar
Paris St-G........ (1) 2-0 (0) .... Malmo

Wednesday September 30, 2015

Malmo............ (0) 0-2 (1) .... Real Madrid
Shakhtar .... (0) 0-3 (2) .... Paris St-G

Wednesday October 21, 2015

Malmo............ (1) 1-0 (0) .... Shakhtar
Paris St-G........ (0) 0-0 (0) .... Real Madrid

Tuesday November 3, 2015

Real Madrid.... (1) 1-0 (0) .... Paris St-G
Shakhtar .... (1) 4-0 (0) .... Malmo

Wednesday November 25, 2015

Malmo............ (0) 0-5 (2) .... Paris St-G
Shakhtar .... (0) 3-4 (1) .... Real Madrid

Tuesday December 8, 2015

Paris St-G........ (0) 2-0 (0) .... Shakhtar
Real Madrid.... (3) 8-0 (0) .... Malmo

Group B

	P	W	D	L	F	A	GD	Pts
Wolfsburg	6	4	0	2	9	6	3	12
PSV	6	3	1	2	8	7	1	10
Man United	6	2	2	2	7	7	0	8
CSKA	6	1	1	4	5	9	-4	4

Tuesday September 15, 2015

PSV Eindhoven (1) 2-1 (1) .... Man United
Wolfsburg....... (1) 1-0 (0) CSKA Moscow

Wednesday September 30, 2015

CSKA Moscow (3) 3-2 (0) PSV Eindhoven
Man United .... (1) 2-1 (1) ......Wolfsburg

Wednesday October 21, 2015

CSKA Moscow (1) 1-1 (0) .... Man United
Wolfsburg....... (0) 2-0 (0) PSV Eindhoven

Tuesday November 3, 2015

Man United .... (0) 1-0 (0) CSKA Moscow
PSV Eindhoven (0) 2-0 (0) ....Wolfsburg

Wednesday November 25, 2015

CSKA Moscow (0) 0-2 (0) ......Wolfsburg
Man United .... (0) 0-0 (0) PSV Eindhoven

Tuesday December 8, 2015

PSV Eindhoven (0) 2-1 (0) CSKA Moscow
Wolfsburg....... (2) 3-2 (1) .... Man United

Group C

	P	W	D	L	F	A	GD	Pts
Atl Madrid	6	4	1	1	11	3	8	13
Benfica	6	3	1	2	10	8	2	10
Galatasaray	6	1	2	3	6	10	-4	5
Astana	6	0	4	2	5	11	-6	4

Tuesday September 15, 2015

Benfica .... (0) 2-0 (0) .... Astana
Galatasaray .... (0) 0-2 (2) ...... Atl Madrid

Wednesday September 30, 2015

Astana............ (0) 2-2 (1) .... Galatasaray
Atl Madrid ...... (1) 1-2 (1) .... Benfica

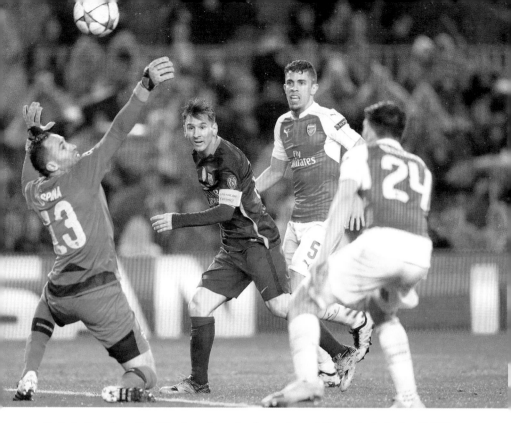

Clockwise from above: Lionel Messi puts Arsenal to the sword; Atletico's Jan Oblak makes a crucial semi-final penalty save from Bayern's Thomas Muller; Memphis Depay's Manchester United suffered a chastening experience in Europe; Kevin De Bruyne was the main man for Manchester City in their run to the last four

Wednesday October 21, 2015
Atl Madrid ...... (2) 4-0 (0) .... Astana
Galatasaray .... (2) 2-1 (1) .... Benfica
Tuesday November 3, 2015
Astana .... (0) 0-0 (0) ...... Atl Madrid
Benfica .... (0) 2-1 (0) .... Galatasaray
Wednesday November 25, 2015
Astana .... (2) 2-2 (1) .... Benfica
Atl Madrid ...... (1) 2-0 (0) .... Galatasaray
Tuesday December 8, 2015
Benfica .... (0) 1-2 (1) ...... Atl Madrid
Galatasaray .... (0) 1-1 (0) .... Astana

Group D

	P	W	D	L	F	A	GD	Pts
Man City	6	4	0	2	12	8	4	12
Juventus	6	3	2	1	6	3	3	11
Seville	6	2	0	4	8	11	-3	6
B M'gladbach	6	1	2	3	8	12	-4	5

Tuesday September 15, 2015
Man City .... (0) 1-2 (0) .... Juventus
Seville .... (0) 3-0 (0) . B M'gladbach

Wednesday September 30, 2015
B M'gladbach . (0) 1-2 (0) .... Man City
Juventus .... (1) 2-0 (0) .... Seville
Wednesday October 21, 2015
Juventus .... (0) 0-0 (0) . B M'gladbach
Man City .... (1) 2-1 (1) .... Seville
Tuesday November 3, 2015
B M'gladbach . (1) 1-1 (1) .... Juventus
Seville .... (1) 1-3 (3) .... Man City
Wednesday November 25, 2015
B M'gladbach . (1) 4-2 (0) .... Seville
Juventus .... (1) 1-0 (0) .... Man City
Tuesday December 8, 2015
Man City .... (1) 4-2 (2) . B M'gladbach
Seville .... (0) 1-0 (0) .... Juventus

Group E

	P	W	D	L	F	A	GD	Pts
Barcelona	6	4	2	0	15	4	11	14
Roma	6	1	3	2	11	16	-5	6
B Leverkusen	6	1	3	2	13	12	1	6
Bate Borisov	6	1	2	3	5	12	-7	5

Wednesday September 16, 2015
B Leverkusen .. (1) 4-1 (1) ... Bate Borisov
Roma .... (1) 1-1 (1) .... Barcelona
Tuesday September 29, 2015
Barcelona .... (0) 2-1 (1) .. B Leverkusen
Bate Borisov ... (3) 3-2 (0) .... Roma
Tuesday October 20, 2015
Bate Borisov ... (0) 0-2 (0) .... Barcelona
B Leverkusen .. (2) 4-4 (2) .... Roma
Wednesday November 4, 2015
Barcelona .... (1) 3-0 (0) .. Bate Borisov
Roma .... (2) 3-2 (0) .. B Leverkusen
Tuesday November 24, 2015
Barcelona .... (3) 6-1 (0) .... Roma
Bate Borisov ... (1) 1-1 (0) .. B Leverkusen
Wednesday December 9, 2015
B Leverkusen .. (1) 1-1 (1) .... Barcelona
Roma .... (0) 0-0 (0) .. Bate Borisov

Group F

	P	W	D	L	F	A	GD	Pts
B Munich	6	5	0	1	19	3	16	15
Arsenal	6	3	0	3	12	10	2	9
Olympiakos	6	3	0	3	6	13	-7	9
Din Zagreb	6	1	0	5	3	14	-11	3

Wednesday September 16, 2015
Din Zagreb ..... (1) 2-1 (0) .... Arsenal
Olympiakos ..... (0) 0-3 (0) Bayern Munich

Tuesday September 29, 2015
Arsenal .... (1) 2-3 (2) .....Olympiakos
Bayern Munich (4) 5-0 (0) ......Din Zagreb
Tuesday October 20, 2015
Arsenal .... (0) 2-0 (0) Bayern Munich
Din Zagreb...... (0) 0-1 (0) .....Olympiakos
Wednesday November 4, 2015
Bayern Munich (3) 5-1 (0) .... Arsenal
Olympiakos..... (0) 2-1 (1) ......Din Zagreb
Tuesday November 24, 2015
Arsenal .... (2) 3-0 (0) ......Din Zagreb
Bayern Munich (3) 4-0 (0) .....Olympiakos
Wednesday December 9, 2015
Din Zagreb...... (0) 0-2 (0) Bayern Munich
Olympiakos..... (0) 0-3 (1) .... Arsenal

Tuesday November 24, 2015
Lyon .... (1) 1-2 (1) .... Gent
Zenit.............. (1) 2-0 (0) ....Valencia
Wednesday December 9, 2015
Gent .... (1) 2-1 (0) ....Zenit
Valencia.......... (0) 0-2 (1) .... Lyon

Round of 16
First legs
Tuesday February 16, 2016
Benfica .... (0) 1-0 (0) ....Zenit
Paris St-G........ (1) 2-1 (1) ....Chelsea
Wednesday February 17, 2016
Gent .... (0) 2-3 (1) ......Wolfsburg
Roma.............. (0) 0-2 (0) ....Real Madrid

Tuesday February 23, 2016
Arsenal .... (0) 0-2 (0) ...... Barcelona
Juventus .... (0) 2-2 (1) Bayern Munich
Wednesday February 24, 2016
Dynamo Kiev .. (0) 1-3 (2) ....Man City
PSV Eindhoven (0) 0-0 (0) ..... Atl Madrid
Second legs
Tuesday March 8, 2016
Real Madrid .... (0) 2-0 (0) ....Roma
Aggregate: 4-0
Wolfsburg....... (0) 1-0 (0) .... Gent
Aggregate: 4-2
Wednesday March 9, 2016
Chelsea.......... (1) 1-2 (1) ....Paris St-G
Aggregate: 2-4
Zenit .... (0) 1-2 (0) .... Benfica
Aggregate: 1-3

Group G

	P	W	D	L	F	A	GD	Pts
Chelsea	6	4	1	1	13	3	10	13
Dynamo Kiev	6	3	2	1	8	4	4	11
Porto	6	3	1	2	9	8	1	10
M. Tel Aviv	6	0	0	6	1	16	-15	0

Wednesday September 16, 2015
Chelsea.......... (2) 4-0 (0) ......M. Tel Aviv
Dynamo Kiev .. (1) 2-2 (1) ....Porto
Tuesday September 29, 2015
M. Tel Aviv...... (0) 0-2 (1) .. Dynamo Kiev
Porto.............. (1) 2-1 (1) ....Chelsea
Tuesday October 20, 2015
Dynamo Kiev .. (0) 0-0 (0) ....Chelsea
Porto.............. (2) 2-0 (0) ......M. Tel Aviv
Wednesday November 4, 2015
Chelsea.......... (1) 2-1 (0) .. Dynamo Kiev
M. Tel Aviv...... (0) 1-3 (0) ....Porto
Tuesday November 24, 2015
M. Tel Aviv...... (0) 0-4 (1) ....Chelsea
Porto.............. (0) 0-2 (1) .. Dynamo Kiev
Wednesday December 9, 2015
Chelsea.......... (1) 2-0 (0) ....Porto
Dynamo Kiev .. (1) 1-0 (0) ......M. Tel Aviv

Group H

	P	W	D	L	F	A	GD	Pts
Zenit	6	5	0	1	13	6	7	15
Gent	6	3	1	2	8	7	1	10
Valencia	6	2	0	4	5	9	-4	6
Lyon	6	1	1	4	5	9	-4	4

Wednesday September 16, 2015
Gent .... (0) 1-1 (0) .... Lyon
Valencia.......... (0) 2-3 (2) ....Zenit
Tuesday September 29, 2015
Lyon .... (0) 0-1 (1) ....Valencia
Zenit.............. (1) 2-1 (0) .... Gent
Tuesday October 20, 2015
Valencia.......... (1) 2-1 (1) .... Gent
Zenit .... (1) 3-1 (0) .... Lyon
Wednesday November 4, 2015
Gent .... (0) 1-0 (0) ....Valencia
Lyon .... (0) 0-2 (1) ....Zenit

Tuesday March 15, 2016
Atl Madrid ...... (0) 0-0 (0) PSV Eindhoven
AET. Agg: 0-0. Atl Madrid won 8-7 on pens
Man City .... (0) 0-0 (0) .. Dynamo Kiev
Aggregate: 3-1

Wednesday March 16, 2016
Bayern Munich (0) 4-2 (2) .... Juventus
AET. 2-2 after 90 mins. Agg: 6-4
Barcelona .... (1) 3-1 (0) .... Arsenal
Aggregate: 5-1

Quarter-finals

Tuesday April 5, 2016
Bayern Munich (1) 1-0 (0) .... Benfica
Barcelona .... (0) 2-1 (1) ...... Atl Madrid

Wednesday April 6, 2016
Paris St-G .... (1) 2-2 (1) .... Man City
Wolfsburg .... (2) 2-0 (0) .... Real Madrid

Second legs

Tuesday April 12, 2016
Man City .... (0) 1-0 (0) .... Paris St-G
Aggregate: 3-2
Real Madrid .... (2) 3-0 (0) .... Wolfsburg
Aggregate: 3-2

Wednesday April 13, 2016
Atl Madrid ...... (1) 2-0 (0) .... Barcelona
Aggregate: 3-2
Benfica .... (1) 2-2 (1) Bayern Munich
Aggregate: 2-3

Semi-finals

Tuesday April 26, 2016
Man City .... (0) 0-0 (0) .... Real Madrid

Wednesday April 27, 2016
Atl Madrid ...... (1) 1-0 (0) Bayern Munich

Second legs

Tuesday May 3, 2016
Bayern Munich (1) 2-1 (0) ...... Atl Madrid
Agg: 2-2. Atl Madrid won on away goals

Wednesday May 4, 2016
Real Madrid.... (1) 1-0 (0) .... Man City
Aggregate: 1-0

Final

Saturday May 28, 2016
Real Madrid.... (1) 1-1 (1) ...... Atl Madrid
AET. 1-1 after 90 mins. Real won 5-3 on pens

Real Madrid celebrate a repeat of their 2014 Champions League final win over rivals Atletico

EURO 2016 QUALIFYING

Group A

	P	W	D	L	F	A	GD	Pts
Czech Rep	10	7	1	2	19	14	5	22
Iceland	10	6	2	2	17	6	11	20
Turkey	10	5	3	2	14	9	5	18
Holland	10	4	1	5	17	14	3	13
Kazakhstan	10	1	2	7	7	18-11		5
Latvia	10	0	5	5	6	19-13		5

September 9, 2014
Czech Rep ...... (1) 2-1 (0) ....Holland
Iceland .... (1) 3-0 (0) ....Turkey
Kazakhstan .... (0) 0-0 (0) .... Latvia
October 10-13, 2014
Holland .... (0) 3-1 (1).....Kazakhstan
Latvia............. (0) 0-3 (0) ....Iceland
Turkey .... (1) 1-2 (1).......Czech Rep
Iceland .... (2) 2-0 (0) ....Holland
Kazakhstan .... (0) 2-4 (2) .....Czech Rep
Latvia............. (0) 1-1 (0) ....Turkey
November 16, 2014
Czech Rep ...... (1) 2-1 (1)............Iceland
Holland .... (3) 6-0 (0) .... Latvia
Turkey ....(2) 3-1 (0) .....Kazakhstan
March 28, 2015
Czech Rep ...... (0) 1-1 (1)............ Latvia
Holland .... (0) 1-1 (1)............Turkey
Kazakhstan .... (0) 0-3 (2) ....Iceland
June 12, 2015
Iceland .... (0) 2-1 (0) ......Czech Rep
Kazakhstan .... (0) 0-1 (0) ....Turkey
Latvia............. (0) 0-2 (0) ....Holland
September 3-6, 2015
Czech Rep ...... (0) 2-1 (1) .....Kazakhstan
Holland .... (0) 0-1 (0) ....Iceland
Turkey .... (0) 1-1 (0) .... Latvia
Iceland .... (0) 0-0 (0) .....Kazakhstan
Latvia............. (0) 1-2 (2) ......Czech Rep
Turkey .... (2) 3-0 (0) ....Holland
October 10-13, 2015
Czech Rep ...... (0) 0-2 (0) ....Turkey
Iceland .... (2) 2-2 (0) .... Latvia
Kazakhstan .... (0) 1-2 (1)...........Holland
Holland .... (0) 2-3 (2) ......Czech Rep
Latvia............. (0) 0-1 (0) ...Kazakhstan
Turkey .... (0) 1-0 (0) ....Iceland

Group B

	P	W	D	L	F	A	GD	Pts
Belgium	10	7	2	1	24	5	19	23
Wales	10	6	3	1	11	4	7	21
Bosnia-Hz	10	5	2	3	17	12	5	17
Israel	10	4	1	5	16	14	2	13
Cyprus	10	4	0	6	16	17	-1	12
Andorra	10	0	0	10	4	36-32	0	

September 9, 2014
Andorra........ (1) 1-2 (1)............ Wales
Bosnia-Hz..... (1) 1-2 (1)........... Cyprus
October 10-13, 2014
Belgium........... (3) 6-0 (0) ....Andorra
Cyprus............. (0) 1-2 (2) .... Israel
Wales .... (0) 0-0 (0) .....Bosnia-Hz
Andorra........... (1) 1-4 (2) .... Israel
Bosnia-Hz........ (1) 1-1 (0) ....Belgium
Wales .... (2) 2-1 (0) .... Cyprus
November 16, 2014
Belgium........... (0) 0-0 (0) .... Wales
Cyprus............. (3) 5-0 (0) ....Andorra
Israel .... (2) 3-0 (0) .....Bosnia-Hz

March 28-31, 2015
Andorra........... (0) 0-3 (1)....... Bosnia-Hz
Belgium........... (2) 5-0 (0) .... Cyprus
Israel............... (0) 0-3 (1)........... Wales
Israel............... (0) 0-1 (1)........... Belgium
June 12, 2015
Andorra........... (1) 1-3 (2) .... Cyprus
Bosnia-Hz....... (2) 3-1 (1)............. Israel
Wales .... (1) 1-0 (0) .... Belgium
September 3-6, 2015
Belgium........... (2) 3-1 (1)....... Bosnia-Hz
Cyprus............. (0) 0-1 (0) .... Wales
Israel............... (4) 4-0 (0) ....Andorra
Bosnia-Hz....... (3) 3-0 (0) ....Andorra
Cyprus............. (0) 0-1 (0) .... Belgium
Wales .... (0) 0-0 (0) .... Israel
October 10-13, 2015
Andorra........... (0) 1-4 (2) .... Belgium
Bosnia-Hz....... (0) 2-0 (0) .... Wales
Israel............... (0) 1-2 (0) .... Cyprus
Belgium........... (0) 3-1 (0) .... Israel
Cyprus............. (2) 2-3 (2) .... Bosnia-Hz
Wales .... (0) 2-0 (0) ....Andorra

Group C

	P	W	D	L	F	A	GD	Pts
Spain	10	9	0	1	23	3	20	27
Slovakia	10	7	1	2	17	8	9	22
Ukraine	10	6	1	3	14	4	10	19
Belarus	10	3	2	5	8	14	-6	11
Luxembourg	10	1	1	8	6	27-21	4	
Macedonia	10	1	1	8	6	18-12	4	

September 8, 2014
Luxembourg... (1) 1-1 (0) .... Belarus
Spain.............. (3) 5-1 (1)..... Macedonia
Ukraine .... (0) 0-1 (1)..... Slovakia
October 9-12, 2014
Belarus............ (0) 0-2 (0) ....Ukraine
Macedonia .... (1) 3-2 (2) ... Luxembourg
Slovakia .... (1) 2-1 (0) .... Spain
Belarus............ (0) 1-3 (0) ....Slovakia
Luxembourg.... (0) 0-4 (2) .... Spain
Ukraine .... (1) 1-0 (0) ..... Macedonia
November 15, 2014
Luxembourg... (0) 0-3 (1)...........Ukraine
Macedonia ...... (0) 0-2 (0) ......Slovakia
Spain.............. (2) 3-0 (0) .... Belarus
March 27, 2015
Macedonia ...... (1) 1-2 (1)........ Belarus
Slovakia .... (3) 3-0 (0) ... Luxembourg
Spain............... (1) 1-0 (0) ....Ukraine
June 14, 2015
Belarus............. (0) 0-1 (1)........... Spain
Slovakia .... (2) 2-1 (0) ... Macedonia
Ukraine .... (0) 3-0 (0) ... Luxembourg
September 5-8, 2015
Luxembourg... (0) 1-0 (0) ..... Macedonia
Spain............... (2) 2-0 (0) ..... Slovakia
Ukraine .... (3) 3-1 (0) .... Belarus
Belarus............. (1) 2-0 (0) ... Luxembourg
Macedonia .... (0) 0-1 (0) .... Spain
Slovakia .... (0) 0-0 (0) ....Ukraine
October 9-12, 2015
Macedonia ...... (0) 0-2 (0) ....Ukraine
Slovakia .... (0) 0-0 (0) .... Belarus
Spain............... (1) 4-0 (0) ... Luxembourg
Belarus............ (0) 0-0 (0) ..... Macedonia
Luxembourg.... (0) 2-4 (3) ... Slovakia
Ukraine .... (0) 0-1 (1)........... Spain

Group D

	P	W	D	L	F	A	GD	Pts
Germany	10	7	1	2	24	9	15	22
Poland	10	6	3	1	33	10	23	21
Ireland	10	5	3	2	19	7	12	18
Scotland	10	4	3	3	22	12	10	15
Georgia	10	3	0	7	10	16	-6	9
Gibraltar	10	0	0	10	2	56-54	0	

September 7, 2014
Georgia.......... (1) 1-2 (1)...........Ireland
Germany .... (1) 2-1 (0) .... Scotland
Gibraltar......... (0) 0-7 (1)............ Poland
October 11-14, 2014
Ireland .... (3) 7-0 (0) ....Gibraltar
Poland.............. (0) 2-0 (0) ....Germany
Scotland .... (1) 1-0 (0) .... Georgia
Germany .... (0) 1-1 (0) ....Ireland
Gibraltar.......... (0) 0-3 (2) .... Georgia
Poland.............. (1) 2-2 (1) .... Scotland
November 14, 2014
Georgia........... (0) 0-4 (0) .... Poland
Germany .... (3) 4-0 (0) ....Gibraltar
Scotland .... (0) 1-0 (0) ....Ireland
March 29, 2015
Georgia........... (0) 0-2 (2) ....Germany
Ireland .... (1) 1-1 (0) .... Poland
Scotland .... (4) 6-1 (1)...........Gibraltar
June 13, 2015
Gibraltar.......... (0) 0-7 (1)...........Germany
Poland.............. (0) 4-0 (0) .... Georgia
Ireland .... (1) 1-0 (0) .... Scotland
September 4-7, 2015
Georgia........... (1) 1-0 (0) .... Scotland
Germany .... (2) 3-1 (1).......... Poland
Gibraltar.......... (0) 0-4 (1)...........Ireland
Ireland .... (0) 1-0 (0) .... Georgia
Poland.............. (4) 8-1 (0) ....Gibraltar
Scotland .... (2) 2-3 (2) ....Germany
October 8-11, 2015
Georgia........... (3) 4-0 (0) ....Gibraltar
Ireland .... (1) 1-0 (0) ....Germany
Scotland .... (1) 2-2 (1) .... Poland
Germany .... (0) 2-1 (0) .... Georgia
Gibraltar.......... (0) 0-6 (2) .... Scotland
Poland.............. (2) 2-1 (1)...........Ireland

Group E

	P	W	D	L	F	A	GD	Pts
England	10	10	0	0	31	3	28	30
Switzerland	10	7	0	3	24	8	16	21
Slovenia	10	5	1	4	18	11	7	16
Estonia	10	4	1	5	9	9	-5	10
Lithuania	10	3	1	6	7	18-11	10	
San Marino	10	0	1	9	1	36-35	1	

September 8, 2014
Estonia............ (0) 1-0 (0) ....Slovenia
San Marino ..... (0) 0-2 (0) .... Lithuania
Switzerland..... (0) 0-2 (0) .... England
October 9-14, 2014
England............ (2) 5-0 (0) .....San Marino
Lithuania.......... (1) 1-0 (0) .... Estonia
Slovenia .... (0) 1-0 (0) ... Switzerland
Estonia............. (0) 0-1 (0) .... England
Lithuania........ (0) 0-2 (2) ....Slovenia
San Marino ..... (0) 0-4 (3) ... Switzerland
November 15, 2014
England............ (0) 3-1 (0) ....Slovenia
San Marino ..... (0) 0-0 (0) .... Estonia
Switzerland..... (0) 4-0 (0) .... Lithuania

March 27, 2015
England......... (2) 4-0 (0) .... Lithuania
Slovenia .... (1) 6-0 (0) .....San Marino
Switzerland.... (2) 3-0 (0) .... Estonia
June 14, 2015
Estonia .... (1) 2-0 (0) .....San Marino
Lithuania........ (0) 1-2 (0) .... Switzerland
Slovenia .... (1) 2-3 (0) .... England
September 5-8, 2015
Estonia .... (0) 1-0 (0) .... Lithuania
San Marino .... (0) 0-6 (2) .... England
Switzerland.... (0) 3-2 (1).........Slovenia
England......... (0) 2-0 (0) .... Switzerland
Lithuania........ (1) 2-1 (0) .....San Marino
Slovenia .... (0) 1-0 (0) .... Estonia
October 9-12, 2015
England......... (1) 2-0 (0) .... Estonia
Slovenia .... (1) 1-1 (0) .... Lithuania
Switzerland.... (1) 7-0 (0) .....San Marino
Estonia .... (0) 0-1 (0) .... Switzerland
Lithuania........ (0) 0-3 (2) .... England
San Marino .... (0) 0-2 (0) ....Slovenia

Group F

	P	W	D	L	F	A	GD	Pts
N Ireland	10	6	3	1	16	8	8	21
Romania	10	5	5	0	11	2	9	20
Hungary	10	4	4	2	11	9	2	16
Finland	10	3	3	4	9	10	-1	12
Faroe Islands	10	2	0	8	6	17	-11	6
Greece	10	1	3	6	7	14	-7	6

September 7, 2014
Faroe Islands.. (1) 1-3 (0) .... Finland
Greece............ (0) 0-1 (1)............Romania
Hungary........ (0) 1-2 (0) .... N Ireland
October 11-14, 2014
Finland............ (0) 1-1 (1)............ Greece
N Ireland........ (2) 2-0 (0) .. Faroe Islands
Romania......... (1) 1-0 (0).........Hungary
Faroe Islands.. (0) 0-1 (1)...........Hungary
Finland............ (0) 0-2 (0) ....Romania
Greece............ (0) 0-2 (1).... N Ireland
November 14, 2014
Greece............ (0) 0-1 (0) .. Faroe Islands
Hungary........ (0) 1-0 (0) .... Finland
Romania......... (0) 2-0 (0) .. N Ireland
March 29, 2015
Hungary........ (0) 0-0 (0) ....Greece
N Ireland........ (2) 2-1 (0) ....Finland
Romania......... (1) 1-0 (0) .. Faroe Islands
June 13, 2015
Faroe Islands.. (1) 2-1 (0) ....Greece
Finland............ (0) 0-1 (1)...........Hungary
N Ireland........ (0) 0-0 (0) .... Romania
September 4-7, 2015
Faroe Islands.. (1) 1-3 (1)... N Ireland
Greece............ (0) 0-1 (0) ....Finland
Hungary........ (0) 0-0 (0) .... Romania
Finland............ (1) 1-0 (0) .. Faroe Islands
N Ireland........ (1) 1-1 (0)...........Hungary
Romania......... (0) 0-0 (0) ....Greece
October 8-11, 2015
Hungary........ (0) 2-1 (1)... Faroe Islands
N Ireland........ (1) 3-1 (0) ....Greece
Romania......... (0) 1-1 (0) ....Finland
Faroe Islands.. (0) 0-3 (2) .... Romania
Finland............ (0) 1-1 (1)... N Ireland
Greece............ (1) 4-3 (1)...........Hungary

Group G

	P	W	D	L	F	A	GD	Pts
Austria	10	9	1	0	22	5	17	28
Russia	10	6	2	2	21	5	16	20
Sweden	10	5	3	2	15	9	6	18
Montenegro	10	3	2	5	10	13	-3	11
Liechtenstein	10	1	2	7	2	26	-24	5
Moldova	10	0	2	8	4	16	-12	2

September 8, 2014
Austria .... (1) 1-1 (1)...........Sweden
Montenegro... (1) 2-0 (0) ....Moldova
Russia .... (1) 4-0 (0) .. Liechtenstein
October 9-12, 2014
Liechtenstein . (0) 0-0 (0) ... Montenegro
Moldova......... (1) 1-2 (1)............Austria
Sweden.......... (0) 1-1 (1)............Russia
Austria .... (1) 1-0 (0) ... Montenegro
Russia .... (0) 1-1 (0) ....Moldova
Sweden.......... (1) 2-0 (0) .. Liechtenstein
November 15, 2014
Austria .... (0) 1-0 (0) ....Russia
Moldova......... (0) 0-1 (0) .. Liechtenstein
Montenegro... (0) 1-1 (1)...........Sweden
March 27, 2015
Liechtenstein . (0) 0-5 (2) ....Austria
Moldova......... (0) 0-2 (0) ....Sweden
Montenegro..... 0-3 ....Russia
Match forfeited – abandoned at 0-0
June 14, 2015
Liechtenstein . (1) 1-1 (1)..........Moldova
Russia .... (0) 0-1 (1)............Austria
Sweden.......... (3) 3-1 (0) ... Montenegro
September 5-8, 2015
Austria .... (0) 1-0 (0) ....Moldova
Montenegro... (1) 2-0 (0) .. Liechtenstein
Russia .... (1) 1-0 (0) ....Sweden
Liechtenstein . (0) 0-7 (3) ....Russia
Moldova......... (0) 0-2 (1)... Montenegro
Sweden.......... (1) 1-4 (2) ....Austria
October 9-12, 2015
Liechtenstein . (0) 0-2 (1)...........Sweden
Moldova......... (0) 1-2 (0) ....Russia
Montenegro... (1) 2-3 (0) ....Austria
Austria .... (1) 3-0 (0) .. Liechtenstein
Russia .... (2) 2-0 (0) ... Montenegro
Sweden.......... (1) 2-0 (0) ....Moldova

Group H

	P	W	D	L	F	A	GD	Pts
Italy	10	7	3	0	16	7	9	24
Croatia	10	6	3	1	20	5	15	20
Norway	10	6	1	3	13	10	3	19
Bulgaria	10	3	2	5	14	9	5	11
Azerbaijan	10	1	3	6	7	18	-11	6
Malta	10	0	2	8	3	16	-13	2

Croatia deducted 1pt

September 9, 2014
Azerbaijan...... (0) 1-2 (1)..........Bulgaria
Croatia .... (0) 2-0 (0) ....Malta
Norway .... (0) 0-2 (1).............. Italy
October 10-13, 2014
Bulgaria .... (0) 0-1 (1)............Croatia
Italy.................. (1) 2-1 (0) ....Azerbaijan
Malta .... (0) 0-3 (2) ....Norway
Croatia .... (4) 6-0 (0) ....Azerbaijan
Malta .... (0) 0-1 (0) .... Italy
Norway .... (1) 2-1 (1)..........Bulgaria
November 16, 2014
Azerbaijan...... (0) 0-1 (1)...........Norway
Bulgaria .... (1) 1-1 (0) ....Malta
Italy.................. (1) 1-1 (0) ....Croatia
March 28, 2015
Azerbaijan...... (2) 2-0 (0) ....Malta
Bulgaria .... (2) 2-2 (1)................ Italy
Croatia .... (1) 5-1 (0) ....Norway
June 12, 2015
Croatia .... (1) 1-1 (1)................ Italy
Malta .... (0) 0-1 (0) ....Bulgaria
Norway .... (0) 0-0 (0) .....Azerbaijan
September 3-6, 2015
Azerbaijan...... (0) 0-0 (0) ....Croatia
Bulgaria .... (0) 0-1 (0) ....Norway
Italy.................. (0) 1-0 (0) ....Malta
Italy.................. (1) 1-0 (0) ....Bulgaria
Malta .... (0) 2-2 (1)......Azerbaijan
Norway .... (0) 2-0 (0) ....Croatia
October 10-13, 2015
Azerbaijan...... (1) 1-3 (2) .... Italy
Croatia .... (2) 3-0 (0) ....Bulgaria
Norway .... (1) 2-0 (0) ....Malta
Bulgaria .... (1) 2-0 (0) ....Azerbaijan
Italy.................. (2) 2-1 (1)...........Norway
Malta .... (0) 0-1 (1)...........Croatia

Group I

	P	W	D	L	F	A	GD	Pts
Portugal	8	7	0	1	11	5	6	21
Albania	8	4	2	2	10	5	5	14
Denmark	8	3	3	2	8	5	3	12
Serbia	8	2	1	5	8	13	-5	4
Armenia	8	0	2	6	5	14	-9	2

September 7, 2014
Denmark....... (0) 2-1 (0) ....Armenia
Portugal......... (0) 0-1 (0) ....Albania
October 11-14, 2014
Albania .... (1) 1-1 (0) ....Denmark
Armenia .... (0) 1-1 (0) .... Serbia
Denmark....... (0) 0-1 (0) .... Portugal
Serbia.............. (0) 0-3 (0) ....Albania
Match forfeited – abandoned at 0-0
November 14, 2014
Portugal......... (0) 1-0 (0) ....Armenia
Serbia.............. (1) 1-3 (0) ....Denmark
March 29, 2015
Albania .... (0) 2-1 (1)..........Armenia
Portugal......... (1) 2-1 (0) .... Serbia
June 13, 2015
Armenia .... (1) 2-3 (1) .... Portugal
Denmark....... (1) 2-0 (0) .... Serbia
September 4-7, 2015
Denmark....... (0) 0-0 (0) ....Albania
Serbia.............. (0) 0-0 (0) ....Armenia
Albania .... (0) 0-1 (0) .... Portugal
Armenia .... (0) 0-0 (0) ....Denmark
October 8-11, 2015
Albania .... (0) 0-2 (0) .... Serbia
Portugal......... (0) 1-0 (0) ....Denmark
Armenia .... (0) 0-3 (2) ....Albania
Serbia.............. (0) 1-2 (1)........ Portugal

Playoff round
November 12-17, 2015
Norway .... (0) 0-1 (1)..........Hungary
Bosnia-Hz...... (0) 1-1 (0) ....Ireland
Sweden.......... (1) 2-1 (0) ....Denmark
Ukraine .... (1) 2-0 (0) ....Slovenia
Second legs
Hungary........ (1) 2-1 (0) ....Norway
Hungary won 3-1 on aggregate
Ireland .... (1) 2-0 (0) .. Bosnia-Hz
Ireland won 3-1 on aggregate
Denmark....... (0) 2-2 (1)...........Sweden
Sweden won 4-3 on aggregate
Slovenia .... (1) 1-1 (0) ....Ukraine
Ukraine won 3-1 on aggregate

Group A

	P	W	D	L	F	A	GD	Pts
France	3	2	1	0	4	1	3	7
Switzerland	3	1	2	0	2	1	1	5
Albania	3	1	0	2	1	3	-2	3
Romania	3	0	1	2	2	4	-2	1

June 10-19, 2016

France............ (0) 2-1 (0) .... Romania
Albania .... (0) 0-1 (1).... Switzerland
France............ (0) 2-0 (0) ....Albania
Romania........ (1) 1-1 (0) .... Switzerland
Romania........ (0) 0-1 (1)............Albania
Switzerland .... (0) 0-0 (0) ....France

Group B

	P	W	D	L	F	A	GD	Pts
Wales	3	2	0	1	6	3	3	6
England	3	1	2	0	3	2	1	5
Slovakia	3	1	1	1	3	3	0	4
Russia	3	0	1	2	2	6	-4	1

June 11-20, 2016

Wales.............. (1) 2-1 (0) ....Slovakia
England.......... (0) 1-1 (0) ....Russia
Russia .... (0) 1-2 (2) ....Slovakia
England.......... (0) 2-1 (1)...............Wales
Russia .... (0) 0-3 (2) ....Wales
Slovakia .... (0) 0-0 (0) ....England

Group C

	P	W	D	L	F	A	GD	Pts
Germany	3	2	1	0	3	0	3	7
Poland	3	2	1	0	2	0	2	7
N Ireland	3	1	0	2	2	2	0	3
Ukraine	3	0	0	3	0	5	-5	0

June 12-21, 2016

Poland............ (0) 1-0 (0) .... N Ireland
Germany .... (1) 2-0 (0) ....Ukraine
Ukraine .... (0) 0-2 (0) .... N Ireland
Germany .... (0) 0-0 (0) ....Poland
N Ireland .... (0) 0-1 (1)...........Germany
Ukraine .... (0) 0-1 (0) ....Poland

Group D

	P	W	D	L	F	A	GD	Pts
Croatia	3	2	1	0	5	3	2	7
Spain	3	2	0	1	5	2	3	6
Turkey	3	1	0	2	2	4	-2	3
Czech Rep	3	0	1	2	2	5	-3	1

June 12-21, 2016

Turkey............ (0) 0-1 (1)..........Croatia
Spain.............. (0) 1-0 (0) ....Czech Rep
Czech Rep ...... (0) 2-2 (1)..........Croatia
Spain.............. (2) 3-0 (0) ....Turkey
Croatia .... (1) 2-1 (1)............. Spain
Czech Rep ...... (0) 0-2 (1)..............Turkey

Group E

	P	W	D	L	F	A	GD	Pts
Italy	3	2	0	1	3	1	2	6
Belgium	3	2	0	1	4	2	2	6
Ireland	3	1	1	1	2	4	-2	4
Sweden	3	0	1	2	1	3	-2	1

June 13-22, 2016

Belgium.......... (0) 0-2 (1)................Italy
Ireland .... (0) 1-1 (0) ....Sweden
Italy................ (0) 1-0 (0) ....Sweden
Belgium.......... (0) 3-0 (0) ....Ireland
Italy................ (0) 0-1 (0) ....Ireland
Sweden .... (0) 0-1 (0) .... Belgium

Group F

	P	W	D	L	F	A	GD	Pts
Hungary	3	1	2	0	6	4	2	5
Iceland	3	1	2	0	4	3	1	5
Portugal	3	0	3	0	4	4	0	3
Austria	3	0	1	2	1	4	-3	1

June 14-22, 2016

Austria .... (0) 0-2 (0) ....Hungary
Portugal.......... (1) 1-1 (0) ....Iceland
Iceland .... (1) 1-1 (0) ....Hungary
Portugal.......... (0) 0-0 (0) ....Austria
Hungary.......... (1) 3-3 (1)........ Portugal
Iceland .... (1) 2-1 (0) ....Austria

Knockout stages

Round of 16

Saturday June 25-27, 2016

Switzerland.... (0) 1-1 (1)............Poland
AET, 1-1 after 90 mins. Poland 5-4 on pens
Wales.............. (0) 1-0 (0) .... N Ireland
Croatia .... (0) 0-1 (0) .... Portugal
AET, 0-0 after 90 minutes
France .... (0) 2-1 (1)............Ireland
Germany .... (2) 3-0 (0) ....Slovakia
Hungary.......... (0) 0-4 (1)............Belgium

Italy................ (1) 2-0 (0) .... Spain
England.......... (1) 1-2 (2) ....Iceland

Quarter-finals

Thursday June 30-July 3, 2016

Poland............ (1) 1-1 (1).......... Portugal
AET. 1-1 after 90 mins. Portugal 5-3 pens
Wales.............. (1) 3-1 (1)..........Belgium
Germany .... (0) 1-1 (0)................Italy
AET. 1-1 after 90 mins. Germany 6-5 pens
France .... (4) 5-2 (0) ....Iceland

Semi-finals

Monday July 6-7, 2016

Portugal.......... (0) 2-0 (0) .... Wales
Germany .... (0) 0-2 (1)..............France

Final

Sunday July 10, 2016

Portugal.......... (0) 1-0 (0) ....France
AET. 0-0 after 90 minutes

Eder's cracking strike settles the Euro 2016 final

Qualifying Group A – winner

	Fred	Coral	Lads	Sky
France	10-11	5-6	5-6	5-6
Holland	5-4	11-8	11-8	11-8
Sweden	8	13-2	7	8
Bulgaria	40	40	33	50
Belarus	250	250	200	200
Luxembourg	1500	2500	1500	1000

Qualifying Group B – winner

	Fred	Coral	Lads	Sky
Portugal	4-7	1-2	8-15	8-13
Switzerland	8-5	13-8	6-4	11-8
Hungary	12	14	16	14
Faroe Is	200	125	350	250
Latvia	500	150	500	500
Andorra	2500	2500	1000	2000

Qualifying Group C – winner

	Fred	Coral	Lads	Sky
Germany	1-7	1-7	1-10	1-8
Czech Rep	5	11-2	8	11-2
Norway	22	20	20	20
N Ireland	28	33	33	40
Azerbaijan	1000	250	500	500
San Marino	2500	5000	5000	2000

Qualifying Group D – winner

	Fred	Coral	Lads	Sky
Wales	15-8	2	2	15-8
Serbia	9-4	5-2	9-4	9-4
Austria	13-5	9-4	5-2	5-2
Ireland	5	5	9-2	11-2
Georgia	150	80	150	125
Moldova	100	50	66	80

Qualifying Group E – winner

	Fred	Coral	Lads	Sky
Poland	7-4	15-8	7-4	13-8
Denmark	9-4	9-4	21-10	2
Romania	5-2	3	11-4	11-4
Montenegro	15-2	11-2	6	8
Armenia	40	33	40	50
Kazakhstan	250	150	200	200

Qualifying Group F – winner

	Fred	Coral	Lads	Sky
England	1-3	2-5	1-4	1-3
Slovakia	11-2	4	11-2	5
Scotland	8	9	9	9
Slovenia	11	11	16	12
Lithuania	150	100	200	150
Malta	500	500	1000	750

Qualifying Group G – winner

	Fred	Coral	Lads	Sky
Spain	8-15	8-15	2-5	1-2
Italy	11-8	11-8	7-4	13-8
Israel	50	50	50	50
Albania	80	50	66	66
Macedonia	250	150	200	250
Liechtenstein	1000	2500	2000	1000

Qualifying Group H – winner

	Fred	Coral	Lads	Sky
Belgium	1-4	2-7	2-7	2-7
Bosnia-Hz	4	7-2	3	7-2
Greece	10	15-2	10	9
Cyprus	150	150	250	200
Estonia	250	200	350	500
Gibraltar	-	-	-	-

Qualifying Group I – winner

	Fred	Coral	Lads	Sky
Croatia	11-10	11-10	5-4	1
Ukraine	13-5	3	5-2	5-2
Turkey	4	4	4	9-2
Iceland	7	13-2	7	7
Finland	28	14	14	40
Kosovo	-	-	-	-

Key qualifying fixtures

Sunday September 4, 2016
Czech Republic..... v .... N Ireland
Malta .... v .... Scotland
Slovakia .... v .... England

Monday September 5, 2016
Serbia.................. v ....Ireland
Wales .... v .... Moldova

Thursday October 6, 2016
Austria .... v .... Wales
Ireland .... v .... Georgia

Saturday October 8, 2016
England.............. v ....Malta
N Ireland............ v ....San Marino
Scotland............. v .... Lithuania

Sunday October 9, 2016
Moldova.............. v ....Ireland
Wales.................. v .... Georgia

Tuesday October 11, 2016
Germany .... v .... N Ireland
Slovakia.............. v .... Scotland
Slovenia .... v .... England

Friday November 11, 2016
England.............. v .... Scotland
N Ireland............ v ....Azerbaijan

Saturday November 12, 2016
Austria .... v ....Ireland
Wales.................. v .... Serbia

Friday March 24, 2017
Ireland .... v .... Wales

Sunday March 26, 2017
England.............. v .... Lithuania
N Ireland............ v ....Norway
Scotland............. v ....Slovenia

England and Scotland last met in qualifying in November 1999

Saturday June 10, 2017
Azerbaijan.......... v .... N Ireland
Scotland.............. v .... England

Sunday June 11, 2017
Ireland .... v ....Austria
Serbia.................. v .... Wales

Friday September 1, 2017
Lithuania............. v .... Scotland
Malta .... v .... Scotland
San Marino .... v .... N Ireland

Saturday September 2, 2017
Georgia............... v ....Ireland
Wales.................. v ....Austria

Monday September 4, 2017
England.............. v ....Slovakia
N Ireland............ v ....Czech Republic
Scotland............. v ....Malta

Tuesday September 5, 2017
Ireland .... v .... Serbia
Moldova.............. v .... Wales

Thursday October 5, 2017
England.............. v ....Slovenia
N Ireland............ v ....Germany
Scotland............. v ....Slovakia

Friday October 6, 2017
Georgia............... v .... Wales
Ireland .... v .... Moldova

Sunday October 8, 2017
Lithuania............. v .... England
Norway................ v .... N Ireland
Slovenia .... v .... Scotland

Monday October 9, 2017
Wales.................. v ....Ireland

To the right of each fixture are results for the corresponding league match in each of the last six seasons. The most recent result – 2015-16 – is on the right. The results cover matches in the Premier League, Championship, League One, League Two, National League, Scottish Premiership, Scottish Championship, Scottish League One and Scottish League Two.

Where Scottish clubs have met more than once at the same venue in the same season, results are separated by an oblique stroke with the most recent to the right. The Scottish Premiership will split into top- and bottom-six sections later in the season. These fixtures cover the period until the split.

Please note that TV coverage and postponements will cause alterations to the fixture list.

	2010-11	2011-12	2012-13	2013-14	2014-15	2015-16
Friday August 5, 2016						
Championship						
Fulham v Newcastle	1-0	5-2	2-1	1-0	-	-
Saturday August 6, 2016						
Championship						
Birmingham v Cardiff	-	1-1	0-1	-	0-0	1-0
Blackburn v Norwich	-	2-0	-	-	1-2	-
Bristol City v Wigan	-	-	-	-	-	-
Derby v Brighton	-	0-1	0-0	1-0	3-0	2-2
Huddersfield v Brentford	4-4	3-2	-	-	2-1	1-5
Ipswich v Barnsley	1-3	1-0	1-1	1-1	-	-
Nottm Forest v Burton	-	-	-	-	-	-
Reading v Preston	2-1	-	-	-	-	1-2
Rotherham v Wolves	-	-	-	3-3	1-0	1-2
League One						
Bolton v Sheffield United	-	-	-	-	-	-
Bradford v Port Vale	0-2	1-1	0-1	1-0	1-1	1-0
Bury v Charlton	-	1-2	-	-	-	-
Millwall v Oldham	-	-	-	-	-	3-0
Northampton v Fleetwood Town	-	-	3-1	1-0	-	-
Oxford v Chesterfield	0-0	-	0-1	0-1	-	-
Rochdale v Peterborough	2-2	-	-	-	0-1	2-0
Scunthorpe v Bristol Rovers	-	-	-	1-1	-	-
Shrewsbury v MK Dons	-	-	2-2	0-0	-	-
Southend v Gillingham	2-2	1-0	0-1	-	-	1-1
Swindon v Coventry	-	-	2-2	2-1	1-1	2-2
Walsall v AFC Wimbledon	-	-	-	-	-	-
League Two						
Accrington v Doncaster	-	-	-	-	-	-
Blackpool v Exeter	-	-	-	-	-	-
Cambridge U v Barnet	-	-	-	1-1	-	2-1
Cheltenham v Leyton Orient	-	-	-	-	-	-
Crawley Town v Wycombe	-	-	-	-	-	0-0
Grimsby v Morecambe	-	-	-	-	-	-
Hartlepool v Colchester	1-0	0-1	0-0	-	-	-
Newport County v Mansfield	1-0	1-0	2-0	1-1	0-1	1-0
Plymouth v Luton	-	-	-	-	0-1	0-1
Portsmouth v Carlisle	-	-	1-1	-	3-0	1-0
Stevenage v Crewe	1-1	-	2-2	1-0	-	-
Yeovil v Notts County	2-1	1-0	0-0	-	1-1	1-0

Results cover matches from Premier League to National League and Scottish Premiership to League Two

	2010-11	2011-12	2012-13	2013-14	2014-15	2015-16
National League						
Barrow v Aldershot	-	-	-	-	-	1-3
Boreham Wood v Forest Green	-	-	-	-	-	0-1
Bromley v Tranmere	-	-	-	-	-	0-1
Dag & Red v Southport	-	-	-	-	-	-
Eastleigh v Guiseley	-	-	-	-	-	1-1
Gateshead v Chester	-	-	-	3-2	2-1	1-0
Macclesfield v Torquay	3-3	1-2	-	-	1-0	1-2
Maidstone v York	-	-	-	-	-	-
North Ferriby v Braintree	-	-	-	-	-	-
Sutton United v Solihull Moors	-	-	-	-	-	-
Woking v Lincoln	-	-	1-1	0-0	3-1	3-1
Wrexham v Dover	-	-	-	-	1-1	0-1
Scottish Premiership						
Kilmarnock v Motherwell	0-1/3-1	0-0/2-0	1-2/2-0	0-2	2-0/1-2	0-1
Partick v Inverness CT	-	-	-	0-0	3-1/1-0	2-1/1-4
Rangers v Hamilton	4-0	-	-	-	-	-
Ross County v Dundee	0-3/0-1	1-1/3-0	1-1	-	2-1/1-0	5-2
Scottish Championship						
Ayr v Raith	-	2-1/1-1	-	-	-	-
Dundee United v Queen of Sth	-	-	-	-	-	-
Dunfermline v Dumbarton	-	-	4-0/3-4	-	-	-
Falkirk v Hibernian	-	-	-	-	1-0/0-3	0-1/1-1
St Mirren v Morton	-	-	-	-	-	1-1/3-1
Scottish League One						
Alloa v Peterhead	2-2/0-0	2-1/3-1	-	-	-	-
Brechin v Stenhousemuir	0-0/3-1	2-0/1-0	7-2/1-2	0-1/1-3	1-0/2-1	1-2/1-0
East Fife v Albion	-	2-0/1-2	1-2/2-0	-	0-0/1-0	-
Livingston v Stranraer	-	-	-	-	-	-
Queens Park v Airdrieonians	-	-	-	-	-	-
Scottish League Two						
Annan v Stirling	-	-	5-2/0-1	4-4/1-2	-	1-1/2-2
Arbroath v Berwick	3-2/2-1	-	-	-	2-0/5-0	3-1/1-2
Clyde v Montrose	2-0/1-1	1-0/1-2	1-2/1-0	0-3/1-1	1-2/2-0	3-1/3-3
Cowdenbeath v Elgin	-	-	-	-	-	-
Edinburgh City v Forfar	-	-	-	-	-	-

Sunday August 7, 2016

	2010-11	2011-12	2012-13	2013-14	2014-15	2015-16
Championship						
QPR v Leeds	1-2	-	-	1-1	-	1-0
Sheffield Weds v Aston Villa	-	-	-	-	-	-
Scottish Premiership						
Hearts v Celtic	2-0/0-3	2-0/0-4	0-4	1-3/0-2	-	2-2/1-3
St Johnstone v Aberdeen	0-1/0-0	1-2	1-2/3-1	0-2	1-0/1-1	3-4/3-0

Tuesday August 9, 2016

	2010-11	2011-12	2012-13	2013-14	2014-15	2015-16
National League						
Aldershot v Maidstone	-	-	-	-	-	-
Braintree v Eastleigh	-	-	-	-	1-5	2-0
Chester v Dag & Red	-	-	-	-	-	-
Dover v Boreham Wood	-	-	-	-	-	2-1
Forest Green v Sutton United	-	-	-	-	-	-
Guiseley v Wrexham	-	-	-	-	-	3-1
Lincoln v North Ferriby	-	-	-	-	-	-
Solihull Moors v Woking	-	-	-	-	-	-
Southport v Gateshead	5-1	1-3	2-1	2-1	0-1	1-2
Torquay v Bromley	-	-	-	-	-	3-7
Tranmere v Barrow	-	-	-	-	-	0-1
York v Macclesfield	-	-	-	-	-	-

Results cover matches from Premier League to National League and Scottish Premiership to League Two

Friday August 12, 2016

Championship

	2010-11	2011-12	2012-13	2013-14	2014-15	2015-16
Brighton v Nottm Forest	-	1-0	0-0	1-3	2-3	1-0

Saturday August 13, 2016

Premier League

	2010-11	2011-12	2012-13	2013-14	2014-15	2015-16
Arsenal v Liverpool	1-1	0-2	2-2	2-0	4-1	0-0
Bournemouth v Man United	-	-	-	-	-	2-1
Burnley v Swansea	2-1	-	-	-	0-1	-
Chelsea v West Ham	3-0	-	2-0	0-0	2-0	2-2
Crystal Palace v West Brom	-	-	-	3-1	0-2	2-0
Everton v Tottenham	2-1	1-0	2-1	0-0	0-1	1-1
Hull v Leicester	0-1	2-1	0-0	-	0-1	-
Man City v Sunderland	5-0	3-3	3-0	2-2	3-2	4-1
Middlesbrough v Stoke	-	-	-	-	-	-
Southampton v Watford	-	4-0	-	-	-	2-0

Championship

	2010-11	2011-12	2012-13	2013-14	2014-15	2015-16
Aston Villa v Rotherham	-	-	-	-	-	-
Barnsley v Derby	1-1	3-2	1-1	1-2	-	-
Brentford v Ipswich	-	-	-	-	2-4	2-2
Burton v Bristol City	-	-	-	-	-	-
Leeds v Birmingham	-	1-4	0-1	4-0	1-1	0-2
Newcastle v Huddersfield	-	-	-	-	-	-
Norwich v Sheffield Weds	-	-	-	-	2-0	-
Preston v Fulham	-	-	-	-	-	1-2
Wigan v Blackburn	4-3	3-3	-	2-1	1-1	-
Wolves v Reading	-	-	-	-	1-2	1-0

League One

	2010-11	2011-12	2012-13	2013-14	2014-15	2015-16
AFC Wimbledon v Bolton	-	-	-	-	-	-
Charlton v Northampton	-	-	-	-	-	-
Chesterfield v Swindon	-	-	-	-	0-3	0-4
Coventry v Shrewsbury	-	-	0-1	0-0	-	3-0
Fleetwood Town v Scunthorpe	-	-	-	0-1	2-2	2-1
Gillingham v Bury	1-1	-	-	-	-	3-1
MK Dons v Millwall	-	-	-	-	-	-
Oldham v Walsall	1-1	2-1	1-1	0-1	2-1	1-0
Peterborough v Bradford	-	-	-	2-1	2-0	0-4
Port Vale v Southend	1-1	2-3	1-2	-	-	3-1
Sheffield United v Rochdale	-	3-0	-	-	1-0	3-2

League Two

	2010-11	2011-12	2012-13	2013-14	2014-15	2015-16
Barnet v Accrington	2-0	0-0	1-1	-	-	1-2
Carlisle v Plymouth	1-1	-	-	-	2-0	0-2
Colchester v Cambridge U	-	-	-	-	-	-
Crewe v Portsmouth	-	-	1-2	-	-	-
Doncaster v Crawley Town	-	-	0-1	-	0-0	-
Exeter v Hartlepool	1-2	0-0	-	0-3	1-2	1-0
Leyton Orient v Newport County	-	-	-	-	-	1-0
Luton v Yeovil	-	-	-	-	-	1-1
Mansfield v Cheltenham	-	-	-	0-2	1-1	-
Morecambe v Blackpool	-	-	-	-	-	-
Notts County v Stevenage	-	1-0	1-2	0-1	-	1-0
Wycombe v Grimsby	-	-	-	-	-	-

Results cover matches from Premier League to National League and Scottish Premiership to League Two

	2010-11	2011-12	2012-13	2013-14	2014-15	2015-16
National League						
Aldershot v Wrexham	-	-	-	2-0	1-1	0-1
Braintree v Macclesfield	-	-	0-3	0-1	0-1	1-0
Chester v Maidstone	-	-	-	-	-	-
Dover v North Ferriby	-	-	-	-	-	-
Forest Green v Gateshead	1-1	2-1	1-0	1-0	1-1	0-1
Guiseley v Dag & Red	-	-	-	-	-	-
Lincoln v Sutton United	-	-	-	-	-	-
Solihull Moors v Bromley	-	-	-	-	-	-
Southport v Woking	-	-	1-2	1-1	2-5	2-2
Torquay v Barrow	-	-	-	-	-	2-2
Tranmere v Eastleigh	-	-	-	-	-	1-2
York v Boreham Wood	-	-	-	-	-	-
Scottish Premiership						
Aberdeen v Hearts	0-1/0-0	0-0	0-0/2-0/1-1	1-3	-	1-0/0-1
Dundee v Rangers	-	-	-	-	-	-
Hamilton v Kilmarnock	2-2/1-1	-	-	-	0-0/0-0	0-1/0-4
Inverness CT v Ross County	-	-	3-1/2-1	1-2	1-1/1-1	2-0
Motherwell v St Johnstone	4-0	0-3/3-2/5-1	1-1/3-2	4-0/2-1	0-1/1-1	2-0/1-2
Scottish Championship						
Dumbarton v Dundee United	-	-	-	-	-	-
Hibernian v Dunfermline	-	0-1/4-0	-	-	-	-
Morton v Falkirk	0-0/2-2	3-2/0-0	1-2/2-0	0-2/1-1	-	1-1/0-1
Queen of Sth v Ayr	-	4-1/2-1	2-0/2-0	-	-	-
Raith v St Mirren	-	-	-	-	-	1-1/4-3
Scottish League One						
Airdrieonians v Livingston	0-1/2-4	-	1-3/0-2	-	-	-
Albion v Brechin	-	1-2/0-1	1-2/3-1	-	-	3-1/4-1
Peterhead v East Fife	2-2/0-2	-	-	-	-	-
Stenhousemuir v Queens Park	-	-	-	-	-	-
Stranraer v Alloa	-	2-3/0-4	3-2/1-2	-	-	-
Scottish League Two						
Berwick v Annan	2-2/2-3	0-1/1-3	3-1/0-2	4-2/1-4	2-0/2-2	0-2/3-2
Elgin v Edinburgh City	-	-	-	-	-	-
Forfar v Cowdenbeath	-	2-2/1-0	-	-	-	0-1/1-1
Montrose v Arbroath	3-0/0-5	-	-	-	1-5/3-0	3-0/0-2
Stirling v Clyde	-	-	0-1/2-0	1-1/4-1	-	0-1/1-2

Sunday August 14, 2016

Championship						
Cardiff v QPR	2-2	-	-	-	-	0-0

League One						
Bristol Rovers v Oxford	-	0-0	0-2	1-1	-	0-1

Tuesday August 16, 2016

Championship						
Aston Villa v Huddersfield	-	-	-	-	-	-
Brentford v Nottm Forest	-	-	-	-	2-2	2-1
Brighton v Rotherham	-	-	-	-	1-1	2-1
Burton v Sheffield Weds	-	-	-	-	-	-
Leeds v Fulham	-	-	-	-	0-1	1-1
Norwich v Bristol City	3-1	-	-	-	-	-
Preston v Derby	1-2	-	-	-	-	1-2
Wigan v Birmingham	2-1	-	-	0-0	4-0	-
Wolves v Ipswich	-	-	0-2	-	1-1	0-0

Results cover matches from Premier League to National League and Scottish Premiership to League Two

League One

	2010-11	2011-12	2012-13	2013-14	2014-15	2015-16
AFC Wimbledon v Scunthorpe	-	-	-	3-2	-	-
Charlton v Shrewsbury	-	-	-	-	-	-
Chesterfield v Walsall	-	1-1	-	-	1-0	1-4
Coventry v Bury	-	-	2-2	-	-	6-0
Gillingham v Swindon	-	3-1	-	2-0	2-2	0-0
MK Dons v Bradford	-	-	-	2-3	1-2	-
Oldham v Northampton	-	-	-	-	-	-
Peterborough v Millwall	-	0-3	1-2	-	-	5-3
Port Vale v Rochdale	-	-	2-2	-	1-0	4-1
Sheffield United v Southend	-	-	-	-	-	2-2

League Two

	2010-11	2011-12	2012-13	2013-14	2014-15	2015-16
Barnet v Blackpool	-	-	-	-	-	-
Carlisle v Cheltenham	-	-	-	-	1-0	-
Colchester v Grimsby	-	-	-	-	-	-
Crewe v Hartlepool	-	-	2-1	-	-	-
Doncaster v Cambridge U	-	-	-	-	-	-
Exeter v Crawley Town	-	-	-	-	-	2-2
Leyton Orient v Stevenage	-	0-0	0-1	2-0	-	3-0
Luton v Newport County	1-1	2-0	2-2	-	3-0	1-1
Mansfield v Yeovil	-	-	-	-	-	0-1
Morecambe v Portsmouth	-	-	-	2-2	3-1	1-1
Notts County v Plymouth	2-0	-	-	-	-	0-2
Wycombe v Accrington	1-2	-	0-1	0-0	2-2	0-1

National League

	2010-11	2011-12	2012-13	2013-14	2014-15	2015-16
Barrow v Chester	-	-	-	-	-	3-2
Boreham Wood v Tranmere	-	-	-	-	-	0-0
Bromley v Aldershot	-	-	-	-	-	1-3
Dag & Red v Lincoln	-	-	-	-	-	-
Eastleigh v Dover	-	-	-	1-0	0-1	2-5
Gateshead v York	0-3	3-2	-	-	-	-
Macclesfield v Southport	-	-	2-2	2-2	3-0	0-0
Maidstone v Braintree	-	-	-	-	-	-
North Ferriby v Guiseley	-	-	-	-	-	-
Sutton United v Torquay	-	-	-	-	-	-
Woking v Forest Green	-	-	2-0	2-1	1-0	2-1
Wrexham v Solihull Moors	-	-	-	-	-	-

Wednesday August 17, 2016

Championship

	2010-11	2011-12	2012-13	2013-14	2014-15	2015-16
Barnsley v QPR	0-1	-	-	2-3	-	-
Cardiff v Blackburn	-	-	3-0	-	1-1	1-0
Newcastle v Reading	-	-	1-2	-	-	-

League One

	2010-11	2011-12	2012-13	2013-14	2014-15	2015-16
Bristol Rovers v Bolton	-	-	-	-	-	-
Fleetwood Town v Oxford	-	-	3-0	1-1	-	-

Saturday August 20, 2016

Premier League

	2010-11	2011-12	2012-13	2013-14	2014-15	2015-16
Leicester v Arsenal	-	-	-	-	1-1	2-5
Liverpool v Burnley	-	-	-	-	2-0	-
Man United v Southampton	-	-	2-1	1-1	0-1	0-1
Stoke v Man City	1-1	1-1	1-1	0-0	1-4	2-0
Sunderland v Middlesbrough	-	-	-	-	-	-
Swansea v Hull	1-1	-	-	1-1	3-1	-
Tottenham v Crystal Palace	-	-	-	2-0	0-0	1-0
Watford v Chelsea	-	-	-	-	-	0-0
West Brom v Everton	1-0	0-1	2-0	1-1	0-2	2-3
West Ham v Bournemouth	-	-	-	-	-	3-4

Results cover matches from Premier League to National League and Scottish Premiership to League Two

	2010-11	2011-12	2012-13	2013-14	2014-15	2015-16
Championship						
Birmingham v Wolves	1-1	-	2-3	-	2-1	0-2
Blackburn v Burton	-	-	-	-	-	-
Bristol City v Newcastle	-	-	-	-	-	-
Derby v Aston Villa	-	-	-	-	-	-
Fulham v Cardiff	-	-	-	1-2	1-1	2-1
Huddersfield v Barnsley	-	-	2-2	5-0	-	-
Nottm Forest v Wigan	-	-	-	1-4	3-0	-
QPR v Preston	3-1	-	-	-	-	0-0
Reading v Brighton	-	3-0	-	0-0	2-1	1-1
Rotherham v Brentford	-	-	-	3-0	0-2	2-1
Sheffield Weds v Leeds	-	-	1-1	6-0	1-2	2-0
League One						
Bolton v Fleetwood Town	-	-	-	-	-	-
Bradford v Coventry	-	-	-	3-3	3-2	0-0
Bury v Oldham	-	0-0	0-1	-	-	1-1
Millwall v Sheffield United	0-1	-	-	-	-	1-0
Northampton v AFC Wimbledon	-	1-0	2-0	2-2	2-0	1-1
Oxford v Peterborough	-	-	-	-	-	-
Rochdale v MK Dons	1-4	1-2	-	-	2-3	-
Scunthorpe v Gillingham	-	-	-	-	2-1	0-0
Shrewsbury v Chesterfield	0-0	-	-	-	-	1-2
Southend v Bristol Rovers	-	1-1	0-0	1-1	-	-
Swindon v Port Vale	-	5-0	-	5-2	1-0	2-2
Walsall v Charlton	2-0	1-1	-	-	-	-
League Two						
Accrington v Exeter	-	-	0-3	2-3	2-3	4-2
Blackpool v Wycombe	-	-	-	-	-	-
Cambridge U v Carlisle	-	-	-	-	5-0	0-0
Cheltenham v Doncaster	-	-	-	-	-	-
Crawley Town v Barnet	-	1-0	-	-	-	0-3
Grimsby v Leyton Orient	-	-	-	-	-	-
Hartlepool v Notts County	1-1	3-0	2-1	-	-	2-3
Newport County v Crewe	-	-	-	-	-	-
Plymouth v Mansfield	-	-	-	1-1	2-1	3-0
Portsmouth v Colchester	-	-	2-3	-	-	-
Stevenage v Luton	-	-	-	-	1-2	0-0
Yeovil v Morecambe	-	-	-	-	-	2-4
National League						
Boreham Wood v Chester	-	-	-	-	-	0-0
Braintree v Aldershot	-	-	-	1-0	1-1	1-2
Bromley v Gateshead	-	-	-	-	-	3-0
Dover v Barrow	-	-	-	-	-	3-1
Forest Green v York	2-1	1-1	-	-	-	-
Lincoln v Southport	-	2-0	1-0	1-0	1-0	3-1
North Ferriby v Torquay	-	-	-	-	-	-
Solihull Moors v Guiseley	-	-	-	0-3	0-1	-
Sutton United v Macclesfield	-	-	-	-	-	-
Tranmere v Maidstone	-	-	-	-	-	-
Woking v Dag & Red	-	-	-	-	-	-
Wrexham v Eastleigh	-	-	-	-	3-0	2-3
Scottish Premiership						
Aberdeen v Partick	-	-	-	4-0	2-0/0-0	0-0
Dundee v Hamilton	-	0-1/2-2	-	0-0/1-0	2-0/1-1	4-0/0-1
Hearts v Inverness CT	1-1	2-1	2-2/2-3	0-2	-	2-0
Rangers v Motherwell	4-1/6-0	3-0/0-0	-	-	-	-
Ross County v Kilmarnock	-	-	0-0/0-1	1-2/2-1	1-2/2-1	3-2
St Johnstone v Celtic	0-3/0-1	0-2	2-1/1-1	0-1/3-3	0-3/1-2/0-0	0-3/2-1

Results cover matches from Premier League to National League and Scottish Premiership to League Two

	2010-11	2011-12	2012-13	2013-14	2014-15	2015-16
Scottish Championship						
Dundee United v Ayr	-	-	-	-	-	-
Morton v Dumbarton	-	-	3-0/0-3	2-0/3-0	-	0-0/2-0
Queen of Sth v Falkirk	1-5/0-1	1-5/0-0	-	2-0/1-2	3-0/1-0	2-2/2-2
Raith v Dunfermline	2-0/2-1	-	1-3/1-1	-	-	-
St Mirren v Hibernian	1-0/0-1	2-3/1-0	1-2/0-1	0-0/2-0	-	1-4/2-2
Scottish League One						
Airdrieonians v Stranraer	-	-	-	3-2/1-1	3-3/1-1	0-1/1-1
Alloa v East Fife	3-2/1-3	-	1-1/1-1	-	-	-
Brechin v Queens Park	-	-	-	-	-	-
Livingston v Stenhousemuir	4-1/2-1	-	-	-	-	-
Peterhead v Albion	-	-	-	1-1/2-0	-	1-1/5-1
Scottish League Two						
Annan v Clyde	0-2/1-0	1-0/1-0	1-3/0-1	1-2/0-1	2-1/0-1	2-3/3-3
Berwick v Forfar	-	-	-	-	-	-
Cowdenbeath v Edinburgh City	-	-	-	-	-	-
Elgin v Arbroath	3-5/3-2	-	-	-	1-1/2-1	2-0/4-1
Stirling v Montrose	-	-	1-3/3-1	3-1/2-2	-	1-0/7-0

Sunday August 21, 2016

	2010-11	2011-12	2012-13	2013-14	2014-15	2015-16
Championship						
Ipswich v Norwich	1-5	-	-	-	0-1	-

Saturday August 27, 2016

	2010-11	2011-12	2012-13	2013-14	2014-15	2015-16
Premier League						
Chelsea v Burnley	-	-	-	-	1-1	-
Crystal Palace v Bournemouth	-	-	-	-	-	1-2
Everton v Stoke	1-0	0-1	1-0	4-0	0-1	3-4
Hull v Man United	-	-	-	2-3	0-0	-
Leicester v Swansea	2-1	-	-	-	2-0	4-0
Man City v West Ham	2-1	-	2-1	2-0	2-0	1-2
Southampton v Sunderland	-	-	0-1	1-1	8-0	1-1
Tottenham v Liverpool	2-1	4-0	2-1	0-5	0-3	0-0
Watford v Arsenal	-	-	-	-	-	0-3
West Brom v Middlesbrough	-	-	-	-	-	-
Championship						
Barnsley v Rotherham	-	-	-	-	-	-
Birmingham v Norwich	-	-	-	-	0-0	-
Blackburn v Fulham	1-1	3-1	-	-	2-1	3-0
Brentford v Sheffield Weds	1-0	1-2	-	-	0-0	1-2
Bristol City v Aston Villa	-	-	-	-	-	-
Burton v Derby	-	-	-	-	-	-
Cardiff v Reading	2-2	3-1	-	-	2-1	2-0
Huddersfield v Wolves	-	-	2-1	-	1-4	1-0
Ipswich v Preston	2-1	-	-	-	-	1-1
Newcastle v Brighton	-	-	-	-	-	-
Nottm Forest v Leeds	1-1	0-4	4-2	2-1	1-1	1-1
Wigan v QPR	-	2-0	2-2	0-0	-	-
League One						
Bradford v Oldham	-	-	-	2-3	2-0	1-0
Charlton v Bolton	-	-	3-2	0-0	2-1	2-2
Chesterfield v Millwall	-	-	-	-	-	1-2
Coventry v Northampton	-	-	-	-	-	-
MK Dons v Peterborough	1-0	-	-	0-2	3-0	-
Port Vale v Scunthorpe	-	-	-	-	2-2	1-1
Rochdale v AFC Wimbledon	-	-	0-1	1-2	-	-

Results cover matches from Premier League to National League and Scottish Premiership to League Two

	2010-11	2011-12	2012-13	2013-14	2014-15	2015-16
Sheffield United v Oxford	-	-	-	-	-	-
Shrewsbury v Gillingham	0-0	2-0	-	2-0	-	2-2
Southend v Fleetwood Town	-	-	1-1	2-0	-	2-2
Swindon v Bristol Rovers	2-1	0-0	-	-	-	-
Walsall v Bury	-	2-4	1-1	-	-	0-1
League Two						
Accrington v Morecambe	1-1	1-1	2-0	5-1	2-1	2-2
Barnet v Carlisle	-	-	-	-	-	0-0
Blackpool v Plymouth	-	-	-	-	-	-
Cambridge U v Luton	0-0	1-1	2-2	1-1	0-1	1-3
Cheltenham v Crewe	3-2	0-1	-	-	-	-
Crawley Town v Notts County	-	-	0-0	1-0	2-0	0-1
Doncaster v Yeovil	-	-	1-1	2-1	3-0	-
Exeter v Portsmouth	-	-	-	1-1	1-1	1-1
Grimsby v Stevenage	-	-	-	-	-	-
Hartlepool v Newport County	-	-	-	3-0	2-2	1-0
Leyton Orient v Mansfield	-	-	-	-	-	1-0
Wycombe v Colchester	-	0-0	-	-	-	-
National League						
Aldershot v North Ferriby	-	-	-	-	-	-
Barrow v Braintree	-	0-4	0-1	-	-	2-0
Chester v Sutton United	-	-	-	-	-	-
Dag & Red v Wrexham	-	-	-	-	-	-
Eastleigh v Solihull Moors	-	-	-	-	-	-
Gateshead v Boreham Wood	-	-	-	-	-	2-1
Guiseley v Bromley	-	-	-	-	-	2-0
Macclesfield v Lincoln	1-1	-	2-1	3-1	3-0	1-1
Maidstone v Forest Green	-	-	-	-	-	-
Southport v Tranmere	-	-	-	-	-	2-2
Torquay v Dover	-	-	-	-	2-0	2-3
York v Woking	-	-	-	-	-	-
Scottish Premiership						
Celtic v Aberdeen	9-0/1-0	2-1	1-0/4-3	3-1/5-2	2-1/4-0	3-1/3-2
Hamilton v Ross County	-	5-1/0-2	-	-	4-0/2-2	1-3
Inverness CT v St Johnstone	1-1/2-0	0-1	1-1/0-0	1-0/2-0	2-1/2-0	0-1
Kilmarnock v Rangers	2-3/1-5	1-0	-	-	-	-
Motherwell v Dundee	-	-	1-1	-	1-3/0-1	3-1
Partick v Hearts	-	-	-	1-1/2-4	-	0-4
Scottish Championship						
Ayr v St Mirren	-	-	-	-	-	-
Dundee United v Raith	-	-	-	-	-	-
Dunfermline v Queen of Sth	1-0/6-1	-	-	-	-	-
Falkirk v Dumbarton	-	-	3-4/1-3	1-2/2-0	1-1/3-3	2-1/1-0
Hibernian v Morton	-	-	-	-	-	1-0/0-3
Scottish League One						
Albion v Alloa	-	-	0-3/1-5	-	-	-
East Fife v Brechin	1-3/0-0	1-1/2-2	2-2/0-3	1-3/1-2	-	-
Queens Park v Livingston	-	-	-	-	-	-
Stenhousemuir v Airdrieonians	1-3/1-0	1-1/0-3	-	1-1/1-2	1-0/0-2	2-1/3-2
Stranraer v Peterhead	-	2-1/0-3	-	-	5-0/2-0	0-4/1-5
Scottish League Two						
Arbroath v Stirling	-	4-2/2-0	-	-	-	2-0/1-1
Clyde v Cowdenbeath	-	-	-	-	-	-
Edinburgh City v Berwick	-	-	-	-	-	-
Forfar v Elgin	-	-	-	-	-	-
Montrose v Annan	1-1/0-1	2-3/1-1	0-0/5-1	0-2/2-1	2-0/2-1	1-1/0-5

Results cover matches from Premier League to National League and Scottish Premiership to League Two

	2010-11	2011-12	2012-13	2013-14	2014-15	2015-16

Monday August 29, 2016

National League

	2010-11	2011-12	2012-13	2013-14	2014-15	2015-16
Boreham Wood v Maidstone	-	-	-	-	-	-
Braintree v Torquay	-	-	-	-	2-0	0-0
Bromley v Eastleigh	-	-	-	1-2	-	2-2
Dover v Aldershot	-	-	-	-	3-0	5-2
Forest Green v Southport	0-0	2-3	0-1	3-1	5-3	2-1
Lincoln v Gateshead	-	1-0	1-1	0-1	1-1	1-1
North Ferriby v Barrow	-	-	-	-	-	-
Solihull Moors v Macclesfield	-	-	-	-	-	-
Sutton United v Dag & Red	-	-	-	-	-	-
Tranmere v Guiseley	-	-	-	-	-	2-1
Woking v Chester	-	-	-	0-1	1-0	5-2
Wrexham v York	1-1	0-3	-	-	-	-

Saturday September 3, 2016

League One

	2010-11	2011-12	2012-13	2013-14	2014-15	2015-16
AFC Wimbledon v Chesterfield	-	-	1-0	1-1	-	-
Bolton v Southend	-	-	-	-	-	-
Bristol Rovers v Walsall	2-2	-	-	-	-	-
Bury v Port Vale	0-1	-	-	-	-	1-0
Fleetwood Town v Coventry	-	-	-	-	0-2	0-1
Gillingham v Sheffield United	-	-	-	0-1	2-0	4-0
Millwall v Bradford	-	-	-	-	-	0-0
Northampton v MK Dons	-	-	-	-	-	-
Oldham v Shrewsbury	-	-	1-0	1-2	-	1-1
Oxford v Rochdale	-	-	3-0	1-1	-	-
Peterborough v Swindon	5-4	-	-	1-0	1-2	1-2
Scunthorpe v Charlton	-	1-1	-	-	-	-

League Two

	2010-11	2011-12	2012-13	2013-14	2014-15	2015-16
Carlisle v Accrington	-	-	-	-	1-0	2-0
Colchester v Exeter	5-1	2-0	-	-	-	-
Crewe v Doncaster	-	-	1-2	-	1-1	3-1
Luton v Wycombe	-	-	-	-	2-3	0-2
Mansfield v Cambridge U	1-0	1-2	3-1	-	0-0	0-0
Morecambe v Leyton Orient	-	-	-	-	-	0-1
Newport County v Barnet	-	-	-	-	-	0-3
Notts County v Grimsby	-	-	-	-	-	-
Plymouth v Cheltenham	-	1-2	2-0	1-1	3-0	-
Portsmouth v Crawley Town	-	-	1-2	-	-	3-0
Stevenage v Hartlepool	-	2-2	1-0	-	1-0	2-0
Yeovil v Blackpool	-	-	-	1-0	-	-

National League

	2010-11	2011-12	2012-13	2013-14	2014-15	2015-16
Aldershot v Tranmere	-	-	-	-	-	0-0
Barrow v Bromley	-	-	-	-	-	1-1
Chester v Forest Green	-	-	-	1-2	1-4	1-2
Dag & Red v Boreham Wood	-	-	-	-	-	-
Eastleigh v North Ferriby	-	-	-	-	-	-
Gateshead v Sutton United	-	-	-	-	-	-
Guiseley v Braintree	-	-	-	-	-	1-1
Macclesfield v Woking	-	-	0-0	3-2	2-1	2-1
Maidstone v Wrexham	-	-	-	-	-	-
Southport v Dover	-	-	-	-	2-2	0-0
Torquay v Lincoln	2-0	-	-	-	1-0	1-3
York v Solihull Moors	-	-	-	-	-	-

Results cover matches from Premier League to National League and Scottish Premiership to League Two

Saturday September 10, 2016

Premier League					
Arsenal v Southampton	-	-	6-1	2-0	1-0	0-0
Bournemouth v West Brom	-	-	-	-	-	1-1
Burnley v Hull	4-0	1-0	0-1	-	1-0	1-0
Liverpool v Leicester	-	-	-	-	2-2	1-0
Man United v Man City	2-1	1-6	1-2	0-3	4-2	0-0
Middlesbrough v Crystal Palace	2-1	0-0	2-1	-	-	-
Stoke v Tottenham	1-2	2-1	1-2	0-1	3-0	0-4
Sunderland v Everton	2-2	1-1	1-0	0-1	1-1	3-0
Swansea v Chelsea	-	1-1	1-1	0-1	0-5	1-0
West Ham v Watford	-	1-1	-	-	-	3-1

Championship					
Aston Villa v Nottm Forest	-	-	-	-	-	-
Brighton v Brentford	1-0	-	-	-	0-1	3-0
Derby v Newcastle	-	-	-	-	-	-
Fulham v Birmingham	1-1	-	-	-	1-1	2-5
Leeds v Huddersfield	-	-	1-2	5-1	3-0	1-4
Norwich v Cardiff	1-1	-	-	0-0	3-2	-
Preston v Barnsley	1-2	-	-	-	1-0	-
QPR v Blackburn	-	1-1	-	0-0	-	2-2
Reading v Ipswich	1-0	1-0	-	2-1	1-0	5-1
Rotherham v Bristol City	-	-	-	2-1	-	3-0
Sheffield Weds v Wigan	-	-	-	0-3	2-1	-
Wolves v Burton	-	-	-	-	-	-

League One					
AFC Wimbledon v Sheffield United	-	-	-	-	-	-
Bolton v MK Dons	-	-	-	-	-	3-1
Bristol Rovers v Rochdale	2-1	-	2-1	1-2	-	-
Bury v Shrewsbury	1-0	-	2-2	-	1-0	2-2
Fleetwood Town v Charlton	-	-	-	-	-	-
Gillingham v Bradford	2-0	0-0	3-1	0-1	1-0	3-0
Millwall v Coventry	3-1	3-0	-	-	-	0-4
Northampton v Walsall	-	-	-	-	-	-
Oldham v Chesterfield	-	5-2	-	-	0-0	1-0
Oxford v Swindon	-	2-0	-	-	-	-
Peterborough v Port Vale	-	-	-	0-0	3-1	2-3
Scunthorpe v Southend	-	-	-	2-2	-	1-0

League Two					
Carlisle v Leyton Orient	0-1	4-1	1-4	1-5	-	2-2
Colchester v Blackpool	-	-	-	-	-	2-2
Crewe v Exeter	-	-	-	-	-	-
Luton v Grimsby	1-0	1-1	1-1	0-0	-	-
Mansfield v Barnet	-	-	-	-	-	1-1
Morecambe v Doncaster	-	-	-	-	-	-
Newport County v Cheltenham	-	-	-	0-1	1-1	-
Notts County v Accrington	-	-	-	-	-	1-1
Plymouth v Cambridge U	-	-	-	-	2-0	1-2
Portsmouth v Wycombe	-	-	-	2-2	1-1	2-1
Stevenage v Crawley Town	-	-	1-2	2-0	-	0-1
Yeovil v Hartlepool	0-2	0-1	1-0	-	-	1-2

Results cover matches from Premier League to National League and Scottish Premiership to League Two

National League

	2010-11	2011-12	2012-13	2013-14	2014-15	2015-16
Aldershot v Chester	-	-	-	2-0	0-1	3-1
Barrow v Boreham Wood	-	-	-	-	-	0-0
Braintree v Gateshead	-	3-1	2-1	0-0	1-0	0-0
Bromley v Macclesfield	-	-	-	-	-	1-0
Dover v Forest Green	-	-	-	-	0-0	0-1
Eastleigh v Southport	-	-	-	-	2-1	1-0
Guiseley v Woking	-	-	-	-	-	4-4
North Ferriby v Maidstone	-	-	-	-	-	-
Solihull Moors v Dag & Red	-	-	-	-	-	-
Torquay v York	-	-	2-1	0-3	-	-
Tranmere v Lincoln	-	-	-	-	-	3-2
Wrexham v Sutton United	-	-	-	-	-	-

Scottish Premiership

	2010-11	2011-12	2012-13	2013-14	2014-15	2015-16
Aberdeen v Inverness CT	1-2/1-0	2-1/0-1	2-3	1-0/0-1	3-2/1-0	2-2
Celtic v Rangers	1-3/3-0	1-0/3-0	-	-	-	-
Dundee v Kilmarnock	-	-	0-0/2-3	-	1-1/1-0	1-2/1-1
Hearts v Hamilton	2-0	-	-	-	-	2-0
Partick v St Johnstone	-	-	-	0-1	0-0/3-0	2-0
Ross County v Motherwell	-	-	0-0/3-0	1-2	1-2/3-2	3-0/1-3

Scottish Championship

	2010-11	2011-12	2012-13	2013-14	2014-15	2015-16
Ayr v Morton	-	0-1/0-0	-	-	1-0/1-1	-
Dumbarton v Hibernian	-	-	-	-	3-6/1-2	2-1/3-2
Dunfermline v Dundee United	-	1-4	-	-	-	-
Raith v Falkirk	2-1/1-2	1-0/2-2	2-1/0-0	1-1/2-4	0-0/2-2	1-2/2-2
St Mirren v Queen of Sth	-	-	-	-	-	1-0/2-1

Scottish League One

	2010-11	2011-12	2012-13	2013-14	2014-15	2015-16
Albion v Stenhousemuir	-	1-1/1-0	4-4/4-3	-	-	2-0/1-1
Alloa v Livingston	2-2/1-3	-	-	1-0/0-3	1-0/2-2	0-3/1-3
Brechin v Airdrieonians	3-1/1-2	1-1/1-1	-	4-3/1-1	1-1/0-0	1-2/3-3
East Fife v Stranraer	-	-	0-1/1-1	1-2/1-1	-	-
Peterhead v Queens Park	-	1-1/2-1	1-0/0-2	2-1/1-0	-	-

Scottish League Two

	2010-11	2011-12	2012-13	2013-14	2014-15	2015-16
Annan v Forfar	-	-	-	-	-	-
Berwick v Elgin	6-2/4-0	1-1/3-3	0-0/2-1	2-3/2-3	1-1/0-2	2-3/2-0
Clyde v Arbroath	1-1/0-3	-	-	-	2-5/1-1	0-2/1-2
Montrose v Cowdenbeath	-	-	-	-	-	-
Stirling v Edinburgh City	-	-	-	-	-	-

Tuesday September 13, 2016

Championship

	2010-11	2011-12	2012-13	2013-14	2014-15	2015-16
Aston Villa v Brentford	-	-	-	-	-	-
Brighton v Huddersfield	2-3	-	4-1	0-0	0-0	2-1
Derby v Ipswich	1-2	0-0	0-1	4-4	1-1	0-1
Fulham v Burton	-	-	-	-	-	-
Leeds v Blackburn	-	-	3-3	1-2	0-3	0-2
Norwich v Wigan	-	1-1	2-1	-	0-1	-
Preston v Cardiff	0-1	-	-	-	-	0-0
QPR v Newcastle	-	0-0	1-2	-	2-1	-
Reading v Birmingham	-	1-0	-	2-0	0-1	0-2
Rotherham v Nottm Forest	-	-	-	-	0-0	0-0
Sheffield Weds v Bristol City	-	-	2-3	-	-	2-0
Wolves v Barnsley	-	-	3-1	-	-	-

Results cover matches from Premier League to National League and Scottish Premiership to League Two

	2010-11	2011-12	2012-13	2013-14	2014-15	2015-16
National League						
Boreham Wood v Aldershot	-	-	-	-	-	0-1
Chester v Guiseley	-	-	-	-	-	1-1
Dag & Red v Dover	-	-	-	-	-	-
Forest Green v Eastleigh	-	-	-	-	1-1	2-1
Gateshead v North Ferriby	-	-	-	-	-	-
Lincoln v Solihull Moors	-	-	-	-	-	-
Macclesfield v Wrexham	-	-	2-0	3-2	2-2	0-0
Maidstone v Bromley	-	-	-	-	-	-
Southport v Barrow	2-4	2-1	5-2	-	-	2-1
Sutton United v Braintree	-	-	-	-	-	-
Woking v Torquay	-	-	-	-	3-2	2-2
York v Tranmere	-	-	-	-	2-0	-

Saturday September 17, 2016

	2010-11	2011-12	2012-13	2013-14	2014-15	2015-16
Premier League						
Chelsea v Liverpool	0-1	1-2	1-1	2-1	1-1	1-3
Crystal Palace v Stoke	-	-	-	1-0	1-1	2-1
Everton v Middlesbrough	-	-	-	-	-	-
Hull v Arsenal	-	-	-	0-3	1-3	-
Leicester v Burnley	4-0	0-0	2-1	1-1	2-2	-
Man City v Bournemouth	-	-	-	-	-	5-1
Southampton v Swansea	-	-	1-1	2-0	0-1	3-1
Tottenham v Sunderland	1-1	1-0	1-0	5-1	2-1	4-1
Watford v Man United	-	-	-	-	-	1-2
West Brom v West Ham	3-3	-	0-0	1-0	1-2	0-3
Championship						
Barnsley v Reading	0-1	0-4	-	1-1	-	-
Birmingham v Sheffield Weds	-	-	0-0	4-1	0-2	1-2
Blackburn v Rotherham	-	-	-	-	2-1	1-0
Brentford v Preston	-	1-3	1-0	1-0	-	2-1
Bristol City v Derby	2-0	1-1	0-2	-	-	2-3
Burton v Brighton	-	-	-	-	-	-
Cardiff v Leeds	2-1	1-1	2-1	-	3-1	0-2
Huddersfield v QPR	-	-	-	1-1	-	0-1
Ipswich v Aston Villa	-	-	-	-	-	-
Newcastle v Wolves	4-1	2-2	-	-	-	-
Nottm Forest v Norwich	1-1	-	-	-	2-1	-
Wigan v Fulham	1-1	0-2	1-2	-	3-3	-
League One						
Bradford v Bristol Rovers	-	2-2	4-1	-	-	-
Charlton v AFC Wimbledon	-	-	-	-	-	-
Chesterfield v Northampton	2-1	-	3-0	0-0	-	-
Coventry v Oldham	-	-	2-1	1-1	1-1	1-1
MK Dons v Oxford	-	-	-	-	-	-
Port Vale v Gillingham	0-0	2-1	0-2	2-1	2-1	1-1
Rochdale v Fleetwood Town	-	-	0-0	1-2	0-2	1-0
Sheffield United v Peterborough	-	-	-	2-0	1-2	2-3
Shrewsbury v Scunthorpe	-	-	0-1	-	-	2-2
Southend v Millwall	-	-	-	-	-	0-4
Swindon v Bury	-	-	0-1	-	-	0-1
Walsall v Bolton	-	-	-	-	-	-
League Two						
Accrington v Portsmouth	-	-	-	2-2	1-1	1-3
Barnet v Colchester	-	-	-	-	-	-
Blackpool v Carlisle	-	-	-	-	-	-
Cambridge U v Morecambe	-	-	-	-	1-2	7-0

Results cover matches from Premier League to National League and Scottish Premiership to League Two

	2010-11	2011-12	2012-13	2013-14	2014-15	2015-16
Cheltenham v Notts County	-	-	-	-	-	-
Crawley Town v Luton	1-1	-	-	-	-	2-1
Doncaster v Newport County	-	-	-	-	-	-
Exeter v Plymouth	1-0	-	1-1	3-1	1-3	2-1
Grimsby v Crewe	-	-	-	-	-	-
Hartlepool v Mansfield	-	-	-	2-4	1-0	2-1
Leyton Orient v Yeovil	1-5	2-2	4-1	-	3-0	1-1
Wycombe v Stevenage	0-1	0-1	-	-	2-2	1-0
National League						
Boreham Wood v Torquay	-	-	-	-	-	0-1
Chester v Braintree	-	-	-	0-2	2-3	1-0
Dag & Red v North Ferriby	-	-	-	-	-	-
Forest Green v Bromley	-	-	-	-	-	2-1
Gateshead v Solihull Moors	-	-	-	-	-	-
Lincoln v Barrow	-	2-1	0-0	-	-	2-2
Macclesfield v Eastleigh	-	-	-	-	2-0	1-2
Maidstone v Guiseley	-	-	-	-	-	-
Southport v Aldershot	-	-	-	1-0	1-3	1-1
Sutton United v Tranmere	-	-	-	-	-	-
Woking v Wrexham	-	-	2-0	2-1	1-1	0-1
York v Dover	-	-	-	-	-	-
Scottish Premiership						
Dundee v Aberdeen	-	-	1-3/1-1	-	2-3/1-1/1-1	0-2
Inverness CT v Celtic	0-1/3-2	0-2	2-4/1-3	0-1	1-0/1-1	1-3
Kilmarnock v Partick	-	-	-	2-1/1-2	3-0/2-2	2-5/0-2
Motherwell v Hamilton	0-1/1-0	-	-	-	0-4/4-0	3-3
Rangers v Ross County	-	-	-	-	-	-
St Johnstone v Hearts	0-2	2-0/2-1	2-2	1-0/3-3	-	0-0
Scottish Championship						
Dumbarton v St Mirren	-	-	-	-	-	1-0/2-1
Falkirk v Dundee United	-	-	-	-	-	-
Hibernian v Ayr	-	-	-	-	-	-
Morton v Dunfermline	2-1/0-2	-	4-2/0-1	-	2-1/2-0	-
Queen of Sth v Raith	1-3/0-2	1-3/1-0	-	0-1/1-0	2-0/2-1	1-1/1-2
Scottish League One						
Airdrieonians v East Fife	1-1/2-2	1-3/2-0	-	1-3/2-1	-	-
Livingston v Brechin	2-0/0-0	-	-	-	-	-
Queens Park v Alloa	-	1-3/1-2	-	-	-	-
Stenhousemuir v Peterhead	3-1/4-2	-	-	-	1-2/2-1	4-3/1-4
Stranraer v Albion	3-2/1-3	-	1-1/3-2	-	-	0-1/0-0
Scottish League Two						
Arbroath v Annan	0-2/2-1	-	-	-	3-2/1-1	0-2/2-1
Cowdenbeath v Berwick	-	-	-	-	-	-
Edinburgh City v Montrose	-	-	-	-	-	-
Elgin v Clyde	0-1/0-1	0-3/1-1	2-1/4-2	1-0/3-1	1-0/2-0	1-1/1-0
Forfar v Stirling	-	2-2/4-3	-	-	2-1/4-0	-

Saturday September 24, 2016

Premier League						
Arsenal v Chelsea	3-1	0-0	1-2	0-0	0-0	0-1
Bournemouth v Everton	-	-	-	-	-	3-3
Burnley v Watford	3-2	2-2	1-1	0-0	-	-
Liverpool v Hull	-	-	-	2-0	0-0	-
Man United v Leicester	-	-	-	-	3-1	1-1
Middlesbrough v Tottenham	-	-	-	-	-	-
Stoke v West Brom	1-1	1-2	0-0	0-0	2-0	0-1
Sunderland v Crystal Palace	-	-	-	0-0	1-4	2-2
Swansea v Man City	-	1-0	0-0	2-3	2-4	1-1
West Ham v Southampton	-	1-1	4-1	3-1	1-3	2-1

Results cover matches from Premier League to National League and Scottish Premiership to League Two

	2010-11	2011-12	2012-13	2013-14	2014-15	2015-16
Championship						
Aston Villa v Newcastle	1-0	1-1	1-2	1-2	0-0	0-0
Brighton v Barnsley	-	2-0	5-1	1-2	-	-
Derby v Blackburn	-	-	1-1	1-1	2-0	1-0
Fulham v Bristol City	-	-	-	-	-	1-2
Leeds v Ipswich	0-0	3-1	2-0	1-1	2-1	0-1
Norwich v Burton	-	-	-	-	-	-
Preston v Wigan	-	-	-	-	-	-
QPR v Birmingham	-	-	-	1-0	-	2-0
Reading v Huddersfield	-	-	-	1-1	1-2	2-2
Rotherham v Cardiff	-	-	-	-	1-3	2-1
Sheffield Weds v Nottm Forest	-	-	0-1	0-1	0-1	1-0
Wolves v Brentford	-	-	-	0-0	2-1	0-2
League One						
AFC Wimbledon v Shrewsbury	-	3-1	-	-	2-2	-
Bolton v Bradford	-	-	-	-	-	-
Bristol Rovers v Port Vale	-	0-3	2-0	-	-	-
Bury v Chesterfield	1-1	1-1	-	0-2	-	1-0
Fleetwood Town v MK Dons	-	-	-	-	0-3	-
Gillingham v Coventry	-	-	-	4-2	3-1	0-0
Millwall v Rochdale	-	-	-	-	-	3-1
Northampton v Southend	2-1	2-5	3-3	2-1	1-1	-
Oldham v Swindon	2-0	-	0-2	2-1	2-1	2-0
Oxford v Charlton	-	-	-	-	-	-
Peterborough v Walsall	4-1	-	-	0-0	0-0	1-1
Scunthorpe v Sheffield United	3-2	1-1	1-1	-	1-1	0-1
League Two						
Carlisle v Wycombe	-	2-2	-	-	2-3	1-1
Colchester v Accrington	-	-	-	-	-	-
Crewe v Blackpool	-	-	-	-	-	1-2
Luton v Doncaster	-	-	-	-	-	-
Mansfield v Grimsby	0-2	2-1	2-0	-	-	-
Morecambe v Crawley Town	-	6-0	-	-	-	3-1
Newport County v Cambridge U	1-1	0-1	6-2	-	1-1	0-1
Notts County v Leyton Orient	3-2	1-2	1-1	0-0	1-1	0-1
Plymouth v Hartlepool	0-1	-	-	1-1	2-0	5-0
Portsmouth v Barnet	-	-	-	-	-	3-1
Stevenage v Exeter	-	0-0	-	-	1-0	0-2
Yeovil v Cheltenham	-	-	-	-	-	-
National League						
Aldershot v Gateshead	-	-	-	1-2	1-2	1-2
Barrow v York	0-0	0-0	-	-	-	-
Braintree v Forest Green	-	1-5	3-1	1-1	1-2	1-1
Bromley v Dag & Red	-	-	-	-	-	-
Dover v Lincoln	-	-	-	-	1-2	4-1
Eastleigh v Sutton United	-	-	-	-	-	-
Guiseley v Macclesfield	-	-	-	-	-	0-3
North Ferriby v Southport	-	-	-	-	-	-
Solihull Moors v Boreham Wood	-	-	-	-	-	-
Torquay v Maidstone	-	-	-	-	-	-
Tranmere v Woking	-	-	-	-	-	1-0
Wrexham v Chester	-	-	-	0-2	1-0	3-0
Scottish Premiership						
Aberdeen v Rangers	2-3/0-1	1-2	-	-	-	-
Celtic v Kilmarnock	1-1	2-1	0-2/4-1	4-0	2-0/4-1	0-0
Hamilton v St Johnstone	1-2/0-0	-	-	-	1-0/1-1	2-4
Hearts v Ross County	-	-	2-2/4-2	2-2/2-0	-	2-0/1-1
Inverness CT v Dundee	-	-	4-1	-	0-0/1-1	1-1/4-0
Partick v Motherwell	-	-	-	1-5	3-1/2-0	1-0

Results cover matches from Premier League to National League and Scottish Premiership to League Two

Scottish Championship						
Dundee United v Morton	-	-	-	-	-	-
Dunfermline v St Mirren	-	0-0/1-1	-	-	-	-
Falkirk v Ayr	-	0-0/3-2	-	-	-	-
Queen of Sth v Hibernian	-	-	-	-	1-0/0-2	0-3/1-0
Raith v Dumbarton	-	-	2-2/3-2	2-1/1-3	3-1/2-1	1-0/0-0

Scottish League One						
Airdrieonians v Albion	-	4-0/1-0	-	-	-	1-1/1-1
Brechin v Peterhead	4-2/3-1	-	-	-	1-1/2-2	1-1/5-1
East Fife v Livingston	2-4/1-3	-	-	-	-	-
Queens Park v Stranraer	1-3/3-3	2-0/3-2	-	-	-	-
Stenhousemuir v Alloa	0-1/2-3	-	0-2/1-1	-	-	-

Scottish League Two						
Annan v Edinburgh City	-	-	-	-	-	-
Arbroath v Cowdenbeath	-	1-1/1-1	-	-	-	-
Clyde v Forfar	-	-	-	-	-	-
Montrose v Berwick	1-1/1-1	3-5/1-1	3-1/1-3	1-1/0-0	2-1/0-2	4-1/1-0
Stirling v Elgin	-	-	1-4/1-1	1-1/2-2	-	3-1/0-0

Tuesday September 27, 2016

Championship						
Barnsley v Aston Villa	-	-	-	-	-	-
Birmingham v Preston	-	-	-	-	-	2-2
Blackburn v Sheffield Weds	-	-	1-0	0-0	1-2	2-2
Brentford v Reading	-	-	-	-	3-1	1-3
Bristol City v Leeds	0-2	0-3	2-3	-	-	2-2
Burton v QPR	-	-	-	-	-	-
Cardiff v Derby	4-1	2-0	1-1	-	0-2	2-1
Huddersfield v Rotherham	-	-	-	-	0-2	2-0
Ipswich v Brighton	-	3-1	0-3	2-0	2-0	2-3
Nottm Forest v Fulham	-	-	-	-	5-3	3-0
Wigan v Wolves	2-0	3-2	-	-	0-1	-

League One						
Bradford v Fleetwood Town	-	-	1-0	-	2-2	2-1
Charlton v Oldham	1-1	1-1	-	-	-	-
Chesterfield v Gillingham	3-1	-	0-1	-	3-0	1-3
MK Dons v Bury	-	2-1	1-1	-	-	-
Port Vale v Millwall	-	-	-	-	-	0-2
Rochdale v Bolton	-	-	-	-	-	-
Sheffield United v Bristol Rovers	-	-	-	-	-	-
Shrewsbury v Peterborough	-	-	-	2-4	-	3-4
Southend v Oxford	2-1	2-1	1-0	3-0	1-1	-
Swindon v Northampton	-	1-0	-	-	-	-
Walsall v Scunthorpe	-	2-2	1-4	-	1-4	0-0

League Two						
Accrington v Mansfield	-	-	-	1-1	2-1	1-0
Barnet v Morecambe	1-2	0-2	4-1	-	-	0-0
Blackpool v Portsmouth	-	1-1	-	-	-	-
Cambridge U v Yeovil	-	-	-	-	-	3-0
Cheltenham v Stevenage	1-0	-	-	-	0-1	-
Crawley Town v Colchester	-	-	3-0	1-0	0-0	-
Doncaster v Carlisle	-	-	0-2	-	-	-
Exeter v Notts County	3-1	1-1	-	-	-	1-1
Grimsby v Newport County	2-0	2-2	3-0	-	-	-
Hartlepool v Luton	-	-	-	-	1-2	1-4
Leyton Orient v Plymouth	2-0	-	-	-	-	1-3
Wycombe v Crewe	2-0	-	-	-	-	-

Results cover matches from Premier League to National League and Scottish Premiership to League Two

Wednesday September 28, 2016

Championship

	2010-11	2011-12	2012-13	2013-14	2014-15	2015-16
Newcastle v Norwich	-	1-0	1-0	2-1	-	6-2

League One

	2010-11	2011-12	2012-13	2013-14	2014-15	2015-16
Coventry v AFC Wimbledon	-	-	-	-	-	-

Saturday October 1, 2016

Premier League

	2010-11	2011-12	2012-13	2013-14	2014-15	2015-16
Burnley v Arsenal	-	-	-	-	0-1	-
Everton v Crystal Palace	-	-	-	2-3	2-3	1-1
Hull v Chelsea	-	-	-	0-2	2-3	-
Leicester v Southampton	-	3-2	-	-	2-0	1-0
Man United v Stoke	2-1	2-0	4-2	3-2	2-1	3-0
Sunderland v West Brom	2-3	2-2	2-4	2-0	0-0	0-0
Swansea v Liverpool	-	1-0	0-0	2-2	0-1	3-1
Tottenham v Man City	0-0	1-5	3-1	1-5	0-1	4-1
Watford v Bournemouth	-	-	-	6-1	1-1	0-0
West Ham v Middlesbrough	-	1-1	-	-	-	-

Championship

	2010-11	2011-12	2012-13	2013-14	2014-15	2015-16
Birmingham v Blackburn	2-1	-	1-1	2-4	2-2	0-0
Brentford v Wigan	-	-	-	-	3-0	-
Bristol City v Nottm Forest	2-3	0-0	2-0	-	-	2-0
Burton v Cardiff	-	-	-	-	-	-
Fulham v QPR	-	6-0	3-2	-	-	4-0
Ipswich v Huddersfield	-	-	2-2	2-1	2-2	0-0
Leeds v Barnsley	3-3	1-2	1-0	0-0	-	-
Preston v Aston Villa	-	-	-	-	-	-
Reading v Derby	2-1	2-2	-	0-0	0-3	0-1
Rotherham v Newcastle	-	-	-	-	-	-
Sheffield Weds v Brighton	1-0	-	3-1	1-0	0-0	0-0
Wolves v Norwich	-	2-2	-	-	1-0	-

League One

	2010-11	2011-12	2012-13	2013-14	2014-15	2015-16
AFC Wimbledon v Gillingham	-	3-1	0-1	-	-	-
Bolton v Oxford	-	-	-	-	-	-
Bury v Scunthorpe	-	0-0	2-1	2-2	-	1-2
Charlton v Rochdale	3-1	1-1	-	-	-	-
Chesterfield v Bradford	2-2	-	2-2	-	0-1	0-1
Fleetwood Town v Sheffield United	-	-	-	-	1-1	2-2
Northampton v Bristol Rovers	-	3-2	1-0	0-0	-	2-2
Oldham v MK Dons	1-2	2-1	3-1	1-2	1-3	-
Port Vale v Coventry	-	-	-	3-2	0-2	1-1
Shrewsbury v Swindon	-	2-1	0-1	2-0	-	0-1
Southend v Peterborough	-	-	-	-	-	2-1
Walsall v Millwall	-	-	-	-	-	0-3

League Two

	2010-11	2011-12	2012-13	2013-14	2014-15	2015-16
Barnet v Leyton Orient	-	-	-	-	-	3-0
Cambridge U v Accrington	-	-	-	-	2-2	2-3
Carlisle v Colchester	4-1	1-0	0-2	2-4	-	-
Cheltenham v Luton	-	-	-	-	1-1	-
Crawley Town v Blackpool	-	-	-	-	-	-
Crewe v Mansfield	-	-	-	-	-	-
Grimsby v Hartlepool	-	-	-	-	-	-
Newport County v Stevenage	-	-	-	-	2-0	2-2
Notts County v Morecambe	-	-	-	-	-	2-2
Plymouth v Yeovil	0-0	-	-	-	-	1-0
Portsmouth v Doncaster	2-3	3-1	0-1	-	-	-
Wycombe v Exeter	-	3-1	0-1	1-1	2-1	1-0

Results cover matches from Premier League to National League and Scottish Premiership to League Two

	2010-11	2011-12	2012-13	2013-14	2014-15	2015-16
National League						
Boreham Wood v Wrexham	-	-	-	-	-	0-1
Chester v Dover	-	-	-	-	3-1	1-1
Dag & Red v Tranmere	2-2	-	-	-	0-1	-
Forest Green v Barrow	2-3	3-0	1-1	-	-	4-0
Gateshead v Torquay	-	-	-	-	3-1	1-2
Lincoln v Braintree	-	3-3	3-0	2-0	3-2	2-0
Macclesfield v North Ferriby	-	-	-	-	-	-
Maidstone v Solihull Moors	-	-	-	-	-	-
Southport v Bromley	-	-	-	-	-	5-3
Sutton United v Guiseley	-	-	-	-	-	-
Woking v Eastleigh	-	-	-	-	1-1	2-1
York v Aldershot	-	-	0-0	-	-	-
Scottish Premiership						
Dundee v Celtic	-	-	0-2	-	1-1/1-2	0-0
Hamilton v Inverness CT	1-3/1-2	-	-	-	0-2/0-2	3-4/0-1
Kilmarnock v Aberdeen	2-0	2-0/1-1	1-3/1-1	0-1	0-2/1-2	0-4
Motherwell v Hearts	1-2	1-0/3-0	0-0	2-1/4-1	-	2-2/1-0
Rangers v Partick	-	-	-	-	-	-
Ross County v St Johnstone	-	-	1-2/1-0	1-0	1-2/1-0	2-3/0-1
Scottish Championship						
Ayr v Dunfermline	-	-	-	2-4/1-1	0-1/0-2	1-2/0-2
Dumbarton v Queen of Sth	-	-	-	0-1/0-3	0-4/0-0	0-2/4-2
Hibernian v Dundee United	2-2	3-3/0-2	2-1	1-1/1-3	-	-
Morton v Raith	0-1/0-0	1-1/1-3	1-0/1-0	1-1/0-0	-	1-2/0-1
St Mirren v Falkirk	-	-	-	-	-	2-3/0-0
Scottish League One						
Albion v Queens Park	2-1/1-2	-	-	2-1/1-0	1-0/2-1	-
Alloa v Airdrieonians	2-3/1-0	-	-	-	-	-
East Fife v Stenhousemuir	6-0/1-1	1-3/1-1	3-2/1-2	1-0/1-2	-	-
Peterhead v Livingston	0-0/3-0	-	-	-	-	-
Stranraer v Brechin	-	-	0-2/3-2	3-0/1-2	2-2/0-2	1-0/2-0
Scottish League Two						
Berwick v Clyde	2-1/1-1	0-2/3-0	2-1/3-3	0-1/3-0	4-0/0-0	0-5/3-0
Cowdenbeath v Stirling	5-1/1-0	2-0/4-1	-	-	-	-
Edinburgh City v Arbroath	-	-	-	-	-	-
Elgin v Annan	2-0/2-3	3-0/1-2	2-2/3-1	2-3/2-3	0-0/4-5	3-2/2-2
Forfar v Montrose	-	-	-	-	-	-

Tuesday October 4, 2016

	2010-11	2011-12	2012-13	2013-14	2014-15	2015-16
National League						
Aldershot v Forest Green	-	-	-	2-2	1-1	0-3
Barrow v Macclesfield	-	-	1-0	-	-	1-1
Braintree v Boreham Wood	-	-	-	-	-	0-2
Bromley v Woking	-	-	-	-	-	2-1
Dover v Sutton United	-	-	-	-	-	-
Eastleigh v Maidstone	-	-	-	-	-	-
Guiseley v York	-	-	-	-	-	-
North Ferriby v Chester	-	-	-	-	-	-
Solihull Moors v Southport	-	-	-	-	-	-
Torquay v Dag & Red	-	1-0	2-1	0-1	-	-
Tranmere v Gateshead	-	-	-	-	-	3-1
Wrexham v Lincoln	-	2-0	2-4	0-1	1-1	3-1

Results cover matches from Premier League to National League and Scottish Premiership to League Two

Saturday October 8, 2016

League One

	2010-11	2011-12	2012-13	2013-14	2014-15	2015-16
Bradford v Shrewsbury	1-2	3-1	-	2-1	-	1-1
Bristol Rovers v Fleetwood Town	-	-	0-0	1-3	-	-
Coventry v Chesterfield	-	-	-	-	0-0	1-0
Gillingham v Oldham	-	-	-	0-1	3-2	3-3
Millwall v Charlton	-	-	0-0	0-0	2-1	-
MK Dons v Port Vale	-	-	-	3-0	1-0	-
Oxford v AFC Wimbledon	-	1-0	3-2	2-1	0-0	1-0
Peterborough v Bury	-	-	-	-	-	2-3
Rochdale v Southend	-	-	4-2	0-3	-	4-1
Scunthorpe v Northampton	-	-	-	1-1	-	-
Sheffield United v Walsall	-	3-2	1-0	1-1	1-1	2-0
Swindon v Bolton	-	-	-	-	-	-

League Two

	2010-11	2011-12	2012-13	2013-14	2014-15	2015-16
Accrington v Cheltenham	2-4	0-1	2-2	0-1	1-1	-
Blackpool v Cambridge U	-	-	-	-	-	-
Colchester v Newport County	-	-	-	-	-	-
Doncaster v Barnet	-	-	-	-	-	-
Exeter v Grimsby	-	-	-	-	-	-
Hartlepool v Crawley Town	-	-	0-1	-	-	1-2
Leyton Orient v Portsmouth	-	-	1-0	-	-	3-2
Luton v Crewe	-	-	-	-	-	-
Mansfield v Notts County	-	-	-	-	-	5-0
Morecambe v Carlisle	-	-	-	-	0-1	1-2
Stevenage v Plymouth	-	-	-	-	1-0	2-1
Yeovil v Wycombe	-	1-0	-	-	-	0-1

National League

	2010-11	2011-12	2012-13	2013-14	2014-15	2015-16
Aldershot v Solihull Moors	-	-	-	-	-	-
Barrow v Maidstone	-	-	-	-	-	-
Braintree v York	-	0-1	-	-	-	-
Bromley v Lincoln	-	-	-	-	-	2-0
Chester v Torquay	-	-	-	-	0-2	4-1
Eastleigh v Dag & Red	-	-	-	-	-	-
Gateshead v Dover	-	-	-	-	1-2	2-3
Guiseley v Southport	-	-	-	-	-	1-1
Macclesfield v Boreham Wood	-	-	-	-	-	0-0
North Ferriby v Forest Green	-	-	-	-	-	-
Sutton United v Woking	-	-	-	-	-	-
Tranmere v Wrexham	-	-	-	-	-	1-2

Friday October 14, 2016

Championship

	2010-11	2011-12	2012-13	2013-14	2014-15	2015-16
Nottm Forest v Birmingham	-	1-3	2-2	1-0	1-3	1-1

Saturday October 15, 2016

Premier League

	2010-11	2011-12	2012-13	2013-14	2014-15	2015-16
Arsenal v Swansea	-	1-0	0-2	2-2	0-1	1-2
Bournemouth v Hull	-	-	-	-	-	-
Chelsea v Leicester	-	-	-	-	2-0	1-1
Crystal Palace v West Ham	-	2-2	-	1-0	1-3	1-3
Liverpool v Man United	3-1	1-1	1-2	1-0	1-2	0-1
Man City v Everton	1-2	2-0	1-1	3-1	1-0	0-0
Middlesbrough v Watford	2-1	1-0	1-2	2-2	1-1	-
Southampton v Burnley	-	2-0	-	-	2-0	-
Stoke v Sunderland	3-2	0-1	0-0	2-0	1-1	1-1
West Brom v Tottenham	1-1	1-3	0-1	3-3	0-3	1-1

Results cover matches from Premier League to National League and Scottish Premiership to League Two

	2010-11	2011-12	2012-13	2013-14	2014-15	2015-16
Championship						
Aston Villa v Wolves	0-1	0-0	-	-	-	-
Barnsley v Fulham	-	-	-	-	-	-
Blackburn v Ipswich	-	-	1-0	2-0	3-2	2-0
Brighton v Preston	-	-	-	-	-	0-0
Cardiff v Bristol City	3-2	3-1	2-1	-	-	0-0
Derby v Leeds	2-1	1-0	3-1	3-1	2-0	1-2
Huddersfield v Sheffield Weds	1-0	0-2	0-0	0-2	0-0	0-1
Newcastle v Brentford	-	-	-	-	-	-
Norwich v Rotherham	-	-	-	-	1-1	-
QPR v Reading	3-1	-	1-1	1-3	-	1-1
Wigan v Burton	-	-	-	-	-	0-1
League One						
AFC Wimbledon v Swindon	-	1-1	-	-	-	-
Bolton v Oldham	-	-	-	-	-	-
Bristol Rovers v Gillingham	-	2-2	0-2	-	-	-
Charlton v Coventry	-	-	-	-	-	-
Fleetwood Town v Peterborough	-	-	-	-	1-1	2-0
Northampton v Millwall	-	-	-	-	-	-
Oxford v Bradford	2-1	1-1	0-2	-	-	-
Rochdale v Bury	-	3-0	-	1-0	-	3-0
Scunthorpe v MK Dons	-	0-3	0-3	-	1-1	-
Sheffield United v Port Vale	-	-	-	2-1	1-0	1-0
Southend v Chesterfield	2-3	-	3-0	3-0	-	0-1
Walsall v Shrewsbury	-	-	3-1	1-0	-	2-1
League Two						
Accrington v Blackpool	-	-	-	-	-	-
Barnet v Exeter	-	-	1-2	-	-	2-0
Cambridge U v Grimsby	1-1	0-1	0-0	1-2	-	-
Carlisle v Hartlepool	1-0	1-2	3-0	-	3-3	1-0
Cheltenham v Crawley Town	-	3-1	-	-	-	-
Doncaster v Colchester	-	-	1-0	-	2-0	2-0
Leyton Orient v Luton	-	-	-	-	-	0-1
Mansfield v Wycombe	-	-	-	2-2	0-0	0-2
Morecambe v Stevenage	0-0	-	-	-	0-0	1-4
Notts County v Crewe	-	-	1-1	4-0	2-1	-
Plymouth v Portsmouth	-	-	-	1-1	3-0	1-2
Yeovil v Newport County	-	-	-	-	-	1-0
Scottish Premiership						
Aberdeen v Ross County	-	-	0-0/0-1	1-0	3-0/4-0	3-1/0-4
Celtic v Motherwell	1-0/4-0	4-0/1-0	1-0	2-0/3-0	1-1/4-0	1-2/7-0
Hearts v Dundee	-	-	0-1/1-0	-	-	1-1
Inverness CT v Rangers	1-1	0-2/1-4	-	-	-	-
Partick v Hamilton	-	1-1/2-0	4-0/1-0	-	1-2/5-0	1-1/2-2
St Johnstone v Kilmarnock	0-3/0-0	2-0	2-1/2-0	3-1	1-2/0-0	2-1
Scottish Championship						
Dumbarton v Ayr	3-2/1-2	-	-	-	-	-
Falkirk v Dunfermline	0-1/1-2	-	2-2/1-0	-	-	-
Queen of Sth v Morton	2-0/1-4	4-1/2-1	-	2-0/3-0	-	2-2/1-0
Raith v Hibernian	-	-	-	-	1-3/2-1	1-2/2-1
St Mirren v Dundee United	1-1/1-1	2-2	0-1/0-0	4-1	0-3/1-1	-
Scottish League One						
Airdrieonians v Peterhead	2-2/1-0	-	-	-	0-2/1-3	1-0/3-4
Brechin v Alloa	3-1/3-2	-	1-3/3-2	-	-	-
Livingston v Albion	-	-	-	-	-	-
Queens Park v East Fife	-	-	-	-	3-0/1-0	0-2/3-0
Stenhousemuir v Stranraer	-	-	0-0/1-2	1-0/1-1	2-2/1-0	1-0/1-5

Results cover matches from Premier League to National League and Scottish Premiership to League Two

	2010-11	2011-12	2012-13	2013-14	2014-15	2015-16
Scottish League Two						
Arbroath v Forfar	-	4-1/0-1	1-1/3-1	3-0/2-3	-	-
Cowdenbeath v Annan	-	-	-	-	-	-
Edinburgh City v Clyde	-	-	-	-	-	-
Montrose v Elgin	0-1/1-0	3-0/2-3	2-2/4-1	3-3/0-3	2-3/2-1	2-0/3-1
Stirling v Berwick	-	-	6-3/1-0	3-1/2-1	-	1-3/2-1

Tuesday October 18, 2016

	2010-11	2011-12	2012-13	2013-14	2014-15	2015-16
Championship						
Barnsley v Newcastle	-	-	-	-	-	-
Birmingham v Rotherham	-	-	-	-	2-1	0-2
Blackburn v Nottm Forest	-	-	3-0	0-1	3-3	0-0
Brighton v Wolves	-	-	2-0	-	1-1	0-1
Cardiff v Sheffield Weds	-	-	1-0	-	2-1	2-2
Derby v Brentford	-	-	-	-	1-1	2-0
Fulham v Norwich	-	2-1	5-0	1-0	1-0	-
Ipswich v Burton	-	-	-	-	-	-
Leeds v Wigan	-	-	-	2-0	0-2	-
Preston v Huddersfield	-	1-0	-	-	-	2-1
QPR v Bristol City	2-2	-	-	-	-	1-0
Reading v Aston Villa	-	-	1-2	-	-	-

	2010-11	2011-12	2012-13	2013-14	2014-15	2015-16
League One						
Bradford v Southend	0-2	2-0	2-2	-	-	2-0
Bury v AFC Wimbledon	-	-	-	1-1	2-0	-
Chesterfield v Fleetwood Town	-	-	1-2	2-1	3-0	0-0
Coventry v Oxford	-	-	-	-	-	-
Gillingham v Walsall	-	-	-	2-2	0-0	1-2
Millwall v Bolton	-	-	2-1	1-1	0-1	-
MK Dons v Bristol Rovers	2-0	-	-	-	-	-
Oldham v Scunthorpe	-	1-2	1-1	-	3-2	2-4
Peterborough v Northampton	-	-	-	-	-	-
Port Vale v Charlton	-	-	-	-	-	-
Shrewsbury v Sheffield United	-	-	1-2	2-0	-	1-2
Swindon v Rochdale	1-1	-	-	-	2-3	2-1

Saturday October 22, 2016

	2010-11	2011-12	2012-13	2013-14	2014-15	2015-16
Premier League						
Arsenal v Middlesbrough	-	-	-	-	-	-
Bournemouth v Tottenham	-	-	-	-	-	1-5
Burnley v Everton	-	-	-	-	1-3	-
Chelsea v Man United	2-1	3-3	2-3	3-1	1-0	1-1
Hull v Stoke	-	-	-	0-0	1-1	-
Leicester v Crystal Palace	1-1	3-0	1-2	-	0-1	1-0
Liverpool v West Brom	1-0	0-1	0-2	4-1	2-1	2-2
Man City v Southampton	-	-	3-2	4-1	2-0	3-1
Swansea v Watford	1-1	-	-	-	-	1-0
West Ham v Sunderland	0-3	-	1-1	0-0	1-0	1-0

	2010-11	2011-12	2012-13	2013-14	2014-15	2015-16
Championship						
Aston Villa v Fulham	2-2	1-0	1-1	1-2	-	-
Brentford v Barnsley	-	-	-	-	-	-
Bristol City v Blackburn	-	-	3-5	-	-	0-2
Burton v Birmingham	-	-	-	-	-	-
Huddersfield v Derby	-	-	1-0	1-1	4-4	1-2
Newcastle v Ipswich	-	-	-	-	-	-
Norwich v Preston	1-1	-	-	-	-	-
Nottm Forest v Cardiff	2-1	0-1	3-1	-	1-2	1-2
Rotherham v Reading	-	-	-	-	2-1	1-1
Sheffield Weds v QPR	-	-	-	3-0	-	1-1
Wigan v Brighton	-	-	-	0-1	2-1	-
Wolves v Leeds	-	-	2-2	-	4-3	2-3

Results cover matches from Premier League to National League and Scottish Premiership to League Two

	2010-11	2011-12	2012-13	2013-14	2014-15	2015-16
League One						
Bradford v Sheffield United	-	-	-	2-0	0-2	2-2
Bury v Bolton	-	-	-	-	-	-
Chesterfield v Scunthorpe	-	1-4	-	1-1	4-1	0-3
Coventry v Rochdale	-	-	-	-	2-2	0-1
Gillingham v Charlton	-	-	-	-	-	-
Millwall v Fleetwood Town	-	-	-	-	-	1-0
MK Dons v Southend	-	-	-	-	-	-
Oldham v Bristol Rovers	1-1	-	-	-	-	-
Peterborough v AFC Wimbledon	-	-	-	-	-	-
Port Vale v Oxford	1-2	3-0	3-0	-	-	-
Shrewsbury v Northampton	3-1	1-1	-	-	1-2	-
Swindon v Walsall	0-0	-	2-2	1-3	3-3	2-1
League Two						
Blackpool v Doncaster	-	2-1	-	1-1	-	0-2
Colchester v Morecambe	-	-	-	-	-	-
Crawley Town v Accrington	-	1-1	-	-	-	0-3
Crewe v Yeovil	-	-	0-1	-	1-0	-
Exeter v Cambridge U	-	-	-	-	2-2	1-0
Grimsby v Cheltenham	-	-	-	-	-	0-1
Hartlepool v Leyton Orient	0-1	2-1	2-1	-	-	3-1
Luton v Mansfield	2-0	0-0	2-3	-	3-0	1-0
Newport County v Plymouth	-	-	-	1-2	2-0	1-2
Portsmouth v Notts County	-	-	0-2	-	-	4-0
Stevenage v Carlisle	-	1-0	1-1	1-3	1-0	0-1
Wycombe v Barnet	4-2	-	0-0	-	-	1-1
National League						
Boreham Wood v North Ferriby	-	-	-	-	-	-
Dag & Red v Macclesfield	-	2-0	-	-	-	-
Dover v Braintree	-	-	-	-	1-0	0-0
Forest Green v Guiseley	-	-	-	-	-	3-0
Lincoln v Eastleigh	-	-	-	-	1-2	3-0
Maidstone v Gateshead	-	-	-	-	-	-
Solihull Moors v Tranmere	-	-	-	-	-	-
Southport v Sutton United	-	-	-	-	-	-
Torquay v Aldershot	0-1	1-0	4-3	-	1-1	0-2
Woking v Barrow	-	-	3-1	-	-	2-2
Wrexham v Bromley	-	-	-	-	-	2-0
York v Chester	-	-	-	-	-	-
Scottish Premiership						
Aberdeen v Motherwell	1-2	1-2	3-3/0-0	0-1/0-1	1-0/2-1	1-1/4-1
Celtic v Hamilton	3-1/2-0	-	-	-	0-1/4-0	8-1
Hearts v Rangers	1-2/1-0	0-2/0-3	-	-	2-0/2-2	-
Inverness CT v Kilmarnock	1-3	2-1/1-1	1-1/1-1	2-1	2-0/3-3	2-1/3-1
Partick v Ross County	1-1/1-1	0-1/0-1	-	3-3/2-3	4-0/1-3	1-0
St Johnstone v Dundee	-	-	1-0	-	0-1/1-0	1-1
Scottish Championship						
Ayr v Queen of Sth	-	1-0/1-1	2-4/1-5	-	-	-
Dundee United v Dumbarton	-	-	-	-	-	-
Dunfermline v Hibernian	-	2-2/2-3	-	-	-	-
Falkirk v Raith	0-0/2-1	2-0/2-3	0-2/1-1	3-1/2-1	0-1/1-0	1-0/2-2
Morton v St Mirren	-	-	-	-	-	0-0/0-1

Results cover matches from Premier League to National League and Scottish Premiership to League Two

	2010-11	2011-12	2012-13	2013-14	2014-15	2015-16
Scottish League One						
Airdrieonians v Queens Park	-	-	-	-	-	-
Albion v Peterhead	-	-	-	1-2/0-0	-	1-0/1-1
Livingston v Alloa	3-3/4-0	-	-	3-2/2-0	4-0/0-0	0-1/0-0
Stenhousemuir v Brechin	0-0/1-3	1-1/2-1	3-1/3-3	3-2/4-2	0-2/2-2	2-2/0-0
Stranraer v East Fife	-	-	2-6/3-1	2-0/2-0	-	-

Tuesday October 25, 2016

	2010-11	2011-12	2012-13	2013-14	2014-15	2015-16
National League						
Bromley v Dover	-	-	-	0-4	-	1-1
Dag & Red v Aldershot	-	2-5	0-0	-	-	-
Eastleigh v Torquay	-	-	-	-	1-2	3-2
Guiseley v Gateshead	-	-	-	-	-	0-2
Lincoln v Boreham Wood	-	-	-	-	-	3-1
Macclesfield v Chester	-	-	-	3-2	3-1	1-2
Solihull Moors v Forest Green	-	-	-	-	-	-
Southport v York	4-0	1-1	-	-	-	-
Sutton United v Maidstone	-	-	-	-	-	-
Tranmere v North Ferriby	-	-	-	-	-	-
Woking v Braintree	-	-	1-4	1-0	1-0	1-1
Wrexham v Barrow	1-1	2-0	3-0	-	-	4-1

Wednesday October 26, 2016

	2010-11	2011-12	2012-13	2013-14	2014-15	2015-16
Ladbrokes Premiership						
Dundee v Partick	2-1/3-2	0-1/0-3	-	-	1-1/1-0	1-1
Hamilton v Aberdeen	0-1/1-1	-	-	-	3-0/0-3	1-1
Kilmarnock v Hearts	1-2/2-2	0-0/1-1	1-0/0-1	2-0/4-2	-	2-2
Motherwell v Inverness CT	0-0	3-0/0-1	4-1/3-0	2-0/2-1	0-2/2-1	1-3
Rangers v St Johnstone	2-1/4-0	0-0	-	-	-	-
Ross County v Celtic	-	-	-	1-4	0-5/0-1	1-4

Saturday October 29, 2016

	2010-11	2011-12	2012-13	2013-14	2014-15	2015-16
Premier League						
Crystal Palace v Liverpool	-	-	-	3-3	3-1	1-2
Everton v West Ham	2-2	-	2-0	1-0	2-1	2-3
Man United v Burnley	-	-	-	-	3-1	-
Middlesbrough v Bournemouth	-	-	-	3-3	0-0	-
Southampton v Chelsea	-	-	2-1	0-3	1-1	1-2
Stoke v Swansea	-	2-0	2-0	1-1	2-1	2-2
Sunderland v Arsenal	1-1	1-2	0-1	1-3	0-2	0-0
Tottenham v Leicester	-	-	-	-	4-3	0-1
Watford v Hull	1-2	1-1	1-2	-	-	-
West Brom v Man City	0-2	0-0	1-2	2-3	1-3	0-3
Championship						
Barnsley v Bristol City	4-2	1-2	1-0	-	2-2	-
Blackburn v Wolves	3-0	1-2	0-1	-	0-1	1-2
Brighton v Norwich	-	-	-	-	0-1	-
Cardiff v Wigan	-	-	-	-	1-0	-
Derby v Sheffield Weds	-	-	2-2	3-0	3-2	1-1
Fulham v Huddersfield	-	-	-	-	3-1	1-1
Ipswich v Rotherham	-	-	-	-	2-0	0-1
Leeds v Burton	-	-	-	-	-	-
Preston v Newcastle	-	-	-	-	-	-
QPR v Brentford	-	-	-	-	-	3-0
Reading v Nottm Forest	1-1	1-0	-	1-1	0-3	2-1

Results cover matches from Premier League to National League and Scottish Premiership to League Two

	2010-11	2011-12	2012-13	2013-14	2014-15	2015-16
League One						
AFC Wimbledon v Bradford	-	3-1	2-1	-	-	-
Bolton v Port Vale	-	-	-	-	-	-
Bristol Rovers v Peterborough	2-2	-	-	-	-	-
Charlton v Chesterfield	-	3-1	-	-	-	-
Fleetwood Town v Gillingham	-	-	2-2	-	1-0	2-1
Northampton v Bury	2-4	-	-	0-3	2-3	-
Oxford v Millwall	-	-	-	-	-	-
Rochdale v Oldham	1-1	3-2	-	-	0-3	0-0
Scunthorpe v Swindon	-	-	3-1	-	3-1	6-0
Sheffield United v MK Dons	-	2-1	0-0	0-1	0-1	-
Southend v Shrewsbury	0-2	3-0	-	-	1-0	0-1
Walsall v Coventry	-	-	4-0	0-1	0-2	2-1
League Two						
Accrington v Newport County	-	-	-	3-3	0-2	2-2
Barnet v Hartlepool	-	-	-	-	-	1-3
Cambridge U v Portsmouth	-	-	-	-	2-6	1-3
Carlisle v Crawley Town	-	-	0-2	1-1	-	3-1
Cheltenham v Blackpool	-	-	-	-	-	-
Doncaster v Wycombe	-	-	-	-	-	-
Leyton Orient v Crewe	-	-	1-1	2-0	4-1	-
Mansfield v Stevenage	-	-	-	-	1-0	2-1
Morecambe v Exeter	-	-	0-3	2-0	0-2	1-1
Notts County v Luton	-	-	-	-	-	3-2
Plymouth v Colchester	2-1	-	-	-	-	-
Yeovil v Grimsby	-	-	-	-	-	-
National League						
Aldershot v Guiseley	-	-	-	-	-	1-0
Barrow v Eastleigh	-	-	-	-	-	1-0
Boreham Wood v Woking	-	-	-	-	-	1-1
Braintree v Solihull Moors	-	-	-	-	-	-
Chester v Lincoln	-	-	-	3-3	4-0	2-3
Dover v Tranmere	-	-	-	-	-	0-0
Forest Green v Dag & Red	-	-	-	-	-	-
Gateshead v Wrexham	0-1	1-4	0-1	0-3	3-1	2-1
Maidstone v Macclesfield	-	-	-	-	-	-
North Ferriby v Bromley	-	-	-	-	-	-
Torquay v Southport	-	-	-	-	0-0	1-0
York v Sutton United	-	-	-	-	-	-
Scottish Premiership						
Aberdeen v Celtic	0-3	0-1/1-1	0-2	0-2/2-1	1-2/0-1	2-1/2-1
Hamilton v Dundee	-	1-6/3-1	-	0-3/1-1	2-1	1-1/2-1
Inverness CT v Hearts	1-3/1-1	1-1/1-0	1-1	2-0/0-0	-	2-0/0-0
Motherwell v Ross County	-	-	3-2/2-0	3-1/2-1	2-2/1-1	1-1/1-2
Rangers v Kilmarnock	2-1/2-1	2-0/0-1	-	-	-	-
St Johnstone v Partick	-	-	-	1-1/1-1	2-0	1-2/1-2
Scottish Championship						
Dumbarton v Dunfermline	-	-	0-2/0-1	-	-	-
Dundee United v Falkirk	-	-	-	-	-	-
Hibernian v St Mirren	2-0/1-1	1-2/0-0	2-1/3-3	2-0/2-3	-	1-1/3-1
Morton v Ayr	-	4-1/3-1	-	-	0-1/2-1	-
Raith v Queen of Sth	0-1/0-1	0-2/3-1	-	2-1/3-2	3-4/3-0	1-0/2-0

Results cover matches from Premier League to National League and Scottish Premiership to League Two

	2010-11	2011-12	2012-13	2013-14	2014-15	2015-16
Scottish League One						
Alloa v Albion	-	-	5-1/4-1	-	-	-
Brechin v Livingston	1-3/1-0	-	-	-	-	-
East Fife v Airdrieonians	3-3/0-1	2-0/2-0	-	1-0/0-0	-	-
Peterhead v Stranraer	-	1-3/1-1	-	-	1-4/1-2	1-1/0-0
Queens Park v Stenhousemuir	-	-	-	-	-	-
Scottish League Two						
Annan v Montrose	2-2/2-1	2-1/1-2	2-1/1-1	2-1/1-0	2-2/4-3	3-2/3-3
Berwick v Arbroath	4-1/0-4	-	-	-	1-2/3-1	2-2/3-0
Clyde v Stirling	-	-	2-1/1-2	2-1/1-0	-	0-1/3-1
Elgin v Cowdenbeath	-	-	-	-	-	-
Forfar v Edinburgh City	-	-	-	-	-	-

Sunday October 30, 2016

	2010-11	2011-12	2012-13	2013-14	2014-15	2015-16
Championship						
Birmingham v Aston Villa	1-1	-	-	-	-	-

Saturday November 5, 2016

	2010-11	2011-12	2012-13	2013-14	2014-15	2015-16
Premier League						
Arsenal v Tottenham	2-3	5-2	5-2	1-0	1-1	1-1
Bournemouth v Sunderland	-	-	-	-	-	2-0
Burnley v Crystal Palace	1-0	1-1	1-0	-	2-3	-
Chelsea v Everton	1-1	3-1	2-1	1-0	1-0	3-3
Hull v Southampton	-	0-2	-	0-1	0-1	-
Leicester v West Brom	-	-	-	-	0-1	2-2
Liverpool v Watford	-	-	-	-	-	2-0
Man City v Middlesbrough	-	-	-	-	-	-
Swansea v Man United	-	0-1	1-1	1-4	2-1	2-1
West Ham v Stoke	3-0	-	1-1	0-1	1-1	0-0
Championship						
Aston Villa v Blackburn	4-1	3-1	-	-	-	-
Brentford v Fulham	-	-	-	-	2-1	3-0
Bristol City v Brighton	-	0-1	0-0	-	-	0-4
Burton v Barnsley	-	-	-	-	-	0-0
Huddersfield v Birmingham	-	-	1-1	1-3	0-1	1-1
Newcastle v Cardiff	-	-	-	3-0	-	-
Norwich v Leeds	1-1	-	-	-	1-1	-
Nottm Forest v QPR	0-0	-	-	2-0	-	0-0
Rotherham v Preston	-	-	-	0-0	-	0-0
Sheffield Weds v Ipswich	-	-	1-1	1-1	1-1	1-1
Wigan v Reading	-	-	3-2	3-0	2-2	-
Wolves v Derby	-	-	1-1	-	2-0	2-1
Scottish Premiership						
Celtic v Inverness CT	2-2	2-0/1-0	0-1/4-1	2-2/5-0/6-0	1-0/5-0	4-2/3-0
Dundee v Motherwell	-	-	1-2/0-3	-	4-1	2-1/2-2
Hearts v St Johnstone	1-1/1-0	1-2/2-0	2-0/2-0	0-2	-	4-3/0-3/2-2
Kilmarnock v Hamilton	3-0	-	-	-	1-0/2-3	1-2/0-1
Partick v Aberdeen	-	-	-	0-3/3-1	0-1	0-2/1-2
Ross County v Rangers	-	-	-	-	-	-
Scottish Championship						
Ayr v Hibernian	-	-	-	-	-	-
Dunfermline v Raith	2-2/2-1	-	3-1/1-0	-	-	-
Falkirk v Morton	2-1/1-0	1-0/0-2	0-1/4-1	3-1/1-1	-	1-0/1-0
Queen of Sth v Dundee United	-	-	-	-	-	-
St Mirren v Dumbarton	-	-	-	-	-	1-2/1-0

Results cover matches from Premier League to National League and Scottish Premiership to League Two

	2010-11	2011-12	2012-13	2013-14	2014-15	2015-16
Scottish League One						
Albion v Airdrieonians	-	7-2/0-1	-	-	-	1-3/1-2
Alloa v Stenhousemuir	1-0/1-2	-	0-2/1-0	-	-	-
Livingston v East Fife	1-1/4-3	-	-	-	-	-
Peterhead v Brechin	0-5/1-1	-	-	-	1-1/3-0	2-3/4-1
Stranraer v Queens Park	1-0/2-1	2-3/2-3	-	-	-	-
Scottish League Two						
Annan v Arbroath	1-2/3-0	-	-	-	0-1/2-0	2-2/4-1
Berwick v Cowdenbeath	-	-	-	-	-	-
Clyde v Elgin	1-1/3-3	1-2/0-2	2-2/1-1	2-1/4-0	2-1/0-2	4-2/1-0
Montrose v Edinburgh City	-	-	-	-	-	-
Stirling v Forfar	-	2-4/2-2	-	-	2-2/0-1	-

Saturday November 12, 2016

	2010-11	2011-12	2012-13	2013-14	2014-15	2015-16
League One						
Bradford v Rochdale	-	-	2-4	-	1-2	2-2
Bury v Southend	1-0	-	-	1-1	0-1	3-2
Chesterfield v Sheffield United	-	0-1	-	-	3-2	0-3
Coventry v Scunthorpe	1-1	-	1-2	-	1-1	1-2
Gillingham v Northampton	1-0	4-3	2-0	-	-	-
Millwall v Bristol Rovers	-	-	-	-	-	-
MK Dons v Walsall	1-1	0-1	2-4	1-0	0-3	-
Oldham v AFC Wimbledon	-	-	-	-	-	-
Peterborough v Bolton	-	-	5-4	-	-	-
Port Vale v Fleetwood Town	-	-	0-2	-	1-2	0-0
Shrewsbury v Oxford	3-0	2-2	-	-	2-0	-
Swindon v Charlton	0-3					
League Two						
Blackpool v Notts County	-	-	-	-	-	-
Colchester v Leyton Orient	3-2	1-1	2-1	1-2	2-0	-
Crawley Town v Cambridge U	3-0	-	-	-	-	1-0
Crewe v Plymouth	-	3-2	-	-	-	-
Exeter v Doncaster	-	-	-	-	-	-
Grimsby v Barnet	-	-	-	2-1	3-1	-
Hartlepool v Cheltenham	-	-	-	0-1	2-0	-
Luton v Accrington	-	-	-	-	2-0	0-2
Newport County v Carlisle	-	-	-	-	2-1	1-0
Portsmouth v Mansfield	-	-	-	1-1	1-1	0-0
Stevenage v Yeovil	-	0-0	0-2	-	-	0-0
Wycombe v Morecambe	2-0	-	2-2	1-0	0-1	0-2
National League						
Bromley v Boreham Wood	-	-	-	-	-	1-2
Dag & Red v Gateshead	-	-	-	-	-	-
Eastleigh v York	-	-	-	-	-	-
Guiseley v Torquay	-	-	-	-	-	4-3
Lincoln v Aldershot	0-3	-	-	0-1	3-0	2-0
Macclesfield v Forest Green	-	-	1-2	1-2	2-2	4-1
Solihull Moors v Dover	-	-	-	-	-	-
Southport v Maidstone	-	-	-	-	-	-
Sutton United v Barrow	-	-	-	-	-	-
Tranmere v Chester	-	-	-	-	-	2-0
Woking v North Ferriby	-	-	-	-	-	-
Wrexham v Braintree	-	5-1	1-1	2-3	3-0	2-2

Results cover matches from Premier League to National League and Scottish Premiership to League Two

	2010-11	2011-12	2012-13	2013-14	2014-15	2015-16
Scottish Championship						
Dumbarton v Morton	-	-	1-5/0-3	3-1/2-0	-	1-2/0-0
Dundee United v Dunfermline	-	0-1/3-0	-	-	-	-
Hibernian v Falkirk	-	-	-	-	0-1/3-3	1-1/2-2
Queen of Sth v St Mirren	-	-	-	-	-	0-2/1-0
Raith v Ayr	-	0-1/2-2	-	-	-	-
Scottish League One						
Airdrieonians v Brechin	1-1/2-2	2-3/4-1	-	3-1/2-1	4-0/1-1	1-0/0-2
Albion v Stranraer	1-2/1-0	-	2-1/2-3	-	-	0-2/0-1
East Fife v Alloa	4-1/3-1	-	0-1/2-1	-	-	-
Queens Park v Peterhead	-	1-1/0-1	0-0/0-3	0-5/0-2	-	-
Stenhousemuir v Livingston	1-2/0-3	-	-	-	-	-
Scottish League Two						
Arbroath v Clyde	3-2/2-0	-	-	-	4-0/3-1	0-1/0-1
Cowdenbeath v Montrose	-	-	-	-	-	-
Edinburgh City v Annan	-	-	-	-	-	-
Elgin v Stirling	-	-	3-1/1-2	4-0/2-3	-	1-0/2-1
Forfar v Berwick	-	-	-	-	-	-

Saturday November 19, 2016

	2010-11	2011-12	2012-13	2013-14	2014-15	2015-16
Premier League						
Crystal Palace v Man City	-	-	-	0-2	2-1	0-1
Everton v Swansea	-	1-0	0-0	3-2	0-0	1-2
Man United v Arsenal	1-0	8-2	2-1	1-0	1-1	3-2
Middlesbrough v Chelsea	-	-	-	-	-	-
Southampton v Liverpool	-	-	3-1	0-3	0-2	3-2
Stoke v Bournemouth	-	-	-	-	-	2-1
Sunderland v Hull	-	-	-	0-2	1-3	-
Tottenham v West Ham	0-0	-	3-1	0-3	2-2	4-1
Watford v Leicester	3-2	3-2	2-1	0-3	-	0-1
West Brom v Burnley	-	-	-	-	4-0	-
Championship						
Barnsley v Wigan	-	-	-	0-4	-	0-2
Birmingham v Bristol City	-	2-2	2-0	-	-	4-2
Blackburn v Brentford	-	-	-	-	2-3	1-1
Brighton v Aston Villa	-	-	-	-	-	-
Cardiff v Huddersfield	-	-	1-0	-	3-1	2-0
Derby v Rotherham	-	-	-	-	1-0	3-0
Fulham v Sheffield Weds	-	-	-	-	4-0	0-1
Ipswich v Nottm Forest	0-1	1-3	3-1	1-1	2-1	1-0
Leeds v Newcastle	-	-	-	-	-	-
Preston v Wolves	-	-	-	0-0	-	1-1
QPR v Norwich	0-0	1-2	0-0	-	-	-
Reading v Burton	-	-	-	-	-	-
League One						
AFC Wimbledon v Bury	-	-	-	0-1	3-2	-
Bolton v Millwall	-	-	1-1	3-1	2-0	-
Bristol Rovers v MK Dons	1-2	-	-	-	-	-
Charlton v Port Vale	-	-	-	-	-	-
Fleetwood Town v Chesterfield	-	-	1-3	1-1	0-0	0-1
Northampton v Peterborough	-	-	-	-	-	-
Oxford v Coventry	-	-	-	-	-	-
Rochdale v Swindon	3-3	-	-	-	2-4	2-2
Scunthorpe v Oldham	-	1-2	2-2	-	0-1	1-1
Sheffield United v Shrewsbury	-	-	1-0	2-0	-	2-4
Southend v Bradford	4-0	0-1	2-2	-	-	0-1
Walsall v Gillingham	-	-	-	1-1	1-1	3-2

Results cover matches from Premier League to National League and Scottish Premiership to League Two

	2010-11	2011-12	2012-13	2013-14	2014-15	2015-16
League Two						
Accrington v Stevenage	1-0	-	-	-	2-2	0-0
Barnet v Crewe	2-1	2-0	-	-	-	-
Cambridge U v Wycombe	-	-	-	-	0-1	1-0
Carlisle v Exeter	2-2	4-1	-	-	1-3	1-0
Cheltenham v Portsmouth	-	-	-	2-2	1-1	-
Doncaster v Hartlepool	-	-	3-0	-	-	-
Leyton Orient v Blackpool	-	-	-	-	-	-
Mansfield v Crawley Town	1-4	-	-	-	-	4-0
Morecambe v Luton	-	-	-	-	3-0	1-3
Notts County v Newport County	-	-	-	-	-	4-3
Plymouth v Grimsby	-	-	-	-	-	-
Yeovil v Colchester	4-2	3-2	3-1	-	0-1	-
National League						
Aldershot v Macclesfield	0-0	1-2	-	1-0	0-1	0-3
Barrow v Solihull Moors	-	-	-	0-2	1-3	-
Boreham Wood v Southport	-	-	-	-	-	0-2
Braintree v Tranmere	-	-	-	-	-	0-0
Chester v Bromley	-	-	-	-	-	1-1
Dover v Guiseley	-	-	-	-	-	0-0
Forest Green v Lincoln	-	0-2	3-0	4-1	3-3	3-1
Gateshead v Eastleigh	-	-	-	-	2-3	2-1
Maidstone v Woking	-	-	-	-	-	-
North Ferriby v Sutton United	-	-	-	-	-	-
Torquay v Wrexham	-	-	-	-	2-1	0-1
York v Dag & Red	-	-	3-2	3-1	0-2	2-2
Scottish Premiership						
Hamilton v Hearts	0-4/0-2	-	-	-	-	3-2/0-0
Inverness CT v Aberdeen	2-0/0-2	2-1/0-2	1-1/3-0	3-4/0-0	0-1/1-2	2-1/3-1
Kilmarnock v Celtic	1-2/0-4/0-2	3-3/0-6	1-3	2-5/0-3	0-2	2-2/0-1
Motherwell v Partick	-	-	-	1-0/4-3	1-0/0-0	2-1/3-1
Rangers v Dundee	-	-	-	-	-	-
St Johnstone v Ross County	-	-	1-1/2-2	4-0/0-1	2-1	1-1/1-1
Scottish Championship						
Ayr v Falkirk	-	2-2/1-0	-	-	-	-
Dumbarton v Raith	-	-	4-2/1-2	2-4/3-3	2-1/2-2	3-3/2-3
Hibernian v Queen of Sth	-	-	-	-	0-0/0-1	1-0/2-0
Morton v Dundee United	-	-	-	-	-	-
St Mirren v Dunfermline	-	2-1/4-4	-	-	-	-
Scottish League One						
Airdrieonians v Alloa	0-1/0-2	-	-	-	-	-
Brechin v Albion	-	1-4/2-1	1-0/2-0	-	-	0-1/2-1
East Fife v Queens Park	-	-	-	-	2-2/0-0	0-2/1-1
Livingston v Peterhead	1-0/5-1	-	-	-	-	-
Stranraer v Stenhousemuir	-	-	1-1/1-1	1-0/1-1	0-2/3-2	1-2/3-1
Scottish League Two						
Annan v Elgin	0-1/2-2	1-1/1-1	2-0/2-2	2-1/2-0	3-3/2-3	1-1/4-2
Clyde v Berwick	1-4/2-0	1-4/2-2	2-1/2-1	1-0/3-3	3-3/0-3	1-1/2-1
Edinburgh City v Cowdenbeath	-	-	-	-	-	-
Montrose v Forfar	-	-	-	-	-	-
Stirling v Arbroath	-	0-1/1-1	-	-	-	3-1/1-0

Results cover matches from Premier League to National League and Scottish Premiership to League Two

Tuesday November 22, 2016

League One						
Bolton v Coventry	-	-	-	-	-	-
Bradford v Northampton	1-1	2-1	1-0	-	-	-
Bristol Rovers v Charlton	2-2	-	-	-	-	-
Fleetwood Town v Shrewsbury	-	-	-	-	-	0-0
Millwall v AFC Wimbledon	-	-	-	-	-	-
MK Dons v Chesterfield	-	6-2	-	-	1-2	-
Oxford v Gillingham	0-1	0-0	0-0	-	-	-
Peterborough v Scunthorpe	-	-	-	-	1-2	0-2
Port Vale v Oldham	-	-	-	1-0	0-1	1-1
Rochdale v Walsall	3-2	3-3	-	-	4-0	1-2
Sheffield United v Bury	-	4-0	1-1	-	-	1-3
Southend v Swindon	-	1-4	-	-	-	0-1

League Two						
Cheltenham v Colchester	-	-	-	-	-	-
Crewe v Morecambe	2-1	0-1	-	-	-	-
Grimsby v Carlisle	-	-	-	-	-	-
Hartlepool v Accrington	-	-	-	2-1	1-1	1-2
Leyton Orient v Exeter	3-0	3-0	-	-	-	1-3
Luton v Portsmouth	-	-	-	-	1-1	1-2
Mansfield v Blackpool	-	-	-	-	-	-
Newport County v Wycombe	-	-	-	2-0	0-2	1-0
Notts County v Cambridge U	-	-	-	-	-	1-2
Plymouth v Barnet	-	0-0	2-1	-	-	2-1
Stevenage v Doncaster	-	-	1-2	-	-	-
Yeovil v Crawley Town	-	-	2-2	-	2-1	2-1

National League						
Aldershot v Eastleigh	-	-	-	-	0-2	1-2
Barrow v Guiseley	-	-	-	1-0	1-0	1-1
Boreham Wood v Sutton United	-	-	-	-	-	-
Braintree v Bromley	-	-	-	-	-	1-0
Chester v Southport	-	-	-	2-2	2-0	0-0
Dover v Woking	-	-	-	-	2-1	2-0
Forest Green v Tranmere	-	-	-	-	-	0-2
Gateshead v Macclesfield	-	-	2-2	2-2	2-1	0-3
Maidstone v Dag & Red	-	-	-	-	-	-
North Ferriby v Wrexham	-	-	-	-	-	-
Torquay v Solihull Moors	-	-	-	-	-	-
York v Lincoln	-	2-0	-	-	-	-

Saturday November 26, 2016

Premier League						
Arsenal v Bournemouth	-	-	-	-	-	2-0
Burnley v Man City	-	-	-	-	1-0	-
Chelsea v Tottenham	2-1	0-0	2-2	4-0	3-0	2-2
Hull v West Brom	-	-	-	2-0	0-0	-
Leicester v Middlesbrough	0-0	2-2	1-0	2-0	-	-
Liverpool v Sunderland	2-2	1-1	3-0	2-1	0-0	2-2
Man United v West Ham	3-0	-	1-0	3-1	2-1	0-0
Southampton v Everton	-	-	0-0	2-0	3-0	0-3
Swansea v Crystal Palace	3-0	-	-	1-1	1-1	1-1
Watford v Stoke	-	-	-	-	-	1-2

Results cover matches from Premier League to National League and Scottish Premiership to League Two

	2010-11	2011-12	2012-13	2013-14	2014-15	2015-16
Championship						
Aston Villa v Cardiff	-	-	-	2-0	-	-
Barnsley v Nottm Forest	3-1	1-1	1-4	1-0	-	-
Brentford v Birmingham	-	-	-	-	1-1	0-2
Brighton v Fulham	-	-	-	-	1-2	5-0
Derby v Norwich	1-2	-	-	-	2-2	-
Huddersfield v Wigan	-	-	-	1-0	0-0	-
Ipswich v QPR	0-3	-	-	1-3	-	2-1
Newcastle v Blackburn	1-2	3-1	-	-	-	-
Preston v Burton	-	-	-	-	-	-
Reading v Bristol City	4-1	1-0	-	-	-	1-0
Rotherham v Leeds	-	-	-	-	2-1	2-1
Wolves v Sheffield Weds	-	-	1-0	-	3-0	2-1
League One						
AFC Wimbledon v Fleetwood Town	1-0	-	2-1	2-0	-	-
Bury v Millwall	-	-	-	-	-	1-3
Charlton v Sheffield United	-	1-0	-	-	-	-
Chesterfield v Bristol Rovers	-	-	2-0	3-1	-	-
Coventry v MK Dons	-	-	1-1	1-2	2-1	-
Gillingham v Rochdale	-	-	1-2	-	1-0	2-0
Northampton v Bolton	-	-	-	-	-	-
Oldham v Peterborough	0-5	-	-	5-4	1-1	1-5
Scunthorpe v Oxford	-	-	-	1-0	-	-
Shrewsbury v Port Vale	2-2	1-0	-	0-0	-	1-1
Swindon v Bradford	-	0-0	-	1-0	2-1	4-1
Walsall v Southend	-	-	-	-	-	1-0
League Two						
Accrington v Yeovil	-	-	-	-	-	2-1
Barnet v Notts County	-	-	-	-	-	3-1
Blackpool v Newport County	-	-	-	-	-	-
Cambridge U v Cheltenham	-	-	-	-	1-2	-
Carlisle v Mansfield	-	-	-	-	2-1	1-2
Colchester v Crewe	-	-	1-2	1-2	2-3	2-3
Crawley Town v Grimsby	0-1	-	-	-	-	-
Doncaster v Leyton Orient	-	-	2-0	-	0-2	-
Exeter v Luton	-	-	-	-	1-1	2-3
Morecambe v Plymouth	-	2-2	2-3	2-1	2-1	0-2
Portsmouth v Stevenage	-	-	0-0	-	3-2	1-1
Wycombe v Hartlepool	-	5-0	-	2-1	1-0	2-1
National League						
Bromley v York	-	-	-	-	-	-
Dag & Red v Barrow	-	-	-	-	-	-
Eastleigh v Chester	-	-	-	-	3-2	1-0
Guiseley v Boreham Wood	-	-	-	-	-	1-1
Lincoln v Maidstone	-	-	-	-	-	-
Macclesfield v Dover	-	-	-	-	1-0	0-0
Solihull Moors v North Ferriby	-	-	-	-	-	-
Southport v Braintree	-	0-4	0-2	0-4	0-2	1-1
Sutton United v Aldershot	-	-	-	-	-	-
Tranmere v Torquay	-	-	-	-	-	2-1
Woking v Gateshead	-	-	2-1	1-2	3-0	1-1
Wrexham v Forest Green	2-1	1-2	2-1	2-0	0-0	2-2
Scottish Premiership						
Aberdeen v Kilmarnock	0-1/5-0	2-2/0-0	0-2/1-0	2-1/2-1	1-0	2-0/2-1
Celtic v St Johnstone	2-0	0-1/2-0/1-0	1-1/4-0	2-1/3-0	0-1	3-1/3-1
Dundee v Inverness CT	-	-	1-4/1-1	-	1-2/0-1	1-1/1-1
Hearts v Motherwell	0-2/0-0/3-3	2-0/0-1	1-0/1-2	0-1	-	2-0/6-0
Partick v Rangers	-	-	-	-	-	-
Ross County v Hamilton	-	1-0/5-1	-	-	0-1/2-1	2-0/2-1

Results cover matches from Premier League to National League and Scottish Premiership to League Two

Tuesday November 29, 2016
National League

	2010-11	2011-12	2012-13	2013-14	2014-15	2015-16
Boreham Wood v Braintree	-	-	-	-	-	1-0
Chester v North Ferriby	-	-	-	-	-	-
Dag & Red v Torquay	-	1-1	2-2	0-1	-	-
Forest Green v Aldershot	-	-	-	3-1	1-3	0-0
Gateshead v Tranmere	-	-	-	-	-	1-4
Lincoln v Wrexham	-	1-2	1-2	2-0	1-1	1-1
Macclesfield v Barrow	-	-	2-0	-	-	1-2
Maidstone v Eastleigh	-	-	-	-	-	-
Southport v Solihull Moors	-	-	-	-	-	-
Sutton United v Dover	-	-	-	-	-	-
Woking v Bromley	-	-	-	-	-	2-0
York v Guiseley	-	-	-	-	-	-

Saturday December 3, 2016
Premier League

	2010-11	2011-12	2012-13	2013-14	2014-15	2015-16
Bournemouth v Liverpool	-	-	-	-	-	1-2
Crystal Palace v Southampton	-	0-2	-	0-1	1-3	1-0
Everton v Man United	3-3	0-1	1-0	2-0	3-0	0-3
Man City v Chelsea	1-0	2-1	2-0	0-1	1-1	3-0
Middlesbrough v Hull	2-2	1-0	2-0	-	-	1-0
Stoke v Burnley	-	-	-	-	1-2	-
Sunderland v Leicester	-	-	-	-	0-0	0-2
Tottenham v Swansea	-	3-1	1-0	1-0	3-2	2-1
West Brom v Watford	-	-	-	-	-	0-1
West Ham v Arsenal	0-3	-	1-3	1-3	1-2	3-3

Championship

	2010-11	2011-12	2012-13	2013-14	2014-15	2015-16
Birmingham v Barnsley	-	1-1	0-5	1-1	-	-
Blackburn v Huddersfield	-	-	1-0	0-0	0-0	0-2
Bristol City v Ipswich	0-1	0-3	2-1	-	-	2-1
Burton v Rotherham	2-4	1-1	2-0	-	-	-
Cardiff v Brighton	-	1-3	0-2	-	0-0	4-1
Fulham v Reading	-	-	2-4	-	2-1	4-2
Leeds v Aston Villa	-	-	-	-	-	-
Norwich v Brentford	-	-	-	-	1-2	-
Nottm Forest v Newcastle	-	-	-	-	-	-
QPR v Wolves	-	1-2	-	-	-	1-1
Sheffield Weds v Preston	-	2-0	-	-	-	3-1
Wigan v Derby	-	-	-	1-3	0-2	-

National League

	2010-11	2011-12	2012-13	2013-14	2014-15	2015-16
Aldershot v Boreham Wood	-	-	-	-	-	1-2
Barrow v Southport	1-1	2-2	3-2	-	-	1-0
Braintree v Sutton United	-	-	-	-	-	-
Bromley v Maidstone	-	-	-	-	-	-
Dover v Dag & Red	-	-	-	-	-	-
Eastleigh v Forest Green	-	-	-	-	2-2	3-2
Guiseley v Chester	-	-	-	-	-	3-3
North Ferriby v Gateshead	-	-	-	-	-	-
Solihull Moors v Lincoln	-	-	-	-	-	-
Torquay v Woking	-	-	-	-	1-0	0-1
Tranmere v York	-	-	-	-	1-1	-
Wrexham v Macclesfield	-	-	0-0	1-0	2-2	2-3

Scottish Premiership

	2010-11	2011-12	2012-13	2013-14	2014-15	2015-16
Hamilton v Partick	-	1-0/2-2	1-0/0-2	-	3-3/1-1	0-0/1-2
Kilmarnock v Dundee	-	-	0-0/1-2	-	1-3	0-4/0-0
Motherwell v Celtic	0-1/2-0	1-2/0-3	0-2/2-1/3-1	0-5/3-3	0-1	0-1/1-2
Rangers v Aberdeen	2-0	2-0/1-1	-	-	-	-
Ross County v Hearts	-	-	2-2	2-1/1-2	-	1-2/0-3
St Johnstone v Inverness CT	1-0/0-3	2-0/0-0	0-0/1-0	4-0/0-1	1-0/1-1	1-1/1-0

Results cover matches from Premier League to National League and Scottish Premiership to League Two

Scottish Championship

	2010-11	2011-12	2012-13	2013-14	2014-15	2015-16
Dundee United v Hibernian	1-0/3-0	3-1	3-0/2-2	2-2	-	-
Dunfermline v Ayr	-	-	-	5-1/3-0	4-2/2-1	0-2/3-2
Falkirk v St Mirren	-	-	-	-	-	3-0/3-2
Queen of Sth v Dumbarton	-	-	-	1-2/3-1	3-0/2-1	1-0/6-0
Raith v Morton	1-0/2-2	1-1/5-0	3-3/2-1	2-1/2-1	-	2-1/3-2

Scottish League One

	2010-11	2011-12	2012-13	2013-14	2014-15	2015-16
Albion v Livingston	-	-	-	-	-	-
Alloa v Stranraer	-	1-0/3-1	3-0/4-1	-	-	-
Peterhead v Airdrieonians	5-1/2-4	-	-	-	1-1/0-1	2-0/1-0
Queens Park v Brechin	-	-	-	-	-	-
Stenhousemuir v East Fife	1-1/0-2	2-1/1-0	3-0/2-1	1-1/1-1	-	-

Scottish League Two

	2010-11	2011-12	2012-13	2013-14	2014-15	2015-16
Arbroath v Edinburgh City	-	-	-	-	-	-
Berwick v Stirling	-	-	4-1/1-0	1-1/4-0	-	1-2/1-0
Cowdenbeath v Clyde	-	-	-	-	-	-
Elgin v Montrose	3-2/1-0	3-1/2-1	6-1/3-2	3-3/2-3	0-1/4-0	2-0/1-1
Forfar v Annan	-	-	-	-	-	-

Saturday December 10, 2016

Premier League

	2010-11	2011-12	2012-13	2013-14	2014-15	2015-16
Arsenal v Stoke	1-0	3-1	1-0	3-1	3-0	2-0
Burnley v Bournemouth	-	-	-	1-1	-	-
Chelsea v West Brom	6-0	2-1	1-0	2-2	2-0	2-2
Hull v Crystal Palace	1-1	0-1	0-0	0-1	2-0	-
Leicester v Man City	-	-	-	-	0-1	0-0
Liverpool v West Ham	3-0	-	0-0	4-1	2-0	0-3
Man United v Tottenham	2-0	3-0	2-3	1-2	3-0	1-0
Southampton v Middlesbrough	-	3-0	-	-	-	-
Swansea v Sunderland	-	0-0	2-2	4-0	1-1	2-4
Watford v Everton	-	-	-	-	-	1-1

Championship

	2010-11	2011-12	2012-13	2013-14	2014-15	2015-16
Aston Villa v Wigan	1-1	2-0	0-3	-	-	-
Barnsley v Norwich	0-2	-	-	-	-	-
Brentford v Burton	-	-	-	-	-	-
Brighton v Leeds	-	3-3	2-2	1-0	2-0	4-0
Derby v Nottm Forest	0-1	1-0	1-1	5-0	1-2	1-0
Huddersfield v Bristol City	-	-	1-0	-	-	1-2
Ipswich v Cardiff	2-0	3-0	1-2	-	3-1	0-0
Newcastle v Birmingham	2-1	-	-	-	-	-
Preston v Blackburn	-	-	-	-	-	1-2
Reading v Sheffield Weds	-	-	-	0-2	2-0	1-1
Rotherham v QPR	-	-	-	-	-	0-3
Wolves v Fulham	1-1	2-0	-	-	3-0	3-2

League One

	2010-11	2011-12	2012-13	2013-14	2014-15	2015-16
Bolton v Gillingham	-	-	-	-	-	-
Bradford v Charlton	-	-	-	-	-	-
Bristol Rovers v Bury	-	-	-	1-1	-	-
Fleetwood Town v Walsall	-	-	-	-	0-1	0-1
Millwall v Shrewsbury	-	-	-	-	-	3-1
MK Dons v AFC Wimbledon	-	-	-	-	-	-
Oxford v Oldham	-	-	-	-	-	-
Peterborough v Chesterfield	-	-	-	-	1-0	2-0
Port Vale v Northampton	1-1	3-0	2-2	-	-	-
Rochdale v Scunthorpe	-	1-0	-	0-4	3-1	2-1
Sheffield United v Swindon	-	-	2-0	1-0	2-0	1-1
Southend v Coventry	-	-	-	-	-	3-0

Results cover matches from Premier League to National League and Scottish Premiership to League Two

	2010-11	2011-12	2012-13	2013-14	2014-15	2015-16
League Two						
Cheltenham v Exeter	-	-	3-0	1-0	1-2	-
Crewe v Crawley Town	-	1-1	2-0	1-0	0-0	-
Grimsby v Portsmouth	-	-	-	-	-	-
Hartlepool v Cambridge U	-	-	-	-	2-1	0-0
Leyton Orient v Accrington	-	-	-	-	-	0-1
Luton v Carlisle	-	-	-	-	1-0	3-4
Mansfield v Colchester	-	-	-	-	-	-
Newport County v Morecambe	-	-	-	2-3	0-1	1-2
Notts County v Wycombe	-	1-1	-	-	-	0-0
Plymouth v Doncaster	-	-	-	-	-	-
Stevenage v Blackpool	-	-	-	-	-	-
Yeovil v Barnet	-	-	-	-	-	2-2
Scottish Premiership						
Aberdeen v St Johnstone	0-1/0-2	0-0/0-0	2-0	0-0/1-0/1-1	2-0/0-1	1-5/1-1
Dundee v Ross County	0-0/2-0	1-2/1-1	0-1/0-2	-	1-1	3-3/5-2
Inverness CT v Hamilton	0-1/1-1	-	-	-	4-2	0-2/0-1
Motherwell v Kilmarnock	0-1/1-1	0-0	2-2	2-1/1-2	1-1/3-1	1-0/0-2
Partick v Celtic	-	-	-	1-2/1-5	0-3	0-2/1-2
Rangers v Hearts	1-0/4-0	1-1/1-2	-	-	1-2/2-1	-
Scottish Championship						
Ayr v Dundee United	-	-	-	-	-	-
Dunfermline v Morton	2-0/1-3	-	2-2/1-4	-	1-2/0-4	-
Falkirk v Queen of Sth	3-1/0-3	1-0/3-0	-	2-1/1-0	1-1/1-1	0-0/3-1
Hibernian v Dumbarton	-	-	-	-	0-0/3-0	4-2/4-0
St Mirren v Raith	-	-	-	-	-	1-2/1-2
Scottish League One						
Airdrieonians v Stenhousemuir	1-0/2-2	5-2/0-3	-	0-1/1-1	2-0/2-1	0-1/1-1
Brechin v East Fife	1-3/2-3	0-2/1-3	2-1/6-0	2-0/3-0	-	-
Peterhead v Alloa	1-0/4-1	1-1/0-1	-	-	-	-
Queens Park v Albion	0-1/2-1	-	-	1-1/4-0	0-1/0-1	-
Stranraer v Livingston	-	-	-	-	-	-
Scottish League Two						
Annan v Cowdenbeath	-	-	-	-	-	-
Edinburgh City v Stirling	-	-	-	-	-	-
Elgin v Berwick	1-2/3-2	4-1/4-0	3-1/1-2	2-0/1-3	2-1/3-3	4-1/1-0
Forfar v Arbroath	-	1-1/2-4	1-1/2-4	1-1/0-2	-	-
Montrose v Clyde	8-1/3-1	4-0/5-0	2-3/1-1	0-2/0-2	0-3/0-1	2-0/2-1
Tuesday December 13, 2016						
Premier League						
Bournemouth v Leicester	-	-	-	0-1	-	1-1
Crystal Palace v Man United	-	-	-	0-2	1-2	0-0
Middlesbrough v Liverpool	-	-	-	-	-	-
Sunderland v Chelsea	2-4	1-2	1-3	3-4	0-0	3-2
West Brom v Swansea	-	1-2	2-1	0-2	2-0	1-1
West Ham v Burnley	-	1-2	-	-	1-0	-
Championship						
Birmingham v Ipswich	-	2-1	0-1	1-1	2-2	3-0
Blackburn v Brighton	-	-	1-1	3-3	0-1	0-1
Bristol City v Brentford	-	-	-	1-2	-	2-4
Burton v Huddersfield	-	-	-	-	-	-
Cardiff v Wolves	-	-	3-1	-	0-1	2-0
Fulham v Rotherham	-	-	-	-	1-1	4-1
Leeds v Reading	0-0	0-1	-	2-4	0-0	3-2
Norwich v Aston Villa	-	2-0	1-2	0-1	-	2-0
Nottm Forest v Preston	2-2	-	-	-	-	1-0
QPR v Derby	0-0	-	-	2-1	-	2-0
Sheffield Weds v Barnsley	-	-	2-1	1-0	-	-
Wigan v Newcastle	0-1	4-0	2-1	-	-	-

Results cover matches from Premier League to National League and Scottish Premiership to League Two

Wednesday December 14, 2016

Premier League	2010-11	2011-12	2012-13	2013-14	2014-15	2015-16
Everton v Arsenal	1-2	0-1	1-1	3-0	2-2	0-2
Man City v Watford	-	-	-	-	-	2-0
Stoke v Southampton	-	-	3-3	1-1	2-1	1-2
Tottenham v Hull	-	-	-	1-0	2-0	-

Saturday December 17, 2016

Premier League	2010-11	2011-12	2012-13	2013-14	2014-15	2015-16
Bournemouth v Southampton	1-3	-	-	-	-	2-0
Crystal Palace v Chelsea	-	-	-	1-0	1-2	0-3
Everton v Liverpool	2-0	0-2	2-2	3-3	0-0	1-1
Man City v Arsenal	0-3	1-0	1-1	6-3	0-2	2-2
Middlesbrough v Swansea	3-4	-	-	-	-	-
Stoke v Leicester	-	-	-	-	0-1	2-2
Sunderland v Watford	-	-	-	-	-	0-1
Tottenham v Burnley	-	-	-	-	2-1	-
West Brom v Man United	1-2	1-2	5-5	0-3	2-2	1-0
West Ham v Hull	-	2-1	-	2-1	3-0	-

Championship	2010-11	2011-12	2012-13	2013-14	2014-15	2015-16
Birmingham v Brighton	-	0-0	2-2	0-1	1-0	1-2
Blackburn v Reading	-	-	-	0-0	3-1	3-1
Bristol City v Preston	1-1	-	-	1-1	0-1	1-2
Burton v Newcastle	-	-	-	-	-	-
Cardiff v Barnsley	2-2	5-3	1-1	-	-	-
Fulham v Derby	-	-	-	-	2-0	1-1
Leeds v Brentford	-	-	-	-	0-1	1-1
Norwich v Huddersfield	-	-	-	-	5-0	-
Nottm Forest v Wolves	-	-	3-1	-	1-2	1-1
QPR v Aston Villa	-	1-1	1-1	-	2-0	-
Sheffield Weds v Rotherham	-	-	-	-	0-0	0-1
Wigan v Ipswich	-	-	-	2-0	1-2	-

League One	2010-11	2011-12	2012-13	2013-14	2014-15	2015-16
AFC Wimbledon v Port Vale	-	3-2	2-2	-	-	-
Bury v Oxford	3-0	-	-	1-1	0-1	-
Charlton v Peterborough	3-2	-	2-0	-	-	-
Chesterfield v Bolton	-	-	-	-	-	-
Coventry v Sheffield United	0-0	-	1-1	3-2	1-0	3-1
Gillingham v MK Dons	-	-	-	3-2	4-2	-
Northampton v Rochdale	-	-	3-1	0-3	-	-
Oldham v Southend	-	-	-	-	-	2-5
Scunthorpe v Millwall	1-2	-	-	-	-	0-0
Shrewsbury v Bristol Rovers	-	1-0	-	-	-	-
Swindon v Fleetwood Town	-	-	-	-	1-0	1-1
Walsall v Bradford	-	-	-	0-2	0-0	2-1

League Two	2010-11	2011-12	2012-13	2013-14	2014-15	2015-16
Accrington v Plymouth	-	0-4	1-1	1-1	1-0	2-1
Barnet v Stevenage	0-3	-	-	-	-	3-2
Blackpool v Luton	-	-	-	-	-	-
Cambridge U v Crewe	-	-	-	-	-	-
Carlisle v Yeovil	0-2	3-2	3-3	-	-	3-2
Colchester v Notts County	2-1	4-2	0-2	0-4	0-1	-
Crawley Town v Newport County	2-3	-	-	-	-	2-0
Doncaster v Grimsby	-	-	-	-	-	-
Exeter v Mansfield	-	-	-	0-1	1-2	2-3
Morecambe v Cheltenham	1-1	3-1	0-0	0-1	0-0	-
Portsmouth v Hartlepool	-	-	1-3	1-0	1-0	4-0
Wycombe v Leyton Orient	-	4-2	-	-	-	0-2

Results cover matches from Premier League to National League and Scottish Premiership to League Two

National League						
Boreham Wood v Barrow	-	-	-	-	-	0-2
Chester v Aldershot	-	-	-	1-1	1-0	8-2
Dag & Red v Solihull Moors	-	-	-	-	-	-
Forest Green v Dover	-	-	-	-	0-0	3-1
Gateshead v Braintree	-	2-2	1-2	1-0	3-1	2-3
Lincoln v Tranmere	-	-	-	-	-	1-0
Macclesfield v Bromley	-	-	-	-	-	2-0
Maidstone v North Ferriby	-	-	-	-	-	-
Southport v Eastleigh	-	-	-	-	1-2	0-4
Sutton United v Wrexham	-	-	-	-	-	-
Woking v Guiseley	-	-	-	-	-	0-1
York v Torquay	-	-	0-2	1-0	-	-

Scottish Premiership						
Celtic v Dundee	-	-	2-0/5-0	-	2-1/5-0	6-0/0-0
Hamilton v Rangers	1-2/0-1	-	-	-	-	-
Hearts v Partick	-	-	-	0-2/2-4	-	3-0/1-0
Kilmarnock v Inverness CT	1-2/1-1	3-6/4-3	1-2	1-2/2-0	1-2	2-0/2-1
Ross County v Aberdeen	-	-	2-1	1-0/1-1	0-1	2-0/2-3
St Johnstone v Motherwell	0-2/1-0	0-3	1-3/2-0	2-0/3-0	2-1	2-1/2-1

Scottish Championship						
Dumbarton v Falkirk	-	-	0-2/0-2	1-1/2-1	0-3/1-0	0-5/1-1
Morton v Hibernian	-	-	-	-	-	0-1/0-0
Queen of Sth v Dunfermline	2-0/1-3	-	-	-	-	-
Raith v Dundee United	-	-	-	-	-	-
St Mirren v Ayr	-	-	-	-	-	-

Scottish League One						
Alloa v Queens Park	-	1-0/4-0	-	-	-	-
Brechin v Stranraer	-	-	3-0/2-2	1-1/1-3	1-2/1-3	2-0/1-0
East Fife v Peterhead	2-1/3-1	-	-	-	-	-
Livingston v Airdrieonians	2-1/2-0	-	0-2/4-1	-	-	-
Stenhousemuir v Albion	-	3-0/1-2	1-0/0-1	-	-	0-1/1-3

Scottish League Two						
Arbroath v Elgin	2-0/3-5	-	-	-	1-0/3-3	0-3/2-3
Berwick v Montrose	1-0/0-1	1-2/2-2	1-4/4-0	1-1/5-0	2-2/3-3	2-1/1-0
Clyde v Edinburgh City	-	-	-	-	-	-
Cowdenbeath v Forfar	-	3-1/2-0	-	-	-	2-1/1-4
Stirling v Annan	-	-	5-1/2-1	0-2/1-1	-	1-0/2-1

Saturday December 24, 2016

Ladbrokes Premiership						
Dundee v Hearts	-	-	1-0/1-0	-	-	1-2/0-1
Hamilton v Celtic	1-1	-	-	-	0-2	1-2/1-1
Kilmarnock v St Johnstone	1-1	1-2/0-0	1-2	0-0/1-2	0-1	2-1/3-0
Motherwell v Aberdeen	1-1/2-1	1-0/1-0	4-1	1-3/2-2	0-2	1-2/2-1
Rangers v Inverness CT	1-1/1-0	2-1	-	-	-	-
Ross County v Partick	0-2/0-0	2-2/3-0	-	1-3/1-1	1-0/1-2	1-0/1-0

Scottish Championship						
Ayr v Dumbarton	1-0/2-0	-	-	-	-	-
Dundee United v St Mirren	1-2	1-1/0-0	3-4	4-0/3-2	3-0	-
Dunfermline v Falkirk	1-1/3-0	-	0-1/0-2	-	-	-
Hibernian v Raith	-	-	-	-	1-1/1-1	2-0/1-0
Morton v Queen of Sth	2-0/0-4	2-2/2-2	-	0-2/1-1	-	2-0/3-2

Results cover matches from Premier League to National League and Scottish Premiership to League Two

	2010-11	2011-12	2012-13	2013-14	2014-15	2015-16
Scottish League One						
Albion v East Fife	-	0-3/1-1	0-3/1-1	-	2-0/2-3	-
Alloa v Brechin	2-2/2-2	-	2-2/0-1	-	-	-
Livingston v Queens Park	-	-	-	-	-	-
Stranraer v Airdrieonians	-	-	-	3-1/1-1	1-0/1-0	1-3/4-0
Scottish League Two						
Annan v Berwick	1-1/2-3	2-2/1-1	3-2/2-2	3-2/4-0	2-0/4-2	1-0/1-0
Cowdenbeath v Arbroath	-	0-0/2-3	-	-	-	-
Edinburgh City v Elgin	-	-	-	-	-	-
Montrose v Stirling	-	-	3-2/2-2	1-2/0-0	-	1-3/1-1

Monday December 26, 2016

	2010-11	2011-12	2012-13	2013-14	2014-15	2015-16
Premier League						
Arsenal v West Brom	2-3	3-0	2-0	1-0	4-1	2-0
Burnley v Middlesbrough	3-1	0-2	0-0	0-1	-	1-1
Chelsea v Bournemouth	-	-	-	-	-	0-1
Hull v Man City	-	-	-	0-2	2-4	-
Leicester v Everton	-	-	-	-	2-2	3-1
Liverpool v Stoke	2-0	0-0	0-0	1-0	1-0	4-1
Man United v Sunderland	2-0	1-0	3-1	0-1	2-0	3-0
Southampton v Tottenham	-	-	1-2	2-3	2-2	0-2
Swansea v West Ham	-	-	3-0	0-0	1-1	0-0
Watford v Crystal Palace	1-1	0-2	2-2	-	-	0-1
Championship						
Aston Villa v Burton	-	-	-	-	-	-
Barnsley v Blackburn	-	-	1-3	2-2	-	-
Brentford v Cardiff	-	-	-	-	1-2	2-1
Brighton v QPR	-	-	-	2-0	-	4-0
Derby v Birmingham	-	2-1	3-2	1-1	2-2	0-3
Huddersfield v Nottm Forest	-	-	1-1	0-3	3-0	1-1
Ipswich v Fulham	-	-	-	-	2-1	1-1
Newcastle v Sheffield Weds	-	-	-	-	-	-
Preston v Leeds	1-2	-	-	-	-	1-1
Reading v Norwich	3-3	-	0-0	-	2-1	-
Rotherham v Wigan	-	-	-	-	1-2	-
Wolves v Bristol City	-	-	2-1	3-1	-	2-1
League One						
Bolton v Shrewsbury	-	-	-	-	-	-
Bradford v Scunthorpe	-	-	-	-	1-1	1-0
Bristol Rovers v Coventry	-	-	-	-	-	-
Fleetwood Town v Bury	-	-	-	2-1	-	2-0
Millwall v Swindon	-	-	-	-	-	2-0
MK Dons v Charlton	2-0	1-1	-	-	-	1-0
Oxford v Northampton	3-1	2-0	2-1	2-0	1-1	0-1
Peterborough v Gillingham	-	-	-	2-0	1-2	1-1
Port Vale v Walsall	-	-	-	1-0	1-1	0-5
Rochdale v Chesterfield	-	1-1	1-1	2-2	1-0	2-3
Sheffield United v Oldham	-	2-3	1-1	1-1	1-1	3-0
Southend v AFC Wimbledon	-	2-0	1-3	0-1	0-1	-
League Two						
Cheltenham v Barnet	1-1	2-0	1-0	-	-	-
Crewe v Carlisle	-	-	1-0	2-1	-	-
Grimsby v Accrington	-	-	-	-	-	-
Hartlepool v Blackpool	-	-	-	-	-	-
Leyton Orient v Crawley Town	-	-	0-1	2-3	4-1	2-0
Luton v Colchester	-	-	-	-	-	-

Results cover matches from Premier League to National League and Scottish Premiership to League Two

The Football Annual 2016-17

	2010-11	2011-12	2012-13	2013-14	2014-15	2015-16
Mansfield v Morecambe	-	-	-	1-2	1-0	2-1
Newport County v Portsmouth	-	-	-	1-2	1-0	0-1
Notts County v Doncaster	-	-	0-2	-	2-1	-
Plymouth v Wycombe	-	-	0-1	0-3	0-1	0-1
Stevenage v Cambridge U	-	-	-	-	3-2	2-0
Yeovil v Exeter	1-3	2-2	-	-	-	0-2

National League

	2010-11	2011-12	2012-13	2013-14	2014-15	2015-16
Aldershot v Woking	-	-	-	2-1	0-1	0-1
Barrow v Gateshead	1-3	1-2	0-2	-	-	0-0
Braintree v Dag & Red	-	-	-	-	-	-
Bromley v Sutton United	-	-	-	-	-	-
Dover v Maidstone	-	-	-	-	-	-
Eastleigh v Boreham Wood	-	-	-	-	-	1-0
Guiseley v Lincoln	-	-	-	-	-	0-1
North Ferriby v York	-	-	-	-	-	-
Solihull Moors v Chester	-	-	-	-	-	-
Torquay v Forest Green	-	-	-	-	3-3	4-1
Tranmere v Macclesfield	-	-	-	-	-	0-1
Wrexham v Southport	2-1	2-0	2-2	1-0	0-0	0-1

Scottish League One

	2010-11	2011-12	2012-13	2013-14	2014-15	2015-16
Peterhead v Stenhousemuir	2-2/0-3	-	-	-	1-0/2-0	2-2/4-1

Scottish League Two

	2010-11	2011-12	2012-13	2013-14	2014-15	2015-16
Forfar v Clyde	-	-	-	-	-	-

Wednesday December 28, 2016
Ladbrokes Premiership

	2010-11	2011-12	2012-13	2013-14	2014-15	2015-16
Aberdeen v Hamilton	4-0/1-0	-	-	-	3-0	1-0/3-0
Celtic v Ross County	-	-	4-0	2-1/1-1	0-0	2-0/2-0/1-1
Hearts v Kilmarnock	0-3/0-2	0-1	1-3/0-3	0-4/5-0	-	1-1/1-0
Inverness CT v Motherwell	1-2/3-0	2-3	1-5/4-3	2-0/1-2	3-1	0-1/1-2
Partick v Dundee	1-0/0-0	0-1/0-0	-	-	1-1	0-1/2-4/1-2
St Johnstone v Rangers	0-2	0-2/1-2/0-4	-	-	-	-

Friday December 30, 2016
Championship

	2010-11	2011-12	2012-13	2013-14	2014-15	2015-16
Brighton v Cardiff	-	2-2	0-0	-	1-1	1-1
Ipswich v Bristol City	2-0	3-0	1-1	-	-	2-2
Reading v Fulham	-	-	3-3	-	3-0	2-2

League One

	2010-11	2011-12	2012-13	2013-14	2014-15	2015-16
MK Dons v Swindon	2-1	-	2-0	1-1	2-1	-

League Two

	2010-11	2011-12	2012-13	2013-14	2014-15	2015-16
Cheltenham v Wycombe	1-2	-	4-0	1-1	1-4	-
Hartlepool v Morecambe	-	-	-	2-1	0-2	2-0

Saturday December 31, 2016
Premier League

	2010-11	2011-12	2012-13	2013-14	2014-15	2015-16
Arsenal v Crystal Palace	-	-	-	2-0	2-1	1-1
Burnley v Sunderland	-	-	-	-	0-0	-
Chelsea v Stoke	2-0	1-0	1-0	3-0	2-1	1-1
Hull v Everton	-	-	-	0-2	2-0	-
Leicester v West Ham	-	1-2	-	-	2-1	2-2
Liverpool v Man City	3-0	1-1	2-2	3-2	2-1	3-0
Man United v Middlesbrough	-	-	-	-	-	-
Southampton v West Brom	-	-	0-3	1-0	0-0	3-0
Swansea v Bournemouth	-	-	-	-	-	2-2
Watford v Tottenham	-	-	-	-	-	1-2

Results cover matches from Premier League to National League and Scottish Premiership to League Two

	2010-11	2011-12	2012-13	2013-14	2014-15	2015-16
Championship						
Aston Villa v Leeds	-	-	-	-	-	-
Barnsley v Birmingham	-	1-3	1-2	0-3	-	-
Brentford v Norwich	-	-	-	-	0-3	-
Derby v Wigan	-	-	-	0-1	1-2	-
Huddersfield v Blackburn	-	-	2-2	2-4	2-2	1-1
Newcastle v Nottm Forest	-	-	-	-	-	-
Preston v Sheffield Weds	-	0-2	-	-	-	1-0
Rotherham v Burton	3-3	0-1	3-0	-	-	-
Wolves v QPR	-	0-3	-	-	-	2-3
League One						
Bolton v Scunthorpe	-	-	-	-	-	-
Bradford v Bury	1-0	-	-	-	-	2-1
Bristol Rovers v AFC Wimbledon	-	1-0	1-0	3-0	-	3-1
Fleetwood Town v Oldham	-	-	-	-	0-2	1-1
Millwall v Gillingham	-	-	-	-	-	0-3
Oxford v Walsall	-	-	-	-	-	-
Peterborough v Coventry	-	1-0	-	1-0	0-1	3-1
Port Vale v Chesterfield	1-1	-	0-2	-	1-2	3-2
Rochdale v Shrewsbury	-	-	-	-	-	3-2
Sheffield United v Northampton	-	-	-	-	-	-
Southend v Charlton	-	-	-	-	-	-
League Two						
Crewe v Accrington	0-0	2-0	-	-	-	-
Grimsby v Blackpool	-	-	-	-	-	-
Leyton Orient v Cambridge U	-	-	-	-	-	1-3
Luton v Barnet	-	-	-	2-1	-	2-0
Mansfield v Doncaster	-	-	-	-	-	-
Newport County v Exeter	-	-	-	1-1	2-2	1-1
Notts County v Carlisle	0-1	2-0	1-0	4-1	-	0-5
Plymouth v Crawley Town	-	1-1	-	-	-	2-1
Stevenage v Colchester	-	0-0	0-2	2-3	-	-
Yeovil v Portsmouth	-	-	1-2	-	-	1-1
Scottish Premiership						
Dundee v St Johnstone	-	-	1-3/2-2	-	1-1/0-2	2-1/2-0
Hamilton v Motherwell	0-0	-	-	-	5-0/2-0	1-0/0-1
Hearts v Aberdeen	5-0	3-0/3-0	2-0	2-1/1-1	-	1-3/2-1
Partick v Kilmarnock	-	-	-	1-1/1-1	1-1/1-4	2-2/0-0
Rangers v Celtic	0-2/0-0	4-2/3-2	-	-	-	-
Ross County v Inverness CT	-	-	0-0/1-0	0-3/1-2	1-3	1-2/0-3
Scottish Championship						
Dumbarton v Dundee United	-	-	-	-	-	-
Falkirk v Hibernian	-	-	-	-	1-0/0-3	0-1/1-1
Queen of Sth v Ayr	-	4-1/2-1	2-0/2-0	-	-	-
Raith v Dunfermline	2-0/2-1	-	1-3/1-1	-	-	-
St Mirren v Morton	-	-	-	-	-	1-1/3-1
Scottish League One						
East Fife v Livingston	2-4/1-3	-	-	-	-	-
Queens Park v Stranraer	1-3/3-3	2-0/3-2	-	-	-	-
Stenhousemuir v Alloa	0-1/2-3	-	0-2/1-1	-	-	-
Scottish League Two						
Berwick v Edinburgh City	-	-	-	-	-	-
Clyde v Annan	0-2/0-2	0-0/1-1	2-1/2-3	2-1/0-3	1-1/1-0	4-2/2-1
Stirling v Cowdenbeath	1-3/3-4	1-1/0-2	-	-	-	-

Results cover matches from Premier League to National League and Scottish Premiership to League Two

Sunday January 1, 2017

National League

	2010-11	2011-12	2012-13	2013-14	2014-15	2015-16
Boreham Wood v Eastleigh	-	-	-	-	-	1-1
Chester v Solihull Moors	-	-	-	-	-	-
Dag & Red v Braintree	-	-	-	-	-	-
Forest Green v Torquay	-	-	-	-	2-1	3-1
Gateshead v Barrow	3-0	2-0	0-1	-	-	1-1
Lincoln v Guiseley	-	-	-	-	-	1-0
Macclesfield v Tranmere	-	-	-	-	-	1-2
Maidstone v Dover	-	-	-	-	-	-
Southport v Wrexham	0-1	0-0	1-4	1-2	0-1	3-2
Sutton United v Bromley	-	-	-	-	-	-
Woking v Aldershot	-	-	-	1-2	1-2	2-1
York v North Ferriby	-	-	-	-	-	-

Monday January 2, 2017

Premier League

	2010-11	2011-12	2012-13	2013-14	2014-15	2015-16
Bournemouth v Arsenal	-	-	-	-	-	0-2
Crystal Palace v Swansea	0-3	-	-	0-2	1-0	0-0
Everton v Southampton	-	-	3-1	2-1	1-0	1-1
Man City v Burnley	-	-	-	-	2-2	-
Middlesbrough v Leicester	3-3	0-0	1-2	1-2	-	-
Stoke v Watford	-	-	-	-	-	0-2
Sunderland v Liverpool	0-2	1-0	1-1	1-3	0-1	0-1
Tottenham v Chelsea	1-1	1-1	2-4	1-1	5-3	0-0
West Brom v Hull	-	-	-	1-1	1-0	-
West Ham v Man United	2-4	-	2-2	0-2	1-1	3-2

Championship

	2010-11	2011-12	2012-13	2013-14	2014-15	2015-16
Birmingham v Brentford	-	-	-	-	1-0	2-1
Blackburn v Newcastle	0-0	0-2	-	-	-	-
Bristol City v Reading	1-0	2-3	-	-	-	0-2
Burton v Preston	-	-	-	-	-	-
Cardiff v Aston Villa	-	-	-	0-0	-	-
Fulham v Brighton	-	-	-	-	0-2	1-2
Leeds v Rotherham	-	-	-	-	0-0	0-1
Norwich v Derby	3-2	-	-	-	1-1	-
Nottm Forest v Barnsley	2-2	0-0	0-0	3-2	-	-
QPR v Ipswich	2-0	-	-	1-0	-	1-0
Sheffield Weds v Wolves	-	-	0-0	-	0-1	4-1
Wigan v Huddersfield	-	-	-	2-1	0-1	-

League One

	2010-11	2011-12	2012-13	2013-14	2014-15	2015-16
AFC Wimbledon v Millwall	-	-	-	-	-	-
Bury v Sheffield United	-	0-3	0-2	-	-	1-0
Charlton v Bristol Rovers	1-1	-	-	-	-	-
Chesterfield v MK Dons	-	1-1	-	-	0-1	-
Coventry v Bolton	-	-	-	-	-	-
Gillingham v Oxford	0-0	1-0	0-1	-	-	-
Northampton v Bradford	2-0	1-3	0-1	-	-	-
Oldham v Port Vale	-	-	-	3-1	1-1	1-1
Scunthorpe v Peterborough	-	-	-	-	2-0	0-4
Shrewsbury v Fleetwood Town	-	-	-	-	-	1-1
Swindon v Southend	-	2-0	-	-	-	4-2
Walsall v Rochdale	0-0	0-0	-	-	3-2	0-3

Results cover matches from Premier League to National League and Scottish Premiership to League Two

	2010-11	2011-12	2012-13	2013-14	2014-15	2015-16
League Two						
Accrington v Hartlepool	-	-	-	0-0	3-1	3-1
Barnet v Plymouth	-	2-0	1-4	-	-	1-0
Blackpool v Mansfield	-	-	-	-	-	-
Cambridge U v Notts County	-	-	-	-	-	3-1
Carlisle v Grimsby	-	-	-	-	-	-
Colchester v Cheltenham	-	-	-	-	-	-
Crawley Town v Yeovil	-	-	0-1	-	2-0	0-1
Doncaster v Stevenage	-	-	1-1	-	-	-
Exeter v Leyton Orient	2-1	3-0	-	-	-	4-0
Morecambe v Crewe	1-2	1-2	-	-	-	-
Portsmouth v Luton	-	-	-	-	2-0	0-0
Wycombe v Newport County	-	-	-	0-1	1-2	0-2
Scottish League One						
Airdrieonians v Albion	-	4-0/1-0	-	-	-	1-1/1-1
Brechin v Peterhead	4-2/3-1	-	-	-	1-1/2-2	1-1/5-1
Scottish League Two						
Arbroath v Montrose	4-0/4-1	-	-	-	3-1/2-2	3-1/0-0
Elgin v Forfar	-	-	-	-	-	-

Saturday January 7, 2017

	2010-11	2011-12	2012-13	2013-14	2014-15	2015-16
League One						
Bradford v Chesterfield	0-1	-	0-0	-	0-1	2-0
Bristol Rovers v Northampton	-	2-1	3-1	1-0	-	0-1
Coventry v Port Vale	-	-	-	2-2	2-3	1-0
Gillingham v AFC Wimbledon	-	3-4	2-2	-	-	-
Millwall v Walsall	-	-	-	-	-	0-1
MK Dons v Oldham	0-0	5-0	2-0	2-1	7-0	-
Oxford v Bolton	-	-	-	-	-	-
Peterborough v Southend	-	-	-	-	-	0-0
Rochdale v Charlton	2-0	2-3	-	-	-	-
Scunthorpe v Bury	-	1-3	1-2	2-2	-	2-1
Sheffield United v Fleetwood Town	-	-	-	-	1-2	3-0
Swindon v Shrewsbury	-	2-1	2-0	3-1	-	3-0
League Two						
Accrington v Cambridge U	-	-	-	-	2-1	1-1
Blackpool v Crawley Town	-	-	-	-	-	-
Colchester v Carlisle	1-1	1-1	2-0	1-1	-	-
Doncaster v Portsmouth	0-2	3-4	1-1	-	-	-
Exeter v Wycombe	-	1-3	3-2	0-1	2-1	0-2
Hartlepool v Grimsby	-	-	-	-	-	-
Leyton Orient v Barnet	-	-	-	-	-	2-0
Luton v Cheltenham	-	-	-	-	1-0	-
Mansfield v Crewe	-	-	-	-	-	-
Morecambe v Notts County	-	-	-	-	-	4-1
Stevenage v Newport County	-	-	-	-	2-1	2-1
Yeovil v Plymouth	1-0	-	-	-	-	0-0
National League						
Aldershot v Southport	-	-	-	5-1	1-2	1-2
Barrow v Lincoln	-	1-0	1-2	-	-	1-0
Braintree v Chester	-	-	-	3-0	1-3	2-0
Bromley v Forest Green	-	-	-	-	-	2-2
Dover v York	-	-	-	-	-	-
Eastleigh v Macclesfield	-	-	-	-	4-0	1-0
Guiseley v Maidstone	-	-	-	-	-	-
North Ferriby v Dag & Red	-	-	-	-	-	-
Solihull Moors v Gateshead	-	-	-	-	-	-
Torquay v Boreham Wood	-	-	-	-	-	1-2
Tranmere v Sutton United	-	-	-	-	-	-
Wrexham v Woking	-	-	3-1	2-0	1-2	1-3

Results cover matches from Premier League to National League and Scottish Premiership to League Two

	2010-11	2011-12	2012-13	2013-14	2014-15	2015-16
Scottish Championship						
Ayr v Dunfermline	-	-	-	2-4/1-1	0-1/0-2	1-2/0-2
Hibernian v Dundee United	2-2	3-3/0-2	2-1	1-1/1-3	-	-
Morton v Dumbarton	-	-	3-0/0-3	2-0/3-0	-	0-0/2-0
Raith v Falkirk	2-1/1-2	1-0/2-2	2-1/0-0	1-1/2-4	0-0/2-2	1-2/2-2
St Mirren v Queen of Sth	-	-	-	-	-	1-0/2-1
Scottish League One						
Albion v Brechin	-	1-2/0-1	1-2/3-1	-	-	3-1/4-1
East Fife v Stenhousemuir	6-0/1-1	1-3/1-1	3-2/1-2	1-0/1-2	-	-
Peterhead v Livingston	0-0/3-0	-	-	-	-	-
Queens Park v Airdrieonians	-	-	-	-	-	-
Stranraer v Alloa	-	2-3/0-4	3-2/1-2	-	-	-
Scottish League Two						
Annan v Forfar	-	-	-	-	-	-
Cowdenbeath v Berwick	-	-	-	-	-	-
Edinburgh City v Arbroath	-	-	-	-	-	-
Montrose v Elgin	0-1/1-0	3-0/2-3	2-2/4-1	3-3/0-3	2-3/2-1	2-0/3-1
Stirling v Clyde	-	-	0-1/2-0	1-1/4-1	-	0-1/1-2

Saturday January 14, 2017

	2010-11	2011-12	2012-13	2013-14	2014-15	2015-16
Premier League						
Burnley v Southampton	-	1-1	-	-	1-0	-
Everton v Man City	2-1	1-0	2-0	2-3	1-1	0-2
Hull v Bournemouth	-	-	-	-	-	-
Leicester v Chelsea	-	-	-	-	1-3	2-1
Man United v Liverpool	3-2	2-1	2-1	0-3	3-0	3-1
Sunderland v Stoke	2-0	4-0	1-1	1-0	3-1	2-0
Swansea v Arsenal	-	3-2	0-2	1-2	2-1	0-3
Tottenham v West Brom	2-2	1-0	1-1	1-1	0-1	1-1
Watford v Middlesbrough	3-1	2-1	1-2	1-0	2-0	-
West Ham v Crystal Palace	-	0-0	-	0-1	1-3	2-2
Championship						
Birmingham v Nottm Forest	-	1-2	2-1	0-0	2-1	0-1
Brentford v Newcastle	-	-	-	-	-	-
Bristol City v Cardiff	3-0	1-2	4-2	-	-	0-2
Burton v Wigan	-	-	-	-	-	1-1
Fulham v Barnsley	-	-	-	-	-	-
Ipswich v Blackburn	-	-	1-1	3-1	1-1	2-0
Leeds v Derby	1-2	0-2	1-2	1-1	2-0	2-2
Preston v Brighton	-	-	-	-	-	0-0
Reading v QPR	0-1	-	0-0	1-1	-	0-1
Rotherham v Norwich	-	-	-	-	1-1	-
Sheffield Weds v Huddersfield	0-2	4-4	1-3	1-2	1-1	3-1
Wolves v Aston Villa	1-2	2-3	-	-	-	-
League One						
AFC Wimbledon v Oxford	-	0-2	0-3	0-2	0-0	1-2
Bolton v Swindon	-	-	-	-	-	-
Bury v Peterborough	-	-	-	-	-	3-1
Charlton v Millwall	-	-	0-2	0-1	0-0	-
Chesterfield v Coventry	-	-	-	-	2-3	1-1
Fleetwood Town v Bristol Rovers	-	-	0-3	3-1	-	-
Northampton v Scunthorpe	-	-	-	1-1	-	-
Oldham v Gillingham	-	-	-	1-0	0-0	2-1
Port Vale v MK Dons	-	-	-	1-0	0-0	-
Shrewsbury v Bradford	3-1	1-0	-	2-1	-	1-1
Southend v Rochdale	-	-	3-1	1-1	-	2-2
Walsall v Sheffield United	-	3-2	1-1	2-1	1-1	1-1

Results cover matches from Premier League to National League and Scottish Premiership to League Two

	2010-11	2011-12	2012-13	2013-14	2014-15	2015-16
League Two						
Barnet v Doncaster	-	-	-	-	-	-
Cambridge U v Blackpool	-	-	-	-	-	-
Carlisle v Morecambe	-	-	-	-	1-1	2-3
Cheltenham v Accrington	1-2	4-1	0-3	1-2	2-1	-
Crawley Town v Hartlepool	-	-	2-2	-	-	0-0
Crewe v Luton	-	-	-	-	-	-
Grimsby v Exeter	-	-	-	-	-	-
Newport County v Colchester	-	-	-	-	-	-
Notts County v Mansfield	-	-	-	-	-	0-2
Plymouth v Stevenage	-	-	-	-	1-1	3-2
Portsmouth v Leyton Orient	-	-	2-3	-	-	0-1
Wycombe v Yeovil	-	2-3	-	-	-	0-0
Scottish Championship						
Dumbarton v Hibernian	-	-	-	-	3-6/1-2	2-1/3-2
Dundee United v Queen of Sth	-	-	-	-	-	-
Dunfermline v St Mirren	-	0-0/1-1	-	-	-	-
Falkirk v Ayr	-	0-0/3-2	-	-	-	-
Morton v Raith	0-1/0-0	1-1/1-3	1-0/1-0	1-1/0-0	-	1-2/0-1
Scottish League One						
Airdrieonians v East Fife	1-1/2-2	1-3/2-0	-	1-3/2-1	-	-
Alloa v Peterhead	2-2/0-0	2-1/3-1	-	-	-	-
Brechin v Queens Park	-	-	-	-	-	-
Livingston v Albion	-	-	-	-	-	-
Stenhousemuir v Stranraer	-	-	0-0/1-2	1-0/1-1	2-2/1-0	1-0/1-5
Scottish League Two						
Arbroath v Berwick	3-2/2-1	-	-	-	2-0/5-0	3-1/1-2
Clyde v Montrose	2-0/1-1	1-0/1-2	1-2/1-0	0-3/1-1	1-2/2-0	3-1/3-3
Cowdenbeath v Edinburgh City	-	-	-	-	-	-
Elgin v Annan	2-0/2-3	3-0/1-2	2-2/3-1	2-3/2-3	0-0/4-5	3-2/2-2
Forfar v Stirling	-	2-2/4-3	-	-	2-1/4-0	-

Friday January 20, 2017

	2010-11	2011-12	2012-13	2013-14	2014-15	2015-16
League One						
Port Vale v Bury	0-0	-	-	-	-	1-0

Saturday January 21, 2017

	2010-11	2011-12	2012-13	2013-14	2014-15	2015-16
Premier League						
Arsenal v Burnley	-	-	-	-	3-0	-
Bournemouth v Watford	-	-	-	1-1	2-0	1-1
Chelsea v Hull	-	-	-	2-0	2-0	-
Crystal Palace v Everton	-	-	-	0-0	0-1	0-0
Liverpool v Swansea	-	0-0	5-0	4-3	4-1	1-0
Man City v Tottenham	1-0	3-2	2-1	6-0	4-1	1-2
Middlesbrough v West Ham	-	0-2	-	-	-	-
Southampton v Leicester	-	0-2	-	-	2-0	2-2
Stoke v Man United	1-2	1-1	0-2	2-1	1-1	2-0
West Brom v Sunderland	1-0	4-0	2-1	3-0	2-2	1-0
Championship						
Aston Villa v Preston	-	-	-	-	-	-
Barnsley v Leeds	5-2	4-1	2-0	0-1	-	-
Blackburn v Birmingham	1-1	-	1-1	2-3	1-0	2-0
Brighton v Sheffield Weds	2-0	-	3-0	1-1	0-1	0-0
Cardiff v Burton	-	-	-	-	-	-
Derby v Reading	1-2	0-1	-	1-3	0-3	1-1
Huddersfield v Ipswich	-	-	0-0	0-2	2-1	0-1
Newcastle v Rotherham	-	-	-	-	-	-
Norwich v Wolves	-	2-1	-	-	2-0	-
Nottm Forest v Bristol City	1-0	0-1	1-0	-	-	1-2
QPR v Fulham	-	0-1	2-1	-	-	1-3
Wigan v Brentford	-	-	-	-	0-0	-

Results cover matches from Premier League to National League and Scottish Premiership to League Two

	2010-11	2011-12	2012-13	2013-14	2014-15	2015-16
League One						
Bradford v Millwall	-	-	-	-	-	1-0
Charlton v Scunthorpe	-	2-2	-	-	-	-
Chesterfield v AFC Wimbledon	-	-	2-0	2-0	-	-
Coventry v Fleetwood Town	-	-	-	-	1-1	1-2
MK Dons v Northampton	-	-	-	-	-	-
Rochdale v Oxford	-	-	2-0	3-0	-	-
Sheffield United v Gillingham	-	-	-	1-2	2-1	0-0
Shrewsbury v Oldham	-	-	1-0	1-2	-	0-1
Southend v Bolton	-	-	-	-	-	-
Swindon v Peterborough	1-1	-	-	2-1	1-0	1-2
Walsall v Bristol Rovers	6-1	-	-	-	-	-
League Two						
Accrington v Carlisle	-	-	-	-	3-1	1-1
Barnet v Newport County	-	-	-	-	-	2-0
Blackpool v Yeovil	-	-	-	1-2	-	-
Cambridge U v Mansfield	1-5	1-2	4-1	-	3-1	1-1
Cheltenham v Plymouth	-	2-1	2-1	1-3	0-3	-
Crawley Town v Portsmouth	-	-	0-3	-	-	0-0
Doncaster v Crewe	-	-	0-2	-	2-1	3-2
Exeter v Colchester	2-2	1-1	-	-	-	-
Grimsby v Notts County	-	-	-	-	-	-
Hartlepool v Stevenage	-	0-0	0-2	-	1-3	1-2
Leyton Orient v Morecambe	-	-	-	-	-	1-0
Wycombe v Luton	-	-	-	-	1-1	0-1
National League						
Boreham Wood v Solihull Moors	-	-	-	-	-	-
Chester v Wrexham	-	-	-	0-0	2-1	3-2
Dag & Red v Bromley	-	-	-	-	-	-
Forest Green v Braintree	-	0-2	4-1	0-2	1-1	1-0
Gateshead v Aldershot	-	-	-	0-0	1-1	3-2
Lincoln v Dover	-	-	-	-	1-0	2-3
Macclesfield v Guiseley	-	-	-	-	-	1-0
Maidstone v Torquay	-	-	-	-	-	-
Southport v North Ferriby	-	-	-	-	-	-
Sutton United v Eastleigh	-	-	-	-	-	-
Woking v Tranmere	-	-	-	-	-	4-1
York v Barrow	0-0	3-1	-	-	-	-
Scottish League Two						
Arbroath v Annan	0-2/2-1	-	-	-	3-2/1-1	0-2/2-1
Berwick v Clyde	2-1/1-1	0-2/3-0	2-1/3-3	0-1/3-0	4-0/0-0	0-5/3-0
Edinburgh City v Forfar	-	-	-	-	-	-
Montrose v Cowdenbeath	-	-	-	-	-	-
Stirling v Elgin	-	-	1-4/1-1	1-1/2-2	-	3-1/0-0

Saturday January 28, 2017

	2010-11	2011-12	2012-13	2013-14	2014-15	2015-16
Championship						
Aston Villa v Bristol City	-	-	-	-	-	-
Brighton v Newcastle	-	-	-	-	-	-
Derby v Burton	-	-	-	-	-	-
Fulham v Blackburn	3-2	1-1	-	-	0-1	2-1
Leeds v Nottm Forest	4-1	3-7	2-1	0-2	0-0	0-1
Norwich v Birmingham	-	-	-	-	2-2	-
Preston v Ipswich	1-0	-	-	-	-	1-2
QPR v Wigan	-	3-1	1-1	1-0	-	-
Reading v Cardiff	1-1	1-2	-	-	1-1	1-1
Rotherham v Barnsley	-	-	-	-	-	-
Sheffield Weds v Brentford	1-3	0-0	-	-	1-0	4-0
Wolves v Huddersfield	-	-	1-3	-	1-3	3-0

Results cover matches from Premier League to National League and Scottish Premiership to League Two

	2010-11	2011-12	2012-13	2013-14	2014-15	2015-16
League One						
AFC Wimbledon v Rochdale	-	-	1-2	0-3	-	-
Bolton v Charlton	-	-	2-0	1-1	1-1	0-0
Bristol Rovers v Swindon	3-1	1-1	-	-	-	-
Bury v Walsall	-	2-1	1-1	-	-	2-3
Fleetwood Town v Southend	-	-	0-0	1-1	-	1-1
Gillingham v Shrewsbury	2-0	0-1	-	1-1	-	2-3
Millwall v Chesterfield	-	-	-	-	-	0-2
Northampton v Coventry	-	-	-	-	-	-
Oldham v Bradford	-	-	-	1-1	2-1	1-2
Oxford v Sheffield United	-	-	-	-	-	-
Peterborough v MK Dons	2-1	-	-	2-1	3-2	-
Scunthorpe v Port Vale	-	-	-	-	1-1	1-0
League Two						
Carlisle v Barnet	-	-	-	-	-	3-2
Colchester v Wycombe	-	1-1	-	-	-	-
Crewe v Cheltenham	8-1	1-0	-	-	-	-
Luton v Cambridge U	2-0	0-1	3-2	0-0	3-2	0-0
Mansfield v Leyton Orient	-	-	-	-	-	1-1
Morecambe v Accrington	1-2	1-2	0-0	1-2	1-1	1-0
Newport County v Hartlepool	-	-	-	2-0	2-2	0-0
Notts County v Crawley Town	-	-	1-1	1-0	5-3	4-1
Plymouth v Blackpool	-	-	-	-	-	-
Portsmouth v Exeter	-	-	-	3-2	1-0	1-2
Stevenage v Grimsby	-	-	-	-	-	-
Yeovil v Doncaster	-	-	2-1	1-0	0-3	-
National League						
Aldershot v York	-	-	0-2	-	-	-
Barrow v Forest Green	3-0	1-1	2-2	-	-	2-2
Braintree v Lincoln	-	1-0	0-3	0-2	1-3	1-3
Bromley v Southport	-	-	-	-	-	0-0
Dover v Chester	-	-	-	-	2-0	0-0
Eastleigh v Woking	-	-	-	-	2-2	2-1
Guiseley v Sutton United	-	-	-	-	-	-
North Ferriby v Macclesfield	-	-	-	-	-	-
Solihull Moors v Maidstone	-	-	-	-	-	-
Torquay v Gateshead	-	-	-	-	2-2	0-2
Tranmere v Dag & Red	2-0	-	-	-	2-3	-
Wrexham v Boreham Wood	-	-	-	-	-	1-0
Scottish Premiership						
Aberdeen v Dundee	-	-	2-0/1-0	-	3-3	2-0/1-0
Celtic v Hearts	3-0/4-0	1-0/5-0	1-0/4-1	2-0	-	0-0/3-1
Inverness CT v Partick	-	-	-	1-2/1-0	0-4	0-0/0-0
Kilmarnock v Ross County	-	-	3-0	2-0/2-2	0-3/1-2	0-4/0-2
Motherwell v Rangers	1-4/0-5	0-3/1-2	-	-	-	-
St Johnstone v Hamilton	2-0/1-0	-	-	-	0-1	4-1/0-0
Scottish Championship						
Ayr v Morton	-	0-1/0-0	-	-	1-0/1-1	-
Dunfermline v Dundee United	-	1-4	-	-	-	-
Queen of Sth v Hibernian	-	-	-	-	1-0/0-2	0-3/1-0
Raith v Dumbarton	-	-	2-2/3-2	2-1/1-3	3-1/2-1	1-0/0-0
St Mirren v Falkirk	-	-	-	-	-	2-3/0-0

Results cover matches from Premier League to National League and Scottish Premiership to League Two

	2010-11	2011-12	2012-13	2013-14	2014-15	2015-16
Scottish League One						
Albion v Alloa	-	-	0-3/1-5	-	-	-
East Fife v Stranraer	-	-	0-1/1-1	1-2/1-1	-	-
Livingston v Brechin	2-0/0-0	-	-	-	-	-
Peterhead v Queens Park	-	1-1/2-1	1-0/0-2	2-1/1-0	-	-
Stenhousemuir v Airdrieonians	1-3/1-0	1-1/0-3	-	1-1/1-2	1-0/0-2	2-1/3-2
Scottish League Two						
Annan v Stirling	-	-	5-2/0-1	4-4/1-2	-	1-1/2-2
Clyde v Arbroath	1-1/0-3	-	-	-	2-5/1-1	0-2/1-2
Elgin v Edinburgh City	-	-	-	-	-	-
Forfar v Cowdenbeath	-	2-2/1-0	-	-	-	0-1/1-1
Montrose v Berwick	1-1/1-1	3-5/1-1	3-1/1-3	1-1/0-0	2-1/0-2	4-1/1-0

Tuesday January 31, 2017

	2010-11	2011-12	2012-13	2013-14	2014-15	2015-16
Premier League						
Arsenal v Watford	-	-	-	-	-	4-0
Bournemouth v Crystal Palace	-	-	-	-	-	0-0
Burnley v Leicester	3-0	1-3	0-1	0-2	0-1	-
Man United v Hull	-	-	-	3-1	3-0	-
Middlesbrough v West Brom	-	-	-	-	-	-
Sunderland v Tottenham	1-2	0-0	1-2	1-2	2-2	0-1
Swansea v Southampton	-	-	0-0	0-1	0-1	0-1
West Ham v Man City	1-3	-	0-0	1-3	2-1	2-2
Championship						
Barnsley v Wolves	-	-	2-1	-	-	-
Birmingham v Reading	-	2-0	-	1-2	6-1	2-1
Brentford v Aston Villa	-	-	-	-	-	-
Bristol City v Sheffield Weds	-	-	1-1	-	-	4-1
Burton v Fulham	-	-	-	-	-	-
Cardiff v Preston	1-1	-	-	-	-	2-1
Huddersfield v Brighton	2-1	-	1-2	1-1	1-1	1-1
Ipswich v Derby	0-2	1-0	1-2	2-1	0-1	0-1
Nottm Forest v Rotherham	-	-	-	-	2-0	2-1
Wigan v Norwich	-	1-1	1-0	-	0-1	-

Wednesday February 1, 2017

	2010-11	2011-12	2012-13	2013-14	2014-15	2015-16
Premier League						
Liverpool v Chelsea	2-0	4-1	2-2	0-2	1-2	1-1
Stoke v Everton	2-0	1-1	1-1	1-1	2-0	0-3
Championship						
Blackburn v Leeds	-	-	0-0	1-0	2-1	1-2
Newcastle v QPR	-	1-0	1-0	-	1-0	-
Scottish Premiership						
Celtic v Aberdeen	9-0/1-0	2-1	1-0/4-3	3-1/5-2	2-1/4-0	3-1/3-2
Dundee v Kilmarnock	-	-	0-0/2-3	-	1-1/1-0	1-2/1-1
Hamilton v Inverness CT	1-3/1-2	-	-	-	0-2/0-2	3-4/0-1
Hearts v Rangers	1-2/1-0	0-2/0-3	-	-	2-0/2-2	-
Partick v St Johnstone	-	-	-	0-1	0-0/3-0	2-0
Ross County v Motherwell	-	-	0-0/3-0	1-2	1-2/3-2	3-0/1-3

Saturday February 4, 2017

	2010-11	2011-12	2012-13	2013-14	2014-15	2015-16
Premier League						
Chelsea v Arsenal	2-0	3-5	2-1	6-0	2-0	2-0
Crystal Palace v Sunderland	-	-	-	3-1	1-3	0-1
Everton v Bournemouth	-	-	-	-	-	2-1
Hull v Liverpool	-	-	-	3-1	1-0	-

Results cover matches from Premier League to National League and Scottish Premiership to League Two

	2010-11	2011-12	2012-13	2013-14	2014-15	2015-16
Leicester v Man United	-	-	-	-	5-3	1-1
Man City v Swansea	-	4-0	1-0	3-0	2-1	2-1
Southampton v West Ham	-	1-0	1-1	0-0	0-0	1-0
Tottenham v Middlesbrough	-	-	-	-	-	-
Watford v Burnley	1-3	3-2	3-3	1-1	-	-
West Brom v Stoke	0-3	0-1	0-1	1-2	1-0	2-1
Championship						
Barnsley v Preston	2-0	-	-	-	1-1	-
Birmingham v Fulham	0-2	-	-	-	1-2	1-1
Blackburn v QPR	-	3-2	-	2-0	-	1-1
Brentford v Brighton	0-1	-	-	-	3-2	0-0
Bristol City v Rotherham	-	-	-	1-2	-	1-1
Burton v Wolves	-	-	-	-	-	-
Cardiff v Norwich	3-1	-	-	2-1	2-4	-
Huddersfield v Leeds	-	-	2-4	3-2	1-2	0-3
Ipswich v Reading	1-3	2-3	-	2-0	0-1	2-1
Newcastle v Derby	-	-	-	-	-	-
Nottm Forest v Aston Villa	-	-	-	-	-	-
Wigan v Sheffield Weds	-	-	-	1-0	0-1	-
League One						
Bradford v Gillingham	1-0	2-2	0-1	1-1	1-1	1-2
Charlton v Fleetwood Town	-	-	-	-	-	-
Chesterfield v Oldham	-	1-1	-	-	1-1	1-2
Coventry v Millwall	2-1	0-1	-	-	-	2-1
MK Dons v Bolton	-	-	-	-	-	1-0
Port Vale v Peterborough	-	-	-	0-1	2-1	1-1
Rochdale v Bristol Rovers	3-1	-	2-1	2-0	-	-
Sheffield United v AFC Wimbledon	-	-	-	-	-	-
Shrewsbury v Bury	0-3	-	0-0	-	5-0	2-0
Southend v Scunthorpe	-	-	-	0-1	-	2-1
Walsall v Northampton	-	-	-	-	-	-
League Two						
Accrington v Notts County	-	-	-	-	-	3-2
Barnet v Mansfield	-	-	-	-	-	1-3
Blackpool v Colchester	-	-	-	-	-	0-1
Cambridge U v Plymouth	-	-	-	-	1-0	2-2
Cheltenham v Newport County	-	-	-	0-0	0-1	-
Crawley Town v Stevenage	-	-	1-1	1-1	-	2-1
Doncaster v Morecambe	-	-	-	-	-	-
Exeter v Crewe	-	-	-	-	-	-
Grimsby v Luton	2-0	0-1	4-1	1-2	-	-
Hartlepool v Yeovil	3-1	0-1	0-0	-	-	2-1
Leyton Orient v Carlisle	0-0	1-2	4-1	4-0	-	1-2
Wycombe v Portsmouth	-	-	-	0-1	0-0	2-2
National League						
Barrow v Tranmere	-	-	-	-	-	3-4
Boreham Wood v Dover	-	-	-	-	-	3-0
Bromley v Torquay	-	-	-	-	-	0-2
Dag & Red v Chester	-	-	-	-	1-0	-
Eastleigh v Braintree	-	-	-	-	1-0	0-2
Gateshead v Southport	1-0	2-3	2-2	2-2	1-1	0-1
Macclesfield v York	-	-	-	-	-	-
Maidstone v Aldershot	-	-	-	-	-	-
North Ferriby v Lincoln	-	-	-	-	-	-
Sutton United v Forest Green	-	-	-	-	-	-
Woking v Solihull Moors	-	-	-	-	-	-
Wrexham v Guiseley	-	-	-	-	-	3-3

Results cover matches from Premier League to National League and Scottish Premiership to League Two

	2010-11	2011-12	2012-13	2013-14	2014-15	2015-16
Scottish Premiership						
Aberdeen v Partick	-	-	-	4-0	2-0/0-0	0-0
Hamilton v Kilmarnock	2-2/1-1	-	-	-	0-0/0-0	0-1/0-4
Inverness CT v Dundee	-	-	4-1	-	0-0/1-1	1-1/4-0
Motherwell v Hearts	1-2	1-0/3-0	0-0	2-1/4-1	-	2-2/1-0
Rangers v Ross County	-	-	-	-	-	-
St Johnstone v Celtic	0-3/0-1	0-2	2-1/1-1	0-1/3-3	0-3/1-2/0-0	0-3/2-1
Scottish Championship						
Dumbarton v St Mirren	-	-	-	-	-	1-0/2-1
Dundee United v Raith	-	-	-	-	-	-
Falkirk v Dunfermline	0-1/1-2	-	2-2/1-0	-	-	-
Hibernian v Ayr	-	-	-	-	-	-
Queen of Sth v Morton	2-0/1-4	4-1/2-1	-	2-0/3-0	-	2-2/1-0
Scottish League One						
Airdrieonians v Peterhead	2-2/1-0	-	-	-	0-2/1-3	1-0/3-4
Alloa v Livingston	2-2/1-3	-	-	1-0/0-3	1-0/2-2	0-3/1-3
Brechin v Stenhousemuir	0-0/3-1	2-0/1-0	7-2/1-2	0-1/1-3	1-0/2-1	1-2/1-0
Queens Park v East Fife	-	-	-	-	3-0/1-0	0-2/3-0
Stranraer v Albion	3-2/1-3	-	1-1/3-2	-	-	0-1/0-0
Scottish League Two						
Arbroath v Forfar	-	4-1/0-1	1-1/3-1	3-0/2-3	-	-
Berwick v Annan	2-2/2-3	0-1/1-3	3-1/0-2	4-2/1-4	2-0/2-2	0-2/3-2
Cowdenbeath v Elgin	-	-	-	-	-	-
Edinburgh City v Clyde	-	-	-	-	-	-
Stirling v Montrose	-	-	1-3/3-1	3-1/2-2	-	1-0/7-0

Sunday February 5, 2017

	2010-11	2011-12	2012-13	2013-14	2014-15	2015-16
League One						
Swindon v Oxford	-	1-2	-	-	-	-

Saturday February 11, 2017

	2010-11	2011-12	2012-13	2013-14	2014-15	2015-16
Premier League						
Arsenal v Hull	-	-	-	2-0	2-2	-
Bournemouth v Man City	-	-	-	-	-	0-4
Burnley v Chelsea	-	-	-	-	1-3	-
Liverpool v Tottenham	0-2	0-0	3-2	4-0	3-2	1-1
Man United v Watford	-	-	-	-	-	1-0
Middlesbrough v Everton	-	-	-	-	-	-
Stoke v Crystal Palace	-	-	-	2-1	1-2	1-2
Sunderland v Southampton	-	-	1-1	2-2	2-1	0-1
Swansea v Leicester	2-0	-	-	-	2-0	0-3
West Ham v West Brom	2-2	-	3-1	3-3	1-1	1-1
Championship						
Aston Villa v Ipswich	-	-	-	-	-	-
Brighton v Burton	-	-	-	-	-	-
Derby v Bristol City	0-2	2-1	3-0	-	-	4-0
Fulham v Wigan	2-0	2-1	1-1	-	2-2	-
Leeds v Cardiff	0-4	1-1	0-1	-	1-2	1-0
Norwich v Nottm Forest	2-1	-	-	-	3-1	-
Preston v Brentford	-	1-3	1-1	0-3	-	1-3
QPR v Huddersfield	-	-	-	2-1	-	1-1
Reading v Barnsley	3-0	1-2	-	1-3	-	-
Rotherham v Blackburn	-	-	-	-	2-0	0-1
Sheffield Weds v Birmingham	-	-	3-2	4-1	0-0	3-0
Wolves v Newcastle	1-1	1-2	-	-	-	-

Results cover matches from Premier League to National League and Scottish Premiership to League Two

	2010-11	2011-12	2012-13	2013-14	2014-15	2015-16
League One						
AFC Wimbledon v Charlton	-	-	-	-	-	-
Bolton v Walsall	-	-	-	-	-	-
Bristol Rovers v Bradford	-	2-1	3-3	-	-	-
Bury v Swindon	-	-	0-1	-	-	2-2
Fleetwood Town v Rochdale	-	-	0-3	0-0	1-0	1-1
Gillingham v Port Vale	3-0	1-1	1-2	3-2	2-2	0-2
Millwall v Southend	-	-	-	-	-	0-2
Northampton v Chesterfield	1-2	-	0-0	1-3	-	-
Oldham v Coventry	-	-	0-1	0-0	4-1	0-2
Oxford v MK Dons	-	-	-	-	-	-
Peterborough v Sheffield United	-	-	-	0-0	1-2	1-3
Scunthorpe v Shrewsbury	-	-	0-0	-	-	2-1
League Two						
Carlisle v Blackpool	-	-	-	-	-	-
Colchester v Barnet	-	-	-	-	-	-
Crewe v Grimsby	-	-	-	-	-	-
Luton v Crawley Town	1-2	-	-	-	-	0-1
Mansfield v Hartlepool	-	-	-	1-4	1-1	3-1
Morecambe v Cambridge U	-	-	-	-	0-2	2-4
Newport County v Doncaster	-	-	-	-	-	-
Notts County v Cheltenham	-	-	-	-	-	-
Plymouth v Exeter	2-0	-	1-0	1-2	3-0	1-2
Portsmouth v Accrington	-	-	-	1-0	2-3	0-0
Stevenage v Wycombe	0-2	1-1	-	-	1-3	2-1
Yeovil v Leyton Orient	2-1	2-2	3-0	-	0-3	0-1
National League						
Aldershot v Barrow	-	-	-	-	-	0-1
Braintree v North Ferriby	-	-	-	-	-	-
Chester v Gateshead	-	-	-	1-1	1-0	4-2
Dover v Wrexham	-	-	-	-	2-0	2-1
Forest Green v Boreham Wood	-	-	-	-	-	1-0
Guiseley v Eastleigh	-	-	-	-	-	1-4
Lincoln v Woking	-	-	0-2	2-2	0-2	2-3
Solihull Moors v Sutton United	-	-	-	-	-	-
Southport v Dag & Red	-	-	-	-	-	-
Torquay v Macclesfield	1-3	3-0	-	-	1-1	1-0
Tranmere v Bromley	-	-	-	-	-	4-0
York v Maidstone	-	-	-	-	-	-
Scottish League One						
Alloa v East Fife	3-2/1-3	-	1-1/1-1	-	-	-
Brechin v Airdrieonians	3-1/1-2	1-1/1-1	-	4-3/1-1	1-1/0-0	1-2/3-3
Livingston v Stranraer	-	-	-	-	-	-
Peterhead v Albion	-	-	-	1-1/2-0	-	1-1/5-1
Stenhousemuir v Queens Park	-	-	-	-	-	-
Scottish League Two						
Annan v Edinburgh City	-	-	-	-	-	-
Clyde v Cowdenbeath	-	-	-	-	-	-
Forfar v Elgin	-	-	-	-	-	-
Montrose v Arbroath	3-0/0-5	-	-	-	1-5/3-0	3-0/0-2
Stirling v Berwick	-	-	6-3/1-0	3-1/2-1	-	1-3/2-1

Results cover matches from Premier League to National League and Scottish Premiership to League Two

Tuesday February 14, 2017

Championship

	2010-11	2011-12	2012-13	2013-14	2014-15	2015-16
Aston Villa v Barnsley	-	-	-	-	-	-
Brighton v Ipswich	-	3-0	1-1	0-2	3-2	0-1
Derby v Cardiff	1-2	0-3	1-1	-	2-2	2-0
Fulham v Nottm Forest	-	-	-	-	3-2	1-3
Leeds v Bristol City	3-1	2-1	1-0	-	-	1-0
Norwich v Newcastle	-	4-2	0-0	0-0	-	3-2
Preston v Birmingham	-	-	-	-	-	1-1
QPR v Burton	-	-	-	-	-	-
Reading v Brentford	-	-	-	-	0-2	1-2
Rotherham v Huddersfield	-	-	-	-	2-2	1-1
Sheffield Weds v Blackburn	-	-	3-2	3-3	1-2	2-1
Wolves v Wigan	1-2	3-1	-	-	2-2	-

League One

	2010-11	2011-12	2012-13	2013-14	2014-15	2015-16
AFC Wimbledon v Coventry	-	-	-	-	-	-
Bolton v Rochdale	-	-	-	-	-	-
Bristol Rovers v Sheffield United	-	-	-	-	-	-
Bury v MK Dons	-	0-0	1-4	-	-	-
Fleetwood Town v Bradford	-	-	2-2	-	0-2	1-1
Gillingham v Chesterfield	0-2	-	1-1	-	2-3	1-2
Millwall v Port Vale	-	-	-	-	-	3-1
Northampton v Swindon	-	1-2	-	-	-	-
Oldham v Charlton	0-0	0-1	-	-	-	-
Oxford v Southend	0-2	0-2	2-0	0-2	2-3	-
Peterborough v Shrewsbury	-	-	-	1-0	-	1-1
Scunthorpe v Walsall	-	0-1	1-1	-	2-1	0-1

League Two

	2010-11	2011-12	2012-13	2013-14	2014-15	2015-16
Carlisle v Doncaster	-	-	1-3	-	-	-
Colchester v Crawley Town	-	-	1-1	1-1	2-3	-
Crewe v Wycombe	3-0	-	-	-	-	-
Luton v Hartlepool	-	-	-	-	3-0	2-1
Mansfield v Accrington	-	-	-	2-3	0-1	2-3
Morecambe v Barnet	2-2	0-1	4-1	-	-	4-2
Newport County v Grimsby	2-1	0-0	0-0	-	-	-
Notts County v Exeter	0-2	2-1	-	-	-	1-4
Plymouth v Leyton Orient	1-4	-	-	-	-	1-1
Portsmouth v Blackpool	-	1-0	-	-	-	-
Stevenage v Cheltenham	4-0	-	-	-	5-1	-
Yeovil v Cambridge U	-	-	-	-	-	2-3

Saturday February 18, 2017

Championship

	2010-11	2011-12	2012-13	2013-14	2014-15	2015-16
Barnsley v Brighton	-	0-0	2-1	0-0	-	-
Birmingham v QPR	-	-	-	0-2	-	2-1
Blackburn v Derby	-	-	2-0	1-1	2-3	0-0
Brentford v Wolves	-	-	-	0-3	4-0	3-0
Bristol City v Fulham	-	-	-	-	-	1-4
Burton v Norwich	-	-	-	-	-	-
Cardiff v Rotherham	-	-	-	-	0-0	2-2
Huddersfield v Reading	-	-	-	0-1	3-0	3-1
Ipswich v Leeds	2-1	2-1	3-0	1-2	4-1	2-1
Newcastle v Aston Villa	6-0	2-1	1-1	1-0	1-0	1-1
Nottm Forest v Sheffield Weds	-	-	1-0	3-3	0-2	0-3
Wigan v Preston	-	-	-	-	-	-

Results cover matches from Premier League to National League and Scottish Premiership to League Two

	2010-11	2011-12	2012-13	2013-14	2014-15	2015-16
League One						
Bradford v Bolton	-	-	-	-	-	-
Charlton v Oxford	-	-	-	-	-	-
Chesterfield v Bury	2-3	1-0	-	4-0	-	3-0
Coventry v Gillingham	-	-	-	2-1	1-0	4-1
MK Dons v Fleetwood Town	-	-	-	-	2-1	-
Port Vale v Bristol Rovers	-	1-0	4-0	-	-	-
Rochdale v Millwall	-	-	-	-	-	0-1
Sheffield United v Scunthorpe	0-4	2-1	3-0	-	4-0	0-2
Shrewsbury v AFC Wimbledon	-	0-0	-	-	2-0	-
Southend v Northampton	1-1	2-2	1-2	2-0	2-0	-
Swindon v Oldham	0-2	-	1-1	0-1	2-2	1-2
Walsall v Peterborough	1-3	-	-	2-0	0-0	2-0
League Two						
Accrington v Colchester	-	-	-	-	-	-
Barnet v Portsmouth	-	-	-	-	-	1-0
Blackpool v Crewe	-	-	-	-	-	2-0
Cambridge U v Newport County	0-1	1-1	0-0	-	4-0	3-0
Cheltenham v Yeovil	-	-	-	-	-	-
Crawley Town v Morecambe	-	1-1	-	-	-	1-1
Doncaster v Luton	-	-	-	-	-	-
Exeter v Stevenage	-	1-1	-	-	0-0	3-3
Grimsby v Mansfield	7-2	0-0	4-1	-	-	-
Hartlepool v Plymouth	2-0	-	-	1-0	3-2	1-2
Leyton Orient v Notts County	2-0	0-3	2-1	5-1	0-1	3-1
Wycombe v Carlisle	-	1-1	-	-	3-1	1-1
National League						
Barrow v Torquay	-	-	-	-	-	4-0
Boreham Wood v York	-	-	-	-	-	-
Bromley v Solihull Moors	-	-	-	-	-	-
Dag & Red v Guiseley	-	-	-	-	-	-
Eastleigh v Tranmere	-	-	-	-	-	0-1
Gateshead v Forest Green	1-1	1-0	1-1	1-1	2-4	0-1
Macclesfield v Braintree	-	-	2-1	0-1	1-0	3-1
Maidstone v Chester	-	-	-	-	-	-
North Ferriby v Dover	-	-	-	-	-	-
Sutton United v Lincoln	-	-	-	-	-	-
Woking v Southport	-	-	2-3	2-0	1-2	1-2
Wrexham v Aldershot	-	-	-	2-1	3-1	3-0
Scottish Premiership						
Celtic v Motherwell	1-0/4-0	4-0/1-0	1-0	2-0/3-0	1-1/4-0	1-2/7-0
Dundee v Rangers	-	-	-	-	-	-
Hearts v Inverness CT	1-1	2-1	2-2/2-3	0-2	-	2-0
Kilmarnock v Aberdeen	2-0	2-0/1-1	1-3/1-1	0-1	0-2/1-2	0-4
Partick v Hamilton	-	1-1/2-0	4-0/1-0	-	1-2/5-0	1-1/2-2
Ross County v St Johnstone	-	-	1-2/1-0	1-0	1-2/1-0	2-3/0-1
Scottish Championship						
Dumbarton v Ayr	3-2/1-2	-	-	-	-	-
Dunfermline v Queen of Sth	1-0/6-1	-	-	-	-	-
Morton v Falkirk	0-0/2-2	3-2/0-0	1-2/2-0	0-2/1-1	-	1-1/0-1
Raith v Hibernian	-	-	-	-	1-3/2-1	1-2/2-1
St Mirren v Dundee United	1-1/1-1	2-2	0-1/0-0	4-1	0-3/1-1	-

Results cover matches from Premier League to National League and Scottish Premiership to League Two

	2010-11	2011-12	2012-13	2013-14	2014-15	2015-16
Scottish League One						
Airdrieonians v Livingston	0-1/2-4	-	1-3/0-2	-	-	-
Albion v Stenhousemuir	-	1-1/1-0	4-4/4-3	-	-	2-0/1-1
East Fife v Brechin	1-3/0-0	1-1/2-2	2-2/0-3	1-3/1-2	-	-
Queens Park v Alloa	-	1-3/1-2	-	-	-	-
Stranraer v Peterhead	-	2-1/0-3	-	-	5-0/2-0	0-4/1-5
Scottish League Two						
Arbroath v Stirling	-	4-2/2-0	-	-	-	2-0/1-1
Berwick v Forfar	-	-	-	-	-	-
Cowdenbeath v Annan	-	-	-	-	-	-
Edinburgh City v Montrose	-	-	-	-	-	-
Elgin v Clyde	0-1/0-1	0-3/1-1	2-1/4-2	1-0/3-1	1-0/2-0	1-1/1-0

Friday February 24, 2017

	2010-11	2011-12	2012-13	2013-14	2014-15	2015-16
Championship						
Burton v Blackburn	-	-	-	-	-	-

Saturday February 25, 2017

	2010-11	2011-12	2012-13	2013-14	2014-15	2015-16
Premier League						
Chelsea v Swansea	-	4-1	2-0	1-0	4-2	2-2
Crystal Palace v Middlesbrough	1-0	0-1	4-1	-	-	-
Everton v Sunderland	2-0	4-0	2-1	0-1	0-2	6-2
Hull v Burnley	0-1	2-3	0-1	-	0-1	3-0
Leicester v Liverpool	-	-	-	-	1-3	2-0
Man City v Man United	0-0	1-0	2-3	4-1	1-0	0-1
Southampton v Arsenal	-	-	1-1	2-2	2-0	4-0
Tottenham v Stoke	3-2	1-1	0-0	3-0	1-2	2-2
Watford v West Ham	-	0-4	-	-	-	2-0
West Brom v Bournemouth	-	-	-	-	-	1-2
Championship						
Aston Villa v Derby	-	-	-	-	-	-
Barnsley v Huddersfield	-	-	0-1	2-1	-	-
Brentford v Rotherham	-	-	-	0-1	1-0	2-1
Brighton v Reading	-	0-1	-	1-1	2-2	1-0
Cardiff v Fulham	-	-	-	3-1	1-0	1-1
Leeds v Sheffield Weds	-	-	2-1	1-1	1-1	1-1
Newcastle v Bristol City	-	-	-	-	-	-
Norwich v Ipswich	4-1	-	-	-	2-0	-
Preston v QPR	1-1	-	-	-	-	1-1
Wigan v Nottm Forest	-	-	-	2-1	0-0	-
Wolves v Birmingham	1-0	-	1-0	-	0-0	0-0
League One						
AFC Wimbledon v Walsall	-	-	-	-	-	-
Bristol Rovers v Scunthorpe	-	-	-	0-0	-	-
Charlton v Bury	-	1-1	-	-	-	-
Chesterfield v Oxford	1-2	-	2-1	3-0	-	-
Coventry v Swindon	-	-	1-2	1-2	0-3	0-0
Fleetwood Town v Northampton	-	-	1-0	2-0	-	-
Gillingham v Southend	0-0	1-2	1-0	-	-	1-1
MK Dons v Shrewsbury	-	-	2-3	3-2	-	-
Oldham v Millwall	-	-	-	-	-	1-2
Peterborough v Rochdale	2-1	-	-	-	2-1	1-2
Port Vale v Bradford	2-1	3-2	0-0	2-1	2-2	1-1
Sheffield United v Bolton	-	-	-	-	-	-

Results cover matches from Premier League to National League and Scottish Premiership to League Two

League Two						
Barnet v Cambridge U	-	-	-	2-2	-	0-0
Carlisle v Portsmouth	-	-	4-2	-	2-2	2-2
Colchester v Hartlepool	3-2	1-1	3-1	-	-	-
Crewe v Stevenage	0-1	-	1-2	0-3	-	-
Doncaster v Accrington	-	-	-	-	-	-
Exeter v Blackpool	-	-	-	-	-	-
Leyton Orient v Cheltenham	-	-	-	-	-	-
Luton v Plymouth	-	-	-	-	0-1	1-2
Mansfield v Newport County	3-3	5-0	3-4	2-1	1-0	3-0
Morecambe v Grimsby	-	-	-	-	-	-
Notts County v Yeovil	4-0	3-1	1-2	-	1-2	2-0
Wycombe v Crawley Town	-	-	-	-	-	2-0
National League						
Aldershot v Bromley	-	-	-	-	-	1-1
Braintree v Maidstone	-	-	-	-	-	-
Chester v Barrow	-	-	-	-	-	1-2
Dover v Eastleigh	-	-	-	1-2	2-1	1-2
Forest Green v Woking	-	-	3-1	2-2	2-1	1-2
Guiseley v North Ferriby	-	-	-	-	-	-
Lincoln v Dag & Red	-	-	-	-	-	-
Solihull Moors v Wrexham	-	-	-	-	-	-
Southport v Macclesfield	-	-	3-2	4-1	1-1	3-1
Torquay v Sutton United	-	-	-	-	-	-
Tranmere v Boreham Wood	-	-	-	-	-	0-2
York v Gateshead	2-1	1-2	-	-	-	-
Scottish Premiership						
Aberdeen v Ross County	-	-	0-0/0-1	1-0	3-0/4-0	3-1/0-4
Celtic v Hamilton	3-1/2-0	-	-	-	0-1/4-0	8-1
Inverness CT v Rangers	1-1	0-2/1-4	-	-	-	-
Motherwell v Dundee	-	-	1-1	-	1-3/0-1	3-1
Partick v Hearts	-	-	-	1-1/2-4	-	0-4
St Johnstone v Kilmarnock	0-3/0-0	2-0	2-1/2-0	3-1	1-2/0-0	2-1
Scottish Championship						
Ayr v St Mirren	-	-	-	-	-	-
Dundee United v Morton	-	-	-	-	-	-
Falkirk v Dumbarton	-	-	3-4/1-3	1-2/2-0	1-1/3-3	2-1/1-0
Hibernian v Dunfermline	-	0-1/4-0	-	-	-	-
Queen of Sth v Raith	1-3/0-2	1-3/1-0	-	0-1/1-0	2-0/2-1	1-1/1-2
Scottish League One						
Albion v Queens Park	2-1/1-2	-	-	2-1/1-0	1-0/2-1	-
Alloa v Airdrieonians	2-3/1-0	-	-	-	-	-
Livingston v Stenhousemuir	4-1/2-1	-	-	-	-	-
Peterhead v East Fife	2-2/0-2	-	-	-	-	-
Stranraer v Brechin	-	-	0-2/3-2	3-0/1-2	2-2/0-2	1-0/2-0
Scottish League Two						
Annan v Clyde	0-2/1-0	1-0/1-0	1-3/0-1	1-2/0-1	2-1/0-1	2-3/3-3
Arbroath v Cowdenbeath	-	1-1/1-1	-	-	-	-
Berwick v Elgin	6-2/4-0	1-1/3-3	0-0/2-1	2-3/2-3	1-1/0-2	2-3/2-0
Forfar v Montrose	-	-	-	-	-	-
Stirling v Edinburgh City	-	-	-	-	-	-

Results cover matches from Premier League to National League and Scottish Premiership to League Two

Tuesday February 28, 2017

League One

	2010-11	2011-12	2012-13	2013-14	2014-15	2015-16
Bolton v Bristol Rovers	-	-	-	-	-	-
Bradford v MK Dons	-	-	-	1-0	2-1	-
Bury v Coventry	-	-	0-2	-	-	2-1
Millwall v Peterborough	-	2-2	1-5	-	-	3-0
Northampton v Oldham	-	-	-	-	-	-
Oxford v Fleetwood Town	-	-	1-2	0-2	-	-
Rochdale v Port Vale	-	-	2-2	-	1-0	2-1
Scunthorpe v AFC Wimbledon	-	-	-	0-0	-	-
Shrewsbury v Charlton	-	-	-	-	-	-
Southend v Sheffield United	-	-	-	-	-	3-1
Swindon v Gillingham	-	2-0	-	2-2	0-3	1-3
Walsall v Chesterfield	-	3-2	-	-	1-0	1-2

League Two

	2010-11	2011-12	2012-13	2013-14	2014-15	2015-16
Accrington v Wycombe	1-1	-	0-2	1-1	1-1	1-1
Blackpool v Barnet	-	-	-	-	-	-
Cambridge U v Doncaster	-	-	-	-	-	-
Cheltenham v Carlisle	-	-	-	-	0-0	-
Crawley Town v Exeter	-	-	-	-	-	0-2
Grimsby v Colchester	-	-	-	-	-	-
Hartlepool v Crewe	-	-	3-0	-	-	-
Newport County v Luton	1-1	0-1	5-2	-	1-0	3-0
Plymouth v Notts County	1-1	-	-	-	-	1-0
Portsmouth v Morecambe	-	-	-	3-0	3-0	3-3
Stevenage v Leyton Orient	-	0-1	0-1	0-1	-	2-2
Yeovil v Mansfield	-	-	-	-	-	0-1

National League

	2010-11	2011-12	2012-13	2013-14	2014-15	2015-16
Bromley v Braintree	-	-	-	-	-	1-2
Dag & Red v Maidstone	-	-	-	-	-	-
Eastleigh v Aldershot	-	-	-	-	1-0	1-1
Guiseley v Barrow	-	-	-	2-1	2-3	3-1
Lincoln v York	-	0-2	-	-	-	-
Macclesfield v Gateshead	-	-	0-4	0-2	1-1	1-0
Solihull Moors v Torquay	-	-	-	-	-	-
Southport v Chester	-	-	-	0-0	0-0	1-2
Sutton United v Boreham Wood	-	-	-	-	-	-
Tranmere v Forest Green	-	-	-	-	-	1-1
Woking v Dover	-	-	-	-	6-1	0-1
Wrexham v North Ferriby	-	-	-	-	-	-

Wednesday March 1, 2017

Ladbrokes Premiership

	2010-11	2011-12	2012-13	2013-14	2014-15	2015-16
Dundee v Partick	2-1/3-2	0-1/0-3	-	-	1-1/1-0	1-1
Hamilton v Aberdeen	0-1/1-1	-	-	-	3-0/0-3	1-1
Hearts v Ross County	-	-	2-2/4-2	2-2/2-0	-	2-0/1-1
Inverness CT v Celtic	0-1/3-2	0-2	2-4/1-3	0-1	1-0/1-1	1-3
Kilmarnock v Motherwell	0-1/3-1	0-0/2-0	1-2/2-0	0-2	2-0/1-2	0-1
Rangers v St Johnstone	2-1/4-0	0-0	-	-	-	-

Scottish Championship

	2010-11	2011-12	2012-13	2013-14	2014-15	2015-16
Ayr v Raith	-	2-1/1-1	-	-	-	-
Dumbarton v Queen of Sth	-	-	-	0-1/0-3	0-4/0-0	0-2/4-2
Falkirk v Dundee United	-	-	-	-	-	-
Morton v Dunfermline	2-1/0-2	-	4-2/0-1	-	2-1/2-0	-
St Mirren v Hibernian	1-0/0-1	2-3/1-0	1-2/0-1	0-0/2-0	-	1-4/2-2

Results cover matches from Premier League to National League and Scottish Premiership to League Two

Saturday March 4, 2017

Premier League

	2010-11	2011-12	2012-13	2013-14	2014-15	2015-16
Leicester v Hull	1-1	2-1	3-1	-	0-0	-
Liverpool v Arsenal	1-1	1-2	0-2	5-1	2-2	3-3
Man United v Bournemouth	-	-	-	-	-	3-1
Stoke v Middlesbrough	-	-	-	-	-	-
Sunderland v Man City	1-0	1-0	1-0	1-0	1-4	0-1
Swansea v Burnley	1-0	-	-	-	1-0	-
Tottenham v Everton	1-1	2-0	2-2	1-0	2-1	0-0
Watford v Southampton	-	0-3	-	-	-	0-0
West Brom v Crystal Palace	-	-	-	2-0	2-2	3-2
West Ham v Chelsea	1-3	-	3-1	0-3	0-1	2-1

Championship

	2010-11	2011-12	2012-13	2013-14	2014-15	2015-16
Birmingham v Leeds	-	1-0	1-0	1-3	1-1	1-2
Blackburn v Wigan	2-1	0-1	-	4-3	3-1	-
Bristol City v Burton	-	-	-	-	-	-
Derby v Barnsley	0-0	1-1	2-0	2-1	-	-
Fulham v Preston	-	-	-	-	-	1-1
Huddersfield v Newcastle	-	-	-	-	-	-
Ipswich v Brentford	-	-	-	-	1-1	1-3
Nottm Forest v Brighton	-	1-1	2-2	1-2	0-0	1-2
QPR v Cardiff	2-1	-	-	-	-	2-2
Reading v Wolves	-	-	-	-	3-3	0-0
Rotherham v Aston Villa	-	-	-	-	-	-
Sheffield Weds v Norwich	-	-	-	-	0-0	-

League One

	2010-11	2011-12	2012-13	2013-14	2014-15	2015-16
Bolton v AFC Wimbledon	-	-	-	-	-	-
Bradford v Peterborough	-	-	-	1-0	0-1	0-2
Bury v Gillingham	5-4	-	-	-	-	0-1
Millwall v MK Dons	-	-	-	-	-	-
Northampton v Charlton	-	-	-	-	-	-
Oxford v Bristol Rovers	-	3-0	0-2	0-1	-	1-2
Rochdale v Sheffield United	-	2-5	-	-	1-2	2-0
Scunthorpe v Fleetwood Town	-	-	-	0-0	0-2	1-0
Shrewsbury v Coventry	-	-	4-1	1-1	-	2-1
Southend v Port Vale	1-3	3-0	0-0	-	-	1-0
Swindon v Chesterfield	-	-	-	-	3-1	1-0
Walsall v Oldham	1-1	0-1	3-1	1-0	2-0	1-1

League Two

	2010-11	2011-12	2012-13	2013-14	2014-15	2015-16
Accrington v Barnet	3-1	0-3	3-2	-	-	2-2
Blackpool v Morecambe	-	-	-	-	-	-
Cambridge U v Colchester	-	-	-	-	-	-
Cheltenham v Mansfield	-	-	-	1-2	1-1	-
Crawley Town v Doncaster	-	-	1-1	-	0-5	-
Grimsby v Wycombe	-	-	-	-	-	-
Hartlepool v Exeter	2-3	2-0	-	0-2	2-1	0-2
Newport County v Leyton Orient	-	-	-	-	-	2-3
Plymouth v Carlisle	1-1	-	-	-	1-0	4-1
Portsmouth v Crewe	-	-	2-0	-	-	-
Stevenage v Notts County	-	0-2	2-0	0-1	-	0-2
Yeovil v Luton	-	-	-	-	-	3-2

National League

	2010-11	2011-12	2012-13	2013-14	2014-15	2015-16
Aldershot v Lincoln	2-2	-	-	2-3	1-0	1-2
Barrow v Sutton United	-	-	-	-	-	-
Boreham Wood v Bromley	-	-	-	-	-	2-3

Results cover matches from Premier League to National League and Scottish Premiership to League Two

	2010-11	2011-12	2012-13	2013-14	2014-15	2015-16
Braintree v Wrexham	-	0-0	1-5	3-0	1-0	1-0
Chester v Tranmere	-	-	-	-	-	0-1
Dover v Solihull Moors	-	-	-	-	-	-
Forest Green v Macclesfield	-	-	1-1	2-3	3-1	2-1
Gateshead v Dag & Red	-	-	-	-	-	-
Maidstone v Southport	-	-	-	-	-	-
North Ferriby v Woking	-	-	-	-	-	-
Torquay v Guiseley	-	-	-	-	-	1-1
York v Eastleigh	-	-	-	-	-	-

Scottish Championship

	2010-11	2011-12	2012-13	2013-14	2014-15	2015-16
Dundee United v Ayr	-	-	-	-	-	-
Dunfermline v Dumbarton	-	-	4-0/3-4	-	-	-
Hibernian v Morton	-	-	-	-	-	1-0/0-3
Queen of Sth v Falkirk	1-5/0-1	1-5/0-0	-	2-0/1-2	3-0/1-0	2-2/2-2
Raith v St Mirren	-	-	-	-	-	1-1/4-3

Scottish League One

	2010-11	2011-12	2012-13	2013-14	2014-15	2015-16
Airdrieonians v Stranraer	-	-	-	3-2/1-1	3-3/1-1	0-1/1-1
Brechin v Alloa	3-1/3-2	-	1-3/3-2	-	-	-
East Fife v Albion	-	2-0/1-2	1-2/2-0	-	0-0/1-0	-
Queens Park v Livingston	-	-	-	-	-	-
Stenhousemuir v Peterhead	3-1/4-2	-	-	-	1-2/2-1	4-3/1-4

Scottish League Two

	2010-11	2011-12	2012-13	2013-14	2014-15	2015-16
Clyde v Forfar	-	-	-	-	-	-
Cowdenbeath v Stirling	5-1/1-0	2-0/4-1	-	-	-	-
Edinburgh City v Berwick	-	-	-	-	-	-
Elgin v Arbroath	3-5/3-2	-	-	-	1-1/2-1	2-0/4-1
Montrose v Annan	1-1/0-1	2-3/1-1	0-0/5-1	0-2/2-1	2-0/2-1	1-1/0-5

Tuesday March 7, 2017

Championship

	2010-11	2011-12	2012-13	2013-14	2014-15	2015-16
Birmingham v Wigan	0-0	-	-	0-1	3-1	-
Blackburn v Cardiff	-	-	1-4	-	1-1	1-1
Bristol City v Norwich	0-3	-	-	-	-	-
Derby v Preston	3-0	-	-	-	-	0-0
Fulham v Leeds	-	-	-	-	0-3	1-1
Huddersfield v Aston Villa	-	-	-	-	-	-
Ipswich v Wolves	-	-	0-2	-	2-1	2-2
Nottm Forest v Brentford	-	-	-	-	1-3	0-3
QPR v Barnsley	4-0	-	-	2-0	-	-
Reading v Newcastle	-	-	2-2	-	-	-
Rotherham v Brighton	-	-	-	-	1-0	2-0
Sheffield Weds v Burton	-	-	-	-	-	-

Saturday March 11, 2017

Premier League

	2010-11	2011-12	2012-13	2013-14	2014-15	2015-16
Arsenal v Leicester	-	-	-	-	2-1	2-1
Bournemouth v West Ham	-	-	-	-	-	1-3
Burnley v Liverpool	-	-	-	-	0-1	-
Chelsea v Watford	-	-	-	-	-	2-2
Crystal Palace v Tottenham	-	-	-	0-1	2-1	1-3
Everton v West Brom	1-4	2-0	2-1	0-0	0-0	0-1
Hull v Swansea	2-0	-	-	1-0	0-1	-
Man City v Stoke	3-0	3-0	3-0	1-0	0-1	4-0
Middlesbrough v Sunderland	-	-	-	-	-	-
Southampton v Man United	-	-	2-3	1-1	1-2	2-3

Results cover matches from Premier League to National League and Scottish Premiership to League Two

	2010-11	2011-12	2012-13	2013-14	2014-15	2015-16
Championship						
Aston Villa v Sheffield Weds	-	-	-	-	-	-
Barnsley v Ipswich	1-1	3-5	1-1	2-2	-	-
Brentford v Huddersfield	0-1	0-4	-	-	4-1	4-2
Brighton v Derby	-	2-0	2-1	1-2	2-0	1-1
Burton v Nottm Forest	-	-	-	-	-	-
Cardiff v Birmingham	-	1-0	2-1	-	2-0	1-1
Leeds v QPR	2-0	-	-	0-1	-	1-1
Newcastle v Fulham	0-0	2-1	1-0	1-0	-	-
Norwich v Blackburn	-	3-3	-	-	3-1	-
Preston v Reading	1-1	-	-	-	-	1-0
Wigan v Bristol City	-	-	-	-	-	-
Wolves v Rotherham	-	-	-	6-4	5-0	0-0
League One						
AFC Wimbledon v Northampton	-	0-3	1-1	0-2	2-2	1-1
Bristol Rovers v Southend	-	1-0	2-3	0-0	-	-
Charlton v Walsall	0-1	1-0	-	-	-	-
Chesterfield v Shrewsbury	4-3	-	-	-	-	7-1
Coventry v Bradford	-	-	-	0-0	1-1	1-0
Fleetwood Town v Bolton	-	-	-	-	-	-
Gillingham v Scunthorpe	-	-	-	-	0-3	2-1
MK Dons v Rochdale	1-1	3-1	-	-	2-2	-
Oldham v Bury	-	0-2	1-2	-	-	0-1
Peterborough v Oxford	-	-	-	-	-	-
Port Vale v Swindon	-	0-2	-	2-3	0-1	1-0
Sheffield United v Millwall	1-1	-	-	-	-	1-2
League Two						
Barnet v Crawley Town	-	1-2	-	-	-	4-2
Carlisle v Cambridge U	-	-	-	-	0-1	4-4
Colchester v Portsmouth	-	-	2-2	-	-	-
Crewe v Newport County	-	-	-	-	-	-
Doncaster v Cheltenham	-	-	-	-	-	-
Exeter v Accrington	-	-	2-0	0-1	1-2	2-1
Leyton Orient v Grimsby	-	-	-	-	-	-
Luton v Stevenage	-	-	-	-	2-0	0-1
Mansfield v Plymouth	-	-	-	0-1	1-0	0-0
Morecambe v Yeovil	-	-	-	-	-	2-1
Notts County v Hartlepool	3-0	3-0	2-0	-	-	1-0
Wycombe v Blackpool	-	-	-	-	-	-
National League						
Bromley v North Ferriby	-	-	-	-	-	-
Dag & Red v Forest Green	-	-	-	-	-	-
Eastleigh v Barrow	-	-	-	-	-	3-1
Guiseley v Aldershot	-	-	-	-	-	0-4
Lincoln v Chester	-	-	-	1-1	0-1	2-1
Macclesfield v Maidstone	-	-	-	-	-	-
Solihull Moors v Braintree	-	-	-	-	-	-
Southport v Torquay	-	-	-	-	2-1	0-1
Sutton United v York	-	-	-	-	-	-
Tranmere v Dover	-	-	-	-	-	0-1
Woking v Boreham Wood	-	-	-	-	-	0-0
Wrexham v Gateshead	2-7	2-1	1-1	3-2	0-3	4-0

Results cover matches from Premier League to National League and Scottish Premiership to League Two

	2010-11	2011-12	2012-13	2013-14	2014-15	2015-16
Scottish Premiership						
Aberdeen v Motherwell	1-2	1-2	3-3/0-0	0-1/0-1	1-0/2-1	1-1/4-1
Celtic v Rangers	1-3/3-0	1-0/3-0	-	-	-	-
Hearts v Hamilton	2-0	-	-	-	-	2-0
Partick v Inverness CT	-	-	-	0-0	3-1/1-0	2-1/1-4
Ross County v Kilmarnock	-	-	0-0/0-1	1-2/2-1	1-2/2-1	3-2
St Johnstone v Dundee	-	-	1-0	-	0-1/1-0	1-1
Scottish Championship						
Ayr v Falkirk	-	2-2/1-0	-	-	-	-
Dumbarton v Raith	-	-	4-2/1-2	2-4/3-3	2-1/2-2	3-3/2-3
Dundee United v Hibernian	1-0/3-0	3-1	3-0/2-2	2-2	-	-
Morton v Queen of Sth	2-0/0-4	2-2/2-2	-	0-2/1-1	-	2-0/3-2
St Mirren v Dunfermline	-	2-1/4-4	-	-	-	-
Scottish League One						
Albion v Airdrieonians	-	7-2/0-1	-	-	-	1-3/1-2
Alloa v Stenhousemuir	1-0/1-2	-	0-2/1-0	-	-	-
Livingston v East Fife	1-1/4-3	-	-	-	-	-
Peterhead v Brechin	0-5/1-1	-	-	-	1-1/3-0	2-3/4-1
Stranraer v Queens Park	1-0/2-1	2-3/2-3	-	-	-	-
Scottish League Two						
Annan v Elgin	0-1/2-2	1-1/1-1	2-0/2-2	2-1/2-0	3-3/2-3	1-1/4-2
Arbroath v Clyde	3-2/2-0	-	-	-	4-0/3-1	0-1/0-1
Berwick v Cowdenbeath	-	-	-	-	-	-
Forfar v Edinburgh City	-	-	-	-	-	-
Montrose v Stirling	-	-	3-2/2-2	1-2/0-0	-	1-3/1-1

Tuesday March 14, 2017

League One						
AFC Wimbledon v MK Dons	-	-	-	-	-	-
Bury v Bristol Rovers	-	-	-	2-1	-	-
Charlton v Bradford	-	-	-	-	-	-
Chesterfield v Peterborough	-	-	-	-	3-2	0-1
Coventry v Southend	-	-	-	-	-	2-2
Gillingham v Bolton	-	-	-	-	-	-
Northampton v Port Vale	0-0	1-2	2-0	-	-	-
Oldham v Oxford	-	-	-	-	-	-
Scunthorpe v Rochdale	-	1-0	-	3-0	2-1	1-1
Shrewsbury v Millwall	-	-	-	-	-	1-2
Swindon v Sheffield United	-	-	0-0	2-1	5-2	0-2
Walsall v Fleetwood Town	-	-	-	-	1-0	3-1
League Two						
Accrington v Leyton Orient	-	-	-	-	-	1-0
Barnet v Yeovil	-	-	-	-	-	3-4
Blackpool v Stevenage	-	-	-	-	-	-
Cambridge U v Hartlepool	-	-	-	-	2-1	1-1
Carlisle v Luton	-	-	-	-	0-1	1-2
Colchester v Mansfield	-	-	-	-	-	-
Crawley Town v Crewe	-	1-1	2-0	1-2	1-1	-
Doncaster v Notts County	-	-	0-1	-	0-0	-
Exeter v Cheltenham	-	-	0-1	1-1	1-0	-
Morecambe v Newport County	-	-	-	4-1	3-2	1-2
Portsmouth v Grimsby	-	-	-	-	-	-
Wycombe v Plymouth	-	-	1-1	0-1	0-2	1-2

Results cover matches from Premier League to National League and Scottish Premiership to League Two

Friday March 17, 2017

Championship

	2010-11	2011-12	2012-13	2013-14	2014-15	2015-16
Sheffield Weds v Reading	-	-	-	5-2	1-0	1-1

Saturday March 18, 2017

Premier League

	2010-11	2011-12	2012-13	2013-14	2014-15	2015-16
Bournemouth v Swansea	-	-	-	-	-	3-2
Crystal Palace v Watford	3-2	4-0	2-3	-	-	1-2
Everton v Hull	-	-	-	2-1	1-1	-
Man City v Liverpool	3-0	3-0	2-2	2-1	3-1	1-4
Middlesbrough v Man United	-	-	-	-	-	-
Stoke v Chelsea	1-1	0-0	0-4	3-2	0-2	1-0
Sunderland v Burnley	-	-	-	-	2-0	-
Tottenham v Southampton	-	-	1-0	3-2	1-0	1-2
West Brom v Arsenal	2-2	2-3	1-2	1-1	0-1	2-1
West Ham v Leicester	-	3-2	-	-	2-0	1-2

Championship

	2010-11	2011-12	2012-13	2013-14	2014-15	2015-16
Birmingham v Newcastle	0-2	-	-	-	-	-
Blackburn v Preston	-	-	-	-	-	1-2
Bristol City v Huddersfield	-	-	1-3	-	-	4-0
Burton v Brentford	-	-	-	-	-	-
Cardiff v Ipswich	0-2	2-2	0-0	-	3-1	1-0
Fulham v Wolves	2-1	5-0	-	-	0-1	0-3
Leeds v Brighton	-	1-2	1-2	2-1	0-2	1-2
Norwich v Barnsley	2-1	-	-	-	-	-
Nottm Forest v Derby	5-2	1-2	0-1	1-0	1-1	1-0
QPR v Rotherham	-	-	-	-	-	4-2
Wigan v Aston Villa	1-2	0-0	2-2	-	-	-

League One

	2010-11	2011-12	2012-13	2013-14	2014-15	2015-16
Bolton v Northampton	-	-	-	-	-	-
Bradford v Swindon	-	0-0	-	1-1	1-2	1-0
Bristol Rovers v Chesterfield	-	-	3-2	0-0	-	-
Fleetwood Town v AFC Wimbledon	1-1	-	1-1	0-0	-	-
Millwall v Bury	-	-	-	-	-	1-0
MK Dons v Coventry	-	-	2-3	1-3	0-0	-
Oxford v Scunthorpe	-	-	-	0-2	-	-
Peterborough v Oldham	5-2	-	-	2-1	2-2	1-2
Port Vale v Shrewsbury	1-0	2-3	-	3-1	-	2-0
Rochdale v Gillingham	-	-	1-1	-	1-1	1-1
Sheffield United v Charlton	-	0-2	-	-	-	-
Southend v Walsall	-	-	-	-	-	0-2

League Two

	2010-11	2011-12	2012-13	2013-14	2014-15	2015-16
Cheltenham v Cambridge U	-	-	-	-	3-1	-
Crewe v Colchester	-	-	3-2	0-0	0-3	1-1
Grimsby v Crawley Town	0-0	-	-	-	-	-
Hartlepool v Wycombe	-	1-3	-	1-2	1-3	1-0
Leyton Orient v Doncaster	-	-	0-2	-	0-1	-
Luton v Exeter	-	-	-	-	2-3	4-1
Mansfield v Carlisle	-	-	-	-	3-2	1-1
Newport County v Blackpool	-	-	-	-	-	-
Plymouth v Morecambe	-	1-1	2-1	5-0	1-1	2-0
Stevenage v Portsmouth	-	-	2-1	-	1-0	0-2
Yeovil v Accrington	-	-	-	-	-	1-0

Results cover matches from Premier League to National League and Scottish Premiership to League Two

	2010-11	2011-12	2012-13	2013-14	2014-15	2015-16
National League						
Aldershot v Sutton United	-	-	-	-	-	-
Barrow v Dag & Red	-	-	-	-	-	-
Boreham Wood v Guiseley	-	-	-	-	-	1-0
Braintree v Southport	-	0-0	1-3	1-0	0-2	1-0
Chester v Eastleigh	-	-	-	-	0-1	1-0
Dover v Macclesfield	-	-	-	-	0-1	2-1
Forest Green v Wrexham	3-0	1-0	0-0	1-1	0-1	0-0
Gateshead v Woking	-	-	2-1	0-2	0-0	1-5
Maidstone v Lincoln	-	-	-	-	-	-
North Ferriby v Solihull Moors	-	-	-	-	-	-
Torquay v Tranmere	-	-	-	-	-	0-1
York v Bromley	-	-	-	-	-	-
Scottish Premiership						
Aberdeen v Hearts	0-1/0-0	0-0	0-0/2-0/1-1	1-3	-	1-0/0-1
Dundee v Celtic	-	-	0-2	-	1-1/1-2	0-0
Inverness CT v Ross County	-	-	3-1/2-1	1-2	1-1/1-1	2-0
Kilmarnock v Partick	-	-	-	2-1/1-2	3-0/2-2	2-5/0-2
Motherwell v St Johnstone	4-0	0-3/3-2/5-1	1-1/3-2	4-0/2-1	0-1/1-1	2-0/1-2
Rangers v Hamilton	4-0	-	-	-	-	-
Scottish Championship						
Dunfermline v Ayr	-	-	-	5-1/3-0	4-2/2-1	0-2/3-2
Falkirk v Morton	2-1/1-0	1-0/0-2	0-1/4-1	3-1/1-1	-	1-0/1-0
Hibernian v Dumbarton	-	-	-	-	0-0/3-0	4-2/4-0
Queen of Sth v St Mirren	-	-	-	-	-	0-2/1-0
Raith v Dundee United	-	-	-	-	-	-
Scottish League One						
Airdrieonians v Stenhousemuir	1-0/2-2	5-2/0-3	-	0-1/1-1	2-0/2-1	0-1/1-1
Albion v Peterhead	-	-	-	1-2/0-0	-	1-0/1-1
East Fife v Alloa	4-1/3-1	-	0-1/2-1	-	-	-
Queens Park v Brechin	-	-	-	-	-	-
Stranraer v Livingston	-	-	-	-	-	-
Scottish League Two						
Berwick v Arbroath	4-1/0-4	-	-	-	1-2/3-1	2-2/3-0
Clyde v Edinburgh City	-	-	-	-	-	-
Cowdenbeath v Montrose	-	-	-	-	-	-
Elgin v Forfar	-	-	-	-	-	-
Stirling v Annan	-	-	5-1/2-1	0-2/1-1	-	1-0/2-1

Sunday March 19, 2017

	2010-11	2011-12	2012-13	2013-14	2014-15	2015-16
League Two						
Notts County v Barnet	-	-	-	-	-	4-2

Tuesday March 21, 2017

	2010-11	2011-12	2012-13	2013-14	2014-15	2015-16
National League						
Aldershot v Dag & Red	-	1-1	1-0	-	-	-
Barrow v Wrexham	0-1	3-1	0-1	-	-	2-0
Boreham Wood v Lincoln	-	-	-	-	-	1-1
Braintree v Woking	-	-	1-1	2-0	0-0	2-1
Chester v Macclesfield	-	-	-	2-1	1-0	0-2
Dover v Bromley	-	-	-	0-2	-	2-3
Forest Green v Solihull Moors	-	-	-	-	-	-
Gateshead v Guiseley	-	-	-	-	-	3-0
Maidstone v Sutton United	-	-	-	-	-	-
North Ferriby v Tranmere	-	-	-	-	-	-
Torquay v Eastleigh	-	-	-	-	2-0	0-1
York v Southport	2-0	1-2	-	-	-	-

Results cover matches from Premier League to National League and Scottish Premiership to League Two

Saturday March 25, 2017

League One

	2010-11	2011-12	2012-13	2013-14	2014-15	2015-16
AFC Wimbledon v Southend	-	1-4	0-4	0-1	0-0	-
Bury v Fleetwood Town	-	-	-	2-2	-	3-4
Charlton v MK Dons	1-0	2-1	-	-	-	0-0
Chesterfield v Rochdale	-	2-1	1-1	2-2	2-1	0-0
Coventry v Bristol Rovers	-	-	-	-	-	-
Gillingham v Peterborough	-	-	-	2-2	2-1	2-1
Northampton v Oxford	2-1	2-1	1-0	3-1	1-3	1-0
Oldham v Sheffield United	-	0-2	0-2	1-1	2-2	1-1
Scunthorpe v Bradford	-	-	-	-	1-1	0-2
Shrewsbury v Bolton	-	-	-	-	-	-
Swindon v Millwall	-	-	-	-	-	2-2
Walsall v Port Vale	-	-	-	0-2	0-1	2-0

League Two

	2010-11	2011-12	2012-13	2013-14	2014-15	2015-16
Accrington v Grimsby	-	-	-	-	-	-
Barnet v Cheltenham	3-1	2-2	0-0	-	-	-
Blackpool v Hartlepool	-	-	-	-	-	-
Cambridge U v Stevenage	-	-	-	-	1-1	1-0
Carlisle v Crewe	-	-	0-0	2-1	-	-
Colchester v Luton	-	-	-	-	-	-
Crawley Town v Leyton Orient	-	-	1-0	2-1	1-0	3-2
Doncaster v Plymouth	-	-	-	-	-	-
Exeter v Yeovil	2-3	1-1	-	-	-	3-2
Morecambe v Mansfield	-	-	-	0-1	2-1	1-2
Portsmouth v Newport County	-	-	-	0-2	0-1	0-3
Wycombe v Notts County	-	3-4	-	-	-	2-2

National League

	2010-11	2011-12	2012-13	2013-14	2014-15	2015-16
Bromley v Chester	-	-	-	-	-	3-0
Dag & Red v York	-	-	0-1	2-0	2-0	1-0
Eastleigh v Gateshead	-	-	-	-	2-2	1-2
Guiseley v Dover	-	-	-	-	-	0-1
Lincoln v Forest Green	-	1-1	1-2	2-1	1-2	0-1
Macclesfield v Aldershot	2-0	0-1	-	1-1	0-0	0-2
Solihull Moors v Barrow	-	-	-	0-2	3-4	-
Southport v Boreham Wood	-	-	-	-	-	0-3
Sutton United v North Ferriby	-	-	-	-	-	-
Tranmere v Braintree	-	-	-	-	-	1-2
Woking v Maidstone	-	-	-	-	-	-
Wrexham v Torquay	-	-	-	-	0-0	3-1

Scottish Championship

	2010-11	2011-12	2012-13	2013-14	2014-15	2015-16
Ayr v Dumbarton	1-0/2-0	-	-	-	-	-
Dundee United v Dunfermline	-	0-1/3-0	-	-	-	-
Hibernian v Falkirk	-	-	-	-	0-1/3-3	1-1/2-2
Morton v St Mirren	-	-	-	-	-	0-0/0-1
Raith v Queen of Sth	0-1/0-1	0-2/3-1	-	2-1/3-2	3-4/3-0	1-0/2-0

Scottish League One

	2010-11	2011-12	2012-13	2013-14	2014-15	2015-16
Alloa v Queens Park	-	1-0/4-0	-	-	-	-
Brechin v East Fife	1-3/2-3	0-2/1-3	2-1/6-0	2-0/3-0	-	-
Livingston v Airdrieonians	2-1/2-0	-	0-2/4-1	-	-	-
Peterhead v Stranraer	-	1-3/1-1	-	-	1-4/1-2	1-1/0-0
Stenhousemuir v Albion	-	3-0/1-2	1-0/0-1	-	-	0-1/1-3

Scottish League Two

	2010-11	2011-12	2012-13	2013-14	2014-15	2015-16
Annan v Cowdenbeath	-	-	-	-	-	-
Arbroath v Montrose	4-0/4-1	-	-	-	3-1/2-2	3-1/0-0
Clyde v Stirling	-	-	2-1/1-2	2-1/1-0	-	0-1/3-1
Edinburgh City v Elgin	-	-	-	-	-	-
Forfar v Berwick	-	-	-	-	-	-

Results cover matches from Premier League to National League and Scottish Premiership to League Two

Saturday April 1, 2017

Premier League

	2010-11	2011-12	2012-13	2013-14	2014-15	2015-16
Arsenal v Man City	0-0	1-0	0-2	1-1	2-2	2-1
Burnley v Tottenham	-	-	-	-	0-0	-
Chelsea v Crystal Palace	-	-	-	2-1	1-0	1-2
Hull v West Ham	-	0-2	-	1-0	2-2	-
Leicester v Stoke	-	-	-	-	0-1	3-0
Liverpool v Everton	2-2	3-0	0-0	4-0	1-1	4-0
Man United v West Brom	2-2	2-0	2-0	1-2	0-1	2-0
Southampton v Bournemouth	2-0	-	-	-	-	2-0
Swansea v Middlesbrough	1-0	-	-	-	-	-
Watford v Sunderland	-	-	-	-	-	2-2

Championship

	2010-11	2011-12	2012-13	2013-14	2014-15	2015-16
Aston Villa v Norwich	-	3-2	1-1	4-1	-	2-0
Barnsley v Sheffield Weds	-	-	0-1	1-1	-	-
Brentford v Bristol City	-	-	-	3-1	-	1-1
Brighton v Blackburn	-	-	1-1	3-0	1-1	1-0
Derby v QPR	2-2	-	-	1-0	-	1-0
Huddersfield v Burton	-	-	-	-	-	-
Ipswich v Birmingham	-	1-1	3-1	1-0	4-2	1-1
Newcastle v Wigan	2-2	1-0	3-0	-	-	-
Preston v Nottm Forest	1-2	-	-	-	-	1-0
Reading v Leeds	0-0	2-0	-	1-0	0-2	0-0
Rotherham v Fulham	-	-	-	-	3-3	1-3
Wolves v Cardiff	-	-	1-2	-	1-0	1-3

League One

	2010-11	2011-12	2012-13	2013-14	2014-15	2015-16
Bolton v Chesterfield	-	-	-	-	-	-
Bradford v Walsall	-	-	-	0-2	1-1	4-0
Bristol Rovers v Shrewsbury	-	1-0	-	-	-	-
Fleetwood Town v Swindon	-	-	-	-	2-2	5-1
Millwall v Scunthorpe	3-0	-	-	-	-	0-2
MK Dons v Gillingham	-	-	-	0-1	4-2	-
Oxford v Bury	1-2	-	-	2-1	2-1	-
Peterborough v Charlton	1-5	-	2-2	-	-	-
Port Vale v AFC Wimbledon	-	1-2	3-0	-	-	-
Rochdale v Northampton	-	-	0-0	3-2	-	-
Sheffield United v Coventry	0-1	-	1-2	2-1	2-2	1-0
Southend v Oldham	-	-	-	-	-	0-1

League Two

	2010-11	2011-12	2012-13	2013-14	2014-15	2015-16
Cheltenham v Morecambe	1-1	1-2	2-0	3-0	1-1	-
Crewe v Cambridge U	-	-	-	-	-	-
Grimsby v Doncaster	-	-	-	-	-	-
Hartlepool v Portsmouth	-	-	0-0	0-0	0-0	0-2
Leyton Orient v Wycombe	-	1-3	-	-	-	1-1
Luton v Blackpool	-	-	-	-	-	-
Mansfield v Exeter	-	-	-	0-0	2-3	0-2
Newport County v Crawley Town	0-1	-	-	-	-	0-3
Notts County v Colchester	2-0	4-1	3-1	2-0	2-1	-
Plymouth v Accrington	-	2-2	0-0	0-0	1-0	1-0
Stevenage v Barnet	4-2	-	-	-	-	0-0
Yeovil v Carlisle	1-0	0-3	1-3	-	-	0-0

National League

	2010-11	2011-12	2012-13	2013-14	2014-15	2015-16
Boreham Wood v Macclesfield	-	-	-	-	-	0-0
Dag & Red v Eastleigh	-	-	-	-	-	-
Dover v Gateshead	-	-	-	-	1-0	4-0
Forest Green v North Ferriby	-	-	-	-	-	-
Lincoln v Bromley	-	-	-	-	-	0-1
Maidstone v Barrow	-	-	-	-	-	-
Solihull Moors v Aldershot	-	-	-	-	-	-

Results cover matches from Premier League to National League and Scottish Premiership to League Two

	2010-11	2011-12	2012-13	2013-14	2014-15	2015-16
Southport v Guiseley	-	-	-	-	-	2-0
Torquay v Chester	-	-	-	-	0-1	2-0
Woking v Sutton United	-	-	-	-	-	-
Wrexham v Tranmere	-	-	-	-	-	2-2
York v Braintree	-	6-2	-	-	-	-

Scottish Premiership

	2010-11	2011-12	2012-13	2013-14	2014-15	2015-16
Dundee v Aberdeen	-	-	1-3/1-1	-	2-3/1-1/1-1	0-2
Hamilton v St Johnstone	1-2/0-0	-	-	-	1-0/1-1	2-4
Hearts v Celtic	2-0/0-3	2-0/0-4	0-4	1-3/0-2	-	2-2/1-3
Inverness CT v Kilmarnock	1-3	2-1/1-1	1-1/1-1	2-1	2-0/3-3	2-1/3-1
Partick v Ross County	1-1/1-1	0-1/0-1	-	3-3/2-3	4-0/1-3	1-0
Rangers v Motherwell	4-1/6-0	3-0/0-0	-	-	-	-

Scottish Championship

	2010-11	2011-12	2012-13	2013-14	2014-15	2015-16
Dumbarton v Morton	-	-	1-5/0-3	3-1/2-0	-	1-2/0-0
Dunfermline v Hibernian	-	2-2/2-3	-	-	-	-
Falkirk v Raith	0-0/2-1	2-0/2-3	0-2/1-1	3-1/2-1	0-1/1-0	1-0/2-2
Queen of Sth v Dundee United	-	-	-	-	-	-
St Mirren v Ayr	-	-	-	-	-	-

Scottish League One

	2010-11	2011-12	2012-13	2013-14	2014-15	2015-16
Alloa v Albion	-	-	5-1/4-1	-	-	-
Brechin v Livingston	1-3/1-0	-	-	-	-	-
East Fife v Queens Park	-	-	-	-	2-2/0-0	0-2/1-1
Peterhead v Airdrieonians	5-1/2-4	-	-	-	1-1/0-1	2-0/1-0
Stranraer v Stenhousemuir	-	-	1-1/1-1	1-0/1-1	0-2/3-2	1-2/3-1

Scottish League Two

	2010-11	2011-12	2012-13	2013-14	2014-15	2015-16
Annan v Arbroath	1-2/3-0	-	-	-	0-1/2-0	2-2/4-1
Cowdenbeath v Clyde	-	-	-	-	-	-
Elgin v Berwick	1-2/3-2	4-1/4-0	3-1/1-2	2-0/1-3	2-1/3-3	4-1/1-0
Montrose v Edinburgh City	-	-	-	-	-	-
Stirling v Forfar	-	2-4/2-2	-	-	2-2/0-1	-

Tuesday April 4, 2017

Premier League

	2010-11	2011-12	2012-13	2013-14	2014-15	2015-16
Arsenal v West Ham	1-0	-	5-1	3-1	3-0	0-2
Burnley v Stoke	-	-	-	-	0-0	-
Hull v Middlesbrough	2-4	2-1	1-0	-	-	3-0
Leicester v Sunderland	-	-	-	-	0-0	4-2
Man United v Everton	1-0	4-4	2-0	0-1	2-1	1-0
Swansea v Tottenham	-	1-1	1-2	1-3	1-2	2-2
Watford v West Brom	-	-	-	-	-	0-0

Championship

	2010-11	2011-12	2012-13	2013-14	2014-15	2015-16
Aston Villa v QPR	-	2-2	3-2	-	3-3	-
Barnsley v Cardiff	1-2	0-1	1-2	-	-	-
Brentford v Leeds	-	-	-	-	2-0	1-1
Brighton v Birmingham	-	1-1	0-1	1-0	4-3	2-1
Derby v Fulham	-	-	-	-	5-1	2-0
Huddersfield v Norwich	-	-	-	-	2-2	-
Ipswich v Wigan	-	-	-	1-3	0-0	-
Preston v Bristol City	0-4	-	-	1-0	1-1	1-1
Reading v Blackburn	-	-	-	0-1	0-0	1-0
Rotherham v Sheffield Weds	-	-	-	-	2-3	1-2
Wolves v Nottm Forest	-	-	1-2	-	0-3	1-1

Wednesday April 5, 2017

Premier League

	2010-11	2011-12	2012-13	2013-14	2014-15	2015-16
Chelsea v Man City	2-0	2-1	0-0	2-1	1-1	0-3
Liverpool v Bournemouth	-	-	-	-	-	1-0
Southampton v Crystal Palace	-	2-0	-	2-0	1-0	4-1

Results cover matches from Premier League to National League and Scottish Premiership to League Two

Championship

	2010-11	2011-12	2012-13	2013-14	2014-15	2015-16
Newcastle v Burton	-	-	-	-	-	-

Scottish Premiership

	2010-11	2011-12	2012-13	2013-14	2014-15	2015-16
Aberdeen v Inverness CT	1-2/1-0	2-1/0-1	2-3	1-0/0-1	3-2/1-0	2-2
Celtic v Partick	-	-	-	1-0	1-0/2-0	1-0
Kilmarnock v Rangers	2-3/1-5	1-0	-	-	-	-
Motherwell v Hamilton	0-1/1-0	-	-	-	0-4/4-0	3-3
Ross County v Dundee	0-3/0-1	1-1/3-0	1-1	-	2-1/1-0	5-2
St Johnstone v Hearts	0-2	2-0/2-1	2-2	1-0/3-3	-	0-0

Saturday April 8, 2017

Premier League

	2010-11	2011-12	2012-13	2013-14	2014-15	2015-16
Bournemouth v Chelsea	-	-	-	-	-	1-4
Crystal Palace v Arsenal	-	-	-	0-2	1-2	1-2
Everton v Leicester	-	-	-	-	2-2	2-3
Man City v Hull	-	-	-	2-0	1-1	-
Middlesbrough v Burnley	2-1	0-2	3-2	1-0	-	1-0
Stoke v Liverpool	2-0	1-0	3-1	3-5	6-1	0-1
Sunderland v Man United	0-0	0-1	0-1	1-2	1-1	2-1
Tottenham v Watford	-	-	-	-	-	1-0
West Brom v Southampton	-	-	2-0	0-1	1-0	0-0
West Ham v Swansea	-	-	1-0	2-0	3-1	1-4

Championship

	2010-11	2011-12	2012-13	2013-14	2014-15	2015-16
Birmingham v Derby	-	2-2	3-1	3-3	0-4	1-1
Blackburn v Barnsley	-	-	2-1	5-2	-	-
Bristol City v Wolves	-	-	1-4	1-2	-	1-0
Burton v Aston Villa	-	-	-	-	-	-
Cardiff v Brentford	-	-	-	-	2-3	3-2
Fulham v Ipswich	-	-	-	-	1-2	1-2
Leeds v Preston	4-6	-	-	-	-	1-0
Norwich v Reading	2-1	-	2-1	-	1-2	-
Nottm Forest v Huddersfield	-	-	6-1	1-0	0-1	0-2
QPR v Brighton	-	-	-	0-0	-	2-2
Sheffield Weds v Newcastle	-	-	-	-	-	-
Wigan v Rotherham	-	-	-	-	1-2	-

League One

	2010-11	2011-12	2012-13	2013-14	2014-15	2015-16
AFC Wimbledon v Bristol Rovers	-	2-3	3-1	0-0	-	0-0
Bury v Bradford	0-1	-	-	-	-	0-0
Charlton v Southend	-	-	-	-	-	-
Chesterfield v Port Vale	2-0	-	2-2	-	3-0	4-2
Coventry v Peterborough	-	2-2	-	4-2	3-2	3-2
Gillingham v Millwall	-	-	-	-	-	1-2
Northampton v Sheffield United	-	-	-	-	-	-
Oldham v Fleetwood Town	-	-	-	-	1-0	1-0
Scunthorpe v Bolton	-	-	-	-	-	-
Shrewsbury v Rochdale	-	-	-	-	-	2-0
Swindon v MK Dons	0-1	-	1-0	1-2	0-3	-
Walsall v Oxford	-	-	-	-	-	-

League Two

	2010-11	2011-12	2012-13	2013-14	2014-15	2015-16
Accrington v Crewe	3-2	0-2	-	-	-	-
Barnet v Luton	-	-	-	1-2	-	2-1
Blackpool v Grimsby	-	-	-	-	-	-
Cambridge U v Leyton Orient	-	-	-	-	-	1-1
Carlisle v Notts County	1-0	0-3	0-4	2-1	-	3-0
Colchester v Stevenage	-	1-6	1-0	4-0	-	-
Crawley Town v Plymouth	-	2-0	-	-	-	1-1
Doncaster v Mansfield	-	-	-	-	-	-

Results cover matches from Premier League to National League and Scottish Premiership to League Two

	2010-11	2011-12	2012-13	2013-14	2014-15	2015-16
Exeter v Newport County	-	-	-	0-2	2-0	1-1
Morecambe v Hartlepool	-	-	-	1-2	0-1	2-5
Portsmouth v Yeovil	-	-	1-2	-	-	0-0
Wycombe v Cheltenham	2-1	-	1-1	1-2	2-1	-

National League

	2010-11	2011-12	2012-13	2013-14	2014-15	2015-16
Aldershot v Torquay	1-0	0-1	1-0	-	2-0	0-0
Barrow v Woking	-	-	2-0	-	-	2-1
Braintree v Dover	-	-	-	-	3-0	1-0
Bromley v Wrexham	-	-	-	-	-	3-1
Chester v York	-	-	-	-	-	-
Eastleigh v Lincoln	-	-	-	-	4-0	1-1
Gateshead v Maidstone	-	-	-	-	-	-
Guiseley v Forest Green	-	-	-	-	-	0-1
Macclesfield v Dag & Red	-	0-1	-	-	-	-
North Ferriby v Boreham Wood	-	-	-	-	-	-
Sutton United v Southport	-	-	-	-	-	-
Tranmere v Solihull Moors	-	-	-	-	-	-

Scottish Premiership

	2010-11	2011-12	2012-13	2013-14	2014-15	2015-16
Aberdeen v Rangers	2-3/0-1	1-2	-	-	-	-
Celtic v Kilmarnock	1-1	2-1	0-2/4-1	4-0	2-0/4-1	0-0
Hamilton v Ross County	-	5-1/0-2	-	-	4-0/2-2	1-3
Hearts v Dundee	-	-	0-1/1-0	-	-	1-1
Inverness CT v St Johnstone	1-1/2-0	0-1	1-1/0-0	1-0/2-0	2-1/2-0	0-1
Partick v Motherwell	-	-	-	1-5	3-1/2-0	1-0

Scottish Championship

	2010-11	2011-12	2012-13	2013-14	2014-15	2015-16
Ayr v Queen of Sth	-	1-0/1-1	2-4/1-5	-	-	-
Dundee United v Falkirk	-	-	-	-	-	-
Dunfermline v Raith	2-2/2-1	-	3-1/1-0	-	-	-
Morton v Hibernian	-	-	-	-	-	0-1/0-0
St Mirren v Dumbarton	-	-	-	-	-	1-2/1-0

Scottish League One

	2010-11	2011-12	2012-13	2013-14	2014-15	2015-16
Airdrieonians v Brechin	1-1/2-2	2-3/4-1	-	3-1/2-1	4-0/1-1	1-0/0-2
Albion v Stranraer	1-2/1-0	-	2-1/2-3	-	-	0-2/0-1
Livingston v Alloa	3-3/4-0	-	-	3-2/2-0	4-0/0-0	0-1/0-0
Queens Park v Peterhead	-	1-1/0-1	0-0/0-3	0-5/0-2	-	-
Stenhousemuir v East Fife	1-1/0-2	2-1/1-0	3-0/2-1	1-1/1-1	-	-

Scottish League Two

	2010-11	2011-12	2012-13	2013-14	2014-15	2015-16
Berwick v Stirling	-	-	4-1/1-0	1-1/4-0	-	1-2/1-0
Clyde v Annan	0-2/0-2	0-0/1-1	2-1/2-3	2-1/0-3	1-1/1-0	4-2/2-1
Edinburgh City v Cowdenbeath	-	-	-	-	-	-
Elgin v Montrose	3-2/1-0	3-1/2-1	6-1/3-2	3-3/2-3	0-1/4-0	2-0/1-1
Forfar v Arbroath	-	1-1/2-4	1-1/2-4	1-1/0-2	-	-

Thursday April 13, 2017

League One

	2010-11	2011-12	2012-13	2013-14	2014-15	2015-16
Bury v Rochdale	-	2-4	-	0-0	-	0-0

Friday April 14, 2017

Championship

	2010-11	2011-12	2012-13	2013-14	2014-15	2015-16
Brentford v Derby	-	-	-	-	2-1	1-3
Burton v Ipswich	-	-	-	-	-	-
Huddersfield v Preston	-	3-1	-	-	-	3-1
Norwich v Fulham	-	1-1	0-0	1-2	4-2	-
Nottm Forest v Blackburn	-	-	0-0	4-1	1-3	1-1
Rotherham v Birmingham	-	-	-	-	0-1	0-0
Sheffield Weds v Cardiff	-	-	0-2	-	1-1	3-0
Wolves v Brighton	-	-	3-3	-	1-1	0-0

Results cover matches from Premier League to National League and Scottish Premiership to League Two

	2010-11	2011-12	2012-13	2013-14	2014-15	2015-16
League One						
Bradford v Oxford	5-0	2-1	1-2	-	-	-
Coventry v Charlton	-	-	-	-	-	-
Gillingham v Bristol Rovers	-	4-1	4-0	-	-	-
Millwall v Northampton	-	-	-	-	-	-
MK Dons v Scunthorpe	-	0-0	0-1	-	2-0	-
Peterborough v Fleetwood Town	-	-	-	-	1-0	2-1
Port Vale v Sheffield United	-	-	-	1-2	2-1	2-1
Shrewsbury v Walsall	-	-	1-0	0-1	-	1-3
Swindon v AFC Wimbledon	-	2-0	-	-	-	-
League Two						
Blackpool v Accrington	-	-	-	-	-	-
Colchester v Doncaster	-	-	1-2	-	0-1	4-1
Crawley Town v Cheltenham	-	4-2	-	-	-	-
Crewe v Notts County	-	-	1-2	1-3	0-3	-
Exeter v Barnet	-	-	2-2	-	-	1-1
Hartlepool v Carlisle	0-4	4-0	1-2	-	0-3	2-3
Luton v Leyton Orient	-	-	-	-	-	1-1
Portsmouth v Plymouth	-	-	-	3-3	2-1	1-2
Stevenage v Morecambe	2-0	-	-	-	1-1	4-3
Wycombe v Mansfield	-	-	-	0-1	2-1	1-0
National League						
Boreham Wood v Dag & Red	-	-	-	-	-	-
Braintree v Guiseley	-	-	-	-	-	0-1
Bromley v Barrow	-	-	-	-	-	5-0
Dover v Southport	-	-	-	-	2-2	1-2
Forest Green v Chester	-	-	-	3-0	2-1	2-1
Lincoln v Torquay	0-2	-	-	-	1-3	2-0
North Ferriby v Eastleigh	-	-	-	-	-	-
Solihull Moors v York	-	-	-	-	-	-
Sutton United v Gateshead	-	-	-	-	-	-
Tranmere v Aldershot	-	-	-	-	-	3-1
Woking v Macclesfield	-	-	5-4	3-2	0-0	2-5
Wrexham v Maidstone	-	-	-	-	-	-

Saturday April 15, 2017

	2010-11	2011-12	2012-13	2013-14	2014-15	2015-16
Premier League						
Crystal Palace v Leicester	3-2	1-2	2-2	-	2-0	0-1
Everton v Burnley	-	-	-	-	1-0	-
Man United v Chelsea	2-1	3-1	0-1	0-0	1-1	0-0
Middlesbrough v Arsenal	-	-	-	-	-	-
Southampton v Man City	-	-	3-1	1-1	0-3	4-2
Stoke v Hull	-	-	-	1-0	1-0	-
Sunderland v West Ham	1-0	-	3-0	1-2	1-1	2-2
Tottenham v Bournemouth	-	-	-	-	-	3-0
Watford v Swansea	2-3	-	-	-	-	1-0
West Brom v Liverpool	2-1	0-2	3-0	1-1	0-0	1-1
Championship						
Aston Villa v Reading	-	-	1-0	-	-	-
Bristol City v QPR	1-1	-	-	-	-	1-1
Newcastle v Leeds	-	-	-	-	-	-
Wigan v Barnsley	-	-	-	2-0	-	1-4
League One						
Chesterfield v Southend	2-1	-	0-1	2-1	-	3-0
Oldham v Bolton	-	-	-	-	-	-

Results cover matches from Premier League to National League and Scottish Premiership to League Two

	2010-11	2011-12	2012-13	2013-14	2014-15	2015-16
League Two						
Grimsby v Cambridge U	1-1	2-1	0-1	0-1	-	-
Newport County v Yeovil	-	-	-	-	-	0-0
Scottish Premiership						
Dundee v Hamilton	-	0-1/2-2	-	0-0/1-0	2-0/1-1	4-0/0-1
Kilmarnock v Hearts	1-2/2-2	0-0/1-1	1-0/0-1	2-0/4-2	-	2-2
Motherwell v Inverness CT	0-0	3-0/0-1	4-1/3-0	2-0/2-1	0-2/2-1	1-3
Rangers v Partick	-	-	-	-	-	-
Ross County v Celtic	-	-	1-1/3-2/1-1	1-4	0-5/0-1	1-4
St Johnstone v Aberdeen	0-1/0-0	1-2	1-2/3-1	0-2	1-0/1-1	3-4/3-0
Scottish Championship						
Ayr v Dundee United	-	-	-	-	-	-
Dumbarton v Dunfermline	-	-	0-2/0-1	-	-	-
Falkirk v St Mirren	-	-	-	-	-	3-0/3-2
Hibernian v Queen of Sth	-	-	-	-	0-0/0-1	1-0/2-0
Raith v Morton	1-0/2-2	1-1/5-0	3-3/2-1	2-1/2-1	-	2-1/3-2
Scottish League One						
Alloa v Brechin	2-2/2-2	-	2-2/0-1	-	-	-
East Fife v Peterhead	2-1/3-1	-	-	-	-	-
Queens Park v Albion	0-1/2-1	-	-	1-1/4-0	0-1/0-1	-
Stenhousemuir v Livingston	1-2/0-3	-	-	-	-	-
Stranraer v Airdrieonians	-	-	-	3-1/1-1	1-0/1-0	1-3/4-0
Scottish League Two						
Annan v Berwick	1-1/2-3	2-2/1-1	3-2/2-2	3-2/4-0	2-0/4-2	1-0/1-0
Arbroath v Edinburgh City	-	-	-	-	-	-
Clyde v Elgin	1-1/3-3	1-2/0-2	2-2/1-1	2-1/4-0	2-1/0-2	4-2/1-0
Montrose v Forfar	-	-	-	-	-	-
Stirling v Cowdenbeath	1-3/3-4	1-1/0-2	-	-	-	-

Monday April 17, 2017

	2010-11	2011-12	2012-13	2013-14	2014-15	2015-16
Championship						
Barnsley v Brentford	-	-	-	-	-	-
Birmingham v Burton	-	-	-	-	-	-
Blackburn v Bristol City	-	-	2-0	-	-	2-2
Brighton v Wigan	-	-	-	1-2	1-0	-
Cardiff v Nottm Forest	0-2	1-0	3-0	-	2-1	1-1
Derby v Huddersfield	-	-	3-0	3-1	3-2	2-0
Fulham v Aston Villa	1-1	0-0	1-0	2-0	-	-
Ipswich v Newcastle	-	-	-	-	-	-
Leeds v Wolves	-	-	1-0	-	1-2	2-1
Preston v Norwich	0-1	-	-	-	-	-
QPR v Sheffield Weds	-	-	-	2-1	-	0-0
Reading v Rotherham	-	-	-	-	3-0	1-0
League One						
AFC Wimbledon v Peterborough	-	-	-	-	-	-
Bristol Rovers v Oldham	1-0	-	-	-	-	-
Charlton v Gillingham	-	-	-	-	-	-
Fleetwood Town v Millwall	-	-	-	-	-	2-1
Northampton v Shrewsbury	2-3	2-7	-	-	1-1	-
Oxford v Port Vale	2-1	2-1	2-1	-	-	-
Rochdale v Coventry	-	-	-	-	1-0	0-0
Scunthorpe v Chesterfield	-	2-2	-	1-1	2-0	1-1
Sheffield United v Bradford	-	-	-	2-2	1-1	3-1
Southend v MK Dons	-	-	-	-	-	-
Walsall v Swindon	1-2	-	0-2	1-1	1-4	1-1

Results cover matches from Premier League to National League and Scottish Premiership to League Two

	2010-11	2011-12	2012-13	2013-14	2014-15	2015-16
League Two						
Accrington v Crawley Town	-	0-1	-	-	-	4-1
Barnet v Wycombe	0-1	-	1-0	-	-	0-2
Cambridge U v Exeter	-	-	-	-	1-2	0-1
Carlisle v Stevenage	-	1-0	2-1	0-0	3-0	1-0
Cheltenham v Grimsby	-	-	-	-	-	3-1
Doncaster v Blackpool	-	1-3	-	1-3	-	0-1
Leyton Orient v Hartlepool	1-0	1-1	1-0	-	-	0-2
Mansfield v Luton	0-0	1-1	2-2	-	1-0	0-2
Morecambe v Colchester	-	-	-	-	-	-
Notts County v Portsmouth	-	-	3-0	-	-	2-1
Plymouth v Newport County	-	-	-	0-0	0-0	1-0
Yeovil v Crewe	-	-	1-0	-	1-1	-
National League						
Aldershot v Dover	-	-	-	-	3-1	1-1
Barrow v North Ferriby	-	-	-	-	-	-
Chester v Woking	-	-	-	0-2	2-3	1-2
Dag & Red v Sutton United	-	-	-	-	-	-
Eastleigh v Bromley	-	-	-	2-1	-	2-0
Gateshead v Lincoln	-	3-3	1-1	3-1	3-3	2-0
Guiseley v Tranmere	-	-	-	-	-	2-2
Macclesfield v Solihull Moors	-	-	-	-	-	-
Maidstone v Boreham Wood	-	-	-	-	-	-
Southport v Forest Green	4-0	1-3	1-2	2-0	0-1	0-1
Torquay v Braintree	-	-	-	-	1-5	0-0
York v Wrexham	1-1	0-0	-	-	-	-

Tuesday April 18, 2017

	2010-11	2011-12	2012-13	2013-14	2014-15	2015-16
League One						
Bolton v Bury	-	-	-	-	-	-

Saturday April 22, 2017

	2010-11	2011-12	2012-13	2013-14	2014-15	2015-16
Premier League						
Arsenal v Sunderland	0-0	2-1	0-0	4-1	0-0	3-1
Bournemouth v Middlesbrough	-	-	-	0-0	3-0	-
Burnley v Man United	-	-	-	-	0-0	-
Chelsea v Southampton	-	-	2-2	3-1	1-1	1-3
Hull v Watford	0-0	3-2	0-1	-	-	-
Leicester v Tottenham	-	-	-	-	1-2	1-1
Liverpool v Crystal Palace	-	-	-	3-1	1-3	1-2
Man City v West Brom	3-0	4-0	1-0	3-1	3-0	2-1
Swansea v Stoke	-	2-0	3-1	3-3	2-0	0-1
West Ham v Everton	1-1	-	1-2	2-3	1-2	1-1
Championship						
Brentford v QPR	-	-	-	-	-	1-0
Bristol City v Barnsley	3-3	2-0	5-3	-	2-2	-
Burton v Leeds	-	-	-	-	-	-
Huddersfield v Fulham	-	-	-	-	0-2	1-1
Newcastle v Preston	-	-	-	-	-	-
Norwich v Brighton	-	-	-	-	3-3	-
Nottm Forest v Reading	3-4	1-0	-	2-3	4-0	3-1
Rotherham v Ipswich	-	-	-	-	2-0	2-5
Sheffield Weds v Derby	-	-	2-2	0-1	0-0	0-0
Wigan v Cardiff	-	-	-	-	0-1	-
Wolves v Blackburn	2-3	0-2	1-1	-	3-1	0-0

Results cover matches from Premier League to National League and Scottish Premiership to League Two

	2010-11	2011-12	2012-13	2013-14	2014-15	2015-16
League One						
Bradford v AFC Wimbledon	-	1-2	5-1	-	-	-
Bury v Northampton	1-1	-	-	1-1	2-1	-
Chesterfield v Charlton	-	0-4	-	-	-	-
Coventry v Walsall	-	-	5-1	2-1	0-0	1-1
Gillingham v Fleetwood Town	-	-	2-2	-	0-1	5-1
Millwall v Oxford	-	-	-	-	-	-
MK Dons v Sheffield United	-	1-0	1-0	0-1	1-0	-
Oldham v Rochdale	1-2	2-0	-	-	3-0	2-3
Peterborough v Bristol Rovers	3-0	-	-	-	-	-
Port Vale v Bolton	-	-	-	-	-	-
Shrewsbury v Southend	1-1	2-1	-	-	1-1	1-2
Swindon v Scunthorpe	-	-	1-1	-	3-1	2-1
League Two						
Blackpool v Cheltenham	-	-	-	-	-	-
Colchester v Plymouth	1-1	-	-	-	-	-
Crawley Town v Carlisle	-	-	1-1	0-0	-	0-1
Crewe v Leyton Orient	-	-	1-1	1-2	1-1	-
Exeter v Morecambe	-	-	0-3	1-1	1-1	1-1
Grimsby v Yeovil	-	-	-	-	-	-
Hartlepool v Barnet	-	-	-	-	-	1-1
Luton v Notts County	-	-	-	-	-	0-2
Newport County v Accrington	-	-	-	4-1	1-1	0-2
Portsmouth v Cambridge U	-	-	-	-	2-1	2-1
Stevenage v Mansfield	-	-	-	-	3-0	0-2
Wycombe v Doncaster	-	-	-	-	-	-
National League						
Boreham Wood v Gateshead	-	-	-	-	-	2-3
Braintree v Barrow	-	1-0	2-3	-	-	1-1
Bromley v Guiseley	-	-	-	-	-	2-0
Dover v Torquay	-	-	-	-	2-2	5-0
Forest Green v Maidstone	-	-	-	-	-	-
Lincoln v Macclesfield	2-1	-	2-3	1-0	2-0	5-3
North Ferriby v Aldershot	-	-	-	-	-	-
Solihull Moors v Eastleigh	-	-	-	-	-	-
Sutton United v Chester	-	-	-	-	-	-
Tranmere v Southport	-	-	-	-	-	1-0
Woking v York	-	-	-	-	-	-
Wrexham v Dag & Red	-	-	-	-	-	-
Scottish Championship						
Dundee United v St Mirren	1-2	1-1/0-0	3-4	4-0/3-2	3-0	-
Dunfermline v Falkirk	1-1/3-0	-	0-1/0-2	-	-	-
Hibernian v Raith	-	-	-	-	1-1/1-1	2-0/1-0
Morton v Ayr	-	4-1/3-1	-	-	0-1/2-1	-
Queen of Sth v Dumbarton	-	-	-	1-2/3-1	3-0/2-1	1-0/6-0
Scottish League One						
Airdrieonians v Alloa	0-1/0-2	-	-	-	-	-
Albion v East Fife	-	0-3/1-1	0-3/1-1	-	2-0/2-3	-
Brechin v Stranraer	-	-	3-0/2-2	1-1/1-3	1-2/1-3	2-0/1-0
Livingston v Queens Park	-	-	-	-	-	-
Peterhead v Stenhousemuir	2-2/0-3	-	-	-	1-0/2-0	2-2/4-1
Scottish League Two						
Berwick v Montrose	1-0/0-1	1-2/2-2	1-4/4-0	1-1/5-0	2-2/3-3	2-1/1-0
Cowdenbeath v Arbroath	-	0-0/2-3	-	-	-	-
Edinburgh City v Annan	-	-	-	-	-	-
Elgin v Stirling	-	-	3-1/1-2	4-0/2-3	-	1-0/2-1
Forfar v Clyde	-	-	-	-	-	-

Results cover matches from Premier League to National League and Scottish Premiership to League Two

Sunday April 23, 2017

Championship						
Aston Villa v Birmingham	0-0	-	-	-	-	-

Saturday April 29, 2017

Premier League						
Crystal Palace v Burnley	0-0	2-0	4-3	-	0-0	-
Everton v Chelsea	1-0	2-0	1-2	1-0	3-6	3-1
Man United v Swansea	-	2-0	2-1	2-0	1-2	2-1
Middlesbrough v Man City	-	-	-	-	-	-
Southampton v Hull	-	2-1	-	4-1	2-0	-
Stoke v West Ham	1-1	-	0-1	3-1	2-2	2-1
Sunderland v Bournemouth	-	-	-	-	-	1-1
Tottenham v Arsenal	3-3	2-1	2-1	0-1	2-1	2-2
Watford v Liverpool	-	-	-	-	-	3-0
West Brom v Leicester	-	-	-	-	2-3	2-3

Championship						
Barnsley v Burton	-	-	-	-	-	1-0
Birmingham v Huddersfield	-	-	0-1	1-2	1-1	0-2
Blackburn v Aston Villa	2-0	1-1	-	-	-	-
Brighton v Bristol City	-	2-0	2-0	-	-	2-1
Cardiff v Newcastle	-	-	-	1-2	-	-
Derby v Wolves	-	-	0-0	-	5-0	4-2
Fulham v Brentford	-	-	-	-	1-4	2-2
Ipswich v Sheffield Weds	-	-	0-3	2-1	2-1	2-1
Leeds v Norwich	2-2	-	-	-	0-2	-
Preston v Rotherham	-	-	-	3-3	-	2-1
QPR v Nottm Forest	1-1	-	-	5-2	-	1-2
Reading v Wigan	-	-	0-3	1-2	0-1	-

League Two						
Accrington v Luton	-	-	-	-	2-2	1-1
Barnet v Grimsby	-	-	-	2-1	1-3	-
Cambridge U v Crawley Town	2-2	-	-	-	-	0-3
Carlisle v Newport County	-	-	-	-	2-3	0-1
Cheltenham v Hartlepool	-	-	-	2-2	1-0	-
Doncaster v Exeter	-	-	-	-	-	-
Leyton Orient v Colchester	4-2	0-1	0-2	2-1	0-2	-
Mansfield v Portsmouth	-	-	-	2-2	1-2	1-1
Morecambe v Wycombe	0-3	-	0-1	1-1	1-3	0-1
Notts County v Blackpool	-	-	-	-	-	-
Plymouth v Crewe	-	0-1	-	-	-	-
Yeovil v Stevenage	-	0-6	1-3	-	-	2-2

National League						
Aldershot v Braintree	-	-	-	2-1	1-3	2-1
Barrow v Dover	-	-	-	-	-	2-1
Chester v Boreham Wood	-	-	-	-	-	2-2
Dag & Red v Woking	-	-	-	-	-	-
Eastleigh v Wrexham	-	-	-	-	2-2	1-1
Gateshead v Bromley	-	-	-	-	-	3-1
Guiseley v Solihull Moors	-	-	-	0-3	3-0	-
Macclesfield v Sutton United	-	-	-	-	-	-
Maidstone v Tranmere	-	-	-	-	-	-
Southport v Lincoln	-	2-2	4-2	0-1	3-3	2-2
Torquay v North Ferriby	-	-	-	-	-	-
York v Forest Green	2-1	1-0	-	-	-	-

Results cover matches from Premier League to National League and Scottish Premiership to League Two

	2010-11	2011-12	2012-13	2013-14	2014-15	2015-16
Scottish Championship						
Ayr v Hibernian	-	-	-	-	-	-
Dundee United v Dumbarton	-	-	-	-	-	-
Dunfermline v Morton	2-0/1-3		2-2/1-4		1-2/0-4	
Falkirk v Queen of Sth	3-1/0-3	1-0/3-0	-	2-1/1-0	1-1/1-1	0-0/3-1
St Mirren v Raith	-	-	-	-	-	1-2/1-2
Scottish League One						
Alloa v Stranraer	-	1-0/3-1	3-0/4-1	-	-	-
Brechin v Albion	-	1-4/2-1	1-0/2-0	-	-	0-1/2-1
East Fife v Airdrieonians	3-3/0-1	2-0/2-0	-	1-0/0-0	-	-
Livingston v Peterhead	1-0/5-1	-	-	-	-	-
Queens Park v Stenhousemuir	-	-	-	-	-	-
Scottish League Two						
Annan v Montrose	2-2/2-1	2-1/1-2	2-1/1-1	2-1/1-0	2-2/4-3	3-2/3-3
Arbroath v Elgin	2-0/3-5	-	-	-	1-0/3-3	0-3/2-3
Clyde v Berwick	1-4/2-0	1-4/2-2	2-1/2-1	1-0/3-3	3-3/0-3	1-1/2-1
Cowdenbeath v Forfar	-	3-1/2-0	-	-	-	2-1/1-4
Edinburgh City v Stirling	-	-	-	-	-	-
Sunday April 30, 2017						
League One						
AFC Wimbledon v Oldham	-	-	-	-	-	-
Bolton v Peterborough	-	-	1-0	-	-	-
Bristol Rovers v Millwall	-	-	-	-	-	-
Charlton v Swindon	2-4	-	-	-	-	-
Fleetwood Town v Port Vale	-	-	2-5	-	1-0	1-2
Northampton v Gillingham	2-1	1-1	1-2	-	-	-
Oxford v Shrewsbury	3-1	2-0	-	-	0-2	-
Rochdale v Bradford	-	-	0-0	-	0-2	1-3
Scunthorpe v Coventry	0-2	-	1-2	-	2-1	1-0
Sheffield United v Chesterfield	-	4-1	-	-	1-1	2-0
Southend v Bury	1-1	-	-	0-0	1-1	4-1
Walsall v MK Dons	1-2	0-2	1-0	0-3	1-1	-
Saturday May 6, 2017						
Premier League						
Arsenal v Man United	1-0	1-2	1-1	0-0	1-2	3-0
Bournemouth v Stoke	-	-	-	-	-	1-3
Burnley v West Brom	-	-	-	-	2-2	-
Chelsea v Middlesbrough	-	-	-	-	-	-
Hull v Sunderland	-	-	-	1-0	1-1	-
Leicester v Watford	4-2	2-0	1-2	2-2	-	2-1
Liverpool v Southampton	-	-	1-0	0-1	2-1	1-1
Man City v Crystal Palace	-	-	-	1-0	3-0	4-0
Swansea v Everton	-	0-2	0-3	1-2	1-1	0-0
West Ham v Tottenham	1-0	-	2-3	2-0	0-1	1-0
League Two						
Blackpool v Leyton Orient	-	-	-	-	-	-
Colchester v Yeovil	0-0	2-2	2-0	-	2-0	-
Crawley Town v Mansfield	2-0	-	-	-	-	0-1
Crewe v Barnet	7-0	3-1	-	-	-	-
Exeter v Carlisle	2-1	0-0	-	-	2-0	2-2
Grimsby v Plymouth	-	-	-	-	-	-
Hartlepool v Doncaster	-	-	1-1	-	-	-
Luton v Morecambe	-	-	-	-	2-3	1-0
Newport County v Notts County	-	-	-	-	-	0-1
Portsmouth v Cheltenham	-	-	-	0-0	2-2	-
Stevenage v Accrington	2-2	-	-	-	2-1	1-1
Wycombe v Cambridge U	-	-	-	-	1-0	1-0

Results cover matches from Premier League to National League and Scottish Premiership to League Two

Scottish Championship						
Dumbarton v Falkirk	-	-	0-2/0-2	1-1/2-1	0-3/1-0	0-5/1-1
Hibernian v St Mirren	2-0/1-1	1-2/0-0	2-1/3-3	2-0/2-3	-	1-1/3-1
Morton v Dundee United	-	-	-	-	-	-
Queen of Sth v Dunfermline	2-0/1-3	-	-	-	-	-
Raith v Ayr	-	0-1/2-2	-	-	-	-
Scottish League One						
Airdrieonians v Queens Park	-	-	-	-	-	-
Albion v Livingston	-	-	-	-	-	-
Peterhead v Alloa	1-0/4-1	1-1/0-1	-	-	-	-
Stenhousemuir v Brechin	0-0/1-3	1-1/2-1	3-1/3-3	3-2/4-2	0-2/2-2	2-2/0-0
Stranraer v East Fife	-	-	2-6/3-1	2-0/2-0	-	-
Scottish League Two						
Berwick v Edinburgh City	-	-	-	-	-	-
Elgin v Cowdenbeath	-	-	-	-	-	-
Forfar v Annan	-	-	-	-	-	-
Montrose v Clyde	8-1/3-1	4-0/5-0	2-3/1-1	0-2/0-2	0-3/0-1	2-0/2-1
Stirling v Arbroath	-	0-1/1-1	-	-	-	3-1/1-0

Sunday May 7, 2017

Championship						
Aston Villa v Brighton	-	-	-	-	-	-
Brentford v Blackburn	-	-	-	-	3-1	0-1
Bristol City v Birmingham	-	0-2	0-1	-	-	0-0
Burton v Reading	-	-	-	-	-	-
Huddersfield v Cardiff	-	-	0-0	-	0-0	2-3
Newcastle v Barnsley	-	-	-	-	-	-
Norwich v QPR	1-0	2-1	1-1	-	-	-
Nottm Forest v Ipswich	2-0	3-2	1-0	0-0	2-2	1-1
Rotherham v Derby	-	-	-	-	3-3	3-3
Sheffield Weds v Fulham	-	-	-	-	1-1	3-2
Wigan v Leeds	-	-	-	1-0	0-1	-
Wolves v Preston	-	-	-	2-0	-	1-2

Saturday May 13, 2017

Premier League						
Bournemouth v Burnley	-	-	-	1-1	-	-
Crystal Palace v Hull	0-0	0-0	4-2	1-0	0-2	-
Everton v Watford	-	-	-	-	-	2-2
Man City v Leicester	-	-	-	-	2-0	1-3
Middlesbrough v Southampton	-	2-1	-	-	-	-
Stoke v Arsenal	3-1	1-1	0-0	1-0	3-2	0-0
Sunderland v Swansea	-	2-0	0-0	1-3	0-0	1-1
Tottenham v Man United	0-0	1-3	1-1	2-2	0-0	3-0
West Brom v Chelsea	1-3	1-0	2-1	1-1	3-0	2-3
West Ham v Liverpool	3-1	-	2-3	1-2	3-1	2-0

Sunday May 21, 2017

Premier League						
Arsenal v Everton	2-1	1-0	0-0	1-1	2-0	2-1
Burnley v West Ham	-	2-2	-	-	1-3	-
Chelsea v Sunderland	0-3	1-0	2-1	1-2	3-1	3-1
Hull v Tottenham	-	-	-	1-1	1-2	-
Leicester v Bournemouth	-	-	-	2-1	-	0-0
Liverpool v Middlesbrough	-	-	-	-	-	-
Man United v Crystal Palace	-	-	-	2-0	1-0	2-0
Southampton v Stoke	-	-	1-1	2-2	1-0	0-1
Swansea v West Brom	-	3-0	3-1	1-2	3-0	1-0
Watford v Man City	-	-	-	-	-	1-2

Results cover matches from Premier League to National League and Scottish Premiership to League Two

Premier League

Champions	Leicester
Champions League	Arsenal
	Tottenham
	Manchester City
Europa League	Manchester United
	Southampton
	West Ham
Relegated	Newcastle
	Norwich
	Aston Villa

Championship

Champions	Burnley
Promoted	Middlesbrough
Playoff winners	Hull
Relegated	Charlton
	MK Dons
	Bolton

League One

Champions	Wigan
Promoted	Burton
Playoff winners	Barnsley
Relegated	Doncaster
	Blackpool
	Colchester
	Crewe

League Two

Champions	Northampton
Promoted	Oxford United
	Bristol Rovers
Playoff winners	AFC Wimbledon
Relegated	Dagenham & R
	York

National League

Champions	Cheltenham
Playoff winners	Grimsby
Relegated	Halifax
	Altrincham
	Kidderminster
	Welling

National League North

Champions	Solihull Moors
Playoff winners	North Ferriby
Relegated	Lowestoft
	Hednesford
	Corby Town

National League South

Champions	Sutton United
Playoff winners	Maidstone United
Relegated	Havant & W
	Hayes & Yeading
	Basingstoke Town

Community Shield

Winners	Arsenal
Beaten finalists	Chelsea

FA Cup

Winners	Manchester United
Beaten finalists	Crystal Palace

League Cup

Winners	Manchester City
Beaten finalists	Liverpool

Football League Trophy

Winners	Barnsley
Beaten finalists	Oxford United

FA Trophy

Winners	Halifax
Beaten finalists	Grimsby

Barnsley enjoyed two successful trips to Wembley in 2015-16

Ross County saw off second-tier Hibernian in the League Cup final

Scottish Premiership	
Champions	Celtic
Europa League	Aberdeen
	Hearts
Relegated	Dundee United

Scottish Championship	
Champions	Rangers
Relegated	Livingston
	Alloa

Scottish League One	
Champions	Dunfermline
Promoted	Ayr United
Relegated	Cowdenbeath
	Forfar

Scottish League Two	
Champions	East Fife
Promoted	Queen's Park
Relegated	East Stirling

Edinburgh City promoted into League Two

Scottish Cup	
Winners	Hibernian
Beaten finalists	Rangers

Scottish League Cup	
Winners	Ross County
Beaten finalists	Hibernian

Scottish Challenge Cup	
Winners	Rangers
Beaten finalists	Peterhead

Champions League	
Winners	Real Madrid
Beaten finalists	Atletico Madrid

Europa League	
Winners	Seville
Beaten finalists	Liverpool

Uefa Super Cup	
Winners	Barcelona
Beaten finalists	Seville

Fifa Club World Cup	
Winners	Barcelona
Beaten finalists	River Plate

West Ham backers were jumping for joy in 2015-16

Premier League

West Ham	+37.90	Liverpool	-2.20
Leicester	+24.32	Watford	-2.59
Stoke	+12.87	Newcastle	-2.64
Swansea	+9.26	Sunderland	-3.55
Southampton	+8.11	Arsenal	-4.71
West Brom	+2.98	Man City	-8.03
Man Utd	+1.76	Norwich	-8.33
Tottenham	+1.04	Everton	-11.10
Crystal Palace	+0.57	Chelsea	-13.76
Bournemouth	-1.63	Aston Villa	-27.97

Championship

Burnley	+10.27	Derby	-2.18
Brighton	+6.82	Charlton	-5.10
Brentford	+5.92	Bristol City	-5.28
Birmingham	+5.52	Nottm Forest	-6.92
Middlesbrough	+4.30	Wolves	-8.67
Rotherham	+4.15	QPR	-9.40
Leeds	+3.58	Huddersfield	-12.28
Hull	+3.04	Fulham	-12.90
Cardiff	+1.32	Blackburn	-15.19
Ipswich	+0.97	MK Dons	-15.40
Preston	-1.17	Reading	-16.21
Sheff Wed	-2.00	Bolton	-26.25

All profit & loss figures calculated to a £1 level stake at best bookmakers' odds published in the Racing Post on match day

League One

Burton	+18.78	Gillingham	+1.23
Millwall	+10.72	Blackpool	+1.02
Walsall	+9.83	Chesterfield	-0.17
Barnsley	+9.74	Bury	-0.85
Scunthorpe	+8.34	Shrewsbury	-0.90
Bradford	+5.85	Southend	-2.93
Wigan	+3.72	Crewe	-4.25
Rochdale	+3.65	Sheff Utd	-7.25
Coventry	+2.49	Fleetwood	-11.41
Swindon	+1.97	Colchester	-12.01
Port Vale	+1.91	Oldham	-12.30
Peterborough	+1.53	Doncaster	-13.95

League Two

Northampton	+23.93	Cambridge Utd	+0.66
Accrington	+12.92	Mansfield	-1.17
Plymouth	+11.68	Leyton Orient	-2.53
Luton	+10.94	Wycombe	-2.63
Bristol Rovers	+10.13	Portsmouth	-3.74
Exeter	+7.42	Newport County	-6.43
Barnet	+6.47	Dag & Red	-7.53
Hartlepool	+4.85	Stevenage	-8.20
Wimbledon	+2.72	Yeovil	-8.33
Carlisle	+2.30	Morecambe	-10.32
Crawley	+1.70	Notts County	-10.70
Oxford Utd	+1.05	York	-22.03

National League

Braintree	+16.03	Halifax	-0.77
Cheltenham	+13.06	Aldershot	-1.26
Gateshead	+10.43	Boreham Wood	-4.89
Macclesfield	+9.10	Torquay	-6.80
Southport	+8.95	Chester	-6.95
Woking	+6.34	Wrexham	-7.36
Dover	+6.12	Lincoln	-7.85
Forest Green	+4.21	Altrincham	-8.95
Eastleigh	+3.42	Grimsby	-9.18
Tranmere	+2.14	Kidderminster	-9.95
Bromley	+1.49	Welling	-12.20
Barrow	+1.08	Guiseley	-12.60

Scottish Premiership

Motherwell	+29.14	Ross County	-2.09
St Johnstone	+14.73	Celtic	-3.59
Aberdeen	+6.98	Hamilton	-3.73
Inverness CT	+5.28	Partick	-5.36
Hearts	+5.12	Dundee	-8.28
Kilmarnock	-1.20	Dundee Utd	-12.60

Scottish Championship

Raith	+13.69	Alloa	-0.70
Falkirk	+7.61	Rangers	-3.91
Dumbarton	+6.70	Morton	-4.54
Livingston	+1.50	Queen of the South	-8.08
Hibernian	-0.42	St Mirren	-8.80

Scottish League One

Airdrieonians	+11.31	Dunfermline	+1.86
Ayr	+8.85	Albion	+1.53
Stranraer	+6.70	Peterhead	+0.57
Cowdenbeath	+6.37	Stenhousemuir	-5.96
Brechin	+3.01	Forfar	-13.62

Scottish League Two

East Stirling	+9.63	Queen's Park	+1.25
Berwick	+5.95	Elgin City	+1.22
East Fife	+5.77	Montrose	-1.00
Annan	+5.64	Stirling	-1.78
Clyde	+2.36	Arbroath	-4.65

SOCCERBASE.COM

Italian Serie A

Sassuolo	+17.74	Lazio	-3.53
Juventus	+8.30	Genoa	-4.13
Udinese	+7.52	Atalanta	-4.16
Bologna	+7.25	Milan	-6.11
Roma	+3.50	Torino	-7.09
Chievo	+3.20	Frosinone	-8.48
Napoli	-0.13	Carpi	-8.50
Inter	-0.37	Palermo	-12.20
Fiorentina	-0.83	Sampdoria	-12.26
Empoli	-2.36	Verona	-17.65

Spanish Primera Liga

Atletico Madrid	+10.61	Sporting Gijon	-1.89
Real Sociedad	+7.16	Real Betis	-2.90
Celta Vigo	+5.89	Espanyol	-4.45
Villarreal	+5.32	Granada	-5.21
Valencia	+5.24	Malaga	-5.92
Real Madrid	+2.81	Eibar	-7.17
Las Palmas	+2.60	Getafe	-10.38
Levante	-0.83	Seville	-10.63
Barcelona	-0.86	Deportivo	-15.00
Athletic Bilbao	-0.98	Rayo Vallecano	-16.69

German Bundesliga

Mainz	+24.97	Bayer Leverkusen	-0.60
B M'gladbach	+9.82	Schalke	-2.64
Darmstadt	+9.60	Hannover	-3.50
Hamburg	+8.60	Ingolstadt	-3.95
Hertha Berlin	+4.32	Eintracht Frankfurt	-5.11
Cologne	+2.90	Augsburg	-5.45
Borussia Dortmund	+0.99	Hoffenheim	-9.78
Werder Bremen	+0.95	Wolfsburg	-10.38
Bayern Munich	+0.63	Stuttgart	-12.45

French Ligue 1

Angers	+15.22	Nantes	-2.92
Caen	+13.07	Reims	-4.30
Nice	+12.52	Guingamp	-5.19
Bastia	+9.67	Rennes	-5.60
Paris St-Germain	+4.86	Lorient	-6.18
Monaco	+3.56	Bordeaux	-7.23
Montpellier	+1.13	GFC Ajaccio	-7.95
St-Etienne	+1.02	Marseille	-14.00
Lyon	-0.36	Toulouse	-17.57
Lille	-1.80	Troyes	-18.00

Multiple bets

Selections	2	3	4	5	6	7
Doubles	1	3	6	10	15	21
Trebles		1	4	10	20	35
Fourfolds			1	5	15	35
Fivefolds				1	6	21
Sixfolds					1	7
Sevenfolds						1
Full cover	3	7	15	31	63	127

Patent (3 selections, 7 bets) 3 singles, 3 doubles, 1 treble

Trixie (3 selections, 4 bets) 3 doubles, 1 treble

Yankee (4 selections, 11 bets) 6 doubles, 4 trebles, 1 four-fold

Lucky 15 (4 selections, 15 bets) 4 singles, 6 doubles, 4 trebles, 1 four-fold

Canadian (5 selections, 26 bets) 10 doubles, 10 trebles, 5 four-folds, 1 five-fold

Lucky 31 (5 selections, 31 bets) 5 singles, 10 doubles, 10 trebles, 5 four-folds, 1 five-fold

Heinz (6 selections, 57 bets) 15 doubles, 20 trebles, 15 four-folds, 6 five-folds, 1 six-fold

Lucky 63 (6 selections, 63 bets) 6 singles, 15 doubles, 20 trebles, 15 four-folds, 6 five-folds, 1 six-fold

Super Heinz (7 selections, 120 bets) 21 doubles, 35 trebles, 35 four-folds, 21 five-folds, 7 six-folds, 1 seven-fold

Goliath (8 selections, 247 bets) 28 doubles, 56 trebles, 70 four-folds, 56 five-folds, 28 six-folds, 8 seven-folds, 1 eight-fold

INDEX OF TEAMS

Index of teams **255**

Odds conversion

Odds-on As %	Decimal	Fractional	Odds-against Decimal	As %
50.00%	2.00	Evens	2.00	50.00%
52.38%	1.91	11-10	2.10	47.62%
54.55%	1.83	6-5	2.20	45.45%
55.56%	1.80	5-4	2.25	44.44%
57.89%	1.73	11-8	2.38	42.11%
60.00%	1.67	6-4	2.50	40.00%
61.90%	1.62	13-8	2.63	38.10%
63.64%	1.57	7-4	2.75	36.36%
65.22%	1.53	15-8	2.88	34.78%
66.67%	1.50	2-1	3.00	33.33%
69.23%	1.44	9-4	3.25	30.77%
71.43%	1.40	5-2	3.50	28.57%
72.22%	1.38	13-5	3.60	27.78%
73.33%	1.36	11-4	3.75	26.67%
73.68%	1.36	14-5	3.80	26.32%
75.00%	1.33	3-1	4.00	25.00%
76.92%	1.30	10-3	4.33	23.08%
77.78%	1.29	7-2	4.50	22.22%
80.00%	1.25	4-1	5.00	20.00%
81.82%	1.22	9-2	5.50	18.18%
83.33%	1.20	5-1	6.00	16.67%
84.62%	1.18	11-2	6.50	15.38%
85.71%	1.17	6-1	7.00	14.29%
86.67%	1.15	13-2	7.50	13.33%
87.50%	1.14	7-1	8.00	12.50%
88.24%	1.13	15-2	8.50	11.76%
88.89%	1.13	8-1	9.00	11.11%

Ante-post odds of recent champions

Premier League		Best odds
2015-16	Leicester	5,000-1
2014-15	Chelsea	19-10
2013-14	Manchester City	23-10
Championship		**Best odds**
2015-16	Burnley	14-1
2014-15	Bournemouth	25-1
2013-14	Leicester	14-1
League One		**Best odds**
2015-16	Wigan	7-1
2014-15	Bristol City	8-1
2013-14	Wolves	4-1
League Two		**Best odds**
2015-16	Northampton	14-1
2014-15	Burton	16-1
2013-14	Chesterfield	8-1
National League		**Best odds**
2015-16	Cheltenham	11-1
2014-15	Barnet	18-1
2013-14	Luton	9-2
Scottish Premiership		**Best odds**
2015-16	Celtic	1-33
2014-15	Celtic	1-33
2013-14	Celtic	1-40
Scottish Championship		**Best odds**
2015-16	Rangers	4-5
2014-15	Hearts	7-2
2013-14	Dundee	15-8
Scottish League One		**Best odds**
2015-16	Dunfermline	9-2
2014-15	Morton	5-1
2013-14	Rangers	1-10
Scottish League Two		**Best odds**
2015-16	East Fife	13-2
2014-15	Albion	6-1
2013-14	Peterhead	15-8

Correct scores 2015-16

	Prem	Chmp	Lg1	Lg2	Conf	SCP	SCh	SLg1	SLg2
1-0	37	58	57	62	57	16	26	18	20
2-0	27	35	46	26	39	17	10	7	12
2-1	25	57	43	45	44	25	13	12	15
3-0	18	25	25	20	13	7	7	7	7
3-1	15	13	20	22	32	9	10	7	13
3-2	10	9	13	17	15	4	6	5	5
4-0	9	11	5	6	8	3	3	4	1
4-1	6	7	9	7	12	2	2	7	4
4-2	3	5	4	4	3	1	3	2	5
4-3	0	1	3	2	1	1	2	1	0
0-0	32	57	44	40	38	15	10	8	10
1-1	41	85	62	67	71	22	18	18	20
2-2	29	29	25	31	27	12	11	10	6
3-3	5	1	6	2	4	3	2	1	3
4-4	0	0	1	1	1	0	0	0	0
0-1	33	35	47	43	59	20	19	17	14
0-2	9	27	23	34	22	9	7	9	8
1-2	28	45	48	51	43	21	12	13	6
0-3	14	11	9	11	9	6	3	4	6
1-3	11	14	12	13	11	8	1	6	7
2-3	7	8	15	16	14	3	3	4	4
0-4	3	2	8	1	6	6	1	4	2
1-4	3	5	5	10	3	3	3	2	1
2-4	2	1	2	5	0	3	1	1	3
3-4	2	1	2	6	3	2	0	1	0
Other	11	10	18	10	17	10	7	12	8

Home/draw/away percentages 2015-16

	Prem	Chmp	Lg1	Lg2	Conf	SPL	Sct 1	Sct 2	Sct 3
Home	41	41	43	39	43	41	47	43	48
Draw	28	31	25	26	26	23	23	21	22
Away	31	28	32	36	32	36	30	36	31

Unders & overs percentages 2015-16

	Prem	Chmp	Lg1	Lg2	Conf	SPL	Sct 1	Sct 2	Sct 3
<1.5	27	27	27	26	28	22	31	24	24
>1.5	73	73	73	74	72	78	69	76	76
<2.5	47	54	51	49	52	43	50	43	47
>2.5	53	46	49	51	48	57	50	57	53
<3.5	69	79	73	72	72	69	69	63	66
>3.5	31	21	27	28	28	31	31	37	34
<4.5	87	91	86	86	87	86	84	80	82
>4.5	13	9	14	14	13	14	16	20	18

Asian handicaps

Conceding handicap				Receiving handicap	
Result of bet	Result of game	Handicap		Result of game	Result of bet
Win	Win	**0**		Win	Win
No bet	Draw	**Scratch**		Draw	No bet
Lose	Lose			Lose	Lose
Win	Win	**0,0.5**		Win	Win
Lose half	Draw	**0.25**		Draw	Win half
Lose	Lose			Lose	Lose
Win	Win	**0.5**		Win	Win
Lose	Draw			Draw	Win
Lose	Lose			Lose	Lose
Win	Win by 2+	**0.5,1**		Lose by 2+	Lose
Win half	Win by 1	**0.75**		Lose by 1	Lose half
Lose	Draw			Draw	Win
Lose	Lose			Win	Win
Win	Win by 2+	**1**		Lose by 2+	Lose
Return stake	Win by 1			Lose by 1	Return stake
Lose	Draw			Draw	Win
Lose	Lose			Win	Win